John Hicks

Carmel, California

THE
SELECTED
LETTERS
OF
MARIANNE
MOORE

BONNIE COSTELLO

GENERAL EDITOR

CELESTE GOODRIDGE

AND

CRISTANNE MILLER

ASSOCIATE EDITORS

ALFRED A. KNOPF

NEW YORK

1997

THE
SELECTED
LETTERS
OF
MARIANNE
MOORE

THIS IS A BORZOI BOOK
PUBLISHED BY ALFRED A. KNOPF, INC.

http://www.randomhouse.com/

Portions of this work were first published in *The Partisan Review*, *Poetry Calendar*,
and *The Yale Review*.

Grateful acknowledgment is made to the following for permission to reprint previously
published material:
Alfred A. Knopf, Inc., and *Faber and Faber Limited*: Excerpt from "Esthetique du Mal"
from *The Collected Poems* by Wallace Stevens, copyright 1947 by Wallace Stevens.
Rights in the United Kingdom administered by Faber and Faber Limited, London.
Reprinted by permission of Alfred A. Knopf, Inc., and Faber and Faber Limited.
The Estate of James Merrill: Excerpt from "Upon a Second Marriage" from *The Country of a Thousand Years of Peace and Other Poems* by James Merrill, copyright © 1958
by James Merrill. (Alfred A. Knopf, Inc., 1958, originally published in *Poetry*, February 1956). Reprinted by permission of the Estate of James Merrill.

Library of Congress Cataloging-in-Publication Data

Moore, Marianne, 1887–1972.
    [Correspondence. Selections]
    The selected letters of Marianne Moore / Bonnie Costello, general
editor ; Celeste Goodridge and Cristanne Miller, associate editors.
      p.   cm.
    Includes index.
    ISBN 0-679-43909-9
    1. Moore, Marianne, 1887–1972—Correspondence. 2. Women poets,
American—20th century—Correspondence. I. Costello, Bonnie.
II. Goodridge, Celeste. III. Miller, Cristanne. IV. Title.
PS3525.05616Z48   1997
811'.52—dc21   96-52200
[B]   CIP

Manufactured in the United States of America
First Edition

Contents

Illustrations

Introduction

O N July 9, 1959, T. S. Eliot wrote to Marianne Moore: "One of the books which obviously must in the fullness of time be published ... will be the *Letters* of Marianne Moore." We are pleased to fulfill his prediction. Marianne Moore's correspondence makes up the largest and most broadly significant collection of any modern poet. It documents the first two-thirds of this century, reflecting shifts from Victorian to modernist culture, the experience of the two world wars, the Depression and postwar prosperity, and the changing face of the arts in America and Europe. Moore wrote letters daily for most of her life—long, intense letters to friends and family; shorter, but always distinctive letters to an ever-widening circle of acquaintances and fans. At the height of her celebrity, she would occasionally write as many as fifty letters a day. Both Moore and her correspondents appreciated the value of their exchange, so that an extraordinary number of letters, approximately thirty thousand, have been preserved. Our selection was made from archives in over one hundred libraries and as many private collections. This volume, then, represents only a tiny sampling of the rich record of Moore's thought and experience. It is Moore's poetry that draws us to her letters, of course. But in making this selection we have tried to present the life and mind of a woman whose interests extended to all the arts, to religion, politics, and psychology, to fashion, sports, and the domestic arts, moving freely between high culture and popular culture, and whose family and friendships remained as important as her professional life. Moore's correspondence is unique in the extent of its extraliterary interests and passionate engagement with the world at large. From her college adventures, her travels, and the flurry of her artistic and social activities, there seems to have been no lull. What has struck us most in reading through Moore's letters is the vitality and fullness of the long life they record.

While Moore's literary correspondence is significant for the picture it gives us of literary culture, of equal importance is the family correspondence. These letters provide a rare, intimate portrait of the artistic, social, and psychological development of a poet. Moore's family members were closely involved in her life of writing and were often the sources of her literary ideas. Here, selection has been especially difficult since the family correspondence is extraordinary in its volume, its continuity over most of the years of her life, and in its detail. Whenever she was separated from her mother or brother for more than a few days, Moore wrote them letters. The Rosenbach Museum and Library, which houses the correspondence between members of the Moore family, lists over 13,500 leaves (often written in small hand on both sides) in this correspondence between the years 1905 (when Moore entered college) and 1947 (when Moore's mother died and her brother virtually stopped saving the poet's letters). Although some of these letters are to aunts or cousins and some are from her brother John Warner's wife and children, the vast majority of this correspondence consists of letters between Moore, her mother, and her brother. To give a more practical idea of the volume of this correspondence, during her college years Moore wrote at least two or three letters home a week, from between two and fifty-four pages in length. Over the course of the thirty-five years following her graduation, except when the three Moores lived together or so close that they could see each other almost daily, they continued to write an average of between one and three letters a week, some of these also quite lengthy. Although few of Moore's letters from the mid-1940s on have been saved, it is clear from her brother's side of the correspondence that the poet continued to write him at least once a week in richly textured detail during these decades as well. We publish here less than 5 percent of Moore's college correspondence, about 8 percent of her family correspondence between 1910 and 1947, and nearly 25 percent of the small number of late letters to her brother that were saved. We have tried to represent the close links between Moore's family life and her career as a poet, between her imagination and her most intimate human ties. The vicissitudes of this correspondence, along with shifting family circumstances and location, mean that not all periods of the relationship are represented. The greatest number of family letters appear in the first two chapters, when the family circle most fully defined Moore's life.

Moore's list of correspondents included some of the most renowned poets and artists of this century. These letters provide a glimpse of modernist aesthetic values taking shape, art being made in the context of personal and public life. Again, we have only been able to represent a fraction of this profound body of writing. For example, Moore's relationship with Ezra Pound began in 1918 and continued regularly until 1968. They began to correspond in the formative years of modernism, sustained a sparring relationship throughout years of economic crisis, fascism, and war, and remained loyal friends during Pound's incarceration at St. Elizabeths and after his release and return to Italy. Of the more than one hundred letters available, we have selected twenty-one. Moore's correspondence with T. S. Eliot began in 1921 and continued with varied intensity until 1964. Approximately one hundred letters have been preserved, of which twelve are published here. Of the more than sixty extant letters to H.D. [Hilda Doolittle], we have selected twelve. One of the richest exchanges is that with Bryher (Winifred Ellerman), whom Moore met through H.D. From 1920 to 1970 Moore wrote approximately five hundred letters to Bryher, each one compelling for its attention to contemporary issues and themes, its descriptive power, or its literary insight. Bryher's activities as writer, editor, and patron of the arts, her efforts against fascism, and her wide travels stimulated intense responses from the poet. Twenty-six of these letters are published here. Similarly, from 1934, when Moore met Elizabeth Bishop in front of the New York Public Library, until 1971 (a year before Moore's death), she wrote over two hundred letters to Bishop, of which twenty-four are represented here. In these and other cases, we have selected letters from periods of the most intense correspondence, generally early on in the relationships or in times of high activity. More occasional but important literary relationships include those with William Carlos Williams, Wallace Stevens, E. E. Cummings, Edith Sitwell, and younger writers such as Louise Bogan, Allen Ginsberg, and W. H. Auden. As she traveled to give readings, judged poetry contests, or received books for review or comment, Moore came into contact with a great many of the writers gaining prominence after her. Her correspondence with these figures—among them May Sarton, Louis Zukofsky, Langston Hughes, John Berryman, Robert Lowell, Ted Hughes, James Merrill, and Mona Van Duyn—is significant for the reach of connections it defines, but precisely because the correspondence was so vast by the 1950s, these letters often lack the depth of her more enduring relationships, and for that reason we have not included them.

Moore's correspondence not only highlights her artistic contributions, but also reveals the major role she played in shaping the art of her time. As editor of *The Dial* from 1925 to 1929, Moore corresponded with an even wider range of writers. While these letters are often interesting, we have included only a few of them because they concern details of editing and evaluation best read in the full context of the *Dial* archive at the Beinecke Library. We have, however, represented letters that reflect the internal relations between the *Dial* editorial board and staff and the personal challenges Moore met as editor. Moore's involvement in the publication of her contemporaries and younger poets extended well beyond the *Dial* years. Her correspondence with Ronald Lane Latimer of the Alcestis Press, Morton Dauwen Zabel of *Poetry*, and T. C. Wilson of *The Westminster Magazine*, for instance, show her continuing interest in the shaping of literary culture. Beyond the literary world, Moore formed close and lively friend-ships that give further dimension to her letters. Her involvement in other art forms is well documented in her long correspondence with Monroe Wheeler of the Museum of Modern Art, to whom she wrote over two hun-dred letters (we have included fifteen). He frequently invited her to join him for evenings of film or theater, sent her books, and gave her a subscrip-tion to the Metropolitan Museum of Art *Bulletin*. Wheeler's wide travels be-came another important subject of their correspondence, as he sent back regular tokens of exotic places he had visited. Moore's friendship with il-lustrator and artist Edward McKnight Kauffer, an intimate friend of T. S. Eliot's, is informed by her deep compassion for his troubled nature. Lincoln Kirstein, who early published Moore's work in *The Hound & Horn*, often in-vited her to openings of Balanchine ballets. Moore visited Alfred Stieglitz's 291 gallery in 1915, and the two remained in contact until the photogra-pher's death. Joseph Cornell sent her playful letters pasted with images from her poems, and these provoked a reciprocal energy. The artist George Plank, a family friend from Moore's early days in Carlisle, Pennsylvania, il-lustrated her publication of *The Pangolin and Other Verse*. Through Eliza-beth Bishop she met the painter Loren MacIver, who with her husband, Lloyd Frankenberg, would become a close friend. With the sculptor Mal-vina Hoffman she spent memorable summers in Maine. Many of these people lived in New York, and it is clear that Moore saw them often and spoke with them frequently on the telephone. But the medium of the letter was for her a way of recording affection and gratitude or memorializing events. Exquisite description often became a means of reciprocation for the treasured gifts her friends bestowed on her. Moore also kept up long-term exchanges with friends who were not themselves public figures, though they took a keen interest in the arts and sometimes served as patrons. Among these, we have selected just twenty-two from the over nine hundred letters she wrote to Hildegarde Watson, as well as a sampling of her exten-sive correspondence with Louise Crane and Kathrine Jones.

In general, we have chosen those letters that seemed to us most valu-able for their thought or wit, letters that highlight the multiple aspects of Moore's mind and imagination, in preference to letters that may provide significant biographical or bibliographical fact, but whose content is less compelling. Such a small sampling of letters cannot hope to represent a nar-rative, but we have sought to highlight continuities and key events in the letters so as to suggest the contours of a life. The range of inquiry and en-thusiasm in Moore's published writing is even clearer in her letters. They reveal Moore's aesthetic predilections, influences, sources for poems, and lines of development and are literary texts in their own right, full of re-markable description and wit, felicitous and original phrasing, and pro-found political, moral, and spiritual reflection.

In preparing these letters for publication, we have sought original, sent letters, though in a few cases we have had to rely on carbons or drafts retained by the poet. We have tried to follow the text, while recognizing that it is neither possible nor desirable to transcribe the letters exactly as they were written. Moore's many handwritten letters were especially problematic. In the early years, for instance, it is difficult to distinguish periods and commas from dashes, paragraph breaks are often ambiguous, and the generally passionate, notational style is not transcribable as printed text. We have silently corrected what seemed to us inadvertencies (spelling errors, missing punctuation, etc.) while preserving much of Moore's idiosyncrasy. We have retained the poet's use of English spelling, for instance, as well as her abbreviations, unusual punctuation, and unique greetings and closings. Economy of space and ease of reading have informed our editing throughout. Marginal comments have been inserted where Moore marks them in the text, with such indicators deleted. We have omitted addresses from the tops of the letters (except where a change of address occurs), and we have provided information about the sources of copy text in an appendix. We have not reproduced any enclosures from the letters, though we have indicated their presence in a footnote when it has direct bearing on the letter. As the focus of this volume is Moore's correspondence generally, we have not reproduced some of the features that make her family correspondence remarkable. For example, we have omitted her mother Mary Warner Moore's marginal comments on, revisions of, or additions to Moore's letters. Similarly, we have omitted Warner's later practice of responding to his sister's letters by writing in the margins or over the lines of her text. During Moore's years as editor of *The Dial*, its owner, James Sibley Watson, also responded to her queries directly in the margins of her letters. We have not included his comments. In only a very few instances have we omitted material from the body of the letter, however. These include the excerpting of three very long early letters to Warner (February 1, 2, and 4, 1909) and the omission of a few long quotations from poems by Moore or another poet that have been published elsewhere. Moore's letters often included sketches, paste-ons, and other visual materials that we have not been able to reproduce, except for an occasional facsimile. We have indicated in brackets where a drawing was inserted.

Secondary information in the volume is designed to enhance rather than intrude on a reading of Moore's letters. The introductions to each section of this volume preview the correspondence and provide basic information about Moore's life and relationships. A general glossary and a family glossary contain information on all included correspondents, and on those people mentioned in the letters who had a special connection with Moore. We have also added here information on most of the journals and magazines Moore refers to in her letters. Missing first or last names have been added in editorial brackets in most cases when an acquaintance is first introduced, but first names have not been inserted for those included in the Glossary of Names. In order to include as many of Moore's letters as possible in this single volume, we have limited annotation to information needed to clarify the letter that could not be represented in our chapter introductions or our glossary. We have left it to the reader to follow the rich web of allusions, trace the many connections to poems, and pursue the complex bibliographic history recorded here.

Since this is the first major publication of Moore's letters, we decided that a broad, one-volume selection featuring her writing would be most appropriate and in keeping with the tradition recently established in editing her contemporaries. Many exciting (and more complete) two-way volumes will undoubtedly follow. In producing the present volume we have worked collaboratively throughout, though Cristanne Miller had primary responsibility for the family correspondence and Bonnie Costello and Celeste Goodridge shared work on the literary correspondence. We have also accumulated many debts. In particular, we wish to acknowledge the ground-breaking work of Patricia Willis, who first organized the Moore archive at the Rosenbach Museum and Library and nurtured a generation of Moore critics before moving on to the Beinecke Library, another major repository of Moore letters, where she is curator of American Literature. Laurence Stapleton of Bryn Mawr College was instrumental in initiating the project of *The Selected Letters* and offered much helpful advice, as did Christopher Ricks of Boston University. Eileen Moran's 1985 dissertation, *Selected Letters of Marianne Moore to Hildegarde Watson,* was a valuable resource and notes for the letters to Watson draw directly on her work. Rodney Phillips at the Berg Collection of the New York Public Library, Leo Dolenski at the Canaday Library at Bryn Mawr, Mary Jane Mackechnie at the Vassar College Library, the staff of the Harry Ransom Research Center, the Houghton Library at Harvard, Columbia University Library, Stanford University Library, Pennsylvania State University Library, the Lilly Library at Indiana University, the University of Chicago Library, the University of Buffalo Library, the Huntington Library, the University of Virginia Library, the Denison Library at Scripps College, the Getty Research Center Library, and the Amherst Library have all been generous in providing copies of their holdings and in responding to questions. Many individuals provided information and copies of letters in their private collections. In particular, we would like to thank Valerie Eliot for her help, along with John Bodley's, in selecting and publishing letters to T. S. Eliot in her private possession and in the Faber & Faber archive. The late Lincoln Kirstein, Grace Schulman, James Laughlin, Guy Rotella, and Chester Page all generously sent copies of letters they or their friends had received from Moore. We would also like to thank the many libraries and individuals who provided copies of letters we were not able to include. Fifi Oscard, literary agent, and Harry Ford, editor at Knopf, made the book a public reality and gave excellent advice at every stage. For clerical and research assistance we are grateful to Hilary Younkin, Jennilee Giguiere, Cynthia Johnson, Maggie Hermes, Ann Keniston, and Louise Harrison. Boston University, Pomona College, Bowdoin College, and the American Philosophical Society provided financial support at various stages of the project. Our most heartfelt thanks go to Evelyn Feldman, of the Rosenbach Museum, who offered help at every stage of this project, and to the Moore family, who have been active and supportive throughout. In particular, this volume would not have been possible without the initiative, effort, and generosity of Moore's literary executor, Marianne Craig Moore.

THE
SELECTED
LETTERS
OF
MARIANNE
MOORE

1887–1909
Beginnings: Childhood and the Bryn Mawr Years

MARIANNE MOORE was born in 1887 and grew up with her brother, John Warner (called Warner), and her mother, Mary Warner Moore. Her father, John Milton Moore, suffered a nervous breakdown before her birth which precipitated the separation of her parents; Moore never met him. Following this breakdown, Moore's mother and brother moved into the home of her maternal grandfather (the Reverend John Riddle Warner) in Kirkwood, Missouri, where Marianne was born and spent her early childhood. After the Reverend John Riddle Warner's death in 1894, the Moores lived with maternal relatives outside Pittsburgh for over a year before moving to nearby Carlisle, Pennsylvania (in 1896). In 1899 Mary Warner Moore began teaching at the Metzger Institute, a private girls' school across the street from their house, which Marianne attended through high school. In 1905 she entered Bryn Mawr College, and in 1909 she graduated with her A.B.

Although the young Marianne Moore corresponded with a few relatives—especially her mother's cousin Mary Shoemaker—and a few classmates, the vast bulk of her early correspondence is with her mother and brother, or in letters jointly addressed to her family and to Mary Norcross, daughter of a prominent local pastor and her mother's closest friend. The family letters begin in 1904, when Warner left home to attend Yale College, and continue without interruption until the end of Marianne's life, except when all three members of the family were close enough for almost daily visits. Between the years 1905 and 1909, while Marianne was at Bryn Mawr and Warner at Yale and then teaching at a boys' school in Elizabeth, New Jersey, the Moore family sent their letters round-robin, each adding to the letters they received, with Mary Warner Moore collecting all letters in

Carlisle once they had gone full circle. While Marianne wrote an occasional private note to her brother or purely business note to her mother, most letters were addressed generally. She wrote at least three times a week and sometimes daily, occasionally sending letters twenty-five pages or longer.

Apart from the frequency of the exchange, this vast early correspondence is most remarkable for its extreme playfulness and for an extravagant nicknaming that eventually developed into what Mary Warner Moore called "a vocabulary that amounts to a foreign language" (to JWM, March 31, 1911). Similarly, Warner responded to reading his sister's poems in a 1920 *Dial* with the comment: "I was . . . greatly impressed with the fundamental grasp of 'Life' in them and expressed too in our own special 'language' but so marvelously handled that the 'aliens' could and can understand them & enjoy them" (May 1, 1920). An early and representative example of this "special language" took the form of a teasing rivalry in which gators (represented by Marianne and first Metzger, then Bryn Mawr students) and turtles (represented by Warner and Yale students; Yale is "Turtletown") compete for the upper hand. In 1904 and 1905 Warner sent several elaborate cartoons depicting gators undone by a turtle, and Marianne responded with jokes, stories, and even a dramatic Shakespearian scene in which a Macbeth-like turtle steals a pie and laments his transgression (February 23, 1905). In all permutations of the family naming, Moore typically referred to herself as male, and is given a male pronoun by both her mother (often) and her brother (consistently).

While each introduction lists the primary names each family member or friend received in the letters reprinted here from that period, a brief mention of the characteristics of this name play is useful. In the early letters, Marianne most often takes the name "Fangs" (varied, for example, as "General Hamilcar" or "Launcelot Barca Fangs"), "Gator," or "Uncle" and "Brother"—to her mother and brother, respectively. Warner is most often "Biter," "Toad," or "Turtle," and their mother is "Fawn" (hence Carlisle as "Fawndale"), "Mouse," or "Bunny"—and often referred to as Warner's and Marianne's mischievous child. Marianne and Warner often referred to themselves by the same names ("Weaz," "Pidge") and even more often as the same species (usually dogs), and all three—although especially Warner and Marianne—are occasionally "Fish." These names appear to stem from a variety of sources, including Roman history, children's books, and family outings or playful responses to daily events at home. While no particular event or source is traceable for most of these very early names, Fangs is the name of a dog in Sir Walter Scott's *Ivanhoe*, and "Gator" may be explained in a memento written by Mary Warner Moore describing how she first met her husband; there she mentioned a flood in the alley between her friends' and the Moore family's houses that "gave rise to the term *alley-gator*," presumably because of the frequent visits between the two households (August

29, 1941). Mary Norcross's special place in the family circle is marked by her inclusion for several years in the address of family letters and by their exclusive reference to her by playful nicknames, "Beaver" and "Rustles"—in reference to her weaving and other artistic activities and interests.[1]

These family names reveal a more general playfulness as well. For example, Mary Warner Moore is frequently "Mice" as well as "Mouse," and Marianne and her brother often referred to themselves as third-person characters—primarily "Barca" or "Barka" and "Willow," for Marianne—whose fictional and real exploits they delight in recounting. In several letters, Marianne substitutes "Fishes" for "Fish's" (corrected silently in this volume). Increasingly as they grew older, both she and Warner also periodically resorted to slang spellings—for example, "ast" for "asked." Instances of Moore's broad humor abound in these names, spellings, coinages, and in jokes she made up or repeated in her letters. As an early example, the twelve-year-old Marianne wrote her Uncle Ira and Cousin Mary Shoemaker, "I have a new riddle. A knight started out for London, from Liverpool; he had colic; when, and where?"; the answer, enclosed in a miniature envelope, was "In the middle of the knight" (November 15, 1899).

Moore was serious, however, about her schooling. By July 1904 she had already taken preliminary entrance exams for Bryn Mawr, having been tutored by, among others, Mary Norcross, who also influenced Moore in her decision to attend Bryn Mawr, Norcross's alma mater.[2] Moore blossomed at Bryn Mawr College, reveling in both the social life and the atmosphere of academic stimulation; despite severe homesickness at first, for example, Moore almost immediately wrote home that "I am still at the top of the wave" (September 29, 1905). In the spring of her second year, Moore was advised not to major in English (see May 9[7?], 1907). In response to this advice and to her peers' comments about her writing being unclear, Moore wrote "*a plea*":

> *Make it long, and write it soon.*
> *Oh yes; be sure*
> *To make it obvious.*
> *I can't endure it,*
> *Hearing that my friends*
> *"Quite like things—so obscure."*   (May 20, 1907)

1. In the letters printed here, Norcross is included as part of the "family" only when she is mentioned specifically in a letter's heading or opening remarks. The interchangeability of "Dear Family" and headings that specifically include "Rustles" or "Beaver" as part of the family group, however, suggests that both Warner and Marianne may have intended to include her in the more general heading as well.

2. Bryn Mawr was known for its rigorous entrance requirements, and Moore passed thirteen of the fifteen exams by the opening of the term. In a class of 112, she was one of 37 who entered without "conditions," i.e., work that was made up by taking courses for no credit.

Not an outstanding student in terms of grades, Moore was nonetheless enthusiastic about several of her courses, including those in English, in her major (law, history, and politics), and in biology. She also contributed frequently to the Bryn Mawr student literary magazine, the *Tipyn O'Bob*, or *Tip (Typ)*, and participated fully in the social life of Bryn Mawr, writing home at length about student "teas," infatuations, dances (where different student classes were assigned the role of "stags" or "girls"), field hockey games, theatrical performances, and lectures, as well as public exhibitions and performances she attended in Philadelphia and elsewhere.

Called "Marianna" by her friends, Moore appears to have been popular and made friendships in college that she maintained throughout her life. Among her closest friends were Marcet Haldeman, with whom she carried on an extensive correspondence about the imagination and the poetry they both wrote during the semester that Marcet was not at Bryn Mawr; Peggy James, daughter of psychologist William James and, for most of one year, the object of Moore's most intense affection and most frequent complaint; and Frances Browne, a friend with whom Moore twice traveled to Europe half a century later, during the 1960s.

Although Moore spoke of herself as primarily a writer of prose during her college years, her mother spoke of her as a poet from her early childhood on. On March 12, 1895, Mary Warner Moore wrote to her cousin Mary Shoemaker that the seven-year-old Marianne had "compose[d] odes and sonnets for your benefit; one of which I copy as follows: 'The shadows now they slowly fall: making the earth a great dark ball.' 'Pussy in the cradle lies—and sweetly dreams of gnats and flies.' If 'brevity is the soul of wit' surely this point is early reached in the aspirations of our young poetess." In 1895 Moore also wrote a verse note to "St. Nicklus" (page 7). On December 28 of the following year, she wrote again to Mary Shoemaker:

> You would have laughed surely, could you have heard my daughter's lament that the *poetry* was for Warner, rather than her. She *dotes on poetry* to a perfectly horrible degree. I know we shall yet have a poetess in the family, and finish our day languishing in an attic (prior to the ages when posterity & future generations will be singing our praises).

Apparently, Moore read more fiction than poetry during her college years, yet at one point she wrote home that "there is a fancy copy [of Browning] in the drawing room which I read when waiting for the mail and the metre of some of the long poems sticks in my head so it bothers me" (December 16, 1907). Even when most interested in prose, Moore included ditties or verse she had written in letters home, and her mother and brother commented on them. By the end of her senior year, Moore had also submitted

MM and John Warner Moore,
St. Louis, 1895

MM and John Warner Moore,
Carlisle, Pennsylvania, c. 1898

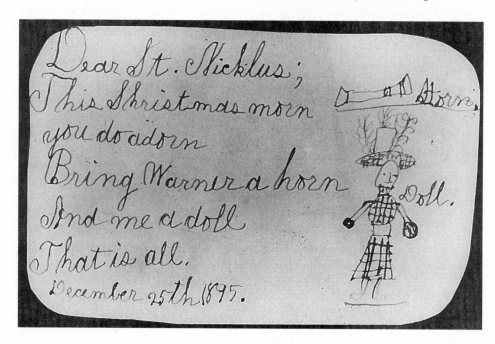

poems and a story to the *Atlantic*, as indicated in letters to her family thanking Norcross for typing the poems (April 20, April 22, and May 1, 1909).

During these early years, Moore wrote repeatedly of other interests that flourished in her later years and appear in her mature poetry. These interests are remarkable for their eclecticism and for the care with which Moore wrote about them, even in the midst of the whirl of college activities. Her early letters reveal not just her broad use of animal analogies and enthusiastic appreciation of the contemporary arts—especially painting, opera, and other forms of vocal music, and theater—but also her attention to details of clothing and gift exchanges, to local, national, and international politics, and to interesting language of all kinds, the latter demonstrated through her use of dialogue and quotation. As these letters also reveal, Moore's extensive reading played a distinctive role in her self-expression. Her early enthusiasm for Robert Louis Stevenson, for example, leads her to allude to or quote him frequently in letters and to exclaim, "One cannot read Stevenson own a family and be an ass" (January 15, 1907). Some incidents detailed in letters of those years later reappear as poems themselves. For example, on February 11, 1906, Moore wrote about an ice-skating expedition during which a young boy introduced himself by saying, "I am John Andrews. My father wrote the English History"—eventually the source for "'He Wrote the History Book'" (published 1916).

During her final semester at Bryn Mawr, Moore enthusiastically considered options for employment. Family response to anything that would take her away from home, however, was cool, and she apparently did not have a clear sense of her own direction beyond wanting to learn to type—a skill she had been told she must acquire if she wanted to write. And Moore knew by this time that she did want to write. Moore's years at Bryn Mawr served as a period of literary apprenticeship, during which it was common for her friends to comment on each other's poems and stories. This experience of serious exchange between friends as well as within her family may have given Moore confidence in her abilities, which was a help in the years of relative literary isolation following her graduation. As she later wrote to Bryher, "My experience [at Bryn Mawr] gave me security in my determination to have what I want" (see August 31, 1921).

To John Warner Moore   *Friday, June 16, 1905*

Dear Biter,

I recall distinctly how, eighteen gator months ago on the eighteenth of this month you were feebly but persistently trying to emerge from the fragments of a tiny freckled egg the size of a ping-pong ball. I was just going to tell the Fawn how you looked but think you are the one most interested. You were small, all your proportions being like those of an Aspinwall toad. Your tail was like a bee's honey sucker and your flippers were mere carets (^). Your eyes were quite large and china-blue. Your trap was corn yellow inside as could easily be seen when you would open it with fright or with the instinct of catching a fly. In the course of your development the rapidity with which you learned to really make sounds and catch flies was amazing.

As you know a phenomenon long peculiar to your race and that of the basilisks and salamanders is the appearance in the head at an uncertain date of a jewel which is symbolical of wisdom and which varies in color according to the disposition of the fortunate acquisitor. Now, I doubt not, you have long been expecting such this jewel but I can assure that it will by no means appear till another eighteen turtle years have passed.

When Barca saw the match-safe I had fashioned for you he submitted to me the following verse. The authorship is unmistakable but the worth of the production is doubtful.

> Ep(is)ode
> *(the tree planting)*
> *My lusty Barka, let us spy,*
> *Upon those turtles drawing nigh.*
> *But what is that they slowly bear?*
> *It is an elm-tree straight and fair.*
> *See how they sink it in the ground*
> *With never an angry word or sound.*
> *Let's not uproot the harmless tree*
> *But hasten back to the "Cocoas Three."*

It's fine that you've ended up so well with history.

My examinations have been heard from and we are satisfied and more. I got Merit in Algebra, Geometry and German translation. English Composition, I passed and failed in English and German Grammar and History.

With love eternal   Your affectionate brother,   Fangs

P.S. I was at a croquet party at C. Warren's yesterday and there met a friend of Constance from Lansdown. I had a dream last night which may thereby be accounted for. I did not dream that I was a tomato plant and you a rubber-plant but I dreamt you and Constance and I were sitting on the grass near Metzger tennis-court. You had to go up the hill for the hammock or something of the kind and as you ascended Constance said, "My, Warner's as straight as a ramrod. Isn't he?"

The Fawn has finished my hat and it surely is pretty.

With love, F.

To Mary Warner Moore   *[Pembroke East, Bryn Mawr College, Pa.]*
Sabbath, Septem[ber] 24, 1905

Dear Mouse,

I studied English and History on the way here, so stand even better chances for the examinations than I did.

When I arrived in Philadelphia the Beaver's train was in, and as I did not see her I seated myself in the waiting room. After about five minutes I spotted the Beaver as she passed by. I then had a sandwich in the station and we got the 8:15 out here. The college buildings seem enchanted, they are so absolutely perfect. Rockefeller is "magnificent," and words in which to describe the library, fail me. The library is not finished at the rear but it is easy to see what it will be. The two tall towers face Taylor and the wings which form the cloister garden are parallel with Pembroke.

I am delighted with the situation of my room although I will not be able to see the clock.

I am having the time of my life. All sorts and conditions of girls abound here but I have met only two besides the five at our table. One of the five is Henrietta Sharp, one a St. Louis girl, two, dandy Washington girls prepared in Boston, and the last a most interesting clipper from New York. The latter knows M. [Margaret] Shearer, being prepared at the Brearley school.

We have a nice room and the food is very good.

The Beaver showed me all the proofs of her pictures that have been finished and there are three fine ones.

Most of the girls here have been diligently studying all morning.

We met Miss Virginia Stoddard and she is exceedingly attractive; Radley will be a nice place this year for Miss Stoddard is to be warden there and many freshmen will be there it seems.[3]

3. Radley and Pembroke East are dormitories; MM lived in Pembroke East (later abbreviated as both "Pembroke" and "East").

We went to the Baptist church this morning and heard a strong sermon.

You can ease the minds of all those who have been solicitous about my being homesick by letting them know that one could as well be homesick here as a frog could be unhappy in a pond.

Please send me the slippers Mrs. Rose gave me if they are not in the trunk; also, my overshoes. Also a large sheet or so of medium heavy brown paper; also the cuticura that is in the old loom-room on the washstand, and a box of Vinolia salve which is I think, in the top-drawer of the chest in the bath-room. *And don't send the rug.*

We did not get my trunk Saturday night but I haven't needed anything and I will have it tomorrow.

The Beaver showed me the stuff Aunt Ann got for a pillow for Toad and it is beautiful. On a light green ground are large peacock eyes.

Don't work at anything of mine for a while and take trolly rides. My skirt has been an immense satisfaction but I dreamt last night I was going up and down stairs vainly trying to hold it up from the dust. There are positively no mosquitoes.

> *With love for his good little mouse,*   Uncle

The Beaver is now asleep so I must join her.

I don't believe I have the big silk spool with me.

Tomorrow the Beaver is going to see Toad in Philadelphia.

Don't write to Biter, I will forward your letter with one from me.

To Mary Norcross   *Sabbath afternoon [October 8, 1905]*

Dearest Beaver,

I got your letter this morning and it's the biggest kind of a comfort. I don't consider leaving for a moment but as is natural don't see how I am ever to live here for two or three months.[4] I force myself to eat and force people to entertain me. That is I don't hesitate to visit them and let them know I am blue. At times I feel quite self-possessed so things may get brighter. If I could control myself perfectly of course I shouldn't be homesick and I shouldn't wail to you this way. But things must get better. Don't imagine that I sit solitary and unoccupied thinking of home and my woes. I do everything in my power to make things go right. It seems unpardonable of me to be homesick when the Fawn and you and Biter are not sick or dying. For a while it made me desperate to see the things you'd done for me and the

---

4. On October 6, 1905, MM had written Norcross that she was so homesick she had stopped eating, and was afraid she would soon be sick.

places where we'd gone about, and my pictures. I loathed my room, my clothes and everything I had. But enough of this. Everything will be all right. I am terribly fond of Judith Boyer, Dorothy Smith, and Sarah [Jacobs]. The two former take care of me and Sarah has a refreshing way about her.

I can hardly wait for next Sabbath to come when I can lie on my couch and read *Pil's Progress*, Milton or the Bible. I think I'd better go out now, though, and get Sarah for a walk. The sun in my room is fine just now. I hope the Fawn hasn't sent my white hat. Helen assures me they don't wear hats or gloves. I am so glad to have the Bi. [Biology] instruments.

With love, Fangs

Today I saw my first bright spots in life.

I'm afraid you think I've been contemptible weak but my sensations are occasionally indescribably horrible.

I have just come from our walk and feel, one longed for, blissful minute, happy. I try to know Sarah as well as possible without being obnoxious so I will have someone in my own class that I can depend upon. Helen has been truly my good angel but I am going to try not to bother her much after this.

I draw water in my pitcher and pour it out quite gaily now and can't believe that this morning I looked sadly at the hound and thought I should never be able to support this bitter existence in exile any longer. Everything was without joy and I looked with wonder and curiosity at girls who were either smiling or eating. I should feel like hanging myself for having written to you but your letter gave me such a start to the good that I can't be sorry. Do we need to wear hats when walking on Sunday?

With love, Fangs

To Mary Warner Moore and John Warner Moore

Thursday, November 2, 1905

Dearest Family,

Yesterday evening as I was going to dinner whom should I see to my surprise and joy but Miss Rulison? She spoke to me and then went over to Miss Thomas's table. Later in the evening when I was in my kimona ready for bed she came to see me, asked me how I liked college and whether the work seemed hard. She thinks my room is a very nice one, and that my pictures are unusually choice. Miss Rulison looked terribly tired last night but said she had been well. She left this morning and said she didn't expect to be back for a long time. At dinner by classes we cheered her and nineteen hundred. It was great fun.

I decided to ask Babe to the play so hurried over to Miss Baldwin's right after luncheon. Babe said she couldn't go on account of some important association party at school. I must confess I was relieved if terribly disappointed for the gym. is going to be fearfully crowded. The Self. Gov. conference will be this Saturday and 1905 has a reunion so extra space will be scarce.

Last Sabbath two Sophomores from [Pembroke] West, unpretentious but nice through and through, came to see me. I called on them after coming from Miss Baldwin's and am to play tennis with one of them before breakfast tomorrow.

I paid my bill and they said the receipt would be sent to Carlisle.

The teas yesterday afternoon were so nice. The Rockefeller girls are perfect gems.

The cast for the play has been published and we are all excited over it.

Miss Delano and another member of the Ford-Anderson crowd have been very nice to me.

A Sophomore here in West is going to lend me her white hockey sweater for lantern night (next Thursday). We have to wear white dresses, so pile on underclothes and a white sweater if we have one. Isn't Miss Fauvre kind? I feel perfectly at liberty to borrow from her, so don't feel uneasy.

Rustles thought Gertrude Congdon very unattractive. I don't take to her greatly but have gotten to know and like her to a comfortable extent.

10 P.M.

I got over to see Miss Anthony before dinner this evening and had a nice visit of five or six minutes. We talked about weaving mostly and were just discussing college work when Miss Hall looking most impressive in an elaborate white cloth and silk dress made her appearance and I left. Is it necessary to call on people that give teas if three or four give one together?

The English work is a joy. I am familiar with a good many of the principles laid stress on but some burst upon me in all their glory. It gives me a headache to hear Miss Hoyt talk but I only have her occasionally.

Fire drill is the worst institution we have here. The gong is outside my door and when it goes off the sound smites my angel ear with diabolical suddenness. I played two halves of hockey today but did not distinguish myself. I know I can't make a team for only the Rosemary girls have a show but I am well satisfied to wait till next year, for the sport is the same in practising and one has more liberty. Match games between the classes are being played almost every day now and excitement runs high. Two 1909 girls are subs on the varsity. Isn't that great? I have procured a brand new hockey stick for .75 from a girl that can't play although she had expected to. When I was putting my royal balance away Barca asked how many cents that would make and upon hearing nearly turned into a pair of automobile goggles. He wondered how long it took Uncle Biter to earn so much.

I don't know how lively it will be here Thanksgiving but know I will get along alright. I am so absolutely satisfied with life on Friday afternoons and Sabbaths that I expect to enjoy every hour of vacation. Helen Haugh-wout will be here too; Leona Labold will be also but I am not going to let that worry me. How much does it cost to go from here to Fawndale and back and from Turtletown here and back? Claude Siesel often speaks of William Scholle who lives on Crown Street. She said she had asked him about Toad. She is going to New Haven for the Yale Princeton game and if Biter runs across her I want him to act Sir Chesterfield Dog. I don't care a great deal for Claude but respect her, like her ways and feel truly grateful to her for her friendliness and generosity to me.

Ellinor will be here the 19th. The weather is getting positively bitter. Miss Witherspoon one of the sophomores I went to see has a dandy room without much in it but everything pretty and good. She has the most per-fectly marked soft calfskin on a large table and a thick rattlesnake skin reaching from the ceiling to the floor. The calfskin is uneven giving the beast's shape and has little ears and eyeholes. It is a great fad here to have skins for tablecovers or to have them over the backs of chairs or on the floor. One girl has the most beautiful leopard skin rug. A great many of the girls have Atlantic City plush bears and every girl I know has a China animal or grotesque likeness of one. The Fawn would attract great attention here by reason of her spots and velvet ears. Although I don't favour the sacrilegious term used I must record that Caroline Kamm pronounced the Fawn (from the Monhegan pictures) "perfectly dear." Your Uncle, Fawn, blinked and slipped his tail through his claws. I must go swimming right away before any sediment or alluvium taints the water. Good night. In Merion they have to register 6 baths a week. Isn't that funny? We maintain that we are such a nice class of girls we don't need any such regulation.

The more work I do in [John] Genung's [*The*] *Working Principles of Rhetoric* the more I realize how much the Fawn needs the book in English work, for everything is clear and there are scores of good and suggestive paragraphs given so the Fawn would not have to do any illustrative work herself. I should suggest the Fawn's levying a tax on all English pupils then buy the book for the Library and assign reading in it. I should think the Fawn could get a chance at the book herself often enough to save her buy-ing one. As I have intimated before, Miss Hoyt is a perfect savage but she knows her subject. Judith Boyer says not one of the readers is a lady and that Miss Daly and Miss Hatcher and Miss Crandall ought to be shaken to death. She says it is a shame to have such a weak department in a place like this. I like Miss Marsh very much and believe what Miss Hoyt says so, I of course stood up for the disgraceful department although I was so amused and tick-led I could hardly voice any sensible or convincing opinion.

Do you suppose I would be allowed to put new strings on my window shades? Would it be all right for me to call on Bernice Stuart? I should like to very much.

Sometimes I can't realize that I am really here, that I have gotten in and that I am wandering through the enchanted land as I had pictured to myself. The things I worked at and planned for, with the Fawn in the summer and the things the Fawn did alone bring back my state of mind exactly. I feel just as rich with my clothes and the conveniences added to them as I had imagined and feel just as criminal enjoying them all myself when you have all never seen them and doing pleasant things all the time as I had thought I would. I just wish you could all visit me—you would love my room I know and admire the disposal of my personal effects in the cupboard.

I have among my best friends a following of servants. Kate to whom Rustles introduced me at the gym. is so nice to me. I see her almost every day and hobnob to the best of my ability. Maggie says I'm the "smartest girl in college keeping everything so nice and getting my room set right so early in the morning." Williams always beams at me when he opens the door for me and acted as if it were a favour to move my old bookcase out and my new one in. Lyddia is most attentive at the table and doesn't raise the dish rapidly after you've had one spoonful the way the other maid does.

Don't worry about Miss Wallace. I treated her *white*. I'll tell you all about it some time.

My splendiferous letter has just arrived. So Sir Fleance [JWM] has been [to] the playhouse, to the Globe. And he would have snouted over his brother Launcelot if he could have gone too? Launcelot is going to the playhouse tomorrow night.

I am caused anguish by the poor noble Fawn's efforts on my coat and by her anxiety to get the wash off. I don't need clean clothes at all. Fawn *never* mend my clothes. I get up a few minutes early almost [every] morning to mend so my things [are] all kept in applepie order and I don't know when they're fixed it takes so little time. Leone Robinson lives in Roc[kefeller Hall]. I believe you had the impression she was here. I am rejoiced that the little Fawn had a little drive. I can just imagine the Fawn and Beaver rolling along those familiar roads. I wonder if the leaves are as pretty everywhere as they are here. Let the whole Family take sleep and exercise. This sounds very grand and unpractical but I am trying strenuously to do it and think it is possible. I have general plans and stick to them. When hockey practice comes, I go out, when time for private reading comes I do that not working on the next day's work every spare minute the way I did in school. Thus far I haven't gotten to bed very early but am going to do so. Self. Gov. Conference people are floating about already. Coming from Miss Baldwin's yesterday a very smart looking girl was tearing along at a great rate carrying a suitcase, umbrella, tennis racket and large package. It seemed unconventional but I offered to carry something. The girl seemed pleased and willing. She asked if I was 1909? She said she was simply beside herself to get back; that she hadn't been back last year. She asked me if I was just crazy about everything. She said she had heard that 1909 was simply a stunning class etc. She left me at Roc. and I went on my way rejoicing.

The nine Baltimore girls were invited to dinner at the Deanery yesterday. Helen Scott (whose mother was here when Rustles was) went from Pem. She says Miss Thomas is perfectly lovely the most delightful the most wonderful person she has ever met. She said the dinner was beautiful. They had Japanese dinner cards; ice cream at the end in the form of owls and when they left Miss Garret[5] gave them each a little feather owl. They had grapefruit with candied cherries first, later partridges on toast, peas, some curious nut salad and a thousand wonderful things I forget about. Helen said that they talked Henry James, Europe and woman suffrage. She said Miss Thomas thought it most strange that a "broadminded charming" man like Cardinal Gibbons should not favour woman suffrage. Miss Garret and Miss Thomas were in Rome when the Pope died and they told all about the funeral ceremonies and the impressive procession of cardinals. Miss Thomas was much incensed at Mrs. Rorer's *Ladies' Home Journal* article and said that because Mrs. Rorer had not been allowed to see the kitchens in the Halls she took this contemptible and spiteful method of revenge. Helen said when they first went in to dinner they couldn't say a word and that Miss Thomas had to talk at them just the way she does in chapel but that after dinner when they sat round the open fire they all became very much at ease and very talkative.

The Fawn must not write such long letters. She likes to do it I know but it means so much. She is really tired from the steady application although she enjoys it and then all her time is gone. The same might be said to each of us I know, but as for myself I simply can't help writing and try to be careful about getting my work done. I never do slight it for letter writing. If I can't write home when I want to very much I will have to let college go for one can't live by books alone and intercourse with strangers.

I hope Rustles doesn't find work toilsome or discouraging. As Miss Randolph says when I get fusstious in lab., "Well you just work along and I think you'll find that it all works out right." I like Miss Randolph ever so much.

I can't decide whether Mary Withington likes me or not but as I don't have to I won't. Goodbye till Sabbath. Afternoon. I've just come back from town. I had a good treatment and feel quite ready for hockey which comes at 4:00 in half an hour. I got through treatment by 3:15 so went over to Wana[maker]'s and looked around. The hats all look like moulds for fancy cakes; many are entirely covered with feathers and some with fur. I didn't see anything that could compare with my hat. There were ravishing remnants of silk. Collars and stocks seem to be straight bands or else bands with

5. Mary Garrett, companion of Martha Carey Thomas, moved into the Deanery in 1904.

a long single tab. I was surprised to see that rather narrow stiff ribbon bows are being worn at the neck. There were a whole lot of straight collars and cuffs of heavy cotton or poplin with a few tight straight stitches in imitation of hardanger embroidery for .18 a set. They looked so clean and plain I believe I should have gotten a set if I'd had the money along and the resolution. I think I shall put my summer hat away now for I feel queer when no one else wears one. I got my critical paper this morning and found a merit on it. I am neither elated nor discouraged. Miss Donnelly spent the whole hour this morning talking about these papers and critical work in general. I never enjoyed an hour so much. Miss Donnelly said originality was necessary to successful work and that as it was undoubtedly a question of effort we should acquire it if we hadn't it. She said always begin enthusiastically and don't balance things disinterestedly. She said there were three kinds of criticism, that which pronounces judgement like Arnold's and Johnson's; that which analyzes impersonally; and the model, personal kind like Pater's. She said we must have personal adventures with the book or subject to be criticized. That the chief fault of our papers was lack of unity and that it was caused by a lack of definite opinion, that we stated things as they were presented by her and various writers on the [subject?] and hence had a mixture of points of view. She said we must pose the subject. As [Robert Louis] Stevenson says if you want to paint a portrait you don't run around and paint first on one side and then on another or have the model turn first one way and then another. She said we must consider the one who reads the paper too and write accordingly. We must have some gentle reader in mind (at present) with an understanding of the subject about like our own. When she said "*gentle* reader" there was a perfect shout. Some good papers and some bad ones were read. Once Miss Donnelly said, "Now I don't know what else to say about this except that it's quite silly (silli)." And many such charming remarks were made. She ended up by saying "After all this harsh criticism, the papers were unusually good." Imagine Miss Hoyt saying this.

Our next paper is "Our personal interest in the history of language and its present use."

Evening. For about an hour after dinner tonight 1906 sang to 1905 with a few songs and cheers from all the classes. 1906 sat on the floor and windowseat of the first big landing of the stairs here in East and 1905 stood above against the railing facing them. It was simply indescribable. All the Oral songs and supper songs and rush songs were given and one or two solos with choruses. Mary Withington made me a long visit afterward. We are going together to call on Miss Ransome. In the game this afternoon between the alumnae and the varsity, Janet Stores *1909*, Mrs. Andrews, and Gertrude Hill 1907 did fine work. I didn't go for when I found our team was to have no practising I hurried back to work. We have composed our cheer, songs and healths for the play. Won't it be exciting?

The composition of my letters is unutterable wretched but I see all the faults when they are written down and hope in this case you prefer quantity to quality.

To Mary Warner Moore and John Warner Moore

> *Pembroke East [Bryn Mawr College, Pa.]*   *December 11, 1906*

Dearest Family,

There have been many hiatuses in my trains of thought recently and I am 10 times sorry for some of them. The Johnstons couldn't come. Elsie telegraphed Thursday and a letter came Friday. I wrote to Elsie and thought so clearly how relieved you would be and revolved things in my own mind so completely I never realized till the letter came tonight how abstracted I'd been in not speaking of my great fortune.

Moreover I meant to mail a letter to Fawndale at 5:30 today and instead, stayed at Gym for 2 classes to make up. I wonder where I'll soon be at.

I do hope Henrietta will take the cape. She said her mother wrote immediately saying her mother was willing if her father was but pappá has not been heard from.

I am willing to have the visit postponed for Miss Kate's sake but I was perfectly mute when I first heard of such funny business.

I am not in 1907's show and am sorry (we cut out the thing I was in). But I may have some other chance.

I am overjoyed that you like my limerick. I've been afraid to give them such a slight thing. I added 2 lines and it now goes.

> *"O lovely beast, O beast" they cry*
> *"How red your tongue, how green your eye.*
> *We'll bring you flies, we'll bring you flowers*
> *If you don't bark in quiet hours."*
> *"I fear—, I fear you flatter me,*
> *Yet laudes, canta more," sighed he.*

It's a huge joke in college about 1907's

> Canta laudes, collegio
> Omnibus clarissimo.

All the odd classes loathe the song & words, and 1907 squeaks it out on all occasions. My drawing of the gator I enclose or rather, the first draught ("from life"). Margaret has been great to me and asked me to write a story for next *Tip*. I am more than mystified as she has one already. I have been wondering if it will be in the December number or if it has been cut out. I said I would try one, but I don't know whether I shall.

Before gym, I finished Gertrude's picture. It's about 6 × 5. The draw-ing and composition is pretty good but the paint looks hard. It's all in brown. I shall offer to give the thing to Gertrude & if she won't do that, I'll charge .50.

I'll go to town early on Saturday I think & get the white material and meet the Fish 10:23 at his train. If we miss each other, I'll go to the parcel checking place. We'll take the 12:15 for here and come to my room. I am glad to hear the coat's being fixed. My English work is encouraging on the whole. I am so much interested I have decided to do as much English as poss. His-tory is discouraging. We had 3 questions in our quiz. I got merit, passed & failed, that is, on the average passed. I think I worked too hard before hand. Dr. Andrews wrote at the end, Try to express yourself more clearly and ac-curately and so I hope I may get along better at Midyears. The Fish's letter was much enjoyed this morning and the mousie's tonight.

I find I have a letter addressed home with Elsie's enclosed which I forgot to send.

To Mary Warner Moore and John Warner Moore *January 17, 1907*

Dearest Family,

It is about two and the Fish's letter has come with the Mouse's. In re-gard to the two letters I spoke of one only enclosed the Mouse's. I hear my story has first place in the *Tip*. Isn't that exciting? I am thankful about these quizzes [being] over. I may go bobbing tomorrow. Gertrude [Congdon] has invited me. You get a horse and attach him to the sled and go round de country.

Mary read my characterization. She said, "My! You do notice things. You have her finely." Rather funny isn't it,—the whole thing?

Terry Helburn *Tip* editor asked me for something Tuesday. I gave her a weekly, "A Bit of Tapestry."

She said she liked the atmosphere but that the story didn't compose. She talked with me some time. I said it would break my heart to make it a love-story but I would. She has that one now and I don't know just what will happen.

All my first rubbish I have recovered. It was brought back before I asked for it. You see this pen doesn't work, either. Perhaps it will.

With dearest love,   Fangs

Don't you worry about me I'm rested.

I am very grateful for *The Merchant of Venice.*

To Mary Warner Moore and John Warner Moore

Jan[uary] 31, 1906 [1907]

Dearest Family,

I am much excited about getting home tomorrow. I still think myself extravagant to come but I think I "need a change." History goes up this afternoon. Uh!

Law was not bad this morning. We had lots and lots of time and the paper was funny beyond words.

For example, would it be assault if a woman crossed a field and seeing a fierce bull brandished her red parasol at him and he tore off sustaining a severe shock to the nerves after which the owner indignant seized the woman and precipitated her into a field? Also, if a man saw a girl across a two-mile gully and hurled a rock at her.

After Law I talked to Frances & Mildred and Frances Jackson and went for a skate. After skating I went to tell Marcet Haldeman I can't go to tea with her to the Muzzy's and Mary Nearing met me and I went in for a chat. Mary and Barbara Spofford made a snow woman who sits in an attitude of repose with her hands clasped round her knees. We criticized it, talked of our careers after leaving and of our Majors. Mary was peevish because she's dropping Economics which she took as elective and substituting French and she's written her course book wrong. Mary said she supposed I'd write when I got through college which pleased me though I said all my distempers were on account of writing. Mary said she thought I could play the author if I really tried. It's very discomforting to have her talk the way she does about doing things herself. She talks in such genuinely unaffected indifference I want to shake her.

Well to return [to] yesterday morning I did Italian in Denbigh [Hall]. Frances and Shirley looked all over college for me to get me to go to *Hamlet* (Forbes-Robertson).[6] Wasn't it a shame. Also Grace Hutchins came to get me to go bobbing. Worse luck. I could have gone bobbing in the morning and to *Hamlet* in the afternoon. Well in the afternoon I fooled with Ellen Thayer & Gertrude Hill and Margaret Blodgett in Gertrude's and Margaret's room. They explained to me a picture they have of 14 animals going along two by 2. Each animal represented a girl at their table Freshman year. Esther was the lion, 2 knowing looking hippos were Eunice & Ellen, the black and white ostrich was Margaret Morison and so on.

I then fooled in Susanne and Frances Lord's room with Frances Jackson and Emma Sweet and Emily Storer and the owners. Frances Jack and I then lay down in Frances' window seat and we read Rossetti and Stevenson's letters for a while when I retired to my den to do Torts. I found a note from

6. Sir Johnston Forbes-Robertson (1853–1937), a famous Shakespearean actor who frequently appeared in the United States as Hamlet, a favorite role.

Barbara to the effect that Mary and Alta and she would like to have me come to a supper party with them at 6:30. Mary and Alta had gone to *Hamlet* and came back laden with the food. Apples, canned peas, bread, chicken, butter etc. I *never* have had such fun. The food was great (and the grape-juice) and the company *just right*. Mary did *Hamlet* all over for us by way of illustrating her criticisms and she acts as well as Marjorie.

We told silly stories and Mary mourned that her family would now say "Mary what's happened?" as her Freshman sister has got H.C. in Psyche. and Mary has got only Credit. Mary's eye has been bothering her. The pupil is enlarged with cold and she spends almost all her time playing round. She gets good marks by magic it seems to me. She is very sensitive about what she calls "bothering" and I had to *force* her to stay over here one night. It reminds me of Mr. Rochester in *Jane Eyre* somehow. She was very funny last night so thoroughly energetic and yet using such an unhappy child drawl when asked about anything.

I am much amused at the Fish. I'm extremely glad he approves of Mary as she is so much to my taste but I really don't see what can be done.

I have my basket all packed and will send it this afternoon. The letter I'll wait to send till I can put in my History mark.

I am very anxious [to] know wherein the Mouse disapproves of me. I am very foolhardy and indifferent about the best way of doing, at times but I think I'll come out all right. I'll feel badly if you are really "down on me" but if you are just sorry that I'm apt for getting into pickles, I'll take heart. I *must* stop.

With dearest love,   Fangs

MERIT

Ah!!!!

don't use this sacred sheet

To Mary Warner Moore, John Warner Moore, and Mary Norcross
Feb[ruary] 14 [1907] ♥   *11 A.M.*

Dearest Bunny, Fish, and Beaver,

Things here are so-so. I have only *passed* Comp. (but so did Mary and May Putnam and Carlie Minor (all in my division and all sharks). I will have at most then, 7½ M's but I have enough with that.

My basket arrived yesterday and the things are beautiful, not at all mussed. The apples too, are great.

I'm sorry about this letter of the Fish's being delayed. I'll never forget another.

Isn't it amazing my figuration in the *Tip*? I was so surprised at the stray verses. People say the nice things they always say to "authors" but what I like is, that it's nice people that say them.

Louise Milligan whom I admire really more than Margie and like about as I like Ellen, said she liked this (my Robin Hood story) ever so much and quoted me passages, even. Ha!

I feel as if some questions had been asked me that I have forgotten to answer. On Monday I don't remember just what I was doing (Italian and gym for 2 things).

I have been doing Ital. today will do some this P.M. and go to Law.

Mildred Pressinger sent me a valentine and Mary Nearing. Mary's has a good ink picture of a minstrel, and this

> *Little love and lady fair,*
> *I would play thee a sweet air*
> *But my fingers are, I swear,*
> *Tangled all in red-gold hair*

> *I would write thee many a ream*
> *Of sonnets, but though strange it seem,*
> *Mine eyes are blinded by the gleam*
> *That from sun-kissed hair doth stream*

I wrote for her this following, the other day in division meeting, because she wouldn't play the violin or show me her literary efforts.

> *She played; and played divinely so they say.*
> *But as she played not every day*
> *She cannot play for me and you,*
> *She has "forgotten all she knew."*

I I

> *But now she draws; and draws quite well.*
> *She cannot mind because I tell*
> *She tears things up—but still I know*
> *Exactly how they used to go.*

(Mary destroyed all the pictures of Margie she'd done for me.)

I I I

> *And then she writes good verses too*
> *I wouldn't be like her, would you?*
> *I wouldn't be " " because—*
> *Because I wouldn't. Did I pause?*

IV

And when she grabs things from one's sight,
And will not play and do what's right,
She does it for one's good I find
She never means to be unkind.

Hers of course is a reply direct to the "writing" and "playing." I wrote her 2 valentines—one,

> *Before gaining my emission*
> *from this place of erudition*
> *I should like to write a Valentine to you.*
> *But I have an awful fear*
> *that you'd call it insincere*
> *And I've had to leave the matter—*
> *Leave it here.*

(She accused me of being insincere one day.)

The real one I wrote was an appreciation of Howard Pyle's [*The*] *Wonder Clock*[7] that Mary likes.

I

> *I passed the bedroom and her frock*
> *Depending from the closet-lock;*
> *I stirred the winking fire.*

II

> *The flames had gone from blue to red*
> *And Mary had strayed off to bed.*
> *The glow was dying down*

III

> *And falling cinders gave a clink*
> *As I began in crimson ink*
> *A Valentine to her*

IV

> *As I stood up to get a light*
> *(The firelight danced yet was not bright*
> *Despite the feeble coals),*
> *My paper floated to the grate*

7. Howard Pyle (1853–1911), illustrator and author of children's books.

> *I watched it—for I was too late*
> *I watched my rhymes blaze high.*

There's a dance Saturday (not dress up). I'm going to take Ellen and Mary is going to take Margie. I didn't want to take Margie. I can play round with her better if not "attached."

I wrote Ellen this valentine

> *"Lady, lady is it true*
> *That you love me as I love you*
> *No of course it isn't true*
> *But say it is, my lady, do"*

I sent none to Margie tho Mary did her a stunner; a pink and blue decorated one with a double lettered sonnet in ink.[8]

I am very grateful for the gold buttons and handkerchiefs and collar. To Frances I wrote this:

> *I tried to make a picture*
> *But it was a fearful mixture*
> *Of things bad.*
>
> *I tried to make a verse*
> *But it was infinitely worse*
> *And I had to throw that*
> *jingle quite away*
>
> *Love me Frances just this time*
> *And someday I will make a rhyme*
> *That will really say the nice*
> *things I can mean.*

To Mildred,

> *You will not be my Valentine*
> *Your heart is gone I fear*
> *But come take hands, I give you mine*
> *Let's ramble off from here*

> *With dearest love,*   Fangs

To Mary Warner Moore and John Warner Moore

February 19, 1906 [1907]

Dearest Family,

The Fawn's and the Fish's letter came this morning. It will be great to have the Beaver visit me. I can easily "sleep out." Cousin Annie's book ar-

8. MM imitated Mary's handwriting in large block letters down the side of the page.

rived last night and I've been perusing it. I find I am ostentatious and love cheap jewelry that Margie is artistic and direct about things that Mary has concentration and discernment and changing varieties of cleverness.

I am so sorry about the letter and the basket. As you know this really isn't my way of doing things.

I shan't be able to write stories much now as I need every minute to work. I'm bound I'll work up if I do *nothing* else.

Miss Fullerton said on my weekly "you have narrative and descriptive ability I think but you must pay more attention to the requirements." She also said I was "incoherent" and had no idea of how to manage situations. I try now to do the grind style of work and though it's not exciting it's worth while.

I worked the weekly over a little and gave it to Mary. Mary likes it but expects too much of me. As I am on your minds I may as well say that I've given up "writing" entirely. What I can adapt to *Tip* from English, I will but nothing else. I don't know why I am so possessed to write. I know it's not because of what nice things people say and it's not for the doing itself, for I *cannot* express myself.

I want to do St. Augustine and Monhegan and Canada and Switzerland and fairie stories and many things I haven't seen but will wait many days.

I shall go to dancing today. I try hard to learn it but am not very apt.

Margie was at gym yesterday and I talked to her a while. She borrowed a pin of me. Carlie Minor is one of the nicest, simplest highest-minded most humorous people I know and I shall visit her more.

The pictures at the acad. are great this year. There are Saint Gaudens and Rodin sculptures. I must go on Friday no matter what happens.

Louise Foley gave a tea last night for Margaret Ames. Marg. is a wonder and was really nice to me.

With dearest love, Fangs

I'm eager to know about my dress but know you haven't forgot it Bunny.

To Mary Warner Moore, John Warner Moore, and Mary Norcross
March 17, 1907

Dearest Mother, Fish and Beaver,

My little fountain pen, like the friar, is somewhat unsatisfactory but I make him work anyhow.

> The Poet
> *dug him a grave with*
> *AN EASTERbrook pen*
> *Jumped in,*

> *Said, "NOT Alright;*
> *John JUMP AGAIN."*

I've been reading *Treasure Island*—finished it yesterday. It is the very most enlivening, inspiring tale I've ever read. The feeling all through it is so nice and fresh. All the descriptions are so vigorous and Stevenson seems to be in his enthusiastic youthful attitude again. I'm more and more convinced that good writing depends on simple, sensitive depiction of the small things of life with an attitude on the part of the writer which never changes unless it changes unconsciously. All the sort of thing in *Treasure Island* is so much to my taste, the "shadows of the pines falling in patterns across the deck," the trees in shore, one being a "giant of a vegetable," and the wreck with its dripping webs of seaweed and all the water descriptions that I am eager to let the friendly world enjoy some of the Fish's and *my* childhood experiences. We ought to write a story about Kirkwood and the oaks and jays and the leaf-fires with the flames bursting out of the sulphur smoke.

It is sweet of you Mouse, to be making a guimpe.[9] I hardly think you ought.

3 P.M. I've just been out walking with Frances (B). She is "it" for me.

To Mary Warner Moore   *May 9 (7?), 1907*

Dearest Bunny,

I am so sorry about my wash. You had lots of trouble about it. I haven't sent it, and shan't till Thursday or Friday when English is over. My letter saying I would not, is probably lost. What can have happened [to] my letters? I think it's very, very strange for I know they have been addressed properly. English tomorrow, History a week from Thursday, Italian next Monday. I saw L.M.D. [Lucy Martin Donnelly] yesterday. She advises me not to major in Eng. if I want to be sure of my degree. She says I have ideas and often do nice work for her but that my work is uneven, and my papers are untidy, that I *might* fail and she would "hate awfully to have me fail." She says however that she should like to have me in her class. I am not going to take English therefore, but Law, History and Politics. It's too late in the day for Biology. I had an interview with Miss Fullerton this morning.

She hadn't one favorable comment on 4 weeklies and said not one of them "composed" or was just the thing asked for but she was very flattering in her solicitation not to underrate me papers and almost obsequious in asking what I meant, etc. She says she thinks narrative and descriptive would be good for me to take but she doesn't implore me to take it or promise me a merit this semester.

9. A short-sleeved shirt worn with a jumper.

Miss Donnelly was *very* friendly with me. Asked me about the Milton in my hand, remarked on the "charming Miltonian flower" (an anemone) that marked the place and talked about college work in general and the sonnet we are to write. She said, "you won't have any trouble about that. You write sonnets do you not?" I smiled, I trust not too diffusely and said I had tried versification of various sorts but found it difficult to produce things at definite times and with a serious end in view but that I enjoyed the effort. "It's good fun, is it not?" she said and as I bowed myself out, "Good luck to you."

Basket-ball games are the order of the day but it rained yesterday. Esther and Eunice and Bunny invited Frances & Mildred and me to tea in Esther's room. Her small brother (17) was there and the food was rich and various. Ellen and Gertrude Hill, and M. Blodgett, and Dorothy Forster were also present and at 5:15 about, Margr. and Anna came over from the tea-house and presented us with cake and chocolate.

Margaret had her hair in rather a new and mawkish style with a hair-ribbon but made up for it in the evening when 1907 sallied to the Dean's reception. I am no longer rated a bird of Margaret's, (from my haughty and independent walking in life, I suppose). People are pretty funny. I think it's much nicer for the "Doodle-Doo" herself (or the "Bryn Mawr Phoenix") to have people "funny" so I encourage them.[10]

I think I told in one of my letters of "the Bird News" edited by "The Bored" M. Blodgett.

Help!—Mad Anna (a calumny) set a thief to catch a thief James (Jeggy Pames) Francis Flunkmore (Passmore) and Lulie Foolie (Foley).

Of course the paper is very much an attack on Peggy James & Anna. It deals with all college crushes and comes out daily on the bulletin board.

I must stop & learn my 65 lls of Milton. I'm pretty scared.

                                                    L.L.L.   Fangs

I'll write when I send my basket.

To Mary Warner Moore and John Warner Moore

Oct[ober] 24 [1907]

Dearest Family,

I was cheered at dinner last night by the reading of a Fawn and a "fisshle" letter. (The mail sometimes comes at 6:30 instead of 7). I am much touched Mouse that you planned the story for me and of course I shall do it. I can hardly wait to. Between lectures I scratch, in the hope that every "little bit helps"—and I have written, what I like better than anything I have ever

10. The phoenix was the class of 1909's chosen insignia.

writ before, a thing called "The Nature of a Literary Man." Perhaps, "Pym." It expresses nothing but a series of individual impressions in "my latest style" and is crystal-clear. If it doesn't come out, I shall not know what to think. It is what James calls the record of "a generation of nervous moods" but has a satisfactory solution.

I shall send my wash home on Friday.

Peggy [James] is a "darling" pure and simple. I never have made the acquaintance of such a sweet child, in my life. I can never reconcile her fearfully intellectual appearance, and Vernon Whitford eyes with her perfect lack of artifice and experience. I went to Ruth Babcock's tea yesterday and had a nice time. And it's great to have Frances back. She came up last night and laughed at my pedantic books and the scatterment of papers and note books on the desk end of my couch. Speaking of Peggy, a bit of very characteristic diction on her part is "are you feeling all right today, honestly? Well if you don't go to bed, I shall come and put you to bed."

4:30—

Mary Worthington was not well today and cut laboratory. She asked me to tell Miss R[ansome]. I did some of her work and went to tell her about it afterward. Peggy came in from Psychology all frosty with excitement. "I am the biggest *goat*," she said "that ever was. I promised Dr. Feree to do original research work in psychology and he says we will report and have our reports printed with our names at the end. *Hee!* I can't do *any*thing in Science," Peggy explained to me "but he thinks I can on account of my Dad."

Well—good by— Fangs

I go to hockey—

To Mary Warner Moore and John Warner Moore

January 12, 1907 [1908]

Dearest family,

I got my letter yesterday and after reading it, placed it reflectively in the envelope and began work.

I will answer the Fish first and then deal with the old man himself (Fangs). Martha and Louise have been away since Friday so I haven't had a proper chance to talk to them. Martha has a coy rather deferential manner however when she talks to me which makes me sure she was in no way vexed or "turned away" by our recent advances.[11]

Yesterday morning in town (I went on the 8:30) I exchanged the

11. JWM had some romantic interest in Martha, and MM encouraged the friendship.

favrile pitcher after a harangue and making of the fur fly. They had not heard from any "*Miss Norcross.*"

I then looked round for hats and got a blue one at Stetson's for $9. reduced from I don't know what. The girl couldn't find out. It is perhaps large and too much in style but Peggy insists that it is "*very* simple" and very becoming. It curves up slightly in front and turns down slightly in the back after the present fashion. Has ribbon (beautiful ribbon) coming up over the front and tying and going back and two blue wings which slant back close to the crown and just reach the edge of the brim at the back. The felt is beautiful and the shape of the hat good in the untrimmed hat. (Mine is bound with blue velvet.)

I also got a pair of heavy gloves (1.25) and had my treatment. From 2 to half past I spent "settling" Marcet [Haldeman] who had been hauled to the Doctor's to see about her eyes and was mad and tired. I then went to the library and set myself down by Frances Browne. I spent an hour talking to Tink [Cornelia] Meigs who is a sub librarian, (about Marcet) then worked till 6. All evening I worked—at the library. I have given Peggy up on the principle that, let them alone and they'll come home bringing their tails behind them. Plattie [Anna Platt?] tells a tale of [a] little guide's son in the Adirondacks who scolded a squirrel vociferously for stealing his father's corn and then when the squirrel darted away, said, "Good-by, tail."

Well as I was saying, me feelings are hurt, as Marcet said (for my sake, of course) "Peggy took her tongue off the wax (in lab.) and said *specially*, to me, 'Marianna is *spoiled.* Everyone tells her she's different from everyone else and though I like the way she dresses, she *knows* she dresses well.' She then shut up and went on working. You won't like it, but I thought I ought to tell you"—concluded Marcet. Of course I am not pleased for whatever I may be, I am not vain—and if Peg doesn't see that, I can't hope to please her or depend on her for a just easy judgement on me. It makes me think that when she is talking to me she is thinking of things behind what she says.

I met her though, going to the Library last night and we walked round the campus at her suggestion for 15 or 20 minutes and then went in and worked till 10 and had the most jovial of times jesting anon and behaving in high feather despite the fact of its being the week before exams. Peggy was curious I guess about Marcet's "fall-out" and asked me about her and then went on a rampage saying how erratic Marcet was and volatile and how hard a master she was in lab. They work, the two of them alone together.

I said Marcet was sort of stirred up, that she had been lecturing me on my conduct etc. though her difficulty was not with me, that she wasn't mad at me at all. (Peg had asked if she were.) Peg said "Oh? Marcet has a great admiration for you really."

"Has she?" said I "well I guess her words of advice are then for my good."

"Well she's been worried about you," said Peggy. "She told me the other day to look after you. She thinks I'm a *beau*, but I don't care."

"Oh no she doesn't" said I. "No she doesn't."

I guess I can regain Peggy's regard, in time. But at present she feels much removed and "disappointed" in me. Marcet said, "I don't wonder Peggy is disappointed in you. She is too young not to be. For your looks *do* lead people to expect a lot of you." I think it's cruel, don't you? But what are "*affaires de coeur*" anyhow if we can't be real and in earnest.

I have been having a *very* nice time though. Frances is back in my "fold" again which is of course satisfactory. I am perfectly open with her about Peggy. I say, I like Peg., and like her as a friend but that I have bothered too much about catering to her likes and fancies and I shall let her be friends now if she wants to be or if she is old enough to forgive me things. Frances called me an old upper-classman but, very evidently stands quite in awe of my opinion and says I *am* no fool, that's certain—(which is a comfort sure!).

The history reading is fascinating and I am having a better and better time, tho having "aged" methinks in [a] fortnight.

I have two good stories in mind but shall save them of course. ~~It is queer that I get excited about one every once and a while no matter how weary I am of the business.~~ It is really pleasant not to get all disgusted with things and have them as castor-oil in the memory.

This morning I went to Friends meeting—and took up on the way and there, with Ruth George and Louise Milligan. Mr. Rufus Jones spoke on, "If ye leave father and mother and brother and sister for my sake" ye lose nothing. This afternoon I began this letter, then paid with Louise Hyman, a short visit on Mrs. Williamson and her Mother. Then I dawdled, talked to Hono and Frances and looked ruefully at the slim pile of *Tip* material awaiting Martha from me then went to supper.

After breakfast I played round with Plattie and she showed me some beautiful photographs and loaned me one of a dark eyed Sicilian boy, an artist's model—and Judith [and] I talked some too.

Mary Worthington leads evening meeting tonight so I must go.

I found in my room yesterday when I came from town, underclothes from Strawbridges which I have "disposed of."

10 P.M. Evening meeting was fairish. It was on Progress and women— explained that we would have to have ideals before men would call us progressive and more than house-cats. I don't see the application to a religious meeting. I said, "we are provoked with people for calling us unprogressive when often we fall short ourselves & fail in realizing our *individual* ideals and just stop—comfortable—inventing all manner of excuses for our faint-heartedness and laziness."

Afterward at 8, I met Peg and Mary and Dorothy Nearing coming into East. I held the door for them and then walked on upstairs.

"Oh don't you want to hear some music?" called Peggy. "Yes I'd love to," said I. All the music rooms were occupied and we went into one to ask if it would be used long. Annie Jones 1910 was in there and she played all evening for us, *wonderfully* and whistled accompanying herself. She is very Western but friendly and kind and I like her more than I can say.

With dearest love,/Good night—   Fangs

I am much pleased about Prof. Baldwin.

I forgot to look for reduced underwear and to go to Hoskin's but I can do that after Exams.

To Mary Warner Moore, John Warner Moore, and Mary Norcross

Jan[uary] 13 [18?]—1908

Dear Mousie and Fish and Beaver,

I got "the epistle" today and the Mouse's special. I have been *awful busy* but very happy (perhaps for that reason). History certainly is *great*. I am doing Napoleon now—Frederick the great yesterday and Voltaire and Rousseau and Montesquieu.

Thank you Mouse for Mrs. Clarke's letter and Emily's. Emily is sitting up in bed and very jolly and is writing letters herself. She is really not badly off—so I hesitate Mouse to write her a "condolence." Besides, I don't know her nearly well enough to know how comfortable she would be as to an invitation from me to visit. I know you have no faith in my standards of knowing people well—but I don't think I had best ask her, yet. But I appreciate Mouse your taking time for the thought and letter.

I shall live up to the best in myself as best I can, and I will not be "imperious, defiant, exacting, gloomy, savage, self-absorbed, distrustful, and solitary," like Nap.[Napoleon]—as a result, I feel sure my forbearance with Marcet's recent spasms and volatility in the midst of her distresses has helped me to a slight feeling of ascension and if I can only proceed, (without a view to glory) in philanthropy, I will soon be on my feet.

Peggy is perfectly charming, scintillating, quiet, witty and responsive, as ever and if I am patient and rid my actions of all view to effect, I shall be all right if I am as nice [as] I ought to be, with the training and family I have. I am very brief and affectionate in all my words, to the capriciously young animal (I was going to say stag!) (I am so puzzled I almost put quotations for brackets—) and am satisfied.

Tip. material is in but I owe 300 words. Carlie gave me a beautiful sketch of a Roman father and son over the remains of a banquet—the former gives the latter a poisoned cup, "and smiled for he knew a traitor was dead." (*Tip.* is not yet out for December.) I have read the proof of my story through and am scared for you to see it. It will shock you—it is so abandoned. I don't see how Terry and Martha let it go in, or could call it effective. It is so full of italicized words and suggested obsecrations—and raggednesses. I have some very "pleasant" freshmen acquaintances—girls I never would try to get to know but who cause me [to] smile to myself when I have been talking to them.

I read till 4 today—then went to 1910 dancing—then to the Hall tea—and then Tink came to see me—after dinner I studied with F. Browne & Hono in the Library, then came home and am now en route to bed. It gets late so fast and I vow I will rise at 6:30 all week. My quiz is *this* Friday. I am happy in the possession of a broadbent calendar and my course-book!

I said to Martha at dinner that I had heard from the Fish and he had had a good time here and thought it *very* good of her to come and talk to him with me.

She said, rather accusing and rather indulgently "You *know* I enjoyed it Mariana." I turned it off "beautifully" (!) by saying well Martha you know that discussion we had with Margaret Bailey last year about "families" and how little "interested we were in them and how scared we were of them" etc. "Oh but that doesn't apply to brothers" Martha said. "Brothers are great fun to talk to." "Well" I said "you never can tell what they are going to say and you feel sometimes like asking to have something repeated and then you think you might not understand much better if it *were* repeated and so on." "Oh no, that's nice" Martha concluded.

Personally, I like all the Fish said but I was vexed that he kept harping on Mathematics and admitted so reluctantly that he took English and Philos. They are Martha's specialties so she could take more interest in someone who was working in them. We *did* though say something on them I believe.

It is 11!

With dearest love,   Fangs

Everyone likes me hat and I am in high "feather."

To Marcet Haldeman   *January 26, 1907 [1908]*

Dear Marcet,

If you knew with what a bound I seized on your letter and devoured it you would smile. I wish you had not had to say "last subtlety."[12] I feel like a cork on the water that is bobbing about, and of no earthly use when I am being depended on by no one, for anything.

12. MH had written to MM on January 23, 1908: "This last bit of subtlety would be the last favor."

MM, c. 1909, Bryn Mawr College

John Warner Moore, 1904–5,
Yale University

MM, Bryn Mawr graduation, 1909

Let me favour you with a personal—(given me once {and composed for me} when I never knew what was the matter and used to grump round like a sick bear).

> *"Did you say the heavens frown?*
> *Surely they are falling down;*
> *For I heard them just now split,*
> *Where the forkéd lightning hit*
> *Never such a roaring wind*
> *Since wild Aeolus went blind*
> *Stone walls crashing round my head*
> *Clinging ivies black and dead*
> *Trees rock madly, and uproot*
> *The rotten earth and at my foot*
> *A star falls down and burns my toes*
> *Thank heaven it only grazed my nose."*

I shall come out with things in plain terms sometime but this inscrutable mad dash at an interpretation of my feelings is what fits the present moment.

To return to the subtlety, all is O.K.—"my 'allies' read with me and smile."

I have lost my heart to Frances Stewart and call her my lady-love. She really has more character and more soul and more sympathy than anyone I ever knew.

Just at present I am a prey to the ills of the flesh and to contending factions of despair, but I keep things to myself. My work is not up to the scratch—that is, I get all over the ground and then want to jump overboard and exclaim, "the fates refuse to favour." And in addition to perfectly reasonable ailments, I suffer with a bad tooth and a cough and so on and people scowl when I bestow upon them the radiating influence of a smile but like Prosper le Gai, I bide my time.[13]

You must read my story. Martha [Plaisted] and Louise [Foley] both said they thought it was "evolved" successfully—which made me in my late valentine's phraseology, "very happy."

I shall love college madly, after midyears, never fear, when I am not dying with fatigue and the cursed unrest which accompanies an outward calm.

Your letter gave me quite a brace.

As to my friends that don't like me I have quite a comfortable feeling for I am unconstitutionally unselfassertive,—and "nice" to them.

I have been reading the old ballads in *Ivanhoe* and *Robin Hood* and

13. Prosper le Gai is the central character in Isoult Pietosa de Bréauté's, *The Forest Lovers* (1898).

they are sweet. I intend to try a good gay-landlord story when I feel more up to it.

College is packed with refreshing medium brilliant people, like Cad (Helen Cadbury) and Kate Ecob and May Putnam, and I like them but I can't be bothered with the cultivation experiment till after midyears. (If I can't eat cake I enjoy a fast for a time, especially as it aids the cause, exams.)

with my best, "*yours* truly," Marianne

P.S. My attitude *has* been perfectly rotten. I have always thought that my nose turned up too much and that my hair sagged in a horrible way and so on, and I do now. But as far as attitude goes, I have been what the spirits of the air say I have, a nice enough ordinary mortal but with a twisted exalted idea of "his" own insight and sympathetic ways—and unique attitude— which disgusts the child who "tries in vain to understand." And I am fearfully subdued, accordingly. I begin to be grateful to my preceptors in an objective way which seems pretty queer to me, all things considered.

As looks go I am a fearful sight just now with a sort of convict-on-an-ash-heap air to me but in vacation I shall sew, on my new lavender low-necked dress, the "rich, old lace" which my mother gave me to put on it, and when the new term begins I shall sing in chapel with the most lusty.

(I prithee bear with me. A sheet of unwrit paper is too much for me. Heaven knows it is not a sense of obligation that reduces me to staggers anon at "the short story," and introspective inflictions upon those psychologically {and "feelingly"}, inclined.)

M.C.M.

To Marcet Haldeman   *February 9, 1908*

Dear Marcet,

I fear this is not a legitimate "favour" for me to be asking,—but please do write to me sometime, if it's all right for you to.

The amount of plain simple, monotonous living one has to do, in travelling the highroad to fortune, is revolting.

I try jollying people up, and reading things I like, and working like a dog for a while and then there's a sticking point—what *is* the use? If I ever find out, I shall feel that I have attained Heaven.

Marianne

I have no more intention of "committing suicide" than I have of flying— as I have a kindergarten habit of saying—but I do feel the starch of life getting weak occasionally. I often think I have such a terrific grasp of things that everything looks small—a great part of the time in fact; then accompanied by thunder and lightning I find myself an idiot with such a worm-like point of view and *so* little spunk——(when people make themselves salt in a wound——unconsciously of course) that I fairly curse the day I was born.

It's fearful of me to write you such a violent "disassociated" lot of rant but you will condone it. I know you will.

Marianne

P.S. You *will* be disappointed in me for my godless point of view after all we've said and after all my vaunted faith in my ability to carry things through to the bitter end. I vow I will come out on top sometime. But I cannot pretend every minute of the time that I know how it feels to be doing it. Consciousness of any kind gets to the point where it is absolutely unbearable.

Do tell me about the kind of country around you and if you sew any and, all what you're doing. I refuse absolutely to speak to anyone on any subject pertaining to myself——except you——so have no fears for the "innocent."

Have a story coming out next month (!)

To Marcet Haldeman *February 11, 1908*

Marcet! my dear fairy,[14]

If you only knew! If you only knew! I was sitting on my couch, in my stick-candy dress, my coat on, my eyes *glued* to the 146th page Scribner's edition of the *Tragic Comedians*——when there was a gentle knock at my door.

Come *in?* I called. Hilda Sprague-Smith——to get me to take a walk. Ill-tempered, my brain a furnace, everything quivering about me, and never in all my life, feeling less gregarious, I was up against it. I shook my head and chewed a smile. Finally I said peevishly, "Oh I don't *want* to go, Hilda." Lacy then brought me a letter at which I sprang, (yours). I cut it open with my book mark, then waited——for Hilda to go——my glance hanging stupid and glittery——anywhere you care to have it. Finally I sprang up, with my hand to my descending rubric hair——and said, "Come! I'll walk round the campus, (*once*)." I could run my dearest friend through the body if she had as little sense and curiosity regarding letters as some *people*. After this lengthy

14. This address is connected to that in another letter ("Dear Marcet, behind the casement"), both perhaps playful allusions to Keats's "Ode to a Nightingale," in which "magic casements" open in "faery lands forlorn." Later in this letter, MM alludes to Keats's "Endymion" and to Shakespeare's *Romeo and Juliet* (a production of which was under way at Bryn Mawr) and *The Two Gentlemen of Verona* (the song "Who Is Silvia?").

introductory *entwicklung*—I can say that I have just read your letter. I should like to see anyone approach you—. *By Eros!*

Don't you think I manifest vigour? for a raving poet in a decline, with nothing in his mind but an image stamped there of Avernus, rivals and enemies strewn about indiscriminately—crying *"Parce, parce"*—as he comes to join them. Well. Life is Heaven and Hell and hurricane and halcyon "wind," all in one. I have "encysted" myself as far as the general world goes. I fairly sparkle inside now and then, to think how real is the world of fancy, (when people sit like dolts, about, taking your words for their evenly milled face value).

Je-rusalem "tinges of mist" and "faint color" are not in it with the future.

You are responsible for this—and my ever dear *dear* George Meredith. I have thought of you all along in reading him. They say of me, you know, or did in the old days of *stupid* unapproachable, *capable* Margarets,

> *one I love two I love*
> *three I love I say etc.*

Well—when I read vigorous George with his heavenly passion, I could stake my most valuable and durable "heart" on getting one draught more of joy out of life. He gives you such a boundless lot of faith in life in the worthwhile-ness of life and your power to cut stars out of paper, all alone, anytime you just *feel* "starry." I am sorry you have to think upon my Sunday's broken growl of anguish. I don't mind your knowing that I slip into a black frenzy occasionally but I insult your understanding by *retailing* you the mess of it, and not taking for granted that I have your sympathy unconsciously whether or not I say I need it and why.

Frances is sweet *sweet*. Now and then "understanding" seems to me, the whole thing—it is bound to. I then look at her—caressingly and wander away with myself to the imaginary owls that reside in each man's imaginary forest.

Last evening from half-past 5 to half-past six, we strolled about the campus, getting me the *Tragic Comedians* in Denbigh—cursed barren place—and ending in the Library. We went up silently as thieves, into the Deanery Tower and stood on the roof and watched the sunset—most *marvellous*—and Frances wondered "if you ever *do* find out what you want when you see a thing like that." I could have kissed her. And then we came home.

Silvia—where is Silvia? in all this. At the bottom of it I fear. She will not do. She cannot reach. I feel like molten lead inside once and a while. It's terrible to the place where you feel. Sampson! wake up. You stand trying to conjure up for yourself a phantom Delilah. Dig your poor sensitive mortal's foot into the earth and *run* with yourself till you are a *man*. You hate to see what is ideality and sympathy and aestheticism and the rest of it, shrink and shrink and shrink, and fade and twist and vanish—while you strain your eyes to the point of blindness and then you stammer with a blink. "I must be dreaming." (But man alive, dreams are vivid, as you know.)

I really don't know myself—but shall with the help of Heaven be getting on with myself famously in a short time. It is beyond my comprehension how I am willing to believe that you take an interest in this venomous introspection and can do it without feeling depressed or without irritably dispatching me a *dart*. But that is another story—of course.

I've never seen the world—the actual—with so little touch of illusion about it. The *upper* air though is divine.

Peggy [James]—to return, is *comme usual.* I get nervous as a horse though when [I] get to touching certain parts of her. I don't believe she has "understanding" or the shadow of it. Alas some deficiencies do not however keep one from being a Circe, if the instinct to please, and a gentle, feeling aspect and a mind over which passions show color as they run, are present. I hate to make Peggy an *objet d'art* and it is her fault that I do—but if she *can*not acknowledge me a man without giving me a black, she *can*not.

I never condescend to feel sorry for myself. It's not sporting—(and Heavens! what*ever* I am I *must* be a sport). She (M.M.J.) led evening meeting, Sunday, on contentment—said women were said to suffer from a subtle discontent which men did not—was all wrong. We could train ourselves. I went to see her afterward or rather she invited me. I was not set on fire by our philosophical disquisition however. Yesterday she—the same—came over and said as "Mary" had a cold and was in bed and was not game for the Walkuere [Valkyrie] (tonight)—she thought she would not go either if I didn't think it was "squealing." I was like Meredith's damsel, "cool and clear-headed (so long as she did not put her ear to my heart").[15] I rose and with the heaviest scented formality I have ever used, and a twitching rather fond smile, said "*No*. I do *not*—think you will be 'squealing.' I think it is nice... for you [to] stay. And if there is anything Mary has which you are unable to provide her with—I'd like to get it for her—if I can." My subdued tones provoked no violent "hissing" down the corridor—and here, like the artist, "I forget."[16]

I *must* stop. But am though inane like Bunyan's Fair Countenance, Pliable etc. as ever.[17]

Yours with love,   Marianne

15. George Meredith, *The Egoist.*

16. Robert Browning, "Memorabilia."

17. John Bunyan, *The Pilgrim's Progress.* A foil to Obstinate, Pliable says, "Don't revile; if what the good Christian says is true, the things he looks after are better than ours; my heart inclines to go with my neighbor." He later steps out of the Slough of Despond and returns home, refusing the struggle.

To Marcet Haldeman   *February 28, 1908*

Dear Marcet,

The pressure upon you is constant and I do not wonder that you come to ask yourself if dreams good and bad are not the whole stuff hope is made of. I know the feeling—the patient-impatience the vague sense of mocking disgust, the whole thing. There is nothing fundamental, the matter with aspiration; a man has to have at least one silver hope to hang by, to live. It is a superstitious hatred of failing in the trivial that tends to hurt one's underlying mettle. IT *does not do.* Self-possession and a spirit of forgiveness are the things to hold to, if you want *really*, to be master of your fate. By self-possession, I mean courage and patience. By the other, a real Christ-like desire to aid, tolerate and endure,—without any desire to dazzle. It is weakness, to want to "do it in a day" or to want to *show* poor jesting Pilate the enormousness and hideousness of his folly. I am considering here the problem of satisfying your highest *individual* desire—not taking into account the glory incidentally accruing. Do tell me when you feel inclined, just how heavy the prospect does appear to you. You will never be dragging me into a net; (for a good deal of balance and varied insight, I think I should be allowed to be depended upon—though tremendous initiative and the great, sudden thought, the genius to help I know well that I lack).

I don't wonder you throw down your hat in vengeful impatience when I begin to talk about Peggy. She is *nothing* to me. She has been nearest to what I like most though of anything that I have yet come upon and with a little idealization can attain proportions of some magnitude—that is the history of the whole business. She is like the sparkle on a wave, that out of the most favorable environment, washes up and down placid and incapable of exciting emotion. When you feel that you can define a person's charm you feel that you are capable of providing an environment which will preserve it. This leaves out [of] account however the fundamental facts of practical, selective, year-in-year-out, inter association—the which I am beginning to learn as I grow older.

Peggy is a child brought up on the hearth-rug of a king, used to seeing kindness done, full of theoretic philanthropy lacking however in constant progressive self-sacrificing philosophy—shrinking—in contact—from the touch of the very beggar whom in the goodness of her heart, she goes out and puts her arm about.

I do not exaggerate the importance of ideals smashed early, in life, enough, to be bitter. It does not do to make sorrows of trivialities. A passionate irritable person of my variety however tends to breathe fire and scrape sparks from the ground, from the mere excess of animal spirits, from a little waywardness of vitality.

They build very decorative fires in the library now-a-days and all moves cheerily. "Just wish though, I knew" where I was coming out. "Ruling spirits" is [a] tough accusation.

There was a mass meeting last night to rouse enthusiasm for the building over of the gym. There is a debate tonight on income-tax (ruler-class). Such are the passing shows of the hour.

"Is it that you want to write or is it that you have something to say?" I came on in *The Atlantic* yesterday. I have come to the conclusion—that I "want to write" but that shortly I *will* have something to say. My "style" is execrable. I slave, and then talk a page of rot to every half-line of sense, but the thing is too much a solace, a fascination, a weapon-to-wield "etc.," to crush into invisibility.

I've just come from lab, and am in the library meditating to the crackling of the fire but am so tired the pleasure of the task and the congeniality of the warm lonely atmosphere are insufficient to keep the pen from stumbling. I should not have adequately stated my ideas however if I had been talking so "vanity let it be."

Think I am going to go to bed early for a few nights and have my pictures taken some day—am I *not* hard up for diversion?

With love,   Marianne

To Marcet Haldeman   *March 15, 1908*

Dear Marcet,

Your letter revived me with a start from a rather subdued state of mental examination.[18] I have lived on a shifting sea sprinkled as it were with Oscar Wilde's mixture of joy and sorrow. I am now going in with a vengeance for the real thing. A trifle hard, I sometimes feel I am,—but so determined am I that someday, I will achieve an all-embracing paternalism that on the whole I find myself at peace with life.

One comes daily in contact with so much that is dashing and at the same time invigorating and inspiring that the whole thing, life heaven and everything seems a play with summer lightning.

I experienced great joy in your off-hand praise of my "turn of the phrase." In fact I could think of nothing but your words, for some minutes. I shall send you my story "The Boy and the Churl" though I feel no excitement about stories done. [They] are like trees which you paused to gaze at and admired extravagantly, but which have grown dead, characterless and uninteresting as you look back on them. I don't seem able to get anything out, which feels like *me*. You asked me about my letters. My letters are bet-

18. MH had written to MM encouraging her flights of fancy but warning her to distinguish these from "life."

ter than my stories I suppose because I am not self-conscious. Because I am thinking of *"you"* (whoever you are). In my stories I can't get the artistic point of view. I think "how supercilious that sounds." "Mother will think I'm going to the bad." "Warner will think I am sentimental getting 'soft'." "Peggy will think that pretentious." "If I say that, Martha [Plaisted] will think me undeveloped, crude——" etc. I fear to handle, red-hot stuff—you see—and hesitation in literatics is ruin.

The mandolin club played for dancing in the Gym, last night. It was really a heartsome frolic. I danced with Georgina [Biddle]—to whom I am really quite attached—and Frances Browne and Ruth Babcock and "Hilda" [Spraguesnulty] and Henrietta Riggs and "Peggy" and others. Peggy sleeps sweetly in her "cradle." I should like to make her happy by being more than negative—speaking in a whisper flatters the sleeper too much—without doing the same, a service. But such is the necessity of the case.

Peggy still seems to cherish a grievance—(and to be taken as one would *not*, is rather hard on a haughty self-righteous snob like your friend) but "loving Pilate" is taking root. Self-preservation is not the end and aim of life anyhow. In Peggy's case I have "hit the nail on the point instead of on the head" but one may be lightly chastened without being killed. I care for Peggy, "like all wild Wales" and don't pretend to *scorn* her. (I am sure you understand.) But all in a particular way. I have *learned* that the child on the hearth is not the hero, leaning on his sword. Do some children ever *get* to be heroes? Some do not and only fools desire them to—"and there you are." Uncle Henry [James] is nice in *his* way too. (His way a bit limited methinks, like the flushing and interpositional M. Margaret's.)

I sputter like a roasting "crab." *Pardonnez*-moi. I've read this over. I don't ring true. In the matter of Peggy I sound annoyed and martyrish. I am *not* though. *"By Justice."*

To Mary Warner Moore, John Warner Moore, and Mary Norcross
March 29, 1908   Sabbath 4 P.M.

Dear Mousie, and Family,

I was much shocked to hear of Uncle Watson's[19] death. I hope the Mouse was not called on for more helping than she can stand—that sounds unsympathetic—I'm afraid.

I got the Mouse's card and the Fish's letter with the Beaver's. (I don't know anything *about* pigeons.)

In town I went to Tyndale's and got the basket. It was only $2. dollars instead of 4. Also tickets for *A Doll's House*. [Alla] Nazimova is the wonderful Russian actress so much talked of, to be here some time. They say she is

19. John Watson Craig, MWM's uncle.

the best modern. Margaret Franklin suggested it and as it is a matinee and Ibsen, I thought it a good thing to do—tickets $.75 cents (family circle).

Friday afternoon was the gym. contest. In the morning Miss Sissen searched me out and told me to come down at 11 and she would help me practise up, to be in it, in Mary Rand's place. I had never been to dancing, Fridays, so had never tried one dance, the Maid of the Mist. It had been my ambition to acquire it, on seeing it suddenly for the first time last Tuesday so I was tickled to death. It was acquired (with some difficulty) from 11 to 12 and in the afternoon, I "performed"—with the others. I was scared, but all went well. Frances Stewart shook me by the hand on achieving it which I vastly appreciated. She is about the most thoughtful, and quietly thoughtful person I have ever known I think. My hair began to fall out a while ago and she gave me some tonic she has and sent home for another bottle—and has sundry times furnished me with pills, and recently with a very efficacious ointment (I got poison ivy on my cheek and neck {*slightly*}) and so on.

Miss Reilley and Miss Parris and Esther Williams (back on a visit) and Jack [Frances Jackson] and the judge sat on the platform—other guests above round the gallery. Georgina won the fencing foil to my delight.

The dancing is really as pretty as anything one often sees I think. I wish you could see it—I'll see what I can do when I get home.

Louise Foley has been over in the village for a week in a nice house utilized by the college as a rest-cure. I went to see her this morning. She read me some poetry she had written—we decided that people simple and cordial surpassed all with pretentions to subtlety and mystery. Louise said, "I am getting old. I don't like people that hold you off at a distance, any more." I think that's a good deal the way I feel, myself.

There also took place a hockey show Friday by 1909 and 1911 to 1908 and 10 in the gym in an alcove beyond the swimming pool. It was a combination of *Lohengrin* and *Siegfried*. The subject the new gym-fund. The Rhine maidens wore bathing suits and green bathing tails—Lohengrin, Frances Browne, wore a gorgeous [costume] made up of green with a white scarf and a white winged helmet. The raft approached slowly (towed by a rope) with him on it and he sprang to the bank. It was Really most realistic—saying, I swan I thought I'd never get here—way down upon the Swanee river. Elsa dear, I *am* afraid to *go* into the brine, with accidents occurring every day upon the Rhine—and so on. The Seniors now sing outside. I thoroughly enjoy it. Louise begged me to stay with her this morning and I didn't get back till twelve. Tonight, I am going to the Musseys' for Supper. Mary Waller invited me. They give a special girl, that is, permission to invite two or three others. I seem to stand high in Mary's favour for some reason. Why the simple and childish invariably make hits with the clever, when their endeavor receives cold response from the "easy" is a mystery—a situational curiosity—which has for many years off and on interested me. My high wave just at present is, I well know, due to a determination to be *slow*, on my part, which makes a phrase now and then come home, to the unprejudiced hearer—the whole idea of Mary's regard rather entertains me. She calls me Meredithian, says I have his (Meredith's) wit and insight, entertain one, size things up in a phrase and so on. I accept the flattery gratefully as it is the pleasantest a "litterateur" could have and more to my taste than any I am ever like to have (in days less golden than the present—) and inwardly "Shrug my shoulders, shake my head, cast up my eyes, but say nothing."

It is very nice having Esther back. She is Greek as ever, in appearance, and "clean-looking" to a degree unrivalled by the present generation. I don't take to her though. She is hard to get on with—not fluent or what is behind fluency with most of *us*, (here at college) sympathetic. But *Peggy* has my respect forever. She has done what I did not *think* she would, (hauled Esther up to see Henrietta Sharp). She is also going to have tea for them (both). She has the courage of her convictions. I like it in her very much as I say for she is undetermined, in most things—and does what comes to her with the strongest call, at the moment—and studies in the romantic adventures are not in her line just now—(sympathetic as Miss Donnelly would say). She is given over altogether to delving and realism.

On Saturday I glanced at the new academy exhibit. I liked a Childe Hassam, *Newport Cat-boats*, a [Pascal Adolphe Jean] Dagnan-Bouveret, *Swedish Peasant Boy*, [John H.] Twachtman, *Sailing in the Mist*, Joseph De Camp (a friend of Frances Stewart's), *The little hotel*—a Tarbell of a woman in white—and various others.

I've been out walking (alone)! from two-o'clock on in the rain. It was great.

I haven't been able to get Sir Gibbie [Charles Gibbons] yet.

With dearest love,   Fangs

What am I to do about a hat—for spring?

10 P.M. I have just come from the Musseys'. They are wonderful. I am keen on "socialistic" agitation though.

We got supper (and cleared it away). I went out to the kitchen for Mrs. Mussey in the course of the meal, and Dr. Mussey was there getting something. He said, "I'm glad I've met you Miss Moore, I've been wanting to say helloa to you for two years"—which pleased me, as I like him.

I said, "I—have felt much the same way Dr. Mussey. I thought I should make your acquaintance in college but—"

"I got away too quick—didn't I?"—he finished.

I need my clean clothes. I don't like to seem anxious as I know they are sent as soon as soonest, but I can do without stockings. I am sorry I don't seem able to keep them mended. They seem to go right to pieces though—I think they must be inferior stuff.

w. love,   Fangs

My letters certainly are foolish.

To Mary Warner Moore and John Warner Moore   *April 2, 1908*

Dear Family,

Poor Mouse, with Carola, an unswept house, mending clothes, school and the rest of it.[20]

I shall be leaving the 15th. Ha! I wish you could have heard [Antonio] Scotti yesterday.[21] Scotti, [Emma] Eames, and [Enrico] Caruso all sang, Scotti being villain, the other two hero and heroine. Scotti and [Alois] Burgstaler have the most natural voices and most natural satisfactory manner of any singers I have ever heard. Burgstaler was of course a different kind of character. But both have the same dignified dramatic conception and the same spontaneity. The scene (the first) was a church—Scotti strode meditatively about all in black, white wig, black cape and so on, his sword pushing his cloak out stiffly occasionally; diamond watch chain lorgnette affairs on his waist coat.

Ladies, escorted, came in, in rose pink yellow, and green the embodiment of picturesqueness. A procession passed, (outside apparently) with men at arms in red-and-yellow costumes curiously mosaiced in Italian fashion and then the cardinal, or Pope (?) under a canopy with a yellow mitred hat, followed by two men with torches; he stopped—there was a subdued sustained burst of as magnificent singing as I have ever heard—and he passed on. Seeing it "hearing it," as they say, alone was great too. My literary prospects are of course infinitesimal but on the score of *pleasure*, the quill for me. I am fired anew by my late success, my story which I have just read, in the proof and 2 "poems"—verses about six lines long apiece which I drew from a clear sky as it were, for nothing. I mean the construction was not the puzzle that of prosody is and I merely wrote them down and gave them in. Poetry is such a sensitive kind of production too, that it always tickles me to be "accepted." I mean you feel much more foolish in writing bad poetry than in writing bad prose, and more *doubly* foolish as poetry is unconscious.

9:30. I have just been to the gym for a physical appointment, and now I am my own bird again—no obligations save the self imposed. My chest is A+ Miss Applebee says. But my height 4 ft 5 [5′4″?] and my weight only 98. Miss Applebee says it is a disgrace that your weight ought to go into your height twice (or the other way about) and was most kindly and persistently

20. Carola was the wife of Claus Craig, MWM's cousin.
21. MM saw Giacomo Puccini's *Tosca.*

solicitous prescribing stuff to eat, tonics, slow eating, sleep everything in fact. She finally pinned me down to raw eggs and said I *had* to eat one a day. "Oh the wardens *hate* me" she said—for they have to order them "you see."

I am glad not to go to Frances'. I decided it was not to be, before the Mouse's letter.

Let Uncle go *alone* for a hat—Mousie. You haven't the benefit of my judgement—(a sample of my judgement, I mean) in the winter hat I got but I think I can get a good one. It embarrasses me moreover to have my private processes supplemented though Aunt Mary is very conservative and un-push-y, always.

I went to Hilda Sprague-Smith's to tea yesterday "to meet Esther" but Esther left very early apparently. In the evening I went to Christian Union. Esther led, on the 10 talents. The text is as suggestive as with the exposition given, I think. I then studied till 9, read "Victor," a short story of [Arthur] Quiller-Couch's till 9:30 and went to bed. It is great and I did not regret my departing from my ordinary path.

To Mary Warner Moore and John Warner Moore   *Sabbath April 5, 1908*

Dear Family,

Skim milk! oh the false pride, the impatient ambition of the youth is as faint starlight beside the shine upon the golden cross of endurance of the man. Think on *that*, star fish, and dig the earth with a rebellious rhinoceros horn.[22]

I hate Mouse to have you so eternally delving, doing work menial, wearing and uninteresting in addition to bearing the incubus of Metzger. I am *idle*, pleasure-bent and wailing at fatigue, at *that*. I wonder how long it will take me to turn into something of account. I get quite impatient sometimes. All the girls here, that are any account, are so practical. Even those tending to the ethereal. Mabel O'Sullivan writes, with Margaret Franklin and Martha the best prose, and poetry in college, is teaching and living narrowly, spending as she can with woe, a small fortune in clean shirt-waists, tutoring in Shakespeare, and punctuation and French and Latin and Greek, for entrance exams, the embodiment of sprouting scholarliness and intelligence. Rattling off rules for punctuation and comparing notes with other authorities in a way to make you dizzy.

Writing is all I care for, or for what I care most, and writing is such a puling profession, if it is not a great one, that I occasionally give up. You ought I think to be *didactic* like Ibsen, or poetic like "Sheats" [Shelley/Keats?], or pathetic like [J. M.] Barrie or witty like Meredith to justify

22. JWM had been sarcastic about their youth in his letter of April 3, saying that she got all the "cream" so he had to be satisfied with "skim milk."

your embarking as selfconfidently as the concentrated young egoist who is a writer, must. Writing is moreover a selfish profession and a wearing (on the investigator himself).

A well—

I got no hat yesterday—at Wanamaker's, and Gimbel's there was *nothing*, at Stetson's a hat which I almost came down to, a brown shiny, fine straw with pale yellow inch rim, trimmed with feathers. The hat is $6 (itself) the feathers could be removed and dull brown ribbon substituted (beautiful ribbon) which would make the cost 9.50 instead of 15 as it is now. The shape is becoming but the hat is *big* and I was afraid to get it.

At Keebler's a plain hat place I saw a panama hat "mushroom" shape with a black band, for $10. I should like to get it, if you are willing. It is white, and *plain*. There is nothing on it—and you desire things so *dressy* or rather suitable to all occasions that I was afraid to get *it*. What attracts me, is good material and both these hats are so beautiful I feel as if I should feel comfortable under either. The Stetson one would just suit the pongee suit. But it would not naturally be the thing for blue.

I like very much the plain 3-cornered sailor and should invest in such (black) if you would allow me.

The Ibsen play was in Georgina's dialect, "the most hairliftin' piece o' actin'" I have ever seen. It was not sensational—just mentally consternating with the pathos the joy the illusioning of *dis*illusioning life, all concentrated. It gives you harrowing experiences in their real setting, from which moral inspiration comes, in real life.

It is a play (*A Doll's House*) in which the Mouse would take great satisfaction. It is typically, for women—the principle, is for all, individual liberty, and manliness enough to sacrifice for the people you love even your honor. The end however, would be harrowing to any man, of spirit.

Frances understands about my not going home with her.

12:30

I have just come from church.

I got home from town yesterday at halfpast six. After dinner Rosalind Mason 1911 came to see me, then Marion Crane, and then Frances Stewart and then it was ten, so I "went light on the studying." Frances certainly is worth many a push, of these dandelions so thick about here. Rosalind was very funny. She is almost witless in her eccentricities and informality—and in a way almost childish alternates flat compliments with crudities till you give up trying to make the compliments preponderate, as a bad job.

She began (through her nose), "You know you're awfully like an author Marianne, the way you sit, and the way you push your hair back. Majoring in English? *History and Policon!* How bromidic—shouldn't have thought it of you. (She leans forward, from the couch, picks up the Fish's picture.)

"Brother? Thought so. Looks like you. He looks poetic—*is* he? He wears a low collar and men do that, generally are. *What* books have you got there—wait I'll tell you. I can't see but I know what they'd be. Shakespeare—and Keats and Bernard Shaw. No? (well then Ibsen), (she moves over) oh Emerson *I* knew that. This your scrap-book—may I look at it? *May* I? How nicely you print. Why you write like Frances Howard (I cannot *abide* Frances) just exactly. That's Peg. *Didn't* she write that? (Peggy Ayer) (yes, with some flowers). Good for *her*. Mary Taylor comes in. "Well *Rosalind Mason*. They thought you were dead." "Did they? Well, I'm very much engrossed."

Afterwhile she departed.

I got a nice letter from Marcet, last night. She is doing distasteful work, banking, weather[s] a few domestic troubles, looking after a relative's crying baby, and so on. (I have it light).

I have a strong feeling for Scotland, today. I have neither been reading or writing, I suppose it is a bubble in the blood.

The weather is cold but fine as silk and I think I shall take Milton and go out.

Peggy is wearing a dress today that would take a prize—pink gingham with a white yolk [*sic*] very Parisien, with an air of distinction her clothes generally lack.

Frances has taught me a song I am aching to sing you.

> *Blow ye winds that blow*
> *Let us a-roving go*
> *I'll stay no more on*
> > *England's shore*
> *So let the music play*
> *Heighyo heigyo heigh-yé*
> *I can no longer stay*
> *I'm off my love with*
> > *a boxing glove*
> *In the teeth of the raging gale.*

Peggy asked me as she passed me after dinner if I couldn't come over and see her? I dropped over and we had a nice time. Jeanne Kerr was there, a crude uncut one but one Peggy dotes on. We had a fair discussion, on Martha and Louise, fundamentally unprofitable but simple and real. I am developing a passion for the raw,—the unpretentious. It is partly due to grand opera partly to the fact that my eyes are getting to be a little wider open, I think.

It is seven and I must to bed. My writing is *hopeless*. I shall start a new kind, a bromidic kind, as Rosalind Mason would say.

With dearest love,   Fangs

To Marcet Haldeman *May 17, 1908*

Dear Marcet,

I was most happy to get your letter. I hope increased business is to your taste. I must tell you about my story. The Dean spoke of the *Tip* in Chapel and said, a certain story "Philip the Sober" contained the kind of thing that made the college ridiculous to outsiders—phrases such as, "chop-chopping along in the half-dried mud," "Promethean-trained sensibilities"—that it seemed too bad that a girl who showed ability should be guilty of affectation. She said however that there were two excellent poems in the paper by the same author and she read out, "To My Cupbearer." I was flattered that she should take me so much to heart. And anon I intend to try what may be done in the world of letters minus "affectation" in a bald form. I have tried a college story which I think will do for next year and I am strong in the notion of imitating Ibsen, in another, with an English setting. I shall tell you how I come on.

Friday night was Junior-Senior Supper. I sat between Caroline Mc-Cook and Mary Waller. They were both amusing and easy to amuse but their proximity was provocative of no emotion in my cold breast. I was bored with the falseness of my seeming amused at all. They are nice girls. Caroline is venomous egotistical and Mary always flippant but for rear ships in a fleet, they pass. We gave *Romeo* as I told you. Mary was both beautiful and "moving." She walked badly but did runs well. She has awkward hands I think and too wide a smile and lets her hair get in her face but her voice is good and she gets a sincere look on her face when she's casting about for "desperate means" so to speak, that I love. She is wonderful in many ways I think. My part was cut out before the dress rehearsal which disappointed me for a moment. I feel though that big parts as far as feeling goes, are all that matter. I should like to play Juliet. I should probably be inelastic however and insist on thinking it more than acting it.

Mr. King said it was the best thing ever given here and better than *any Romeo and Juliet* he had ever seen. He told the Dean she would never see anything like it for twenty years and she told him afterward we had not disappointed her.

1910 gave to 1908 Wilde's *The Importance of Being Earnest* not long ago. Peggy was John Worthing the hero and Rosalind Romeyn was the heroine. Peggy was herself all over, self-possessed and whimsical, and clear and lazy in her speech, acting absolutely not an atom; but everyone liked her. I liked her better than the others. Elsa Denison was the blasé brother and as disgustingly doublejointed and insinuating and crafty as she only can be, and Rosalind was lisping Mellius' food so I was *much* of the time much bored. Ruth Cabot, spinster, and Hilda Smith servant were admirable and Kate Rotan mother to Rosalind.

Peggy and I are on excellent terms but utterly "uncongenial." We never by any chance hit on a happy thought or remark—and both act as if we were trying to keep from yawning or complaining of our heads or weariness etc. She is a little spoiled I think on the score of her family which I dislike. Personally she is as young and ingenuous as ever. I like to look at her and hear her talk but I also like people to like me. It makes me cross too, to have people stupid and attributing to you things you have not. I think Peggy does to me and many others so often. I think she is a dead failure, physically and intellectually. Again, I think my *kind* of intellectual-ness bores her and when people distinctly and reasonably dislike me I am well pleased to have it so and call the matter done. Peggy is a mixture I think of misapprehensions. She thinks she sees, and doesn't see, but doesn't care. The talent for "not caring" is one of the nicest of the minor ones I think. I like Peggy for having it anyhow but I do not call it a basis for any tremendous admiration. Peggy is stupid I think, in liking crude unintelligent people such as Jeanne Kerr and snobs, such as Mary (W.) and bluffs such as Suzanne, and in not liking clever affectionate *real* people like Frances— but people we must take as we find them.

You were quite right about Peggy in saying she was incapable of situational heights—constitutionally so and that she never would be anything but the family's one charming daughter—and I am a little annoyed that you *were* right. The world is full to crowding however of girls and I shall have to throw for another. (I am joking. I have no notion of being premeditatively fickle.)

L.M.D. my old apparently permanent flame has been burning more brightly again. She invited me to tea—alone, with her and Miss Fullerton. I had a wonderful time. I love to "talk," as you know and Miss Donnelly is fun in a very peculiar way, to talk to. She listens and comments so engagingly.

Frances is just as nice as ever. She rarely plays with me however and I am so abominably busy that I rarely play with *her*.

I have a new dress, the prettiest I have ever had, a white one with innumerable small tucks at the top of the skirt and in the waist but I "rilly" am so blasé as Mr. Johnston says I do not feel much more pleased to have it than not to.

I *must* write to my family.

With love,   Marianne

To Mary Warner Moore and John Warner Moore   *Oct[ober] 28 [1908]*

Dear Family,

I shall hope soon to see you. Meanwhile I slave—with the Deutsch. I am exceedingly humble about it and though I have done 5½ hours today I can't feel that I "know it all." It is positively as bad as Latin. Your incitations are, however, helpful. It was fine to see the Beaver Monday. I did not say I believe how I appreciated the Beaver's letter on the occasion of my first ascent to be slaughtered.

I did about *two* hours of German yesterday and took in a great variety of almost everything else to be taken, Lectures, a Philosophical club tea to meet Dr. Delag. [de Laguna], Dr. Leuba and the other philo-psychologists. That was great—one of the nicest experiences I have had in college. I was just leaving when Dr. Dela. arrived. I at once postponed my departure and we got to talking. I was amazed—to find him utterly lacking in William Morris-ism, but keen for practical rationalism; (saneness; not rationalism in the philosophical sense). He discussed politics and Orals and matters within my ken, I abetting him by fits and starts.

He is for Bryan![23] Going to vote for him. When he said so I said, "Why Dr. Delagoona [de Laguna]!" He said incredulously "Why not?" and then I got him to explain just what he thought. He said [William Howard] Taft had no knowledge of economic theory. Bryan had. He said Bryan had been engaged for some years in managing the Democratic party which was absolutely the best Presidential training possible. I then said Taft had shown himself efficient in his department and was candidate for the Presidency, by force of circumstances not for the sake of exploiting his capabilities on a chance as Bryan was; I said he was anything but self interested etc. Dr. de Laguna laughed and said undoubtedly he was but that Bryan was as far as personal and moral motives went, a good man too, etc.

At length I tore myself away. Hockey was half over but considering I had changed my clothes and got into the game, I thought I was doing well. I play on the first team now. I shall probably be only a sub, in the match games but, First Team practice is not to be beat.

With love,   Fangs

Give my love to Dockey [Reverend Dr. Norcross] and the youngsters.

Don't be disappointed if I don't get through this oral. I shall send my wash next week to the Nest (?) or Manse.[24]

---

23. William Jennings Bryan (1860–1925), Democratic presidential candidate in 1896, 1900, and 1908.

24. The Nest is the family name for Mary Norcross's mountain house in Sterrett's Gap, Pa.; the Manse is the Norcross parsonage in Carlisle.

To Mary Warner Moore and John Warner Moore

[December 12 or 13, 1908]

Dear Family,

I have passed through the multimum of strange adventures, this past week.

Last week, President Thomas described the organizations of the various universities. In Germany the Faculty and fellows elect new members of the faculty and the ambition to have the *greatest* scholars makes the standard apparently high. But Pres. Thomas said the jealousies between professors counteracted the advantage in restricting the appointments. The various lecture courses begin at diffferent times in the year which is amusing I think. Pres. Thomas said when she was there no 2 of her courses began and ended at the same time, some professors preferring a longer spring and others a longer fall vacation.

The sanction of the minister of education to Professorial appointments is really perfunctory I was interested to hear. I supposed he did a good deal of the appointing, himself.

In France Pres. T. says the same system operates, only much worse. In England things are in a very sad way apparently as concerns the rank and file, the garden students. The faculties are good, appointed by the dons and fellows, and faculty, but the tutor system deprives most of the students of good teaching or rather of assurance of good teaching for the tutors are apportioned, hit-or-miss. In Germany that is obviated by their system of giving the same course under 2 or 3 men. That is having the same course given contemporarily. It must annoy the professors but President Thomas said it was a successful way of getting rid of superannuated professors which worked well. At Harvard the new faculty are appointed by a committee of 5. Harvard has gradually lost its pretension to scholarship however the Dean says, through President Elliot who favors the scientific man at all costs. What will become of Harvard when the old learning has died out with some of the present Professors she hinted at but did not say. Unless President Elliot is defeated in trying to get a young scientist.

On a following day we heard how our professors contributed to our tuition, to each $200. How they had to have a strong desire to teach to be willing to be attracted from professions such as law and medicine. Of course the glory compensated poverty, to *some* extent. President Thomas told how a professor ("not a Bryn Mawr professor") was told by the President of the college to which he went that it would be well for him to learn how to manage a furnace and to learn from his mother something about cooking before he came so that he could help his poor wife when she became utterly exhausted. The man was just going to be married, and no servants were to be obtained apparently but at high rates in the town he was going to.

After the Oral, the Dean said she was on the whole encouraged that such a large number of us had got through. She said that the German Oral was harder to pass than the French, that there was really no comparison between the two. She said "the absolutely unreasonable German compounds and the crabbed German text make it very difficult for students to pass it. It is due to the least lovable of the German characteristics. I think," she continued "that the Germans have stood this really barbarous text, as long as they have. It is what we call 'Pan-Germanism,' the feeling that anything which is not German cannot be good. It is in America, Spread-eagleism. But I *think*," she said "we are getting over this. I think the eagle will not flap his wings so much for you as he has done in the past, for *my* generation."

Monday nothing happened. I think I collected material for the *Tip*. Shirley says I can't go off. And I am only too glad to try it, longer. I wrote a poem time before last which has gone through three versions. The last two I shall give you in case it doesn't appear in the *Tip*.

>To an Artificer
>*Not of silver nor of coral,*
>*But of weather-beaten laurel.*
>*Carve it out.*

>## I I
>
>*Make a body long and thin*
>*And carve hairs upon the skin*
>*Make a snout.*

>## I I I
>
>*On the order of a tower*
>*Faintly wrinkled like a flower*
>*On the paws*

>## I V
>
>*Carve out heavy feline toes*
>*Make each claw an eagle's nose.*
>*Carve great jaws.*

>*2.* To a Screen-Maker
>*Not of silver nor of coral*
>*But of weather beaten laurel*
>*Carve it out.*

II

Carve out here and there a face
Fling a symbol out in space
Of grim Doubt.

III

Represent a branching tree
Uniform like tapestry
And no sky.

IV

And devise a rustic bower
And a painted passion flower
Hanging high.

The board said the first was grotesque and I think this, sentimental but I guess this will go in.

Wednesday, we had rather a stiff lecture in philosophy and as we were going out, Dr. de Laguna said to me, "Well Miss Moore, do you think you got anything out of this?" I said I had then I asked him about a beginners' Greek book. I said I thought I would like to look at one when I went to town sometime. The other was a day or so before but it is immaterial. He is pricking his ears forward after class stray inquiries almost every time. He asked me if I was thinking of studying Greek and I said I was. He said, "are you going to be busy now?" I didn't know just what he meant but I said I was not, and mumbled something about not having any more German to do. He said, "well I'd like to give you some advice, if you have a minute to spare. But we'll have to get out of this, for other people will be coming in." We went over to the library to his seminary. We met Dr. Saunders as we went in the side door. Dr. de Laguna scrutinized him, then said in the pleasantest way imaginable, "*How* do you do——" and passed on.

That tea of Mildred Pressinger's was great fun. I will have to reserve it. Dr. de Laguna then proceeded to explain, (having assured me numerous times that I must be afraid of the language) that I must regard the language as if it were spoken. He said, "it's much easier than German, and *much* easier than Latin, but you must regard every sentence as spoken, even if you don't read it aloud." And he said "I'll give you two rules and if you stick to them they'll save you any amount of trouble. Never translate a Greek sentence into written English. Never write a sentence out and *always* write an English sentence out in Greek." He says he learned in 17 weeks in his Junior vacation, at college, and that nothing was more possible. He said of course it was in the summer and he gave four hours a day to it but he said "you can do it—and you can teach yourself." As to remembering, he said, after you have passed out of childhood, you are in the best condition possible, to remember. "It's a popular myth," he said "that children remember better than grown people. You think it's wonderful when a baby 2 or 3 years old remembers you took it on the train, the other day, and you don't think it's wonderful when you remember that you took a journey 8 years ago." "I'm glad you want to learn Greek," he said "and come to me if you want any help and I'll be glad to give it to you." That's just the sort of man he is.

Elsa Meyer, a freshman, was telling me the other day how "awful" nice she thought he was. This girl is a German and *very* intelligent. She has read more philosophy than I have even heard of. But is very shy and small and beetling, in a fashion. She said, I felt so lost when I first came here. I have never been in a school before and I have had teachers that you know, were quite old men, and they were like my father to me. And I went to Dr. de Laguna and I said how I felt about things here, and could he tell me what I ought to study—(she takes General Philosophy) and he was "awful" nice and he said "and if there's anything the girls can['t] help you out with, come to me." She mentioned I believe that she had brothers who were older and as it were constituted preceptors of themselves.

I led evening meeting tonight on Fear. It went tolerably well and I feel much delighted to be once more on the scent of garden studying. I wrote the paper Friday night and yesterday, but even *so* much time to spend on it, seemed ruinous. For I have [a] great assortment of quizzes descending on me.

I am getting very eager for the letter. I don't know when it was I got one but I daresay I am living so fast, I reckon every day a pair of days.

W. love, Fangs

To Mary Warner Moore and John Warner Moore
29 W. 68th St. [New York]   Monday, Feb[ruary] 1, 1909   P.M.

Dear Family,[25]

Art is long, but life is so fast I wonder it does not catch up to it.

. . .

25. MM had gone to New York for the first time, to spend two days with Hilda Sprague-Smith (Bryn Mawr 1909). She wrote five letters about this trip, three of which are quite long; they have been excerpted here, as no single letter gives the full flavor of her detailed responses to this very important trip. The two letters dated February 1 are six and then two pages long; the February 2 letter is forty-nine pages long; and the two letters dated February 4 are fifty-three and forty-two pages long, respectively. At least half to two-thirds of the February 2 and the second February 4 letters describe the play *What Every Woman Knows* by J. M. Barrie (1860–1937), starring Maude Adams. Barrie, the author of *Peter Pan*, was a Moore family favorite.

I have been having a time to dazzle Maecenas.[26] My stay has been *bewitched*, with pleasure. Mr. Sprague-Smith and Miss Veltin[27] I like better than all words could say and I have learned enough to shake even the Fish's firm foundation in the belief that youth is too shallow a cockle shell to contain interest (which will sell). I saw the most interesting man tonight that I have seen while I have been here—Mr. [Louis Kaufman] Anspacher, (a Jew), for all the world like the Tragic comedian. He was on the front row of the platform (at the People's Institute) at this suffrage meeting and I saw Mr. Sprague-Smith speak to him afterward so I asked about him. "He's a very brilliant fellow," Mr. S.-S. said—"Anspacher; he's bringing out a play. He writes very well." My perspicacity was not on a cold scent. I think I can put him in a story that will net me some cold cash . . .

Feb[ruary] 2, 1909, BMC [Pembroke East, Bryn Mawr College, Pa.]
. . . Mrs. S.-S. had just come in and was taking off a furlined coat. She was dressed in a cream lace waist with black jabot effect and had a twisted rope of small pearls onto which was attached a ΦβΚ key. She powwowed over Hilda for a second in a way I should not have liked and the Mouse would not have done—then shook my hand or shook hands first, I can't remember and asked Hilda if she wanted tea. H. said she thought it would be nice—and we went in to the living room, a medium large square room, front, with a big low dome-shaped lampshade (leaded glass in sections) hanging over a table, and big easy chairs about. The maid rolled in a little table (oblong) walnut or mahogany and brought a silver tray with cups and a nickel tea pot, straight and plain, and sugar and cream and lemon. Then a silver dish of raisin cake, (raisin bread) and went out. Mrs. S.-S. did not take tea; shortly after we had had ours, she put some paper in the grate and some sticks on and lit a fire. The mantelpiece was the one drawback to the room, it was tall and yellow, with columns and with variegated tiles. But the fireplaces all through the house, were that hideous type and I guess they can not help it—windows went along the street side of the room, on the walls were a few pictures, a large Japanese print, a drawing by [John White] Alexander in pencil of a little girl an acquaintance of Hilda's. The technique was very interesting—and another Japanese picture, and three medieval colored studies, by Alexander Fisher.
On the mantelpiece were a set of books, divided by a clock—Kipling and Lowell—Kipling tall and red, outside, Lowell green and smaller *inside*.

26. A very wealthy statesman, courtier, and patron of literature of the Augustan Age of Rome and a generous patron of several poets, including Virgil, Propertius, and Horace.
27. Lived with the Sprague-Smiths and was "head of the Veltin School," which several of MM's Bryn Mawr friends attended, including Hilda and Frances Browne.

[MM sketches this arrangement.] A passage kind of lobby led from this living room back to Mrs. S.-S.'s room, lined with closets faced with maple. Innumerable lockers—the place being like the hall at the Manse which leads from the front door to the kitchen.

. . .

I had been so careful not to "blossom out," that I hadn't said anything to Mr. S.-S. at all. But I was put next him at the theatre and we talked long and busily. At dinner, Mrs. S.-S. had said she was so sorry Hilda and I had not been home for *Friday* night that they had had a dinner which would have set us tintillating (to use my word) at which were Mr. Hunter and Mr. Seligman and Commissioner Watchaw (?) and I don't know who else.[28] You know what I think of R. F. Hunter—(and *Socialists at Work*). I had smiled but not "let out." But on the way to *Maude A[dams]*, Mr. S.-S. said, "Are you a Socialist?" I said I was, but not a Marxian—that I guessed I on the whole was opportunist. We then got to talking. I asked about Spargo and Hillquit.[29] Mr. S.-S. says Mr. Hunter is the cleverest and most refined of them all, (very young). Hillquit is clever too but very unpolished, Spargo a dandy (not in the gloves, cane sense) and also Seligman. I dragged in Walter Crane[30] as Hunter gives him in his *Socialists*—and Mr. S.-S. said, "Yes there is a good deal of socialism among the artists. The Bohemian side of the artist has something to do with it and then the artist is in reality proletariat." "Amen," I thought. We discussed the German insurance and labor commissions and democracy vs. monarchy or communism. Mr. S.-S. asked me how B.M. girls went as to general feeling, democratic, or socialist. I said we inherited our politics so largely and we [were] so little informed practically that many of us, didn't yet stand out enough to be counted but that monarchy seemed to appeal to the thoughtful and more practical. And I then expanded what I meant. Of course we all are Socialists, (I say this to you) in so far as we know economics and are halfway moral, and want clean politics. But as I told Mr. S.-S. I should have voted for Taft if I could have and should have voted for Roosevelt, if I could have, however the socialist cause might have been booming ~~for I believe in gradual adaptation to new policy as most do~~ being for no goose scheme with everything turned upside down when we need old dogs for present difficulties. I then inquired of Mr. S.-S. if many of the German Socialists didn't vote Socialist, not to support Socialism but to register

28. Wiles Robert Hunter (1874–1942), a sociologist involved with social reform; Edwin Seligman (1861–1939), professor of political economy at Columbia; Robert Watchorn (1858–1944), Commissioner of Immigration.

29. John Spargo (1876–1966), founder of Prospect House School Settlement and prominent socialist lecturer and writer; Morris Hillquit (1869–1933), author of *History of Socialism in the United States* (1903) and *Socialism in Theory and Practice* (1909).

30. Walter Crane (1845–1915), painter, book illustrator, and socialist.

a protest against present government. He said such was the case—then the play began—and *such* a play. It made me feel the way I used to feel when I first read Meredith—"why does he stop. He could make it twice as long and not impair it."

. . . In New York, I flourished like a bay tree. No extravagance of starch or chiffon was too much for me. I never feel at home, in fact when I'm *not* spending more than my "income" but economy as a feat, is entertaining and when so obligatory becomes natural and pleasant even. I was talking about Mr. S.-S. and the meeting—Judge [Benjamin Barr] Lindsey didn't come for a while and Mr. Slicer (a Unitarian minister) spoke, on the scientific method, (free thought, direct temper and scientific method). It all sounds like heresy but I can see where the truth of the everyday gets into it and helps the people. Mr. Slicer said—"When Huxley was studying, he was in the woods, one time—and saw *two* beetles. They were on a log and appeared at the same time. He clapped his hands down and secured them, one in each hand—then, before he could put them anywhere, he saw a third. He put one of the beetles from his hand into his mouth and caught the third one but the one in his mouth squirted out a poison, he had to spit the beetle out, and at the same time, lost the other two so he had no beetles, but that was scientific method." He was very clever. He said, "I was to have talked to you tonight, but I gave this time to Judge Lindsey. He has given it back to me but if he comes, he shall have it again." Then he said, "Let me have your attention please. Nothing that will happen behind me will surprise you as much as it will me." Again, "what has been determined by activity of protoplasm can not be dissolved by acts of parliament."

He quit when Judge Lindsey came. *He* talked about the courts and children. He was most eloquent (and religious). He said the problem finally reduced to how much love we could show our fellow men. He gave some illustrations where youngsters lied out of terror and he said, "Now was it the boys' fault or was it society's." (Prolonged cheering.) He mimics, admirably and gave the youngster's whiny, teary protests with very curious vigor and realness and his discourse was full of slang—and *very delightful*. He opened with a watermelon story of how boys stole melons from a box-car— and how his sympathetic hearing was presumed on and the youngsters said impertinently, "Oh Judge when you was a boy, did you never swipe a watermelon?" He said, "I said very firmly, 'It is against the rules of the courts for the plaintiff to cross-examine the judge.'" Everybody laughed. "It is against the rules of the court to cross-examine the judge. It is against the rules of the court for the jury to examine the plaintiff, but is it against the rules of the courts for the plaintiff to examine society?" (Roars of applause.) . . . He made numerous references to the Bible in a simple (not goody-Miss

Lizzie Smead-fashion) and the crowd was uproarious at the beginning. Mr. S.-S. had said, Judge Lindsey is going to speak to you, he is known to all of you, and I think if you will, you may give a fitting welcome to him. They shouted unanimously 3 times, "Hooray, hooray, *hooray.*" It was like the cheers at the game if you remember on the end of the 9 Yales. The Judge is small, active with a thin nose, black eyes, hair, moustache—very acute. His address was not literary, but unconsciously impressive enough to be in effect so. He was invited to dinner Monday if he could come but there was a meeting of a town committee of some sort he had to go to.

Monday was the great and glossy day—I thrived then, most. It was on my mind that I hadn't written to you but like John I put it out of my mind—let nothing interfere with "my career." . . . The music hall was not open, till nine, so we went down 5th Avenue to the bank. (I never felt such cold, I nearly perished.) The shops are beau-ti-ful—with natural polished wood backgrounds and panne velvet draperies, a few pieces, of lace or of diamonds or vases, or what not according to the store—we went to Tiffany's to order cards for Hilda. The place is a marvel, obsequious lacqueys at the door—and a maze of jewels and necklaces, vases, and silverware to beat Aladdin—inside a very beautiful display of Favrile glass in one case. Two pieces were dull iridescent blue with silver twisted stripes about them, squat like jars that [I] liked excellently, but some of the pieces are hideous and I think don't pretend to be pretty. The uncut stones and jewel flowers entertained me—a whole carnation, crusted with topaz (pink not very pretty) but the ancient dull gold chains and twisted pearl short necklaces and the lapis lazuli and crystal turned me sea green, and the plain gold hair brushes and belt buckles and shoe buckles and the stained glass lamp shades.

The store is square—everything is accessible, (an improvement over Bailey Banks). We went to the bank, a low, mosaic affair (inside). I sat on an olivewood bench till Hilda got through, then we went out and back to the Mendelsohn. After prolonged telephoning home Hilda picked out 4 seats for Miss V., Mrs. S.-S. and for us and we left. We then went to a studio, the Montross,[31] to see an exhibit of [Dwight] Tryon's. The pictures were not arranged, but the exhibitor, (not a very interesting man) showed us some [Childe] Hassams and two [Willard] Metcalfs which I hugged in spirit. They beat Tryon all to pieces—a funny thing happened, (at the house) the night I arrived—we were in the "parlor" looking at the S.-S.'s Tryon, and the other pictures before dinner and Mr. S.-S. came in and set a little painting on a chair and walked off and said, "What do [you] think of that, Belle?" It was a beauty, of a yellow sunset with a high cliff, to the side. I should be satisfied with a man if he picked a picture as harmonious as that. But Mrs. S.-S. shook her head—No Charlie, it's all out. She picked flaws in it. It had

31. A gallery that frequently exhibited work by Alfred Stieglitz and Oscar Bluemner.

in her judgment, 3 inches too much foreground, for the composition and the cliff she said if it looked as high as the man had it, would be three inches nearer. "Very well," Mr. S.-S. said cheerfully. "I wanted to see what you thought of it. I told Delenban I didn't know but I'd like to bring it home with me." (He got the picture at the Century Club and knowing the artist was allowed to pick it off the wall.) He turned to me—and said, "It looks just *like* Iceland, I was up there a good many years ago, and the sky gets that look. He did it there last summer." I will have you weeping for a self-sufficient man, if I go on. But the episode showed me some things.

The Hassams were two, standing on easels with velvet cloths thrown over them—one of a soft sunlight, morning or afternoon—on the Isle of Shoals, very blue, the other, *Low Tide, the Isle of Shoals* with a deep blue transparent water and firm rusty seaweed sticking to the cracks and reflecting into the left foreground in the water—in a cut out place one of those oblong bath tubs, cut out with a biscuit cutter. It was a wonderful piece of work, so definite and brilliant and yet so imaginative. I have never seen any of his like it. I generally feel complacent about his rocks and think, "oh anybody can do that, with a palette knife and an indifferent mixture of dirty paint"—but these were master ones. I don't see how he has clomb so. The one Metcalf was mediocre, in old fashioned colors, of two tall, spindling poplar trees, set anywhere on any rocks in any gully—outside Washington. The other was a beauty one, of little filmy trees, a regular maze of green forest, with a mossy brook called *Trembling Leaves*. All artists are so indifferent to ridicule in the names they put on their pictures. The Tryons were to be up by the afternoon—we went then to the Macbeth studio.[32] It was much more "tasty"—in the room we entered first was pottery and on the wall a lot of photographs in dull narrow frames of artists, ([Albert] Groll, [William] Sartain, Alexander [John?] La Farge, etc.). This exhibition was of [Henry] Rangers—(awful things like half done Turners). But there were other pictures in another room of nice ones, a girl with lemons that was here at the academy, and a Sartain of a sand dune, (pronounced Sar*tén*) and a [Charlotte] Coman of a valley, with distant hills and a mist and winding stone fences well subordinated that entranced me. It was all blue green but carefully done and for all the world like the rolling land near the mountain—(Miss Coman is the artist, age 75). Mr. Macbeth showed us two more of hers, one was like the first on a small scale, the same farm patch and vista, through blue mist, and another big one, of autumn somewhere, with a blue line of mountains and all the near work reddish, lavender and pink. A red oak if you studied it, was the centre of a middle group of trees and clumps of half cleared forest stood at the sides. The harmoniousness of the picture was remarkable. I seemed appreciative perhaps for Mr. Macbeth got out

32. The Macbeth Gallery in New York often displayed the work of American Impressionists.

some more pictures from a row of cubby holes, (this was in a different room, with a skylight and easels, but nothing hung). A Sartain he showed me, less good than the first, of New Jersey marshes to infinity with slits of pool and stagnant water showing. Then he showed some [Arthur Bowen] Davies, curious things of centaurs and nymphs and white puppy dogs playing on a sward, and tall incongruous trees, by an arbor. He doesn't exhibit in the galleries. He just lacks the deft slash. Rather extravagant and crude he is, though one photograph he showed of a picture of his sent to Paris, was impressive, a jagged cliff in the Yosemite by a pool, the inveterate nymph in a corner. "The immortal Jimmy," Mr. Macbeth said and pulled out a portrait by J.N.C.N.W.[33] My lips parted in a smile but I declare it was not Whistler and too much Whistler for me—*Rose and Brown* was the title. It was a girl, complacent, haughty, like Cromwell, but very classic with soiled flaxen hair like ague cheeks—and wonderful snobbish brows, and hands, folded woodenly. The dress was brown; there was some black about the picture. I smile yet, whenever I think of it. We then left having taken much of Mr. M.'s time. He let me glance at the photographs put in with thumbtacks in a group above the pottery in the hallway, pointed out a man I asked about as a pupil of Whistler's and showed Sartain and the others I mentioned.

. . .

Dr. Wüllner[34] was way beyond my expectations. No fool tremolos, and no great spread eagle of sheet music. He sang from small slips or a small slip, was tall, gray and full of natural emphasis and expression. He beat Burgstaler and Scotti all to pieces. He looked like Carlyle if Carlyle had been combed, and lean, and had brown eyes. His accompanist, Mr. Bos, was as good in his way as *he*. The rhythm was faultless and easy so it was not on your mind (and exceedingly light and rapid at times). The songs were all German, from Goethe and Schumann and Strauss (not so good). A ballad he sang, beyond my wildest dreams—very descriptively but not offensively, like an impersonator or concert singer.

The [Carnegie] Hall was very suitable to concerts, (we sat in the gallery) flanked up along the ceiling with [Robert Frederick] Blum frescoes, vague and full of action, girls dragging lambs and swinging garlands and mainly white. The stage was white with a semicircle of green velvet, set in the white woodwork, (curtains hanging). After the concert, Mrs. S.-S. took me to get me a theatre book. She said she wanted to get me some little thing for Commencement and as I had none, that was the thing for me. I submitted, cordially as possible. We got one at Brentano's then went to the Montross gallery again. We saw the Tryons and some pastels of slim stylish

33. Whistler's initials are J.A.M.W., for James Abbott McNeill Whistler.

34. Ludwig Wüllner (1858–1938), German singer who toured the United States in 1909–10.

girls sitting naturally, on benches, each girl a separate sketch. The Tryons were of sunsets at sea, all small, pearly and without a ship or buoy to flag the interest. Mrs. S.-S. couldn't abide the girls, I couldn't abide the paintings. I asked to see the Hassam again and was reinstated in enthusiasm. We got home, just in time for dinner. I kept on my concert waist and suit skirt as I was going w. Mr. S.-S. to Cooper institute to the Suffrage meeting. We had a beautiful dinner, turkey, stuffed with chestnuts, "wrinkly figs," cranberry in small squares but all in one dish, sweet potatoes, gravy, creamed celery, pistachios, lettuce with watercress, charlotte russe, white of egg sort of dessert, candy and cream puffs (the creampuffs one lifted with the fingers from a dish and ate with a fork). The suffrage meeting was a joy. Mr. Zueblin[35] spoke. (Mr. S.-S. introduced all these speakers.) At the door there were lots of women with tablets and pencils asking names, subscriptions, what not. The "members" have a special door which leads to a cloak room a big place and then to the platform. A young woman came up hurriedly and said, "may I have your name." "I am Mr. *Charles* Sprague-*Smith*," Mr. S.-S. said flushing. It was the first time I have seen him at all ruffled. He said to me, "I won't be kept out of my own *meeting*." He presides very well. Mr. Zueblin was witty, every man I heard speak (officially) was. But he brought up few new arguments. He played with words a little, he said, "You say politics are not clean enough for women. If politics can't be clean enough for women, it is treason. Treason in time of war is met with hanging but traitors in time of peace are more liberally dealt with." Mr. Z. is an easy, tall man, with flat long shoes, very clever fair sized hands and smooth, straight gray hair, very quiet hair, rather old fashioned. He spoke of Miss Jane Addams and the polling place in Chicago how it was a roomy airy salon ten times better than any male polling place in the country. A discussion followed after applause. Mr. S.-S. went around from section to section of the hall, a huge place, calling for questions wh. Mr. Z. answered. Mrs. [Harriot Stanton] Blatch also was on the platform and did considerable talking. (I would say for the Fish's benefit if he doesn't know it, that English women have the municipal vote. My remarks might be misleading about inheritance and labor conditions. The ill state of English women's fortunes is iller than the state of American women's fortunes but practically, England is giving political power to women, as fast as she can—because they are raising such an insupportable dust for it.)

. . .

Next morning I woke up at half past ten—(the metropolitan was off, of course)—as we had our bags to pack in the course of the morning and

35. Charles Zueblin (1866–1924), professor of sociology at the University of Chicago.

[Ignacy Jan] Paderewski to hear, after luncheon! [MM writes an entire line of exclamation marks.]

            . . .

Presently (half-an-hour late) he [Paderewski] appeared. Zounds what a fox hound. I was quite bowled over by him. I had been told that he was old and stouter than in years past, and quite stiff. (If you call gray-hound-deliveration, stiff, he was very stiff.) We were on the right of the stage, in the first tier of boxes so "saw" him. [MM sketches the theater.] He has something about him, of Stevenson, a certain captious, animal, whimsicalness but he never smiled through the performance. He is abandoned, selfish and autocratic to the finger tips, that too I noticed. But with such looks he could be Mephistopheles and fool his critics—or "capture" them to make the word do service. He played a Bach and then a Schumann, and then Chopin. It was a very heavy program. I don't see how he did it. He hurt his finger during the performance *The Ledger* says, so cancelled his engagement in Philadelphia today. (I was going, being extra incontinent as we had to leave before the end of the 6th encore and he played 7, when they say the piano movers came in and took the legs off the piano and toted it off.) Mrs. S.-S. said as we were watching people "Now how do you suppose people could choose seats like those, in the front row? Do [you] suppose they couldn't get any other seats?" "Oh, for sentimental reasons I guess," Miss Veltin said. I giggled to myself, but when the fellow had got done playing I felt very much as if the same music by a different man would have been a slow article. He played a polonaise, Chopin, Op. 53 that I should care to hear again *immediately* he did it so wonderfully. He was not so gymnastic as they say he used to be—I mean technically (not the scales)—his low keys were indescribable. I used to hate the piano, and you know what a "touch" is, in the common phrase, as well as I, an ear-sore in most cases. But I thought of the word with great unction when I. J. had played two numbers. I think it must be the absence of *quality* in music ordinarily that makes it hard to remember . . . I felt as if something ailed his nervous organism that he was so tense about it and then did so well. He must be a fiend incarnate when things rile him. He has that tiger temperament, cold eyes and abandoned viciousness, (in both senses perhaps), but I imagine as long as he lives he will not miss his kill. My state of mind when we went out, you can imagine. Elsie wonders, still what ails me.

            . . .

With dearest love,   Fangs

To Mary Warner Moore and John Warner Moore

Feb[ruary] 14, 1909 ♥

Dear Family,

I hate to think of your taking so hard, my anxieties. To think I could ever come so near the ragged brink though and miss it, makes me squirm. I find I did *not* have to get Merit in Philosophy. I merely had to get half 15 hours, but of course with persistent drawing of Passeds, it's very pleasant to have 10 hours. Mary Allen has 2 too few and Hilda S.-S. failed Philosophy (pretty badly), so there has been a general slaughter. Hilda will get her degree of course, for she can take the exam. at Easter.

Elsie failed English Comp.—(technically. Her critical papers are passed)—so she feels very sore but she got H.C. in one Mathematics and in Latin Comp.—and is so "proud of her High Credits," I feel they should salve her pain. She says not infrequently, "I'm pretty proud of my High Credits. Wouldn't you be?" I said I think I would and that I think I'll go in for one in Philosophy in June, ([J. M.] Barrie like).

I have a verse of not very high character which is coming out in *The Lantern*. I gave it to *Tip*. But Ruth George wrested it away to my ineffable joy.

Ennui I call it—
He often expressed
A curious wish
To be interchangeably
Man and fish
To nibble the bait
Off the hook said he
And then slip away
Like a ghost in the sea.

I am not proud of it, but I like the rhythm and I intend to try, till I do write something. (I intend to try too for H.C. in Philosophy and in Daddy.)[36]

These sporadic poems I don't work over, (though my stories I do), so I smile, (as if I had found a penny) when people tell me how they like them and talk about writing poetry and so on as if it were gymnastics or piano practice.

Miss Shaw spoke last night on the Modern Democratic ideal. I couldn't say how she delighted me. No decent, half-kind, creature could possibly think of fighting suffrage if he or it had heard her arguments. They hold water so that they stand repeating, too. Elsie didn't go, so I gave her an extract today, (we went walking)—and she is "on the fence." (Flourish of

36. MM and her friends referred to physiology professor Joseph Warren as Daddy.

trumpets.) I said when Elsie said for the 12th time she didn't see what difference voting would make in "making people better," I said, if you want to oppose women's voting I said, you merely say you are willing to tramp over people's bodies to get all these luxuries you take so calmly. I said, "if women are going to support children and perhaps unproductive adults they ought to have as much pay as men and ought to work eight hours if men work eight hours, and not work ten." I delivered a cruel flow on the score of men. I said the *men* are all that keep you respectable. Just because they don't *choose* to grind women down more than women *are* ground down, is not the fault of the women. I said, (Educated!) women say, men give us every thing we want why try to get the ballot. I said, "the men give you what you want because they are a high grade of animal. The clothes of every woman in N.Y. a few years ago, belonged to her husband, no widow could legally be buried in the state—a widow inherited ⅔ of her husband's property—(during her life). The cemetery lot came in the property, so the woman had ⅔ of the cemetery lot during her lifetime and to get any use out of it would have to be buried before she was dead." Elsie laughed quizzically. I said also that the eight hour day was all a question of the ballot. Elsie said she didn't see how it could be. I said, "well, in Colorado, the men had an eight hour day, the women, a ten hour day, the women got an eight hour day because they put a bill in as voters (for state legislature). In N.Y. they did not." The philanthropy argument I think was Miss Shaw's best. But I think Elsie "tried not to pay attention"—and didn't see what I was talking about—the idea that if you prevent *all* babies from drinking infected milk, you do more good than if you solicit money and supply 200 with Pasteurized milk. Miss Shaw said, people were bringing up the argument that women would neglect charity (Dr. Lyman Abbott)[37] the idea of the ballot being to obviate the necessity of charity. She quashed the unladylike argument and the time argument. She said the ladies of Colorado get a bill through in one year and the ladies of N.Y. take a trip up the Hudson every year for *seven* years and don't get a bill passed *then*. She said the legislative measures were often more ethical than partisan and that feminine women oughtn't to feel too ignorant to *care* what happened. The point about the industrial school I thought squashing but Elsie did not. That you can't tell girls to stay at home when the girls who are fit to stay at home are a million in three and the girls that need to stay at home or get positions as housemaids have run on the streets all their lives and don't know what clean beds are or what cooking utensils look like. I wasn't as rabid as I sound here, but I was pretty bulldoggy. I said "of course woman suffrage doesn't mean much to you, because you're petted and have money lavished on you and you wouldn't think what a slum looks like and wouldn't think of touching an infected horse-hide or danger-

37. Congregational clergyman (1835–1922), who edited *Outlook*; author of *The Life and Literature of the Ancient Hebrews.*

ous machinery for anything, but a lot of girls that haven't quite your chances could see why it might help some." Elsie said, "Did you see that bunch of flowers Glady Spry had on?" and I could have beat her with a book. But my words sank in, as someone asked Elsie in my presence later what she thought of woman suffrage and she said, "I can't decide."

Pres. Thomas had us at the Deanery after the lecture (the Suffrage Society) and I was struck dumb, the place is so beautiful. It's more educational than an art course. It rambles a little and there is a narrow passage I don't like, but the whole, is an Elysian garden. The reception hall, is a big square place with a tiled floor and gold (burlap!) on the walls and a hammered brass ceiling of which little shows for heavy brown beams go across—and sparsely filled with antique, capacious chairs, inlaid with gilded legs. The bedrooms upstairs are indescribable. The one I left my wraps in had a punctured bed, square, Indian brass (square posts and low head and foot boards) with a pale silk spread (embroidered flat) across it. The bathroom adjoining is a square room, size of my college room, mosaic floor, white tiled walls. All the ceilings through the house are stenciled, the lamps—Favrile glass— and the woodwork the color of the walls. In Pres. T's study the walls are blue and the window frames blue and the chandelier a bunch of (five) pale pepper shaped, conical lobes, greenish yellow. The Dean came in as we were looking at it, (standing in the doorway, Sh. Warner and Mabel Ashley and some Freshman and I) and said, "I think we shall have it done and have the curtains up, by the time of the Senior reception—the first after Easter." This room was adjacent to the "salon" so it was suitable we should be there, (we were encouraged moreover to circulate). I did the talking about the stone in the gymnasium, the stain on the wood, the gargoyles in the cloister and dozens of kindred topics. The Dean was more charming than I've ever known her. The way she has worked too for the gym. excites my admiration. Hours she worked every day in the hottest part of the summer, on the plans, Miss Lawther says. She said finally, "Now, won't you have some lemonade, nuts, cakes (in the *dining*-room). See how you like our grape-juice lemonade." The grape-juice lemonade, nuts, cakes and candy were fine, a tinge of Deanery luxury. The old pieces of furniture decorated with brass and the electric lamps and the windows and rugs and the piano—and red patterned East Indian cover made me gasp. My suffrage experiences in New York hearing Mr. Zueblin stood me in good stead—(he is very well known and apparently universally liked) as I first shook hands, for I feel the ice thin at any party when I have to bow and grin and go and haven't time to get into a mellow conversation.

In the middle narrow passage I speak of there are low dark bookcases on which were various pieces of rainbow peacock glass. In the middle room (centre) from which opened the salon, and the office and the narrow hall was a table (low) but square with all the periodicals neatly arranged in columns and here and there on other tables, upstairs were odd modern books, Nonsense verses etc. The servants were masters—at their tasks— neat, very tall, very sagacious—the maids obsequious and busy, (upstairs). I smiled with satisfaction at the whole affair.

Today I went to church—took a walk with Elsie (after dinner) went to the Musseys', (with Elsie) and am now going to bed—10:15. Elsie is provoked with me because I didn't introduce her round, at the Musseys'. But I introduced her to Mrs. Mussey and after the spiel made a dart for the man to ask him a question which right Elsie had also as none of us knew him. Dr. de Laguna was there and I nosed out a seat near him on the sofa, (next to him) and of course left him to speak to Mr. Meeker afterward so I don't think Elsie has really a *casus belli.* Besides she had 3 years in which to make his acquaintance. Mr. Meeker was very delightful, had a drawl and a shy very humorous way of saying things. But I think Dr. Mussey beats them all. He is sound as a bell. He is crude occasionally, he is so much in earnest, but his clean way of looking at things and his energetic openminded broad-minded face is enough to set you housecleaning yourself. He looks like an inspired fieldhand very square and homespun with respect to ties and shoes. He is the finest type of social evangelism I've seen. He told a funny story (informally). He said a boy was telling about his brothers who had learned to play musical instruments of some kind and he said, "Maurice can play alone but Charles can only play when he plays with the band."

With love, Fangs

I have a story, "The Blue Moth" which I think will do for ye *Tip* this month or next. Shirley said she liked it, most of it, and gave it to Grace Branham to read. It elates me very much for it is like my poem, (what Dr. D. would call a "tentative" story).

Friday afternoon I went painting to Miss Garber's studio by Miss Baldwin's, she invited me, and did 2 bottles a green one and a brown one, very ugly I thought but I had to do what the others were doing. I hope however refined my taste may become, I shall not be perverted into calling cold gingerale-bottle-green "stunning" as Miss G. called it. I appreciated the invitation however and am going again. I expect to do things bigger, too. Small scale studies are very injurious to one's hand.

Don't forget Mrs. Landberton (the address).

To Mary Warner Moore and John Warner Moore *March 16, 1909*

Dear Family,

I have got the Mouse's check. I am too glad for words that the Fish is in comparative prosperity again.

I shall send to the Mouse 9 dollars, I don't need so much. I have broken, one; I got *Dulci Fistula*, for Elsie, (collected B.M. witticisms) (.15). They were, 50, I think but Katherine said at the Book Shop there were only a few left and they'd be glad to sell them at any price—15, anything. It was an inspiration, my thinking of it by way of a suggestive present yet one not beyond my means. I think my story "fluctuates." Shirley was uncertain about it and took it to Miss Crandall without my knowing and *Louise* who is great friends with Miss Crandall tells me Miss Crandall said it was better in suggestion and clutch than anybody's here—imagine my pleasure—but is incoherent. She wanted me to fix it Louise said for *The Lantern*. I am furious not to have it in the *Tip* for I wrote with my eye on its appearance there but such is the tragedy of effort. It may not appear anywhere! I feel as if it probably were a dead seedling—but I'll try it again if they want it. I do seem able though, to dash off poems. I've done two, that seem to satisfy— Ruth and Shirley both rather enlarge on them.

Rhyme on a Jelly Fish

Visible, invisible
A fluctuating charm
An amber-colored amethyst
Inhabits it, your arm
Approaches and it
Opens and it
Closes and
The blue,
Surrounding it
Grows cloudy,
And it floats
Away from you—.

O Longinus

O Longinus,
Blot your name
From every page
We sigh and look and try
To intersperse
With our own thoughts,
A page, a book
But you laugh grim
In silent metre
(Banish *him*—).

This last is so hot cross a production, I couldn't think how it goes.

I wrote a criticism with pain of spirit on [Robert] Browning's *In a Balcony*, the play I almost escaped seeing, for the *Tip*, and it is going in, unless a ghost detains it. I did so with reluctance but Shirley said everybody else had done thankless jobs and I really ought to. So I did, (3 times!).

Shirley rigorizes every fibre in my body though on the score of my story. She can't take the manuscript up and point out what's the matter with [it] and say *that*, and *that* but hands it over and expresses vague dissatisfaction and I flounder with it. It makes no difference however in the eye of real value. Miss Crandall said the end was good; she didn't know just how I got there, but it held.

I went to tea today to the graduate one, Miss Swindler and Miss Crawford gave it, (in Denbigh). Miss Shearer was there to my pleasure, and Miss Bascom came. It has been my dear desire to get to meet her, so I settled down and talked, when duly presented and she was most responsive—(for her). She was practically stranded, so it was very neat, just at the beginning my sidling up. She had on a blue suit, rather green, and a peacock toque, green-blue feathers perfectly exquisite in a stiff brim—and sealskin collar thing and muff—and white chamois gloves. She talked [of] Mrs. Woodbridge, and some new Bacon Shakespeare book, which I knew nothing of, and Dr. [Albert] Schinz's *Anti-Pragmatism* and pictures some, and the *Typ*. She says she likes it, sent one away the other day. I had to do most of the talking. She was rather reticent. But she asked me in [the] middle of my talk what my name was, and said she hadn't heard it, and said when she left she had enjoyed talking, very much.

Norvelle who was there also told me a tale I had been looking forward to. At Cembric's farewell dinner Paderewski and all the stars were there and the Damrosches[38] who are great friends of Norvelle's. Mrs. Damrosch said they asked Paderewski to make a speech. He said it was asking a good deal of him, who was a Polish immigrant to speak, but,—after the dinner, they danced, and had hired musicians. Mr. Kneisel and Mr. Mannis, Mr. Damrosch's son, sent them away and took the violins. Mr. Mannis is 1st violin in the N.Y. Symphony and Paderewski played! Then they had the Merry Widow waltz and every star sang his star opera, *to the waltz*. Caruso, Dalmorès[39] and all—Caruso further busied himself drawing caricatures. Mrs. Damrosch or someone remarked facetiously that 7000 dollars worth of merry widow waltz had been sung. It seems like a dream, doesn't it? (Paderewski playing dances, for confederates to dance to.)

Must, to bed.

With dearest love,   Fangs

---

38. Walter Johannes Damrosch (1862–1950), conductor and composer.

39. Charles Dalmorès (1871–1939), French tenor and member of Oscar Hammerstein's opera company in New York from 1906 to 1910.

To Mary Warner Moore and John Warner Moore   *May 2, 1909*

Dear Family,

I was telling you about Mr. Alexander.[40] He told how he had been an office boy and how he hoped if he was a very good boy and went to church every Sunday, some day he might be a reporter and showed me the picture of the church I told you about, and the *Boston Transcript* and *The Atlantic*, he laid his hand on explanatorily. Talked a little bit about how clean the *Transcript* was and he enjoyed being city editor. He says he would have been an architect if a straw had not turned him onto journalism. Says he takes great interest in plans of houses and studies up the house building papers and so forth, yet he said reporting was hard, he said no one could go through it either without getting a "kind of—*cynical*, hard, point of view" but he said it with such benevolence I smiled to myself. He said about his office here at the *Journal*, the work was deadening and hard, (the clerk work) and he wouldn't like to see anyone that he was interested in, go into it. He got to talking about the reading matter in the *Journal* and said he didn't know as he would read it if he were not connected with the paper, but it was evident he felt a great pride in it. He showed me a picture of one of their contributors marked (by the girl), "not for publication," and the letter I told you about. I couldn't keep from showing that I was very much interested and he asked me if I'd had anything published at which I smiled, felt like telling him that before I was through something "might turn up." But I said I hadn't quite got my ideas boiled down (at all!) (that I had something published occasionally in our college magazine). He gave me a long and salutary and galling speech on the fruitlessness of writing verse and I told him that I wrote it as I guessed all people did for the accessory gratification ~~it lent heavier interests~~, etc., etc.

Fine-ly I let him go. A very crabbed man was at the next desk dictating to a girl something about "married life," "our ideas of" such and such a thing, etc. A great contrast.

Night before last I heard Mr. Dickinson[41] on Ideals of Democracy. He twists his mouth up and lends interest to everything he says by his whimsical smiles. But I didn't learn a thing from him beyond what is in his book. He said in general that because socialism is a pig in a poke that is no reason why we should be unwilling to investigate and see whether we like it or not. He was very dry, he kept characterizing women, and men; he said with regard to the suffrage—there is no reason to believe the universe would be

40. Described in an April 22, 1909, letter as the business manager of the *Ladies' Home Journal*. He invited MM to come to him for advice about a career in writing after MM wrote him to ask for an interview.

41. Goldsworthy Lowes Dickinson (1862–1932), English essayist and lecturer in political science.

overturned if women got the suffrage unless they were led into the fanatic and unseemly support of unfit causes, by their emotions, but there is no reason to suppose that *men* are without emotion.

James Huneker has a new book you may have noticed on *Egoists: A Book of Supermen*—Baudelaire, Flaubert, Huysmans, Stendhal, Ibsen and so forth. His *Visionaries,* seems a little fantastic to me but I haven't seen *Iconoclasts.*[42]

I guess you have been pretty busy. What is Mrs. Kellog like? The fact of their advent is miraculous, in the abstract—(I am getting tinged with Dr. Sander's philosophy) but I hope you won't find them an ever present concern.

Lucinda Van Dyne and the glee club concert I have not yet dwelt on but I think I'll go over and see Elsie. I have neglected her woefully just recently.

Lucinda V. D. was a girl Mr. Johnston told about who tore her clothes to bits every time she was irritated and then the furniture. He also told of 2 men Jesse and Jerry Black. Jerry came in one day having stuck at his task all day with his hand all swollen. He said, "I done harra'd the field and I bruk ma hand."

The Glee Club concert last night was a great affair. Mary Rand who had appendicitis in the middle of the year and has given up graduating till next year came back and was all dressed up in a yellow satin dress with a gold fish net over it and an amber diadem in her hair and very Handy Andy with the "baton" (which is I think an outrage). Mr. & Mrs. Browne invited me & Mildred to sit with them (wasn't it nice?). Reeny & Norvelle are both in the glee club. Miss Reilly & Miss L. and Miss Parris and a girl they called "Ruby" and Mr. Reilly (brother) and a strange man, fearful coxcomb with a waxed mustache, and Dr. Smith all came in late.

Coxcomb to Marion (L.): "who was that very attractive girl talking to Marion (R.)?"

Miss Parris: "that was Miss Rand the leader of the glee club."

C.: "oh" (coxcomb before each reappearance on Mary's part, "Steady there, steady").

I got well acquainted with Mrs. Browne which was pleasant. The concert was as usual very well done and very painful.

This morning I went to church, came home, talked to Elsie for a while after dinner, got a sophomore to take me to Paradise, a perfectly marvelous estate near here with a laurel grotto against a cliff, and natural pools (ap-

42. *Iconoclasts* is subtitled *A Book of Dramatists: Ibsen, Strindberg, Becque, Hauptmann, Sudermann, Hervieu, Gorky, Duse and d'Annunzio, Maeterlinck and Bernard Shaw.*

parently), filled with goldfish and frogs. Columbine and hypaticas and anemones and windflowers and every imaginable wildflower is stuck over the place.

I've just got home and am in the hollow by the athletic field though it's pretty cold and windy. I don't believe I said anything about my white belt. I appreciated it very much.

We had a hockey picnic Friday night on the roof of the gym—1910, 11, & 09—which was a great success, from my point of view as I sat next [to] Miss Applebee.

With dearest love,   Fangs

To Mary Warner Moore, John Warner Moore, and Mary Norcross
May 6, 1909

Dear Family,

Thank you Beaver for the copies of my ASB and Iron Box. I shall see about the children for [the] Garden Party. I don't think I need send them invitations as there are no cards of admission (I shall merely have the amount added [to] my bill).

I went to the Dr.'s today after Imitative Writing. I am trying to finish my report of Christian doctrine by Saturday.

You asked for a list of things I want:

Books, Whistler's *Ten O'Clock* and "The Gentle Art of Making Enemies."
Will Low's *Life of Saint-Gaudens.*[43]
Swinburne (prose)
a rain coat
Pater
Book on Wagner's operas
[Henry Thornton] Wharton's Sappho
Xenophon's treatise on hunting
the "pen" photograph of Stevenson
Watts' *Prometheus*
Botticelli's illustrations to *The Inferno*
Burne-Jones' Paderewski
[Thackeray's] *The Newcomes*
A bar pin on the order of "————" feather, Pleasance lost
The Oxford Book of Verse.

43. Perhaps Will Hicok Low's *A Chronicle of Friendships*, which features Saint-Gaudens, among other artists.

Chopin's waltz e sharp minor

I must quit as it is late.

With dearest love,   Fangs

My story is coming out in the next *Tip.* so a thin stream of sap still trickles through my joints.

1910-1918
From Teacher to Poet

AFTER graduation from Bryn Mawr, Moore returned to Carlisle and took a year-long course in typing, shorthand, and stenography at Carlisle Commercial College. In 1910 she worked for a few months at Melvil Dewey's Lake Placid Club in upstate New York, as a stenographer. On returning to Carlisle, she obtained a position teaching bookkeeping, stenography, commercial law, commercial arithmetic, and English at the Carlisle Indian School. In an unfinished memoir (1969–70), Moore wrote of this experience: "The salary was $2000/year and it seemed self-evident to accept it. With misgiving I did. The commercial students, about 30, were an ideal group, among which were James Thorpe, Gus Wells, Alex Arcasa, Joel Wheelock and Ivy Miller, also some other competent girls. I did not know it but they were my salvation, open-minded, also intelligent." Although this was work Moore apparently did well (another teacher tells her that "somebody said you were the best business teacher they had ever had here. They said the results were better" [to JWM, July 18, 1912]), her family—and she herself—frequently expressed concern that she was being overworked. Consequently, when, in 1914, the department in which she taught was disbanded, the family response was primarily one of relief. Moore then remained without regular formal employment until after she and her mother moved to New York, in the summer of 1918.

Although much less frequent than the earlier family correspondence, Moore's correspondence during these years is still dominated by family letters—primarily to her brother. Between the summer of 1909 and 1914—while Warner was, successively, teaching at a private school in Elizabeth, New Jersey, and then in the seminary at Princeton—she wrote (or Warner saved) at most a few letters a month, although there is voluminous correspondence whenever she and her mother were separated (for example, when Marianne was working at Lake Placid) and to Warner about exceptional trips. In particular, Moore and her mother traveled in 1911 to England, Scotland, and France, and in 1915 Moore made a momentous trip to New York. One sees Moore, in these longer letters, trying out the highly detailed descriptions of landscape and objects of interest for which she later became famous.

While at Lake Placid, Moore wrote at length about her social life; for example, she mentioned "seven suitors" (see August 18, 1910), then later wryly commented that they were "has beens, wilted. . . . I am not 'changing my spots in regard to any of them.' When I 'eventually become wild you will know it'" (September 11, 1910). In general, however, the surviving letters of these years give a less full sense of Moore's inner life than those of her Bryn Mawr years. At the same time, they do make abundantly clear her determination not just to write but to publish her poems. Moreover, despite what might seem to be the relative isolation of living in Carlisle, these letters reveal the remarkable breadth of her reading of avant-garde poetry and criticism, as well as her deep involvement in the contemporary visual arts scene and in public events. She wrote frequently of what she had just heard or read, and of her regular trips to the Harrisburg library. For example, she was reading Ezra Pound by at least 1911, and T. S. Eliot by 1914, and referred to several little magazines she had read, including Wyndham Lewis and Pound's *Blast*, which she called a "wonderful publication—compilation of curses and blessings" (March 2, 1915).

This exposure was aided by the fact that the Moore family had exceptional friends and neighbors in Carlisle. The Benét children (Laura, William Rose, and Stephen Vincent) met Marianne soon after the Moores' arrival in Carlisle, and remained lifelong friends and enthusiastic supporters of her literary endeavors; their grandmother lived across the street from the Moores and the Benét children spent their summers there. The Hays and Cowdray families in Carlisle also shared the Moores' literary and artistic (as well as religious and, to some extent, political) interests, as did the well-educated and influential Norcross family. Mary Norcross's uncle, Sheldon Jackson, was an occasional visitor to Carlisle, and the artist George Plank was a Carlisle acquaintance. With these and other friends and neighbors, Marianne read and exchanged books and journals, participated in local theater performances, church and missionary society events, and suffrage rallies, and generally explored ideas of the world beyond Carlisle. It is, then, perhaps not so surprising that, even while teaching full days, six days a week, at the Indian School, Moore wrote at greater length of her literary aspirations, artistic endeavors (in 1914 she won $2.50 for her drawings of a zebra and a leopard at a fair), community activities, and reading than of the employment that absorbed most of her time.

From 1914 to mid-1916, either Marianne wrote more frequently or

Warner was more careful about saving her letters—perhaps because he was moving less frequently during these years, at his first parsonage following his ordination. In contrast, from September 1916 through early 1918 there are no extant letters from Moore to her family, as they were living together again or in the process of moving. By 1917, however, she had begun what would become some of the more important literary friendships and correspondences of her life—particularly with H.D. (a classmate for one year at Bryn Mawr, now married to Richard Aldington and living in London) and William Carlos Williams. This correspondence began directly in response to Moore's publication in small, mostly avant-garde magazines in 1915 and 1916. For example, H.D. wrote a brief essay on the seven poems Moore published in *The Egoist* in 1915 (a journal H.D. then edited)—to which Moore responded with a personal letter (see August 9, 1916), initiating a lifelong correspondence. Williams, whom Moore had first read in *Others* and had met through mutual friends during brief trips to New York in late 1916 or early 1917, came to visit the Moore family in Chatham (see April 16, 1917). Moore was also corresponding more briefly and formally with editors during these years, as indicated by a May 10, 1918, letter to Harriet Monroe, with whom she also maintained a periodic correspondence until Monroe's death.

While Moore submitted both poems and stories to literary magazines during her college years and in 1910, by 1911 she spoke only of writing poems. From 1909 on, however, she saw herself as a professional writer, repeatedly announcing her intention to sell her work; for example, on August 2, 1909, she wrote, "I have some poems fresh from the pen which I expect to sell," and on February 6, 1911, she announced that she expected to "turn an honest penny by my writings." The family evidently supported this decision; in 1913, for example, Warner wrote, "If your poem is not took by the *Book News*—whatever you do, don't 'quit'" (July 24, 1913). By 1914 Moore had the confidence to respond to the repeated rejections of her work defiantly and creatively. On January 18, after a refusal from H. L. Mencken's *The Smart Set*, she commented, "If they pray to me, I never will give them a poem." On February 8 she joked that Floyd Dell, editor of *The Masses*, "hasn't seen fit to write to me [about her submission of poems]. I guess he is deciding between 10,000 or a salary"; and on March 27, after these poems were refused, "I am writing a poem as an indirect choke pear for all my detractors and sluggard critics—drat them. It is on a couple of fighters"—perhaps a reference to an early version of "To Be Liked by You Would Be a Calamity" (published 1916). By the end of 1915 she had published poetry in *The Egoist, Poetry,* and *Others,* and by 1918 also in *Contemporary Verse, The Chimaera, Bruno's Weekly,* and *The Little Review.*

Moore's December 1915 trip to New York, which she called her "Sojourn in the Whale," was among the most important events of this period (see December 12 and 19, 1915). The Cowdray family invited Marianne and her mother to travel to New York with them for a short visit. Only Marianne went, and there she split her time between exploring New York City with Hall Cowdray, Laura Benét, and college friend Margaret Shearer, attending lectures at the YWCA National Training School, where she and the Cowdrays were staying, and visiting writers and art galleries on her own. Relishing each moment of her visit to this center of writers and artists, the poet stayed on in the city for a few days after the Cowdrays returned to Carlisle. Moore had known about Alfred Stieglitz's photography and his 291 gallery since the spring of 1909, but now visited 291 for the first time and made Stieglitz's acquaintance. This trip also allowed Moore to meet Alfred Kreymborg, who was publishing her poems in *Others*. Through this contact with Kreymborg, Moore had an immediate link to other artists and writers in the city. Moore's delight in her conversations with the writers she met— as well as her confidence in her own opinions, even when they contradicted those of far better-known or older persons—are clear indicators of the direction she saw her life taking.

Although using a variety of names for herself and her brother, Moore referred to both of them primarily as "Weaz" for several years following her graduation from Bryn Mawr. After 1914, however, when the family read Kenneth Grahame's 1908 children's classic *The Wind in the Willows*, their family nicknames changed. Moore, by this time a serious poet, became the poem-writing "Rat" ("the hero of the book," as her mother wrote to Warner on May 24, 1914); Mary Warner Moore became "Mole," the homebody; and Warner became (to Marianne) the dignified and powerful "Badger" and again (now to his mother) the impractical, always in trouble, but well-meaning "Toad." These remained their primary nicknames for the next two decades. The Moore family's love of wordplay is also apparent in their recurring "publication" of mock newspapers: Marianne's "File" (or "Philadelphia Public Rat-Tail File" [November 29, 1914]), mailed to Warner between 1914 and 1916; Warner's *The Badger Hair* of the same years; and an earlier paper called *The Egg* that Warner wrote for a few months in 1911 during his sister and mother's trip abroad (Moore and her mother evidently also "published" a newspaper while on board ship, but no copies of this paper survive). The practice of sending such newspapers may have been an outgrowth of the bulletins or "News Notes" that Moore occasionally appended to her mother's longer letters to Warner. This practice, however, could also have been a sign of Moore's consideration of journalism as a career—an idea in evidence during her last semester at Bryn Mawr and again in 1914, after the business department of the Carlisle Indian School had closed down. For example, on December 16, 1915, after her trip to New York, Marianne wrote Warner about getting an interview at *The Ledger* for a job: "I am just as sure of getting it as I am of eating, if I could only see them. . . . I am prepared to review, 'poetry, fiction, art or theology.' Music and

sport and dancing are the only things I am afraid to tackle." Moore continued to consider the possibility of regular work for newspapers until 1919,
when, after writing a review for the *Times*, she wrote Warner that "I hope
you will not have it in mind to get a hearing for me anywhere else—I think
I could do such work—(am sure of it in fact) but I don't believe I fit in with
the program of the average daily and will have to get at the matter some
other way. . . . [E]ditors for large crowds of people don't want fine distinc-
tions and meditative comment they want something practical and colorless
that would not draw attention to itself or seem contentious. And the more
play I had in what I wrote the more uncompromising I would be, so I will
have to let things go as they are for [a] while" (October 5, 1919).

Especially after she stopped teaching at the Indian School, but
throughout these years, Moore was actively engaged in women's suffrage
activities, writing brief articles for the local paper, participating in local rallies, and attending public lectures on the subject. In 1913, for example, during a trip to Baltimore, Marianne wrote her mother that she had studied
"the Woman Suffrage program which is most interesting. Your Oncle is to
march with the authors and artists and will bring one of the programs"
(February 23, 1913). In response to a letter from Warner advising her
against such public display, she decided not to march. She wrote in later letters, however, of active participation in suffrage events (see September 22,
1915, and October 3, 1915).

In the fall of 1916 Moore and her mother moved to Chatham, New Jersey, to live with Warner in his first parsonage. As they packed up to leave
Carlisle, Marianne wrote her brother (in typical third-person style), anticipating her new family role there: "We all know that Mr. Rat has not such a
predilection for buildings with steeples as for buildings of flatter and more
informal clubhouse type but your athlete must be good, as well as any other
animal and Mr. Rat anticipates administering a helpful claw wherever such
ministrations are acceptable" (August 31, 1916). The letters give little evidence of how Moore actually spent her time during her years in Chatham,
but her conversation notebooks indicate that she made frequent trips into
New York City, now that she was only a short train ride away—even calling
this in her notebook, her "Middle Pullman Period." Through such trips, she
became a regular part of the group of experimental artists and writers cen-
tered there, so that moving to the city was an obvious next step for her by the
time it became clear that the female Moores must move again. In 1918
Warner resigned from the Ogden Memorial Presbyterian Church in
Chatham to be commissioned a chaplain in the U.S. Navy, serving aboard
the battleship USS *Rhode Island,* doing convoy duty across the Atlantic. In
the same year, Warner married Constance Eustis. When Warner left
Chatham, Marianne and her mother moved to 14 St. Luke's Place in New
York City.

To John Warner Moore   *[343 N. Hanover, Carlisle, Pa.]*
Apr[il] 22, 1910

Dear Weaz,

Hammy[1] has been lining a coat with satin grass (providentially) I think, with a view to flitting. I am offered a p'sition at $50.00 a month to start with and "double" that "only too gladly" per authorities in question if worth it.[2] As Bunny says I can't begin to fidget about a raise in pay for at least three months. I haven't even the position yet and don't know whether to fasten on it if I *do* get it. The Adirondack Lodge and Lake proposition rather attracts me. Bunny seems very depressed at the idea of my going and I am not romping at the idea of leaving Dusty behind, nor you for that matter nor Furry. They say the air is fine, (exhilarating) and that though food is expensive the body is more than put in shape by it. Laundry is a dastardly price, 25¢ a waist.

I have a new gray suit and a new gray evening dress so I am ready to cut a dash with duds. My salary would of course be too small to be considered as supplementary to the family income at first. My work would be proofreading of stuff for the bettering of social conditions, private secretary work, and filing statistics or information. I should take my tennis racket and swimming suit and affect great clerical industry. They say they don't want anyone who regards work as a painful necessity. Hah! hah! haw, haw turkey in the straw. They don't know what scaly-scaly they have when they get me.

I've been doing shorthand and selling tickets for *Samson* and snarling at passersby.[3]

I am also enthralled in Christian endeavors. I don't think I could be any busier if I ran the Baldwin Locomotive works.

Tell me what you think of the job.

Yours fraternally,   Hammy

1. Short for "Hamilcar B. Fangs" (MM). Hamilcar was one of Hannibal's generals during the Punic Wars. Below, both "Bunny" and "Dusty" refer to MWM; "Furry" is Mary Norcross.

2. MM had been offered a position as a secretary for Melvil Dewey at Lake Placid in New York.

3. *Samson and Delilah*, an opera by Charles Camille Saint-Saëns (first produced 1877). Throughout 1910 MWM and MM went frequently to the opera house in Carlisle to attend concerts and plays. MM performed in this production of *Samson and Delilah.*

To Mary Warner Moore and John Warner Moore
Lake Placid Club, Essex Co., N.Y.   *Wed[nesday], July 6, 1910*

Dear Family,

I had a nice letter from Weaz this morning on arriving at Mr. Dewey's. The ride up was glorious, the harder the engine puffed the more exhilarated I was. The views are magnificent. I saw a little boy in a blue suit leading a white dog up a lavender hill and if that is not "modern art" may all salamanders be sunstruck. I couldn't possibly tell you about it. I will by degrees. All along the road pine trunks were strewed in the Ravines like a box of matches dropped in a darning basket. Not alone were there mountains but the sand dune effects, white sand topped with green and orange fringe around the top. Up here Lake Placid looks just like the mirrors and looking glasses we used to put round Christmas trees and edge with moss and wooden animals only the animals aren't wooden. I have never seen such Lotus eaters, regular lushiolas and Lofty Lufuses. The men are beauties. I saw a man tonight in white flannel trousers and blue coat with a long white cape on his arm, lined with red, a perfect staggerer. The girls are just as pretty, and all the old women are young, [have] gently waving hair Mrs. Hagerty style, correct waists next door to too small, and languid airs, shapely frog leg hands, and petticoats scalloped and embroidered with real lace on the edge of the scallops. Miss Seymour met me here last night at the Club House and showed me my room for last night and today. Today I went to see the room at Mrs. Wilcox's but I don't like it and I am going to live in the club at Iroquois Tower. It will cost more, about $10. a month more, but Mrs. Wilcox is in the village and very dingy and living "plain" and without busts of nonsense such as golf and Debussy musicals. There are dozens of cottages here, Low Buildings Craftsman style. They lack finish but the effect is perfect and views beyond description. They have concerts twice a week in the Mohawk Club House, have a grand piano and the best musicians obtainable. They play everything they even strike up the *Samson and Delilah.* God rest it! I listened to a concert from the time I finished supper till I began this, Chopin, Wagner, etc. I haven't heard a concert at the Mohawk House, but they have a grand piano and 4 musicians here who hold forth afternoon and evening for about half an hour each time. The hall is half open, a part of the porch looking out on the Lake. A sign modest and distinct requests silence and the leader who plays the piano puts up the number of the selection in a Hymn [slit?] or similar arrangement and you look it up in the catalogue or reference book. Many are scattered round. The food is fine and Miss Seymour is very considerate. I think I shall like the work and the place is a honey pot.

I hope to be settled tomorrow. I ought to have my tennis racket but I will classify or suppress my wants later.

With dearest love, Weaz

My address is Lake Placid Club.

To Mary Warner Moore and John Warner Moore

Sunday July 31 [1910]

Dear Family,

I am spending a wild life, wild and glorious. I lay on the top of Cobble and sunburned for a while and ate blueberries and disturbed what I could find, that was alive, in the pools of rainwater. The water is soft, as soft as velvet. On the way down I met a man a woman and two children. I didn't look down as I stepped out of the path and I nearly tripped. The man said, "My! I thought you were dead."

I have been to all the plays (with Mrs. Heston). Mrs. Heston is the lady who admires Godfrey Dewey[4] so much and is social in her proclivities but very "considerate" (*very* considerate). I was glad to have her go with me for I felt rather distant from home and respectability but when I learned *one* reason for her interest in me I felt vile treachery had been practiced on me. There is a young man here or *was* here who took a fancy to me. He is rich, fair to middling and well dressed and fastidious, and melancholy and reclusive. He made me fidget and gnash with indignation. I don't know when I have been so riled. Mrs. Heston set about matchmaking and if there is a more odious institution in modern society than a matchmaker I should like to see it. Mrs. Heston felt sorry for Mr. Walker and thought she could sacrifice *me;* a nice tidy little quail. I gave her some doctrine, but very politely; she said "You know Mr. Walker is such a nice fellow. There's something youthful about him too. I wonder if you know what I mean. He's humorous, underneath that pall. He's had brain fag you know and been worried over financial troubles. But he's well off, not tremendously wealthy but he expects to stop business and travel in a few years. He says when he's forty." (He looks 35 to me.) "Yes" I said, "I know what you mean but I haven't much sympathy for Mr. Walker. I think wealth is a disadvantage when a man is as melancholy and inactive as Mr. Walker. He owes it to society to be a little more responsive."

"Well" said Mrs. Heston, "he is underneath but he's shy."

"Oh" I said, "I don't mean that he should be more responsive to individuals, I mean in his attitude to life." Shortly after, Saturday afternoon, I met them going to a recital. So was I going. Mr. Walker blushed furiously

4. Godfrey Dewey (1887–1977), author of books on spelling and phonetics.

and Mrs. Heston said "Oh Miss Moore—we've just been talking about you."
I said "Have you?" I was a perfect suck my thumb, and rough when I did
speak. (I continue:) Mr. Walker has gone home. FINIS.

---

7 P.M. I have spent the afternoon with the Norths. Dorothy[5] came up to me
in Arden one night at the theater and asked if I couldn't come over today to
Northgate. I came over after dinner intending to leave early. She suggested
that we take a walk. As we were leaving her mother invited me to supper so
here I am, waiting for Dorothy to dress for supper. On returning from our
walk we went out in the canoe (the Norths have rented one), and went up
the lake to Placid, pulled up the canoe and crossed the carry to take a look
at the lake (Placid). It was more fun than anything I've done since I've been
here.

I want to thank Weaz for the $5.00. It was most beneficent and
thoughtful. I have had just 5¢ in my pocket. But pay day is here and I ought
to get something.

The Crawley Plays were not much. The company is not so "tasty" as
Ben Greet's[6] though perhaps I've seen Ben at his best. The theater is indescribable. It alone is worth the price of admission in itself. Splendid tall
trunks and leaves and thick shrubs and evergreens and the sky showing way
up above.

With dearest love,   Fangs

I mended my blue cape last night, (the hood) and it looks well.

I return skein of thread (1) and I think I'll want more of the other.

To Mary Warner Moore and John Warner Moore   *Thursday,*
                                                    August 18, 1910

Dear Family,

I cut a dash and plunge in debt and neglect the quill. I have a dollar or
so but instead of hoarding my cash I got a tennis racket and some shoes and
a Hampton's magazine. I wanted to play right off, with Dorothy North and
thought sending my racket was precarious and one more straw on Bunny.
The game was fine. We played at 5 yesterday. Monday afternoon (at 5) I
went canoeing with Dorothy and Tuesday and yesterday we played tennis
and today is my half holiday.

Last night I took supper with the Clarksons. The Clarksons have

5. Bryn Mawr friend, class of 1909.
6. Ben Greet (1857–1936), English actor and manager of a theater company that
toured the United States. MM saw his performance of *The Tempest* in 1907, and his
name is a common reference in family letters.

moved into the quiet comfortable dining room (Bryn Mawr white rabbit style) and they asked me to come eat with them as they have an extra place. After supper we went to the annual Float at Lakeside. All the people who have energy decorate their boats with Japanese lanterns skeleton frames etc. Each float represents a picture or phrase and the line moves along before a reviewing stand. There was one dandy, the red cross camp with a fir tree and soldiers and nurses etc. sitting about. Most of them were on 2 canoes or boats. One was "Elaine," a couple of boats supporting a platform *and* Elaine; a red flag a lantern etc. on the order of the "Voyage to Arras." "Cream of Wheat" was good, and "The Late Prize Fight" was the funniest thing I have ever seen. (A man in a striped jersey engaging on a large platform, with another.) Clarence Graham and Miss Bement had a float on 2 canoes, entitled "The Inferno or Home Sweet Home," a tripod with red Fourth of July fire in it and a lot of imps in scarlet seated about.

The boat houses and wharves were all decorated with lanterns. It was a pretty sight. There was one float, "The Volcano," which was very amusing, a thing like a tepee that let forth rockets and kept rumbling. Firecrackers were going off in a tin box, inside.

I have 7 suitors. What do you think of that? They are all dandies.

Miss Seymour asked me about my back the other day. She said I walked sometimes as if my back weren't straight and she thought this (sedentary) sort of work were very bad for me. I reasoned with her (I never felt better) (I never felt so well) and I explained that I *knew* my back was crooked and that my doctor said as long as I kept in tone and didn't have back ache I needn't bother. If she agrees to let me try it as long as I want to, I will. Otherwise I guess you will refund my permit to become wild, and receive me.

Mouse will you send me some more of that chiffon ruching the deeper of the two if possible. [MM sketches examples.] I need it for my gray crepe dress.

Cousin Mary sent me some lovely white chamois gloves. I admired hers when she was here and she said "if you like these I am going to send you some. I was wishing I could give you some little memento of this trip and I'll just get you those." Wasn't it kind?

With dearest love,   Fangs

To Mary Warner Moore and John Warner Moore

Sunday, Aug[ust] 21 [1910]

Dear Family,

I went to "the show" Friday night. Mrs. Heston asked me and Miss Sawyer. We drove and came back by carriage. It was an exhibition of moving pictures, 1st half stationary, of Alaska, last half, Walkover Shoe factory at Brockton, Mass., an exhibition before the Pres. of the French Republic, and logging in the Italian alps.

The pictures were wonderful. Such coloring I have never seen. Some of them were lurid but the changing color ones made you hold your breath—*Sunset on the Columbia River,* for example. The river was perfectly light. Gradually a glow spread up, behind it and the line of trees on the shore and made a great bloody path in the water. Also the moonlight, was magnificent. One sailboat picture just made you feel as if you were at Monhegan. He spent considerable time on the Muir glacier showing changing lights and crevasses. The "exhibition" was splendid (the goings on before the President in Paris). Moorish dances were performed, grain ground, arts and sciences exhibited and the best of all, the elephant's bath. In a sort of wooded pleasure ground like Holly or Boiling Springs a huge pool was prepared. A trellis stood behind it and a chute extended from the top of the trellis down to the pool. In turn the elephants appeared at the top gradually crept forward extending their fore legs over the edge of the chute and zip, shot into the water, throwing the foam almost to the top of the toboggan. Each elephant driver ran to the steps where they came out to meet his elephant. *The Logging in the Italian Alps* was what we saw, Mouse, at home. The man in front of me was very amusing. He said to a little boy, "Look out Joe, or you'll get your feet wet." "Now hold onto your hats." At the end he said, "*My!* I'm glad *that's* over."

It was such a cold night, they had fires built all along the edge of the theater and I wore my sweater, gray coat and blue cape. Miss Sawyer brought newspapers which she spread out and we didn't take cold. Yesterday was the day that broke records. I cleaned the store house and worked on D.C. French Version (of Penal Code). At 1, Mr. Jaffrey from Theanoguen telephoned Miss Seymour that a yellow cat was over here and had been eating chipmunks and he had it in his bathroom and everybody was indignant and they wanted it disposed of. This cat had been at Cedars the week before occupying Miss Seymour's porch and she had given it to Mr. Graham to dissect. He was busy working on his float at the time, and let it get away. Miss Seymour looked savage; as savage as she can. Perhaps determined is a better word. She said "Miss Hewitt when you go to dinner, (at Lakeside she dines) tell Clarence Graham this is his last chance to dissect a yellow cat. If he doesn't do it, it's gone." Miss Seymour said she had sent the cat to Mr. Gallop (L.E.) several times to have it killed and this time it was going to be done.

"Well," I said, "I'd like to have it if Mr. Graham doesn't want it. Only I have no instruments. I wonder if Mr. Graham would lend me his." Miss Seymour said, "All right. Miss Hewitt tell Clarence if he will call up Miss Moore at 2 o'clock at Theanoguen she'll arrange with him what's to be done about the cat, for Mr. Jaffrey has agreed to keep her till 2, in his bathroom."

"Clarence" called me up and said he didn't want the cat. He was going to the woods and if I wanted I could have his instruments and chloroform which I would find in the laboratory. I put the cat in my room, did
some errands at Forest Hill, got Miss Seymour to let me off when I should
have done my necessary work. I took an hour first to get a box from Cedars
and the chloroform and go home, put the cat in the box, a comfort over it,
and table on top and then rushed back. I had a letter (10 carbon copies of
each sheet) to write for Mr. Dewey and that took me till a quarter of six. I
was in despair. But I got Mr. Graham's instruments and beat it. The cat was
dead. I threw the things off my table and bed. Set the table on the floor, tied
the pussy to the table spreading the paws, made an anterior and a posterior
transverse cut and a longitudinal, dissected one leg thoroughly. I saw what
I wanted to know apropos of Maxy's leg, location of arteries etc.[7] Took out
heart and lungs and examined ribs. I then went to Theanoguen boiler room,
borrowed an iron coal shovel, dug a hole down the slope from Iroquois
Tower and buried the cat. As I was digging moiling and rooting, clinking
against stones and tearing roots, Mr. West came along and his wife. He said,
"Digging for treasure?" I said "no, I'm digging a grave. It looks like the
opening chapter to a Maurice Hewlett story doesn't it?" They lamented the
cat and Mr. West said, "I took a picture of her this morning. I'll show it to
you if it comes out." Two men came along and also inquired at a distance
what I was doing. One is a young fellow, manufacturer or something. He
said, "I wish I'd known you were doing it, (dissecting) and I'd have helped
you. I like to do that sort of thing." People are all fine to me. I am spoiled to
death. Mr. Western at the boat house thinks a great deal of me but is very
casual. I like him but don't get acquainted as there . . . [Letter is incomplete.]

I am keen to go to West Point. The 30th of October will suit. (I don't mean
that I think they will set the game to please me.)

To Mary Warner Moore and John Warner Moore   *Tues[day],*
                                                       August 23 [1910]

Dear Family,
    I got a rubber coat today, a Bronx, 4.50. It matches the lily pad. It is
light and strong. It has the funniest tag on it (very [word]). "If this coat
should appear damp on the inside after wearing, do not assume that it leaks.
This condition is often caused by the condensation of moisture on the inside
of the coat from the heat of the body, on the same principle that moisture
appears on the outside of a pitcher of ice water in a warm room. To deter-

7. Max was a lame dog owned by the Moores.

mine whether the coat leaks or not place it over a barrel or pail and pour a quantity of water in the bag thus made, allowing it to remain several hours. If the water comes through the coat leaks, but not otherwise." Cogent isn't it?

Dorothy North has gone away to Lake Raquette and Mrs. North and she told me to take the canoe whenever I wanted it. I took it to go across the lake for my coat. I couldn't paddle at all. I was much embarrassed. I got there eventually and I improved coming home but Mr. Weston laughed when I landed and said, "You're just a little girl" in an indulgent tone and I felt very sore. I am going out with Miss Bryant a friend of the Norths, at 5 to-morrow.

Paul the bell boy waits on Mrs. Peeler and me and is "fine." I said tonight, "Paul can't you wait on us before the rest come?" He nodded. "Feed you any time." He changes from his bell boy's uniform into his white suit 3 times a day and Mrs. Peeler said, "Paul you dress more than anyone I have ever seen." Yes he said "Every meal."

I've made friends with the "actresses" the girls who have bleached hair and wear white coats over black evening dresses and call, "George bring my chewing gum it's in the pocket of my coat on the bed." They live here in the tower. George is Yale 1903 and very unusual. He has read Dumas and standard English, doesn't read popular novels, has "Billy" Phelps' list of reading or had, he said and read it through as he had occasion crossing off books as he got through with them. He is married to one of the girls and is very "demonstrative" at the same time has much sensitivity and originality. I am very much pleased with him. He has a strong sense of humor. A boy who harangued Biology with me for an hour tonight, the one who said he would have dissected the cat with me if he had time, was reading French and peacemealing [piecemealing] it out to us. He finally said have you ever read "Le Duc de ————" " "Ever read the duke of Coney Island?" said George. "It's fine." I could write for an hour if I had time. This boy went to Cornell. He was discussing Mendel, the Mendelian law, and botany and staining and a little bit of everything. At length he described to me different cuts of spider webs, a collection a man had, a Cornell professor. "Oh," he said, "They're wonderful. He's about the top notch in spiders."

I don't know whether I'll stay all winter. I want to but it's doubtful whether I fit the place. I asked Miss Seymour definitely the other day if they wanted me and she surprised me by saying she couldn't tell yet. She would know in a few weeks. She said I had made some pretty serious mistakes. I know that I have, and I have made up my mind to improve but the things she jumped on me for were things I had no idea I was responsible for. I was perfectly unaware of my shortcoming or I could have repaired it and it made me furious. I explained this but she still thought I should have had gumption to know I was responsible for this and that and until I can convince her that anything I know I am told to do, I can do, I don't know how things will go. She says she knows I have ability but she doesn't know whether it's for this sort of work or not, a mass of details. And I don't know either for I have to work doubly hard on all this truck which seems like nonsense when I could work on something higher class with less effort. Pictures for instance. But there is a lot I haven't tried, D.C. work etc. and have no doubt I can come up to the scratch on the other. I won't leave because they don't want me if anything I can do can prevent it. I know well enough I can "please" if I set about it so I am getting busy. Miss Seymour feels the friction. I never let an opportunity pass, to rub it in, to apprise her of the fact that I see things to a finish and do what I understand to do. She likes me personally and is very kind. She gave me some pills the other day when I had a cold, that fixed me up instantly.

With best love,   Weaz

I have lots of money. Don't send any.

I have just got your letter. Thank you for the money. I don't really need it. Shall I send it back or simply not cash it? I hate to have you impoverishing yourself. *Don't send the racket.* I wrote in my last letter about the dress. I'll probably be here this winter though it is rather [precarious?] to say so. My back is well, never better.

To John Warner Moore   *[343 N. Hanover, Carlisle, Pa.]*
November 13, 1910

Dear Weaz,

I don't know that I should care to live in New York even with you. I don't know *where* I should like to live unless in a nautilus shell. There is certainly a great deal of satisfaction to be got out of a very little money if you know how to prospect but New York is not a promising field. Think awhile and give us the result of your deliberation.

My aim in life at present is to become "beautiful" and sagacious. You can imagine how productive of husks and "joy beans" that program is to the most facile pup on earth but I am not so despicable as I make out. I hope your waggings prosper. Every dog his own leash adjuster is my motto. For *you.*

I took a long walk yesterday 9 miles from Holly to Boiling Springs with the Cowdrays, Miss Mary Bosler, Miss Clurie McKeehan and Miss Kendall and Margaret Shearer. We sampled the air and determined the toughness of our muscles. It certainly was no mean stroll.

I laughed till the stiffness was extracted from my frame, last night—at [Thomas] De Quincey. He is a sly cove and a wise.

I hear Yale has been losing in football—my sympathy.

Your inseparable wall-toad,   Poisonous

To John Warner Moore   *[March 3, 1911]*

Dear Pussy eyes,

There are three smells in our house, of superlative vileness and endurance, smoke from the parlor home-hearth equipment, the smell of ash wood drying in the kitchen oven, and of the clean clothes home from the wash. *Dies irae! Solvet Saeclum in favillae.*[8]

We have just been out to the Indian School and bought a collar of elks teeth and two vases. Between sorties I work on my poems. If some of them don't materialize this time in breakfast food, I'll kick my scrapbasket to California. I am going to try the *Sunset*. (I "don't see why not.") In other works, I am hopping slowly, but unequivocally, from my perch.

With love,   Weaz

"Tiny!" Little pussy eyes junior shall be wapwalloped.[9]

To John Warner Moore   *Glasgow   Tuesday, June 20, [1911]*

Dear Ouzel,

The old oaken bucket[10] has come up with a gator in it, in the precincts of Glasgow. It is a great old place, "not so select as Edinburgh," Mrs. Bain informs us, but there is enough forthcoming to content fringe-fangs.

We enrouted from Ambleside to Keswick yesterday. It was a perfectly glorious ride. We had a good coachman who cracked his whip and rounded up to the station in fine style when we got to Keswick and dropped a word now and again on the mounds of stones on famous highwaymen as we went along and the haunted houses and the peaks and streams and even roses. He pointed out Nab Cottage where Coleridge lived and the Swan near Grasmere, an Inn where Wordsworth drank a Bunny B. (wink!) or similar beverage and a house where Shelley lived. We walked up a part of the Dunmail Raise a long pull between two mountains, inspected the gills and becs and tarns and toddling lambs. The fells are covered with sheep, in fact there are so many Bunny felt slight incentive to paddle them. We also saw Wythburn Church, next to smallest in England.

At Keswick we had two hours, about. We fed at the Keswick station hotel. Had an excellent fish, cold chicken, bread, apple tarts, cheese and crackers. They call crackers over here, "biscuits" and petrol or gasoline for cars

8. "Day of anger! The ages dissolve into ashes [or dust]." A famous medieval hymn of repentance.

9. A response to MWM, who had written on the same page that MM "lays about him with all his tiny arm radius" when writing JWM.

10. Reference to "The Old Oaken Bucket," a popular poem by Samuel Woodworth.

and motors, "motor spirits." "Pratts Motor Spirits" is a prevalent ad. even in Ambleside.

We had a good deal of fun in Ambleside with an English Congregational Minister and family. Mr. Taylor was our standby and Mr. Caisely a Scotchman and Miss Brooks, an American. But that is a chapter in itself. Mr. Taylor said, "He's not got much under his hat, that chap." And after a moment of vicious reflection he said, "He's a *thorough cad*"—"a half-inch toff." The man would ask us, "Hev you heard of William Morris?" Or "You're really more Scotch or Irish than American. You say, 'Ver'ra,'" or, "'and hev you good water in America. Do you get nice streams from the Rocky Mountains?'" All this incensed Mr. Taylor and us too but the fellow was too much a dolt to boomerang.

Mr. Taylor, Mr. Caisley and the elder Mr. Walmsley went on an all day walk up Fairfield Mountain peak. Mr. Taylor had no nails or rubber plugs in his heels and had a terrible time. He is stout and predisposed to thirst. He said, "When I got to the top of that mountain, I had a thirst—well it would have been worth 20 shillings to any landlord round about." Mr. Caisley lives in Newcastle. He rode to Penrith on his wheel Saturday between showers. It rained cats and dogs when he got to Penrith. But there he got the train to Newcastle. This he wrote to Miss Brooks. He said "The heavens opened but I caught the train at Penrith and was dry from there till I got home. Tell Mr. Taylor I was *very* dry." He added "Please *don't* remember me to the *bigoted nonentity*."

I got some decent paper in Glasgow as you see.

We are at a tidy boarding house, the only boarders in it with a breakfast room to ourselves. We also have a bathtub at disposal for which, *praise be*. We went to the Art Galleries the first thing this morning. By the way, we took in the museum at Keswick, in which was a collection of etchings from the South Kensington Museum, also a collection of English birds, (these are very prevalent, these collections). I identified a bullfinch and a ring "ouzel." I had seen both at Ambleside and on the train I saw from the window, a pheasant and a grouse and three skylarks. Mr. Taylor got me at Ambleside 2 little books on local birds which I appreciate as much as anything I've been given. There was a picture in it of *Guillemots* a species of gull. Miss Brooks said "How do you pronounce those; g-u-i," etc. Mr. Taylor said "As lads we used to call them 'gilly-mots'—I really suppose it's French."

We saw also at Keswick, Southey's gloves, clogs, and some autograph verses, one about Lodore a waterfall near Ambleside, a lock of Wordsworth's hair, some photographs of music stones, stones you tap that give a sound in a scale, and some embroidery and photographs of Matthew Arnold. I had a very nice time Sunday night at Ambleside, sitting by the fire in the kitchen. Mr. Walmsley told me some anecdotes of Ruskin and read me some letters from Ruskin to Miss Susie Beever. The kitchen is very old fashioned and the fireplace a grate, with shelves on each side and oven arrangement for cooking and standing a tea kettle. We also saw at Keswick Greeta Hall where Southey lived and harbored Coleridge. It's a dismal place about the size of the Hayses house and used for a girls' boarding school.

We ran into Mrs. Sprout and 2 people we met on the steamer. They were in the car coming across town in Phila. 2 women in black with a tall young man.

At last, here we went to the Art Galleries. There we saw—!!!Rembrandt, a soldier; Millais' sheepfold and another, 3 Corots, Velasquez! a gentleman, several Turners, a Dürer, a moorish thing by Arthur Melville one of the best in the gallery, Burne-Jones' the *Danaë and the Brazen Tower*, some Romneys and [Henry] Raeburns and [Meindert] Hobbemas and Titians; and Whistler's *Carlyle* a magnificent thing and the Lord knows what in the way of Assyrian and Greek copies and the best geological and biological demonstrations I have ever seen in my life. Bryn Mawr is a pimple to the whole thing. We saw a *roc's* egg!! (= crocodilius Mississippiensis).

With love,   Weaz

To John Warner Moore   *Oxford   July 5 [1911]*

Dear Weaz,

Oxford for fat rich olfactory impressions. I never have seen such a place. It's a Persian garden in terms of modern student life. Everything we have seen is a rush light in comparison (and a garbled metaphor). It's the savour of use on everything that makes it doubly impressive! I thought I was "rolling" a little in Warwick, but I clean tumbled and had to be fetched when we got above 3 blocks from the railway station *here*. Warwick is swarmed over by tourists and petty tradesmen; though Kenilworth is a fine sight it is trampled down metaphorically speaking. Warwick castle and Warwick castle grounds are not like anything else. The grass is beautiful and the shrubs and cedar trees ancestral pagodas in themselves and the peacocks make your hair stand on end. One spread his tail and tottered about a little before us, every feather perfect and the green on his neck enough to make you faint. And the portraits and statuary and the collection of arms in the house are very fine. I shan't be satisfied now till we have an armoury, (if we have to sack Abbotsford to fit it out). The Roman swords were the only ones I've seen and the chain mail was particularly fine. We had splendid coaching from Warwick to Kenilworth and also to Stratford. The private estates are beautiful. The Lucy estate was an eye opened. Millions of bunnies playing around holes in the roots of trees and deer, brown and red, the descendants of the ones the Shakespeares poached, and streams and 2 stone boars on the gate. It was all like a fairytale. The whole place was I should say about the size of Carlisle and dotted with these fawns and deer. We got to Oxford Tuesday. We visited the colleges today, with a guide. Each college has its chapel and dining hall, quadrangle and garden & library; some have two quadrangles. In Pembroke we saw Dr. Johnson's portrait by [Joshua] Reynolds in the masters and fellows commons and Dr. Johnson's teapot and his desk in the library. The colleges buy buildings of one another and are in every way distinct. The quadrangles are beyond description with shaved grass ovals and wide yellow gravel paths around them. And all the windows have windowboxes with flowers in them of uniform color. The gardens are young parks, entirely secluded with high walls around and gravel paths and old trees and banked shrubs. One (Trinity) has a walk of limes in it. Some of the quadrangles are entirely gravel with traces of bonfires in the centre, from celebrations of victories. The river is the nicest thing of all, a mere streamlet, but bordered by magnificent trees and a nicely kept path and there are swans on it, one black fellow we noticed with a red beak and it is full of fish. The water is so clear you can see every movement of the fins and of the swans' "webs." In the back park to Magdalen there were 30 or 40 fawns feeding. The boating seems tame; it is on the order of creeping on the water or nosing like a fish. You pole along but it is shady and the air felt cool today when the air in the town was roasting. We saw the Burne-Jones tapestry, and Christchurch College dining room. The portraits on the walls, the vaulted ceiling, and the trenchers on the serving tables, are indescribable. The Burne-Jones tapestry was chiefly blue and red and all the workmanship of the finest imaginable. The reredos in the Exeter Chapel is inlaid with gold or rather the mosaics are gilded and the whole thing is very rich and quiet, quieter in fact than most of the chapels.

We went to the Bodleian yesterday. It is small but choice, the atmosphere of rarity fairly stifles you. The librarian was very pompous and decrepit. He called to one of his underlings, (one of his 50) "*Mis*ter—will you pull down theese shade—or *get* someone to do it." He then mumbled out a few more directions. They have some manuscripts at the B. of Shelley's and Milton's, a lock of Shelley's hair and the Sophocles taken from his hand when he was drowned and so forth. They have an Alfred the Great Manuscript and part of the *Iliad* on Papyrus, an old Euclid, an illuminated book on Animals (in Latin); the page open was about Salamanders "kinds of lizards with arms . . . against whom the fire was not powerful to inflict injury." They have a book bound in some silk of a waistcoat of Charles I.

In the portrait gallery they have a chair made from the wood of the *Golden Hind* on which Sir Francis Drake sailed round the world and some Elizabethan trenchers or roundels—dessert plates, wooden the size of a bread and butter plate with verses on them. I copied out a few which I will give you when we get home.

The boys here are a very deluxe lot apparently. (And *roll* in hansoms.) Hansoms designate the doors of closing halls, as ants an anthill. I don't mean they take hansoms to and fro about the town, but going to the station. They ride wheels and horses and punt on the river and disport white flannels & loud ties and socks. Such a combination of taste and seasickness I never have seen. Green socks with orange clocks, lavender socks and flannel coats with wide rainbow stripes of orange light blue and dark blue, but they look scholarly and their shoes and flannels are immaculate. They go in pairs spinning down a crowded street on bicycles carrying nets filled with tennis balls, (like a shopping bag filled with sponges). I have maybe overdrawn this a little but it's "what they look like." (I'll say this though, they are polite and their accent is curious to the 30nth power plus. You ought to hear them.)

We waggle about so, feeding and seeing there is no time to comment let alone "write," but that you understand.

With love,   Weaz

Special. (Corr. to Egg) Oxford Jul 5: It is a common sight to see Bunny engaged in exploitation of a fruit stall, supervising the lining of a basket with a cabbage leaf and the shaking in of strawberries and to see Mr. Fangs in deep study before a pastry shop.

To John Warner Moore   *London   July 9 [1911]*

Dear Weaz,

Having once seen London you will live in a blaze of glory all your life. It is acre of fungus on acre of fungus, on toad stool, on ant hill and repeated again. 'Buses thread the streets and wheel round each other and across each other and policemen punctuate the town like may beetles. The 'buses are 2-story affairs and most of them motor 'buses; being operated like motor cars, keeping in a rough line, (placarded over with advertisements), though at liberty to pass each other if passengers accumulate and cause undue delay. We went out to Hampton Court yesterday and it took two hours. We took the British Museum tube for half an hour to Shepherd's Bush and then a train car.

Hampton Court is a four ply palace in a garden of the French sort. There is a large vine in a hot house there, 4 or 5 feet round the stem and covering a small trellis under a roof, about the size of the parlor ceiling at home. It was full of grapes which were pruned and trained down through the trellis to hang to the best advantage. The Palace has rooms on rooms, 27 or so full of pictures, some good and some bad. There are wonderful tapestries and a series by [Andrea] Mantegna *The Triumphs of Caesar*, a series of panels in distemper painted for an Italian and bought by Charles I. The palace is on the whole very bare and tawdry but the collection of arms in one room is the most appalling we have seen. Pistols arranged in a great whirl so I took it for a South African igloo flattened out. We got home about supper time and hung out our window, looking at the street after supper. All sorts of people pass. It might be Coney Island for the number of styles you see. Women in ball dresses and cockatoo hats and men in dress suits and cricket costumes and porter's boys and servant maids and what not. We are in a very quiet part of the town, all 4-story residential hotels or boarding houses, with brass knockers and fancy parlors (plush & mirror effects) downstairs. We are in a block between 2 parks, greenery fenced in, and Bury St. is very near the British Museum.

We got some fruit there on the way home from Hampton Court—fine fruit—the best we have had. It has on all the bags, I notice, "only Canary bananas sold at this establishment." Also "families waited on."

We went to Kelmscott from Oxford on Friday. It is 3 quarters of an hour by train from Oxford in a sweltering farm district. The flowers, weeds, birds, were beautiful and we heard a sky lark (saw and heard) but it was a long 2 mile walk to Kelmscott and then we only saw the garden. It was beautiful but the gardener hadn't been there in William Morris's time and we were rather stung on the whole. Oxford is the "apple" so far.

This morning we went to St. Paul's as the Abbey is closed. I was very much disappointed, it is so gaudy and the congregation kept swishing about, in and out like swallows in a barn but it was what I knew it was going to be.

London is too immense to monkey with at all if you can't stay some time and I am glad we hurried ourselves in Scotland.

Bunny is looking over postcards sniffing admiringly but she will probably write later. The Henley regatta is on; finished yesterday and I would have given my snout to have seen it but we didn't go. Harvard and Yale compete with Oxford and Cambridge on the 12th too but we may not go. In field sports, that is.

With love, Weaz

To John Warner Moore *[Paris] Sabbath, August 13, 1911*

Dear Weaz,

I have Bunny in a basket with a cloth over her to keep the heat off, and I have a nest of lettuce in the basket. But Bunny rolls on it and frays the edges without eating very much.

Old Paris is a great place. The names and state of preservation of the place is beyond my highest expectations (or *are*. I am all balled up). The language of the *ville* is amusing. A sweater is a *chemise de sport* and the omnibuses belong to the *voiture Co. Générale.* The town is full of *oiseaux* and poodles, some very mangy, dreary poodles with few patches and dusty ears and plain legs.

All along the Seine there are bookstalls and curio stalls. Little tin traps or boxes are set up on the wall and propped open during the day. The posters and paper covered books in the town, by streets and so on are wonderful, and the cafés. The cafés for the most part consist of wicker tables with round marble tops stood in rows 3 deep along the side walk and you can get beer, soda water (not "sodas"), ices and lemonade. We have more fun than a picnic talking French. The policemen are very polite and very voluble in their directions, but we manage to understand. Things to buy are more expensive here than in London I am sorry to say, for I had rather hoped to pick up trivialities for nothing. But pictures are cheap. I got an 8 x 12 photograph of Rodin's *Penseur* for a franc (20 cents).

There are a great many birds in cages all over the town and small stores with lead soldiers for sale and toys.

We went to the Luxembourg day before yesterday. They have the most beautiful sculpture and jewelry I have ever seen and the paintings are fine. I can't find the Hôtel de Tréville or Palais Cardinal not having sufficiently informed myself before arriving. But I intend to ask at the Odéon bookstore. A young snipper snapper from Washington told us the Odéon was the literary oracle of Paris.

I got a Dumas the evening after we arrived, 2 volumes (*Le Chevalier de Maison-Rouge*). "*Très excitant*" the man told me. People are very kind when they see we don't know French and are explicit.

The Louvre is full of "rotten Rubens." I have never seen such atrocities. Mary de Medicis and Henry IVs floating in Elysian "*déshabille*" amidst cherubs and fat Homeric porters. But if you could see the "antiquities," the Victory [of] Samothrace and some Assyrian things they have. The Assyrian Gallery could put the British Museum in its pocket. We also trained our pig eyes on some Dürers and some drawings in colored chalks.

The Knoxes were here when we arrived. Mary and Miss Louise and a friend. To see their staid respectability in this rat hole was a marvel. We took a taxi from the station (St. Lazare) and when we drove up to dingy cobbles and a running gutter and halting beggars down the street (a way) I *gasped.* But we got out, went through the door into the courtyard and there was a bower full of birds in a cluster of vines and everything apparently tended and clean. A large "*Pension de Famille*" over the door was reassuring. Inside, the table was set and looked very nice with thin glasses and napkins in checked covers. Mlle. Guillet appeared and babbled at us a little. We understood moderately but Mlle. Guillet fetched Mlle. Agé who speaks English. We are now very casual with our phrases but my dear boy, it was an experience.

There is a very nice man here (of the type of Mr. Taylor whom we met in England). He said he had a phrase book which was very helpful and that he would let me see it. He said if you want to say something to the "garsong" in the morning you can say, "Common Tallay voo?" and it tells you the names and prices of things.

I was reading Bunny's letter to you and she said "Can you read it?" I said "No. I'm in kindergarten but pretend I can read and sit with the paper up-side-down under my paws, slobbering over it and looking with wise pig eyes, but haven't learned my letters yet."

Napoleon's Tomb was wonderful. I didn't like the red granite it was made of but the general impression was just what I had expected.

I am very much interested to hear of Ralph's engagement. There is a New Haven girl here. A girl and her mother. I don't know their names but they are very nice people—the nicest in the place except the "garsong" gentleman.

Dear Bunny reads the guide book (on Sunday) with the utmost *sang froid* and says "(I think we'll have to go up the Arc de Triomphe—upstairs.)"

I wish I knew what to get for people. I am most desperate. But I intend to make an exhaustive "hunt" tomorrow. Bunny spits so emphatically on everything except the million dollar baby rattles and turkey down fans, I don't know what to do with her, unless I slip her leash over a picket in the fence and go without her.

There is a little tawny freckle-haired dog in the pension and 2 cats (an angora and a tiger). The tiger and the flea (Lily) are great friends. They are about of a size.

The American Express is the paradise of the city. They have a reading room upstairs and sterilized water in a large aquarium sort of jug, and maps (of London and Paris) to give away, luxurious chairs and a commanding view of the city and "English is spoken." (oh ma soul.) I'll climb on my galleon with no feeble star points.

This may be my last, if so though, it will be an account of the vigorous snouting among these eelgrasses. We have had Spotted Flank with us every evening (and day).[11] The British Museum in London was our only respite. He could not go [to] the classical corridors and bibliographical collections. He enjoys the cafés and his straw. He is always ordering the *garçon* to bring him "*une paille.*"

With love,   Weaz

Spotted "*Flanque*" has an "Englishmen on the Continent: How to make yourself understood" and pretty work he makes of the language.

11. Spotted Flank is another third-person pseudonym for MM.

To John Warner Moore   343 N. Hanover Street   Carlisle, Pa.
Sunday, November 23, 1913

Dear Pidge:

I asked Longears this morning if she was playing possum or turkle. She said, "Turkle. Me not like Amellican possum. It has an ugly tail." I said, "Why it couldn't have a hairy tail. Its tail is like that, so its offspring can twine their tails round it." "Yes," Longears said. "It has good points. It just happens me never play possum." That was some letter Longears wrote you on the mummy and grasshopper. Ask Longears if she is practising for publication.

I finished a poem yesterday. There is a great deal of work on it and I have been putting it off. I am going to be very harsh with somebody if I do not get it printed sometime. I brought home *McClure's* from school, for Nov. and Dec. with a view to reading [Owen Johnson's] *The Salamander* when I had mended some of my gear, and finished my poem. I didn't get to *McClure's* till evening and then Honey came down to say Miss Anna was going to read her club paper on Selma Lagerlöf, to Mrs. Benét, and the Cowdrays and us if we cared to hear it. It was a splendid paper, and gave me an idea [of] the "field" of Nils and Gösta Berling[12] and other of S.L.'s books that I hadn't dreamed about or cared about. Miss Anna promises to lend me the books. I am very much pleased with *The Life of the Spider,* by [Jean-Henri] Fabré, (translated by Alexander Teixeira de Mattos, F.Z.S.). For example a description of two dung-beetles. "Hardly has he begun, by dint of great effort of his frontal shield and bandy legs, to roll the sphere backwards, when a colleague appears and hypocritically offers his services. The other knows that in this case, help and services, besides being quite unnecessary, will mean partition and dispossession, and he accepts the enforced collaboration without enthusiasm. But so that their respective rights may be clearly marked, the legal owner, invariably retains his original place, that is to say he pushes the ball with his forehead, whereas the compulsory guest pulls it towards him. And thus it jogs along . . . amid interminable vicissitudes, flurried falls, grotesque tumbles, till it reaches the place chosen to receive the treasure. . . . The dishonest partner makes untold efforts to play upon the other['s] credulity, turns it round, embracing it, propping himself against it, with fraudulent heroic exertions and pretends to be frantically supporting it on a non-existent slope."

I now am going to fold the corners of the mercerized, pictorial blanket, around your rabbit's rotundity, as it is night.

With love, Pidge

---

12. Lagerlöf wrote many novels about these characters, including *Gösta Berling's Saga, The Story of Gösta Berling,* and *The Wonderful Adventures of Nils.*

To John Warner Moore   *Sunday, Jan[uary] 11, [1914]*

Dear Bruno,

I seem to be having trouble with my arithmetic.[13] I am much obliged for the problems tendered and understand them. I can't make anything of section, 634 P. 641 though (I got problem 1, page 245). I can't get (2) and (4) page 245 and (1) and (2) page 246. Sometime I'd like to have them though I will not be to them till next week (Jan. 19).

Longears and I have been on considerable of a tear. One thing we have done. We have selected a lamp standard at Gehrings. It is plain and well weighted and is a fine thing I think [MM sketches the lamp]. But we have to get one without a shade as he has a red glass affair on it which simulates the infernal regions. He has written for another but hasn't heard yet.

I spent most of yesterday putting my room in order, writing a letter to Brentano's ordering some paper, and writing to Mrs. Grosvenor.

Friday I was pulverizing the clouds with my hooves. I tried to buy a piece of black Zuni pottery about 5 inches across that had belonged in the studio, and Mr. Miller gave it to me. I went to ask Mr. Friedman about it first and incidentally regretted that the work of my students hadn't been satisfactory in any case but one. (He had written me about it.) I added some opprobrium and I said "well Mr. Friedman, I'm discouraged. I am not going to quit unless you tell me to but I'm discouraged." He said, "Well I don't know what you're doing here anyhow—a girl that's a graduate from Bryn Mawr." That is rather strong from Sourball.

with love,   Pins

To John Warner Moore   *October 4, 1914*

Dear Badger,

What did *you* say about the war today? I hope not "to sit tight and not rush to the door of your hole at the first rustle of an unfamiliar tread."

Kel [the Reverend Kellog] harangued a long time to great point and said that peace is not the only alternative in the case of loyalty to God.

You didn't say anything about making a frame of *Badger honey* for the Conovers, or coming home again before Christmas. What about that? Mole and me were invited to Hall [Cowdray]'s today for dinner with Margaret, and had a very pleasant time. Margaret is a thinker and much "funnier" than I ever hoped she could be. You know how witty Conway is when he feels lightsome.

I play tennis every day now and am more the man, for doing it.

13. JWM often helped MM work out math problems that she would then assign to her students at the Indian School.

Mole pin points me a good deal but my ribs would never show. They draw in from every opprobrious attack.

Are you pug wrinkling for any cause? I hope not.

I had a fine letter from Lizard's Beetle coat yesterday. (Mr. Plank.) He feels with England on the war just about as if we were in it. He has had a fine time visiting with the breed of beetlewings in London—Yeats, Ezra Pound and others.

Rat meanwhile is throwing every energy into a war poem.

with love,   Rat

To Harriet Monroe   *April 8, 1915*

Dear Miss Monroe:

Unless you object, I should like to use as a title for my poems, "Tumblers, Pouters and Fantails"; and I like the order in which you have arranged the poems.

Please use as a title for the David poem, "That Harp You Play So Well," and be kind enough to print "To an Intra-Mural Rat" without quotations. I have seen the phrase in print—"Intra Mural Rat"—and I should quote it rather than appear to trespass but it had occurred to me independently and I see no reason for quoting it.

Might "Counseil to a Bachelor" read,

"Counseil to A Bachelor"   A in Capitals
Elizabethan Trencher Motto—Bodleian Library: } Italics
(with title, and modification of second line)? }
I am sorry your rates are lower than they have been but I can easily understand that it might be necessary to make them so.

Since I last wrote to you, poems of mine have been accepted for publication by *The Egoist*. I do not know whether or not they have been printed and should you wish to say that work of mine has not appeared previous to the appearance of those poems selected by you for publication in *Poetry*, I should be willing.

Sincerely yours,   Marianne Moore

I thank you for your suggestions as to title and am grateful for criticism, even adverse.

To John Warner Moore   *May 9, 1915*

Dear Badger,

Willow has exhibited his coon at two drug stores for 50 cents in each case and was only induced by his Uncle Snapper to liberate it, by the promise of an American Traveller next summer (a year from this summer).[14] What you say about his hanging 'round a stable is perfectly true. He let his tail into Bunstable Blacktail's milkpail a few nights ago the hired man told them. Bunstable now has three additions to his family, Snapper, Bullawee, and Chicky (a rabbit).

My poems came out this week to the polite oh's and ah's of the neighborhood—Mole is very much disgusted with me for owning up to them, or at least to consenting to discuss the matter. Miss Rose just returned from N. York, says she told Billy [Benét] that "that English paper called me an imagist" and he said he would advise me not to let myself be influenced too much by the Imagists. I'll have to tell Billy or rather show him that it's like getting married; I am sorry to disappoint him, but it is not possible to meet his views on the subject and please myself.

Mrs. Benét is all cordiality and all the Roses are, in fact. Honey took us to Harrisburg last week. We saw the Capitol which I was most anxious to have Eunice see; Mrs. Benét explained the Barnard[15] statues and we drew Eunice's attention to the floor, with the exception of which Mole says the capitol is a mass of iniquity. Rat obtained leave of absence for a few minutes to get out two or three books, [Richard] Curle on Conrad [*The Last Twelve Years of Joseph Conrad*], Amy Lowell, "Imagist" and [Samuel] Butler's *Notebooks*. Then we were taken to reservoir park to see the Judas trees and the golf course and then up the river to Rockland, Mrs. Benét and Eunice, simultaneously, en route, taking us to Rose's for [the] dog. Eunice entertained the party, took Mole home some candy and a plaster mouse. We had a fine time. I took Eunice in the evening to Charlie Goodyear's pupils' recital which was not an unmixed treat. Tuesday Miss Winnie Woods invited us to tea to meet Mrs. Coche, (Mr. Plank's newly married sister) and Mrs. Glass.[16] Miss Martha Hench was there and Miss Mary Shearer and about 10 more. Mrs. Coche is a fine girl, neither spoiled nor homely, rather tall with dark hair and a level head. I perceived no superfluous bells either external or mental. She has Cousin Mary Shoemaker's very settled manner but is less stony, and she is thin.

With love, Rat

14. "Uncle Snapper" may be MM herself or JWM; "Willow" is also MM. "American Traveller" could refer either to the monthly journal *American Traveller's Gazette* or to Henry Tanner's *The American Traveller; or, Guide Through the United States* (1834). Bunstable Blacktail is probably a neighbor. A few weeks earlier, MM acquired a raccoon, and several family letters refer to this event.

15. George Grey Barnard (1863–1938), sculptor.

16. Mrs. Glass was also George Plank's sister, and lived in Carlisle.

Tell me what "transpired" at your supper with Margaret Morison. I am going to send her a copy of my poems when I get hold of an extra one.

You can see them at the Ratt. Ask for or look for, *Poetry* for May.

To John Warner Moore   *Sept[ember] 22, [19]15*

Dear Badger,

I'm glad you are "prospering." You are a noble fellow.

We have had a busy day. Hall Cowdray and I went to the fair to distribute suffrage leaflets and talk to farmers. We found that our Headquarters' banner stretched between two maple trees had blown off at one corner. I climbed on a chair and onto the roof of the neighboring "portable house" and secured it, and then descended with considerably more glibness than I had ascended.

Saturday we called on Mrs. Russell. Mrs. Russell lamented Richard's introduction to V.M.I. [Virginia Military Institute?], played for us, allowed me to examine the books, and showed us their old furniture, some of the finest things I have ever seen, a rushbottomed, bulbous legged Dutch day couch, like the French chaise lounge, and a dressing table with a top which lifted up by a hinge; the space below the top was a jewel case, oval, the exact size of the table lined with blue velvet. Mrs. Russell also has an alarm jewel box. If you pick it up by the handle it jingles like a fire engine bell till you set it down. (Excellent idea.) The Russells have some rare writing tables and the finest Windsor chairs, arm chairs, I've ever seen. A mixture of mahogany apple and walnut, finished dull. The wood is light, not quite like maple.

Today I did so much talking Hall said I ought to go on the stump. The people surely were respectful and every man but three said they would vote for suffrage in November.

Yesterday Honey took me to Hbg. [Harrisburg] to return books while she bought a hat and suit. Miss Anna and Mrs. George H. and Blaine went also. I brought home Hueffer's [Ford Madox Ford's] *Memories and Impressions,* a pearl of a book in which Hueffer tells about the Pre-Raphaelites and his grandfather who looked "exactly like the king of hearts on a pack of cards," and Morris who said, "Mary those six eggs were bad. I ate them but don't let it happen again." He says they all looked like old fashioned sea captains and Morris was gratified beyond measure on several occasions at being stopped by sailors and questioned with regard to their shipping with him. I also got [George] Moore's *Hail and Farewell* (*Ave,* rather), Evelyn Innes and the last Imagist Poet anthology. Also read Ezra Pound's article on Vorticism in last year's *Fortnightly Review* which I have been after, for some time. When I got to the hat shop I still had an hour I think at least a half hour before Honey got through. When we came out Kauffman's indulgent look of amusement was one of the funniest things I've ever seen. He said, "Blaine says he could buy 800 hats in the time you were in there." Yesterday I played tennis with M. Bosler, Gayle Strohm and Almeda Jones. Afterwards Almeda and Gayle sang for us, over here, and it surely was an experience. Good music.

Richard Aldington mentioned me in *Greenwich Village* for July. Not very emphatically but I am obliged to him. *Greenwich Village* is a clever magazine—(non-political).

w. love,   Rat

I took in none of the animals but a little black bantam rooster, with drooping wing, very aggressive.

To John Warner Moore   *October 3, [19]15*

Dear Badger,

The Bell has come, paused, and proceeded.[17]

Yesterday Mole and I hung around the house, re-establishing order and writing a few letters.

Alfred Kreymborg is going to use some of my poems in the December *Others*. He added a *postscript* to the effect that he thought my work "an amazing output and absolutely original if with his 'uneddicated consciousness' he might judge"—*which* caused Mole's lip to curl. I said to Mole, "now with what poems I have published and my general well-being, I could publish a book anytime." Mole said "I wouldn't publish." I said, "Never?" Mole said, "After you've changed your style." "Huh!" I said, "you would omit all these things I prize so much?" "Yes," said Mole, "they're ephemeral."

Life last week had a paragraph on *Others* by [John Barrett] Kerfoot. He said the new poetry was revolutionary and you might not like it, but it was worth the price of a Wednesday matinee, to find out, or something like that. Alfred contributed a long criticism of Duchamp the author of the *Nude Descending a Stair Case*, to the Buldy [*Bulletin?*] last Saturday.

I have just finished [Benvenuto] Cellini's memoirs and if anything is calculated to make Don Quixote "look like a Cumberland timetable," they are. He had a "large hairy dog black as mulberry," which stood by him on many occasions and his intrepidity is beyond belief. He says on one occasion, "swelling like an asp, I resolved on a desperate thing" and again, "I

17. The Philadelphia Liberty Bell was on tour as a publicity event for the women's suffrage movement. MM and MWM, as described in the accompanying "File," helped decorate the Court House for the event and joined the "parade." MM also passed out leaflets.

clothed myself with patience than which nothing is harder to me." You will have to read it for yourself.

With love,   Winks

To John Warner Moore   *October 10, [19]15*

Dear Winks,

Moley beats me this I know,
for my spare ribs tell me so.

Mole is not a little condemnatory of me because I exerted myself so, to prepare for the lady who is visiting Mrs. Glass and who knows the Aldingtons—Miss Rhodes.[18] We suggested last week that she and Mrs. Glass come to tea today at 2 as they had to get home at 4 to receive the children from school. Miss Rhodes came alone saying Mrs. Glass had had to go to Harrisburg. She is a perfectly delightful lady, rather tall with gray hair and she wore a lovely hat black velvet with gray silk bows or rather ribbon side wing effects. She told me all about my confederates. Said Mrs. Aldington kept her house spotless and that Mr. Aldington has dispensed with a hat, that the Whitalls had two houses one in town and one in the country and that their father had made a prodigious pile of money, in the cement business, that James Whitall was writing a novel superintended by George Moore, that John Cournos was poor as poor but very interesting, growing daily more so, that Mr. Plank was asked at a very regal dinner one time, where there were a lot of the aristocracy, how he came to start on his career and he told them with great gusto that he had been born "in jail" (his father was a sheriff) and how he had sold mackerel and washed windows, and they assured him that such a thing could never have happened in England. I learned also, to my great satisfaction, that Dora Marsden[19] whom I abominate, and who contributes to *The Egoist*, pays for a front page every month, on which to air her views about Truth and Reality and that if it weren't for her financial support, *The Egoist* couldn't exist.

To my disgust I learn that Yeats has interested himself in spiritualism and is busying himself about that to the exclusion of everything else. Miss Rhodes deplored the fact that such a cheap brainless fakirism should have secured a toehold on him. Ask Mole when she got her little bull, Bealnambo?

Yesterday I dispatched my second installment of Missionary moneys and I suppose I have escaped jail by a miracle, the second time also.

18. H.D. and Richard Aldington were married in 1913.
19. Dora Marsden began *Freewoman: A Weekly Feminist Review* in 1911. The name of this publication was later changed to *The Egoist*.

Parade of the Un-enfranchised Animals--Bunny Longears trims the Court House with a large grasshopper's wing of yellow muslin. Mr. Rat weights the party banner with stones gathered from a distant gutter, street paving having been rather prevalent during the last two months. Mr. Willow Beekman joins the parade on his sheltie, with four rats following at his heels. He is warned to be as dignified as possible so that his entrance in the parade will not appear ~~like~~ an intrusion.

POETRY

The File Poet

Regret to think, how

   short a time

A summer chicky is

   in its prime.

Mosquito and Centipede
(written for the File)

With naked hand and

   slippered toe,

Consign them to the

   world below.

Editorial

The editor of the file regrets to note among rabbits, a tendency to wear what is knowing rather than what is becoming. Take, for example,

the matter of rhinestone whiskers and high heels. The rabbit's paw is round, a little like a walnut shell. It is foolish to crowd it into a cornucopia and make the whole contrivance conspicuous by ~~by~~ applying a design of rhinestone whiskers, sun's rays, rat's eye beadings or anything of the sort. Moreover it is a matter of extreme difficulty, to keep all four "soldier hats" on at once. The rabbits are officially discouraged from their imprudence.

Personals, apropos of the garden...........

The Mole does not want any violets. She "does not want any violets anywhere." This may seem strange but it is true.

A very small toad is made welcome at Mole End. Nobody knows anything about him. It is presumable that he is an orphan.

QUESTION BOX

The Editor of the File:
   Sir:

   Will you kindly tell me how to say, "I wonder," in French.

   I am, Sir, yours faithfully,

   ad astra per aspera.

permission to Mr. B. Mackenny and the Rev. J. W. B.

a. a. p. a.:

   Je me demande, is, we think, the expression that you desire.
         The Editor
            per T. We

The Editor,
   Sir:

   Will you kindly furnish me with the answer to this famous riddle. Some rats and I have had a dispute about it. And was it Frederic the Great who sent the riddle to Voltaire?
            2 Years.

~~2/1~~
      ~~Xff~~
         P
   "Venez à San Souci

   Oui, G a"

2 Years:

      Yes. The reading of the riddle is as follows:

   "Venez a souper, San Souci."

   "Oui, j'ai grand appetit."

      Readers of the File are requested to append their full names to questions submitted to the Editor.
I
Is the File worth while?
You are referred by

I have received a peacock from Edwin [Howard], a large Japanese print of bird on tree with gold tail—very beautiful; it is an old master I think Hokusai, or some such.

I patterned after you and walked home with Miss Rhodes as I was lending her some books and magazines. It will be a pretty intrepid fellow that will buzz around Rat, now to annoy him; freshened up as he is, and full of life.

With love,   Rat

To John Warner Moore   *December 12, [19]15*

Dear Badger,

Yesterday from 10–12:30 Mr. Norcross, Florence's brother, paid tribute to us, and the day before from 10 to one. Mole says while anyone wants anything of us we "*dare*" not be too tired to give it.

I'll have to tell you about the expedition in installments.[20] I suppose Mole told you that I had met J. B. Kerfoot. Wednesday morning I went to "291" to see as I thought, some of Alfred Stieglitz's photography. He had an exhibition up of [Oscar] Bluemner, a modern architect. Mr. Stieglitz was exceedingly unemotional, and friendly and finally after telling me how he was hated, said I might come back and look at some of the things standing with their faces to the wall in a back room. I enjoyed them. He has a magnificent little thing of the sea in dark blue and some paintings of mountains by a man named [Marsden] Hartley, also some Picabias and Picassos and so on. He told me to come back and he would show me some other things. I stopped at the Modern Gall. on my way home to see some Van Goghs and some of Mr. Stieglitz's magazines and at one I got back to the Training School. Zaroubi Himurjian took us for luncheon to a Turkish restaurant, the Constantinople. We had soup and pieces of meat roasted on skewers and meat fried in grapeleaves and rice and pastry and ice cream. We then saw some ancient Chinese rugs at an Armenian wholesale rug place and an importer there took us to see the processes of silk making. The demonstrator was a "parvenu" as Zaroubi said who buzzed on about reels and filatures and dyevats punctuating his story with asides to his stenographer. Finally he said, "Minnie is my taxi waiting?" "I have a luncheon engagement at the Astor House for 12 o'clock and I'm now half an hour late but might as well complete the story. This is the last process." Finally he took his coat and stick and hat and sailed off telling the stenographer, that if anyone wanted him,

20. MM had gone to New York with Hall Cowdray and her family. They apparently met Zaroubi Himurjian, an architect and painter, and a close friend of Alfred Stieglitz's, at the YWCA Training School, where they stayed.

he would be in *"the palm room."* Zaroubi said, "Oh the intellectual dude! And his taxi was not there!" And it wasn't. We then paid a visit to the brass shop near Allen Street and saw Brides and Grooms in the windows and got back just after 4. Alfred Kreymborg was waiting for me, by appointment and I never was so surprised to see anyone. He is middle height, quiet, dignified, dry, unpuffed up, very deliberate and kind; he was dressed in [a] black suit with the suspicion of a white check in it like your 1913 suit you got at Kronenberg's and was wearing a new pair of shoes, very plain and rather fashionable, nothing deluxe. I asked him if he had expected to have a meeting of the people he spoke about in his letter and he said he would like to but couldn't be sure. He was just up, had been sick for some time and so had Mrs. Kreymborg but that there were a good many out of town people in town. I told him I had seen his *Studies in Love and Life* [*Love and Life, and Other Studies*] and his article on Duchamp in *The Transcript*. He nearly sank down in a fit, when I spoke of *Studies of Love and Life*! He said, I feel as if I ought to go home. Those are worthless things I did them when I was 18. I hate to think there are any of them about etc. Where do you see them? etc. He also deprecated *The Transcript* article and said, "It was very tired, it dragged towards the end but I couldn't do any better so I let it go." He then explained how the pictures of Duchamp and some other celebrity had been mixed and how *The Transcript* sassed him for objecting to the slip till Duchamp himself remonstrated. He gave me the back numbers of *Others* and told me about half a dozen people in N.Y. said he "couldn't live with him" when I asked him what Floyd Dell was like, said Duchamp was a lovely fellow and Alanson Hartpence. Said he knew Horace Holley[21] and Mr. Kerfoot and Mr. Stieglitz. He said, "Did you tell Mr. Stieglitz you knew me?" I said "no, I didn't know he knew Mr. Kerfoot or you or any of the men who are interested in poetry." He then said how good Mr. Stieglitz had been to him, and given him things and how he (A.K.) had printed Mr. Kerfoot's criticism of *Others* in the November number and so forth. He then said the madame and he wanted me to come to dinner some time. He said, "I have to go round to the studio of a man who lives near here, Mr. [Adolf] Wolff's, perhaps you have seen his poems—he has been at Blackwells Island[22] for a while and has just come out. What plans have you for tonight? Could you come round with me for a moment to his studio and then go on to the house for supper? We have nothing prepared but I can go out and get a few chops. I am sure you wouldn't be intruding at Mr. Wolff's. We have nothing private to talk over and I won't be there long." "Mr. Wolff," he said "is changed in a great many ways since being on Blackwells Island and he has put lots of what he saw, into his poems. Here is one." He read a poem on identification

21. Secretary of the National Spiritual Assembly of the Baha'is of the United States and Canada and author of books about Bahaism (1887–1960).
22. An insane asylum located in New York City.

and another about men carrying buckets, bent like patriarchs and so on. I said I would ask Hall if it would be convenient for me to go home with him. "But" I said, "if you have been sick perhaps I'd better not go. Suppose I come another time." "Not at all" he said, "we want you and it's not a party it's just us," and so forth. Hall was loath to consent but I got assent after introducing Alfred to her. On the way to Mr. Wolff's, Alfred said, "Are you often here?" I said, "no this [is] the first time, to go round by myself. I have been through New York on the way to other places and my brother used to be here or near here teaching and he took me round once to make a call but I didn't know where I was." "You have never been to N. York before!" Alfred could hardly take in the enormity of it. He said "I'd like to see your brother when he comes. You say he's often here? Send anyone round. Remember we want your brother when he comes to town, etc." At last we arrived at the Studio on Madison Ave. Alfred said "I'm afraid Adolf lives in a palace." We then moved a house or two farther on. "This is almost as bad" he said "but this is the place." We went up four flights of a spic and span apartment and "Adolf" appeared in a blouse I think but I can't be sure, leaning over the banisters. He greeted me when introduced very limply, in a harmless casual way and said we could not come into the apartment proper as the floor was not dry enough to walk on. It has just been stained I think but it was a gorgeous place in point of situation and atmosphere, (it was a front room). There was nothing in it, but 2 pictures on the wall, a modern oil in rather deep colors of a German street and a small thing I didn't notice. We were shown into the studio on the opposite side of the passage, also front. It was full of plaster statues the best things I have seen for a long time and the only things of their kind, done all, in right angles—they are full of drollery and wit however and some were very powerful. One I liked particularly of a mother holding two children—the first child sitting on the mother's lap with his feet straight out in front of him and the second child sitting on the first, in the same position. [MM sketches the statue.] He also had a cat that I liked. Mr. Wolff himself is stout, moderately genial, naive, and dry with black hair and beard. Alfred said, "Adolf your poems have made a hit with the highbrows, they're all quoting you." "*Is* it posseebal?" Mr. Wolff said unconcernedly but genially. Afterwhile we left and he said, "Miss Moore: Come and see me."

The Kreymborgs live at 29 Bank Street, Greenwich Village. You take the Madison Ave. car to 14th St.—that is Madison Ave. runs into 14th, change at 14th and go along 14 to 8th Avenue. Then get out and walk: turn to the left and then to the right in a sort of zig zag (anyone there, knows where Bank Street is). Alfred pointed out the old fashioned houses and it took about 2 minutes to get to his own. He opened the door and said, "I've brought Miss Moore." Whereupon "Mrs. Kreymborg" advanced with the most glowing expression and said "I'm so glad, give me your coat. Alfred you help Miss Moore to take her things off. Put them here. Supper's almost ready. I am so sorry Mrs. Kreymborg isn't here but she'll be back any moment." We smiled and Alfred led me round the room slowly showing me things. The room is large, the walls are pale yellow and nothing is "extravagant." A small kitchenette opens from the room with folding doors which they keep open as the kitchen is an enlarged cupboard the width of the room. In one corner of the living room next to the far end of the kitchen is a round fumed oak table on which we ate and framing the corner is a book case full of the things we have, the Brownings in lamb skin and Tennyson and Shelley and against the other side of the kitchen partition is another book case with some larger sets, Turgenev, Molière etc. An old fashioned white fire place, which is closed up is in the middle of the room opposite the doors from the hall, (with the small classics as noted, on the right,) and a desk and old Remington typewriter on the left. Over the desk (which is a table) is a magnificent photograph of Whitman with autographs and on the street wall between the windows is an enormous full length gilt mirror. Against the hall wall, (opposite the fireplace bookcase and Whitman) is a wide, low couch covered with pillows and one cute little orange velvet one and there is a painting on that wall of a girl in [a] green dress against a dull yellow background framed in a heavy gilt, regulation oil painting frame. They have a few chairs—one wicker I think and some straight ones. Presently they gave me [a] towel and told me "the first room at the top of the stairs on the right" and after I came down Alfred went up and presently we sat down to supper. (When we had first come in, Alfred had said he would go out for some chops but I prevented him and as it turned out they are on a vegetable diet and can't eat meat for a while, or anything but chicken.) We had potatoes and lima beans and salsify and carrots I think, beautifully cooked and applesauce and bread [and] jam. They gave me six times more than I could eat. They have pretty china with a small red and green design on it, and silver spoons like ours and pepper in the pot and paper napkins and a dish of fruit. I said, while Alfred was out, "It is such a pleasure to know you and Mr. Kreymborg and to be here but I am afraid it will tire you to have me since you have both been sick." "Not a bit," Mrs. Kreymborg said, "Don't you think of it. We're enjoying it so." A.K. came in at [that] moment and I said, "I was just telling Mrs. Kreymborg that it is a great delight to know you both and find you—as you are." "What did you think we were like?" he said. "Oh, " I said, "very tall, with dark hair, very intimidating." Alfred grinned and gave a sniff—"Shall I tell her?" he said. "Gertrude told me to go and see you and if you were nice, to bring you home to supper." "Otherwise not," I said. They laughed.

On the way down, Alfred had told me about Amy Lowell and the Poetry Society. He said "there is a poetry society in town, where they wear evening dress and give dinners and have celebrities speak. You haven't heard of it? Well, doesn't amount to anything. You want to keep away from it." I said I supposed that Amy Lowell had been to it and he said "Yes, we had her at a meeting one night. She's impossible. About so wide—and she can't talk about anything but herself. Seemed to take no interest in anything but her own work, and 'Pound.' She has had a falling out with him—I think she's made it up but she told us all about it. She doesn't go, with the crowd." I said I liked some of her work and he said "So do I but she was a great disappointment." Alfred then went on to say that he liked Ezra Pound personally though his work had fallen short and then I enlarged on the Aldingtons. Alfred said, "It is interesting to see how people's impressions of other people differ. This is in confidence, but I have had all sorts of trouble to get Richard Aldington to do anything for the magazine. I wrote to him and he didn't answer the letter and then I wrote to him again and got a very uncalled for disagreeable sort of letter that had no justification so far as I could see. I replied and told him what I thought and now things are straightened out and he's sent me something but I asked him to tell the others, Flint[23] and [John Gould] Fletcher and H.D. to send some things and he has taken no notice of it." I said "Should you object to my writing to them and telling them about you and the magazine not mentioning of course that fact that you had talked of them?" "Not at all," he said. "I should be glad if you would. So I can do something for them possibly." After supper they showed me pictures, some photographs by Mr. Stieglitz and [Edward] Steichen, of Shaw, Anatole France and others, that Mr. Stieglitz had given them and some of the most superb pictures of snow and engines and boats that I have ever seen. Alfred said "Are you fond of Japanese prints? We have a hundred and one things to show you." (I am just waiting for you to see the pictures, old bird.) I asked if "Mrs. K." wrote poetry and Alfred said music is our other bug. (Mrs. K. plays the piano and he plays the mandolin.) She was wearing a blue crepe (turquoise blue) dress short sleeves and small round, low neck and sewed on a curtain while Alfred read a few things. She has brown hair and eyes and [the] loveliest smile I ever have seen. To be continued. Don't you skip.

Weaz

Sojourn in the Whale: part II[24]   *December 19, [19]15*

Dear Winks,

I was telling you about my passage of the Red Sea, or rather my experience in the whale. I had an extremely good time Wednesday night—the

23. F. S. Flint, English poet and translator (1885–1960), editor of the *Imagist Anthology*.

24. This is actually the third letter of the four-part sequence MM writes about this trip, although neither of the first two is titled.

night I took dinner with the Kreymborgs. Friday morning, I repaired to the Daniel Gallery and saw an exhibition of things by William and Marguerite Zorach, paintings and embroideries. As the *Times* says, the embroideries "recall the great periods of embroidery" and the pictures gave me a chill they were so good. They have one waterfall and arrangement in stripes, that is as rhythmical as a zebra and as realistic as Maupassant. I met Mr. [Alanson] Hartpence who selects the work for the gallery and makes sales for the artists in some cases and "knows the ground." "Mr. K" had told me to introduce myself if I went to the Gallery. I did, and Mr. Hartpence was exceedingly cordial and thoughtful about showing me round. He is a positive dogmatist on art theory. I told the Kreymborgs what he said to me in comment on my comments and they were greatly amused and said there was not a soul, who had yet been discovered at least, who could talk "over" him or assert anything. (More of him, later.) I then went to 291. Mr. Stieglitz had told me to come back, that he would show me some things and Alfred had told me to ask to see his Congo things. He had nothing to show me yet, but gave me *Camera Work* to cut and look at. One number is entitled, "What is 291?" and contains an article by Hodge Kirnon the elevator man (colored) which is considered one of the best in the book. Mr. Kerfoot also has one in it and Alfred has one. Alfred had asked me if I had told Mr. Stieglitz that I knew him (Alfred) (and I *had* been delighted to see him and Mr. Kerfoot and "the gang" as contributors in a copy of *Camera Work* that I had seen at the Modern Gallery). So I told Mr. Stieglitz how pleased I had been at the above circumstance and said I had also seen some wonderful photographs at the Kreymborgs; (by him and by Steichen). I said I had not known there was anything in existence like Steichen's photograph of Gordon Craig—I said at all events I had never seen anything like it. "Well, there *is* nothing like it," he said. He told me to come in and take my coat off and look at the copies of *Camera Work*. He opened his knife and handed it to me, a plain nickel one with a ring in the end. Previously, however, while I had been examining some things against the wall, he said, "Mr. Kerfoot is here now." He went back to the aerial pocket wherever it was in which he had left Mr. Kerfoot after giving me the books and indicating the couch where I could sit (by the window) and I had a fear that Mr. Kerfoot would conclude his business at the door and "fly away" for I saw nothing of him despite the announcement that he was imminent. Presently Mr. Stieglitz came in with as nearly an approach to a selfconscious manner as it would be possible to attribute to him and said, "Miss Moore, Mr. Kerfoot," without however looking back at Mr. Kerfoot. He then went on attending with other matters, going into a nearby "pantry" and thence to the front of the studios or apartments or whatever you would call them. Mr. Kerfoot is burly—just Mr. Conover's build though a little taller, dressed in a green tweed coat which he drew off, and tan shoes (unministered to), and he had a cocked hat of some sort suitable to weather and a cane I think (I can't be sure). He has gray eyes and rather pugnacious though decent moustache and no flummeries. He drew up to the stove, a little barrel shaped affair with a tall jointed pipe, and kept darting venomous glances at me from that stronghold for a few minutes. There is a great deal [of] the type of humor about him that there is about Dr. Davis, he'll play you for about 5 minutes and then lay aside all posturing and state frankly what he thinks. He is an awful tease, though for some reason he is so direct that he is not annoying. I said, "Mr. Kerfoot you have given me a great deal of pleasure. I was just saying to Mr. Stieglitz that I had been surprised to find you in *Camera Work* and that Mr. Kreymborg was also, was a friend of Mr. Stieglitz's." (By the way, when I had mentioned Alfred Mr. Stieglitz had said, "Yes, he's one of my children.") I said, "I told Mr. Kreymborg that I had been delighted when I came on your notice of *Others* in *Life* and Mr. Kreymborg said he had put it in the front of the November *Others*. I thought it very generous of you to speak of *Others* for it is an experiment. You don't often speak of magazines do you?" "Never," he said "there has never been a notice of a magazine in *Life* before, so far as I know. I haven't taken any interest in poetry. This is the first time I have been able to see anything in it." I said "Of course some of it is trash, but what delights me is that the authors of it are willing to admit that it might be trash." "Oh yes" he said "that must be understood. It's absolutely essential that they *should* admit it." I can't remember what he said exactly but it was something like that. I asked him if he knew *The Egoist;* he said not. I told him how I liked his review of Shaw (ptomaine and caviar) and of Julian Street (*Abroad at Home*) quoting; and we had a discussion of the word "haunting," both Mr. Stieglitz and Mr. Kerfoot downing me saying that a haunting quality was not the earmark of good art—but of bad art. I said I meant the sort of thing that annoyed you till you had to trace it to the source where you had first encountered it and he said, "Oh that's a different thing—that's another sort of 'haunt.'" He asked me if I liked *The [New] Republic.* I said Yes and he said he had started out with it but had given it up, it was too "deep" for him. Then he said, "Who is that fellow, one of the editors of *The Republic;* he has been writing off and on, recently,—I can't think of his name." "Hackett?" I said. "That's the man," he said. I like him. He's the only one that writes for *The Republic* that excites my interest. I said, "I like him. In fact I like him so much I think it would be impossible for me to resent his mood or it would, if he continues to write about things as he has written about them in the past. He said something about the lavendered atmosphere of Bryn Mawr that amused me but that's a trifle. I don't take that into consideration." "Well, you wouldn't hold that against him," Mr. Kerfoot said. "I think his mind works in an interesting way." "It does," I said. "I think he has just come over here from somewhere recently, hasn't he? He had an article on 'Lincoln and Immigrants' that made me think so." "I don't know" Mr. Kerfoot said. "I met him once and I have met his brother but I don't know where he is now." I said "He had an article in *The Republic* on Mrs. Gerould[25] that delighted me. I was disappointed that you liked her so much (his "Vain Oblations"), and Francis Hackett said in *The Republic* just about what I should have liked to say." "He didn't like her you say—I haven't seen Hackett's article," Mr. Kerfoot remarked. "O," I said "he roasted her." "Roasted her, did he?" Mr. Kerfoot looked extremely delighted. "Well," he said, "in those stories Mrs. Gerould has succeeded in arousing a genuine sense of fear—a creepy feeling. Now in Poe's tales I am always conscious of the fact that the machinery is going round. I am interested but I am conscious of the fact that I am being horrified to order. In producing that sensation of horror Mrs. G. has done a notable thing." I said, "I am compelled to agree with you Mr. Kerfoot. It is Mrs. Gerould's attitude of intellectual superiority that I object to. Mr. Hackett was satirizing her point of attitude in her article on the "Decay of Culture" in *The Atlantic Monthly*, not her ability as [a] writer of short stories. On the ground of craftsmanship, she can't be taken exception to." "Well," Mr. Kerfoot said, "that may be but you mustn't let that enter in to your estimate [of] a book. I try to know as little as possible about the people I am reviewing, so that I won't be influenced. It's distracting." I then quoted "Hackett" saying how he "grieved to see the sharp visaged New English spinster encounter the bustling crowds of the subway and lose a few beads of jet from her reticule" and so on. I then explained that he had had to reply to a complaint brought against him—and that he has said he was sorry to have been so clumsy that his remarks should have been taken personally. It was the lady's mind not her self he had seen in imagination, in N. York. I spoke of the Kreymborgs and said how lovely I thought them and how delighted I was to find them, not literary monstrosities, long haired, speaking a lingo etc. Mr. Kerfoot said he had only met Mrs. Kreymborg once or twice but that Mr. Kreymborg was a fine fellow, "very fine" or something, I forget what, that he had always liked him. I said "he looked as if he had been chastened and ground down by illness and that you felt conscience-stricken for having been so noisy, after talking to him." Mr. Kerfoot look[ed] appreciative. I asked him if he knew Mr. Richardson & F. G. Cooper. He said yes. About Mr. R. he said, "I know him well. He's the only advertising man I have ever known, that I like." I said, "Mr. Conover, a friend of my brother's, is a great friend of Mr. R's and he thinks everything of him. He says, the longer you know him the better you like him." "True" said Mr. Kerfoot. "I've known him a long time and what you say is true"; "he grows on you" or "he wears well." I forget what he said. (I have concocted painfully and w. prayer, a letter to Mr. Conover apropos of the above.) Have no fear. Mr. Stieglitz bore away Mr. Kerfoot to

25. Katharine Gerould (1879–1944), American novelist, essayist, and short story writer. She began teaching at Bryn Mawr in 1901 as a reader in English.

the front room, to tell him something, "*So* rich that he absolutely *must* tell him," he said. I offered to go (having monopolized Mr. Kerfoot anyhow unduly) but he wouldn't hear to it. "Sit still" he said—"don't move." Afterwhile Mr. Kerfoot came back and said he must go and shook hands and said, "I hope I'll meet you again." Afterwhile he drifted in a third time, for his hat I think. I said I had just been reading his impression of 291 and I thought "that was about the way it made you feel." He looked pleased and said goodby. He surely is a crackerjack.

Thursday afternoon the Cowdrays left. Zaroubi and I talked as we went back through the station, I to go to Bruno's (Garret), she to school. I took the Stage, to that gentleman's abode, only to find him out. His garret is over a drugstore on Washington Square. The drug clerk said I might find him at 10 Fifth Avenue. I walked down there into an imposing vestibule-basement entrance where there was a directory of names and entered a marble-lined elevator-equipped place and ascended 4 flights to Mr. Bruno's office. In one room was a cutting table piled with letter copy. File-cases stood about I think and a neat stenographer had been writing to beat the band prior to my entrance. Mr. Bruno came out and invited me in, to the inner lair, sat down on a light yellow folding chair with his back to the window a table in front of him and offered me another on the other side of the table facing him. He had just been shopping and had a pile of about 10 books on the floor beside him, Granville-Barker on Gordon Craig and others. He is, himself, tall and pallid with straight, colorless hair, he smiles brightly and slowly with great reserve power. He wore a black and white checked serge suit and as I said to Alfred, the white checks seemed to dance all over him. I said "I came to see if you have 'Mushrooms' Mr. Bruno. I have just been to your garret and couldn't get in, and the clerk in the drugstore told me to come here." "Real ones?" he said. "The only ones" I said "that I should be sorry to find you hadn't got." He said "I haven't here, but if you have a few minutes to spare, (you can spare 10 minutes?) I shall be through with my work and I shall go back with you." I thanked him and picked up a pamphlet. I said "Mr. Bruno you have printed work in [*Bruno's*] *Weekly* by L.S. or S.L. drawings like Egyptian hieroglyphics that I admire very much. I have wondered who did them. They are very sound." "They are good" he said. "They are done by a German living in Switzerland" and he didn't tell me anymore. "Perhaps you can find something here" he said reaching me a pile of chapbooks and pamphlets. "Look through them." We continued to talk and he didn't seem to be getting any work done. Presently I said "I am hindering you Mr. Bruno, perhaps I had better go. Would it suit you better to have me come again?" "Not at all" he said, "why I am taking you *with* me!" Then he said, "How did you know about me? How did you find me?" I said I had seen advertisements of [*Bruno's*] *Weekly* and that Mr. Kreymborg had told me about him. "You know Mr. Kreymborg?" he said. "And you have met Mrs. Kreymborg?" He told me they had a lovely house in the country ("Grantwood," my boy) and that he had visited them. I told him I thought them lovely. He said, "You select from those what you like and you will accept them from me." (mushrooms, some of his own things, etc.) I said, "I don't wish you to let me make you poor, Mr. Bruno. I should like to pay you for them." He wouldn't let me. He called his stenographer and told her to bring me 2 tickets for the Thimble Theatre performance that night and gave me 2 for the Kreymborgs in case I should see them. I had said I was going there. "And the five last copies of the *Weekly*" he said. The most obsequious girl I have ever seen got the *Weeklies* from a file and procured the tickets. I told Alfred about it afterwards and he said, "Oh he is *powerful.*" A messenger boy came in to say he couldn't find an address and Mr. Bruno said "You *must* find it—go again—you will *have* to find it." As I was leaving he said "I am very stupid but fot haf you done?" I told him about *The Egoist* and he said Mr. Aldington wrote to him every week or something as foolish. He urged me to write for the *Weekly* and said he would pay me "not much but something."

w. love,   Winks

To John Warner Moore   *March 9, 1916*

M'dear Badger,

I hope to go rolling tomorrow. Imagine describing circles with 16 little wheels under you! and no fear of falling, weaving your way in and out among the moving silver skins!

I had a letter from Honey this morning telling how she has lost 6 pounds through exercise, "scrubbings" and under-eating, and on account of "amusements" attended. Also a letter from Billy [Benét] commenting on my contributions to the *Chimaera*. He wants to keep 3, which he may have, though I had to take 2 from Guido Bruno. What he says is very amusing and deserves commendation for it is frank. He says, "The ones I am returning I don't understand and the ones I am keeping, I only partly understand." He says that Robert Frost and Amy Lowell and Don Marquis and Louis Untermeyer and various others are contributing so I think he is being as hospitable as I am being obliging.

Mrs. Gilbert has not written me since leaving me to bask in the entrance of my hole with my check.[26]

26. Mrs. Lyman Gilbert of Harrisburg was preparing a "Memorial library for boys" and hired MM for about a month as a typist. MM called Mrs. Gilbert "a real litterateur without any of the crust," and borrowed books from her (MWM, February 12, 1916; MM, February 13, 1916).

Mole is busy with her silk dress that had to be fixed and is washing curtains apropos of spring. The Rat's one concern in spring is to "out."

I have to get missionary money sent off and the book put in order and half a hundred letters written and then I am ready for midstream.

With love,   Winks

To H.D.   *August 9, 1916*

Dear Mrs. Aldington:

Your letter with the proof has just come.[27] I never expected to be among those writers whose chief recommendation is the introductory letter with which they are published. As I read your article, I wondered and was amazed anew as I proceeded. It is hard to be commended by those for whose opinion we care nothing but when commendation comes from those from whom it is everything, we scarcely dare take it. Why, when you have written "The Shrine" and "The Wind Sleepers," should you be willing to find worth in that which the ordinary reader finds worthless! There are two things that I have always been disappointed not to be able to put into my work—a sense of the sea and a fighting spirit, and it delights me that anything I have written should remind you of the sea or seem to you to set itself in opposition to mediocrity and the spirit of compromise.

Our hearts are lightened today by reports of the Allies' success.

Yours,

To H.D.   *Ogden Memorial Presbyterian Church,   Chatham, N.J.
November 10, 1916*

Dear H.D.:

I have your letter and the article. Everyone thinks the article beautiful. Mary Carolyn Davies says she thinks it is the most beautiful book review she has ever read. Your poem "The Contest" is a beautiful thing, also "Evening" though there is nothing in it to compare, I think, with the last half of "The Contest."

I enjoyed Mr. Cournos's *Not Vodka* and have heard several people speak of it; also Leigh Henry's "stag kings, singing apples, and serpent women." W. L. Phelps[28] has an article in the October *Yale Review* on new

27. See H.D., "Marianne Moore," *The Egoist* 3 (August 1916): 118.
28. American critic and professor of English at Yale (1865–1943).

translations of Russian novels in which he says: "[Fyodor] Sologub is just beginning to be known in England and America largely through the efforts of John Cournos, to whom we owe some admirable translations of the short stories of [Leonid] Andreyev."

I hope Mr. Aldington will be in England through the winter; then perhaps by spring the war will be over. Won't you tell me what the prospects are and please tell Mr. Aldington that I am delighted that he likes my "Talisman." I am encouraged by the fact that Miss [May] Sinclair is interested in my work; I hope your efforts in my behalf are not burdensome and that you are not feeling that there is something interminable about doing anything for anyone?

The part of New Jersey in which we are, is not at all like the coast. It makes me think of Canada. There are small downs or hills covered with long pale grass and dotted with cedar trees. I have never seen so many cedar trees anywhere as there are here or so much untouched woodland. There is a stretch of woods near us composed almost entirely of oaks and hemlocks so that you get a magnificent columnar effect and a uniform floor of leaves and moss and the beech woods are full of sage green stones, and little sprouts of birch and hickory to which a few yellow leaves are still clinging. An old canal runs through this part of the state with ducks and swans on it; there are tow paths at the side and occasional rows of green beehives surmounted by round green stones. There are skating and iceboating on a freshet near here and there is a clubhouse nearby at which we can play tennis and bowl when we like.

If you know of or should hear of a publisher who wishes a translator to translate modern French, Old French, or Provençal, I wonder if you would be willing to let me know? Two friends of mine in Carlisle, a Mr. and Mrs. Lucas, are experts in working with French or any of the modern languages and I have wished for a long time that they might do some translating. Mrs. Lucas was Bryn Mawr 1901; Mr. Lucas has lived in France till about six years ago; Mrs. Lucas lectures on Italian art; Mr. Lucas teaches French. They wish to do translating but feel that the demand for translations is so slight that there is no use in their conferring with publishers. Mr. Knopf has published some French translations but he is more interested in Russian than in French just now and I do not know of anyone else over here, who is publishing translations.

I enclose the article on [Francis] Bacon. If you do not care for it, do not hesitate to return it. Sometime I may have something that you might like better. I should like to try a comparison of George Moore and [Henry] Fielding; also one of Knut Hamsun and [Thomas] Carlyle and one of Wallace Stevens and Compton Mackenzie. I am very much interested also, in William [Carlos] Williams' work, but I am a little afraid to undertake a criticism of it. I feel that I have not seen enough of it to justify my writing one.

Yours,

To William Carlos Williams   *April 16, 1917*

Dear Dr. Williams,

We are looking forward with pleasure to having a visit from you. My mother and brother are anxious to meet you and I should be writing now to appoint a day but that an old gentleman is with us who may be here a week or two. When his visit is over, I shall write to ask what day it would be convenient for you to come. I have enjoyed *The Tempers* and was sorry not to get in a word about it the other night.

Yours,   Marianne Moore

Your compression makes one feel that the Japanese haven't the field to themselves. I went to a ball game with Alfred [Kreymborg] Saturday, he said he had been talking to Mr. [Skip] Cannell's Japanese friend and he said (apropos of I forget just what,) "red flowers, blue flowers, ashes—that is best."

To Harriet Monroe   *May 10, 1918*

Dear Miss Monroe,

Shortly after writing you, I allowed a dealer to have the copies of *Poetry* of which I spoke to you. So return the postage enclosed in your letter.

Poetry's approach to art is different from my own; I feel it therefore to be very good of you to imply that I am not *ipso facto* an alien.

Yours sincerely,   Marianne Moore

1919–1924
Moore in the Modernist Circle

ONCE MOORE and her mother were settled in their St. Luke's Place apartment, Moore became increasingly connected to the literary and artistic community in New York City, attending literary gatherings and going to the theater, or to art exhibits and galleries. These years show the intensity of Moore's engagement in a sphere outside that of her family. The letters convey her voracious and wide-ranging appetite for contemporary art, popular culture, and entertainment.

Among Moore's early acquaintances in New York City were members of the *Dial* staff, including Scofield Thayer and James Sibley Watson, who in 1920 became co-owners of *The Dial*, publishing it as a monthly between 1920 and 1929. Moore reported her first impression of the famously reticent Sibley Watson in a letter to her brother: "Wednesday I was invited to *The Dial*, to meet Mr. Watson, President of the Company. He is very quiet, not very starchy as to appearance but is considered very brilliant. All he said was (in answer to a question of Mr. Thayer's about the tea), he said the janitor made it" (September 26, 1920). Inauspicious as this meeting may have seemed, the two would become lifelong friends. In 1923 Watson introduced Moore to his wife, Hildegarde, who eventually became a close friend with whom Moore corresponded extensively. Through the Watsons she also became acquainted with E. E. Cummings, whose work she reviewed and followed, and Gaston Lachaise, whose alabaster head of Moore is in the Metropolitan Museum of Art in New York City. Attending parties at Lola Ridge's, Alfred Kreymborg's, Paul Rosenfeld's, and others', Moore socialized with leading writers and artists associated with *Broom*, *The Dial*, and *Others*—three of the most important little magazines in New York City at the time.

At the same time, Moore was attentive to her life at home with her mother, to her ambitions to promote her poetry and reviews, and to her part-time work, which began in 1920, at the Hudson Park Branch of the New York Public Library, conveniently located across the street from her apartment. This balance continued throughout her life, as Moore maintained an interest in the world at large while working quietly at home. Noting Moore's intense dedication to her work at this time, Mary Warner Moore wrote of her daughter's "grim sternness" and "monk-like severity," maintaining that "her old merry self-indulgent rollicking days are gone" (October 27, 1919). On the other hand, Mary Warner Moore's letters to Warner frequently described the interest writers and artists were taking in her daughter, indicating to Warner the extent of Moore's involvement with an ever-growing community of transatlantic figures. She reported to Warner that Pound had sent Moore a book of poems as a present (October 27, 1919), and that even before she achieved any degree of fame, several artists had asked to paint Moore's portrait: "M. had an appointment with William Saphier to be painted this morning. . . . This is the 5th person who has asked M. to sit for a study" (to JWM, November 11, 1919). Mary Warner Moore's letters to Warner tended to include more information about Moore than the poet's own letters; although Moore wrote to her brother with some frequency, her family letters at this time are rather brief. While still playful and informative, Moore's letters now began to take the form that was characteristic of later years, focusing on description of objects, animals, and outings or events and avoiding much self-reflection or personal disclosure. Marianne and Warner continued to address each other primarily as "Rat" and "Badger," and they extended their use of nicknames to others as well. Robert McAlmon, for example, is "Piggy" in family letters, until his marriage of convenience to Bryher in 1921 (see February 20, 1921). Moore also acquired a new nickname from Bryher (see December 13, 1920); by the beginning of 1921 Moore was signing letters to Bryher and H.D. "Pterodactyl" and "Dactyl."

In this period, Moore expressed both an intense interest in self-promotion and an equally fierce modesty; this apparent dissonance is most visible when family letters are read in conjunction with letters to correspondents such as T. S. Eliot, Bryher, Ezra Pound, H.D., and Robert McAlmon. What the final record reveals, however, is that Moore was tremendously successful at launching her literary career. These years saw the publication of her first two volumes of poetry: *Poems* (1921) and *Observations* (1924). By 1924, the year she was awarded the prestigious Dial Award, Moore had published eleven poems in *The Dial* and influential reviews of T. S. Eliot's *The Sacred Wood* in 1921, William Carlos Williams's *Kora in Hell* in 1921, Bryher's first novel, *Development*, in 1921, H.D.'s *Hymen* in 1923, and Wallace Stevens's *Harmonium* in 1924.

During these years, Moore continued extensive and important correspondences and friendships with H.D., her former classmate at Bryn Mawr, and William Carlos Williams, whom she met in 1917. Although Moore had already corresponded with H.D. by this time, their correspondence increased after H.D. and Bryher visited her in New York City in 1920–21. Over the years, their letters are largely taken up with detailed responses to and praise of each other's work, comments about gifts sent to each other, family news, and publishing efforts on each other's behalf. Moore's correspondence with Williams, which spanned five decades, was also under way by this point. Williams quickly became a good friend with whom she had frank exchanges about his work and their contemporaries. From the beginning, they were on an equal footing, frequently seeking each other's advice and promoting each other's work through reviews. Moore praised Williams's aesthetic throughout their correspondence, though she later expressed reservations as well, for example, telling him emphatically that some of the "'everyday' images" in his poems were "too everyday to be condoned" (see January 7, 1941). During this period, Moore also began correspondences with Ezra Pound, Bryher, T. S. Eliot, Robert McAlmon, and Monroe Wheeler. Collectively, they map her assessment of the art and ideas of her time and present her perceptive readings of her peers; they also give us new insights into her own aesthetic and artistic project. These early literary correspondences, many of which would become increasingly personal, were in most cases sustained for the rest of her life.

In January 1919 Moore began corresponding with Pound; their letters are characterized from the start by a sense of mutual admiration and intellectual sparring. The correspondence began when Pound wrote to Moore in December 1918 concerning some poems she had submitted to Margaret Anderson's *The Little Review*, poems which he now hoped to publish in a quarterly he planned to start. He inquired if she had a book of verse, and if not, offered to arrange publication for her, as he had for Joyce, Eliot, and others. "You will never sell more than five hundred copies," Pound asserted, "as your work demands mental attention" (December 16, 1918). A day later, Pound wrote to Harriet Shaw Weaver at *The Egoist* to tell her he had a new poet in mind. Moore wrote Pound back immediately that she was not yet ready to publish a volume (see January 9, 1919), but she clearly appreciated the interest he took in her work. Although she did not meet Pound until 1939, their correspondence documents a strong and enduring connection that deepened over the years.

The year 1920 was a full one for Moore; she traveled, made her first contributions to *The Dial*, and met several people who would play crucial roles in her life. She and her mother visited Warner, whose ship, the USS *Mississippi*, was based on the West Coast at the time; they would regularly visit him wherever he was currently working, making subsequent trips in 1922 and 1923 to Bremerton, Washington—journeys that inspired Moore's poem "An Octopus." Their 1920 trip out west allowed them to travel by ship through the recently opened Panama Canal to California (see June 11, 1920). That same year, she became acquainted with Scofield Thayer—a relationship that began on uncertain terms. Mary Warner Moore wrote to Warner at length of Moore's nervousness; for example, after Moore's first meeting with Thayer and Watson at *The Dial*, she commented: "The poor fellow [MM] is so unused to things that the ordinary very mortal young woman assumes to be used to as soon as growed, that he asks in an agony 'Oh! ought I to have invited him to call?'" (September 23, 1920). Five months and several meetings later, Mrs. Moore wrote in similar terms of Moore's uneasiness about the frequent dinners and teas to which Thayer invited her: "*The Dial* has a heinous way of having its contributors entertained socially one at a time after each contribution and on Monday Ratty was laid on this altar, whence for an hour her precious essence went up in smoke to make fragrant the Benedictine apartment of Mr. Thayer. . . . Ratty was so overwrought in resolving to seem low-keyed—elegant and calm— Kam I mean, that he came home a wraith, and has not eaten a full meal since" (February 1, 1921). Moore's friendship with Thayer soon assumed a calmer tone, and they repeatedly expressed their respect for the other's writing and advice.

Moore's 1920 meeting and subsequent correspondence with Bryher (Winifred Ellerman) is one of the highlights of this period. Introduced by H.D., then Bryher's lover, on a 1920 trip through New York City while en route to California, Moore and Bryher began writing to each other in 1920, corresponding extensively until 1969. During the early twenties it was not uncommon for them to exchange two to three letters every month, discussing their own work and commenting on publishing schemes, other writers, mutual friends, films they had seen, animals seen or read about, and daily activities. Bryher's marriage of convenience to McAlmon in 1921 sparked some lively exchanges about the marriage and the institution in general—exchanges that undoubtedly influenced Moore's long poem "Marriage" (1923). Over the years, as they became closer friends, their subjects broadened to include more news of friends and family, illness, politics, and World War II, and exchanges about gifts received and sent.

Bryher's central role in the publishing of Moore's *Poems* (1921) is well known. On July 7, 1921, Moore received copies of *Poems*, published by Harriet Shaw Weaver of the Egoist Press, with the financial backing of Bryher; H.D., McAlmon, and Bryher were all involved in selecting the poems. Although Moore professed great surprise and some dismay at the publication of *Poems* and had indeed written Bryher, Eliot, and Pound that she did not care to publish a collection at present, her letters reveal that she had been considering, at least as early as 1915, the publication of a book of her work.

Moore wrote Warner that "Mr. Rat receives a ms. and one hair from Erskine MacDonald of the *Poetry Review* with an invitation to compete in a book publishing enterprise. The fella is going to issue a series of one-man volumes (60 or 80 poems each). Rat believes he will compete" (February 7, 1915). It is also clear from her first letter to Bryher (see October 15, 1920) that Bryher received some encouragement to go forward with the volume, despite Moore's protests that she had not yet written enough.

Moore's correspondence with T. S. Eliot also began during this period; like Pound and Bryher, he expressed an interest in helping Moore publish her poetry. The exchange began in April 1921, when Eliot wrote to Moore thanking her for her review of *The Sacred Wood*, which had recently appeared in *The Dial*. Eliot's letter, like Pound's early one, makes it clear that Moore was being read with care and taken seriously by her contemporaries. Her exchange with Eliot marked the beginning of a long correspondence, which spanned the years 1921 to 1964, though they did not meet until 1933. Eliot was consistently supportive of Moore's work, aiding her in publishing it over the years, and writing the introduction and suggesting the arrangement of the poems for her *Selected Poems* (1935). There is a studied formality to the early letters they exchanged; by temperament, both were rather reserved. The later letters are less reserved, dealing as they do with mutual friends, family, and illnesses.

Moore's close friendship and correspondence with Monroe Wheeler, which began in 1922 and continued into the 1960s, was important as a channel for Moore's interest in the visual and performing arts. Moore wrote frequently to Wheeler, detailing her responses to new gallery shows and exhibitions. His interest in Asia and Asian art, and his gifts to Moore from China and Japan, inspired some of Moore's richest descriptions.

This period ends with the publication of *Observations* (1924), which Thayer and Lincoln MacVeagh, the director of the Dial Press, invited Moore to publish, and with Moore's receiving the Dial Award for 1924. *Observations* contained fifty-two of the sixty-five poems she had published since 1915 and four unpublished poems; they were arranged in chronological order and included an index and her "Notes," which identified sources, quotations, and debts; she would continue to supply these in subsequent volumes. These years saw Moore launch herself as a poet and immerse herself in the literary and popular culture of her time, making her eminently qualified to become editor of *The Dial*.

To Ezra Pound   *14 St. Luke's Place   New York City   January 9, 1919*

Dear Mr. Pound:

In your letter of December 16th, I have a great deal to thank you for. My contemporaries are welcome to anything they have come upon first and I do not resent unfriendly criticism, much less that which is friendly.

I am glad to give you personal data and hope that the bare facts that I have to offer, may not cause work that I may do from time to time, utterly to fail in interest. Even if they should, it is but fair that those who speak out, should not lie in ambush. I was born in 1887 and brought up in the home of my grandfather, a clergyman of the Presbyterian church. I am Irish by descent, possibly Scotch also, but purely Celtic, was graduated from Bryn Mawr in 1909 and taught shorthand, typewriting and commercial law at the government Indian School in Carlisle, Pennsylvania, from 1911 until 1915. In 1916, my mother and I left our home in Carlisle to be with my brother—also a clergyman—in Chatham, New Jersey—but since the war, Chaplain of the battleship *Rhode Island* and by reason of my brother's entering the navy, my mother and I are living at present in New York, in a small apartment. "Black Earth," the poem to which I think you refer, was written about an elephant that I have, named Melanchthon;[1] and contrary to your impression, I am altogether a blond and have red hair.[2]

The first writing I did was a short story published in 1907 by the Bryn Mawr undergraduate monthly and during 1908 and nine, I assisted with the editing of the magazine and contributed verse to it.

Any verse that I have written, has been an arrangement of stanzas, each stanza being an exact duplicate of every other stanza. I have occasionally been at pains to make an arrangement of lines and rhymes that I liked, repeat itself, but the form of the original stanza of anything I have written has been a matter of expediency, hit upon as being approximately suitable to the subject. The resemblance of my progress to your beginnings is an accident so far as I can see. I have taken great pleasure in both your prose and your verse, but it is what my mother terms the saucy parts, which have most fixed my attention. In 1911, my mother and I were some months in England

1. A figurine, among many MM collected. Philipp Melanchthon (1497–1560), Luther's assistant during the Reformation, originally named Schwarzerd (German for "black earth"), translated his name into Greek.

2. Pound had wondered, in response to reading "Black Earth," if MM was "Ethiopian."

and happening into Elkin Mathews's shop, were shown photographs of you which we were much pleased to see. I like a fight but I admit that I have at times objected to your promptness with the cudgels. I say this merely to be honest. I have no Greek, unless a love for it may be taken as a knowledge of it and I have not read very voraciously in French; I do not know [René] Ghil and [Jules] Laforgue and know of no tangible French influence on my work. Gordon Craig, Henry James, Blake, the minor prophets and Hardy, are so far as I know, the direct influences bearing on my work.

I do not appear. Originally, my work was refused by *The Atlantic Monthly* and other magazines and recently I have not offered it. My first work to appear outside of college was a poem, which one of three, I do not recall—published by *The Egoist* in 1915 and shortly afterward, four or five poems of mine were published by *Poetry*, a fact which pleased me at the time, but one's feeling changes and not long ago when Miss Monroe invited me to contribute, I was not willing to. Alfred Kreymborg has been hospitable and does not now shut the door on me and Miss Anderson has been most kind in sending me copies of a number of *The Little Review* in which some lines of mine have appeared with which I am wholly dissatisfied. Moreover, I am not heartily in sympathy with *The Little Review* though I have supported other magazines for which less could be said. I grow less and less desirous of being published, produce less and have a strong feeling for letting alone what little I do produce. My work jerks and rears and I cannot get up enthusiasm for embalming what I myself, accept conditionally.

Anything that is a stumbling block to my reader, is a matter of regret to me and punctuation ought to be exact. Under ordinary circumstances, it is as great a hardship to me to be obliged to alter punctuation as to alter words, though I will admit that at times I am heady and irresponsible.

I like New York, the little quiet part of it in which my mother and I live. I like to see the tops of the masts from our door and to go to the wharf and look at the craft on the river.

I do not feel that anything phenomenal is to be expected of New York and I sometimes feel as if there are too many captains in one boat, but on the whole, the amount of steady co-operation that is to be counted on in the interest of getting things launched, is an amazement to me. I am interested to know of your having had a hand in the publishing of T. S. Eliot. I like his work. Over here, it strikes me that there is more evidence of power among painters than among writers.

I am glad to have you send the prose to *The Egoist* and to have you keep the two poems that you have, for your quarterly. As soon as I have it, I shall send you something new. Perhaps you would be interested in seeing a poem which I have just given to one of our new magazines here, a proposed experiment under the direction of Maxwell Bodenheim, and a poem of mine which appeared in the Bryn Mawr college *Lantern* last year?

To capitalize the first word of every line is rather slavish and I have substituted small letters for capitals in the enclosed versions of the two poems you have.

I fully agree with you in what you say about the need of being more than defensible when giving offense. I have made

You are right, that swiftmoving sternly
Intentioned swaybacked baboon is nothing to you and the chimpanzee?

to read

You are right about it; that wary,
Presumptuous young baboon is nothing to you and the chimpanzee?

For

And the description is finished. Of the jaguar with the pneumatic
Feet,

read

What is there to look at? and of the leopard, spotted underneath and on
its toes:

Leopards are not spotted underneath, but in old illuminations they are, and on Indian printed muslins, and I like the idea that they are.

its-self may read its self

and I have made

The little dish, dirt brown, mulberry
White, powder blue or oceanic green—is half human and any
Thing peacock is "divine."

to read

the little dishes, brown, mulberry
or sea green are half human and waiving the matter of artistry,
anything which can not be reproduced, is "divine."

Confusion is created by introducing contradictory references to lizards; I have therefore left out stanzas seven and eight and I have made other alterations.

In "A Graveyard," [the change] I have made is to end the line as you suggest and for the sake of symmetry, have altered the arrangement of lines in the preceding stanzas. I realize that by writing consciousness and volition, emphasis is obtained which is sacrificed by retaining the order which

I have, and I am willing to make the change, though I prefer the original order.

Sincerely yours,   Marianne Moore

To John Warner Moore   *Nov[ember] 2, 1919*

Dear Badger,

The pheasant's feather, which Raymond Russell sent you, is very interesting and the fact of his going into detail about the walnut crop. I tried to read *Huckleberry Finn* night before last and was disappointed to find that although there are high spots in it and fine bits of realism, it doesn't hold my interest. There is considerable demand over at the library for "sporty" boy's fiction like [Horatio] Alger's and for stories of fights and trapping but with even the smaller boys there is more interest in airplanes, ships, war, scientific experiments and biography than for fiction. Dan Beard's handy books for example are in great demand. I think *Huckleberry Finn* is the most in demand of its kind. There are three copies. Roosevelt is the subject of the hour upstairs and down. The encyclopedias and *Who's Who* are putty colored at the sections devoted to him. The schools require information about him, have assigned him as a subject, that is, which partly explains it. Every shop in town has had a Roosevelt feature of some sort in the window. The best was Gunther's, a marvellous display of skins hanging forward like tent flaps from the rear of the window, with a typewritten quotation from [Theodore Roosevelt's] *African Game Trails.* An elephant skin, a zebra's skin, a great monkey skin which was thick and fine like squirrel skin, an antelope's skin and two mammoth snake skins. It was a heart-rending sight but all the people seemed to look at it with joyful awe. Lord and Taylor's and various other stores had fifth rate, very tawdry imitations of the Gunther display, and there were thousands of busts and photographs on display good and bad—Yamanaka's had enormous lengths of silk, a red one, a white one, and a blue one hanging in the window and then to fill in the space, a venetian red one which made the whole thing look neither American nor Chinese.

Thursday, I had luncheon at the Bryn Mawr Club with Frances Browne and Miss Whaley. There were so many half acquaintances there that I felt as if I were escaping from a barbed wire entanglement and didn't know which way to turn. Some sort of handy mask ought to be invented or hindoo veil for the city social event. Walter Hampton spoke afterward on *Hamlet* though his announced subject was the return of beauty to the stage. He is a Brooklyn man named [Paul] Dougherty; used to be wealthy and has had a good education though you wouldn't know it. I had a personal, fellow feeling for him when he got through but he is not a great man and nothing of an artist. He told one amusing thing by way of tribute, to Shakespeare. He said when *Hamlet* was announced by the actors entertainment committee for the soldiers they cheered for the first time and during the performance not one left the house—though on other occasions despite the fact that the entertainment was free they nearly left the house in a body and were ordinarily at all times going in and out and very restless. He said they were very unstereotyped in their behavior and when the cast tried to build up applause for Hamlet by having the whole cast appear first without him and then having him appear alone with Horatio, that there was vociferous applause, but no request for Hamlet alone. Hampton said, "I bowed to Horatio as though the success of the play were due wholly to him. There was a burst of applause, the curtain went down and I was flabbergasted. There was not another sound. They had seen *Hamlet* (the play) that was all they wanted. If I had appeared with a dozen, they would have been just as well pleased."

We invited Honey to visit us but she cannot come. Miss Lizzie is so sick. She says Mr. Landis is home with 8 decorations, one the Italian war cross, and a lot of pictures.

The Spring St. Church had a dinner Thursday night to which Mole and I went after I got back from the University Club where I had gone with Frances to hear [Sir] Hugh Walpole,[3] after hearing Hampton at the B. Mawr Club. The dinner was a great success—a fearful undertaking with about two hundred people all seated at once in a big room decorated with lanterns and corn and a table of speakers on a raised dais. Mr. William Coffin was toastmaster and he spoke well. We had roast beef, beans and mashed potatoes, pickles and particolored ice cream.

I am glad you are reconciled to the arrangement made about the house and hope nothing will interfere with it. I hope we can find in time a place where there are rocks and water, near a food supply, somewhere in Rhode Island or Massachusetts but it will take time I suppose. It might be possible to build and I wish we could.

Cousin Annie says that there is a likelihood of the Pittsburgh property's[4] being in demand later when the war strain is mitigated and I hope it will be.

People here have let us pretty much alone though there are various obligations on us that will have to be tackled and somehow or other leisure seems to make away with itself. Some Bryn Mawr students have got up a magazine which they sent me and asked my opinion. Such things are a pleasure but take time.

With love,   Rat

3. English novelist (1884–1941).
4. House owned by MWM, sold in 1922.

To John Warner Moore   *Jan[uary] 16, 1920*

Dear Badger,

Your box came Tuesday and we were absolutely paralyzed at the number and value of things included. I would hate to think of using anything that you could in time put to use yourself and I feel sure the pencils and typewriter ribbon would have come in sometime somewhere. The typewriter ribbon looks and smells like a good one and the blue bond paper is wonderful both in weight and texture. Where did the white ribbon come from? Mole fears it had to do with a funeral but I thought it probably was part of a Christmas decoration or dance perquisite. I am needing some black binding tape for pictures and as Denisons have discontinued making plain black binding it is a great satisfaction to have some plain tape.

The Publishers Weekly came yesterday but I haven't looked at it yet we have been so hopelessly in the claws of business and of interruptions.

My salary has been raised ten dollars a month, as it was before "yielding" me 4 dollars a month, more (as I work but half a day instead of all day). I am now in class C, that is the third grade, instead of the second to which my examinations technically entitle me. That makes my actual salary 51.50, or it would [be] 103.50 dollars if I worked all day. I am very sorry to be promoted over Miss Townsend and Miss Terry who have both been in the library for years and know more about the work practically than I ever will know but Miss Leonard said it was just, to her mind as I understand some things better than they do but that she would not speak of it as it couldn't but discourage them.

Wednesday we went to *The Beggar's Opera* at the Greenwich Village Theater. There were a patchwork lion and unicorn, red & white, on a green curtain at the opening and many pleasing features—beautiful costumes and clever jibes. The dressing room in the theatre is very unique with a sort of oblong living-room window looking out over 7th Ave., a round mirror hung by two tasseled cords, a dressing table with a heliotrope and green porcelain parrot at either side and a couple of benches upholstered in plum colored velvet. Mole said it was an affectation for me to go into it but it was very satisfactory to me that [I] went.

Last night there was a large party in the church gymnasium for Eastern relief with a magyar choir and a boy violinist. I had offered my services to take care of children in the Spring St. nursery while the parents attended the performance. Mole went to the performance but came away and joined me and the other girls who were in charge of the children. It was a very enjoyable experience. The nursery equipment is perfect: I was as much amused by the toys as the children were and we had four or five very peaceable older boys working out puzzles.

At 10, I went to a party up on 16th Street, a jammed unsorted mammoth gathering of celebrities, Art Young, Max Eastman,[5] some Russians, Gaston Lachaise, Scofield Thayer, Lola Ridge, Piggy McAlmon, and many others whom I didn't meet and hardly saw for the lights were dim and at the same time glaring and smoke crowded the atmosphere. Alfred Kreymborg gave the party and gave a marionette play; Art Young did a side-splitting take-off of a Southern Senator and of a German Socialist and as Scofield Thayer remarked to me, "Nature has helped him" for he is stout, gray-haired, grandiloquent looking and wore glasses with a string. I didn't wait for refreshments but left at half past eleven—Piggy gave me two copies of his magazine just out and helped me with my wraps very ignorantly however as he squeezed my muff under his arm till it looked like a tam-o'shanter or typewriter mat. Scofield asked me if I would do a review for him of a book of T. S. Eliot's and I said I would.

Mole was amazed to see me home so soon and asked me what had happened and if I didn't like the party.

Today I went to a children's party at Margaret Franklin's. Margaret was in the class of 1908 at B. Mawr. Her father is editor and owner of the *Review*, and she is a non-partisan League worker agitating for women's admission to the Columbia law school and things of that sort. There were some fine fellows and interesting girls of the social worker type present and the children for whom the party was given.

With love,   Rat

Mole has overworked all week calling, receiving visitors & serving for me but found her glasses Friday.

To John Warner Moore   *U.S.S. Mercy Balboa*   *June 11, 1920*

Dear Badger,

We have had a "big liberty" in Panama City. Liberty at large I think they called it. Have been everywhere and seen everything—first, the Castle which Morgan rid of pirates and this morning, we went to the Commissary and all round the active part of the city. The ruins were far beyond my expectation. H. Tower, the main feature, looks over the sea towards the north side of the gulf of Panama, commanding a view of 4 or 5 pointed islands that look like little blue icebergs—very distinct but clearly defined. Along the shore there is a short line of cocoa palms and several enormous sandbox trees grow beside the tower. One of them is covered with orchid plants and

5. Art Young (1866–1943), American cartoonist; Max Eastman (1883–1969), American editor, essayist, and poet.

one has a straight descending stem like a banyan tree. This was a small tree which grafted itself on the old. Even so it is about 10 inches in diameter. The architecture of the ruin is everything one could wish—a kind of gradually diminished 6-story square white limestone tower. The diminishing is very slight but the principle of it is the principle of a tower made of a nest of children's boxes. The cornices are curved with the utmost skill and toward the land side are the vestiges of a winding stair. Three treads remain and all the way up to the 6th story you can see the sockets in the wall for the missing steps. I was highly delighted to surprise several lizards, two very large, slight bodied ones and several babies. They walked so high on their legs and reared their heads so high, I was amazed.

It is very curious to see banana plants, mango trees, and that tall bush with thick glossy leaves shaped like a guitar, growing everywhere as lustily as poplars or maples. At the market we saw parrots and innumerable parakeets, some in tin slatted cages like revolutionary lanterns, some in reed cages and some in vermilion wire cages. The small parakeets are 50 cents a pair. They have flat hammocks shaped like the seamen's hammocks in the market—some orange, some green, but they are very heavy and I thought I'd better not even price them. Everything we saw seemed to be more expensive than the same things at home except, I suppose, hats and we didn't price them. Panama hats can't be worn on every occasion, and it seems greedy to buy things just because they are beautiful. That sounds very sanctified but the people on the ship are so like a barge full of maniacs on the subject of spending and loading up with products of the ports where we have stopped that I feel as if I couldn't buy a nickel's worth of anything unless I had been needing it a week. We saw 4 or 5 churches some very harmonious, in fact—noble from the outside but choked up inside with tinfoil shrubs and fronds and quantities of crude paper flowers. All the floors were clean and the newly applied calcimine and the plaster tableaux and virgins made me feel as if I were in a Roman Catholic emporium on Barclay Street or a little Baptist church near Steelton or Altoona. I saw no monkeys but the coxswain for the motor sailor bought one for 5 dollars (as he reluctantly admitted to several other sailors) and it rambled about on me last evening as he was taking it below—a gray and black marmoset. It lives in a white duck hat with cotton waste around it and eats bananas.

The trip through the Canal was a revelation and accomplished under the most favorable circumstances. We started through at a quarter of ten and arrived at Balboa at about 4. I was surprised to find the entrance at Colón so narrow and sedgey and to find that we had so much breeze merely as the result of our own motion. The bird life was beyond my expectations. The pelicans were superb and there were little white birds (herons perhaps) emerging every little while and hurrying along the shore before they flew away. I had not expected to find the canal so green or to see so many blue peaks at the far side of Gatun Lake, or to find the Lake so large. The machinery of the locks is very inspiring and all the detail—of grass between the lighting pillars and the cabwindows of the engines picked out in yellow made a great impression on me. We had a fine view of everything. In fact till one o'clock we were on the main deck below the pilot house and though the struggle on the part of those "photographing" to get the highest, most central, most psychological sight of every lock and channel dredge was appalling we enjoyed the progress greatly. You probably noticed a fine lawn and government house surmounting a steep slope by the Miraflores Locks or just before you come to them—with a square fountain like a bed of small closely packed egrets at the side of the house. It was beginning to get hot by the time we got there but it was one of the prettiest things we saw. There were a number of cows grazing along the Canal and one with very long horns was close by on the ridge of the cut (a bull it was). I pointed it out to Mole who said she was horrified at my drowsy attention to it. She said it made her think of Julia when she was about 9 standing stock still with gratitude and saying, "Oh, Aunt Mary Warner it's a cow, I *thought* it was a bull" (when crossing an alley on Hanover Street).

Culebra Cut was a beautiful sight and I would give a good deal to have a picture of the cranes Ajax & Hercules with the pulley lines for the grapnel hanging vertical from the apexes. A pair is much more interesting than just one I think.

We had a deluge of rain at the last bend in the Lake before entering the cut—very much like a storm we had one night at Port au Prince when the sky got as black as midnight and the rain fell as if it had been poured off a carpet. The lightning there was very wicked and like a solid shaft of wriggling fire but the rain in the canal was confined to a small spot and there was no lightning.

I looked around a little in Panama City for weapons and saddle gear but saw only one saddle, a very ornate carved leather affair and the knives were chiefly butcher knives like the scimitars and cleavers they have in plays and very new looking things with agate handles. We bought some things at the Commissary and a grapefruit and 4 oranges (all for 18 cents) but the ship moved into the stream soon after we left and as we couldn't get back to it for luncheon, we ate our grapefruit (much to my disgust) on a concrete bench in the park near the Tivoli. Mole doesn't thrive very well on a continuous breakfast of fried eggs and can't eat much meat in this hot weather and every time I proposed buying some oranges from a bumboatman or negress, prevented me; so on this occasion I hurriedly bought the grapefruit and was annoyed at having to eat it ashore.

Yesterday when we went to the ruins we took an automobile but today we took a street car from Balboa. The car goes through a cemetery and then through huts and little liquor and drygoods shops, fastened to a back gate of one of these huts was the prettiest ocelot I have ever seen pacing two [*sic*] and fro on a leash. It was spotted in stripes as they usually are and about the size of a very small coach dog or an immense rabbit. We passed the Bullring outside the city yesterday, a red tin gingerbread affair like a base-ball grand-stand. The cockpit, we didn't see but as we have been all over town we must have been near it.

I hope you have been cool and that all is well.

With love to all,   Rat

P.S. Don't think by my saying that Mole can't eat very much, that the meals aren't good. The meals are out of the ordinary—immense portions and they try to give us fruit every day—also there is occasionally ice cream.

The colored mess boys are very amusing—every evening that we have been in port and sometimes when under way, they furnish jazz music of the most emphatic order; several dance together and a few try buck and wing dancing or clogg dancing. They take turns at the various instruments and the best performers eye their understudies very jealously.

Coming to the ship yesterday when we left the trolley, we were at a loss how to get to the ship as we had gone ashore at pier one, by the gangway and had been told that we would get a boat at pier 19. There are a lot of army ambulances and trucks around the trolley terminus and I asked a youngster attached to me, which direction the pier was. He was about the age and size of one of Mr. Alfred Budd's boys and evidently was just out of the egg for he said he really didn't know. The driver however came around and said if we got in he would take us, as he was going to 18 himself. It was raining briskly and turned out to be more than half a mile. So we were very much bene-fitted.

On the dock there was a stuffed armadillo and a stuffed iguana (which they pronounce ig*wán*a) also a white and gray marmoset in a cage. The dock hand moved them very rapidly to get at some trunks, and the superinten-dent said, "Don't you break those, that's fine work; if you break that, it means money." The fellow seemed to pay very little attention and kept say-ing "Moankay?" or "monykay?" It was hard to tell which.

We have two large monkeys with white faces on board, one belonging to a sailor and one to a lady. The lady's has been teased and is very cross and irritable. One of the sailors said, "Come on Alfred, you don't mean a word of it," but the poor fellow has a hard berth nagged and dragged by ignorant passengers and children.

We sail tomorrow, so you probably won't hear from us again.

I have just heard that we have an ocelot on board, probably the next thing will be an iguana.

I hope things are not piling up on Constance in view of our arrival. Our round of sight seeing is pretty complete so we are looking forward to retirement.

With love,   Rat

To John Warner Moore   *[14 St. Luke's Place, New York]*
                             September 19, 1920

Dear Badger,

It was a great satisfaction to know that the shoes fit and are right in every way, though it seemed to me they were a long time getting to you. You don't say if you need any high ones or if you like lighter weight leather. Don't get any "seamen's" shoes. The ones we sent aren't very expensive.

We have had a lot of company this week. Mole has been panting, from engagement to engagement and I haven't lifted a finger to sew, cook, or do anything needful in the house—(except Thursday when I was like a performing bear in my heroic exertions to get our things hid and dusted before the arrival of Scofield Thayer who had invited me to dinner with him). We had a very pleasant evening. I was scared to death but he isn't very terrifying at close quarters and asked me to send some work as soon as possible and read me one of the most amusing letters I have ever heard from Ezra Pound's father, Homer L. Pound, asking him to mail a copy of the September *Dial* to Mr. —— Mercer of Doylestown, Pennsylvania, or if he could, to "*run* over to Doylestown," that it would interest him to see Mr. Mercer's house, "a castle of 60 rooms made of concrete and tiles, full of rare books, paintings etc. etc." and "to *run down* to the Washington Square Book Shop to get back for him a photograph of Ezra which the Playboy, *Arens*, had not returned."

Mrs. Conover and Lillian came in Wednesday for a little while. They are so excited about their trip and Mrs. Conover lamented that since we had taken it, we shouldn't have gone together. They are very eager and excited over being on the ship for dinner and asked what to wear, suits, very evening dresses or semi-evening dress. We advised Lillian to wear her dark blue velvet and Mrs. Conover, a net dress which she described.

Yesterday Peggy and Paul DeBoer and the baby came at a quarter of five, Edwin [Howard] had been photographing doorways all afternoon with Mole's assistance and at five Peter's mother invited us to supper, roast chicken and fritters.[6] Edwin wants to know what evening we can go with him to a Chinese restaurant he knows about—someday this week and I have a book review I have to copy for *The Dial*. Adair goes home tomorrow and as she had sent me a month ago, 11 leaves of a friendship calendar for

---

6. Peter was a cat memorialized in MM's poem by that title and belonging to neighbors. Pedro, mentioned later, was JWM's cat.

Gladys [Howard], it seemed about time that the pages were written out, and I was paddled into reviewing a book for the library but soon I'll be working only half a day, and we'll have more time.

You must have had a hard time with the library. Nothing could be more teasing than a lot of unaccounted for books. We got the little blotter, also the bulletins. The sporting news is very excellent I think, very untrammeled and amusing.

Don't send money, as we have all we need and I'll be getting 82 something the first of October.

We have found all our keys, the floor is drying and things are in general more convenient than since we have been home. Night before last Brenda Meland took us upstairs to see their kittens just arrived—a maltese, and several black ones, also an evening dress, hat and a magnificent suit which she had just got at the "Tailored Woman," $160.00, green with Australian opossum collar and cuffs.

Pedro is certainly entitled to his emoluments—he must be very droll to watch.

With love, Rat

I'll send you a copy of *The Dial* if they print my article. Scofield Thayer says Ezra Pound wrote them to by all means get some prose from me.

To Bryher *October 15, 1920*

Dear Miss Bryher,

It was a pleasure to have your letter and your interest in my poems does me a great deal of good. Moreover, it is so easy to comment favorably on work in passing, and leave the matter at that, that I am doubly grateful to you for wishing that something could be done about having the poems published in a volume. I should not care to have published by itself, what I have done so far, but I should like, I think, as I said to H.D. if I were to have a book of prose published, to have the poems published as an appendix. If the poems were to be published by themselves, I think there ought to be more of them and I think that there ought to be among them some that are easy to understand and that are beyond doubt, alluring.

I am so glad that you like New York. I feared that you might begin to find it humdrum before you left for California. My mother and I were not in Santa Barbara but I can see it perfectly from your picture. I hope you have found Carmel a great contrast and that you have been able to wear your riding breeches and do as you please. Have you found any horses? I cannot imagine anything more delightful than riding through the woods by the sea, in California. Unless it were to look at the elephants of which you speak—in Carthage. I hope that I give a false impression of myself in my poems for there is nothing I love more, than the concrete and there is an especial romance I think, about elephants. I have a kodak picture of one, a princess's elephant, on which a friend of mine went sight seeing in Gwalior, with a bell hung against its side by a cord which runs from the front to the hind legs, and a checked cloth on its head. I set great store by it. Of course I like the gazelles too and I have had so much curiosity about the world before the fish age that I am pleased to have reminded you of it.

I have not your book yet but am awaiting it with great interest. Would it be a trouble to you to tell me again to which English magazines you have contributed? and to name the month?

You have done me a service in speaking of [Thomas] Middleton. I have a not very clear recollection of *The Spanish Gipsy* and *A Trick to Catch the Old-One* but have never read *The Changeling* nor *A Chaste Mayd in Cheapside* nor *Women Beware Women* and succeeded a day or two ago in getting them from the library. I am delighted with *Women Beware Women*, and they are all written with a gusto and prodigality of allusion that I find irresistible. Beatrice's "Thou Standing toad-pool" and Yellowhammer's "He's much too verbal, this learning's a great witch," are very amusing I think. I tried to get *The Black Book* and *Father Hubbard's Tale* but they do not seem to be in the library. I am very fond of Captain John Smith's *[A] Description of New England.* I wonder if you are? particularly the parts itemizing the edible and other fishes that are to be found in the pools on the coast.

I have written to H.D. of La Jolla and Balboa but have no addresses for either place and I hope that soon you will have word from a Miss Chamberlain of a possible cottage in Carmel.

You are in the most beautiful part of our country and I hope that you have already begun to feel that part of it belongs to you.

Sincerely yours, Marianne Moore

To John Warner Moore *Sunday, Oct[ober] 17, 1920*

Dear Badger,

We got a telegram from Mrs. Conover this morning saying that they had a fine visit on the *Mississippi.*[7] I am glad you carried it though I suppose the time when they were in Seattle was the strategic time for it. Mrs. Conover sounded very delighted and contented about the whole visit.

I got a great deal of pleasure out of *The Publishers Weekly.* It is a concise, cleverly gotten up publication.

7. JWM's naval ship.

Tuesday evening we go to a supper party at Daisy's[8] for Edwin and the two boys who are with him & Aunt E. at Crestwood. Wednesday, I took tea with Scofield Thayer and the encounter rather knocked me out. Miss Hueby has been most sympathetic, not knowing the cause, and generous, giving us ice cream and muffins and lending us Peter. I have been at work and about as usual but my stomach has been about as much use to me as a feather duster or a rim for spectacles without any glass in it. The food was very simple at the tea, plain tea, toast and square scones like very dainty biscuits. Scofield Thayer lives at the Benedict Club, 80 Washington Square East, a red brick building near the American Book Company; a coon took me up in the elevator and a butler let me in. There is a roomy hall carpeted with a yellow and blue Chinese rug—and at one end a library opens from it and at the other end a "lounge" opens from it with a blue gauze curtain hanging across the door way and a large iron candlestick stands by the door. Scofield has a gorgeous library, about 3 walls full of light calf bindings or blue bindings, a grate full of ashes a foot deep and a yellow desk like yours, not quite so large. He is very quiet friendly polished and amusing, said my letter made a deep impression in the office; I think what he said was that it was very unusual, (in which I said anything that was an involuntary outcome of the mind was singularly remote from money). He said he liked my poems but didn't understand them and that Mr. Watson liked them. He showed me his art treasures (on request), a large black marble, nude, some [Aubrey] Beardsley pen drawings—a "cubist painting" and some drawings of dancers. He has in his art room, a set of real red lacquer, a red lacquer cabinet three little benches and a smoking stand in front of the fireplace. He doesn't smoke and has no chairs—one I think at his desk but that is all.

With love,   Rat

To Bryher   *November 29, 1920*

Dear Bryher:

Thank you for all your care in telling me of modern English writers. I quoted to Mr. Scott what you tell me and he agrees that the field is very restricted.

[Thomas Middleton's] *No Wit, No Help Like a Woman's* is one of the plays that I have not been able to get and I do not know [George Chapman's] *Eastward Ho* nor Petronius but I delight in [Thomas Dekker's] *The Gull's Hornbook*; I have admired it from the first. What you say of [William] Wycherley interests me and I hope you will finish the essay you speak of. He is completely in oblivion so far as the modern world is concerned, I think,

8. Daisy Anderson, neighbor of the Moores' at 12 St. Luke's Place and friend of the Howard family.

and if you could bring him to light it would be a fine thing. I do not know how elastic editors' and publishers' minds are with regard to literature—the essence of literature that is, apart from fashion. I should submit to *The Dial* with assurance, anything that I was thoroughly interested in and be sure of its being welcomed and read with enjoyment whether it were used or not. I am a little in doubt as to the exact nature of the editorial policy. I have not met any of the editors but Scofield Thayer but he is enthusiastic and I think he is sincere in not wishing to miss anything good. Dr. Cross of *The Yale Review* is a book-worm and a great enthusiast over sources; his life of Fielding and his life of Sterne are very complete and show faith in people's being able to enjoy such things; moreover, *The Yale Review* has published some poems, imaginary poems by a Greek or Roman by a Mrs. Crewe which lead me to think that *The Yale Review* might be interested in work which does not specifically treat of modern life and *The Yale Review* has an ambition, I think, to cover a wide field. We expect to have it at the library soon and I shall watch it to see what the trend is. *The Bookman* is a possibility; it also has "ambitions" but it is so inept and woolgathering a publication that I am wasting time in considering it.

Your "Girl-Page" has just come and I hope you do not begrudge me the pleasure I have had from it. The opening is delightful; the treatment throughout is just right, I think, and anything but unpsychological. I am interested in what you say of Mary Frith as the possible model for Moll Cutpurse and the Gallathea incident is exceedingly droll. I like the phrase very much, "the depth of a leaf." ("This root of childishness. . . has scarcely the depth of a leaf") and "brush cloaks, make clean spurs, nay, pull off strait boots" and I like

> *"But you can keep a little tit-mouse page there,*
> *that's good for nothing but to carry toothpicks."*

and I like the exposition of wildness. At the end, "the imagination of a child joined to the freedom of a boy" sums the thing up very well I think. I detest effeminateness and prudishness but "Here's brave wilfulness!" gives me food for thought which is irrelevant and perhaps tiresome. Wilfulness in itself, is an attractive quality but wilfulness fails to take into account the question of attrition and attrition is inevitable.

I have your *Development* at last and hardly know what to say of the pleasure that it has given me.[9] The positiveness and absence of exaggeration in the narration give it an authoritativeness which is very striking and the instinctiveness and intenseness of the wording, give to a great many of the lines, the force of poetry. The passage beginning "The sea was a wide mass of luminous metal" is a very great achievement as description, I think, and the exhibition of the basset hound, the Mrs. North call and the frying-pan

9. Bryher's novel, *Development*, was published in London in 1920.

tea and the waste-of-time aspect of school life are of a piece with the best things in literature. "Camels, vultures, scorpions, and even jackals" is a masterly summary of Egypt as we imagine it and the sense of the land is in all the places which you describe. The exposition of the baffled sense one has of being outside what it is one's birthright to enjoy, is the great feature of the book, I think. The satire in "I don't believe you appreciate travelling, at all," is one of the things that one remembers and the poems are full of power. I especially like "Give me freedom in your woods."

I have always liked fairy-tales; they have never seemed less real to me by reason of the fact that they describe what never could have happened and tennis—not compulsory—is a good half of my life but my experience of childhood playmates—of girls at least—corroborates yours and dolls have always seemed to me, the dreariest, tawdriest things in the world.

Thank you for looking after my interest in the matter of the essays. Do, if I am not burdening you, secure me anything you can.

I am delighted to hear of the elephant; I wish I could see it. How large is it?

Yours sincerely,   Marianne Moore

P.S. Tell H.D. that I have not seen Mrs. [Evelyn] Scott's poem but will set about getting it. I wanted to see it myself but I see Mrs. Scott or anyone else so seldom that I am handicapped in getting what I want. I have not heard anything of *Contact*. Horace Brodsky's "Rainbow" made a stir—perhaps it was merely the suppressing of the first number that made a stir—but I have not seen it.

I am returning "The Girl-Page" to this address and I hope it will reach you safely. Our post-man put quite a bad crease in it but it is otherwise intact.

To Bryher   *December 13, 1920*

Dear Bryher:

I shall like any name you select for me; I am in my family, a weasel, a coach-dog, a water-rat, a basilisk and an alligator and could be an armadillo, a bull-frog or anything that seems suitable to you.

I hope I am on the way to Greece though by a long way around. I like what you say about me and marvel that you can say anything at all for it is true that I have not expressed so far, any of the things that I particularly wish to say. You could not see any education that I have had, with a microscope so I do not know that I am justified in blaming education with my ice-bound state. I should attempt observations in prose I think—nothing absolute. To put my remarks in verse form, is like trying to dance the min-uet in a bathing-suit but for the time-being I have some things to say about acacias and sea-weeds and serpents in plane-trees that will have to appear in fragments. If I seem to take your efforts for me coolly, do not be deceived; your criticism has helped me and in having been the occasion of your illusory sketch of a Petronius-flower-strewn Greece, I find rich satis-faction.

Vachel Lindsay is an unalluring bird of Paradise, isn't he. "The pump-kin in the moonlight" is a little hard to harmonize with the night, light, colour or anything but Vachel Lindsay.

Your advance on the book-seller is highly amusing; I am sorry you did not have time to inquire for *Development*. Let me know without delay, won't you, when *Adventure*[10] is ready?

I wish I could fence. I was not allowed to fence when I was in college because it was thought that it would be bad for my back but I yet hope to learn.

Speaking of education, I was greatly amused last year, by "The Gor-dian Knot" in *The Marionette:* the "wis, wis, wis," of the priests when de-serted by their university background of education, at Alexander's point-blank inquiry about the money and their reliance on formulas inter-mittently and irrespective of anything:

> *"He who would this net untie,*
> *Must A B C D E F G H I."*

Do you remember it?

Yours,   Marianne Moore

I copied the first two paragraphs of your essay on the Girl-Page,—which seemed to me particularly prepossessing,—in case I should be able to show them to anyone who might be interested in the Wycherley. They are very interesting in connection with *Development*, I think.

To H.D.   *January 11, 1921*

Dear Hilda:

I am so glad that California has done you good. You have to forego life on the Acropolis I think, anywhere away from the east. I am like the man in *Life* who was shocked by the rawness of the west, deprecated the women—

---

10. *Adventure*, which became Bryher's travel narrative *West*, was published in 1924.

"attractive of course but crude," supposed that shoe polish had been cut off by the war and then when the frogs' legs were served, the smile appeared, so rare in an easterner but on second thought he said "though superbly cooked, it strikes me that they are a little more bowed than those we get in the east." Well, the main thing is that the climate has agreed with you and that you have all had time to think and to follow your own devices secure from the inroads of eastern harpies. It is so good of you to write about the book. I am distressed to have had you do it. I can well get along without it and have expected to but mentioned it involuntarily as I felt it might be just such a thing as you had read.

I return "The Island" but if you decide not to send it to the magazine you have in mind, return it to me and let me send it to *The Nation, The New Republic* or *The Post Literary Review*. I think any one of these might take it. I was just on the point of sending it to *The New Republic* on my own responsibility so return it to you with reluctance.

I return you fifty cents in stamps as the Pausanias was two dollars fifty cents—not three dollars. If I should turn into a Bennett or a Wells, I have enough clerical supplies on hand to last me two or three years, so do not deplore my expenditure of paper. (My brother moreover has sent me some things, some very spirited blue bond paper among them—which make me like the editor of *Punch*, as if I should like to copy the directory.)

I know of a delightful place in Maine, an island south of Bar Harbor, reached by a tug boat from Boothbay Harbor—Monhegan Island. It is possible to go from New York to Portland; or to go to Boston by night boat and from Boston to Bath, to Boothbay to Monhegan. Frederick Waugh, Elizabeth Stoddard, Rockwell Kent and various painters and writers go there but it is a very sane place none the less. If you go, the place to go is The Tribler Cottages and one has to arrange about accommodations several months in advance. Miss Isabel Tribler is the one to write to, (Monhegan Island, Maine). There is a pine woods on the island, full of colored toadstools; and the smells are indescribable—of wild strawberries, bayberries, cones and so forth. There is a headland a hundred and fifty feet high and there are two smaller ones and too much could not be said for the attractions of the place though I noticed the last time we were there, that the mosquitoes had increased. As for me, I see no island and no novel on my horoscope; I shall have to be in town this summer, I fear. I hope my novel has not taken very firm hold of your mind; all that I can say just now for my writing a novel is that when I read certain of the novels of contemporaries, [Frank Swinnerton's] *September, The Romantic*, [Edgar Lee Masters's] *Mitch Miller*, [Edith Wharton's] *The Age of Innocence*—I feel as if I should have more mastery of the material if I were doing the thing myself, but "the material" so far as I am concerned is not very tangible. A novel must be something more than a collection of jibes and advertisements. So B. is considered "cute"? Please remember me to Mrs. Doolittle. How much better I should have felt if she had been as Mother says she is "a monster of gentleness"—at the Belmont—instead of generosity itself, to the associated harpies.

With love to you all,

P.S. If you write to Miss Tribler, be sure to mention Mother's name—(Mrs. M.W.).

Mina Loy is English, considered very beautiful, was first married to Stephen Haweis the painter, has two children in Florence and lived in Florence for some time. I first met her in 1915 at the Cannells' at tea preparatory to going to the Provincetown Playhouse where she acted in Alfred Kreymborg's *Lima Beans*. She was very beautiful in the play, very rakish previous to the play owing to the necessity of wearing a mixed costume,—some of the properties and also ordinary street clothing. She enunciated beautifully, wore gold slippers, a green taffeta dress, a black Florentine mosaic brooch, long gold earrings and some beautiful English rings. We discussed Gordon Craig whom she knew, George Moore, and the hollowness of fashionable life and I thought her very clever and a sound philosopher. I haven't seen her since. She was married shortly to —[Arthur] Cravan a prize-fighter and editor with Robert Coady, of *The Soil*, lived in Tahiti or one of the South Sea Islands and has lived there until recently, this winter I think when Mr. Cravan was drowned. Mr. McAlmon was telling us about her a few evenings ago—that she is working with the Provincetown Players, writing a novel about her life with Cravan. Mr. McAlmon says she was wrapped up in him "and her novel is all about him." He says he invited her to luncheon several times for fear she would pawn a necklace. I said, "Is she as beautiful as ever?" "Well," he said, "she hasn't got her wardrobe. To tell the truth," he said, "I used to see her in a restaurant before I knew who she was and I thought, 'she has good features, a fine nose and beautiful eyebrows' but I didn't think she was beautiful and I wouldn't have cared if I had never seen her again."

To John Warner Moore   *Jan[uary] 23, 1921*

Dear Badger,

We have anozzer little *Publishers Weekly* worm, and I feel much more independent than when I have to beg the favor of Miss Leonard's *Book Review Digest*.

Mr. Conover is much pleased at having a letter from you. We saw Mrs. Conover, Lillian, and two needlework guild companions in the Waldorf Wednesday. Cousin Samuel[11] took us there to dinner. He was much charmed with Mrs. Conover. I was interested in the hotel as usual but would rather

11. Could be Samuel Kennedy, husband of MWM's cousin Elizabeth ("Lizzie") Warner.

be poor all my life than haunt a hotel and look like those tea-toad, lounge lizard, parlor snake patrons of a hotel (needless to say, I am not talking about the Conovers).

We had a pleasant day at Aunt E.'s Tuesday. It was quiet and we could talk but the cold outdoors was enough to kill a reindeer.

I was a good deal amused by Mole's account of Piggy [McAlmon]'s leave-taking, Wed. night. The poor fellow was much crestfallen at seeing on the table (for review) T. S. Eliot's *The Sacred Wood* which he had rocked to sleep and stoned to death without reading, in the last number of his magazine.

I am straining every nerve to do the review right away and hope nothing will hinder. (H.D.'s friend in California, to my absolute stupefaction, has written me saying that she can't see the use of my being cooped up and kept to work when I might be writing, or riding an elephant. She says she and H.D. are "fording about and *not* riding delicately about on a Tyrian-trapped elephant"—and that H.D. has reminded her that one cannot go on an adventure without gold, and that elephants cost about $5000.00 as she knows for her father has some in connection with a rice mill in Burma, and that the amount for an expedition shall be "extended on the point of a sword" if I will be a "good pterodactyl that will come out of its rock" and write a novel; H.D. wrote too, very much afraid I would take the offer amiss and feel that it was presumptuous, saying that Winifred [Bryher] had been rescued by her from a mansion in a fashionable part of London "refusing to meet any of her class." (Her father is a baronet), and that he often sends her "little sums" for forwarding her "ideas and ideals." This is surely very kind, isn't it? Of course I couldn't write a novel and wrote that I have none in the process of hatching and that I work and live here as much from choice as from necessity but put it better and more gratefully I hope.

With love,   Rat

Mole got a dress at Gimbel's last week for Mary. It is white and very dainty though *small*.

To Bryher   *January 23, 1921*

Dear Bryher,

Your wishing to forward my novel has given me a great deal of happiness and I should like to take the money from the point of a sword but to do this would not drag me from my slough. There is nothing to hinder my doing "my novel" right here if I could do it anywhere. A friend of mine said the other day, "You never go anywhere on Sunday and you say that you work all week and I didn't suppose that I was ever going to see you." But I am telling the truth when I say that if I had all the time in the world, I should not write anything for some years. In order to write as I should have to, I should like to look into certain things and make up my mind with regard to the relevance or irrelevance of certain other things; moreover, the work I am doing and the annoyances to which I am subjected, are to some extent the goose that lays the golden egg and are I am sure, responsible just now, for any gain that I make toward writing. I have no swiftness; this may be hard for you to realize but it is true and I have I think, an intuition as to how I am to succeed if I do succeed. The library is to some extent an incubus and our time is sometimes pre-empted but on the whole we live like anchorites and I could work here better than I could in any other place.

The thought of a story's having as its initiator and attendant spirit, a bona fide baby elephant is so irresistible as to lead me to think I might try to hatch a china egg and I know what it is to be opposed by shyness, scepticism, lethargy and other tiresome qualities and dread to seem stubborn but I beg that you will put up with me.

The pterodactyl has often thought of shortening its hair. (It will send or read you "The Rape of the Lock," a friend's burlesque dealing with this very subject.)[12]

Its craving for peacock blue is the scandal of its rock.

The pterodactyl has an open mind with regard to Freud and child and parent protective measures. It likes Judge Lindsey's "Horses Rights for Women" in his *The Doughboy's Religion*.[13] As much more of this later as you care to have.

The pterodactyl's conscience hurts it; it has done wrong but hopes that no harm will come of it. It is sending to *The Dial*, a stone tablet depicting T. S. Eliot in *The Sacred Wood*.

    Love to H.D. *Your trusting but disobedient,* pterodactyl

Have you seen a review of *Development* in a December *Spectator?*

To John Warner Moore *February 13, 1921*

Dear Badger,

We had a letter from Constance this week in which she enclosed two snapshots of Mary—one of you and Mary. The one where you are holding

12. In a brief, incomplete memoir written in 1969–70, MM wrote: "One Thanksgiving vacation when Mary Nearing and I remained at college instead of returning home, I cut about a foot of my hair off and inspired by this truncated relic, we wrote a play "The Rape of the Lock," in which this souvenir was the dastardly work of a sacred pig. I remember only the line, 'What monarch would not blush to have a wife with hair like a shaving brush.'"

13. Benjamin Barr Lindsey (1869–1943), American judge, author, and reformer whom MM heard speak in 1909; wrote *The Revolt of Modern Youth* and *The Companionate Marriage.*

Mary is one of the best I think we have. The *[National] Geographic* also came. I have wanted one of this number very badly on account of Sir Harry Johnston's article on Haiti and on account of the Fuertes[14] article "The Sport of Kings" on Falconry. I kept it home from the library about a month copying things out of it. Which article did you send it for?

Yesterday was Lincoln's birthday and I worked all day at the library. Last Monday, we spent at the Falconers'. All our things are in good condition and as nice as ever but there are a lot of them. Mrs. Falconer had a glass of warm milk waiting for me which I *had* to drink. They drove us to the tube at three o'clock and the drive did us a great deal of good. Things in the church are evidently not phenomenally prosperous.

Tuesday H.D. and Winifred Bryher (Lady Winifred Ellerman) arrived. They are at the Brevoort and are about to be come after, to go home, by Sir John Ellerman, Winifred's father, but she said "there isn't any danger of his coming before April." We are to have Scofield Thayer and Mr. Watson to tea tomorrow to meet them. Winifred was to come for 3 months and has stayed five. Her father has coal mines and a rice mill in Burma and is interested in shipping and American trade; also in art. I am reviewing her novel *Development* for *The Dial*. She looks as if she were 18 or twenty but is 26, had some beautiful Empress Josephine clothes Hilda says which she discarded for plain silks and suits when she turned artist. She is going to wear a cute black silk dress with short sleeves tomorrow with a figured pattern of little flowers in circles and a high, low neck cut square. Ezra lives near them in London and comes in late sometimes they say, and stays for hours. Miss Bryher says the first time she met him she was staying at Hilda's apartment and she said, "I let him in; I thought it was the bread or the potatoes and I was very sorry I had. He talked to me an hour about a Saxon king and a Danish chief and how one wanted to carry off the other's wife and things went on till but one was left. He said afterward I didn't stand up very well without H.D." I took them to a party the other night to which I was invited and she sat perfectly motionless smiling brightly but saying nothing most of the time so I guess even Ezra was slowed down a little. When there are no strangers about she is most sprightly. Piggy has a bad crush on her and spends as much of his time at the Brevoort as he can so eventually he too was smuggled to the party. H.D. wouldn't leave him and wouldn't go [to] the party unless they both were definitely invited so I took Winifred and then got him invited and went back for him. Winifred wants Mole and me to go over to England with them for the trip and to spend a month or two. She tried most of one evening to get me to promise to take a check for a Mediterranean trip as soon as she got it from her father. She said, "Dactyl if you don't take it delicately with a swish of your tail it will be very awkward. You see my father wants to encourage me to get rid of money. Half of it will be

14. Louis Agassiz Fuertes (1874–1927), artist-naturalist.

his and half of it will be mine." I said I couldn't do it. She said to take it and put it away for some future time as a kind of artist's scholarship, but I refused. I said "You shouldn't be so insistent and you don't like what I write anyhow." "I don't like what you write," she said "but I like you." Now she is full of the idea of our going back with them for a month or so and is going to the White Star line and the Red Star line tomorrow to see about sailings. She said, "you have to make reservations several months ahead and it won't do any harm to inquire. Dadda had to send a clerk to beg a cabin for us when we came over." I don't suppose we can go but I think there is some possibility that we might go. Mole doesn't know what to say about it either. The library might let me go but if there is a possibility of Mole's being more worried than benefitted by going, it would be out of the question.

Peter's family had two artist friends for dinner and invited me in afterward. Peter had retired to their bathroom but we got him in here later on. I guess I didn't tell you I was at tea at Scofield Thayer's apartment last week for tea and nearly perished with excitement and "jeu d'esprit." He has a very dainty valet and a lacquer cabinet with a jade snuff bottle and various kinds of things in it and when he asked me what I thought about Paul Rosenfeld (his musical critic for *The Dial*) and said, "*Entre nous,* I think he's punk," I nearly fainted with surprise at the humanness of the condemnation.

With love,   Rat

To John Warner Moore   *February 20, 1921*

Dear Badger,

Your cable was a great pleasure for we didn't know what changes and delays there were going to be in your sailings and wouldn't have known anyhow just where you were. The bags are beautiful but you ought not to have got so many. I know what a task that bargaining with natives is and how, do what you will, you can't get the things for what they ought to sell them for.

We have had a jammed week—two weeks I ought to say. The worst event is Piggy McAlmon's being married at City Hall on Monday, (an hour or two before our tea), to Winifred "Bryher." The girls arrived at about a quarter past five, Scofield Thayer and Mr. Watson at about twenty minutes past. Hilda just had time before the men came to say that W. had been married to "Robert" a little while before and that that had made them late. The girls looked lovely and the men were graciousness and responsiveness itself, but what an earthquake. Mr. Watson is about seven feet tall very silent and well-appointed, Scofield glittered like the "Shining figure of an Ethiopian," you could almost see the paths in his hair from a brushing, his shirt advertised the powers of his laundress, his batwing tie sat neatly across his collar and his feet also gave evidence of friction. We entered upon conversation in a most strained and cold soup fashion. Scofield commented upon the "sand-blast" out-of-doors and wondered if the girls had been subjected to its annoyances. We touched on California which no one "raved" about though I defended the fuchsias and thistles. Finally the ice gave, and Ezra and Mrs. Asquith[15] and D. H. Lawrence and *The Dial* were discussed. Winifred said *The Dial* was reactionary and hadn't advanced beyond 1912. Scofield asked what writers she thought *had* advanced beyond Yeats and Ezra and George Moore and others. "Why," she said, "Robert McAlmon." From our point of view the tea was lovely and Hilda was a remarkable guest, the most dignified and yet the most informally friendly and entertaining that I guess we have entertained. She told how Ezra had set out to give Winifred fencing lessons. He had had a few in Paris from an Italian. W. had been taught at 6 years old and had fenced all her life, and how Ezra said finally, "I see you're no amateur. We'd better stop, for you have learned the French method while I learned the Italian." She also told how the Ellermans' butler came to the door during a zeppelin raid and said to Winifred's mother, "My lady—the zeppelins."

Mr. Watson said he had heard that Charlie Chaplin was playing in a remarkable movie of his own, *The Kid.* I went uptown to go to a gallery Thursday and seeing the sign on the Strand, went in and was richly repaid—an international news film came first showing wonderful skiing, Edison at work, and scenes in Flanders. *The Kid* was then run and was just over at a quarter of two—leaving me barely time to get home and get some bread & chicken and get to work at two.

Friday we went to one of the nicest plays I have ever seen, Rollo's *Wild Cat,* at which Mole laughed as much as I. It's the story of a young fellow who comes to N. York to spend his grandfather's money on an "artistic production of *Hamlet.*" He acts or tries to act in the play and there [are] many laughs at the expense of Shakespeare. Lola Ridge had us to a little party to meet Laura & William Benét and the Scotts and invited me to an evening party for Friday. I am reviewing Mr. [C. Kay] Scott's *Blind Mice,* a novel for Doran[16] and I have another book to do.

With love,   Rat

---

15. Lady Cynthia Asquith was secretary and companion to J. M. Barrie from 1918 until 1937, and a frequent correspondent and associate of D. H. Lawrence's.

16. George H. Doran Co., a publishing house.

Dear Pago-Pago: O   Know what this is?

    Several things have happened since I wrote you. Your telegram concerning Homer came. We went to Wall Street this morning and Mouse will give you the news. Mr Houston had moved from 37 Wall to 70 Pine, received us very kindly, and says the Allegheny Gas will revive, it's a good house, could not for the time being surmount the depression.

    The Criterion has came out and though they did not send proof and the changes I sent in lieu of proof were not incorporated, the thing reads very well. Ezra has the opening piece--a tribute (in memoriam) to Harold Monro, and T. S. Eliot has a rather interestin Commentary, and there are sousands of reviews. The poem is not of much account and I feel that they need a piece of verse (on the order of my Jerboa or the twenty froggies; I am just beginning to concentrate on the Plumet Basilisk, however, so may not get around to this for a couple of months.) Speaking of frogs, I see Earnest Ratsey's Golliwog won something in a race way up the Sound. There is going to be a Marine Museum; I mean Mariner's Museum costing $10,000,000 and covering 850 acres at Morrison, Virginia. Models of ships and ship machinery will be gathered covering maritime development as far back as investigators find proof of activity. The project was proposed by Archer M Huntington. Every type of small hand and wind propelled boat known to history will be placed on the lake. In the field of model-making the museum will start with the present and work backward. The origin of rope and canvas and other materials will be traced and models of the Monitor and Merrimac and of the first ships that sailed into Jamestown will be included. They plan to be exact and not to hurry and to have the material gathered in about 25 years.

    The church next door has flowered on a tremendous scale. Everything inside has been plastered Nile mud red, they have a lot of new images, a giant palm, and a good deal of singing, by small boys in red gowns with white smocks. The basement is being excavated and a heap of assorted rocks has come out. Beside these rocks was a pile of well-sifted sand rising to a symmetrical point. Mouse says yesterday morning Beble was loose in the court-yard and began to snout the sand and then to dig in it; surprised to find his no resistance, he dug the more enthusiastically, sending the sand in every direction, rejoiced to see how far it would go, then lay on his back in what remained of the pile and rolled and rolled, saddened by the reduced condition of the pile. Nor did he get a beating; he was somewhere else by the time the ignoramus returned to the pile. He real name seems to be Bimbo. Brownie Barker, the market man's Chow has been clipped andd is a picture; very shy because of the funny feeling; but how he feels; like yourself, after a clipping.
    See by the paper Mr Garner says he"can deal with Hoover" and "feels big enough for the job" of governing in view of the President's " weakness." We have had quite a little humor over Mr Lawrence A Greene, our neighbor on the fourth floor. When he came in to collect for Block-Aid, I was typing the Brontë review; ever since,he has been asking me how was business and said he was interested in literary things and Mouse has dropped a bushel over the matter and encouraged me to tell him we had no time and did nothing that was for his ears--especially when he said he would drop in some evening to contimue the conversation. I met him on the street one day when a tennis-player was passing; I commented on the player and he said, "there are tennis-courts right near us in the Park; would you care to play sometime?" I said "yes, I would be delighted." He said, "Have you a racquet?" I says yes. He said what time would suit me and so on, ending with much happiness and better confidence--having in the beginning asked me timidly, "Have you heard from your mother yet? I mean your brother." Mouse shook and slappered her ears over this and kept saying, "etched; he's won out; well, well." But nothing has come of it and I am delighted for the good would not be commensurate with the triviality and annoyance waiting on the bench for half an hour and playing battledore for 20 minutes; and much talk about your brother and the quill.

    Mouse came to me very dutifully to have her pads attended to with salisilic acid. I taped them and said on no account to touch them without my supervision. This morning they were all trimmed and she called my attention to the fact and when I said I had charge of the case, she said be careful, "the hoof will lift" and added"but you have charge of

meaning she would kick me;

Printed version on page 267

Mary Watson spoke with great appreciation of her visit to Crestwood and how she enjoyed being with the children; said Johnnie was in certain ways a little like Sue's Johnnie. Also, I meant to say that May when here last month, seemed very much delighted with the house, surprised to find it so roomy and very much liked the furniture and the way it looks against light walls. She said Leo would be working at the detail of the house when we were at Woodbury and doesn't like to be interrupted, but "he is not to cut off his service to you; and if you want to go any where in the car or take some drives, just tell him and don't spoil him or make a fuss over his work on the house for he revels in praise."

The radio at times has remarkable things on it and we have it as loud as we like-- and "make them suffer like they make us suffer;" then again it is ludicrous indeed. I'll be tweezing gravely for some reasonable thing and it'll say, "now I'm goin to ask you a shivery question and you can't help but agree. What makes you so sweet." or "These are the songs you love best; sung the way you love to hear them. First on tonight's program will be 'Ive a date with an Angel; by the sun-burned boys in the baloon-ball-room at Luna Park, Coney Island--accompanied by our Fourth of Juliars." Ed Wynne's band is the Voorhees Orchestra and they give us last week,"Oh Gee, Oh Joy"and "Roar, Lion, Roar." I don't know whether Mouse likes it or not; anyhow she bears it; said, I think, it was no great strain on the emotions; whereas during one of the pieces up at the Stadium she nearly bit me for rattling a paper and thinking of reading during it.

Tremendous lopings. Wall Street; Wanamaker's; Schulte's, yesterday and day before. Outside Schulte's we were joined by David Lawson, Lola Ridge's hubband. He was very kind, said he would urge us to come to his rooms to tea but he didn't want to have us climb the stairs on a hot day, and so on. He said Lola had been in Mesopotamia but was now visiting Mrs. Floyd and, was going later to Yaddo. He said he had had a letter from Lore-a "Benét. That Mrs. Benét had had an illness and I think an operation on her eyes; she needed the operation before leaving but they had waited so long to go abroad--and had never been abroad--they feared if they didn't go they might never go. Lore-a had seen Masefield De la Mare. Mr. Lawson smiled. "That's Lore-a; that's the one thing to say about it," he added. "She was surprised to find him selling petroleum or petrol--a man like that." Again he smiled; but he said they were delighted with the trip in spite of backsets.

I was greatly intrigued by Mr Pesky in Schulte's; "P.Pesky, Sec'y". I asked him where reptiles were. "Rep-tiles?" he said briskly. "Right here, Miss Mouse. Rep-tiles and lizzeds in this alcove." But I didn't find any; at least no basilisks. I find from the library that newts are moist-skinned flat-tailed animals whereas lizard lizzeds have dry scales and a cylindrical tail.

Today we got Mouse's glasses adjusted, bought her a pair of shoes--brown with lowish heels and a strap and buckle--at Hanan's, next Merowitz's; and got me several things got her a pongee kimona with blue hem and an ice-cream festival chrysanthemum-and-lantern pattern across the shoulders--wondrous flimsy; but its lightness is good, it will wash, and she is wearing it right away. We got for me a tiny blouse--white muslin with pink polka dots, sleeves half-way to the elbow--69¢--that fits me better and looks better on me than anything I've had for several years; and a large baku dark blue hat for 5 dollars reduced from $12.95 which Mouse had been pining to get me at the regular price, but left me go. This is a big deed. I haven't gone anywhere but to church that Mouse hasn't urged me to get a hat, and told me how puny I looked.

I got Mouse from the library Lord Kilbracken's Memoirs and it is a very impressive book, modest, tolerant, and vivid. I had a letter from Ezra today--very, very considerate and attentive--urging also that we have Louis Zukofsky to the house. This is the third approach on the subject and we think in the fall we will let him over. Ezra says he feels that Ford M. Ford and I had been underestimated by him in his previous summaries and he was glad to put in this anthology all of my poems that he had; but that oversight was not his reason. And I appreciated appreciate this very much; though I never felt he slighted me.

A'f'M'ly
Rusty Mongoose

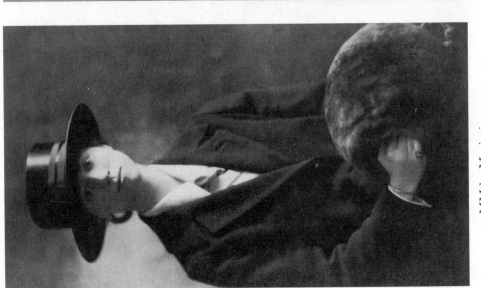

MM by Marjori, 1922

MM by Sardony, 1924

MM by Alice Boughton, c. 1929

To H.D.   *March 27, 1921*

Dear Hilda:

It was a delight to have your letter; I feel much happier now, about all of you. I had a firm picture of you all in my mind and your various responsibilities; like Gordon Craig, "I had not thought of a blue gauze veil"; I hadn't thought of anything so rational and domestically poetic as a little sulking. I had forgotten Robert. I am delighted to think of his being of service either to you or to Bryher. I am still shocked by him. Anyone who is so ignorant as not to know that he was doing Bryher an irreparable injury by doing as he did, is not fit to marry her. What I miss in Robert is a lack of reverence toward mystery—a failure to understand human dignity. William [Carlos Williams's] cavorting about naked for the fun of the thing is a different matter and speaking of liberty, I must tell you what Mother said when I tried to describe to her, some of your snap-shots in the woods. She said: "I'd adore to run through the hedges at Matthew Arnold's, under the big trees, in the deep snow—alone,—or with just a few." I said, "With Mary, perhaps?" (My niece.) "No," said Mother, "she wouldn't enjoy it as much as if she were my age." I meant to tell you this one day while you were in town but I forgot. You reassure me somewhat in what you intimate of Bryher's equipoise, but not enough. You remember in [George Moore's] *Avowals*, [Sir Edmund] Gosse says of the Brontës: "Then you think that Emily was the genius?" and Moore says: "The word is inapplicable to prose writers under forty, besides more than one book is necessary."? It may be that there is no such thing as a love affair in the case of people under forty and that an improvised duet doesn't signify but my intuition doesn't corroborate my wish in this matter. I think [G. K.] Chesterton is right as I said to you the night after the party—at the Brevoort. (There is no such thing as a prudent marriage;) marriage is a Crusade; there is always tragedy in it; in the case of one with so finely adjusted a mechanism as Bryher, one's spiritual motive power is sure to receive a backset, and I can smile only very ironically at Robert's harmonizing so nicely with the family, in his adaptibility to Perdita.

Your "Simaetha" and "Prayer" are beautiful, in *Contact*—especially the "Simaetha." The color is magnificent; the rhymes are structurally strong and the sense of detachment is precise and very much felt. I don't know how you can vivify material that has been toyed with so much; or perhaps I should say, use symbols that have been used by people so much, with disastrous results to themselves. I like Bryher's "Extract"; it is very much herself; and I like William's "Portrait [of a Lady]" better than anything he has done; however uneven the article on the goats may be, there is genius in the "Gna-ha-ha-ha! as in a hat." Don't you think so? The night we repaired with dignity, to Mrs. Head's, I told William that I would review *Kora in Hell* since he wished it, for *Contact*. I have just sent him the review and in writing me about it, he suggests that I send it to *The Bookman;* he speaks heartily of it but evidently does not think of using it in *Contact*, so that I fear you may not see it if I do not send you a copy.

We cannot come over to see you though Cook agonized us this morning with a circular entitled, "The Voyage of Your Dreams." My winglets rose and remained suspended a moment but it is out of the question for us to think of leaving for a year or so. The dactyl is not an oracle—merely Bryher's problem.

Your detail in the poems makes me think of [Benvenuto] Cellini's *Treatise De Oreficio* [Tratto dell'Oreficeria], for which I think as I told you, I have been looking. Also of some African jewelry and articles of handicraft that I saw a few nights ago. An African girl who looks like an Egyptian princess, with narrow eyes and a narrow nose, showed these things, to interest people in a trades school for girls in West Africa; she said the authority on Greek gold ornaments at the South Kensington Museum, thought a pair of old African earrings she had, were early Greek work and when she told of the crude implements with which the Africans make their ornaments, I was dumbfounded. She showed bottles and cans covered with thick, polished scarlet calf-skin—one, square like a perfume bottle with a battered, smooth green cork which slid on a thong which went over the bottle like a handle, and in some cases, the surface of the skin was cut off with a sharp knife in intricate patterns, making an effect like marquetry or the Rajah's breeches; and a whip with a band of leopard skin about an inch from the end of the handle, fur needle-cases shaped like toad stools, with fine stripes of white fur set in, forming circular lines between the dark fur; daggers with barrel shaped hafts of rhinoceros hoof, a section or two of ivory at either side of the rhinoceros, and wooden combs with long, cylindrical teeth like some of the early Greek combs.

I am delighted that you were not annoyed by *The Goddess*.[17] I liked that afternoon; I wish there needn't be so few times of carefree enjoyment.

I have just had a letter from Bryher which makes me very happy. She says her father and mother are pleased with Robert and I hope they are. Perhaps I exaggerate the momentousness of marriage.

When you can, send me anything you have been writing and do send me a picture of Perdita.

Bryher says she fears that Robert finds London not very nutritious. "There does not seem to be a young man in London." She says "you can imagine how that makes me feel. It is absolutely impossible to see anything which you could not create for yourself without seeing it and with the mind that was born in me, Robert should be enjoying London in California at this moment."

17. American film directed by Ralph Ince (1915).

I shall go to the 42nd Street library on Tuesday to look for any press notices which mention Bryher. A true dactyl of course, has not seen anything that may have appeared.

Your address which I wrote on a scrap of paper the day we went to *The Goddess*, I have lost so I shall have to send this in Bryher's care. You will not mind writing it for me again, will you?

We both miss you and shall be missing you till you come back.

Dactyl

To John Warner Moore *April 4, 1921*

Dear Badger,

We were shocked to hear of Mary's operation. If that had to be done, I know the sooner the better. It is good that you can soon be home to see how things are going and Constance will be much happier of course also.

Mole is well. I dragged her to Gimbel's on Monday to see Van Tines merchandise which is being sold at so called half price. We could find nothing worthy, pretty, or needful but some 25 cent straw slippers and a little wooden dog like Mary's. We need a cup and saucer but their reductions to $1.75 $1.95 incensed Mole unspeakably and we did not buy.

Thursday we went to Yvette Guilbert's last recital. It was not so remarkable as the one before, but fine enough. Yvette wore in her first song a bright pink silk dress with gold lace down the front, large blue peacock eyes appearing at intervals in the gold and a blue chiffon scarf embroidered at the edge with pink and a long blue veil from her cap and in her next appearance, a dull blue silk taffeta skirt and pale yellow waist with a gray flower pattern. Her young girls were very punk.

Wednesday Scofield called me up at the library and asked me to come to tea but I couldn't go as I had to work till six so he asked me to have dinner with him. Also asked if we should dine in the village or if he should wear evening dress! I said to wear tails and a gray top hat as I understand that was the latest thing in Paris. We went to a little place where West Houston Street turns toward Macdougal near Borden's milk depot. He couldn't find the place at first as there is no sign out, and asked a man going into a house. He came down his steps and hurried towards the right door. Scofield remarked to me under his breath before thanking the man, "Very efficient." The door had diagonal wires across the glass to protect it and was locked on the inside but promptly opened. We had a good meal in a clean, well managed place (a little like the ball room of a Cape May Hotel) with light pine floors and serviceable Cape May furniture. Mr. Watson Sr. the father of Scofield's partner, an old gentleman with a white beard, has been in Florida for his health and while there killed a large rattlesnake. When he came home, he and his son and grandson and daughter-in-law and Scofield's sister-in-law went to the zoo and when visiting the snakes, the old gentleman was determined to hear the rattlesnake rattle. Young Mr. Watson, who never speaks unless forced to, was obliged to stir the rattles up and to shout to his father continually, "Do you hear it?" while many strangers gathered round to watch. Scofield told this with great gusto. He said Mr. Watson persevered till "the poor rattler was nearly worn out." Also he had a clipping from the *Times* about Bryher which he gave me—a very nauseous, made up story of Mr. McAlmon first a halfback on a Minnesota football team and how he decided to come to New York to be a Bohemian. How Miss Ellerman saw one of his poems then met him and how when he quoted a poem there was nothing to do but call a minister. I told Scofield how it was not funny to me and he said, "Yes it's all very well for me to be amused looking at it from the point of view of an outsider." I said it was an outrage for anyone to marry Winifred Bryher in such style so unromantic—and he said, "You think it was unromantic to be married on Valentine's Day?" and so on. He said on leaving that he would like to bring his friend Mr. Nichol to call—he thinks Mr. Nichol would be congenial to Mole—being a curator of the Metropolitan and opposed to Gaston Lachaise's nudes. He also took one of my Indian-chief tracings to reproduce in *The Dial*.

Today he and Mr. Nichol called but we were out. We went down to the River and lingered in the sun till six and when we came back Peter only was in the vicinity.

We have invited Aunt E., Daisy & Edwin to dinner a week from tomorrow.

With love,   Rat

The pictures of the turtle with red eyes are very amusing and so are the words.

To T. S. Eliot   *April 17, 1921*

Dear Mr. Eliot,

Your letter gives me great pleasure. In *The Sacred Wood*, I met so many enthusiasms of my own that I could not feel properly abashed to be "criticizing" a critic—at least not until it was too late to retreat.

It is a happiness to know that I am not quite a stranger to you; the war makes 1917 seem long ago.

Were I to publish verse I should be grateful indeed for the assistance you offer. Your suggestion tempts me almost beyond my own certain knowledge that I have nothing that ought to appear in book form. For me to be published so, would merely emphasize the meagerness of my production. Not that I have expressed sentiment that I am unwilling to stand by, but should verse of mine that has been published, ever appear again, it ought to be supplementary to something more substantial. But to have friends is the great thing. I value more than I am able to say, your approval. H.D. has been kind; also "Winifred Bryher" and Miss Harriet Weaver.

I am happy indeed that you have met and like Mr. McAlmon and wish that he could immediately be inoculated with a liking for England and experience the transports in being there that some of us have, three thousand miles away.

I should be glad to think that my review of *The Sacred Wood* had given a satisfaction in the least commensurate with that which it has given me.

There is much in *The Sacred Wood* that gives enjoyment besides the few things commented on in the short review—that has been gone over in conversation by my own fireside. It is odd that occasionally, a mere jibe or bit of byplay will remain longer than one's best wit. I have had occasion to quote more than once, your comment on H. G. Wells and Chesterton but I hope sometime to hear you speak yourself upon the main issues of this book.

I am yours most sincerely,   Marianne Moore

To Bryher   *April 18, 1921*

Dear Bryher:

I am happy to have your letters; I am glad to know your feeling about Robert and past recent events, and can be trusted. You don't shock me but the way in which newspaper men have let their imaginations run wild about you, does shock me. I enclose what notices I could find; reluctantly, for they are nauseous and not even racy. Mother especially resents the picture of the little girl who posed for you. I suppose it is not cruelty on the part of outsiders to say things, they are so far away from it all.

What you say is true; the physical is important as well as the spiritual and I don't doubt that a thousand derangements are the result of our misunderstanding of the physical. Freud says his object is to substitute a conscious for an unconscious—a normal for a pathogenic conflict and we must do this if we can. A knowledge of abnormal conditions is a help in understanding normal conditions but as Freud says, our capacity for transferring energy from one field to another is almost infinite and the adjustments of one need to another, involve so many things that it is no easy matter to be absolute as to what course of action we are compelled to adopt for our all round best good.

I am excited to hear of your kodak. I had just seen it advertised in *Kodakery* when I got your letter; the sketch looks just like it. I am so chagrined over my own attempts, I can scarcely bring myself to speak of them. In my excitement, I forgot to autograph any but the last film which couldn't be printed and I did not hold the kodak level. Mother had trouble focussing me, but I shall send you what we took and shall take the next with the utmost care. I surely will get a portrait attachment but don't think I might break into my three hundred for that or a tank. Do you know Stratz's book showing characteristic physical types of women of every nationality? *Die Rassenschönheit des Weibes:* Prof. Dr. C. H. Stratz, published by Ferdinand Enke, Stuttgart, 1920. ($12.00 in America.) I should say that from the point of view of present day aesthetics, the Persians, Parisiennes, Americans and English stand first.

I have had a letter from T. S. Eliot, in which he says he has met Robert and likes him. I haven't heard from Hilda since she landed. Mother wants to know when Perdita's birthday is. Do you know? I got a little jointed wooden dog for her a few days ago like one my niece has. It is a little mongrel but as the *Geographic* dog book says, of the true hound, the stern is carried gaily.

Mr. Thayer no doubt is several mails ahead of me with an article about you and Robert which he says he has forwarded you.[18] He seems to think that your literary predilections will hinder your having any feeling against being brought into print. He likes you extremely and when I was aghast at reference being made to your father, he said he thought the article was so obviously a phantasy, that he didn't see how anyone's feelings could be hurt by it. As to his referring to Hilda and repeating a remark of mine, quoted from your letter, he said he was willing to omit these things. He said that Ezra Pound had written him that Robert hadn't found people in London very conversible and that he would consult Dr. Williams about repeating certain things quoted from him. I don't know what Dr. Williams' reply would have been but I was relieved to have Mr. Thayer tell me over the telephone the next day that he would print nothing at all unless it was authorized by you.

I have decided that I like a quarter to, better than a quarter of, though I say a quarter of. I think what one wishes is the maximum of precision and the maximum of compression. If it is a case of 1. a quarter towards; or 2. it lacks a quarter of or is within a quarter of, a quarter to, seems to me a little the better; but Mother says the manual permits either as an idiom.

I have been to the circus at Madison Square Garden. The great features were a race of whippet hounds, an acrobat in white with a black stripe down either side of him, and bare back riding—several girls and several clowns, each from time to time, alighting on a galloping horse by a backward standing jump. Afterward, I visited the cages—dogs, a goat, a white mule, a lioness with four cubs faintly freckled, tigers, elephants, zebras, gnus, giraffes and sea lions.

Dactyl

18. Thayer mentioned Bryher and McAlmon's marriage in the May *Dial* "Comment."

The Illustrated [London] *News*es have been a great pleasure but bring a thought too, of the care it is to address them and get them off. People in the provinces ought not to be a drag on people who are at the hub.

To John Warner Moore   *April 24, 1921*

Dear Badger,

I am happy about the baby—that all has gone so well—that Constance could have the best care and that Mary could be so wonderfully provided for. I was interested in Mrs. Eustis's card and like Mole, was amused at Mrs. Eustis's being so decisive about her goings and comings. I like Mrs. Eustis and her force of character is on long acquaintance an assistance rather than an interference I should say at least to one with my temperament. Don't have any regrets about the baby's name so far as I am concerned. As Mole says, when a child is continually being called by a name, it should have a name that its mother has a feeling for and though you certainly have a right to consideration, there is nothing to harrow you in having the baby named for Mrs. Cameron while it would be a great sacrifice for Constance not to have her named for Mrs. C. If her hair is red it is a blessing that she isn't a boy, don't you think so? For red hair is to some extent the fashion for girls but for boys, it is an abomination always accompanied with large freckles.

To send so much money is overwhelming but send it since Constance is willing. I hope we won't need to use it up. If I can I will get Mole to take osteopathy. She isn't very well—has a bad eye this week—swollen above and below and doesn't feel very spry. We have been a little too busy perhaps and confused. *The Dial* has kept me busy although I want the work and should be only too displeased if they discarded me, and we have had various other distractions. May Eustis's visit Monday for dinner was a great success and we made a successful trip to the optician's yesterday to see about having Mole's glasses mended. Tuesday, I went again to the Circus. I saw the lions milk (4 very fascinating little cubs), contending and struggling as if the old lion were nothing but a roll of carpet, sliding down the slippery body and staggering up like a football player bucking the line. The hounds were collected in a heap at the back of their enclosure but the stable boy called them out. They barked and showed considerable excitement and friendliness and then returned. He said they hadn't been running so well since people had been feeding them peanuts. There were several new features in the performance and some good ones left out. They had a small procession of pigs— 5 or six which went round the ring with clowns between acts—graduated in size (a kind of auburn) each with its tail in a tight round curl—and each drawing a little cart—the largest was about the size of Max (Frank Butcher's dog). The poodles were a great feature—an African brown one and 4 black ones. They bounced on and off spring boards through hoops, into the arms of the trainer and so on. I got very tired of the foremost lady acrobat for whom "the lights were darkened and drums rolled." As *Life* said, (*quoting* the program) "This miniature marvel of the air, breaks every law of gravity throwing her body over her own shoulders scores of times without pause." *Life* says, "How many laws of gravity she breaks will have to be determined by someone who knows how many laws of gravity there are. As for throwing yourself over your shoulders scores of times without pause— what has been gained by it? You have simply cast your body over your shoulders scores of times without pause etc." I had an interesting time with the kangaroos—holding them up by the front paws and so on. I have done the animals an injustice as my clothes smelt of carbolic acid—not of them.

Scofield sent me from the office, during my absence at the circus, a copy of Stewart Mitchell's poems just out—and he called me up yesterday at the library to ask me to review it. Week before last he invited me to tea and in the course of the conversation I said I had just seen an announcement of Stewart Mitchell's poems in the *Publishers Weekly;* (he didn't say he would give me a copy but must have on mature reflection, decided to). He had written a satire on Piggy McAlmon and Bryher in which he quoted two things I had told him—and he wanted to know if I would object to his using them. I was much taken aback and implored him to leave them out though I said since I had said them to him, I had no right to say whether he should quote or not. I ran the risk of his repeating anything at all that I said. No; he said he thought not; that jokes told informally were "privileged" and he would leave them out, neither would he refer to Sir John Ellerman as a "vigorous rooster" since I objected to that though he liked the phrase. We haggled till half past seven much to my discomfort. Mole was in despair at my not coming home and Scofield had an engagement to dine with somebody but refused to drop the matter with more dispatch so he was probably put to the embarrassment of apologizing. Last night I spent with Oliver Sayler and his wife. Oliver Sayler is an Oberlin fellow who has written 2 books on the theatre. His wife I knew at Bryn Mawr. He hates Scofield like poison, and said Alfred Kreymborg would walk round *The Dial* in circles when he got the *Broom* started. Thus they lash each other.

With love,   Rat

Do you want a striped cotton bathrobe for summer?

To John Warner Moore   *May 1, 1921*

Dear Badger,

Mole assists me to a stray, faded sheet of paper that we got in Scotland just when I was thinking of looking about to see what I could write on.

I have got *The [Publishers] Weekly* and have just finished reading it. I also went to the main library Thursday to hear Lowell Brentano speak on the "economic aspect of book distribution." He is all brains and willing to have you know it wearing his P.B.K. key high up, squarely in the middle of his vest. He spoke of the severity of the postal rates on booksellers and how, when buyers are asked to pay postage on purchases they object regarding this as a kind of "petty graft."

I had 2 cables from Winifred Ellerman this week. One, "please come secretary summer" the other "come summer." We can't go, needless to say. Mr. McAlmon wrote me a delightful letter telling me of having seen bulls in the British Museum and he described a wonderful piece of jewelry that Lady Ellerman has, a squarish turquoise with diamonds set in platinum and a pearl larger than a robin's egg. He said that T. S. Eliot asked him a great many questions about me and said about one of the lines in a poem in *Contact* that he "did not know of any more beautiful cadenced line in the writing of any time." He no doubt had more trouble in extracting praise from Wyndham Lewis for he said, "Lewis likes you too." He enclosed some postcards of a hairy man in the British Museum, of a monkey and young, a camel, 2 Yogis and the discobolus. He also sent me the first number of *The Tyro* a little paper being edited by W. Lewis. W. Lewis explains in an editorial note that a tyro is known as an elemental person usually referred to in Journalism as "the veriest tyro." "All the tyros we introduce to you are the veriest tyros." One of the jokes amused me very much. Mr. Segando: The mood of nostalgia, Philip, is frightened off by the bombastic shadow of my hair. Philip: But I wonder why it ever comes. Mr. S.: Come it must Philip like other moods. Three quarters of my moods move about like well trained servants and when they have gone I find a delicate polish on what was previously dull. Philip: I have one mood that frightens me. Mr. S.: Indeed? Philip: It is one that has one word like Poe's raven. It says create create create. On one of its visits, it threw me into such a state, that I designed a hat for Philippine. She wears it to this day. Mr. S: Oh yes, a charming contrivance. I have often remarked it.

With love, Rat

To Bryher *May 3, 1921*

Dear Bryher:

I cannot come; though on receiving your second cable, the thought immediately occurred to me of coming over and returning the next day, after assuring myself that you and Hilda are well and as when I last saw you at The Brevoort. I should like to do the typing—though you might discharge me for inefficiency. I should enjoy typing some lines that said something after being ankle deep in musical therapeutics and kindergarten plays written by kindergarteners inspired to supplement our inadequate supply of nursery playlets. I should not like at this time, to leave the library unless it were to save a life or unless the situation here, for me, were so unbearable that by staying there wouldn't be anything of me left to go when I did want to go. My large webbed feet have enough freedom here and the facsimile pasture is not so unnutritious as it is lacking in aesthetic allurements. Perhaps you will feed me on detail from time to time and so preserve my exploring faculties until I can use them.

Robert's vitality and compasslike mobility are good things and his relish of what he relishes. I had a delightful letter from him enclosing *The Tyro* and some post cards—one of a hairy man frowning and one of two Yogis—both veritable incarnations of the east. His aloofness from the past is very dire—his tendency to appraise it and never get lost in it; he approaches culture goat fashion; he hasn't the concentric crushing power of the python. As for shades and overtones, I am ruled by them and escape from them with my life by a hairsbreadth and I cannot be much with people who are not as unhealthily impressionable and implacable as I am myself, so I was displeased when I heard of your being married to Robert. I felt that your daily intellectual formula and Robert's were not the same and I felt also, that Robert could not now or later grasp your motives for benefitting him and that was a disappointment to me but when one is honest as you are, in diagnosing situations, half the poison in life is eliminated and I don't fear that you won't work things out well and be happy at the same time. As for John Cournos and T. S. Eliot, I shall be cut in two like Solomon's babe for I like them both. T. S. Eliot sounds self contained and desirous of doing the just and appropriate thing, so it is highly amusing to me that you "disliked the look of him." I do not know the Sweeney poems. I especially like John Cournos. His article on [Jacob] Epstein in *The Studio*, last fall, was commanding. I feel in his writing every little while, the beauty of smothered flame breaking through and the dignity and perseverance which mark the artist, separate him from chirpers and dilettanti. The flame may be more a racial asset than a mark of the artist. I like it of course and am glad to know of your having a possible similar title to it. I am interested in the poems. "We shall smell the fields as the rose leaves fall over us" is a fine line and your detail justifies itself; it is fresh in the old pagan way and pagan feeling is not easy to reconstruct. We have modern feeling that is pagan but it seldom revives antiquity. I am all eagerness to see the novels and am sorry I cannot see them piecemeal as they advance.

My interest was aroused in Casanova last year when I read [Arthur] Symons' essay on him in *Figures of Several Centuries*. If the Secretary parts with any information, share it with me.

The Tyro is a joyous burst of Gulliverism, isn't it? I know Philip and Mr. Segando by heart; Philip certainly, with teeth clenched on the pipe and his elliptical eyes. Will Eccles I fear, is a bad egg.

I am much interested in *The Spectator*'s review (April 2nd) of Congreve's *Love for Love* given by the Phoenix Society; it is by Tarn, *The Spectator*'s dramatic critic. I wonder if you know who he is? He quotes Dryden's lines on Congreve and "manly Wycherley," particularizes as to which of the Company played best and commends Ben Field as the Astrologer; or rather, he says, "Mr. Ben Field amused the audience, many of whom were surely from their demeanor, fresh from the works of our modern dream interpreters."

I have given *The Dial* your address and have asked them to send you a March, an April and a May number. If these numbers should not come or not be properly addressed, let me know. I am anxious to have you see the May number, (though I am not sure you will be pleased with it,) for I have a review in it of *Development*.

Your affectionate,   Dactyl

I have been careful to make a distinction between you and the heroine, Nancy. It may not be very apparent, however.

To Bryher   *May 9, 1921*

Dear Bryher:

You are by no means off the rock; nor shall a husband share it with us.[19] I am impatient to see *Adventure*. Do not corrupt me with offers of typing for the party; I am only too eager to be in England this minute but I cannot come before next year even if by that time it should be too late.

I have done a short review for *The Dial*, of Stewart Mitchell's *Poems*, which will if anything, rouse your disapproval even more than past offenses.

Mother is excited over Stowe House's being sold; and I am, over Dr. A. S. W. Rosenbach's purchase of *A Lytell Treatyse on the Beaute of Women* and [R. Turner's] *The Garland of a Greene Witte*—mentioned in your *Sphere* of March 19th.

Robert is brave to enter Denmark with English only and I don't doubt that there is a dearth of Americans and that he has cause to be plaintive. Mother is glad that he is getting his experience without having it react on you.

19. Bryher's description of MM in *West* (1924) illuminates this reference: "Sitting here like a pterodactyl on a rock afraid to move. I suppose you feel if you fell off it into the sea you'd enjoy swimming among the anemones."

Ezra has written me and speaks most disrespectfully of America. Defiance being a form of dependence according to Freud, we perhaps should be honored.

Bertram Hartman, at whose exhibition I was a few days ago, has some elephants that would delight you: a black one in the centre of a hooked rug, a small one of thin amethyst glass with a green cork fitted into a hole in its back and a light blue china man with a mulberry sash standing on the cork; an old brass one, tailless and tuskless with a Javanese mahout astride his neck, smiling in an exuberant and sinister way; a delft one trumpeting; and a slate one about three inches high and four or five long, treading on a crocodile which bites it. Its eyes are like the tilde (?)—the little wavy mark over n in cañyon and the slab which is part of it, has quartz crystals showing on the under side and feels cold like a grotto, when you pick it up.

I have seen a wonderful movie. If it should be in London, I hope you and Hilda will be sure to see it—*The Cabinet of Dr. Caligari.*[20] It is the only movie except *The Kid* that I have gone to voluntarily in New York. The Hartmans told me about it and Mrs. Lachaise has seen it five times. It is a German film and the settings are modern. All vertical lines slant and the shadows on stairs, on attic floors and through casements, are wonderful; Cesare, the somnambulist on appearing—although standing with legs side by side—looks as if he had but one leg. Later, when he is roused from a trance in total darkness against the back of his cabinet, wedge-shaped lights slant down from his eyes at Lida, the heroine, the exact shape of a dagger that he uses later when intending to kill her. In a scene in an insane asylum, stripes on the ground in a courtyard, radiate from a central point like the rays painted on King Arthur's table on the wall at Winchester, and before you at the back of the stage, are three Romanesque entrances to the building like the openings from which animals came out, in the Coliseum.

Mother asks me to put in a little note for her.

Your affectionate,   Dactyl

No doubt you have my cable?

To Robert McAlmon   *May 9, 1921*

Dear Robert:

It is good of you to tell me what T. S. Eliot said about "Those Various Scalpels." It encourages me for I have admired his work from the first. I was pleased to have a letter from him saying that he liked my review of *The Sacred Wood* and that he had met and liked you.

20. Film directed by Robert Wiene and produced by Erich Pommer (1919).

The post-cards have been a great pleasure, especially the Yogis and the camel, and the hairy man with the fish mouth fascinates me more than words can say.

I am glad Wyndham Lewis liked your "Boar" and "White Males." I remember the Irish stags and liked them from the first. I like the idea of "The Wild Boar" but the technique I think, could be improved. In "Six months rooting had taken all tamed spirit out of the swine," "taken" is too prominent and "tamed" breaks the speed of the sentence; it seems redundant but on examining it, you find that the idea in the word is needed, so a different arrangement of all the words would be better.

I have enjoyed *The Tyro* more than anything I have seen since I saw the first number of *Blast*. I received a prospectus today and shall certainly subscribe. I relished the explanatory note about Tyros and the look of concentrated attention in Philip's eyes is wonderful. I see by the alterations in the text that others tinker at their productions as I do myself. A few nights ago, I went to Bertram Hartman's exhibition of drawings and water-colours and told him about Philip and Mr. Segando. He looked a little sceptical as I repeated the first few lines, but when I came to "create, create, create," he burst out laughing. He has a large linoleum cut of a horse—the mane and tail, complementary half ellipses and the outside defining edge of each is a series of jagged indentations like the teeth of a cross-cut saw, giving a wonderful effect of swirling motion. He has also, half finished, a bright jade green and black hooked rug with a design of arrow heads or wedges in the centre which made me think of the black geometric design on the back of a young locust just after it has come out of the shell. He says that Marsden Hartley has been sick and that all his work is to be sold at auction under Mr. Stieglitz's jurisdiction. I am more sorry than I can say. I think Mr. Hartley could get through without an auction if he had a few grains more of dynamite in his constitution and they could be artificially acquired if he has not got them; it is too bad.

I wonder if you have met W. P. Roberts! I liked his drawings in the British war loan exhibition here last year. It was not the bull mummies but the large stone bull in low relief that I wanted you to see.

I have had a letter from Ezra Pound in which he shows that he is quite out of sympathy with everyone but the French.

Sincerely yours,   Marianne Moore

To Ezra Pound   *May 10, 1921*

Dear Mr. Pound:

You imply that what we are doing in America might be of interest to artists in Europe; it is, of course, important to me.

It is true as Miss Anderson says, that the words "literature" and "obscenity" cannot be used synonymously any more than the words "science" and "immorality" can; and as an artist, James Joyce has been wrongly subjected to indignity by stupid people. I admire the artistry of his poems and was exhilarated by *A Portrait of the Artist* and although *Ulysses* has not held my interest enough to enable me to read a single section of it to the end, I might exert myself specifically on his behalf but I have no impulse to bestow military decorations on his editors and prefer not to be associated with them even as an exception. They are not stupid as Joyce's arraigners are stupid, but they are stupid. I accept mongrel art but a flavor of the exceptional must be there along with the negligible. By the nature of the case, anyone who cares about art, is actuated by egotism but Miss [Margaret] Anderson and Miss [Jane] Heap are not highly endowed enough to make their egotism interesting. *The Dial*, in a review of a recent book, says that the book somehow takes its flavor from the less successful poems and *The Little Review* takes its flavor from its editors. I know that they are by no means to be regarded as identical but when the most has been said for Miss Heap that can be said, I think my general conclusion still applies.

It would give me pleasure to write to you personally of anything that comes up that you might not know of, that I know would interest you. Such books as [George Moore's] *Avowals*, [George Saintsbury's] *Héloïse and Abelard*, [Percy Lubbock's] *The Letters of Henry James*, and [Gordon Craig's] *The Theatre Advancing* are important but immediately on publication, they are common property. I am not at pains to investigate small books of verse and sensational fiction and have been interested most, in the last two years, in technical books such as [Benjamin Ives] Gilman's *Museum Ideals of Purpose and Method*, [Frank Alvah] Parsons' *The Psychology of Dress*, [Ernest] Harold Baynes' book on dogs [*Animal Heroes of the Great War*], *The Earthenware Collector* by G. Woolliscroft Rhead, [John J.] McGraw's and [Christopher] Mathewson's books on baseball and [Bill] Tilden's book on tennis. This last is a little crude as when it says that a tennis racquet is an introduction to any town but it is sound and aggressive both from the point of view of sport and of art.

The chief events of interest in town this winter have been Yvette Guilbert, the circus, *The Cabinet of Dr. Caligari*—a German moving-picture film with a cast and settings of great exotic beauty, and *The Beggar's Opera*.

As for native material, I think we have it in Wallace Stevens, in Dr. Williams, and in E. E. Cummings as poets, and of course we pride ourselves on H.D. You speak of Dr. Williams and I suppose with us, you acclaim his spring poem in the last number of *Contact*, as an achievement. I have a notion that a compliment at second hand would not be a pleasure to him; besides, I have seen him but twice the past year, so I take the liberty of disregarding your injunction. E. E. Cummings is self-conscious and a little complacent but he very plainly has poetic gift, whether one is attracted to him temperamentally or not. As for prose, his article on Lachaise in the February *Dial* of last year, is remarkable I think; the subject may have been a happy one, but if he can write on other topics as well, he deserves a hearing. Alfred Stieglitz, in his published statements and early magazines, is worth owning and Scofield Thayer, in his discernment and interplay of metaphor is very brilliant. I infer from certain letters of Gordon Craig's, which Oliver Sayler has let me read, that Gordon Craig is interested in him and I was amused by the aptness of his comment on George Nathan when he said he ought to be put through a cream separator. We pride ourselves, also, on you and T. S. Eliot. Perhaps space was restricted but I felt that W. C. Blum [James Sibley Watson] might well have cavilled at lack of opportunity to enlarge on the chapter on James in his review in *The Dial*, of *Instigations*. I well remember what you say of [Arnold] Dolmetsch in *Pavannes and Divisions* and feel the force of the statement in your article on [Arthur] Symons in *The Athenaeum* last May—that cadence is not dexterity.

Your post-card from Saint-Raphaël was a great pleasure; your enviable proximity to what is the best of the past is very much felt by those at a distance.

Sincerely yours,

To Robert McAlmon   *June 18, 1921*

Dear Robert:

Your elephant arrived yesterday. The color is gorgeous; I don't see how you think it could be improved and the wavy eyes are a delight. The trunk was broken off just in front of the tusks but I have mended it with waterproof cement and it is as solid as it ever was I hope. I have made it a little carpet of blue chiffon velvet the same color—an inch wide by about six inches long and as it stands on the mantel-piece you would think it was walking along a solid blueglaze ocean. You see, you have selected the proper mahout. I call it Jean Clément, Pierre Noziére. Jean because Anatole France says about the little boy who was selected to represent Buddha, "Little Jean experiences a solemn joy in seeing that he has become an idol" and Clément Pierre Noziére, because his ears stand out as described in *Little Pierre* where Pierre remarked to his mother, "Clément's got butterfly wings."

I hope you are not having too good a time in Paris to explore the old corners. I think it is in the Musée Carnavalet that there is a gold camp set of Napoleon's and Victor Hugo's house in the Place des Vosges had a strong flavor to me of *Les Miserables* and of Dumas. Versailles is just like an old engraving invaded by modern red silk parasols and ladies with white poodles. Perhaps you have seen it?

A painting of Marsden Hartley's—*The Virgin of Guadaloupe*—is reproduced in *The Studio* this month, a kind of modern primitive, very definite and impressive.

I have read James Joyce's *Dubliners* this week for the first time. It is pretty nearly a manual I think, of the fundamentals of composition. I have never been more impressed by a story than by "The Dead" and the finality of the whole thing, the aeolian harplike effect of "Araby" and the characterizations and diction haunt me. "His face had a ravaged look." "His voice seemed winnowed of vigour." "His conversation was mainly about himself; what he had said to such a person and what such a person had said to him and what he had said to settle the matter."

Apropos of freedom in your last letter: I think it is very nice of you to accord a woman as much freedom as she might care to have but I think a woman's keeping her own name seems like clutching at the last straw of self-identification.

Don't miss anything but don't forget that American men have something to show the French, both French men and French women.

Sincerely yours,   Marianne Moore

To Bryher   *July 7, 1921*

Dear Bryher:

I received a copy of my poems this morning with your letter and a letter from Miss Weaver. Now that I am a pterodactyl, it is perhaps well that you even with your hardened gaze, cannot see what it is to be a pterodactyl with no rock in which to hide. In *Variations of Animals and Plants under Domestication*, Darwin speaks of a variety of pigeon that is born naked without any down whatever. I feel like that Darwinian gosling. You say I am stubborn. I agree and if you knew how much more than stubborn I am, you would blame yourself more than you do, on having put a thing through, over my head. I had considered the matter from every point and was sure of my decision—that to publish anything now would not be to my literary advantage; I wouldn't have the poems appear now if I could help it and would not have some of them ever appear and would make certain changes; if Mr. Thayer contributed "When I Buy Pictures," I cannot understand why he did not send "A Graveyard" with it as it is certainly the better of these poems in the July *Dial*. Despite my consternation, the product is remarkably innocuous. I should have used *Observations* I think, as a title but I like *Poems*. I am very much touched by the beauty of all the printing details. I like the paper, type, title-label, the fact that the printing was done at the Pelican Press, there is not a single misprint and nothing could exceed my appreciation of the unstinted care and other outlay bestowed on the book. But what shall I say of your activities as press-agent! Poor Mr. Child, browbeaten into an attempt to launch a review; may I never have to look him in the face! I wrote Ezra not long ago that I "was not at pains to investigate small books of verse" and told T. S. Eliot that I did not wish to reprint work of mine that has been published unless it were supplementary to something substantial! Nothing is reprinted from *Poetry* for which I am glad but under the circumstances how deeply Miss Monroe would value a notice of this opus. Poor Hilda!

To turn to more important matters, when I took *Experiment*[21] to Macmillan's, Mr. Latham said they had not gone on with the book[22] and that he had written to you. He seemed disappointed and was exceedingly grave. He said he was convinced that if the book appeared in its present form, it would not be out two months before you would regret having published it. He said he thought the writing was uneven—some parts were beautifully written, some seemed hurried. I said that I disapproved of certain parts but that I felt that some parts couldn't be improved if you waited a hundred years to publish the book. He agreed, then said again that the injury to your writing was the really vital issue. He seemed personally interested and not callous and publisher-like. I have told him that I thought the first part of Hilda's book might be more explicit and that if it were, I thought the book might make a stir.

My first impression of Hilda is very clear. There is a large forsythia bush on the campus at Bryn Mawr near Taylor Hall, the central building on the campus (an office building and lecture-hall combined) and a main campus path passes along the side of each side of the building. I remember Hilda passing this bush in a great hurry on the path leading from Rockefeller Hall—and the Bryn Mawr village—to Dalton Hall, the science building. She struck me as being extremely humanitarian and detached, as if she would not insult you by coldness in the necessary and at longest, brief moment of mutual inspection but I felt that she was not interested in the life of the moment. I remember her eyes which glittered and gave an impression of great acuteness and were, as I say, sunny and genial at the same time. I remember her seeming to lean forward as if resisting a high wind and have the impression of the toe of one foot turning in a little and giving an effect of positiveness and wilfulness. I thought of her as an athlete, I believe. Hilda's being a nonresident was very much to the loss of the resident members of the class. Katherine Ecob, a classmate of ours, who has no interest whatever in art and never thought of Hilda's having any, has a great affection for her and has chiefly the impression of her social charm and bedrock reliability.

21. This manuscript was probably a version of one of the experimental novels— *Paint It Today* or *Asphodel*—that H.D. was working on at the time.

22. Bryher's *Adventure*.

I am going to send you a couple of books, not recent, one on bears and another one. Have you *The Man Who Did the Right Thing*, (Sir Harry Johnston) and *They Went* by Norman Douglas? Sir Harry is disagreeable but I've learned a great deal from him. The Douglas I haven't read but hear that it is unusual. Roger Fry's *Vision and Design* both excellent and sumptuous, Frank Parsons' *The Psychology of Dress* (psychological and historical comment, very fascinating) and Frank Harris's *Contemporary Portraits, Second Series* are prominent here and I can get you any one of them if you wish. The list of illustrations to Frank Parsons' book takes nine pages and the illustrations seem sparse in the text; there is a great deal of originality in these titles, not diminished to me by the fact that Frank Parsons is regarded as our prize expression of femininity: "Early Fifteenth Century; Religious Scenario with naive humanism in manner and in costumes. Second part of Fifteenth Century; Elemental Impulses seen in Bodies, Faces, Poses, and Costumes. Near the End of the Sixteenth Century; Italian; The Child but the Miniature of the Adult in Dress. James I; if so ordinary and clumsy a prince is thus arrayed, what of the more fastidious? For Unparalleled Insipidity of Pose, the Period of about 1862 is Supreme. By 1869 Redemption from the Impossible was no longer a matter of Speculation. To Behold in Silence is a Privilege, to Comment Superfluous and Senseless. (July 1877)." The cocoon style with small waist and two or three yards of ruffled train. (I explain this, my dear baby dactyl as you would not remember.)

I have seen *The Golem*,[23] a movie said to be a more coherent counterpoint to *The Cabinet of Dr. Caligari* but saw nothing but a *papier-mâché* town in ruins and two rank lovers panting to the metronome. The real value of the play consisted in a picture of the grave of one of Columbus's helmsmen at Prague, a beautifully engraved old stone sunk to one side with a half dead spindling cypress in front of it and a court scene in which four or five men wore actual suits of mediaeval armour and walked about in them nimbly and with not a little grace. Yesterday, I saw a white snake with pink eyes, just acquired at the Bronx, the only albino in America, which I have been wanting to see for a month. *The Times* said it was twelve inches long, eighteen months old and a rattler; that its eyes were pink and that it was absolutely transparent, that you could see its entire mechanism when you held it to the light, (a thing Mother said, "which of course you would do"). We both agreed that if we had not heard of it we would have said that it was a very pale rattler and that its eyes were apricot but of course when the keeper said, "Do you see its little pink eyes?" we assented. It eats mice without any fur and has to be kept in the office as it was nervous when put on exhibition and wouldn't eat. I also saw a mongoose, it has always been the ambition of my life to see one, an immense regal python, a coral snake, a blue racer, tad-

23. MM probably saw the 1920 version of *The Golem*, a German film directed by Paul Wegener. There was an earlier version produced in 1914 by the same director.

poles with legs and a little family of South American boas, silver grey with dark gray diamonds and I noticed that on each side of the head a horizontal dark line continues right through the cornea of the eye; the pupil of course is vertical. I think the best thing we saw was a blue bird of paradise from New Guinea. It comes from a very high altitude, 4000 feet I think and is the only one ever brought here. It kept uttering piercing cries from time to time and looking in a tense way toward the upper corners of the cage; I am afraid it will never get used to being caged. Its head, breast and neck feathers ending in a **V** between the wings are jet black—thick short feathers like seal skin—the wings are a bright, greenish blue, it has two long black, limber tail feathers, rather narrow, a mist of cinnamon brown feathers at each side behind the legs and a similar gauzy looking haze of blue feathers under the tail. The eyes are black with a very conspicuous pure white line above and one exactly parallel, below—eyelids. The toco toucan also gave us a start. It is black with vermilion under the tail and its neck is lemon yellow, the cleanest color I ever saw, with a tinge of light vermilion here and there. The less rare toucan with blue eyes and blue and green bill, I have always liked better but deserted it for the adjoining bird. They fought while we were watching them, locking their bills through the wires and showing the greatest energy. I sound like Barnum and Bailey but must have you get an inkling of these animals since cameras were forbidden. We saw a majestic giraffe with oyster white legs and pale auburn markings. Its pop eyes disaffected me but I could not look away. The Java peacock shed a tail feather which the keeper gave me and I childishly but successfully drew myself up a wire fence around an out-door enclosure and got myself a macaw feather which proved to be not in the best condition. I sprang out more clumsily than I crept in but did not regret my determination as I think macaws should not be kept in a wire-enclosed field.

As for Hilda's part in gathering the poems, I am too much in awe to be articulate; I cannot grasp the benevolence and the compassing of the whole enterprise and Robert too, is prodigious.

Your now naked,   Dactyl

I should like to be very decent to Miss Weaver but so far have ordered only ten copies. I don't know what to do with these and don't know what to do next.

To Robert McAlmon   *July 8, 1921*

Dear Robert:

I have your letter and am interested in what you say of your novel and James Joyce. Joyce has forgotten his acute and more artist-like period when he "damns tradition." *Chamber Music* and *Dubliners* are masterpieces; the effect of originality deriving from propriety in both these books is remarkable and the unaccountable effect of finality despite tentativeness, in the closing sentences of every one of the stories—which haunts you and makes you investigate the mechanism of the writing—is, I know, the result of pruning and "resistance" rather than the result of throwing off the brakes and letting everything take its own course; and the writing is limber and spontaneous besides. Duty and self-inflicted hardship as abstract virtues defeat themselves but when rightly applied, are the essence of perfection. I have just ordered *Dubliners* for Bryher. From what she said of *The Portrait of the Artist*, I think she can't have read *Dubliners*.

The cards are gems. The horse from the Parthenon surely looks as if it belonged to "the Moon goddess." I like horses with clipped manes better than the unclipped horse as a rule, and have supposed it was because they look more business-like but I have no doubt the Parthenon horses account for my taste though I have never studied one of them before. I like the bear rattle and the crafty eye of the elephant in the elephant with the rabbis, also the bronze horse; it is a wonderful example of symmetry and texture. The reliquary is Flemish through and through, isn't it and the tracing on the Greek vases has a speed and vigour that you never get in anything outside of Greece.

As for St. Anthony and the monsters, I agree with you, it seems as if temptation ought to be alluring but I think the idea in these monsters is that the devil would eventually wear him out; his incorruptibleness was the storm-centre of attack and his resistance had to be eaten away since he was proof against any obvious seduction, in fact it was persecution rather than allurement.

I have just received a copy of my poems from Miss Weaver and am more taken aback than I have ever been in my life. The poems ought not to have come out; I know that. As the act of my friends, it is a testimony of affection; if it were the act of an enemy, I should realize that it was an attempt to show how little I had accomplished. The detail of the printing is beautiful and I am pained to think I may seem ungrateful for your work in the matter I realize, has been nothing short of prodigious. I hope T. S. Eliot and the others whose advice I repudiated will not think I have been working up a surprise all by myself. On the other hand, when I look at the book, everything being done to give it dignity of size and a beautiful construction, I am indeed speechless. I hope the burden that it has been and the fatigue it has caused will not make you lastingly hate it.

Can't you belabor the Parisiens without including the Jew? I think the getting spirit of the Jews is the same as ours but they are a little more successful. I have had to do with the very highest type of Jew and I suppose for that reason, I don't feel the force of the general antipathy.

D. H. Lawrence has a magnificent poem on a snake in the July *Dial* and I hear that he has one on a mosquito in the July *Bookman;* I envy you the pleasure of meeting such people. I saw a snake drinking at the zoo yesterday, so am in the spirit of the tribute. He says,

[MM quotes thirty lines from Lawrence's "The Snake."]

This is The End. He calls it "Snake." I have omitted about two thirds of it.

I am glad Bryher wants me to come to Europe for I am coming as soon as I can, and as often.

Yours sincerely,   Marianne Moore

To John Warner Moore   *July 10, 1921*

Dear Badger,

We went to the zoo Wednesday for I thought it was a cool day, and although it was and is as hot as Tophet the sun stayed under a cloud most of the time. The animals are truly worth a trip especially the birds that are usually so uninteresting, the giraffes, marsupials and small herbeaters, and the outdoor waterbirds and the eagles and ravens. We ate our lunch opposite the eagles and the ravens and walked over afterwards just as they were being fed. Some old, tender meat was thrown down (a piece for each, about the size of a mediumsized plantain leaf). One raven hopped joyously toward the meat, picked it up and took a few light energetic hops back with it to a corner and evidently relished it very much. The other one in the tree in a very connoisseur like suspicious way, teased off a few shreds with his beak, holding the main supply tight under one foot and ate a few long sinews and gradually ventured on more. There were a few crowned cranes among the water birds and I looked at them with interest as they are spoken of in Sir Harry Johnston's new novel about Africa, as one of the glories of Africa. They are slate blue with a pompom of centipede's legs on their heads about the size of a silk pompom on a slipper. Mole said "they aren't so wonderful but you've been reading about them and there they are."

About the best thing we saw was a blue bird of paradise from New Guinea—with a jet black head and breast like sealskin—black shoe button eyes with a dazzling white line above and below each eye, two long limber black tail feathers, a haze of cinnamon brown feathers back of each leg and a similar smoketree of bright blue under the tail. We also spent a good deal of time by the toucans—a toco toucan with a canary yellow neck, black body and yellow bill and a blue and black one with blue and green bill. They finally fought locking beaks through the bars of the cage.

The albino snake which we really went to see was in the office. It is a pale wicker color with apricot eyes two neat little nostrils and three rattles. Mole thinks when it has eaten a few more furless mice its spots come out a stronger colour. The keeper had put up some rattlesnakes to ship to Paris in a pine box covered with wire screening and he had in the hall a large packing box of pet snakes from Dr. Kelly the surgeon in Baltimore valued at $150.00. You could see them through the slats, lying in holland bags. We saw in the snake house, also, a stuffed specimen of a frog from the Cameroon in Africa, as big as a derby hat, also Tadpoles with legs, a blue racer snake, a pale blue harmless snake a yard long, maybe more, a coral snake, a family of silver grey boas with darker grey diamonds and clear eyes like rock crystal with a line of the gray marking carried on from the skin through the eye, an immense regal python with eyes as large as Peter's, the color of a russet shoe button, and a mongoose. The mongoose was exactly what you would expect. It had a body rather like a squirrel's or a long light guinea pig's, with rat feet, fine striated fur of a kind of grayish brown not quite as brown as a rat's, with this variegated look and rather long—on the whole it looks like a miniature porcupine and the tail was about five inches long, the fur being full near the root and middle, tapering off to nothing at the end. It was very active stepping around in some light fine hay. Most of the peacocks are at large but two Java peacocks have a house and yard. One of these in the house was moulting and shed a tail feather and some small ones which I got the keeper to give me, remunerating him highly. In this same house was an armadillo with a cylindrical tongue like a pencil which he curled out and in, in a coil like a watchspring. Also, there was a honey badger with a blunt nose and very pleasant little face. We enjoyed the zebras (Grevy's zebra, and Grant's zebra, and Burchell's zebra) and several others and spent a long time in front of the giraffe, a magnificent nubian giraffe with oyster white legs, large crab eyes and pale reddish yellow markings. Its tongue, as Mole said, is just like a lizard's.

Tuesday, I was very much startled to receive from Miss Weaver of *The Egoist*, a little book of poems of mine collected and published by Hilda, Winifred Bryher and Mr. McAlmon. I will send you a copy as soon as I have decided on, and made, some corrections. It is twenty four or five pages bound in a little red and black figured paper cover with a white label and the whole thing is beautifully printed and has no misprints whatever. Miss Weaver wrote to me three months ago to know if I would be willing to publish something "before the reviewers scatter for the summer" and I said no. I had also told T. S. Eliot I didn't wish to publish a book and Ezra and Hilda and Bryher herself. I think it's not to my advantage to publish a book now and think so now that the thing is out as much as I did before. Several poems could have been put in that aren't in—many should be left out that are in and I would make changes in half the poems that are in but as B. wrote me if anything is not right "it is my own fault" for refusing to publish a book—and said if I liked I could prosecute *The Egoist* with the $300 she gave me. She says she has "made" Mr. Harold Child of *The London Times* promise to review it. Hilda will review it for *Poetry*, copies will be sent everywhere, she will "have a try" for *The Saturday Review* and "Robert has written to everybody he has ever known or ever met." She then said, "My now famous dactyl you can prosecute *The Egoist* with that 300.00 if you like." I appreciate the affection of the whole undertaking and said so (also saying how I haven't changed my might [mind?] about my wish to have nothing published for a long time). I enclose T. S. Eliot's letter which I meant to send before.

Dr. Wilson is a bad egg I fear. At least a heavy one to hold. He gave us however quite a graphic picture of the boxing arena in Jersey City which he travelled over to see the Sunday after the bout. We are going to Middletown tomorrow night to stay till Thursday morning.

With love,   Rat

To T. S. Eliot   *July 15, 1921*

Since you were so kind as to propose the collecting and publishing of work of mine, I wish to send you a copy of the book which Miss Bryher has brought out. Its publication was a tremendous surprise to me. I was convinced that other work would have to be done by me before the public would be interested in these poems. I felt that it was not to my literary advantage to publish work but Miss Bryher has been so optimistic as to disagree & to have these poems published without my knowledge. As I have written to her, I am aware that everything has been done to give the dignity of size and a beautiful construction and as the act of a friend it is a testimony of affection but if it were the act of an enemy, I should realize that it was an attempt to show how little I had accomplished; that it would have been made without any contribution of labor on my part in the production, is overawing and inspires gratitude but I dissent as strongly as ever from the fact of its being and for the burden it places on a number. I fear there will be many more to wish that I had been victorious than to congratulate Miss Bryher.

Allow me to wish you all possible good in the completion of your analyses of poetry.

Sincerely yours.

To H.D.   *July 26, 1921*

Dear Hilda,

You are very gentle in permitting suggestions about your icy Balder and your nom de plume. Bryher has set her foot down—no changes; so in discussing matters, we may "lose our day" as a slovenly maid of ours remarked apropos of too much conscientiousness but I like Alka in Aksakoff better than I like Helga and since you speak of the title, it doesn't seem to me entirely like you while the book itself seems so characteristic.[24] It is a pleasure to approach publishers in their reptile houses and if I should prove a mongoose, all concerned would be enriched, so let me take it to one or two.

I am eager to see *Hymen* and wish I might have the honor of reviewing it; Bryher mentioned the possibility. The fish hawk and the white catalpa seem almost a part of it and I like the idea of a blue cover.

As for my Cretan twilight baby or is it a veiled Mohammedan woman, Mother has offered it two fingers and likes everything about it that is individually yours and Bryher's. "Veiled Mohammedan woman" is her term. I am sorry for all your work on the book; the mechanical part alone is slavery and I am very much benefitted by what prompted it though I can't see now more than I did, that I am to set the Thames and the Hudson on fire. And when Bryher says: I don't like your work but I like you, what will the public's sentiments be, who don't even like *me*?

There has been an exhibition of modern work at Wanamaker's that has a great deal of flavor to it—a cross-eyed monk in browns by Max Weber and a wool map of New York in minute stitches, by Marguerite Zorach; the color is lovely; blue, lavender and champagne color, green and much orange. Lachaise has a bronze statuette, still dusty from the chisel, originally called *Pudeur*, which he calls *Standing Figure*—very elegant and demure and four dolphins with long, oval eyes, diving side by side at different heights, with a wave thrown in. Gidding has a beautiful stone facade on its new quarters near 57th Street with an urn over the entrance with two eels in low relief for the handles. There is nothing else of any special interest in town just now.

I am glad you like D. H. Lawrence's "Snake"; he has a story in the August *Metropolitan* about a tailless peacock named Joe-y. It is just like D. H. Lawrence to write about a tailless peacock, isn't it, pathologically humanitarian as he is? He tells how the birds "stepped archly over the filigree snow, moving like small, flat light-bottomed boats" and how later, Joe-y got lost and how he saw him "rowing and struggling in the snow, his eye closing and opening quickly, his crest all battered." He tells how he could not make him eat and put him in a basket and covered him with cloths. He says, "In the night, we heard him thumping about. I got up anxiously with a candle. He had eaten some food and scattered more, making a mess and he was perched on the back of a heavy armchair." Then "he consented after various flappings to sit in a fishbag, with his battered head peeping out with wild uneasiness" while being carried home. As they approached the farm, "he gave

24. H.D. does not name the manuscript, but it may have been *Paint It Today*, which she composed in 1921.

a loud vehement yell, opening his sinister beak and I stood still looking at him as he struggled in the bag, shaken myself by his struggles yet not thinking to release him." I think this is a wonderful little epic of bird nature.

I have recovered from my fever and eat as much steak and candy as I can get my hands on though the doctor said I was not to eat anything but vegetables and fruit.

I kept Perdita's dress, which Mother has been wanting to send so long, and my dog till I could make tatting for it (for it—that is Sparkle, the dog!). We were aghast when we found that we had to ticket the value, to a cent, of everything, and it would be just like someone to put duty on it. If there is any duty on it, please let me know.

Love from us both,

To Bryher   *July 27, 1921*

Dear Bryher:

The bear is here: its name is W. Bryher. Its inquisitive nose is very affectionately and respectfully received by the other animals and its little dagger teeth and curling tongue tip are a profound source of admiration. The smell of the cedar, like Petrarch's cypress in [Walter Savage] Landor, "strengthens the nerves of the brain." The Matterhorn and the yellow anemones and the snow and the blueness are as beautiful as anything I can imagine. I will tell Hilda myself.

I am delighted with Robert's letter and of course shall not speak of having seen it. Also I like his not saying anything when I reproached him for a hasty marriage.

The Prig has just come; when I wrote you last, I hesitated to say that I thought you didn't do Mrs. Trollope[25] very well for fear you would think I couldn't be impersonal but I think in a work of art, one must get at the individuality of a thing one is describing literally. Mrs. Trollope's phrases have a limping, uncertain quality that makes her have to me, an improvised effect. In the United States, "quite a little" is parvenue like "thanking you in advance," and "hoping you are the same." Perhaps I think it is worse than it is because it is a phrase that Mother happens to have an idiosyncrasy against and without any offense against art, you can put a phrase in her mouth that she doesn't like but I remember her satiric air when she pointed out the bad brains of the phrase when I used it once when I was a little girl and it seems out of key. I have taken out "quite," subject to your replacing it for I realize the liberty. When Mrs. Trollope says that being in England was "a tremendous experience for us," Mother might have said exactly that but

25. A pseudonym for MWM in Bryher's *West.*

the phrase gives the impression that we were surprised out of our wits whereas the experience was uniquely congenial and true to the imagination and the realization was tremendous in that way. Mother's talk—talk-out-of-a-book talk—sometimes affords me great glee as when a woman said one day in Carlisle, "Pretty day, isn't it, Mrs. Moore?" and Mother said, "Truly it is a great and beneficent gift," and didn't realize that she had said anything out of the ordinary until I laughed; while very much at variance with the atmosphere of the moment, this sort of talk is not inept. Judging character is a very easy matter when one is interested in a person or thing and I realize that it is not easy when one is remote from the subject. I have pounced on these details for I think it is not good for an artist to be hurried. I have always combatted Robert's facility a little because I have felt that he didn't psychologize his detail enough and the tendency to waive tiny responsibilities in writing predicts a delay in arriving (arriving in no way applying to *Adventure*). I do not mean of course, that things cannot be distorted for the sake of art for they can so long as you don't do violence to the essence of a thing. This is your book and if I act as if it weren't, I hope you will take no notice of what I say. As for the trouble of taking it to Macmillan's, I wouldn't mind going every day with a section. I wonder if you intentionally made the Indian school a reservation. I think in the impression given, it is immaterial.

I don't know Storm Jameson[26] but *The Spectator* gave her a long respectful review.

Amy [Lowell] has put forth a horrid book called *Legends*. W. L. Phelps says the way in which she is developing must be a source of general satisfaction to many.

D. H. Lawrence's "Snake" in the June *Dial* has made me happy for a year.

I have received an anonymous letter castigating me for moderation, asking me to "mix the light wine of dreams with the heavy drink of reality."

Yvor Winters of Summit, New Mexico has sent me a pamphlet of remarkable poems:

The Morning

The dragonfly
Is deaf and blind
That burns across
The morning

. . .

I see my kind
That try to turn:

26. English novelist (1891–1972).

I see one thin
Man running

Where My Sight Goes

The frogs sing
Of everything
And children run
As leaves swing.

And many women pass
Dressed in white,
As thoughts of noon pass
From sea to sea.

And all these things would take
My life from me.

---

another one, a kind of pantomime

> *My life is green water seen*
> *Through a white rose leaf.*
> *It has a sheen.*   and so forth

He says that people who leave their poems in magazines and don't publish them are like people who leave papers in parks.

Mother says I have been tough, ever since we saw *Liliom* by Franz [Ferenc] Molnar, last Wednesday. It is a very intense, very imaginative play and nearly everyone misses the point and thinks it is dreadful to see a rough-neck graphically depicted while the true clod throughout is the meek, stereotyped soldier bound like a dart for success.

Loving,   Dactyl

Suit, necktie twice this width and plain silk shirt. Sorry the pictures are so poor.

To Bryher   *August 31, 1921*

Dear Bryher:

I had already posted you *Adventure* when your letter came, saying to keep it till you decided what had best be done about it; I am so sorry. I shall review *Hymen* if Hilda approves; I am most anxious to see her stories. I should think there would be no trouble about placing them and shall do with them just as she directs.

I have not read [Oswald] Spengler's *Der Untergang des Abendlandes*. I shall try to see *Die Weissen Gotter;* I am especially interested in the Incas though I know nothing about them and I know nothing about Mexico. I have always thought of Cortez as an iron clad monster of the largest variety; picturesque of course on a large scale, too. I am most impatient to read Flaubert's correspondence. I have wanted to read it for some time.

I am highly in favour of a Bat-ears—later, for I should think as you say, that Berlin would interfere. We had one as a neighbor when we were in New Jersey and nothing could exceed his pansylike attractiveness of feature and his general vigour, mental and other. When he had been in a fight with a large bulldog and was still so weak that he had to lie down as soon as he had got to the other side of the street, he limped over to attack another dog.

Robert's picture is very like him I think and I am delighted to have it.

We are just back from a delightful visit to a friend, in the mountains near Carlisle, our old home. I took pictures of nearly everything—a pine tree, two dogs in many positions—an airedale and a collie, an earthenware tea set, a winding path to the house—of logs sunk in the earth and two, out of five fringed gilled newts that I caught in a spring. I even allowed a stinging fly to settle on me and select a place to bite me rather than risk losing one of these lizards in a good position. I had them in a square dish of water belonging to the dogs—on a white cloth. I took a copperhead at our doorstep and the shed skin of another copperhead and caught a grasshopper of the kind I had been looking for—a large fawncoloured one with barred legs but had no more films; I also had to relinquish an immense iron crowfoot about two feet long, belonging to one of the carpenters. A live snake is worth feeling, or perhaps I should say a freshly killed one; it feels like a piece of old fashioned bead work made of infinitesimally small beads or a fine gold mesh bag with nothing in it and is silky like a poppy petal—dry and warm. The one I took was dead so it had not the remarkable bevel that a live copperhead has; the way the muscles of one of these snakes with a bevel, are connected with the spine is wonderful I think, like the complicated orderly appearance of the ropes by which a ship's sails are tethered to the mast. If the prints are good, I shall send you some. I saw a falling star which looked like a sheet of paper on fire and a bat so close that I could see light through its wings—a kind of amber—and could make out the veins and scallops. The most beautiful feature of this ledge in the mountains is a group of immense pines; the ends of the branches look like black fox tails against the dark blue of the sky at night and the stars, the times when I was out, glittered like cut silver.

I don't hate Lloyd George but I loathe Lord Northcliffe.[27]

27. David Lloyd George (1863–1945), British statesman of Welsh extraction who was considered eloquent but unscrupulous and opportunistic. Lord Northcliffe (1865–1922), Irish-born British journalist whose newspaper campaigns during World War I were determining factors in England's conduct of the war and whose support of

I don't see in what way T. S. Eliot is not "with you." It strikes me that he has created a good deal of carnage and I certainly feel that in comparison, I am not a very large rock to heave at the stupidity of the public.

As for dressing down Mr. Latham, temerarious pterodactyl, maybe he will answer back like the echo in [Lucius] Osgood's *Second Reader*, "Foo-o-lish fel-low."

A great many trashy old time novels are being written today, there is no doubt of that and the form annoys one along with the content and I think with you, that in the case of anyone who can write, the idea will completely burst the bottle but I am sure that the play writing expedients of creating suspense and making people feel by the time they have got to the end—that something has happened—strengthen a presentation and we do not want to be in Dostoevsky's plight of attempting to carry milk without putting it in a jar. He belches out life as a smoke stack belches smoke and George Moore is justified in saying, "His farrago is wonderful but I am not won." We haven't his faults but we have our own, tending to exposit astuteness and sensibility without perspective and people are likely to say, "Very charming but not enough horse power." *Robinson Crusoe* is to my mind, the perfect novel both in detail and in conception. Apropos of Antar, I don't misunderstand what you say about disliking sentimentality but it recalls to me something I have thought for some time—that it is normal for young people to have a sentimental attitude to love and that it is abnormal for them to be aware of the sexual aspect of their relations.[28] In beating the drum of sex continually, the psychoanalytical wing of modern thought surely misses the mark; it is as if someone were to say to one of us, in accepting an invitation to tea, "I haven't any illusions about your intellect; my stomach is in good working order and I am here to prove it." Your poor Libyan probably shares my Baucis-Philemon[29] notion of marriage yet I can't but smile at her view of your corruptness. I don't like divorce and marriage is difficult but marriage is our attempt to solve a problem and I can't think of anything better. I think if people have a feeling for being married, they ought to be married and if they have made a mistake, or if one of them is not on a marriage level, there may have to be a separation. An intentional matrimonial grand right and left has no point whatever so far as I can see; in Turkey, monogamy is gaining as it is everywhere else and there is confusion of thought I think in advocating anything different in a plan where there is any kind of civil contract. If we do away with the marriage contract, the case is different but nobody seems to wish to do that since if we do, we get back to cave life. The

Lloyd George in 1916 was instrumental in bringing about the downfall of the Asquith government.

28. MM refers here to some of Bryher's remarks in *Adventure*.

29. Baucis and Philemon, an aged couple who received a visit from Zeus and Hermes, and whose house was then transformed by the gods in return for their hospitality.

canker in the whole situation I think, is that people who have no respect for marriage, insist on the respectability of a marriage contract. When one is at one's wits' end for a solution, I do believe that there is nothing to do but let the elements involved work out slowly.

The net result of my experiences at Bryn Mawr was to make me feel that intellectual wealth can't be superimposed, that it is to be appropriated; my experience there gave me security in my determination to have what I want. I can't very well illustrate, it would take too long, the more since you and Hilda and I are at the antipodes from each other in our notions of education. In an article on the advantage to a musician of university training, a journalist quotes a friend of mine who is a musician as saying that her college experience gave her "a sense of repose and conscious strength" and "developed good taste and the power to think problems through," "breadth of style and a more strongly defined colour sense." At Bryn Mawr the students are allowed to develop with as little interference as is compatible with any kind of academic order and the more I see of other women's colleges, the more I feel that Bryn Mawr was peculiarly adapted to my special requirements.

Master Mouse and the narcissus and the manuscript have arrived. The narcissus, looking as if it had come right from the garden, is hanging on me on an old, old chain which I have never worn for lack of a suitable pendant and I am entranced with Master Musculus Mouse "from the tooth of an elephant." The polish ivory takes is almost incredible. Last year, I lost a white mouse up my sleeve; he bit me and came out at the far side of my collar and involved in mischief by me as he was, I cannot but contrast with him Sir Musculus Mouse, ten thousand times charming. As for that giraffe, he would have made me unspeakably poor. Do you remember the eight cornered tent that Nero insisted on having made, "a wonderful object both for its beauty and costliness" and how Seneca said, "You have now shown yourself to be poor for if you should lose this, you will not be able to procure such another" and how it happened that it actually was lost, in a shipwreck? I paid no duty.

I am delighted with the prints of you and Robert; I do wish that I could get scientific results.

As I told you, Mother drove me to Miss [Alice] Boughton's in June. The proofs were not good but Miss Boughton said she will try again as soon as it is cooler; your friends will be refreshed I am sure, when I am passed around.

I have not read the new version of *Adventure* as it has just come, but what I should like to do is to take it back to Macmillan. I am convinced that their reason for declining it was not commercial but because they misunderstood the Antar part in the way that I misunderstood it myself; my choice of publishers is as follows: Macmillan, Doran, Knopf, Huebsch. As for commission, no compensation would induce me to take the manuscript anywhere if I did not wish to take it and if I took ten manuscripts a month about for you, I should not feel that you were under any obligation to me; do you recall the ten dollars that you sent for postage; I don't remember the postage on anything I have mailed but I know that I could mail things all winter and not exhaust in postage, those ten dollars.

I am sorry that you decided not to answer Mr. Thayer's letter; it was not businesslike to ignore it. When friendship is balanced with pride, the result is never even and those least responsible bear the deficit. You feel that Mr. Thayer is not a gentleman but a ruffian does not allow his victim any lee-way and Mr. Thayer tried to consult you so, although you can take him to task for his attitude to your marriage and for wishing to discuss it, it is not possible I think, to lay on him the whole responsibility of the article.

Don't think I have given up hope of coming over; you say everyone is quitting England for Berlin and I only wish I could fill their places as air fills a newly made vacuum.

I have no poems just now as I am under promise to *Broom* to submit something as quickly as I can get it ready. I have no idea what *Broom* will be but as I told you, I am friendly to Alfred Kreymborg and if you and Hilda are willing to go outside the established magazines, I think you might not regret submitting some things. I have been held up because I wanted to re-vise some poems taken by *The Dial* last spring—three, which resisted the most pertinacious attack.

In regard to Amy Lowell, don't think that I have any less friendly feel-ing for her than you have but that doesn't say that I admire her work.

I have for some time been watching for an opportunity to write to Robert.

When your dress is made, won't you send me a scrap and do send me a picture of your stand-up page curls; they sound very pleasing.

Mother sends her love to you, every one and would love to see Perdita in her rose and wonders if she was plane-sick.

Your affectionate albino-dactyl

To Robert McAlmon   *September 2, 1921*

Dear Robert:

You are right; the intellect has not the last word today—any more than it ever had. Sophistication is no match for nature and as I have written Bryher, I have a respect for nature, blind or conscious. The blind instinctive behavior of old fashioned unenlightened society has many advantages over our conscious behavior today; psychoanalysis is a fascinating study and in some ways a useful one but it pre-empts too much of the mind and people tend to feel that a situation analyzed is a situation solved. In rapping marriage on the head as it sometimes does, it is unscientific—when you consider the evolution of the marriage relation and the instinctive tendency to idealize it, and to explain religion away is ludicrously superficial. Religious conviction, art, and animal impulse, are the strongest factors in life, I think, and any one in the ascendant can obliterate the others. We see different phases of them, for example, Bryher's interest in education and in securing freedom to the race, are a tangent of religion. Religion may be pigeonholed as a transference but religious conviction in operation has always made room for itself over the head of every obstacle. It is apparent that sincerely religious people are contented and are not easily at their wits' end. Perhaps you are not interested in this but since you and Bryher have been frank in giving me your points of view, I venture to speak out.

Do you know what edition of Defoe James Joyce likes best? While visiting in Albany a few weeks ago, I stole more time than is compatible with sociability to read a school edition of *Robinson Crusoe* and have not words in which to express my contentment with the whole thing.

As for assisting Bryher with my private notions or my admirations for anything in literature that she hasn't singled out on her own responsibility, I am like a rain drop on a rubber coat.

I enclose a comment from *The Tribune* on your "little British book of baffling verse."[30] Bryher will be interested. Do you suppose all Americans in French and British clothes are "weird"? This is the second comment to that effect. Has the American exodus into café life modified it any or been lost in the whirl?

Sincerely yours,   Marianne Moore

P.S. I meant to ask Bryher what she thinks of Martin Secker as a publisher. Have you any opinion of him?
I shall read your stories with interest when you send them.

To H.D. and Bryher   *November 10, 1921*

Dear Hilda and Bryher:

My dactyls with flexible wings are here and have adopted me. I paid no duty. I thought they must be dactyls by courtesy—such a coincidence is so remarkable—until I saw them. Perfect they are, with their yellow bodies, green wings, and snake heads; and one rascal a trifle different from the others, has a bony little jaw like a butcher's cleaver. Tell Hanno and Perdita that I am sorry they don't have to wear little shirts that need flexible but-

---

30. *Explorations* (1921), published by the Egoist Press.

tons. I shall have much happiness in wearing them and in the thought that Hilda wears a near relative.

We are so happy to have Perdita and to have H.D. by the pampas grass. Perdita's picture really looks like her; to see such a look of life in "that baby" is a joy; this is our first picture of her, do you realize it? Hanno is entrancing; I wish he could make us a daily visit. His satin skin and bat ears are perfection. I like him best standing in front of H.D. with his head down but all the pictures are delightful; I have never seen such perfect snapshots. Tell him that Strongheart, the dog actor, is playing in *The Silent Call*[31] and don't tell him that I mistook his mushroom for a white madeira leaf.

The De Régnier is exquisite, with its flowered cover, sheafs of wheat and remarkable little index.[32] The subject matter is beautiful—the cypress, the roses, the fountain, the purple train and the double serpent of the caduceus. I like having the title of a poem the first line and thought and feeling are so well fused the sentences seem actually to glide. I marvel to have so much in this tiny book.

I am much excited to hear of your housekeeping. It sounds so alluring that I can hardly connect the idea of famine with it; I hope, however, that food will be more plenty and that Mrs. Doolittle will arrive safely. *Rêve d'Amour* and *Cloches du Matin* are indeed delicious and as you say, hundreds of miles away from The Brevoort. The Gotham is a stately, two-horses-and-a-*coupée*, Notre Dame-like hotel to which I shall recommend you the next time you are here.

Doran returned me *Adventure*, October 29th; I enclose their letter. We took it at once to Knopf. I have not changed anything and I don't object to Trollope as a last name—indeed feel too highly honored. Perhaps the first name might be changed and a word substituted for "create," and I liked "stand up" better than "come up" in the Ezra part but these things are merely suggestions.

Hymen is beautiful in itself and in its blue dress and I am impatient to write about it. Holt has sent me *Helen in Egypt;* doubtless they have written direct. Each of the studies is stately and in harmony with the others and full of beautiful detail—the great lion, the frail gazelle, the doves, flamingoes, scarfs and pillars and Helen a sister to the gulls. "Dead sea fruit" is preferable I think, to being "accepted for worse." *The Nation* for October 26th says in a review of Edna St. Vincent Millay, Anna Wickham,[33] and me, entitled "Women of Wit": "For better or for worse these women have contracted marriages with wit, have committed themselves to careers of brains.

31. Silent film (1921), one of a series by director Larry Trimble that featured the popular "dog actor."

32. Henri de Régnier (1864–1936), French poet and novelist; Bryher probably sent MM *Vestigia flammae* (1921).

33. Pseudonym of Edith Alice Mary Harper (1884–1947), English poet.

17th century England, where all of the three would have been at home, would have prized them well. 20th Century England and America will not do badly to accept their poetry now for better or for worse, since by many a sign it is here to stay a while; almost certainly more of its sort remains to be written and read. It is independent, critical, and keen, a product oftener of the faculties than of the nerves and heart; it is feminine; it is fearless; it is fresh.

["]Not that it is all alike. Marianne Moore, one admits right away, must be taken for worse. She wedded wit, but after divorces from beauty and sense. Her manners are those of the absurder coteries, her fastidiousness is that of the insufferable highbrows. She wrote some pieces for Alfred Kreymborg's *Others* which made that anthology difficult to take seriously, and in the present volume she quite smothers out an occasional passage of distinction with verbiage like this:

> *Those*
> *various sounds consistently indistinct, like intermingled echoes*
> *struck from thin glasses successively at random—the*
> *inflection disguised: your hair, the tails of two*
> *   fighting-cocks head to head in stone—like sculptured scimitars*
> *repeating the curve of your ears in reverse order: your eyes, flowers of ice*

There will be other Marianne Moores, perhaps as there were other Cowleys and Crashaws and Cartwrights in the century of Jonson and Donne. They can and will be endured." The comment on Edna St. Vincent Millay was favorable and very interesting.

The clipping about the restoring of the Temple of Herakles is most interesting and I am glad that "Signor [Benedetto] Croce" approves of such an undertaking. His views on Hegel interest me and his enthusiasm for Dante seems to me infectious without being fanatical and without being repetition. Do you care for him?

I am delighted that you like *Natural History* and will have it sent to Hilda at Territet [Switzerland] for a year. I tried to get you a copy last spring with an article in it on national characteristics of American art but the issue was exhausted. The numbers are four yearly and always reach us late at the library so don't feel that it is lost if it doesn't come promptly. Your check I return as I have not yet broken into the check you sent me before—ten dollars—part of which I shall use for this subscription.

The snake was not alive. I had one, better marked and the embodiment of grace, freshly killed and arranged as if crossing a fallen branch, but dogs or a passerby carried it off by the time I was ready to take it. That was the last picture I have taken. Last week I was ill and that hindered both pleasure and business but I hope to take some pictures soon. About a month ago on Madison Avenue, we saw in a grocer's, a baby ocelot just brought from South America. It was crying like a parrot that has got its head caught between the wires of its cage but we untangled its cord and when Mother picked it up, it closed its eyes and settled down as if for an indefinite nap—growling when we put it on the floor again.

I do not know Margaret Sanger. At one time, apropos of birth control, there was a steady defense of her and great excitement over her in *The Masses*, now *The Liberator*, Max Eastman's paper.

I have not read [Norman Douglas's] *They Went* or *South Wind*.

I was born November 15th, 1887.

I sent *Broom* a poem entitled, "Snakes, Mongooses, Snake-charmers and the Like."

The shops have tried to look wintery and austere but have succeeded only in being dull. The hats are dowdy as if they had been unintentionally crushed and everything seems to be peppered with beads. I saw at Wanamaker's today, a piece of pale gray panne velvet with a minute design of rather large palm leaves in gold thread and Bernard had some time ago, a crinoline—heliotrope and silver flexible cloth, just heavy enough to hang perpendicular, but even these are stereotyped. A small crinoline extension, I mean; and the Pavlova shirts were not crinoline but hoopsturs.

Pavlova[34] is here and we saw her last week in *Amarylla*. First there was a minuet with girls in pink silk crinolines with red rosettes on their skirts and red heels and a marquise in a pink crinoline with silver bodice and peacock blue ostrich feather flowers and fringe on the skirt, pink slippers with blue heels and a black tricorne hat edged with blue fringe. Pavlova was a gypsy exhibited by mountebanks—some in green tights and red boots—some in red tights and yellow boots. They tossed each other about—with great skill I thought when you consider how hard it is to carry people let alone throw them a distance; Pavlova's feet were very graceful as they trailed through the air and [Laurent] Novikoff, one of the men, did some wonderful bounding. There was a scene with fauns and faunesses, with tails wired out so that they vibrated at every step and ludicrous brown cloth hoofs with fur fetlocks. Pavlova danced in white chiffon with several red garlands and hair flowing; and later, as a dragonfly in green iridescent tulle with four long slender wings which she drew up over her head several times. A Pierrot, thin and froglike, with black mask and white ruffles around his neck and at the sleeves, was most amusing, pattering round and round with a mandolin. Finally, Pierrette put a large rose in his mouth which covered up most of his face—the rose did—and he went off. In the last scene with Russian costumes, Pavlova did some formal steps in which her exactness showed to greater advantage than in her eel-like roles and she looked well, in a little white coat with accordion plaited tail and a wide skirt like a round

34. Anna Pavlova (1882–1931), Russian ballerina about whom MM wrote in 1944 for *Dance Index*.

white lampshade with a pink stripe and a green stripe around the hem, and a hat like a bishop's mitre. A thing, however, which I liked as well as any of this conscious art, was an analysis I saw some time ago in the movies, of the movements of football players in a match game—all the movements slowed down by the speedograph so that the players seemed to move like sea-horses or float through the air like scarfs. The ball waved when kicked instead of descending in a perfect ellipse and when the players caught it you felt as if they were catching cobwebs.

If Knopf should not take *Adventure*, I shall take it to Huebsch and then which, Selyer or Boni? I shall gladly get any book that either you or Hilda or Robert is interested in seeing. Love to you each.

Dactyl

To John Warner Moore   *Dec[ember] 18, 1921*

Dear Badger,

We are aghast at what you say of your "journey" in the car, though you enlarge only on the auspiciousness of all the various circumstances. I am by nature very much opposed to prairie schooner experiences as a planned for part of the program but it is not well to labour what is past. I hope the set-tling will not be laborious. San Pedro is such a shaved off little spot I should think Constance would object to it but perhaps the compensations are great enough to ameliorate everything.

I got one copy of *The World's Work* at the library—can get the others later. The girl with the broken rib is not yet back but I held to it that I *would* not work all day this week and have worked only half time. Even so, we have been very busy—I finished a review of H.D.'s book—not a very good one—wrote to her and to Robert. He sent me two copies of his poems—*Explorations* and two copies of his stories *A Hasty Bunch* printed in France. He publishes as a loose leaf or "dainty" in the front of the book a letter from an English publisher who says, "we have never brought such things before our workmen before and do not intend to do it now." This attitude is typical of the book. Much of the detail is accurate and amusing as of a negro preacher who said he couldn't preach on earth and board in heaven—"dis-sembling the world of god" with no material upkeep—and "lawdy lawd how that niggah can eat!" But I am so affronted and depressed by the shal-low calfism and sensuality of the whole performance that I was puzzled as to know what to say. Finally I said that I thanked him for his generosity that I "could say nothing that was not serious and that I knew from reading the stories that he wouldn't take seriously what I would say, so I could say noth-ing." As Mole says, this depriving him of concrete comments is the only way to make him reflect or realize anything amiss in himself. I also wrote Bry-her, who is breathless to know my opinion of the stories, that an artist must respect life as well as crave it and that when he doesn't, satire, humour, and neat phrasing have no point.

Friday *Sour Grapes* arrived from Dr. Williams. It also is a little out of balance but is serious as Robert's book is not. I wrote him last night and yesterday morning we spent hunting Christmas cards, foolish inanities most of them, "to my son"—"to my father" "Howdy, howdy, howdy" "Don't think I'm kidding you when I wish you the very best Christmas you have ever had." Emerging partially from that agony we came home to make out the list of recipients and I had to work last night at the library. I had a teasing committee meeting this week and must address a hundred or so letters but have no more extra writing to do but a poem for *The Nation* which has a contest and which Mole urges me to compete in.

Mr. Kelly has been saving me at my request, *The Evening World,* which has in it Charlie Chaplin's impressions of London and his crossing on the *Olympic.* I am delighted with it, where he tells of meeting his cousin Aubrey, a very "dignified gentleman but with all the earmarks of a Chaplin," and of how worried he was at the thought of meeting the Mayor of Southampton—hurried along to the meeting by his friends. "It doesn't take long to reach any place when that place is holding something fearful for you."

Miss Gregory has just dropped in with a magazine she is returning and one she is lending me. Stayed only a minute.

I don't know that we have seen all the *Bulletin*s though perhaps Mole has "engrossed" them.[35] Yesterday we were passing a holiday shoe display of brocaded mules and bedroom slippers. Mole said, "Aren't moles ugly?" And not seeing the point naturally I didn't say anything, whereat Mole took umbrage and the mistake came out. We have been too busy but are well, nothing to compare however with your exertions.

With love,   Rat

I am trying to get the [Benvenuto] Cellini but don't know yet whether it can be got.

To John Warner Moore   *January 1, 1922*

Dear Badger,

We have your letter, also the *Bulletin* which is as good as ever. I thought the paragraphs on Morgenthau[36] and the missionaries very fine. The Dear

35. The *Bulletin* was a newsletter published on board JWM's ship or at a nearby naval station.

36. Probably refers to Henry Morgenthau (1856–1946), who served as ambassador to Turkey and Mexico. Morgenthau's son, also named Henry (1891–1967), was a policy adviser to Franklin D. Roosevelt.

Queen letter seemed to me not so congenial in the brand of humor offered as might be—bordering now and again on coarseness. I have kept a file of numbers so far, in case I should wish to consult them or of course if you should want something you had not kept. "Secure the chains" is an excelling heading. I think the last time is the one we were apprehensive about.

We are afloat again. I had a cold all week different from anything I have ever had and Mole has had one too and is also "tired with anxiety" says that she hadn't a peaceful moment all week for fear I would not get to Paul Rosenfeld's tea on Saturday. I did get there and it was clear, rather windless, and not too cold and the whole affair was most relishable. All were there when I arrived but the Lachaises. Sherwood and Mrs. Anderson were the guests of honour. Miss Gregory assisted Paul with his tea; Dr. Williams, Dr. Watson, Gilbert Seldes, a Mr. Duncan,[37] and a [Freichman?] girl were the only guests, besides. The Lachaises arrived shortly. Paul made me think of Jack in [Randolph] Caldecott's *The House That Jack Built*, with a large round plate of Turkish cinnamon buns in one hand and a collection of tarts, eclairs and French pastries in the other. He assigned me a fork saying, "you must use my only fork." His quarters are very snug (on Irving Place looking towards Gramercy Park), with a large fireplace, two sofas, windows on two sides, an immense number of books and modern paintings, and a little bedroom with an oldfashioned four poster and telephone in it. His cushions are panne velvet and African brown taffeta with ruffles, and everything is comfort. Also there is the general air of bachelor pertness and conglomerateness in it. He was dressed very modishly and as Mole says is not a lineal descendant of Paul the apostle. I talked a little to Bill Williams forgetting to thank him for his Christmas card; Sherwood Anderson was most friendly, made a determined effort to enlarge on my poems, and said he had three copies. He said he has remarked to Mrs. Anderson that I was the person who was going to get *The Dial* $2000 award and that he was surprised when I hadn't. Mrs. Anderson is a crude, undignified curtain-tassel-swinging woman, well meaning but impossible. She had much curiosity to know if I had met Mrs. Watson said she had heard she was very handsome and vivacious and a great society girl. She said, "I wonder how she does it with [a] husband who is deaf, dumb and blind. Do you suppose he goes along as a sort of lay figure? He seems awfully nice but does he ever talk? Or do you suppose he can and won't?" She said, "I started two or three times to say something & he blinked and said nothing and I felt so queer. I thought I had said something shocking." I said "if you knew him I think you wouldn't feel that." "Can you ever?" she said. When I told Mole this, she said, "that's the poet-wife—raw, insincere, matronizing woman." She is not insincere however; she is just not advantaged. Paul omitted to introduce Gilbert when introducing the others

37. Probably William Cary Duncan (1874–1945), librettist, lyricist, and biographer.

to me, so Gilbert suggested to Paul that he do it. Gilbert conversed actively, a little snobbishly as regards his lesser literary rivals but with much gusto. He is rather slim, small, businesslike and wholesome—very conventional as to dress and more got up than Dr. Watson who was the large dog stepping in without a haircut or a special shine or fancy socks or any knickknacks.

Dr. Williams had licked himself till he had worn the corners off and looked very well. Mrs. Lachaise was dressed in turquoise blue with turquoise blue fey and Miss Gregory looked very nice in dark blue silk with a blue hat trimmed with martin fur. I wore my black velvet suit, peacock petticoat, new turquoise crepe waist, silk hat, black satin and turquoise tie, and black calf oxfords. Mrs. Lachaise invited me to tea for Friday on general principles and to see Mr. Nagel's[38] paintings.

Paul asked several times if we would have more tea and the last time when I said no but that it was delicious he fluttered his hand at me, with a little genial wink, which showed that he was very much pleased with the healthy aspect of his party. Mr. Duncan said he was in the dark about all things aesthetic but he seemed at home so I don't know yet who he is.

Mole was expecting me about 2 hours before I got home & had been to market and to a stationer's and had written several letters and said she supposed that Paul had had a little supper brought in. Dr. Watson's indomitable generosity was brought to light by Sherwood Anderson as an offset to Mrs. A's remarks. He said that Dr. Watson called on the editors of *The Little Review* one time when as it happened they were "busted" and said in leaving, he thought he'd like to contribute something and slipped a bill in her hand and later they found it was for $100. When they brashly asked him later "where he ever got it," he said, "Sometimes I happen to have something with me."

Robert sent me an ivory pansy for Christmas, H.D. a tooled purse, they sent Mole a yard of fine filet lace and me a beautiful Italian lace cover, a copy of an old Sicilian pattern. It has a kind of square, Dutch look and is very becoming to me for summer or spring days.

With love,   Rat

Aunt E. sent me a cute little New Year's card with affectionate remarks written on the back, addressed Toodles Moore.

Wallace Gould's[39] visit Christmas was amazing. He blustered and dogmatized and smoked an insupportable kind of cigarette but Mole said when he left "a child might scatheless stroke his brow." She said that after I had gone to the library he said, "She's a sweet little girl isn't she?" Mole says she said,

38. Edward Nagel (1893–1963), a painter whose work appeared in *The Dial;* the son of Isabel Nagel Lachaise and stepson of Gaston Lachaise.

39. American poet (1882–1940) who published in *The Dial.*

"I think it is pleasant for authors to meet each other" and relapsed into silence. Again when he said Lord Byron was the greatest poet he had ever known, Mole said "it seemed a pity that when he had gone so far as he had, he had not gone farther" and that Wallace Gould was smothered in small back-bitings like Sir Roger when he went to see Sir Leonard with his horses freshly bitted and his carriage painted & was beaten upon by tiny waves of conversations that carried him back so he couldn't say anything.[40] Mole kept him for supper and as he left Mole says he says it was the pleasantest hour he had had since he had been in New York.

To Robert McAlmon   *Seattle [Washington]   July 28, 1922*

Dear Robert,

It was a pleasure to have your letter and I am most interested to know of your work. You don't say who is bringing it out.

I am glad to know that Mina Loy has assembled her family. I wonder if you saw a poem of hers about arctic lights or ice crystals in *The Dial* last summer—a crisp imaginative piece of work?

What you say of intensity interests me. It is in general true that in order to create works of art one has to have leisure. On the other hand I think that one needs to experience resistance in a practical sense, and even that which is poignant to bring out what makes easy reading for others. Too much deprivation of course, means death.

Last winter was as bad as this summer is good. We are out here so as to see my brother. It is a little depressing to me that what is an extreme novelty to us is the daily grind to him but he is so cheerful and noncommittal that I never should have known it if we had not seen it. A thing so mechanically perfect as a battleship is always a pleasure to me and last night, during the crew's movies there was intermission for a searchlight drill.

It encourages me very much that Mary Butts, Anna Wickham and the Sitwells should admire my work. There is something to be said for their reluctance to call it poetry for sometimes I deliberately insert a prose phrase with a view to its standing as prose and I myself should not have called the collection in my book "poems," but "observations," but I also think that if a piece of writing is not ridiculous in itself, yet sounds highflown as prose, it might as well be classified as poetry. I have always admired Anna Wickham and Mary Butts is quite startling I think in impact and untrammeled diction. I was fascinated by a poem of Osbert Sitwell's in *The Spectator*, August a year ago:

40. Reference to an episode involving Sir Roger de Coverly in *The Spectator*.

"The marmoset plays with Zenobra's curls
Clutches the papillon's enamelled sail
Gesticulates with idiot hand, unfurls—
To count the piebald rings upon his tail."

I have not yet seen T. S. Eliot: *The Art of Poetry;* perhaps the publishing has been delayed. I am so sorry to hear he is ill.

I have not seen Dr. Williams since December or January. He called one day but I was not at home.

I had a criticism of George Moore in *Broom* (May), reviewed Charlie Chaplin's: *My Trip Abroad* for Paul Rosenfeld's *Manuscripts*—and have done a criticism of Alfeo Faggi's sculpture.

Apropos of the novel, the most interesting thing I have read is Professor Saintsbury's *The English Novel.* He gives practical suggestions as to how the thing is done, which Sir Percy Lubbock I feel, doesn't pretend to do.

Sincerely yours,   Marianne Moore

You speak of our coming abroad and I am happy to say each day brings us nearer to going but how near I don't know.

To H.D.   *14 St. Luke's Place   N.Y.C.*
             November 18, 1922

Dear Hilda:

What a pleasure to have your letter and to know that the shoes amuse Perdita. They *are* like little real animals, aren't they? They are hair seal.

I sent the essays to Amy Lowell at once on receiving your letter. Surely you don't need to be told that anything I can do about them is a pleasure. Miss Lowell answered at once that she looked forward to reading them and would confer with her publisher.

I have just read your poems in *The American Miscellany* and "The Satyr" is especially beautiful I think—a most contagious, inspired piece of work. I writhe under Conrad Aiken's bungled introduction; one hopes as is true, that with the public, the contents is the main issue. Also, I have just read Bryher's review of *Hymen* in *The Bookman.* I like it better than any review I have seen so far; the independence and concreteness of the interpretation hold one as the usual review expositing the reviewer's theories and his relation to the work in hand, does not. Tell Bryher I think it very shabby of her not to have told me of this review as I am not likely to see *The Bookman.*

John Cournos called a week or so ago and I thought I found in him, many of the qualities I had thought good in his work seven or eight years ago. *Babel* which I have just read, seems to me, tragic in its restlessness and its partial grasp of the old philosophical verities. Life as described in it, however, has verisimilitude and the satire on art group intensities—"take a banana," et cetera, is successful, the more for being mixed with genuine fraternal respect for the motives of the misguided. And the sketch of Tobias Bagg is perfect I think—a most genial little interlude.

Please thank Bryher for her cheque for the *Natural History* subscription.

I have been unable to find for some time, the post-card of the stone serpent which you sent me but found it today. This reminds me of a python we saw at a movie to which I went to see Charlie Chaplin. It was on a ledge of rock below a water-fall; it raised its head snake-charmer fashion and gradually slid over the ledge on which the fall struck to a small pool and rivulet below, where it lay in the shallow water with the mist and fresh water continually playing on it. Mother, who has a modified enjoyment of snakes, was as delighted as I was. We have also paid a visit to the Metropolitan Museum and have seen the faience hippopotamus and the Flemish and Florentine paintings. The dog life in these paintings and the contemporary interpretation in dress fascinate me very much—the Argonauts in black striped hose and short capes while white greyhounds crouch on the marble floors. One other thing, also, quite different from anything I have ever seen before, was a cowboy contest at Madison Square Garden. The program said, "The Management propose to run a fast, snappy program and every contestant is required to lend his assistance in the matter of keeping the program moving and up to the standard set." Nothing was left to be desired in snappiness or action and the purposeful appearance of the contestants both from the point of view of sport and of aesthetics, emphasized the speed in other respects. The shirt of one was checked blue and olive flannel, of another, apple green and one was a batik, lemon and gray—the spreading blot variety worn with white linen trousers. One contestant wore carmine goat's fur chaps with tufts of black goat's fur inserted at regular intervals, on the principle of kings' ermine; the saddles and bridles and spurs were very finely wrought. Some of the saddles were of carved leather with silver bulls' heads inlaid or applied, some were studded with square borders of silver nails or lines of silver hearts, graduated in size, and the exhibitions of skill were amazing, especially in lariat spinning and steer wrestling. Leonard Stroud, whose sister rode in the contest and is champion cow-girl of the west, I think, spun circles of every size, singly and in combination and standing on his head, roped four horses at once.

I hope Bryher is not being thwarted with her novel. The mercilessness of visitors everywhere, makes us very sympathetic.

Love to you each. Dactyl

I have been ill for two or three days but expect to be about tomorrow. The pictures are some I took this summer. The water is Lake Louise; my brother and I won the mixed doubles in the Navy Yard tournament and the little picture of the tennis-court is the scene of our endeavor. This picture of my brother couldn't be more like him, I think. I did not care much for the other one taken at Mount Rainier but had some printed as the lilies and trees give an exact idea of the place.

This blot looks like an illustration of the batik but it was not intended. nor this.[41] You will see the vest pocket Kodak in my hand on the back of the collie.

To Yvor Winters   *December 20, 1922*

Dear Mr. Winters:

Mr. [William Penhallow] Henderson's pictures which we saw two weeks ago were a very great pleasure. The intensity of feeling in them, in choice of subject matter and in the exacting use of it, are commanding—the expression of a life's ideal slowly wrought. The classic, architectural solidity of composition and the technique of the painting—definiteness without harshness—are great achievements; the vibrant atmosphere of the sky in *The Penitente Procession* and the deep sculptured quality of the tree. I care most, I think, for *Lucero's Place, Springtime; Outside the Rinconda Bar, Awa-tsireh* and *The Penitente Procession.* We saw the pastels also, exquisitely imagined and executed. We admired the workmanship of the frames and the various tones of gold used; I have never seen more sensitiveness in presentation. Mrs. [Alice Corbin] Henderson told me also of the exhibition and I hope to write to her shortly.

I expect to buy T. S. Eliot's poem and shall reread the "Gerontion." *The Waste Land* is, I feel, macabre; it suggests that imagination has been compressed whereas experience should be a precipitate. I too, question the rhythmic cohesiveness. "Demotic French," the bats and tower and bursts of imagination do, however, set up an "infectious riot in the mind" and the impression long after reading justifies the poem to me, I think, as a creative achievement. *The Enormous Room* is a remarkable book, I think and I enjoyed it, from the point of view of literature and of psychology. Though it inescapably preserves the flavour of E. E. Cummings' personality, it lacks many things I have objected to.

I hope you will be able to go on with your drawing. It must be an inexpressible pleasure to draw well.

41. MM refers here to two inkblots.

I feel as you do about "The Mysticism of Money" and about "Machinery as Sculpture."[42] I am mystified by your saying that prose fails to hold your interest. For the litterateur, prose is a step beyond poetry I feel, and then there is another poetry that is a step beyond that.

Do not hurry about returning the books.

Sincerely yours,

To John Warner Moore   *Jan[uary] 14, 1923*

Dear Badger,

I am glad your sightseeing party was so ideal; with no disasters; I can see the boys in my mind's eye riding ostriches and picking oranges. The anxiety however, must have been very great. The pictures are wonderful, particularly of the firing with the deck railings down and the one under large guns. The picture of you is fair and the one showing Santa Claus very graphic. This morning at church a Mr. Harlow spoke whom I had been dreading as an old Springstreeter.[43] I thought he would probably recall old days and enlarge on the growth of Christian work day by day in every way but his discourse was a striking contrast to the missionary's old old story. He has been in Turkey and enlarged on the courage and enthusiasm of the martyrs and maltreated Christians, said it was hard to understand the atrocities in the east, when most of the men who died in the European war died with the express intention of making brutality and murder a thing of the past, that he had told Armenians and Syrians at the time of the armistice that they needn't live with the fear of the sword hanging over them any more and that members of their families would never again be tortured and driven into exile, but that things worse had happened, since the armistice, than ever before, and he has come to the conclusion that the meaning of it is that nations are not to be converted and exemplify righteousness wholesale but that individuals will go on being sacrificed and doing the work and that the result will come piecemeal. We spoke to him afterward and he said he would try to see you when he is in California. He was with the New Zealand division during the war and was chaplain of the *Tennessee* (which is the *Memphis* at San Domingo). He is not very prepossessing in appearance but if you could get him to speak or tell a little of his views of the situation in the east you would be richly repaid. His choice of words is "homely" but remarkable, with no bunk of the Y.M.C.A or the "advantaged" theological student.

42. Winters did not think highly of these prose pieces, which appeared in *Broom*.

43. The Moores attended a church on Spring Street, after first moving to New York, but had stopped going there.

Thursday afternoon I went to tea at the *Broom*. Gorham Munson & Kenneth Burke were there. At a proper moment on leaving I attacked G. Munson on the score of my Bacon essay—offered gladly to withdraw it and said I feared he had hesitated to say it wasn't what he needed. He protested that it "had been accepted" and that he wanted it very much and the only reason I hadn't received word of its acceptance was the most unfortunate lack of fixed editorial policy. He has committed suicide in my eyes in not acknowledging it but I "let him go." Glenway Wescott eulogized my poems in public in a most appalling way and no one seemed to resent it, and asked when he could come for [E. E. Cummings's] *The Enormous Room* which he wishes to borrow. I suggested that he come that evening as he happened to have it free when usually prevented by his Jewish patron who has to be read to in the evening. He brought us a German book of Hindoo sculpture to look at. I said I didn't know that I could read it. He said "well the Germans themselves have trouble with it." He says one trouble with Gorham Munson is that "he is nervous because he isn't a poet," and that he feels he must make it up someway by plunging feverishly into all kinds of activities. I smiled. Gorham Munson wears his moustache now with a small curve and tiny waxed points like a machine sharpened lead pencil. Tuesday when we had tea with Glenway Wescott and Monroe Wheeler, they showed us a number of remarkable books and post cards and had food of the most varied and imported variety.

The Verdant Green[44] has arrived and I shall mail it to you as soon as possible.

Friday morning we went to a lecture to which Daisy gave us tickets by Dr. Ditmars[45] at the Waldorf on animal life with moving pictures—nothing painful as at the big movie. We saw frogs' eggs & toads' eggs and salamanders' eggs & snakes' eggs developing. Saw moles, woodchucks, beavers at work, rattlesnakes in the Berkshires flowing like water as Mole said over stones and boulders near their den, saw deer shedding & growing their horns, white peacocks, baby bears, polar bears, buffaloes & bees.

Friday night Mrs. Conover & Lillian came to supper. I didn't get back from the library till six. Mole had had to go down to the market after the lecture to get a chicken & then "clean" the room & cook the dinner & I was afraid she would give out but she is rested today and as rambunctious as ever. The doctor says her urine test is most satisfactory and encouraging. I had feared something might be wrong & am relieved indeed.

Mole had a note from Mr. Cameron thanking her for mailing the Page letters.

With love to all,   Rat

44. *The Adventures of Mr. Verdant Green, an Oxford Freshman* (1853–57), by Cuthbert Bede.

45. Raymond Ditmars (1876–1942), American naturalist.

To John Warner Moore   *March 25, 1923*

Dear Badger,

The map is here, with the news of your manoeuverings and triumph. It is incredible and immeasurably gratifying. I feared you might lose as so many contributory matters enter into such a thing, and feared that the first race would not be compensation if this last one went against you. Certainly the unanimous victory is very impressive and merits notoriety and subdued acknowledgment. I am delighted too to think that soon you will be leaving the mosquito beds and nesting grounds of the basilisk.

Tuesday we went to the Metropolitan with Mr. Wheeler to see the Chinese paintings. We pored over them, read the descriptions and made a complete survey of the collection. The animals were beautiful, a dragon appearing in a cloud, horses, water buffaloes and insects. There is a white falcon which as Mr. Wheeler said somewhat overrating it: "it's like hammered silver." Mr. Wheeler brought us each a bunch of pansies and urged us to have tea with him at the Waldorf but we refused. Night before last he gave a party for Dr. Williams; Gorham Munson & wife, K. Burke, a Mr. & Mrs. [Edward] Goldbeck were there, Davy Lawson & Lola Ridge, and four others. Bill Williams was more than entertaining on the subject of Ezra's affections & his legs which, as he said, "have a double curve in them so he has great trouble to get his pants to hang straight." Mr. Wheeler had his room for a coat room and "entertained" in his landlady's Italian reception room—an immense place with gray walls, gray & black rugs, Italian wrought iron lamp stands, white book cases and so on. For refreshments he had tea or coffee in yellow lustre cups, orange cake, chocolate cake, & sandwiches. He invited me & Bill to Mme. Ney's[46] Tuesday afternoon when she is to play for a few friends. Bill has written a novel or rather satire called *The Great American Novel* published by Ezra—Bill paying $100.00—Ezra publishing one, called *Indiscretions*, I suppose for nothing.

Buffalo is developing and is cuter and cuter—his flower pin eyes are a pretty amber—and now that he sharpens his claws on the hall rug each time we let him out the door, he is not so puny.

I read an amusing article in *Boy's Life* at the library last night on "Putting on a Minstrel Show" in which it said, "Don't pick up the bones or the tambourine or engage in loud talking as it is sure to be heard beyond the curtain" and there were some remarks on "mugging."

I can't get my poem finished and it has cut us off from various breathing spells & exercise we might have had. *The Double Dealer* invites me to contribute but I shall have to decline for the present.

Mr. Harrison's coming Thursday probably with the furnishings com-

46. Elly Ney (1882–1968), German-American pianist who performed in Europe and the United States.

plete of the old igloo—cars, canes, pictures, Mr. Minton's dictionary stand and everything.

With love,   Rat

Mole is deeply anxious about your having bought the hat and other things in Panama but if you *liked* them I don't doubt we will have pleasure in them. I wish you had bought a hat for yourself. Certainly no capital should be put in our wearing apparel that is additional to what we do have. The hat will be here soon no doubt. It hasn't come yet.

To John Warner Moore   *April 8, 1923*

Dear Badger,

The duster is here and an amusing thing it is, with those millions of small two-toned neck feathers, yellow on one side and red on the other and the assortment of piebalds. We have put a screw eye in the end of the handle—you should do the same with yours—and have it hanging on the partition by the fireplace. It came Thursday as I was being shoved and shouldered to a tearoom, by Mole to meet a Miss Jones with whom I was to have had luncheon but I thought the engagement had been postponed.

Tuesday I went to Morristown with W. Williams to see Charles Demuth[47] who is at a sanitarium there. The drive was delightful and I looked about sharply at the chickencoops and cedartrees and polarine stations as we passed, everything looking very much as usual. It took us about an hour from Newark. The *sanitarium* I had never seen before—an immense private mansion on a hill with Italian terraces and box borders garden statuary and so forth. Mr. Demuth is so invalided, he has to stay in his room so we were shown upstairs. He has a small room about twice the size of the Halliday's bathroom, with a high window extending all along one side of it, looking towards some mountains and woods and a broad white windowsill on which were some tulips, geraniums, a small jade cat, a few books and a shaving brush. There was also a bureau and a white iron bed and a pink linen laundry bag hanging by a cupboard door; also a very pretty blue and orange striped cotton bathrobe hanging on the door. We discussed Lancaster, Carlisle, Alice Meynell,[48] Henry James, Gertrude Stein, the flower show, the Williamses plan of going abroad next fall and so on. It was delightful, also heartrending as it doesn't look to me as if Mr. Demuth is going to get well. He is very game, jokes about the cure he is taking and says

47. Charles Demuth (1883–1935), a painter and a close friend of William Carlos Williams's. Demuth suffered from diabetes and, after 1922, spent time off and on at the Morristown Sanitarium for treatment.
48. Alice Meynell (1847–1922), English poet, essayist, and critic of English literature.

if you get too much of the serum all you need to do to counteract it is eat a handful of candy; he has diabetes and the proprietor of the sanitarium has discovered a new cure. On leaving he gave me an Easter egg with a rabbit on it from a box of elaborate candy which someone had given him. (Bill, he omitted!) And Bill circumspectly did not cry out.

Yesterday we called on Mr. Faggi's friend, Miss Rubenstein, whom he asked us to call on about Christmas time. She was out and as she lives near the museum, we went over to look again at the Chinese paintings, stopping first to see the armor. One of the attendants took charge of us and discanted on history, armor making, the relative size of collections, the silk flags hanging from the roof and we were much benefitted. One flag especially took my eye, a crusader's flag, white cross with a narrow circle of green leaves, (the crown of thorns) and pink flames radiating to the corners—(the light of Christianity the man said). We also ate in the museum, 2 muffins, 2 dogs and I ate a custard and then I went to the library, Saturday being a specially loathesome day there (with everybody on the staff there and out for himself in full force) so that there is neither order nor quiet, but things were as good as can be hoped for. When I got home Tuesday, I found Mr. Wheeler had been here & Mole had invited him to a meal. I said "So you have invited him for Tuesday?" "Yes" said Mole, "If I don't send for him Thursday or Friday." The tournament summons is certainly racy.

As for the summer, I am perfectly prepared to win again or lose as the case may be, but I thought it was a pity that we played [tennis] when your arm was not fit & we should be guided entirely by wisdom, not the enthusiasm of the hour.

Rat

We enjoyed the letters from Constance. The pictures are remarkable. The trophy shows clearly and the men are very graphic. The small boat pictures are the most vivid I think though one of the large views of you is unusually good.

To Bryher   *May 5, 1923*

Dear Bryher,

The views of Capri which came a few days ago, make one wonder that the island is not infested with cottages and other alien barnacles. The ones you sent Mother are especially illusive—of the cactus with thorns punctuating the leaf in a diapered pattern and the high part of the coast at a distance. It is so good of you thus to take us about with you (as Burton Holmes is said to have taken his wife on a honeymoon). The photographs are delightful, of Hilda seated Moslem fashion, of Philae and the Nubians in a canoe. I could not even suggest our delight in the Egyptian cards of the painted limestone statues, the servants in leopard skins and the unbeliev-ably intricate and significant jewelry. I am fond of the necklace and pectoral in the Metropolitan, which perhaps you saw when you were here but even they, cannot compare in my mind, with the design in the Cairo pectorals of the cobras and key of life entwined, and of the hawk headed beasts stepping simultaneously on twin captives. It is especially a pleasure to have the little ivory key you sent; it is always so integral a part of every symbolic design.

The colour and symmetry of "The Pelican" please me; I shall hope to see it in print.

We have seen a loan exhibition of very old Chinese paintings at the Metropolitan, which would I think, interest you; one of "spirited horses"— a series of white horses with scarlet pompoms and smoky manes and tails; one of a dragon in the clouds, concealed but for a few claws; *Enjoying the Breeze in a Fishing-Boat* which made me think of the Oxford punt, and one of supremely delicate brush work called *Herd Boys Returning Home* in which two elderly peasants are mounted on water oxen upon whose skin whorls are indicated with minute brush strokes in a darker colour so blended as to be imperceptible except upon scrutiny. We also examined the manuscript of a poem on Wang Wei:[49] "He took ten days to paint a river and five days a rock. A masterpiece cannot be produced in haste or by pressure. It was after bestowing such pains as these that Wang Tsai allowed his work to remain. Powerful is the painting of the Fang Hu mountains of the Kuen Lun Range, and high it is hung on the spotless wall in the lofty hall of your mansion." Since seeing the pictures, my only diversion has been the circus. We are expecting to see [Elmer Rice's] *The Adding Machine* and [George Bernard Shaw's] *The Devil's Disciple*. Eugene O'Neill I have not seen and somewhat mistrust. The greatest novelty of the circus was a troupe of six little elephants, the leader weaving his way through the line which auto-matically turned as he approached the tail of each individual, so there was a constant and orderly reverse motion of the line through the leading ele-phant's eight. Also, as a welcome contrast to Miss Leitzel, there was a new rope dancer, Betty Beeson, "the madcap of the wire" in swansdown and blue chiffon, who did most deftly and poetically, an unbelievable variety of dance steps on a wire. Please give my love to Hilda and do let me know anything either of you writes. I saw a most entrancing vignette of Slains Castle in *The Illustrated* [London] *News* or *The Graphic* a few weeks ago, showing sea-gulls and precipitous rocks.

Affectionately,   a dactyl

The postman has just brought your letter from London. The handkerchief is full of *esprit*, with the rolled hem and the posture of each bird different,

---

49. Wang Wei (699–759), T'ang-period artist and poet who was head of the newly developed "southern school" of landscape painting.

and the very knowing combination of blood red and vermilion. If you were extravagant only in clothes I could make excuse for you but to be so extravagant in gifts is very heinous. I wish I could see your new wardrobe.

The royal wedding interests us even here and I wish I could have been with you at your window.

The Williamses and Monroe Wheeler dined with us recently. The Williamses are both devoted to Robert and full of zeal over a new number of *Contact.*

To John Warner Moore   *May 10 [1923]*

Dear Badger,

"It is pretty that you say" but I think it necessary that various parts of your outline be modified. I agree strongly with Mole that nothing distracting ought to be railroaded through while Constance has her hands so full as they will be in June and July and for us to be in Puget Sound for a short time in the fall seems reasonable to me and richly repaying for the outlay. I am satisfied that you are to stay on the *M[ississippi]* another year for probably your influence is at a point now to count most. It being a fact that you are to stay, I think it would be hard for us not to see you at all if there is any opening for a visit when the strain of connecting would not overbalance the tranquility of the visit. Miss Leonard is very kind & Miss Sharp (my prospective substitute) is dying for a chance to work extra and make more money so I think it could be arranged.

Mole described somewhat our conversation with M[atthew] Josephson[50] and it was an ordeal. He said at one point of the salvos, "well, I hope we can still be friends." "Surely; one's interest in human beings" I said "transcends a difference in tastes." Previous to this, he had said that abroad nobody "studied over" obscenity; that grossness and sensuality were part of life, one didn't make a point of it or avoid it, it was just there like the trees on the street and he thought if I had lived abroad I would have a different feeling about it. I said, "I'm afraid not and what makes me sure I wouldn't is that none of the writers who write the fiction & poems you speak of ever discuss face to face with me any of the questionable matters that they write about. Mr. Burke when I am talking with him never borders upon a discussion of any of the details I object to in his writing because he would be embarrassed." He said, "that is a point I have raised myself in my own mind, but" etc. I said, "Shakespeare exhilarates me; These writers don't. When a piece of work focusses attention so strongly upon his grossness or its funni-

50. American poet, critic, and biographer (1899–1978).

ness that you can think of nothing else then all question of the writer's potential greatness disappears; he's not an artist, & signifies only as [a] moral
problem." More of this and at length he said "Then I wonder what you
think of my book—if you've troubled to read it." I said of course I had read
it & there was much I didn't like—much that I felt was unconscious & instinctive, not meant aggressively but that I deplored & felt was reflected
from the society that perhaps he had happened to be in. He looked down-
cast & somewhat slyly defiant and then I said I liked 2 of his poems in which
I felt that he escaped from impinging influences when I hadn't the feeling
that he was writing with a view to the thing's being read by Gorham Munson & Slater Brown & James Joyce & Scofield Thayer. We laughed outright
but he was displeased & we had a real carnage of skin & fur for 2 hours or
more. Words couldn't do justice to the revolting inanity of it & as I said to
Mole, the man's limitations which should enlist one's pity merely alienate
me. However he will be here again & on that occasion I shall ignore the existence of offal & smelly fishheads and treat him as if he were a little mister
in society & thus eventually fly away from him.

                                                        With love,   Rat

To John Warner Moore   *July 5, 1923*

Dear Badger,

Your telegram of Tuesday night restored us to sanity after the most un-
toward and unjustifiable anxiety, which nevertheless we couldn't help, and
the baby's name [Marianne Craig Moore] excited us immeasurably. I hope
Constance sees "points" in the fact of another little pantalettes. I myself
would as soon have girls as boys though of course in theory the complementary value of a mixture is apparent. It is surely comforting to know that
Constance is well and that May [Eustis] is not tugging on her cord or up to
infidelities when not watched—like a hireling.

Mole has an eye which has made her give up active business today. The
lid and cheek are swollen so she can't open it entirely and we have been
putting ice on it. It began Monday; when we were sitting on the balcony
Tuesday, with Monroe, it got worse and Wednesday the 4th at Bronxville
brought it to a head. I insisted this morning on telephoning Dr. Dodd,
Mole's oculist, but he is on his vacation and the voice of the substitute, like
a mosquito's sting disaffected me so, I gave up seeing a doctor. The swelling
will soon, I think go down of itself. As Mole said when she was persuading
me not to telephone the doctor, nature will cure it and he'll get the money.

Monroe brought us some peaches Tuesday and two beautiful prints
(East Indian, in sepia), one of a garden with fountains and one of two sages
disturbed by a dream of snakes. He is one of the most affectionate and one

of the most self-effacing people I have ever seen and it galls us not a little that Glenway Wescott his adoring beneficiary is not by nature fitted better to share the work of the domestic packhorse. However, as Mole said a little while ago, it is out of our hands; circumstances will shape the growth of each as we can't if we wanted to.

The 4th, at Aunt E.'s was a heartwarming if somewhat depressing experience. Aunt E. cares about us and is always getting half a loaf elsewhere and she doesn't respect Daisy who kowtows to "father's" this and that and goes into retreat annually. I said I had committed the blunder in the library of calling Father Williams "Mr." Aunt E. said privately, "You needn't tell Daisy but you never catch me calling them 'Father.' I call them 'Mister' and they answer up just the same." Edwin was at Loon Lake at a house party. The new house is a tragedy of mediocrities with no weight or poetic subtlety. Mr. Baldwin (Charles Baldwin) who is living with them and draughting for Edwin, is a remarkable boy; unspoiled and gentle though the only child and his parents are very rich. He went to Harvard then was 2 years at Oxford where he studied history and is going to study architecture at Columbia this winter. He gave Aunt E. as a present the one volume English edition of [Alexander] Gilchrist's *Life of William Blake* and had in his room a beautiful old morocco copy of some Latin author. He has a Chinese flute and a hunting horn—both of which he was too shy to play but later he brought out to the porch Stephen Leacock's parody on the Russian theatre and read it out loud to me.

Mole would now like to add a few words.[51]

To Bryher   *July 5, 1923*

Dear Bryher:

I was happy to have your letter this morning; it seems so long since I have heard from you; I feared you might be ill.

All of [Constantin] Brancusi's work I have seen, interests me prodigiously. I feel as Ezra says somewhere in *The Little Review*, that without mathematics, he arrives at a result which is mathematically exact. [Jean] Cocteau also, I have enjoyed and Gertrude Stein for all her strangeness, is really inspiring; I have just read her "Miss Furr and Miss Skeene" reprinted in *Vanity Fair*. Man Ray when he was painting here, made a deep impression on me; I have not followed him recently; I resented a little, his interpretation of you. I envy you the pleasure of meeting James Joyce and his wife. I don't think I know Miss [Sylvia] Beach, or is her shop the Paris book shop? I know Robert's sister has enjoyed being with you. Does she want to see old art or only modern? I am sending you a copy of *Contact* and could

51. MM took dictation from her mother, here, for two pages.

you give me William Bird's address? (I want to order William Williams' *The Great American Novel* that he is publishing.)

I have not read Dorothy Richardson but have just finished [Virginia Woolf's] *Jacob's Room* and *The Voyage Out*. There is amazing imagery in it all and infinite disappointment. I saw at an exhibition of modern paintings at the American Art Galleries not long ago, some beautiful things—Charles Sheeler's *Yachts and Yachting*, a model of a racing yacht—sails set—and photographs of a square-rigged ship, schooners, and racing yachts; a 12th-century stone head of a king with a little fringe of hair on the forehead and long wavy curls carved almost as in low relief Egyptian carvings; African sculpture and a cotton cap with magenta velvet bull's heads appliquéd, one on the front and one on the back, the eyes in red, yellow and white chain stitch with a velvet pupil. Also, I have seen the Martin Johnson animal film—supposedly with the minimum of shooting. It didn't seem so to me. The reticulated giraffes were magnificent, bending to drink and browsing on thorn trees; an elephant in a lily pool, making circles in the water with his trunk; a diana monkey; a tree full of small black monkeys and camels congregated at a water hole.

Do you know and like Mary Butts's work? And what of your own? *The Dial* offered me Vachel Lindsay's *Collected Poems* to review, but he hasn't inspired me and I did not venture. I asked for McGraw's *My Thirty Years in Baseball* but it had been assigned.

Are Hilda and Perdita well and is the Montreux address the proper one?

I was delighted with the article in the May-June *Natural History* Journal on monkeys harvesting the crops.

I think constantly of you each and will let you know when our plans ripen.

Affectionately,   a dactyl

My Florentine book cover has been a source of great pleasure and has been admired and admired.

I have a new green jersey dress with accordion plaited skirt which makes me look like a minor character in a Ben Greet play or Leigh Hunt's grasshopper. You recall his "green vaulter in the sunny grass"?

Mother has a beehive on her eye; I believe she wrote you a note before it made its appearance. She is now under an ice poultice.

To John Warner Moore   *August 5, 1923*

Dear Badger,

We are much delighted to know of your recreation at Bellingham, I was afraid all the facilities for pleasure would be present and only man be vile. (And I am glad we have met the Pipers so we know what the visit would be like and how sincere they are.) I am relieved that Constance is much better; with such a consensus of cares for her & May it is well we are not going to San Pedro. And I feared for Mole to go through Colorado and middle California at this time as the weather bureau shows strong heat in all the middle states and Arizona, and heat has an instant effect on her. We are ready to go except that we have not yet rented the apartments. Mole made curtains for the 4-poster of those octagon spotted Japanese curtains we used to have in Carlisle. We have had them dyed solid green and the room looks remarkably well. There are 4 trunks under the bed, concealed by the curtains.

Mole's teeth are fixed passably well—much better than we had anticipated and in the fall we'll get an appointment with Dr. Todd the Darrs' dentist who is good and not expensive they say. Dr. Baldwin has worked on me 4 times with wonderful results. In the train last summer on the way home, I pulled a facing off a gold tooth when we were eating toffee. Perhaps you remember. I wasn't urging him to fix it up as he said it was merely for looks but when doing the other work, he put a new tooth on of his own accord and also repaired the roots of two very troublesome teeth.

Monroe and Glenway Wescott came to see us yesterday afternoon. Glenway has been in Paris and saw Robert McAlmon whom he says everybody loves for his simplicity and good nature; he saw Ezra who he says wears a pointed beard and side whiskers, which makes him look as if he hadn't been very well shaved; he saw Mina Loy and Gertrude Stein. He says Scofield Thayer is in wrong everywhere, refused an article by M. Loy on G. Stein, was offensively aggressive and insolent when calling on Gertrude Stein and that she "showed him the door." He didn't see Bryher and his high airs and disgruntlement with the present state of affairs was colossal—entertaining Monroe and us very much. He brought me a book of Indian miniatures which he had brought to Monroe but decided to give me and a beautiful silver pendant which Monroe had asked him to get me, of a little man perched among some discs, dark silver about an inch and a half long with some tiny chasing in lines and bars here and there.

Friday after leaving Dr. B. I went downtown to get money at Clarke's and see if there were any high shoes I could get you. At Eggers's & Silk they had a pair of French calf J & M. oxfords (8 A) reduced from $16.00. All I objected to is that they are bluchers[52] but the soles are not thick and they are otherwise plain. They can't be returned but if you can't wear them don't feel badly about it as they were not high priced—they have them without the blucher at the regular price & without the blucher high with hooks at the regular price. I could get them anytime.

---

52. Bluchers are a type of high shoe or half-boot.

Mr. Eggers gave me a pair of waxed laces that he said wear better than leather. We'll be starting Monday.

To Monroe Wheeler   *916 Washington Street*   *Bremerton [Washington]*
                          August 25th [1923]

Dear Monroe,

We are now established at the other end of the town from 1048 Fifth Street, but how kindly we submitted to being transferred you may know, when I learned from a post office clerk that our mail had been sent back to New York. We telegraphed the post master in New York to send it back here, to 916 Washington Street, and if a letter from you was remailed to you, please let it return; we have been so concerned to know if you are well; and unhappy to think of the burdens we laid on you, in leaving.

I wish sometime that you could take the trip from Buffalo to Duluth it was a delightful contrast to all that I had anticipated. In spite of the fact that there was a great herd of people on the boat, we had all the room we wanted and plenty to eat and so much sun and wind that I felt when we got to Duluth, as if I had been in Maine a month. We had the best darkey music I ever listened to and we had the pleasure—for the first time—of hearing the banana masterpiece played by an orchestra. The scenery is tame except for the sunsets and some little lighthouses. We passed a lighthouse on a peninsula one evening about sunset and the yellow shades around the lenses and the white masonry against a stretch of blue water—bright swordfish blue— were very impressive. After we left Mackinac Island, a woman was placed opposite us at luncheon, who gave us an immense amount of amusement. A phi beta kappa key applied securely so it would not get lost in the folds of the dress, led me to fear the worst but I was mistaken. The lady had been at Harbor Springs and I asked if she knew Ivan Swift.[53] ("The poet of the North." He wrote "Faggots of Cedar," "Ashes and Embers" and some other sylvan poems.) She said yes, that he had talked to them one afternoon, about modern poetry. She said, "He talked for I should say, an hour and a half; he got tiresome at the last; all poets do but he told us some interesting things." She then said she didn't like modern poetry and asked me if I did and if I *enjoyed* it, that she had heard five poets read and one especially had antagonized her but she couldn't think of his name—he was from Texas and he had said blusteringly, "Of course Longfellow and Tennyson were poets in a sense but today nobody ever thinks of reading them," and she said, "I felt

53. Poet and painter (1873–1945); founder of Chippewa Cove Woods, an artists' colony near Harbor Springs, Michigan.

like saying, 'I read them and I enjoy them and I haven't yet found any modern poetry that I enjoy or that I could compare with them.'" I said, "Was it Vachel Lindsay?" "Yes" she said vindictively, "that's the man."

We did not shed our naïve natures in leaving New York. When we arrived in St. Paul, I delightedly entered what I thought was the Y.W.C.A. although it looked like the Union League, whereon a negro butler in scarlet waistcoat with little horizontal black stripes said it was the Minnesota Club but he hospitably told us just where to go.

When we got to Seattle we were overwhelmed with joy to see Warner on the dock. After finding and approving this house which a doctor's wife had discovered for us, he went back to Tacoma and will be here on the *Mississippi* Monday afternoon. We have been saving a part of your chocolates and candied fruit until we are a united family—how, I don't know, for you have seen the strength of Mother's and my burglarizing instinct when candy is near. We observed simultaneously, your remarkable thoughtfulness in selecting maple and chocolate and no vanilla flavor but Mother remarked that it was not remarkable at all.

The cards are some I liked when we stopped at Banff. Would you be willing to send the mountain goat to Glenway?

Affectionately yours, Marianne

To Monroe Wheeler   *October 1 [1923?]*

Dear Monroe,

We are so happy to know of your large living-room, fireplace, and rightly equipped kitchen. Christopher Street is not a very exposed street and I should think the gas radiators would be enough. It is good to know your duplex landlady is not a mountebank or a Mrs. Muscat.[54]

Word of your being made Purchasing Manager delights us. It is not surprising but it is gratifying that one's beneficiaries—I should say, *your* beneficiaries—have perception to depend upon you. What a blessing to Frau Franco your ingenuity was, and of course your believing in the restaurant enough to wish to help her. So many people allow their talent to destroy them in leaving always a single eye upon their own art. It is no wonder that experts are so often, anathema to us; their significance really diminishing and being corroded in proportion as they are hoarding the minutes to make an advantageous outburst.

As for *The Dial*—despite estrangements, I have respect for it and the

54. Perhaps Nicol Muschat in Sir Walter Scott's *The Heart of Midlothian* (1818): a "debauched and profligate wretch" murdered by her husband.

last number quite galvanized me into my first ardor. I am overjoyed that Glenway's novel, or part of it, is to be published in it.

I am glad you like "Bowls"; I am surprised to know of *Secession*'s appearing.

Saturday, we went to the county fair at Port Orchard. There were pheasants, ducks two deer and some small elks in a paddock of young balsams and hemlocks—the air like an elixir with resin. The pheasants stepping about in the under brush with the sun on them, were a dazzling sight—their fiery yellow heads, black edged hackles, long speckled tails and red bodies—especially one black and white one an expanse of white feathers running down the back to the tail, covered with hair fine black tracery—each feather veined with two half circles meeting in a point like a church window. There was a kiwi which looked like a tailless white leghorn covered with marabou, Himalaya white rabbits with black noses and ears, many chickens, Holstein cows, goats and a little black kid.

Also, the excitements of the turf were included in the entertainment, three false starts, much waving of the white flag and a negro mounted on Sunshine—who carried off the palm.

I send my love to you both; I cannot say enough of our pleasure in your success.

Marianne

A princely feature of the exhibits in the embroidery pavilion was an immense painting of a waterfall—ledges above ledges of gray rock edged with white monkey fur.

To John Warner Moore   *14 St. Luke's Place [New York]*
                              Nov[ember] 30, 1923

Dear Badger,

We are delighted that the gumdrops were "acceptable" and of course I am proud that you like the [Vachel] Lindsay review. It is full of weak spots but I felt too that it was more natural and readable than most of my reviews. Scofield has been exceedingly kind, expressing the most emphatic confidence in me; Wednesday (when he and Monroe came to tea), he brought me an advance number of the December *Dial* with T. S. Eliot's review in it of my poems—which I shall send you. The review is beautifully written— a very stately natively sweet natured affair. If bolstering by the profession can do one any good it certainly will advantage me. Both Scofield's and Monroe's noses were pushed in the same milk pitcher and they acted as nice as they could which is a great deal, rather painful to their weasel-like struggle for the mastery. Scofield wore a white shirt with very widely separated black lines in it and a black bat wing tie, black suit and black shoes—Monroe the same, barring the black stripe and he wore tan shoes. We had sandwiches, brownies, tea, a fire, candles and every prospect pleasant. At eight I went to the library; things there were very active and I got tired, had a cold already, and Thursday and today I have been a-bed. It has been all right for me but hard for Mole. Tomorrow I shall be on deck.

Your letter came today enclosing the letter from Commander Berthold—a very impressive, astonishing letter I think. I can't believe it was written by the apparently rather hard, proud, nervous automaton we first met at "Dr. Davis's tea" at Everett. Monroe's letter is beautiful I think and the image of him. The two other letters enclosed are alas Janet Lewis's,[55] left by her irresponsibly in the Johnston which "Arthur" [Yvor] Winters lent her. I shall return them to her telling her we have not read them attentively or passed them around.

I am sorry the vaccinations were put off for I know it has been wearing on you to anticipate them. Surely, however, it is not going to be torturing or harmful when it does come.

It is dull and rather cold downstairs and a great pleasure to be upstairs although Mole has taken steps she wouldn't have had to take if I had been up.

It is great news that you will be heading for N. York in March. May nothing change that part of the program.

With love,   Rat

To T. S. Eliot   *December 10, 1923*

Dear Mr. Eliot,

Your letter which reached me in Bremerton, Washington, was a happy surprise for I have long looked upon you as the busiest of editors; and in another sense your article is a surprise for contrary to your assertion that it does me less than justice, quite the reverse is true. I feel that you are especially happy in what you say of rhythm and if I dare appropriate the application which you are so gracious as to make, I should be delighted. In justice to you, it would have been well that when making some corrections in the copy of my poems which I sent you, I had supplied the article "a" in the title "A Talisman" and the article "the" in the phrase "with regard to which the guides are so affirmative." I enjoy the ingenuity and perspicuousness of what you say of "that pleasantry of speech which characterizes the American language" and covet the right to exemplify what you say of simplicity of phrase. Charles Demuth spoke to me recently of the skill and the very per-

55. American poet and novelist (1899–   ); she was later married to Yvor Winters.

fect finish of your writing in this article, and today I received a letter from Mr. Alfeo Faggi, in which he says that he has read and reread your subtly discriminating criticism of my work and hopes that it has compensated me for *dell' ignorante silenzio dei grossolani critici.*

Your "Conspectus of Literature" in *Vanity Fair* gave me pleasure— what you say of intuitions and of the shared excellence of the best work in all countries.

As an assistant in a branch of the public library, I had last year, occasion often to speak of your work in *The Dial*—indeed finally became your expositor in an informal lecture. I distrusted my own rashness but the audience vindicated you most heartily. That you are not officially associated with *The Dial* at present is regretted not only by me.

Sincerely yours,   Marianne Moore

P.S. Nothing would give me greater pleasure than to have your advice, if any more of my work were to be published. For years I have wished to write something in prose but I seem to be no nearer to doing it than heretofore.

To Alyse Gregory   *February 5, 1924*

Dear Miss Gregory:

Your patience with Maxwell Bodenheim, and magnanimity, persuade me that one ought not on the grounds of disgust, to refuse him a hearing. After reading his *Crazy Man* last night, it gave me a start this morning to see the name so considerately quoted in your letter. As for Mr. Bodenheim's being persecuted, the tables are quite turned I think, in his requiring of the public the reading of this book. It almost destroys my belief in a mentality which I have thought his one asset. But with the incentive of your letter, I shall look up some of his other work and try to send you a short general article.

Mother was happy to receive your message; we often speak of you. Your study of D. H. Lawrence was immensely exhilarating to us both.

Sincerely yours,   Marianne Moore

To Bryher   *September 9, 1924*

Dear Bryher:

What enthralling books! *The Origin of Magic and Religion* has just come and *The Egyptian Legends* and *The Wisdom of the Apocrypha* arrived this morning. I am more than fond of the writings of Solomon and of anything Biblical, as you know, and the book of legends is a phenomenon it seems to me; it is so scholarly and so full of entertaining, poetic particular-ization. As for the Perry,[56] far from the title's putting me off, it would lead me to insist on seeing the book, however rebuffed or inconvenienced I might be—if you had not sent it to me. It is amazing of you to think of giv-ing me something more of Dorothy Richardson's but I couldn't allow you to; a neighbor of ours has her work and has offered it to me entire, at my con-venience.

We are most eager to see your poems in *The Transatlantic Review* and feel terribly ostracized by you that you have not told us of them. Monroe Wheeler asked if we had seen them and is bringing us the number. I have been rather lacklustre about speaking of work that I have been doing off and on for two years, but Mother has goaded me into completing it, so I am again at work on it—two poems, "Sea Unicorns and Land Unicorns," and "An Octopus" which is descriptive of Mt. Rainier in Washington. We read Dr. Williams' article on Robert with deep interest; I had the feeling that I had spoken of our pleasure in his enthusiasm. In respect to your liking of [McAlmon's] *Post-Adolescence*, I must tell the truth and admit that friends are continually writing what I resist, but that fact in no way lessens the keenness of my interest; there was much that I cared for in something of Robert's in *The Transatlantic Review*.

It is very exciting to think of you in England. Poor Mother says that in her notebook of 1917, she mentions Eastbourne as one of the places to which we were going. But for that matter, a Baedeker would be a good memoran-dum of the places with which we have romantic associations. I feel no nearer England than before so I have resumed my motto that we are going next year. Warner has arrived—Jacob and his family, apropos of the Bible,—and we are much exhilarated.

Elinor Wylie was married to William Rose Benét about this time last year. She is tall, spare, pale, with black shingled hair, rather wary and sus-picious, with extreme intensity and energy of manner. Should you care to have me send you her recent little book of poems, *Black Armour*? or have you seen it? I felt *Jennifer Lorn* to be facile but brittle and cruel, and I felt that some of the diction was very ready-to-hand. *Punch* seemed to me apt in its criticism: "The manner of telling has a heavy, cosmetic quality which goes far beyond the graceful needs of 18th century make-up." *Punch* also had the best review of Kate Douglas Wiggin's *My Garden of Memories* that I have seen and the two reviews made me curious as to who that member is, of *Punch's* staff of learned clerks. I should so love to send you something in which you might be interested, but suppose I couldn't ask you to give me even a hint of what? I have no gift of finding the right thing in the dark.

Affectionately yours,   a dactyl

56. Possibly Bliss Perry (1860–1954), editor of the *Atlantic Monthly* and author of *And Gladly Teach.*

To William Carlos Williams   *October 9, 1924*

Dear William:

I have just made a humble surrender to Bryher and to Robert McAlmon, of my determination to have made my positively last appearance. That is to say, I have reconsidered my decision about the book in so far as to allow Mr. MacVeagh to publish an American edition[57] and I have been so perplexed and preoccupied the past few weeks, in tumbling the furrow from right to left, that I have not dared take the enjoyable leisure to drop you a line; or Bryher either till just last week, to say what I am going to do. I am perfectly aghast at thought of the work the first edition must have been when I have been so overwhelmed in merely rearranging it. Of course I've added a few things. And also, working under pressure makes the undertaking seem more onerous. When Mr. MacVeagh first suggested an edition last spring, I declined and when in September it seemed as if there might as well be an American edition, I found that the really favorable time for bringing out the book was almost past. To one working subterraneanly it's odd that such things could be.

My brother is now in town (on duty at the Navy Yard) and we're feeling ourselves a rather expanded family—seven as over against two. When you and Florence can come to see us I hope you won't refuse to gratify our insatiable thirst for European experience.

Yours,   Marianne Moore

To H. D.   *October 26, 1924*

Dear Hilda,

The piece of romance which you "found" for me is prized and dwelt upon; the little figure, the color of a fox's brush, is the precise tone, somewhat lighter, of a Scotch coat that I have and the combining of it with the blue and the green is so poetic. Beset with gaieties and business as you must have been in London, how could you think of us? Mother, too, is touched by your thought of her and the exquisite lavender and yellow scarf with its serpentine lines is a delight to us both. It transports one out of the dullness of humdrum occupations as long as one looks at it.

We were happy to find your "Calliope" in *The Saturday Review*,

The   *"see—*
                          I am gone"

is an exquisite paradox—so inescapably a climax. I enjoyed writing—I

57. *Observations* (1924) was published by the Dial Press.

should say trying to write—of *Heliodora* which Miss Gregory allowed me to review briefly for *The Dial*. Your imagery and the sense of nature as you give it—so electric in their actuality—make me think of Schiller's reflection about the world of nature; perhaps you remember! which like Pygmalion's statue, "answered to my youthful daring and understood my heart's quick sound." Of course a *Dial* was sent you? If by chance, not, I should like to send you one.

Perhaps Bryher has told you that The Dial Press has offered to publish an American edition of my little book? The last few weeks in preparing it, I have been breathless and have marvelled to think how endless the care of preparing the first book must have been to you and Bryher and Robert, and what patience it took to assemble from scattered magazines the poems you included.

I have just had a letter from Miss Weaver in which she speaks with delight of seeing you and Bryher and Robert. What wouldn't I give to have been with you. Miss Heap, too, whom I saw a few days ago, spoke so eagerly of meeting you, and what she said of her pleasure, was so vivid, I felt almost as if I had been in Paris, too. We think often of Perdita; as you know, we care so much about her, and our thoughts travel to you both always, with solicitous insistence.

Marianne

1925–1929
Editing *The Dial*

M O O R E's work at *The Dial* between 1925 and 1929 consumed her time and energy as no previous employment had done, and thus marks a distinct chapter in her life. She was profoundly aware of the significance of the magazine in shaping the art and literature of her time, and approached her responsibilities, both of broad judgment and editorial accuracy, with appropriate solemnity. Much of Moore's correspondence during this period is of a business nature, involving particulars of editing and production that are best appreciated in the full context of *The Dial*'s history. We have included only a very few of the hundreds of unique and lively letters which Moore wrote in response to submissions, thoughtfully rejecting, revising, accepting, or soliciting work for publication. We have omitted as well the many letters Moore wrote to the *Dial* owners, staff and contributing editors, discussing her various editorial and production decisions. We have emphasized, instead, those letters that represent something of Moore's own experience as editor of *The Dial*. The overall impact of the *Dial* work on her life and art is best represented in her letters to Warner (to "Badger" from "Rat"), and in those to James Sibley Watson, Scofield Thayer, and Alyse Gregory.

Moore's association with *The Dial* began long before she joined the staff of the magazine. She had met Scofield Thayer in 1920 and Sibley Watson had praised her work in the pages of *The Dial* even before the appearance of *Observations*. As Moore's mother wrote to Warner, Alyse Gregory reported that Dr. Watson had called her "the best writer of poetry we have; (that is we in America). Happily Rat doesn't think so himself" (January 6, 1922). After Moore won the Dial Award in 1924, her association with the magazine was solidified.

When the managing editor, Alyse Gregory, decided to leave (she went to England on account of the health of her husband, Llewelyn Powys, who suffered from tuberculosis), Moore was a natural choice to replace her. She had often offered help. Thayer invited her to become associate editor in April 1925, and she was listed as acting editor in the July issue. Increasingly, Moore was left at the helm. Sibley Watson completed his medical studies around this time (Moore would henceforth refer to him as Doctor Watson) and returned to Rochester, where his energies were divided between research in radiology and experimental filmmaking. Scofield Thayer left for Europe in 1925 and continued to live an expatriate existence, often avoiding New York even when he did visit the States. Thayer resigned as editor in June 1926, and Moore was named editor in the July 1926 issue. Both Watson and Thayer were nominally in charge, however, and indeed Moore turned to them whenever major decisions had to be made or approved.

The first year of Moore's editorship was burdened by trials connected with Thayer's mental decline. This manifested itself particularly in his irrational discontent with the staff (both professional and clerical), and many of Moore's early letters to Watson concern the matter of how to cope with Thayer's whims in demanding the dismissal of worthy employees. Thayer's mental troubles mounted, and his cousin Ellen Thayer consulted Freud (January 7, 1926). The renowned analyst advised reinstating the dismissed employees, using Watson as the arbiter.

While it is clear that Moore deferred to Thayer and Watson on many decisions at *The Dial*, and beyond this, that the *Dial* staff worked cooperatively, Moore's editorship was distinct in certain respects. She shared Thayer's commitment to the aesthetically crafted, but also Watson's enthusiasm for the new, and she managed to synthesize these interests in volumes that resisted the partisanship of their day. Under her editorship, George Saintsbury, a distinguished Victorian man of letters, became a regular contributor. At the same time, she continued to cultivate the bold modernism of Ezra Pound (whom Thayer, before his departure from *The Dial*, had alienated and who won the Dial Award during her editorship). Moore regularly solicited reviews from T. S. Eliot, several of which were published during her tenure. Perhaps the most striking feature of Moore's editorship was her penchant for revising the work of her contributors rather than simply accepting or rejecting it. To Robert Hillyer, Moore wrote (July 14, 1925), upon accepting "Remote":

> May we, however, make so bold, despite the exactions of symmetry, as to ask if you would permit us to publish it without the last line—and would the sequence, to you, be irreparably impaired if the third stanza were omitted?

Hillyer was completely pliant in the matter.

I enclose with this a copy of "Remote" embodying your suggestions. It generally pleases me to cut, and I agree with you that the
apocalyptic third stanza is better out. I am too near this piece to
know whether or not the bold cut of the last line pleases me quite
as much, but I am more than willing to try it that way. The line
was banal? too subjective? I wonder if I damn myself when I say
that the loss of the idea distresses me not at all; it is the break in
pattern that gives me pause. But since that is an effect that I have
often employed deliberately, I dare say my doubt is caused
merely by my not being accustomed to it in this particular poem.

Archibald MacLeish was equally submissive when Moore changed his
"Nocturne in White" to "Nocturne" and omitted four lines. But others resisted. When Moore wrote to Conrad Aiken (May 17, 1929), upon accepting
"You Went to the Verge," "sanctioning, however, the omission of the last
seventeen lines," he withdrew the poem. We do not always know what these
poets felt privately about Moore's revisions, but some freely expressed their
resentment. Among the most entertaining exchanges in the *Dial* collection
(much of which belongs to the Beinecke Library at Yale) is that between
Moore and Maxwell Bodenheim, a confrontation of two very strong wills.
Bodenheim, the enfant terrible of avant-garde poetry in the 1920s, touted
by Williams, Kreymborg, and others, clearly resented Moore's authority.
When she rejected his "In a Garden," "though the first part and the first
part of the last part, are surely very perfect," he vented his envy and rage.
He resented the "harshly exacting, complete-perfection-or-rejection attitude of a magazine which offers a leniently appreciative eye and persistently
numerous acceptances to anything written by Mr. E. E. Cummings, Mr.
Malcolm Cowley, and other poets." After a sequence of rejections, he wrote,
bitterly, "God how I hate you and your mean, unfair, half-blind, apprehen-
sively arbitrarily, literary group."

Hart Crane's letters to his friends also suggest more than a little
chomping at the bit. The "Rt. Rev. Mountjoy," as he called Moore to Slater
Brown (August 19, 1925), was a force he was not always happy to submit to.
She accepted seven of his poems for *The Dial*, several before the appearance
of *White Buildings*, and so played an important part in his emergence as a
major figure. But she was choosy, and often critical even of the poems she
printed. To Watson she wrote (March 9, 1927): "Hart Crane—I am accepting his poem—seems to me vapid and pretentious—not well reefed. In
'Powhatan's Daughter' the thought, the rhythm, and the syntax 'yield'
where they shouldn't yield, and the climax scarcely apologizes for much
that is unpractised." Of "Passage" she wrote to Crane (August 13, 1925):
"We could not but be moved, as you must know, by the rich imagination and
the sensibility in your poem, 'Passage.' Its multiform content accounts, I

suppose, for what seems to us a lack of simplicity and cumulative force. We are sorry to return it." Crane commented to Waldo Frank (August 19, 1925) about this rejection letter: "It seems almost as though Miss Moore might be rather speaking of her own poems in such terms." Perhaps the most famous case involving Moore's practice of revising poems submitted to *The Dial* was that of Crane's "Wine Menagerie," published in *The Dial* as "Again." Crane complained to Charlotte and Richard Rhychtarik (December 1, 1925) that he could hardly own it after her manipulations: "*The Dial* bought my Wine Menagerie poem—but insisted (Marianne Moore did) on changing it around and cutting it up until you would not recognize it." Yet it is clear that Crane respected Moore's talents. He told Yvor Winters (October 5, 1926) that "one goes back" to Marianne Moore, along with Poe, Whitman, Melville, and Frost, "with renewed appreciation of what America really is, or could be." Some of the more irate contributors accused Moore— privately, in letters to their friends, or directly—of prudery and conventionality. Moore resisted publishing excerpts of Joyce's *Finnegans Wake* and hesitated to publish a protest when Samuel Roth printed a pirated edition of *Ulysses* in America. But the breadth of material she included in the pages of *The Dial*, often enthusiastically, belies such accusations. She was the first to print a selection from D. H. Lawrence's *Pansies*, for instance, which he had sent to her surreptitiously through his agent (since the trial of *Lady Chatterley's Lover* his work had been under the eye of Scotland Yard).

Moore's awareness of the "unrest" among writers subjected to her editorial decisions appears in her essay "*The Dial*: A Retrospective":

> To some contributors—as to some non-contributors—*The Dial*, and I in particular, may have seemed quarrelsome, and it is regrettable that manners should be subordinated to matter. Mishaps and anomalies, however, but served to emphasize for me the untoxic soundness of most writers. And today, previous victims of mine have to dread from me, as pre-empting the privilege of the last word, nothing more than solicitude that all of us may write better.

This is the voice of an established woman of letters who knows she has left a permanent mark on the literature of her time.

The work of *The Dial* was extremely taxing for Moore, particularly in its last year, as her letters to her brother make clear. And the finances of the magazine became problematic as Watson and Thayer lost enthusiasm for fund-raising. Watson and Moore agreed to end publication with the July 1929 issue. In the middle of that month (July 15, 1929), she wrote a letter to Thayer that makes clear just how she had valued her time at *The Dial*, despite the difficulties she had encountered there:

You and Doctor Watson for years and years have been devising ways to benefit others, and I, looking on, have admired and approved; but how often have I been taken aback and astonished by being myself brought into the circle and made a chief recipient. Work for *The Dial* has been rewarding from my first timorous day in the office; and certain parts of that work have been the most rewarding of any I have ever had a part in. Can you the better understand why I now feel that it is you and Doctor Watson who should be receiving from everyone associated with *The Dial,* expression of grateful remembrance?

Moore's life was not entirely circumscribed by work at *The Dial.* She and her mother made a trip to England in the summer of 1927, while Warner's ship was in European waters, visiting Alyse Gregory, George Saintsbury, and others.   (Kenneth Burke took over for her.) In the fall of 1928 she made another trip to Virginia (where she would return in the 1930s, while her brother was stationed at the Norfolk Navy Yard in Portsmouth). But her writing during this period chiefly included her forty-two columns for *The Dial.* She did not publish any poems between 1925 and the middle of 1932.

When *The Dial* closed, Moore in a sense began a new life. She moved to Brooklyn in September 1929 and found there abundant energy to fuel her poetry.

To Alyse Gregory, James Sibley Watson, and Scofield Thayer
[14 St. Luke's Place, New York]   December 23, 1924

Dear Miss Gregory, Dr. Watson, and Mr. Thayer,

I have received an advance copy of *The Dial* and am deeply moved by that for which I have no adequate expression—your treatment of those whom you choose to champion.[1] I am chastened by the beauty of Mr. Wescott's article; I had not known that he could write so quietly, concisely, and with so steady a mechanism. That he has the salesman's faculty of showing only the good side of his wares is not for me to comment on at this time.

That you should have also allowed me an entirely personal pleasure, known only to yourselves and me is a gift distinctly memorable. I refer to the collecting of short reviews in this number.

Mr. Thayer as you know allowed me to have a printed sheet of the editorial announcement in this issue. The published announcement, however, comes to me as if I had not seen it before; I do not know how to receive so much. My pleasure which is also terror, in his defense of me, surely could not but augment any aptitude that I may have for work. Recalling *Poetry*'s designation of me as a fanciful acrobat, to be associated with Emily Dickinson's rigorous splendor is rare and trembling praise. Mr. Thayer's brilliant antitheses and criticism will cause me to be read about even if I am not read.

I wish that if ever I may serve *The Dial*, I may do it well, for I am yours sincerely,

Marianne Moore

To George Plank   *March 15, 1925*

Dear Mr. Plank,

Your letter is a great pleasure—as great as if any work that I have so far done, were worthy of your confidence or of *The Dial*'s. The Dial Press published this year, some work of mine called *Observations*, which I shall send to you, when the second edition is ready. I hope this edition will be better than the first which was disappointing in text and format.

It is delightful to think of your English surroundings. I have the feel-

1. MM received the Dial Award for 1924.

ing that they include some of Henry James's former ones, and fond as we are of England, anything pertaining to him, is particularly stirring. As for what you call the dust of London, no one could love it more than we do. I have long looked askance at Ezra Pound's apostasy. H.D. I hear from occasionally; I feel her fineness and her charm, as you do.

We left Carlisle in 1916, to be with my brother when he became pastor of a church in Chatham, New Jersey. During the war in 1917, when he entered the navy, we came to New York temporarily and have been here ever since.[2] I have been in a branch of the library across the street from which my mother and I live, working but four hours a day so that I could do some writing—chiefly reviewing. Honoring as *The Dial* is to my book, I feel that perhaps it was this other work the editors had in mind in making me the award, though in any case their judgment is surely temerarious.

Your designs in *Vogue* from time to time, we welcome—*in Vogue* as well as on it. The ballerinas in the March 15th number have that complementary grace and esprit which are particularly your own. The initial decoration also, of "Society," we attributed to you.

We live in an obscure but very accessible part of New York and my mother and I should be happy to have you come to see us if at any time you should be in New York.

Sincerely yours,   Marianne Moore

To Monroe Wheeler   *April 19, 1925*

Dear Monroe,

It was a pleasure to have your card, and to have your letter saying that you have a home. I hope it can be made Americanly warm. Your remark that it is "still emphatically winter," makes me—with my hairless-mouselike inheritances—shudder.

The Coal and Iron Bank has not outlawed us. I hope its confidence in you is being in some degree an enjoyment and not a confining bugbear. One should not, and you especially, ought not to allow "Conscience to occupy the armchair" as Barrett Wendell[3] would say,—in Paris.

[Ford Maddox Ford's] *No More Parades* is a delightful title, is it not? I also as you know, was delighted with [Gertrude Stein's] "The Making of an American Family" or what I read of it in *The Transatlantic Review*. In Paul Rosenfeld's book *Men Seen*, there is a bit from Marsden Hartley which I value—"You would expect him to land on a lily-pad any moment and smooth his wings with his needle-like legs."

2. MM and MWM moved to New York in 1918.
3. Literary historian (1855–1921), who taught one of Harvard's first courses in American literature.

I saw the Lees a mere moment when returning the Goethes and again when taking Brande's life, for Mrs. Lee to read. I shall watch eagerly for Glenway's article in *Vanity Fair*. E. E. Cummings' tribute to "Hairy Jones" [*The Emperor Jones / The Hairy Ape*] in the May number entertained me for as you know my tendency is not to canonize Eugene O'Neill.

I have been reading Professor Saintsbury, whose ability has somewhat the effect on me of ethyl chloride or a more permanent annihilator. These essays and some strange novels which I have been reading for the library have given me so, the illusion of hurry that thoughts even of my book have lapsed. It ought to be out now, not properly reprinted perhaps but improved. I could not have Garamond type, or a different page size or an omitting of certain poems and you may be repelled by many an ununiformity as I broke some rules that I know of, and may have broken some I did not know of but I shall send you a copy when I have it, also a *Times* with the picture you like. I wish I had the photograph itself to send though I like the dim cut in the newspaper better than the thing it was made from.

Also I have been more concentrated at the library than usual as I am expecting shortly, to give up my work there to do half a day's work at *The Dial* and I should like my housekeeping there at the library not to scandalize my successor.

I hope that all is well with you and Glenway and with those at home and that you will remember my advice about the armchair.

Affectionately, Marianne

I don't think the comment in the March *Dial* was intended other than as friendly raillery.

To Maxwell Bodenheim   *[Dial office, 152 West 13th Street, New York]*
                                  July 6, 1925

Dear Mr Bodenheim:

I was not aware of your having published work other than that which you have deemed worthy of preservation.

In respect to my concept of your concept of woman, I would say that although the words quoted in my review were those of a character in your book rather than your own, you in no way made it apparent that the view expressed was at variance with your own. If I have misled any person, I am glad to think that he may revert to you, yourself, and to your books for his final concept.

In returning your "Poetic Essay," *The Dial* congratulates you upon lines nine to fourteen inclusive.

Sincerely yours, Marianne Moore   Acting Editor

To William Carlos Williams   *[14 St. Luke's Place, New York]*
                                    December 16, 1925

Dear William:

I have your book[4] and your letter. My admiration for "The Destruction of Tenochtitlán" you know, and I am eager to read those chapters which I have not seen. I almost grudge your giving it to me for I know that copies of one's book are not leaves on a tree.

Your hearty invitation to contribute to *The Contact Collection* stirs me but I have not one hour at my command. As for that appropriate pot of gold, neither auburn-haired women remuneratively employed, nor popular doctors have a right, I am sure, to be concerned about it. I must confess that I gravitate toward poetry occasionally rather than towards filling critical gaps caused by my own inadvertences. Speaking of criticism, your review of H.D.'s *Collected Poems* is a triumph. I did go to Gertrude Boyle's exhibition and was greatly impressed by her talent and her courage.

If you knew how any one of my days is spent, and how much I should like to be in *The Collection,* you would know that it is no easy refusal I am making.

Please give my love to Florence.

                                    Sincerely yours,   Marianne Moore

To Scofield Thayer   *[*Dial *office, 152 West 13th Street, New York]*
                           December 28, 1925

Dear Scofield:

I have just received your radiogram and am sorry, exceedingly, to have alarmed you. I did not foresee your not perceiving that my plea for kindness referred to subordinates at *The Dial* and not to myself. Your kindness to me has always been so great and you have benefitted and made happy so many others, that I could not endure that you should by accident of misapprehension, hurt those whom you would if you knew the facts in the case, especially wish to shield and benefit. Although self interest ought not to actuate one, an aspect of the matter, which is wholly unbenevolent, is I must say, ever present to me—the inevitable misrepresenting of yourself to the harsh casually observing public. For an unexplained dismissing of a large part of our staff could not but focus attention upon you.

Mr. Burke's loyalty you doubt and you will discount anything which I may say in praise of him. Nevertheless I do say that if Mr. Burke had been our regularly appointed Assistant Editor—if Ellen that is to say, had not

4. *In the American Grain* (1925).

been here—intrusive as my action would have appeared, I could not have retained my office had I been asked to concur in his dismissal. As it is, convinced though I am of his affection for you and of his pride in *The Dial*, I must needs acquiesce in his leaving, since this was the plan originally agreed upon as expedient. When I said in the letter which you quote, that circumstances might arise in which it would be impossible for me to cooperate, I alluded to the possibility of your suspecting other members of our staff, of disloyalty to you.

Sincerely yours,

To Alyse Gregory   *December 29, 1925*

Dear Alyse:

Your letter came days ago, but your understanding is a renewed consolation day by day. How much I owe to your discerning sympathy. I don't myself think the [George] Santayana alluring and sent it to you only for the light which your writing would reflect upon it. Your review of Paul Morand is a triumph. (I remember writing ferociously and much less alluringly of his *Green Shoots*.) Mr. Powys's review of Mary Agnes Best is surely too, a major briefer mention. Mr. McBride said a little while ago and I agreed with him, that Mr. Powys's briefer mentions have always a special style. I do hope the trouble with his eyes is already past; one is so acutely hampered in having one's eyes not available for hard use. Two copies of [Llewelyn Powys's] *Skin for Skin* did come to *The Dial*. One, we sent to Mr. John Powys for review; the other had been opened without our having been aware of the address. Ellen Thayer was anxious to read it and having read it, and your letter having come at the same time, she forwarded it to Scofield.

With respect to the December *Dial*, the Editor's attack upon us is, I think, somewhat nullified by its cryptic character. Mr. Seldes said over the telephone today, that nobody knows what it is about. This ameliorating statement, S.T. would, I know, take in bad part. Mr. Seldes talks of seeing him in case he goes abroad and I wish he might, for reassurances in person would counteract present irritation.

I am deeply touched by your effort to save me from excessive drudgery. Scofield writes insistently recommending moderation and it is true that although I work all the time, I do not work too hard. And I like the work—really delight in it. In your reference to being happy, you do touch the hidden and essential core of any kind of work. Dr. Watson and Ellen Thayer are matchless in their co-operating helpfulness. Having said so much, I will be frank in saying that there are some things that I am not happy about, but they have not yet made me heart-sick. You know how full each day is, of diverting incidents—Mr. Bodenheim and Mr. Hillyer calling today simultaneously; Mr. Bodenheim to inquire how with my prudery "I" should have selected Mr. Cummings as the recipient of *The Dial* award, followed by Mrs. H. B. Eveline to ask if we were prepared to present to the recipient, the award itself. Alfred Kreymborg called a few days ago to beg the loan of *The Mercure de France* in which a criticism of him has been published and to ask if we could use at once, a pigeon poem of his, called "Pantomime," which he has rashly incorporated in a book. The only place in the make-up which we were at first able to find for it was between S. T. and Yeats! The stately Ailanthus came to our rescue and the pigeon follows Anatole France. I thought one day in being telephoned to by Gilbert Seldes, that I was talking to Gilbert Cannan and while there has been some despair, there has been no little humour in Mr. MacVeagh's financial recriminations and restrictions. Miss Thayer and I are continually proffering our salaries in payment for briefer mentions, (not with success). Miss Thayer did actually, however, advance today to Mr. Bodenheim, payment for a poem to save him from starving, I having promised Mr. MacVeagh to pay for no verse until after January first.

Mother is well and sends you much love. I do hope that you are not over-hospitable; it is so far better that you should be alive. I am going to send to you, as a memento of your gentle hospitality in *The Dial*, Mabel Simpson's *Poems*. (I think we may have an inclusive review of them, of Melville Cane—another of your discoveries—and of my Leon Serabian Herald.)

With love always, and so many kinds of thanks,

P.S. Henry commissioned me a long time ago, to send you his best wishes for Christmas and with sovereign tact, avoided emphasizing the fact that his wife was disappointed to find me at *The Dial* rather than you, when she came in a week or so ago. He said "My wife didn't know you just at first. You see, she was expectin' to see Miss *Greg*'ry and she said afterward, 'Who is that lady? She's awful nice.'"

To James Sibley Watson   *January 7, 1926*

Dear Dr. Watson:

I learned only yesterday morning that you had sent to Mr. Burke, changes which have not been incorporated in your announcement. This disgraceful, distressing error, I cannot reconcile myself to. I recall that last spring, Scofield felt that consolation could have been derived from a sense of guilt on the part of those in the office who had been guilty of grave mistakes. However, my acute misery in this instance seems to me, only futile. When Mr. Burke called here yesterday to decline a briefer mention of the Moscow Art Theatre plays which Mr. Seldes translated and had requested that Mr. Burke review, I asked if the memoranda of these changes, in his handwriting, had merely been attached to a piece of proof and put in a drawer or if they had been given to Miss Thayer; and he said that they had been given to her and that there had been some conversation on the subject. Miss Thayer does not recall this and is profoundly distressed. She says that that whole week, she scarcely knew what she was doing. Her preoccupation with regard to Scofield is very saddening. What I write to him does not give her satisfaction. She feels that the letter which I did not post was too strong; that its substitute was too mild. But all of this is not an excuse, merely a reason, for the omission. Other misfortunes augment my unhappiness—the late appearing of *The Dial;* the oldness of some of the briefer mentions; certain clumsy bits of diction in [Nicolai Leskov's] "The Bear," which escaped me after what seemed hundreds of revisions; and the placing of some of the pictures, to say nothing of Cane and [Adolf] Dehn, which had seemed inevitable, since the poems had to be put in this issue and the pictures were already there.

To revert to Scofield, Ellen has written, (in German), what seems to me an admirable letter to Freud. She says—of course not in this letter—that Mrs. Thayer who is deeply influenced by Mr. [Hermann] Riccius, wonders why, if dismissing certain persons would save Scofield's mind, we will not dismiss them. I feel that letting Mr. Burke go had probably intensified his twist and hope that we can impress upon him that Mr. Burke was sent away in accordance with an agreement made last spring and not because of disloyalty.

Mr. Lewis May asks if we would care for the series of essays on Anatole France, of which he gives us the enclosed list. I should say No.

Sincerely yours,   Marianne Moore

To George Saintsbury   *February 2, 1926*

Dear Mr. Saintsbury:

So much the worse for any one we are tempted to say, for whom the substance of your article, will not "do." This subject so savoury, so seldom rightly treated, is in your hands, nutritive and "garnished." I wish it were not editorially unconstitutional to publish it in *each* of our subsequent issues. Our material for March having gone to press, it will appear in April. I am so happy in the article that I am accused by my family—that is to say, by my mother and brother—of resembling that young man of whom George Meredith says, "a gentle delirium enfolded his brain."

If though proud to serve, our printers should have been unserviceable, please when the proof reaches you, be at liberty to make changes. We enclose a cheque for fifty dollars.

Your having read, "scores of novels over and over again," leads me or perhaps misleads me to remind you that a new edition of Stendhal is by degrees appearing in America. We have received [Stendhal's] *The Charterhouse of Parma*. You will discern what we are wondering. May we send it to you or must we not?

What you say of Xenophon, as a novelist and the delightful picture of him in *The Advancement of Learning*, lead me to wish that you might care to say "a word" on him. *The Cynegeticus* and *The Treatise on Horsemanship* are favourite "novels" of mine and the Loeb translations of the *Minor Works* and of the *Anabasis* have not so far as I know, been noticed in America.

I should be less than honest not to admit that I think more highly of my Christian name than heretofore. In my Scotch Irish ancestry, the name Marian has appeared but when it was given to me, "ne" was added to make it accommodate the names of two aunts, "Mary" and "Anne."

Yours most gratefully,   Marianne Moore   Acting Editor

To Yvor Winters   *14 St. Luke's Place, New York City*
February 3, 1926

Dear Mr. Winters:

I wished to reply at once to your barrage attack upon me, but can also allow myself some surprise that a personal letter should ever be answered, my progress this winter has been so labored. Your metaphor of the crow is amusing the more so that it is perhaps true.[5] Mr. Cummings is surely gifted, but others are also. Some of his writing as I told him one day last fall in the first real conversation I had ever had with him, I could not read. He bowed quite understandingly. But what I said in the January *Dial*, I said without any reservation. Your "backings and turnings" far from seeming ridiculous, are an honour to the writers who occasion them; more than is deserved in certain instances it seems to me, and I am glad that you decline to blush when admitting occasional pangs of jealousy. There is a kind of jealousy of which it would be a shame to be ashamed.

I like "The Barnyard," in which I don't feel the beard to be irrelevant. My objection was to the cadence of the line about the beard. I am tempted to wonder if you might care to reinstate the beard—to substitute it perhaps for the wall of hell, which is confusing to me; but shall not, until I have

---

5. Winters had written to MM on January 12, 1926, in response to her review of Cummings in the January 1926 *Dial*. He compared MM's prose to a crow who picks over the ash heap and leaves the ashes behind.

heard from Doctor Watson. We have been denied the privilege of purchasing more verse for a while, and an exception was made in favour of this particular poem. Could you not allow us to read your criticism of T. S. Eliot?

To hark back to your letter of resistances, to Richard Aldington for instance, may I say that one of the oddest things that pass in panorama before one, is the entanglement of good with ill; it would all but seem that figs do grow on thistles; not that I could for a moment think so, but one is confused to the point of not coming to any decision respecting a good many of the thistles.

A thing that is a surprise to me is that you do not like "The Bear." That, I have the deepest feeling for, as writing and as merely a story.

I look forward very earnestly to your long vacation. Yet I hope the over long schooling of Colorado and Idaho may not be without some pleasure that is genuine. Monroe Wheeler writes that he and Glenway are to remain at least until the autumn, in Villefranche—taking perhaps a short trip to Vienna.

Sincerely yours,

Your "Prayer Beside a Lamp" will appear in the March issue.

To James Sibley Watson   *February 13, 1926*

Dear Doctor Watson:

I am submitting comment to you for the April issue and should be glad of any changes or improvements you might make. May we continue to hope for comment from you for March 15th, for the May issue? Shall I forward you Mr. Bragdon's[6] card of rebuke? I saw the other day, that someone thinks that despite the bizarre poetry we publish, by reason of our publishing Anatole France, *The Dial* is "sacred and apart."

I had read the first six chapters of Miss Gregory's novel before sending it to you and have read the rest only today, and my opinion is modified, but I still think the texture of the writing remarkably fine.

Ellen Thayer and I are summoned tomorrow to meet Mr. Riccius at The Commodore at twelve o'clock. I was greatly cheered by Doctor Freud's evident sanction of our retaining employees at *The Dial*. Perhaps you know of his answer to Ellen's letter of inquiry? in which he said that it would be awkward for her to disregard Scofield's wishes but that it would be unjust to dismiss innocent persons and since there are two directors of *The Dial*, might it not be possible for the other director to frustrate her cousin's

6. Claude Bragdon (1866–1946), architect, art critic, and stage designer.

wishes? He asked particularly that the fact of his reply should be kept a secret.

Sincerely yours,

To James Sibley Watson   *April 12, 1926*

Dear Doctor Watson:

I am enclosing additional manuscripts.

I did deplore and I do, Scofield's letter to the editors. And though I admit that at the time it came, I thought more of the discourtesy to those who were serving him to the utmost than I thought of the bad light that his letter would put him in, even if no one were to think of any word of Scofield's except in light of his own goodness and dignity, we were fully exonerated, I feel, in allowing the letter to be published; because at the time, we were struggling manfully to prevent his turning from the office, nearly the whole staff and thus to prevent a broadcasting of everything that was destructive to him. He was like a child who was striking at parents, friends, and servants and it was to his interest I am sure that we should have received the brunt of his displeasure. And he would not have endured to be thwarted in every direction. Mr. Mitchell in knowing of the letter, knows only the least of our difficulties. Had the letter been our only anxiety, we might have undertaken to persuade Scofield not to publish it. There may be some consolation for us in recalling that when Mr. Mitchell was with Scofield in Bermuda, he might have served Scofield by modifying an acrimonious comment that was written at that time? In thanking Scofield for the Berlin letter, I ventured so far as to say that I regretted that the Sitwells have been so greatly overpraised, and that I regret "also perhaps that they should now be underpraised." It has seemed to me that Scofield did not receive well when he was in America, adverse criticism from me, invariably made in his interest, of things which seemed to me a little egotistical and though I noticed the footnote in question, it did not occur to me that you might see fit to change it. However, perhaps from this on, we ought to take him at his word and if he invites criticism, ought honestly to give it.

I returned the Hamilton and the poem by Kenneth Ellington, the Eliot essay, and George Dillon's story.

(Scofield may object in "First Years," to Mr. [Max] Robin's allusion to the invalids, or to Libau, or there may be something objectionable to him in the fact that Mr. Robin's name coincides with that of the ragged sailor or ragged robin.)

P.S. Ellen received from Scofield on Saturday, a cable in which he says that he is sending "poems and cuts" for the June issue, and today she received a cable correcting the Berlin letter, among which changes there is a modified version of the note about Thomas Mann. He asks also if the note is in good taste, in which he says "If I may risk a personal allusion . . ."

To Scofield Thayer   *[Dial office, 152 West 13th Street, New York]*
May 1, 1926

Dear Scofield:

An issue which nothing could have persuaded me we should ever come to, is that you should wish to put something in *The Dial* that I should oppose your putting in. I have once or twice been frank in admitting that I have not liked things which have appeared in *The Dial*. Upon one occasion when I was asked by you and Miss Gregory to write advertisements for *The Dial*, I could scarcely bring myself to tell you that what stood most in the way, was my dissent from certain things which had appeared in it. To my relief and amazement, you permitted me the confidence that you had not liked them entirely, yourself, and as after that I grew more familiar with your basis of selection, I lost all fear that we should ever disagree in a matter of taste. The present exigency seems to me unbelievable. The question miserably recurrent to me is, why should I be inexorably an obstacle to those whom I am here to serve? Your acquiescence and forbearance—as noted in the cable which has just come—bridging what I cannot surmount, I am pitiably grateful for. Nothing could be more an extravagance than that you have any thought of acting editor in the matter. I am asking you to do this for me and you are doing it precisely as you would do it were my duty but that of tying up the mail. And any kind of printed term that you direct to be used, is powerless to alter the basis upon which we stood when you were here. When you are ready to take back the Editorship, it will be I who am "happy" and justified in being so. But as I am sure I said in my recent letter, I feel that you ought graciously to withhold any such statement as that you are happy in resigning. Propriety and elegance have been characteristic of you and if you are not sorry in resigning, you at least ought not to say so.

With respect to your direction that we "run a dotted line" in the poem, we understand you to mean that we run a real dotted line—not that we insert dots. This is not a question to be answered, unless I am wrong. And the footnote shall be as follows, "Note: Two stanzas have here been omitted." "The Editorship of *The Dial*" shall be substituted for "the office of Editor of *The Dial*."

A proof of your caricature and of the other [Adolf] Dehn drawings, Ellen mailed to you yesterday.

Sincerely yours,   Marianne Moore

To George Saintsbury *May 18, 1926*

Dear Mr. Saintsbury:

If we did not like your Abelard—that is to say your Héloise—I think we should have to stand with the man of whom you say, "recognition of reality is not quite his strongest point." Your unequivocal attitude to the genuine and the spurious is very enlivening, and your distinguishing so firmly between the mystical passion of Saint Theresa and the more human passion of Héloise. We treasure "the impregnable recesses of fantastic memory"— and mention of Leigh Hunt is to me always highly congenial, as is your hypothetically poetic collaborating by Shakespeare and [Michael] Drayton, in "that extraordinary sonnet." What you say of Abelard's Latin verse is to most of us a satisfying pronouncement, and we are grateful for the reading past and present, that most of us have never done.

You have not given us a title and perhaps will suggest one when you send us the proof? We are sending the article to press immediately with a hope of using it in our July issue, although we may be disappointed.

Would it be desirable for us to have, and if so, could you conveniently give us in a foot-note, the publisher and title of the forthcoming book about Abelard of which you speak?

We have followed earnestly and anxiously, your terrible experiences in the May strike[7] and Blake's line[s] have been continually in my mind:

> *"I shall not cease from mental strife*
> *Nor shall my sword sleep in my hand,*
> *Until I see Jerusalem*
> *In England's green and pleasant land."*

I may not be quoting precisely.

Nor until deliverance from the ugly present has come could we ask you to turn from it to *The Victorians.*

A cheque for fifty dollars will go to you in a few days.

Sincerely yours, Marianne Moore Acting Editor

To Monroe Wheeler *14 St. Luke's Place [New York]*
July 18, 1926

Dear Monroe,

Your abounding and multiple goodness to us in the midst of convalescence and society and work (which you don't mention) and the obliterating charm of Europe, touches me so more than words could say, that it is no loss

7. General strike in Britain, May 4–14, 1926.

that I am dumb. The handkerchiefs which came yesterday are the very embodiment of Parisian poetic elegance, the threads are so fine and the typographically exact M's are so the perfection of ordered detail. However ingenious or entertaining colours may be, I cannot quite admit coloured handkerchiefs and the effect of angelic white that these have, does delight one. Since three could be no whiter than one, I ought deeply to reprove you, and the disaster of your probably still unincarcerated *valet de chambre,* seems intolerable. We are accused in America, of wasting string and newspaper, but no one here, I know, would ever be found throwing away the principle and proudest treasure of a lady's wardrobe.

The handkerchief containing the Musée Cluny arrived first—museum and handkerchief reversing appropriate rôles—and in the next mail, came your letter enclosing two other handkerchiefs; the picture of L'Abbaye d'Hautcombe, and the animals. The Cluny was the dearest delight we had in Paris and the place we went oftenest. The Abbaye we have never seen. How beautiful it is in the picture and how glad we are, that you are hearing this glorious music. We are thankful that you *feel* well, but should like to have the feeling corroborated by an adequate weight. I found by the scales in the Houston Street station of the subway a few days ago, that I weigh a little less than a hundred, so I too should like to know what would modify the angles.

I have heard Mr. MacVeagh speak of her, but I have never met Mrs. Robbins. Isn't it strange? What you say of rugged wisps of English ladies is inimitable.

I have just heard from Miss Sergeant of Mr. Winters' and Janet Lewis's marriage. About a year ago, Mr. Winters said he hoped to go abroad in three years; I hope they can both journey over. I have not known of Elizabeth [Madox] Roberts' having tuberculosis. I am so sorry. I hope living in California will restore her. I must send you the July *Dial* which I did speak of sending—in which are the chapter of her novel, William Carlos Williams' "Struggle of Wings" and an editorial "Comment" by Doctor Watson which seems to me very choice.

I have not read, but someday am going to read Mr. Fowler's *Dictionary;* his Comments in the Society for Pure English Tracts are so delightful. (The *Donne's Letters,* to several persons of honor, you and Glenway bought on 4th Avenue and are lending me until your return.)

Perhaps as much as a month ago, your friend Theodore Hatfield called at *The Dial.* He spoke of course delightedly of you and Glenway, said he had just received his doctor's degree, and intended to take a voyage to South America, defraying expenses by acting as table steward.

The animals—first and foremost the snake—are matchless. The composition is interesting but the detail of the eye and scales is unbelievably perfect. The baboons and the white tiger also, are excitingly real.

We are expecting to be in Maine with Warner and his family for part of August.

I don't know how it is that being used to the work at *The Dial* does not aid me to despatch it more rapidly. Every holiday we have had, has been full, from the beginning of the day till the latest ending, with work which I have brought home. And I have not read a book—outside of work—since being at *The Dial*. I am saving the Prodgers[8] and one or two other books for my vacation. Doctor Watson assumes any kind of work or bother I would let him, but I am not willing to undertake work and not do it.

Miss Thayer admires Glenway's poems and Doctor Watson who has not seen them, seems pleased with them from my review.

Mrs. Burke and Mr. Burke have a third daughter, "Frances." Mr. [Edward] Nagle and Mrs. Nagle are in Brittany. Mr. Rosenfeld is spending the summer with the Kreymborgs in Santa Fe. Mr. Cummings has just returned from Paris.

You have all our wishes for health and vigour and for every poetic and enjoyable accessory that Europe can afford.

Affectionately, Marianne

To James Sibley Watson *[Dial office, 152 West 13th Street, New York City]*
March 3, 1927

Dear Doctor Watson:

We were a little late in sending Mr. [Roger] Fry the Bruegel, with which we also sent, on approval, the Demuth. I feel inclined to encourage him to write on anything he proposes, even Ingres. I shall of course wait to reply till I know your wish.

I have been thinking about the manner of protesting against Samuel Roth's unscrupulousness. Miss Yohalem says that a page of Mr. MacVeagh's advertising could be omitted to make room for the protest and Mr. MacVeagh is willing to give up the space if we are positive that it would be safe to publish the protest, but he said he felt that we were being taken advantage of in being asked to publish it—that there is no guarantee that the names which appear were "signatures"—that Miss [Sylvia] Beach, a publisher with no reputation, is trying to make trouble for a rival publisher (who has no reputation) that likely James Joyce received a nominal sum of money and that Mr. Roth could sue us for libel—and lastly that the whole thing was discussed in other magazines in November.

I am sorry I didn't ask you for your final impression of our obligation with regard to the Joyce manuscript. I still feel that the manuscript is bad

8. Perhaps C. H. Prodgers, *Adventures in Bolivia.*

material intrinsically, but I feel also very strongly that your wish in the matter ought to be pre-eminent. If I am obliging you to show me that a perspicacious person would have felt these questions to have been already answered, I will have been most sorry to have brought the matter up again.

If we should publish in the June issue, the [Thomas] Mann pamphlet (or a part of it? We are sending it to you to Rochester) might it be well to publish in the same issue, a review of the Knopf translation of [Mann's] *Der Zauberberg*? In the possibility of our getting Osbert Burdett to review it, should we be justified in cabling Osbert Burdett?

When we next send manuscripts I shall send *The Dial* clippings of which we were speaking.

M. M.

To James Sibley Watson   *March 10, 1927*

Dear Doctor Watson:

In the letter with which you returned Mr. Cummings' play and other manuscripts, you make it plain I think, by your emphasis on "protest," that the decision with regard to the Joyce manuscript is open, so I have read it again and recognize in it, literary ability that I had missed; but surely it lacks what originality and distinction parts of the longer manuscript had; and in so far as readers will be able to catch the author's meaning, we should be discredited I think. We have elected to exclude obscenity when it was dull, and even the advance guard couldn't think that we consider this piece brilliant. You permitted me to oppose Scofield when he fell below what we felt to be his own standard; so for us to like this would be exceedingly grievous to him, the more that he resists Joyce's present method. When Mr. Joyce has written what would make a magazine illustrious and yet chooses to coerce us, showing even for an author, exaggerated unconcern in the matter of reciprocal consideration,—we refraining from self interested requests— our position is, I feel, the more judicial, our liberty being emphasized by the fact that he is no longer in financial straits. Private publication could take what risks courage would recommend, but remembering that I felt detached from *The Dial* by certain juxtapositions of material when I was a subscriber to it, and sometimes a contributor, I am aware of the way the content of the magazine might affect some of our contributors and readers. An irrelevant consideration that irritates me, is that James Joyce possibly & Lewis Galantière surely, I think, will feel that we are being hoodwinked for despite Mr. G.'s insistence that it isn't, this book looks to me like an exception. To argue against taking the article seems contradictory to my assertion that your wish was to decide the matter. My reason for writing is that you may know specifically what has influenced me. I am honest in offering to put the article into *The Dial* if your wish to do so remains unchanged.

To James Sibley Watson   *14 St. Luke's Place, New York City*
May 10, 1927

Dear Doctor Watson:

Dial business accumulates so fast that I am always apologetic in mind when writing you although there is no use being apologetic for what is inevitable. But I do feel that apology is due when I write as today on business purely my own. When the possibility of my going to England arose, I felt no definite measure toward going could be taken till I had a promise from Mr. Burke that he would be responsible for such editorial letter-writing as you cared to have him do, for weeding the manuscripts, and forwarding matters of importance to you, but we find that passage can be reserved no longer. Nothing can be had for June. So we have bought passage for May 26th. We can of course forfeit the reservation and I should rather do it than have my work unprovided for. There is a possibility Mr. Burke thinks, of his being able to come the first week in June, but he will not know definitely till about the 26th. I should like with your approval, to pay Miss Sharp for keeping my work up until Mr. Burke arrives, forwarding urgent manuscripts to you, allowing others to accumulate—but returning obviously inappropriate ones. I have given her many form letters and she knows besides, surprisingly well, the attitude I should probably have, toward the usual enquirer. She also would let nothing slip that ought to be presented to you. The matter has been full of anxiety to me because Ellen, though most happy in her own work, would enjoy doing my work more than she enjoys her own and it has been a real hardship to me to be deliberate not only in suggesting but in openly planning that what I leave behind shall be divided between Miss Sharp and Mr. Burke. (Perhaps I need not say that the real difficulty is a not sufficiently protective and intuitive judgment—a telephone message when a record in writing would be helpful, and a failure to perceive the danger points in dealing for instance with such people as Mr. Santayana.) I said to Ellen a few days ago when I first spoke in the office of the possibility of my being away—that last summer Mr. Burke was so overburdened in having for two or three weeks, both her work and mine to attend to and that I should not be willing to have her do that same thing this year; and fortunately this argument was somewhat satisfactory.

Another matter. This you may feel borders on the meddlesome, but it is so important that I am willing to be open to blame. I wish to make the request of Mr. MacVeagh that no one be dismissed from the staff without presenting the case to you in good season. You might be surprised to know the strength which Miss Hatch and Miss Yohalem are to *The Dial*. I admit that under injustice, Miss Hatch speaks a little freely. After having been left alone in the business office for an afternoon, when asked if she got along all right, she answered that "it was not the first time she had been alone in the office;" and another time when Mrs. MacMillan said in justification of a long absence that she had been attending to some business for her husband, Miss Hatch said, "I'd like to go uptown too, and do an errand for *my* husband." Last summer when I returned I found that Henry had been discharged—without apparent reason. Miss Yohalem would have gone abroad last summer but for the intimation that if she did so she needn't return—though Mr. MacVeagh I think values her more than he does anyone else. So unless you advise me to have nothing to do with the matter, I shall ask Mr. MacVeagh to permit no dismissals without consulting you. Please destroy this and do not trouble to answer it unless you have certain remonstrances to make.

Sincerely yours,

To John Warner Moore   *R.M.S. Coronia*   *July 31 [1927]*

Dear Badger,

(Lest I be thwacked, had I better not write something! to accompany Mice's faithful chronicle.) Poor Mice says, "I wish the boat would go the other way. It seems the same as it did before but instead of going it is coming *back*."

Our visit to The White Nose was a thing we shall never forget; and want not to forget. The house is the embodiment of poetic scholarly seclusion. A lion's skull rests on either side of the book case in the dining room. Flowers and fruit in profusion on the side board, and the china & silver are dainty and elegant and indigenous. Llewelyn [Powys]'s crest is a lion's paw holding a sceptre or mace and this device is on the dinner service (red & white) and on the flat end of the handle of each knife and fork—the work handle being ended with silver, like a walking-stick. Upstairs is a grate fire of peat or coal. There are 3 arm chairs & a sofa, a writing desk a cat & kitten—the most companionable kits I ever saw (both buff tigers). In Alyse's bedroom is a writing table with purple felt cover and a book case & beautiful engravings a kind of seagull-grey-&-black one of a chalk cliff cove that looks like a whale's gill—(Lullworth cove) framed with gold-&-black border. There are figured pink flowered curtains lined with blue at the window & in L.'s bedroom is a pale blue silk brocade down comfort (probably hers) on the bed, & a tray, shaving glass & stand, with a candle. We had each a wicker hamper padded with cotton quilting in which is a galvanized can of hot water that stays boiling hot all night. L. took me to see foolish guillemots & puffins & young seagulls, ravens possibly & possibly a fox, all of which disappointed him but the young gulls (but we found a young kestrel hawk in the path). We were right above the sea which stretched in a kind of primeval panorama for miles in a great curve as far as you could see. He showed me a beach and an iron stake driven in the cliff by smugglers in a tiny vertical chained path up the cliff and a beach cut off by a steep chalk cliff at either side so no one can land on it & we were above another which could be reached by climbing down a chain. We were on bat's head and beyond was Swyre Head & beyond that, the Durdle door. The vegetation on the cliff head close to the edge is a close tough, interlacing needle moss or grass like the felt on a billiard table & further back is longer grass, full of wildflowers, thistles, furze etc. L. pointed out many butterflies & plants, a golden fritillary, a marble white butterfly, wild thyme which I enclose and should be pressed & crushed (as it smells very savoury) ploughman's spikeward, rest harrow, vipers bugloss—pronounced bue-gloss—yarrow, pyramid orchises, scabiosa (i.e. an exquisite pale blue fringed daisy like thing) harebells and much else. Llewelyn said he did admire my review of *The Verdict of Bridlegoose*—more than any attack ever made upon him, that he said to himself as he read it, "From what new & unseen source has this deadly blow been dealt me, by a rapier of Toledo steel?" He spoke admiringly of Scofield & of Dr. Watson—dislikes Mrs. Watson because she was "teased" as he said by Judge Bridlegoose. I called her he said, "my resplendent hostess" & she said—"we've been doing things together for months & that's all he could say about me." "She is that curious phenomenon" he said, "a philistine with a mania for art. But Dr. Watson is talented. *Whudda charming chap* he IS!"

Alyse consented (after a terrible battle) to give us her ex comment as a review & Llewelyn was the perfection of chivalry in withdrawing, if we wished him to, the Maupassant.

At Cambridge the item of greatest importance was Milton's mulberry tree the large branches supported by poles. It is on a mound but was once on the level; and is full of mulberries (green as yet). The garden[er] said when we hoped it would live on, "It may get a new lease of life from the mound." Queens' College with half timbered plaster & brick is matchless with a tiny court in which is Erasmus' tower. We also were amazed at King's Chapel full of hounds & dragons rampant. Llewelyn says a rampant hound in heraldry is a talbard and a winged dragon is a wyvern (pronounced "wivvern").

w. love,   Rat

The King's picture is very pleasing—nicer than I could have imagined. How did you know how to get one & in what way inform them that you wanted it. We shall save it for you. The letter you thot might not get to the boat was waiting for us here (a tuppence-halfpenny owing upon it). Willow wondered compassionately if you could have been "in the hole" to that amount. The telegram was a profound surprise and very cheering to us for we had suffered certain severities in our departure—from Dorchester. The pictures of Oslo are certainly "cute." I wish you could have seen the yachts at the Isle of Wight (Cowes!).[9]

Rat

The vine is thyme & the stiffish stalk is marjoram. (Smell them.)

To T. S. Eliot *[Dial office, 152 West 13th Street, New York]*
August 10, 1927

Dear Mr. Eliot:

When it would be a satisfaction to us to have you speak not only personally but on behalf of *The Dial* upon any subject upon which we could induce you to express opinion, it seems contradictory that we should not feel it to be *The Dial*'s necessity to protest against Mr. Roth's indecorums. However, since your letter will appear in a number of magazines in America, it may be that you were merely not definitely omitting *The Dial*, a thought for which of course we are grateful.

Upon my return recently from England it was a very signal enjoyment to read the review of Edmund Blunden's [*On the Poems of Henry*] *Vaughan*, which you have sent us. To be "excessively harsh" is not to me as perhaps it is not to you, emotionally congenial, but the invigoration one experiences from a reasoned, uncoerced diagnosis of poetry, such as, "The Silurist," is rare and is most to be desired.

My lodgings while in London—my mother's and mine—were but a few doors from *The New* [*sic*] *Criterion* and many times I was tempted to call, with a hope of persuading you to write for *The Dial* the article on poetry which we have been hoping you might care to give us. However, a request is more easily considered when received in writing, and knowing besides that many unjustifiable calls are made by visiting Americans I was able to resist the impulse to add to them another.

I have thought you might be interested in writing upon Crashaw's *Poetical Works*, edited by L. C. Martin and published by the Oxford Press. May we send it to you to examine? Also, should you be willing to look at the *Selected Letters of Baron von Hügel* (1896–1924): Edited with a Memoir by Bernard Holland? I have myself had an interest in Baron von Hügel, though I have not seen this particular volume.

Sincerely yours   Marianne Moore

9. A seaport on the northern coast of the Isle of Wight.

To John Warner Moore   *[14 St. Luke's Place, New York]*
Jan[uary] 22, 1928

Dear Badger,

We read with great interest your table of moneys. I am glad you are getting some good of the 300 dollars. Mouse & I are certainly "getting something out of" the hundreds milked into the pail with such regularity night & morning. I am glad Constance thinks of letting Vevey be the family's headquarters. The idea of not getting genuine cow's milk is monstrous. Monroe has not expatiated on that peculiarity of Villefranche nor on the snow on the palm trees but he did say there is not running water in the house. Have you come on a Miss Clemence Raymond at La Colline? A subscription to *The Dial* as a gift was sent her by Theo. Chanler & refunded him by her since she was already subscribing.

When you see the Jan. 22 *Herald T.* be sure you look at Ford M. Ford's article on Hardy. Not since Scofield insisted on my writing the Williams announcement last Jan. have I been in trouble so deep as with the Hardy comment & though we got done with it Sunday—a week ago—around this time (4 o'clock) the whole week following was a rolling up-hill of casks containing old old bear's grease, & dead clams, & unpurified debris of editorial crab shells. I don't know what sickness infected the office. I made mistakes myself and every single editorial proposal or request concerning press work presented superhuman & insuperable difficulties. My March comment soured on me & had to be half re-written although already set up—& when "handed in" Ellen said "You've cut so much more than you replace that it will be 2 pages now instead of 3. I have remeasured it & it is just two," knowing that that would ruin the make-up & that I would have to write more. "I counted the words" I said, "last night & it comes to 2 pages & 6 lines if we let the first ¶ stand alone on the first page. I'm sorry it's not more than that, but that's enough & I wouldn't mind having the last page blank if we *had* cut it to two for a blank page next the advertisements looks very well." Ellen patiently re-measured & said, "yes—well. I guess that's all right." That was a sample of the whole week. I had also "pigheadedly" selected for reproduction a lady-slipper of Bertram Hartman's instead of a giant near nude bather & many other things were open to discussion. The monthly announcement which I got wrong had not yet been run off due to the delay with the comment so that's all right. And though Ellen remarked that Mr. Hartman's drawing seemed poor—that it didn't "seem to have much reason for being" I said, "well, send him a proof, and if he protests against publishing it, we'll hear it now rather than when the thing's printed. We could even withhold it and not have a plate made. I'd be glad to pay for the proof, rather than have him disappointed. But don't let him know we are doubtful of it." So Ellen wrote him, "we enclose a proof. If you find it disappointing please let us know and we shall not print it. We are sorry it is not just to the original but we hope you will approve of it" or something like that—3 or 4 times as long. Miss Sharp by accident gave me the letter with my letter & I thought Ellen had submitted it to me. I hurried downstairs, & said contritely but imploringly "Ellen would you mind writing another letter? etc" Ellen said "No, but how did you see it?" I said "Why I thought you sent it up to me?" No she said "I didn't but I'm glad you saw [it] if you think it isn't right. But won't *you* write it. I might say something else wrong." No I said, "You write it. Just tell him we enclose proof and will he kindly tell us how to designate it—a drawing or a lady-slipper." If he is displeased he'll tell us without our asking if he is.

So yesterday when all but me had gone, he came in glowing with excitement & enthusiasm. Said "the proof's splendid; I had no idea it would come out so well, & Mrs. Hartman feels the same way about it. Would you try a reproduction of the Jack-in-the-pulpit? I brought it along and I think the 2 would make a nice pair. It was your idea you know. I think it would be a nice effect." etc. I had asked for the Jack but he said it wouldn't reproduce well. So I can tell Ellen of this tomorrow. *Then* Alyse invited Ellen & Miss Nagel to tea Friday but Ellen was "injured" because so many weeks have passed without being invited & she & Miss Nagel refused. Ellen didn't say so in so many words but said she declined partly out of consideration for Miss Gregory—that they have so many engagements and she thought it would conserve her strength—and also she feels cold-hearted towards her for coming up to my palm-tree to see me instead of into the 2nd floor office. Another thing, I left the office Friday morning to take Miss Hatch to visit the city & country school which Frank attends and Ellen can't forgive *any* one for snooping at Frank's school—let alone Miss *Hatch*! "Of all persons!" said Ellen, "what would *she* want to go for?" in Nov. when I attempted to go. So Friday we sneaked away & I said on leaving, if Miss Gregory brings her review, don't urge her to stay till I get back" etc. Ellen said "Is she coming to your room? She would probably go up to your room & I wouldn't even know she's here." So that general pleasantry prevailed. I was so feather-besnooted from all the suspicion, carping & hostility of the morning "work," that I decided to go to the movies Friday afternoon to see C. Chaplin in the circus. It was a wonderful show—marvellous, with a lion-cage scene & tight-rope incidents and a mirror maze and I thoroughly enjoyed myself. Mouse & Anna were "cleaning" when I left & when I got back Anna was gone but who should be sitting in the willow-chair but Ellen. Mole had the candles lit & the room in order but why was Ellen here? Miss Gregory's review had come & she thought I would like to read it & the closing quotation read "the infirmity of noble mind" the s on mind having been scratched out by Miss Gregory, & should it go to press mind or minds? I said it had been deleted with the utmost precision so let it be "mind." After she went Mice found it (it's in Milton) "infirmity of noble *mind*."

Well Sat. morning another injustice. Stewart Mitchell had written in a letter with his review that he sent his very best regards to me & to Dr. Watson & signed the letter "Ever your friend." I thought I would keep it from Ellen so threw it on my desk, easy and said there's nothing special in the note that was with it but if you feel like reading it do. "I *always* want to see what comes," said Ellen & then looked very black & turned from it coldly. So when Raymond Mortimer's letter came, I said to Mouse "I think I won't show this," but [as] it said "I give you *absolute* discretion with regard to spelling, punctuation, etc." I felt I must. He said "Dear Miss Moore, I am a shocking fellow. If you were only here to knock at my door or ring at my telephone, you would find me the most punctual of contributors" etc. Ellen gave me a long, steady, inimical look & said "the London Letter will hold us up; we couldn't possibly get his proof before the 15th. Do you want to tell him we can't send proof?" "No" I said. "Better send it & then if there's not time, let him cable changes or we can apologize later for not having been able to make corrections." Well, I hope these matters are over with. It's not very interesting either, & dwelling on it makes it worse. All made worse by "us" inviting Miss Wallach & Tippy her dog to tea for tomorrow afternoon. But one ought to think of the source of it—Ellen's pent-house spirit & craving for the several bunches of bagged grapes that I seem unlawfully to preempt & no real happiness at anytime from anything.

Aff'ly   Rat

I was reading to Mouse from [Apuleius'] *The Golden Ass* yesterday this part about the jugglers at Athens. "I saw . . . a juggler that swallowed up a knight's sword with [a] very keen edge, & by & by, for a little money that we that looked on gave him, he devoured a hunting-spear with the point downward; and over the blade of the spear, when the haft of the spear turned down, rose through the throat & there appeared on it, . . . a fair boy pleasant & nimble, winding & turning himself in such sort that you would suppose that he had neither bone nor gristle, & verily think he was the natural serpent creeping & sliding where the twigs are cut off on the knotted staff of rough wood which the god of medicine is wont to bear." (How is that?)

Tippy the Irish terrier is the one whose potential puppy Miss Wallach offered me (although there was a ban on pups).

To John Warner Moore   *[March 15, 1928]*

J. W. Badger N.S.N. K.C.G. (Knight Commander of the Gazelles)
Dear Badger,

I consider your trip to Egypt of the utmost importance—mainly by reason of the gazelles, in which unwittingly you were no doubt observing certain antelopes or "impala deer" that can leap 20 or 30 yards at a bound or when at rest can sit up and eat leaves from a tree overhead, like a stick-insect. Many is the time I have seen them—(rare though they are) leaping pampas grass or young thorn trees—in the movies—skimming away in a flock like chippies or sandpipers.

Badger at the Pyramids—and on the Nile and "worshipping the crocodile"! Willow says you certainly could command an audience when you get back. Just let him know when you certainly expect to touch port & he will arrange matters with the Pond lecture bureau. Have you been among camels? Do they seem "reasonable"? Have you seen any domesticated elephants? besides your experiences at the zoo? I suppose the hippos were not mean enough to stay under water till every several watcher had paid over something & that some who spent nothing profited along with those who spent. I understand that Egypt "needs rain" perpetually. Have you seen any mongeese or seen asps anywhere? ("Better let them things alone," Willow remarked.)

Well, Mole wrote you about anything and everything of importance I infer, from a letter I saw yesterday to which I believe she had devoted paws & mind morning before last. She is working—off & on—at her alpaca dress and billy-goated me into inviting Miss Sergeant to tea for tomorrow. And I have called on Lola [Ridge] twice, and persuaded Alyse to go to Doctor Thorburn. She is to go Tuesday. Mr. Riccius called at the office yesterday for an hour or so & seems an Ishmael among Ishmaels. He vehemently denounced Mr. MacVeagh for selfishly & unlawfully milking Scofield; said Scofield was bored with him (Mr. Riccius) and eulogized Mrs. Thayer. He said no one could have been wiser or more intelligent; (in her care of Scofield). Since Ellen had been told by Miss Gregory that Mrs. Thayer feels she (Mrs. T.) threw Scofield into a relapse by saying he wasn't presentable enough to see people and that he oughtn't to come to town for fear he [would] be kidnapped, Ellen listened frowning and said she thought Scofield would improve if apart from his mother; but didn't tell what Miss Gregory had told her. Afterward she said to me, "Of course Aunt Florence may tell him. If she would confide in Miss *Gregory*, she might of course confide in *him*. But she has not been frank with me. She told me she was *afraid* Scofield would be kidnapped, she didn't tell me she told *him* she was afraid he would be kidnapped. I suppose she was afraid I would condemn her." I said "Well, even if Scofield won't see Mr. Riccius, the visit will do

Mrs. Thayer good." "I think it may be very bad for her" said Ellen. "Everyone praises her. She is entirely self-satisfied. She said, 'Mariposa Taylor said to me "Florence, I don't see how you keep well. You must be *very* strong." and I said, "I'm not strong. It's my spirit; I won't give in," and she said, "I think your spirit is wonderful. No one in the world would do for Scofield what you are doing."'"

Don't forget to send us any bulletin of information you compile and don't stint yourself in expenditure in those hot dusty countries. It don't pay. Don't buy things—unless it be cards. I have been too busy to go to the library regularly but this week I got Mouse some copies of *Punch* & of *The Ill[ustrated] [London] News* and she has been buzzing around them—and around me ever since. Spent an entire evening on 6 magazines I understand. Mr. Burke took me to the Philharmonic Thursday night—and exerted himself to be hospitable—urging me to have hot chocolate & endeavoring to find a window on 57th Street where they had real yachts in the window. When I got home Mouse was "reading the news."

Today I read her the life of *Annie Besant* by Geoffrey West and Mouse used her growing powers to read from it to me—a very impressive and curious story of a transition from Episcopalianism to Atheism to Theosophy. I don't know whether it would be good for your mouse to read it or not. Anyway I read it to her.

Mouse caught and cooked a chicken yesterday and dyed a dickey for her new alpaca dress, and at a late hour we climbed into the hay. We paid our income tax—$9.00—this week, finished the Comment, I wrote 3 briefer mentions and had several tedious interviews.

Aff'ly,   Rat

To John Warner Moore   *May 4, 1928*

My Dear Badger; (Ahem:)

Micey is supposed to be taking care of me, and such mouse-caperings and running high jumps as it indulges in, landing on me and circling me;[10] it makes me think of the little gray & white bulldog they have in the circus again this year. He escapes from the clown and runs along a strip of carpet and takes the corner of the rug in his teeth and rolls it back over him, like a golf bag. He is picked up and spanked and immediately runs to the other end of the carpet & does the same thing, rolling up swiftly in the carpet & is spanked. The poor Mouse is *now*, however, unloading a box of wood Mr. Kelley sent over by Walter, & is also stowing away a kind of separate wood-pile.

---

10. MM bracketed the whole first page and added the note "italics for my whole letter."

Mouse first wrote a letter returning my ticket to *Keep Shuffling*—requesting the money.[11] Willow said, "I always thought I'd like to have a mouse secretary—neat, knowing little creatures, they are—and not common." (meaning *usual*)

I believe Mouse told you about Doctor Heckler's trained fleas. Well I got her so interested in them she almost wanted to see them, & asked me a thousand questions—for instance, could I see them or had you to use opera-glasses, how large was the merry-go-round & how large were the vehicles drawn, what was the flea-hotel like, & so on. Doctor Heckler says fleas cannot communicate disease because "fleas do not ail."

In the same place, Hubert's Museum, they have a carriage—, claret-coloured chaise, possibly—which belonged to Fred'k the Great & to the Ex-Kaiser—got through a Pole, who let it be sold at public auction as unclaimed German property. It has two coats of arms enamelled on the door & body of the vehicle, has enormous carriage lamps & coachman's rug of navy blue, & large s-shaped springs, fore & aft, ending in swans' heads.

I am going to stay home today & tomorrow to see if I can get my throat cured, & then be more "careful." Paul Rosenfeld called at 12, Wednesday & stayed till 2. Ellen came in to speak to him and to say she was just hurrying to lunch. The whole matter reminded me a little of the begrudged chicken lunch you acquired, for at two just after Paul departed—indeed she saw him going away—Ellen came back, (in a new dress black with a large yellow spot at intervals, new black suede shoes & Miss Nagel's large string of round amber beads, and a neat little black hat). The dress is short, light & "smart"—got at Abercrombie's because I go there. She said, "I know you would have got out of it; but I am going to a concert with Mr Riccius!" Nothing of this had been intimated though the day before I asked after Mr Riccius. "That's very nice" I said, "I hope you will enjoy it. Mr. Rosenfeld wanted permission to reprint his *Dial* essays and I said of course that he could." "He stayed long enough," said Ellen. "I'm sure he enjoyed it." When she first spoke to him before leaving for lunch another little matter amused me. She said "Do you still have lunch at the tea room at Irving Place Mr. Rosenfeld?" "Yes" he said, "& dinner too. What did you think of [Theodore Fay's] *The Hoboken Blues*? Did you like it better than *The Belt*?" "No" said Ellen, "I didn't like it." "I liked it best," he said. "But *The Big Stick* was even better." "I didn't go to that" Ellen said. "Hildegarde went, & liked it." "What did you think of the [Leonid] Andreyev?" continued Paul. "Perfectly stunning I thought," said Ellen,—"really marvellous." When Ellen left, he said "The Playwright Theatre at Irving Place has been giving experiments this winter. Some of them have been very good." "Is the Andreyev one of them?" I asked. "No" he said "that's at the Cherry Lane Theatre—next

11. MM crossed out *Shuffle Along*, the correct title of this play by Flourney Miller and Aubrey Lyles.

door to you." I said, "Should I go to it?" "No" he said, "I didn't care for it. The settings are beautiful but it's dull & the seats are wood & pitch forward so that you get very tired trying to keep from falling on the people in front of you." Miss Sharp & I have been trying to figure out all winter what Ellen does at Irving Place. Sometimes she will say, "Miss Thayer had an errand at Irving Place. I don't know what she went for." Or "there's a little cafeteria at Irving Place that Miss Thayer likes to go to." I said, "way over there? Too inconvenient." "Well," Miss Sharp would say, "she seems to like it."

Paul ast me to dinner with him & Edmund Wilson. I said "Edmund Wilson & I were locked in mortal combat & that he seemed to think *The Dial* needed discipline, speaking harshly of it on every occasion but that I accepted that as a token of respect & was extremely grateful to him for caring about us so much." Paul laughed merrily. I said I'd be glad to see Mr. Wilson, however, that I had nothing against him, & that everybody at *The Dial* liked him. He said he would arrange it phoning in a day or two. I told him to phone me to my home & gave the number. He gave me *his* number & said he lived at 77 Irving Place but had taken *his* name out of the book too. We then discussed Mr. Cummings' play which Paul was to see that night. I said I didn't care for Mr. Cummings' idea of life & especially of marriage—and for that matter, for other people's idea of it. It just seemed to be a question of which could get the jointly acquired loot from the other without being shot or blackmailed. He shook his head & said, "I don't see how you ever escaped." Do you think (apropos of society)? etc. "Well," I said "those were deep questions. I didn't know what I think." As I said to Mole, Paul sat there meditatively asking me questions as if he were Buddha & I Socrates.

Mole said "when he telephones just tell [him] you aren't able. You'll have to let him know when you are fit for a party." He hasn't phoned but we now plan to have him & Bunny [Edmund] Wilson here for tea when I can "handle" them better.

Rat (aff'ly as always)[12]

That note about coon-bread from Soriano is awfully cute.[13]

I guess I ought to be getting back that letter of Mice's about presents soon. If not I'll start hollering. (Not about presents for *Willow* but about the idea of presents, Xmas and so forth.)

12. Throughout the correspondence of this period, JWM and MM carried on a playful banter about her disrespectful use of abbreviations.

13. JWM included with his April 9, 1928, letter a note from "Soriano" saying "Ship cook has given this Coon bread for you Sir"; he had found the note and warm bread on his desk that morning. JWM frequently wrote of his alliance with the kitchen staff.

To John Warner Moore   *July 29, 1928*

Dear Badger,

Micey is fleaing me and I take pen in hand to tell you that I am very glad you got the "sea-glasses," & that you have seen Amsterdam. The pictures are very impressive. I did not know the place was so notable for art works. I thought Antwerp was the select city for such things. How I wonder did it come to be so hot on the way. Mr. Saintsbury says England is hotter, I think, than he has ever known it; and it has not been cold here. Today however is an ideal summer day, clear, bright, & windy. It cooled off in the night (without any storm however). Very strange.

I I put a few cards & pictures in my post-card book this morning, that have been mixed in with the others. Mice raised a terrible howl and said "if that isn't a pineapple snake between a badger's hind legs!"[14] I ran out of the house at the ball players, too, the third time a ball hit the window sill & got the ball, & beckoned the ball player over & reasoned with him. I guess that bee picture came to the right doghouse.

This week in the office has been a kind of rally day, devoid of prohibition; all incumbents feeling at liberty to play gad-bee & green fly. I have been negotiating for a "Russian Letter"—trying to adopt, that is, a ms. offered by a worthless footpad who has been in Russia & said his piece could be "cut" if desired. I went over the article & submitted changes. (It took Mice & me an afternoon I think.) We were to go to press the next day but thought we could delay. We didn't hear for a week as he had "moved" (to New Jersey). He then returned the piece with half my stipulations erased & 2 pages of hopeless balderdash *added*, and none of the pages copied. So Friday Mice & I strove with it & I got it copied & a letter written him by 11 Friday night telling him to telegraph if he wishes to withdraw the article. It remains to be seen, on Monday, what he will do. (The reason I was in such a fever over it is, that Scofield forbade us to publish 2 foreign letters in one issue unless we had a 3rd in hand for the next issue & in the August issue I risked doing it—as a Paris Letter was already due & I had written 2 special letters saying we expected it by July first. Then, we had 4 visitors at the office Louis Zukofsky, a kind of bohemian tick, & George Dillon, & Charles Norman, and an old rackarhinus, Edward Goldbeck, and Miss Sharp Tuesday night at home & Monroe, Monday.) I am revising a 19-page translation & a 20-page story, copying an article by Mr. Saintsbury, and so on; and I am learning to operate the switchboard as Miss Hatch will have to be alone

14. On April 16, 1928, JWM wrote at length about how dangerous pineapple snakes were, and the animal became a part of the family menagerie for a while. On July 1, for example, MM sketched "Badger, trembling, after having crossed the path of a pineapple snake."

with it for 3 weeks otherwise. We could hire an ousel for an hour a day but I wish "personally" to be able to operate the board.

The Beaver came Wednesday and is a revelation in courage and high principle, and she feels deserted and worked against by the family for they are all against the mountain, fore-legs braced.[15] She told us in detail about this last crisis at the mountain & the funeral and the behavior of the various friends. We had not sent flowers or felt it possible to go but she seems not to misunderstand. Mouse was brave, also tactful, in telling her she ought to face the matter of the mountain fairly. Did she need so large a house and could she take care of it always without depriving others of income, and Mice made it clear that she don't herself like living in the woods.

Miss Yohalem suggested Friday morning our "giving" Miss Sharp something. I agreed & as Miss Sharp had said that very morning that she liked the silver paper knife we gave Miss Yohalem for a wedding present, better than any gift she ever saw, we got a handmade paper knife at Jansen's & Miss Yohalem wrote all names on a card & the knife was presented (in my absence)—in the afternoon. In saying goodbye in the morning, I was (as I read in *Punch*) like a child trying to drop a piece of fly paper in high wind; Miss Sharp obviously repented her plan to leave, and kept asking if there was *any*thing she could do for me. I with the Russian calf's brains before me—& pencil in hand—could only say, "No, I think not. You must dismiss anxiety now & leave as comfortably as possible. Tha's all." Now, leave us know or cable an address to which we can write you August 15 or 17.

Rat

Your data about Amsterdam is very fine.

What Mice says is all very true about seeing the places you describe. But that pineapple snake being detained I would want to *see* for a moment or see a photo of a little rather than a drawing.

To John Warner Moore   *Jan[uary] 27, 1929*

Dear Badger,

As Mouse wrote you, Doctor Watson says Mrs. Thayer & Mr. Riccius feel we ought to give *The Dial* up and would be glad if we could stop with the May issue. I said very well, and by all means let us plan it carefully so we shouldn't disappoint people & end shabbily. He approved, but said not to do anything about stopping till he saw Mrs. Thayer again, and Scofield's doctor; for possibly they would feel it unwise to worry Scofield by stopping; but he didn't know.

15. "The mountain" refers to Mary Norcross's house at Sterrett's Gap.

Pompey [a cat], Willow, Mouse & I have had a conference about it and have about decided that after a little recuperation from present strain & anxiety, I had better go back to the library again. Miss Leonard said something about perhaps raising my salary if I would stay—at the time I went to *The Dial*; and it is possible that instead of 50 a month I could have 55 or 60, but even at my old rate of "earnings," I think the library would be preferable to some other kind of work that would disrupt our leisure more and impose work in free time. As I said to Mouse, the apparent disparity between $2,600 & 720 or 600 is not so appalling when you realize that at present, we work every afternoon & evening without a pause and in the library I worked exactly half a day—(with books to review extra). I suppose if I went back, I'd be given all the books to review, and would be asked advice about every kind of book and writer and I might tire of Miss Carleton, now as before. But I think we would have time and privacy so much greater than anything we've known since I was there, that it would pay us. Anyhow, I don't dread it and as I said to Mole, if I hadn't been forced to go to *The Dial*, I would have been in the library all this time.

I tire under the offensive visits and parasiticism [*sic*] of certain pumpkin-bugs and you know how genteel certain other relationships are! But I'll be glad to keep on if Doctor Watson favours doing it and the others permit him. Things seem to have shaken down, and the writing public respects us and we do a great deal of good, despite leakage of money & strength to innumerable bums. I feel sure you will be back of these ruminations & preparations however discouraging things appear. Doctor Watson shut the doors carefully when laying the matters before me and Ellen merely said when I came out, "I'm sure it was a great satisfaction to you to ask Doctor Watson questions you've had in mind." I said, "Yes. It was. He seemed to understand our difficulties with the announcing and other matters and was exceedingly hearty about everything."

Mouse got me a coat the other day for $95.00, with beaver fur on the collar. It is a pinkish tweed and was said to be $150. It looks very simple and "informal" though—as if Bee or Johnnie might wear it. Mole worked on it about 4 nights & afternoons making it short and cutting thick stuff from under the seams, & fixing the buttons, and so on. I hope it will prove worth it.

Mouse saw in *The World* this morning the following news note:

"The scales rose, quivered, hesitated, and finally held firm at 22 and three quarters pounds . . . James had gained nearly 6 pounds in less than three months," (a young gorilla)—"the zoo's darling as he is today."

Micey has written you in full and I will continue later—when you have read these few remarks.

(Mice is very belligerent about money just now & says, "It's what we waste I would deplore, *only*.") Willow walled up his eyes at this and said he usually priced his nuts etc. before deciding what to order. Mr. Hunger had a man in today, to refute Dr. Barnes & then added a little, "because of this reason," "we must cling to our faith so we will have a faith to cling to," and so on.

Rat

To John Warner Moore　　*Feb[ruary] 24, 1929*

Dear Badger,

I wish you did not have to start work here until the fall; even so, I would feel apprehensive about it. I think some rigid plan should be worked out whereby you need not go *every* day back & forth between Bklyn & Crestwood. This, however, must be left to you. (I don't know what I'd do if *The Dial* were not convenient to us here; a third of the strain is saved by such a circumstance.)

Dr. Watson said in a recent letter he might be in N.Y. about Friday (Washington's birthday) and I larruped myself into going to the office, though thinking that when he realized it was a holiday, he would come Saturday. He was very kind and inclined to keep things going longer if we could *know* that *The Dial* benefits Scofield or provides him refuge when he emerges from solitude; but he seemed to feel that we have to artificially propel things that Scofield would innately enjoy propelling, & he seemed solicitous about my working all the time in an often adverse atmosphere. I said I had at times wished I needn't be in the office anymore, but that actually I preferred to go on than to stop & would only stop because it had come to be *necessary* to stop. He said, "But there would be compensations." However, he thought we might proceed even blindly rather than be violent toward Scofield & I respect him deeply, realizing that he has been non-interested personally for years & would have no compensation but the approval of conscience for persevering; for no one regards his sacrifices or thanks him for exerting himself. I told him to give us warning if possible, but that if he couldn't, no grudge would be felt. I think if Scofield were on the spot and entertainingly active in his machinations, as formerly, that Doc would consent to help him; but I feel very firmly that having done our most, if Scofield must be absent we'd better stop & suffer no selfish regrets in the matter. And you must not marshall pecuniary supplements of all kinds. As Mice says, we lived safely & enjoyably & had our upper bedrooms before I quit the library, & the pleasures we would have in leisurely home life would be so great one durst not contemplate them unless they be certain as a reality.

You will be delighted to know that the talked-of apartment is to be built from one beyond the Mayor's house to Mr. Smith's house, that is from 7 to 11 inclusive—rather than to include us. Perhaps the beelzebubs who are building there will desire to build here, but there is no talk of it yet.

We had tea, or rather supper, at Mary Watson [Craig]'s on Friday on 11th Street & she & Sue [Craig] were marvellously generous & affectionate toward us. I couldn't say how warm my feeling is towards them.

Would you care to have your bed bugged with a Hoover appliance? If so, we will buy one & go over every tuft & dimple. Hand labour however, is out of the question.

*Yrs,** Rat

*respectfully [MM draws an arrow pointing to the asterisk and writes:] (a star, not a bug.)

I said to Mice "Suppose it weighs too much & doesn't get to fly?" "I weighed the paper first," said Mice & in addition am going to have it weighed at the drug-store.

To Ezra Pound   *March 8, 1929*

Dear Mr. Pound:

We now have the [Boris] de Schloezer complete—"The Problem of Style" for two issues, and "A Classic Art" for two issues. (Proof of "The Problem of Style," Part I, you did return to us corrected.)

The airs and violin accompaniments of the two songs would greatly augment our pages but we are locked in the ice so far as expansion of this sort is concerned. We have more work awaiting publication than is wise or comfortable.

I think you do the public greater honour than it deserves, for it seems, so far as I can see, not consciously aware of having or not having musical criteria. The wise few whom we might wish to teach and who decline to be taught, will continue to teach the critics who in turn won't be taught. I may lead an "enclosed life" as Robert McAlmon seemed to think, but aside from *Modern Music* and Lawrence Gilman's concert notes and H. T. Parker in *The Boston Transcript,* I see no musical criticism that appears to be potent.

Mr. Burke, who is of German descent, is by endowment very much a musician and has two pianos—one in town and one in the country. Far from being didactic, he has accepted his post on *The Dial* with a great deal of diffidence and modest backbiting.

Your "how to read" in *The Herald-Tribune* is a source of pride and enjoyment to your adherents and I am surprised that it was not published immediately.

Sincerely yours,   Marianne Moore

Enclosed is a cheque for $5 for the [Alvaro] Guevara review.

To John Warner Moore   *March 27, 1929*

Dear Badger,

Consence forwarded the letter and it is indeed a thing for study and contemplation's daily food. Willow kept twirking his whiskers tensely every line or so, quivering with eagerness and ambition at each development. I am glad the captain lends substance and happiness to the event by giving the men something. It surely is free of corruption, & worth the effort of attention required by deciding to give.[16]

My disease is passed off. We both are active as usual & very much cheered by a telegram from Doc today permitting us to take 8 pages of poems by D. H. Lawrence & a Declamation by Mr. Burke. Mr. Burke was fluttering round the office with his chronicle and Ellen is sceptical of the value of deference towards Doc since my judgement is good & "we know it's what he would approve." Yes I said in matters of taste, but if I were asked myself if I wanted to buy the poems and do it feeling they would never be published, perhaps I'd say I didn't think I could buy, and I might hesitate to buy them even knowing they could be used—that I was opposed to doing anything that would be a hardship to us not to [be] able to *un*do. Ellen said, "well, I think your attitude does good; I'm sure Doctor Watson must appreciate it."

I have been to a luncheon at the Cosmopolitan Club sponsored by a committee of 7 women's colleges in the interest of endowment for women's colleges & I feel the need a very great one unless we want girls to go to co-educational colleges or to learn through correspondence courses, or to get frail instruction from somewhat spineless instructors. The idea was to inform the nation through indirect publicity—stories & articles and some suggestions were very unfit & ludicrous,—"along the line" of "debunking"; any editor will take anything about "debunking" "or anything disputatious" or "*any*thing about sex." Well, I got home at 4 and have had mice hitched & unhitched and she is now reading *The Spectator;* (the Mouse literary Bible at present—or should I say, Westminster Teacher. Baedeker is still the Bible and pilgrim's roll).

Pompino was taken to baby Burke yesterday & Mole says she is delighted. Pompey too seems a little more complacent & busy since he left. I am afraid he was pretty much a pet & not wholly in the notion of sharing.

with love,   Rat

---

16. JWM had written on March 16–17 that both he and Captain White were winners in a boat race; White gave the servicemen involved one to three dollars apiece.

To D. H. Lawrence   *[Dial office, 152 West 13th Street, New York]*
                             March 28, 1929

Dear Mr. Lawrence:

By reason of the delay of one and another, it is only now that we have found that we may have the following poems:

> "When I Went to the Circus"
> "To Let Go or to Hold On"
> "Things Men Have Made"
> "Whatever Man Makes"
> "Work"
> "November by the Sea"
> "Sea-Weed"
> "What Would You Fight For?"
> "Lizard"
> "Censors"
> "Attila"

Next week we shall send a cheque for one hundred and sixty dollars ($160) to Miss Rowe Wright of Curtis Brown. Although it precludes our sending you proof of "When I Went to the Circus," we have embodied this poem in the May issue (withdrawing something to make room for it) and are asking your permission to regard the enclosed typescript as proof. There is not even time, however, for it to be returned to us and should anything be amiss, please cable at our expense. Dialpubco, New York is the address. If for instance there ought to be space before the line beginning, "The elephants," the one word "space" would be sufficient; and if you objected to the title's being set in capitals, the word "low" would indicate the change. If, however, by April 15th, we have not had a cablegram from you we shall know we may proceed without changes. The other poems we should, as we think, like to publish as a group in November; they would appear about the middle of October, but we could publish them sooner if it were to your interest that we should.

We admire exceedingly the sentences:

> *Pensées*, like pansies, have their roots in the earth, and in the perfume there stirs still the faint grim scent of underearth. Certainly in pansy-scent and in violet scent it is so: the blue of the morning mingled with the corrosive smoulder of the ground.

Should the Foreword not have been published before we have brought out this group, might you accord us the privilege of prefixing these two sentences to our group?

One can hardly express the enjoyment given by poems in this book, as feeling and as form of expression, and that we should have for *The Dial* what we have selected, is an eager delight. I admit, there are lines in the book, that are the outcome of certain hurts, and I am not saying that in every case the lines themselves leave no shadow of hurt; one asks for the high beauty that you conceive, inviolateness from reprisal. But taken as a whole, there is an infection of beauty. Wishing for you always the best,

Yours, sincerely,   Marianne Moore

To D. H. Lawrence   *14 St. Luke's Place New York City*
June 22, 1929

c/o Signor S. Orioli   6 Lungarno Corsini
Florence, Italy

Dear Mr. Lawrence:

What a pleasure to know that your *Pansies* will appear without delay, and that the book of reproductions is also to be published soon. I had hoped that *The Dial*, which is to be discontinued with the July issue, would at least complete the year, and that we might have for the November issue, your poem, "November," but the early publishing of the poems, reconciles me to this disappointment. I could not say how much we prize the sentence from the Introduction first written, which will so enrich our presentment of the group—in the July *Dial*.

You speak of the missiles of the crowd. Insults, however, have not the force of insults when overbalanced by what is inviolable. This assertion may seem to have a touch of insincerity in view of my own choosing and selecting; but were we speaking together you would absolve me I am sure. Among Mr. Secker's[17] omissions there are poems perhaps that to me would not be correlated with that artistry of yours in which I delight, and in person you could instruct me about many things.

Your story in *The Criterion*[18] for instance, is startlingly veracious and holds one breathless to the very end; yet were we conversing I should probably be saying that a mind with mere truth as a standard rather than veracity, insists every step of the way that veracity also includes the possibility of an opposite situation. The world has a hundred examples of malaise to one of equilibrium, and perhaps you will forgive the wish of a friend who is but of the laity, that matchless sensibility such as yours should choose to present the rare phases of life which have in them relationships that one would wish to multiply and make eternal. But in what you have written, I have my own

17. Martin Secker, Lawrence's British publisher.
18. "Mother and Daughter."

sense of possession, and despite an unseemly boldness in proffering unasked opinions, I shall always be benefitted and a learner at your hand.

Marianne Moore

My mother has been ill and I have been at home from the office for some weeks, or I should have replied before.

To James Sibley Watson   *July 12, 1929*

Dear Doctor Watson,

You have become accustomed—I fear—to having gifts that *The Dial* confers, accepted gladly; and I am much accustomed to accepting such. But never before have they made me sad.

To say no, to this last great goodness of yours and Scofield's would for me be insincere. I should like to tell you—a long time hence—how sharply the reverse are other surprises that have come within a day or two; and *The Dial*'s gift will be remembered in strange contrast.

But it is a sadness to be always the receiver; besides, the gift is so unbelievably great. I feel as if the wish of an old friend were being realized when she said she hoped I "would win *The Dial* prize every year."

I hope that making others rich will never make you & Scofield poor. To me this last gift is a business responsibility. It is too beautiful a thing to be turned to food and shelter. Should I borrow it for that, I shall still feel I owe it to heaven to make it again a flame that will bless others as you & S. have made it to bless me.

That Mrs. Watson has been ill is bad news. I am so very glad that she is getting well. Please tell her that I am wishing her to have music & flowers; and health most of all. To you both, my lasting gratitude.

1930–1934
The Poet in Brooklyn

When *The Dial* closed, Moore no longer needed to be in Manhattan and she wanted a slower-paced, less intensely social existence, which would be easier on her mother and would allow her the time and seclusion she needed to turn back to her writing. This shift in priorities is reflected in her move from Manhattan to Brooklyn. By 1930 Moore and her mother were ensconced in their Brooklyn apartment at 260 Cumberland Street. The apartment was conveniently near the Navy Yard, where Warner was then stationed. In Brooklyn, Moore was also within easy reach of the cultural resources that fueled her writing in ever complex ways: museums, art galleries, lectures of all kinds, theater, and a wide variety of films. During this period, she embraced this sort of external stimulation, instead of plunging into the whirlwind of socializing with writers and artists which characterized her early years in New York City. She was by no means isolated, however, as friends visited her in Brooklyn and she made regular trips to Manhattan.

Now Moore could finally return to writing poetry full-time. Between June 1932 and November 1934 Moore published eleven new poems, including some of her best-known animal poems: "The Jerboa" (1932), "The Plumet Basilisk" (1932), and "The Frigate Pelican" (1934). We see in these letters that Moore worked from a position of eminence, querying journals in advance about poems she was working on and writers whose work she wished to review; she was also receiving an increasing number of requests for contributions to anthologies and journals. Both Lincoln Kirstein of *The Hound & Horn* and Morton Dauwen Zabel of *Poetry*, for example, wished to publish "The Plumet Basilisk" (to JWM, August 6, 1933).

Her letters document her immersion in her work and reveal the evolution of several new poems. In 1931 she remarked to Williams: "Your letter is received with enthusiasm, and I am under much obligation to you for your invitation to the cock-pit. Since *The Dial* closed I have not done any writing but am as strong for it as ever and have various things in mind. Perhaps like snails' eggs, which have such persistent vitality, they will hatch in time" (March 20, 1931). In 1934 she wrote Warner a spirited description of her progress on the poem "Nine Nectarines and Other Porcelain": "I am writing like a demon with canton-flannel horns, on my Nectarines poem" (June 1, 1934).

The correspondence of this period is filled with information about her process of research for these poems. Moore became increasingly fascinated by animal lore, natural history, and anthropology, frequently attending lectures and readings at the Brooklyn Institute of Arts and Sciences, of which she became a member after her move to Brooklyn. These occasions helped inspire a new kind of writing. Her poems were also informed by her many trips to the American Museum of Natural History in Manhattan, where she took notes and did drawings; by her consultation of books from various libraries; her delving into back issues of magazines, such as the *National Geographic*, for articles that she had heard about or once seen; and by her visits to art exhibits. All of these activities are highlighted throughout her letters, particularly those written to Warner, whom she often addressed as "Pago-Pago," after the capital of Samoa. (Beginning in 1932 he served for almost three years as the chaplain of the U.S. naval base there. His responsibilities included his work as director of education in the school system set up by the American government.) While working on "The Jerboa" and "The Plumet Basilisk," she wrote in great detail to Warner of her visits to the American Museum of Natural History (see July 19, 1932), and in her letters Moore frequently took for herself the name of the poem she was working on at the time or had recently finished, occasionally giving herself the same nickname that she used to refer to the poem; for example, both she and "The Plumet Basilisk" are "Feather," or she is often some version of "Rusty Mongoose" or "Pharaoh's Rat" (from "The Jerboa").

Moore valued firsthand accounts of her subjects, which led her to use her own observations as a naturalist in composing her poems. When she and her mother were visiting Warner in the summer of 1934, when he was stationed at the Norfolk Navy Yard in Portsmouth, Virginia, Moore wrote to Bryher: "There are butterflies here the size of bats and I have been entertained by seeing three grown mocking-bird fledglings—mouse gray with dark gray freckles on the breast—persecute their mother for food. They perch on the gate or stand in a row like penguins in the shade of a bush, chirping without a pause all day, in the tone of a broken carriage-spring; then at night hop up into a pussy-willow tree, about a cat's height from the ground, still chirping, till one after the other, they fall asleep" (August 9,

1934). Moore repeated this wonderful description two years later in the poem "Bird-Witted," which appeared in *The Pangolin and Other Verse* (1936).

While Moore clearly used letters to Warner and her friends as notebook entries that later contributed to her poems, she also wrote to them about the domestic economic situation in the United States. By 1932 she had begun to be concerned about events in Germany. Her letters to Bryher, in particular, are increasingly focused on the rise of fascism, Hitler, and anti-Semitism (see April 4, 1932). She admired Bryher's valiant efforts to help people leave Germany and Austria, writing her: "I have not yet received anything from Heinrich Mann but got testimony from Berlin of the Teuber cruelty and sent it to *The Times*. . . . Your courage, and struggle for the helpless, will be blest, that I know—to more than yourself. But how almost unfaceable and without circumference the wickedness and inhumanity are" (August 26, 1933). Moore's political conservatism is also evident in her letters, and stands in striking contrast to the socialist sympathies of many writers of the thirties. A staunch Republican who supported Hoover over Roosevelt, Moore wrote Morton Zabel (then an associate editor of *Poetry* and one of her new correspondents during this period, with whom she exchanged letters between 1931 and 1963) to tell him what she had heard on the radio: "Of late I have been using the radio [a favorite activity from this time forward] and have been troubled by the porcine self-interest of our country; but was stirred in a different way last night by Mr. Hoover's Des Moines address. I have thought I am a pacificist; but for men who live abroad—who did not fight and do not vote—to voice as they do the assured view of passivism, is a gruesome phase of patriotism" (October 6, 1932). The next day she wrote to Warner about Mr. Hoover's talk in Cleveland, noting that it "was as the fellow said over the radio, a humdinger, crafty and humourous but also deadly serious" (October 7, 1932).

Although Moore would comment on politics in her letters to Zabel, many of her letters to him were concerned with what they both were writing and reading, and friends they had in common. She confided to Zabel that she did not feel she could review H.D.'s *Red Roses for Bronze:* "I wish I need not return it to you unreviewed, but I must. There is beauty in it, I feel, as great as in anything of hers, but trammeled" (December 7, 1931). (Moore and H.D. were in less frequent contact during the early thirties; Moore only wrote to H.D. twice in that decade, but by the early 1940s they had resumed their regular exchanges.) Moore also wrote Zabel about her first meeting with T. S. Eliot in 1933, a meeting to which she had looked forward, but was disappointed by: "T. S. Eliot was in New York for a time, it seems, and I enjoyed meeting him at tea at Edmund Wilson's. The few minutes I was there, the conversation was entirely peripheral. Nevertheless I liked him exceedingly as I am sure you did if you saw him in Chicago" (June 12, 1933).

Warner was given a less delicately encoded version of "the conversation" when Moore noted that what was said was trivial (see June 11, 1933).

Although Moore would not meet Ezra Pound until the end of the decade, they continued to correspond regularly. He still took a keen interest in Moore's publishing ventures, and he respected the work she had done at *The Dial*. In 1931 he wrote to ask her if she might have an interest in taking over the editorship of *Poetry* when Harriet Monroe stepped down. Although Pound continued to advise Moore, during the thirties they were on a more equal footing. That Moore was a central and firmly established figure in their coterie is clear from the fact that Pound solicited her signature for his manifesto against corrupt criticism which he planned to circulate among his friends and associates (see January 18, 1933). In a letter to Moore, Pound had listed some of the tenets of the manifesto, calling for "the critic who causes others to write better" and for "the critic who most focuses attention on the best work" (January 1, 1933). When Moore received the manifesto, replete with her signature, she wrote Pound criticizing the wording of it and told Zabel she was not able to sign it (April 1, 1933). Moore was also deeply critical of his racism and anti-Semitism, warning him to resist such attitudes when he indulged them in his letters and other writing. Yet even when she was most critical of Pound, Moore never forgot how much he had done for her over the years.

Moore's correspondence with Hildegarde Watson began with intensity in 1933. Watson's children were now old enough to be left alone, and she resumed her career as a concert singer (as well as performing in her husband Sibley Watson's film, *Lot in Sodom*). Moore and Hildegarde Watson shared an astonishing range of interests, from poetry and the arts to religion and politics, which sustained their close friendship for over thirty years.

A 1934 event that turned out to be of considerable importance in terms of both poets' futures was Moore's first meeting with Elizabeth Bishop, who was then a senior at Vassar College. While there, Bishop had read some of Moore's poems in *The Dial, Poetry,* and *The Hound & Horn;* learning of Bishop's interest in Moore's work, Fanny Borden ("Aunt Ann"), the Vassar librarian and a family friend of the Moores', arranged for Bishop and Moore to meet outside the third-floor reading room of the New York Public Library that spring. Bishop wrote Moore right away, thanking her for the lengthy visit. A month later, Bishop invited Moore to the circus, which they attended together at the end of April. Late that summer, Moore gave Bishop's name to T. C. Wilson, a young poet and critic with whom she had begun corresponding in 1934, as a potential contributor to his *Westminster Magazine*. Before the year's end, Moore had offered to write something about Bishop and Mary Barnard, another young poet in whom Moore took an interest, for Ann Winslow's anthology, *Trial Balances;* her commentary on Bishop would appear in 1935. Although four years passed before Moore would invite Bishop to address her by her first name, they quickly became good friends who saw each other frequently and corresponded regularly between 1934 and 1971.

These years were simultaneously contemplative and exciting for Moore. Turning back to the writing of poetry, Moore achieved major public recognition when she won the Helen Haire Levinson Prize from *Poetry* in 1933. As in other instances, Warner's response to this event captured its importance in a way that Moore's own comments about it did not: "The *Poetry* award affects me to the very soul. I hardly know just where to touch it first. Perhaps, the best of it is the reliving of the moments in my den in '260' [Cumberland Street, Brooklyn] when we gathered to read Rat's po'ms & listened to Mole read them while I gazed at the steeple with its star slightly tilted awry & watched pigeons circle the spire, against an azure sky" (December 2, 1933). Warner continued to be one of Moore's most faithful witnesses as she went on to publish her work in the decades to come.

To Monroe Wheeler   *260 Cumberland Street Brooklyn*
                          March 18, 1930

Dear Monroe,

It is bad news that what we had almost grown used to as the common tragedy of our country has made its way into your very home. We are so sorry for your father and for the poor treasurer who bore the brunt of the attack. It is hard to rise above the sense of discouragement one has in mere loss, and the cruelty of ruthless attack multiplies it many times.

And at this same time you have been thinking of our pleasure! It would be impossible to say what enjoyment the pictures in the Italian Exhibition give us. *The Crucifixion* (lent by Henry Harris), the [Andrea del] Castagno, the [Alessio] Baldovinetti, the Sasseta, *The Duke of Urbino and His Wife*. The pinks and columbines in the Pisanello *Portrait of a Lady* are a marvel of execution; and in their own ways the *Bust of an Old Woman*, and the dish illustrated beside it are wonders indeed.

I am exceedingly pleased to know that the Buttses have the Holbein portrait—either to have, or to sell. The Havemeyer Collection here in New York is being much discussed. I have not seen it. A few evenings ago I went to a party at Mrs. Draper's. I have seen *Across the World with Mr. and Mrs. Martin Johnson,* and tomorrow I expect to go to a program of four plays and dances by the Chinese actor, Mei Lan-Fang and his company. But all of this is recent. It seems as if the winter had been a year of life absent from living. I shouldn't want to give you detail of it, so will only make the statement that Warner was in the Naval Hospital for many weeks with a dangerous, almost fatally serious carbuncle. For some time he has been allowed to be at home several days at a time and presently is to be given leave of absence in which to recuperate.

I am happy to make corrections in the book and to inscribe it; I wish I could know just what form would be pleasing. I was rather hindered from putting a date because the present time does not coincide with the coming out of the book. The edition was not pirated, and when I think of the enthusiasm, labour, and expense, involved in producing it, I think ill of myself for ever having felt that a liberty was taken. Until the book was brought me in the post, however, I had no knowledge of Bryher's and H.D.'s intention to publish it. Bryher felt me to be unduly retiring; and I, not liking small collections of verse, was very definite in my intention to offer nothing for book publication for a long time.

The copies which you gave me of my poem in *Manikin*, I still have, and should you wish to give one away or wish me to give one away, please don't be reluctant to ask for copies, or to send me directions for mailing a copy.

Despite the distress of Warner's illness, Mother's health is very encouraging. I wish you had told us of your own.

Yours affectionately,   Marianne Moore

To John Warner Moore   *June 24 [1931]*

Dear Pago:

I write you on the typewriter for two reasons—so you can save your eyes to perform the duties you are being hired to perform and so as to "get the good" of Mouse; so you will leave off Mouse's letters and read the typing. I have told Mouse this—that all the much penvipering is useless.

I had her at the movie, sitting in the front row in the balcony with nobody next her but me, but she took it very quietly. In some curious way, I missed the point of the colubrid's ascending the tree after being embroiled with the leopard. The leopard sprang into the tree and the snake was pursuing it; the leopard worked higher and higher in the tree, and then out on a branch and when the twigs became fine let itself fall crashing through the leaves to the ground to escape the snake. And several other things I related out of the proper order. The tiger and crocodile fight lasted some time and the strange feature of it was the way in which they kept turning over and over, the whiteness of both showing at regular intervals, and the gator's stout, limited little legs with webbed claws at the end making slow, futile swimming motions. Mole did seem impressed by the way in which the honey bear toddled up over the body of the snake and then a few feet, and then over the neck. I am sorry you could not have seen the long glaring look of each animal at the other as the tiger and crocodile parted; the tiger standing in a curve about two yards from the crocodile and lowering on him as he turned away.

A rather amusing thing was the collection of animals and imitation cocoa-fibre at the mouth of the theatre, round the ticket-booth—a kodiak bear on its hind legs, that kept nodding, and a nodding mustard yellow tiger with a cotton stockinet snake with red spots; about the size of two garden hoses looped careless round the body several times. They certainly did need a Pharaoh's rat (rusty mongoose) in that jungle. The mongoose I might say, is the ichneumon; or rather, the rusty-backed Egyptian mongoose is called an ichneumon. I have been studying this up.

The weather is bright, cool, and very windy so that it is pleasant on the roof but almost too fresh. I take my jerboa up there and am working like a demon to complete it—except for these shows.

I see that Mrs. Smith at the convention is avoiding "the grilling publicity" and that Mr. Smith[1] admits that Roosevelt has 500 votes. Mr. Hoover's disarmament cuts seem to me very carefully thought out.

In *The Illustrated [London] News* a while ago they had some remarkable photographs of small animals feeding under a flood-light near a home in Pasadena. You will see these in the [*National*] *Geographic* from which they were copied; or perhaps they have already come out. There is a fox eating grapes and a mouse on three legs, carrying its baby in its mouth and its right fore-claws holding a grape which it is also taking away with it.

Thought you might like this dog. [MM pastes a picture of a dog here.] "The Fathers'" sacristy—as the Jordan children call them—is about finished and they have a Spaniard mixing plaster for the inside. He is dressed in white with a scarlet bandana showing above the shirt collar and an edge of red bandana showing under a white skull-cap that he wears. Mole called my attention to him yesterday and the profound care with which he hoed the plaster into the cone of water that he formed. Bibi was so full of excitement he had to be tied, and stood watching with his ears up and five or six strong wrinkles between them. As soon as he was let go, he immediately went to the water barrel and picked up the nozzle of the hose which was dropping over the barrel and dropped it on the ground, doing this several times so that finally the man decided to let the nozzle lay on the ground.

This all is not "strictly private" if you think it would be of interest to Constance and your weazels.

Affly,

To Harriet Monroe   *October 1, 1931*

Dear Miss Monroe,

It was a pleasure to have your letter. I was ill at the time, or I should have replied to it immediately.

I should be sorry indeed to have anything that I write interfere with your set-up or office practice in any way. One detail in quoting seems to me of importance and if I have spoken of it before, please pardon my referring to it again. If, in a series of lines, a line is omitted, the omission ought to be indicated, I feel, by placing dots where the line would have been, not at the end of the previous line, or an impression will be given that that (complete) line is incomplete.

My mother, my brother, and I, each enjoyed our visit with Mr. Zabel. We were lastingly troubled that his vacation had much to mar it; he needed

---

1. Alfred Smith (1873–1944), governor of New York (1919–20 and 1923–28) and Democratic candidate for president in 1928.

rest and invigorating weather when *he* does the serious work that he does, for *Poetry* and in teaching.

I feel deeply your thinking of the work I put on the Pound article, but no one knows better than you, the impetus such writing brings with itself, and the fact that you find the article useful nullifies any sense I might have of unremunerated labor. Have no fear to entrust me with [any] acrimonious word you may receive from Ezra Pound. He is a distinctly dual nature and is so much oftener Bottom than he is Titania that while the worst from him is worse than any other worse, it is not in the least disturbing.

You are very good to suggest sending me other copies. I should like to have, counting the copy that has just come, five copies if I may.

I must ask forgiveness for an error concerning which letters will probably pour in. The snail quotation should have been attributed to Cowper, not to Leigh Hunt. For many years that poem has been to me an oft-repeated enjoyment and by some strange aberration, I got into the way of associating it with Leigh Hunt. My brother and we were reading in Cowper one evening lately—a rare bit of pleasure—, and my eye fell on "The Snail."

When you come to New York I hope you will have leisure and strength to come to see us. The telephone number (not in the directory) is Sterling 3-1123.

Sincerely yours,   Marianne Moore

To Ezra Pound   *November 9, 1931*

Dear Mr. Pound:

I value your indulgence.

The Grand Turk is not explicit, and I have the sense of quotation marks lost in successive copyings—not to mention "Thus the book of the mandates:" in Romans—probably the fault of the printer.[2] A persistent sun spot on the eye must have been responsible for Leigh Hunt instead of Cowper after the snail quotation; I am surprised no one has called me to account for it. Might I say too, that I wish I could have spoken more directly about originality of outlook in your seeing what is poetry in what seems to be prose.

Lemon-yellow-black was my idea of the underwing of the grasshopper but the carmine in connection with the sunset is better. Speaking of minor work, no doubt you recall [John] Skelton's grasshop in "Phyllyp Sparowe." I agree with you that there are substitutes for Calvin but the commentaries on the minor prophets, the letters, trouble about translators, and

2. This is a response to EP's response (EP to MM, October 6, 1931) to MM's review of *The Cantos* in the October 1931 *Poetry*.

so on, have life. "The trappings of the horse have fallen upon the ox." "Perhaps my style is over concise. But I am not at present discussing which is best; the readers of the day are fastidious and not possessed of great acuteness." I saw recently in a newspaper that a man who had written in the front of one of Calvin's books, "This is not true," was complained of by Calvin and put to death, yet such things even if true have nothing to do with style.

With regard to Christianity, abuses—whether in the church or out of it—are just that; but it's a stupidity to "reprove the saints for thinking what they never thought." I am not grounded in Aquinas. On the other hand it is not by the tactics of the opposite camp that I can progress. I know there are beliefs that matter, and am saying so in an article I have been writing on Conrad Aiken for *The Hound & Horn*. Since you advised my writing more, you may approve. I submitted to *The Times*, a review of Alyse Gregory's novel, *Hester Craddock*, and after 19 days got it back with a note to the effect that *The Times* could not use it,—"received a few days ago." *The Herald Tribune* took it at once but through a fortuity; the reviewer for the book was ill—so I am not highly encouraged to try to strengthen the weaklies. I think I do tend toward *The Criterion*. I have thought of writing on Mr. Saintsbury's new introduction to Thackeray for I am interested in fiction, but I had occasion to do with *The Criterion* when at *The Dial*, so know that they know of me, and would feel free to ask me for something if it were needed. I told *The Saturday Review of Literature* I might be interested in writing on the Thackeray and one of the editors replied that "the Thackeray would have to go to one of the regular staff;" a just decision of course.

The title of *The Cantos* article was "Books, Arms, Men." I had asked in the first place to have it "*De Litteris et de Armis, Praestantibusque Ingeniis,*" then saw at once the force of Miss Monroe's request for a simple title and for one not too wide for the page. However, I wish to say that Miss Monroe showed the article favor and made exceptions for it beyond all reason.

Should there not be a moderately priced American edition of *The Cantos*? A number who are interested in them say they have not been able to get them except singly in issues of magazines.

My mother and I are anti-radio but feel that we missed a great deal in not hearing your opera.[3] I have recently seen some remarkable Ming musical instruments in the Brooklyn Museum—flutes and lutes.

When I was at *The Dial*, I had a letter or two from your father and hoped he—both he and your mother—would sometime be in New York and would be able to come to see us. Here in Brooklyn we are not quite so conveniently reached, but do see certain friends should they be willing to take the trouble to come to see us.

Sincerely yours,   Marianne Moore

3. *The Testament,* an opera based on François Villon's poem; first performed in Paris, June 29, 1926.

P.S. The Italian stamps—Roman wolf and Caesar—make a hit with me that the Fascisti do not.

To Morton Dauwen Zabel   *December 7, 1931*

Dear Mr. Zabel,

Immediately after writing to Miss Monroe on Saturday, I received your letter; and today, H.D.'s book.[4] I wish I need not return it to you unreviewed, but I must. There is beauty in it, I feel, as great as in anything of hers, but trammeled. H.D. is to me very touching, as a person and in her work, though she is not asking to be that to me; but effective pronouncement, supposing I achieved it, would be distressing to her. A troubled treatment I tried to avoid in commenting on [Mark Van Doren's] *Jonathan Gentry*, with little success and in the face of deep respect for the book.

You are surrounded by much that is enticing. I have not read [Thomas] Sturge Moore for a long time, but value his prose book, *Art and Life*, and was once deeply impressed by a poem of his on a leopard. *The Panama* I have not seen but read with interest a column on it in one of the newspapers; nor have I seen T. S. Eliot's introduction to Pascal's *Pensées*. Robert Bridges I prize. I suppose you know his address: "The Necessity for Poetry."

I should, I know, like *The Ballet Mécanique*,[5] and I have heard that Charles Laughton[6] is remarkable. I don't get to the theatre but here in Brooklyn I have heard some very unusual music—Mozart and Bach and Haydn. What you have seen and are working with, does give one impetus; it must bring much to your pupils. I hope teaching is not the drain upon you that would seem inevitable. I am glad you have had such enjoyable weather. We had a spectacular snow-storm today which has left not a trace of itself.

Sincerely yours,   Marianne Moore

P.S. I am sending the book to you by this mail. It arrived in perfect condition and I hope nothing will mar it in its return to you.

To Harriet Monroe   *March 14, 1932*

Dear Miss Monroe,

Since receiving your letter I have made diligent effort to reconstruct the pattern of I and II in my group of poems. In "The Student" I succeeded

4. *Red Roses for Bronze* (1931).
5. Avant-garde film (1924) directed by Fernand Léger.
6. English-born actor (1899–1962), who made his first film appearances in 1928.

in halving the two long lines of each stanza but meaning and rhythm suffer, and to multiply lines without multiplying rhymes does, I fear, baffle involuntary expectation. It seems to me more modest to let the pattern remain. I hope what I've done with "The Steeple-Jack" will prove practicable.

I don't know what to do about the title. Since it is not repeated as a running-head I wish, for my own part, that it could be set as two lines—as below—centering "Part of a Play":

PART OF A NOVEL, PART OF A POEM,
PART OF A PLAY.

Sometimes in *The Dial* we used two, three, and even four line titles but they are troublesome, I know, and every exception in type-setting is an expense. I shrink from being one of that class I came to know in my office experience, the kind of person that "when you except to one of his verses, tells you it cost him more labor than all the rest." The mere phrase, "I am always right in my own eyes" would save an editor a good deal of tiresome reading. I do wish when being benefitted, to be a benefit, and perhaps you will see further something to suggest in these matters. Should you prefer to put the title at the bottom of the first page, in an Editor's Note?

I have retyped "The Student" and "The Hero," as there were a number of long-hand changes; and I am making two changes in "The Student" and one change in "The Hero."

I shall be watching for your Editorial in the April issue and I feel that a review such as you contributed to this last one is bound to help an author.

I should like my subscription to begin with the February issue which I haven't seen; though I ask pardon for not writing a separate letter to the Circulation Department.

Again, I can't but say that it was a real disappointment not to be with you on the occasion of the dinner given for you in February. I supposed then, if it had been a week later I should have been able to go, but I am still not more than convalescent and was severely reprimanded for getting up to type these poems. But I had delayed so long in offering them, I thought perhaps even so I was merely being faithful to an intention.

Sincerely yours,   Marianne Moore

To Bryher   *April 4, 1932*

Dear Bryher,

Yes, I have been ill; three weeks in bed with bronchitis, and Mother was ill at the same time. I feel deeply your writing to know if something could be amiss. We are now up and about, but cautious. I do hope you have kept well yourselves, and are escaping the epidemic of which you speak; also that superintending the Villa has not been wearing. The place is full of charm, I know, and I hope it will be as full of happiness for you. And I hope Tunis and N.D. [New Delhi] will show their better side to Mr. Macpherson.

It is a pleasure to know of Hilda's writing. You don't speak of your own writing? And what about the camera? *Red Roses for Bronze* has in it that which is so impressive I marvel to see with what intrepidity reviewers "deal" with the book. I like *The Herald Tribune* review best but thought the quotations in *The Times* happily chosen.

The Mary Butts has come and I am delighted with it. The acute sensitiveness—with the fang of aristocracy in it, so that she is annoying to herself and to others—excites the utmost sympathy. And though she keeps to certain fetishes, the refracting beauties that she insists on finding to look at, and the chamois-like agility of word and idea, are a fine sight. The Swiss setting in *The Last Spring* pleased us as you thought it would. Dorothy Richardson's awareness is a heightened one, but the sense of obstacle, as a thing she has always been meeting, makes one sigh. *A Buried Treasure* I have not read. *The Time of Man* was of interest, I thought, but the conviction remains with me that *Under the Tree,* the book of poems by Elizabeth Roberts that came out before the prose, is the book of hers that is most my taste.

Hitler's defeat indeed seems necessary. Otherwise we might all "leave forever." You would be surprised to know how anxiously the Hindenburg election was awaited and hoped for in America.

I wish I had Perdita's cooking talent. I had wheedled away from cooks, a number of secret recipes, and at intervals try to force the hand of heredity by making something, but have about decided I must take the position that I need time and better facilities. An experienced helper might solve the problem. If I had that, I would not even know her name, I would be so remote from the activities, Mother says.

The Guggenheim awards this year please me in some instances— George Dillon, Ernest Fiene, Marsden Hartley (for painting), and John Flannagan, the sculptor whose animals, like undetectable cobblestones, you may know.[7] Also, there has been a rousing exhibition of American primitives at the Whitney Museum. Some trenchant portraiture—chiefly anonymous; and some histrionic pieces; *The Runaway Horse*—a black trotter without saddle or harness, skirting a cove with boats in it and a blue bridge of sighs at the back—pursued by a coach-dog. A sulky race; two horse-headed iron hitching-posts; and a room of selections from Audubon's elephant folio; *The Snowy Owl, The Great Tern,* and *The Carrion Crow.* Some of the backgrounds are remarkable—a tree of which the leaves were partly

7. Dillon (1906–1968), American poet and editor of *Poetry* (1937–42); Fiene (1894–1965), German-born American artist; Flannagan (1895–1942), American sculptor and medalist.

eaten by caterpillars, each little worm, a portrait; and a tree of the locust variety with long curly pods like banana-skins.

I think I mentioned a Pierre Roy that I saw at the Julien Levy Gallery—an oil—a baton, a fife, and a drummer's stick, tied together tepee-fashion and stood on a table by the sea, together with a conch shell, against a back-ground of sea and fringe of cat-tails and marsh grass; and I like a newspaper reproduction I have seen, of his *Physique Amusante*—a cart-wheel, string of ostrich-eggs, paper snake, and a lithograph in miniature of a locomotive with bell stack.

Also, I have heard a lecture on insects by Dr. Franz Lutz, Curator of Entomology at the Natural History Museum. He has made some curious discoveries; he has found out something about how insects see colors, colors to which they are blind, and the fact that certain plants have ultraviolet in the blossom or at the edge of the blossom; the ability of insects to live at air pressures at which we cannot live. And he is studying, as he can, diseases of insects. He much deplores the poisoning of insect pests instead of rearing the enemy parasite or producing disease bacteria injurious only to the insect pest—since Agricultural Department poisons, poison desirable insects and destroy the productivity of the ground.

My "writing" has been augmented by my illness, for while recuperating I finished a group of poems that I have been working at for some time. Miss Monroe has taken it and when it comes out—fall or summer—I shall send it to you. Unless *Poetry* is one of the magazines you always see? I am sending you the issue of *The Hound & Horn* in which I have a review of Conrad Aiken.

I thank you, dear Bryher, for your care over us and I wish I could know that its benedictions were descending on you and yours. With affectionate greetings to Hilda and Perdita as well,

M. M.

To John Warner Moore   *June 25, 1932*

Poor Mouse, the other half of this sheet was a drawing she had made for one of the children: a mouse with a grape; so I cut it off for her.

When at Bryn Mawr, our insignia was an oval of white-oil cloth about five inches long with a scarlet phoenix hand-stencilled on the centre of it by Mary Nearing. Mouse uses it as a bookmark but lost it one day and kept saying "Where is that *pigeon*?" Also, just now she asked me what was funny in Ed Wynn's[8] saying Firechief gasoline was mighty like a hose? (Too shy to ask before; laughing however, every time.)

8. Ed Wynn (1886–1966), theater and radio comedian with his own show during the 1930s.

I want you to know I am *cured.* Give no further thought to all this fool-ishness about poor Rat; Rat this and Rat that. That is all over now; and never will be again. I understand the matter now. (Dry yourself as carefully at the end of your spine though, as between your toes; and you'd better suggest it for each and all.) The coccyx is the name of the spine-tip.

Will we send you either or both of these books by Dr. Curry? I thought the *Racing Tactics* would no doubt be useful to you; the *Wind and Water* not so good. Saw the notice in *The Times* for June 19th.[9]

Frank, the paper man, is very sorry to know you are away and such a ways away, but "duty" he says. "That's the thing." Mrs. Nowak looked with parrot eye on your large picture and said, "My, I'd like to have one! But I guess they're very expensive pictures." Mouse said afterward with hard wrinkles, "Yes, the picture would do her great credit."

Only two-thirds of a page to say what is boiling in me concerning my jerboa. I think it is maybe the one and only thing I have ever written; and to have it "passed under the clippers"!! But the Mouse is probably right. I told her, however, that it should be read several times before any light comment was passed; one has to get used to a thing, when it comes to one as something a little new and Mouse respectfully said "That is well said." But now is say-ing "Cry-baby; cry-baby."

Well I must git this water-melon to the boat.

R.M.   Rusty Mongoose (Pharaoh's rat)

To Monroe Wheeler   *July 11, 1932*

Dear Monroe,

The hunting-leopard is a delight—rightly speaking, a study; and the production itself is so very remarkable in harmonious contrasts, and definiteness. The whole concept—bony frame and dog claws, with the "useless" claw on the foreleg so well depicted—is more interesting to us than I can tell you. Strange to say, I had just been thinking about this beast in connection with something I am trying to write for *The Hound & Horn*—"The Jerboa"; (I may have mentioned it).

The murals catalogue which came just after you were here, entertains and benefits us greatly; it is surely a revelation beside Puvis de Chavannes' and Pompeii. Benjamin Kopman is a favorite of mine and one has no reason to be ashamed of him here, I think. The Fiene of Brooklyn Bridge seems to me unusually able; also the Nicolaides. The [Grant] Wood is a great success

9. MM pasted a newspaper clipping on the back of the letter briefly describing these two books.

too, I feel, and one warms to anything so genuinely American. Glenn Coleman has that native quality; I suppose you saw the notice of his death, May 9th; I am sorry about it.

George Lynes' Photo-mural is one of the best things in the collection, I think; imaginative and firm. The [Edward] Steichen and Sheeler seem to me, like the [Georgia] O'Keeffe, a little too proficient. The Kirstein and [Julien] Levy introductions also are of interest—so very unperfunctory.

We were rejoiced to know that your voyage was not a nightmare, and of your having a few days alone for your "typographic pursuits;" I hope they are not from week to week deferring to other matters. (You may not get any grapejuice another time because of your dutifulness in acknowledging those few drops.)

Your getting especially for us a copy of *Fear and Trembling* and bringing it, grows in the mind and does perhaps justify your doing so troublingly generous a thing. Considered impersonally, the content is not Glenway at his best, I feel;—is somewhat accusing. But the thing that matters is that one should have a best. Glenway has a gift for seeing things in an unusual way and of expressing what he sees, in an unusual way; and distaste is, as I realize, part of selectiveness. I am not satisfied with the world myself; but as soon as I begin to say so, I find that I am not being cosmic but personal and am constantly in a despair—on the verge of embitterment almost—as a result of world abuses and my own errors.

I saw a few days ago the notice of a novel by a Mr. G[athorne]-Thorne Hardy and wondered if that was not your friend and Glenway's.

We are taking care of Warner's and Constance's radio for them while they are away and have heard some beautiful music—Mozart's *Symphony in G minor*, Brahms' *D major Concerto*, Prokofiev's *Classical Symphony*, and some fine things conducted by Mr. von Hoogstraten, more familiar to me than these others. "Under a brightly shining half-moon in a lightly cloudless sky," according to the announcer, "we are about to have Debussy at his finest, writing with the romantic passion which belongs not in this world and yet not wholly in another. From the Lewisohn Stadium in its ideal setting under the stars, we now hear: *The Afternoon of a Faun*."

I went to the Natural History Museum a few days ago to see the jumping mice and the bower-birds, and was waylaid by the insects—a live tarantula, two live scorpions, a live centipede about eight inches long—orange-red with vermillion legs of a remarkable pattern; it is not one of the putty-colored variety with whisker legs; some live peacock green beetles, gray beetles with a round black disc on each wing; and a variety of cockroaches. A boy who had presented the gray beetles joined me and explained his beetles and conducted me to the reptiles where there is a model of a rattlesnake with an electric button which when pressed shakes the rattle, and also duplicates the rattler's buzz. The Audubon drawings are impressive, but tiered on a wall three stories high, surrounding the stairs, and some were covered by amber glass to protect them from the glare, so they are more a possession than an exhibit. One little spotted bird, standing pigeon-toed, with a waiting expression is a wonderful piece of portraiture; also a raccoon on an unfinished square-ruled background; it is posed on a tree, with each guard-hair depicted, the body color suggested in water-color. The bower-bird number of the *Zoological Bulletin* is one of the most enthralling expositions I have ever read. Just what one would expect, however, of the crow family.

I hope you have been well since getting back, and that you did not find anything of a business nature awaiting you that was exasperating.

Affectionately yours, M. M.

To John Warner Moore *July 19, 1932*

Dear Pago-Pago:

Several things have happened since I wrote you. Your telegram concerning Homer came. We went to Wall Street this morning and Mouse will give you the news. Mr. Houston had moved from 37 Wall to 70 Pine, received us very kindly, and says the Allegheny Gas will revive, it's a good house, could not for the time being surmount the depression.

The Criterion has came out and though they did not send proof and the changes I sent in lieu of proof were not incorporated, the thing reads very well. Ezra has the opening piece—a tribute (in memoriam) to Harold Monro,[10] and T. S. Eliot has a rather interesting Commentary, and there are thousands of reviews. The poem is not of much account and I feel that they need a piece of verse (on the order of my Jerboa or the twenty froggies;[11] I am just beginning to concentrate on the Plumet Basilisk for W. Williams, however, so may not get around to them for a couple of months). Speaking

10. Belgian-born English poet, editor of the *Poetry Review*, and publisher of *Georgian Poetry* (1870–1932).

11. Poem by George Cooper anthologized in Kate Douglas Wiggin's *Pinafore Palace*. "The twenty froggies" may be the family nickname for this poem, which they all enjoyed and referred to in later correspondence.

of frogs, I see Mr. Ernest Ratsey's Golliwog won something in a race way up the Sound. There is going to be a Marine Museum; I mean Mariner's Museum costing $10,000,000 and covering 850 acres at Morrison, Virginia. Models of ships and ship machinery will be gathered covering maritime development as far back as investigators find proof of activity. The project was proposed by Archer M. Huntington. Every type of small hand and wind propelled boat known to history will be placed on the lake. In the field of model-making the museum will start with the present and work backward. The origin of rope and canvas and other materials will be traced and models of the Monitor and Merrimac and of the first ships that sailed into Jamestown will be included. They plan to be exact and not to hurry and to have the material gathered in about 25 years.

The church next door has flowered on a tremendous scale. Everything inside has been plastered Nile mud red, they have a lot of new images, a giant palm, and a good deal of singing, by small boys in red gowns with white smocks. The basement is being excavated and a heap of assorted rocks has come out. Besides these rocks was a pile of well-sifted sand rising to a symmetrical point. Mouse says yesterday morning Bibi was loose in the courtyard and began to snout the sand and then to dig in it; surprised to find his effort met no resistance, he dug the more enthusiastically, sending the sand in every direction, rejoiced to see how far it would go, then lay on his back in what remained of the pile and rolled and rolled, saddened by the reduced condition of the pile. Nor did he get a beating; he was somewhere else by the time the ignoramus returned to the pile. His real name seems to be Bimbo. Brownie Barker, the market man's Chow has been clipped and is a picture; very shy because of the funny feeling; but *how* he feels; like yourself, after a clipping.

See by the paper Mr. Garner[12] says he "can deal with Hoover" and "feels big enough for the job" of governing in view of the President's "weakness." We have had quite a little humor over Mr. Lawrence A. Greene, our neighbor on the fourth floor. When he came in to collect for Block-Aid, I was typing the Brontë review; ever since, he has been asking me how was business and said *he* was interested in literary things and Mouse has dropped a bushel over the matter and encouraged me to tell him we had no time and did nothing that was for his ears—especially when he said he would drop in some evening to continue the conversation. I met him on the street one day when a tennis-player was passing; I commented on the player and he said, "there are tennis-courts right near us in the Park; would you care to play sometime?" I said "yes, I would be delighted." He said, "Have you a racquet?" I says yes. He said what time would suit me and so on, ending with much happiness and better confidence—having in the beginning

12. John Nance Garner (1868–1967), congressman from Texas, who was Speaker of the House in 1931, and later served as vice president (1933–41).

asked me timidly, "Have you heard from your mother yet? I mean your brother." Mouse shook and slappered her ears over this and kept saying, "Ketched; he's won out; well, well." *But* nothing has come of it and I am delighted for the good would not be commensurate with the triviality and annoyance—waiting on the bench for half an hour and playing battledore for 20 minutes; and much talk about your brother and the quill.

Mouse came to me very dutifully to have her pads attended to with salicylic acid. I taped them and said on no account to touch them without my supervision. This morning they were all trimmed and she called my attention to the fact and when I said I had charge of the case, she said be careful, "the hoof will lift" meaning she would kick me; and added "but you have charge of the case." What am I going to do about a thing like that? Too much trimmed off and much truculence and defiance.

Ed Wynn last Tuesday was not so good as previously but I noticed Mouse smiling, though too proud to "give him credit." Especially when he said, "I said to the artist do you paint in the nude much?" and he said, "No, I usually wear a smock." Mouse's ears also veered out of the ear line when he told how the man gave the African chief an egg-cup and the chief said, "I'll keep it for a novelty, but I could never get any hen to sit over that." The funniest thing he said was that "if it wasn't for his spinal column a man could have legs all the way to his neck." Graham McNamee amused me the most with his ad. of the Firechief gasoline. "It's a he-man gasoline bristling with power. Up with the brakes, down with the starter, and the roar of power. July is emergency weather for a motor oil. Firechief Motor Oil will not clog nor harden, etc. Listen for the signal—the siren and bell." I wrote down a little of it but have lost my paper. The thing starts and closes with a little fire siren and a rapid dinging of a bell.

I wrote Dr. Ditmars when I could not find out certain things at the Nat. Hist. Museum about the Jerboa and he replied very kindly. He says they sleep "round" as I described it; that he has also "noted them sleeping on their sides, in a semi-curled position." He says, "The food which you mention—grain, bulbous roots and tiny cactus—are preferred items. The usual body coloration of jerboas is fawn brown, under parts whitish, and the tail 'pad' white." He is going for his vacation, August 15th, to Panama to get a few bushmasters, the b.m. is the generic grandfather of the rattler. They grow to be about 10 feet and are dead poison. Some engineers working on the Canal had killed several nine-foot ones and that is what decided Dr. Ditmars to get some. This reminds me of Frank Buck's film. I asked Mouse what frightened her the most and she said, "Douglas Fairbanks" (of Pickfair), shown starting off on his yacht Invader—in the News Reel; "his personality."

July 5th I went to the Natural History Museum and that was my big day since seeing Doug. Sorry you cannot visit it. I was finding out about the jerboa, the basilisk, and the fawn-breasted bower-bird. First I got among the insects. They had a row of bell-jars illuminated from the back containing various live things; "these animals" the card said, two scorpions in separate jars—each with a couple of cockroaches for food. The scorpions were reddish yellow like very old amber, jointed, with a lobster claw for catching food, and a sting on the tail like a small pin-point. The notice said they do not sting unless attacked. The sign said in very large letters, Live Scorpion, and then: "Many visitors have asked if these scorpions are alive. Yes. They are, but often they do not move for hours at a time. Incidentally they are not insects. They have four pairs of jointed legs and no insect ever has more than 3 pairs of jointed legs." The same was said of the tarantula, an awful big seal brown spider with a silky panne-velvet fur and 4 pairs of legs. Then, there was a centipede about 7 inches long, reddish with vermilion legs and a kind of button head and 2 cockroaches for food. It had been discovered in a shipment of bananas. Another jar was crowded with brilliant emerald green beetles, and in another was a piece of gray and black bark and several long gray beetles were in it, each with a black disc on the wing; harmless. A boy who had presented them, explained them to me and led me to the reptiles where the basilisks are. These diving feather basilisks in which I am interested come from Costa Rica and are different from frilled lizards and from Flying dragons of Malay—little brown newts with yellow flecks on the wings. The newts have at each side of the body a wing supported by six ribs and they are like medium sized butterflies. They plane down through the air, lighting on orchids or spotted leaves, and are exhibited at the Museum on a nut-meg tree—one in air, suspended by a wire, and two on the orchid blossoms with the wings folded in a little, like a half-closed umbrella. The basilisk, however, is the prince (c.f. *basileuns*) of lizards in my estimation— bright green with 8 bands on the tail and three plumes—strictly herbivorous and can run a little way on the water before diving, on the hind legs, tail dragging. *Basiliscus Americanus* Gray.

There are at the Museum two star tortoises, found in Burma and Ceylon, ivory white and seal brown, the under side being the strangest, with a central pattern and two-side paths of marking, like wall-paper put on without reference to matching the figure. I stood and blinked at the turtle and finally made a drawing for I knew I would want later to look at it again. I loitered a while among the reptiles, seeing how they feed, and looking at the series of eggs—crocodile, alligator, turtle, snake, lizard. At one end of the room is a case on a table with four chairs drawn up and inside is the model of a rattler with an enlarged model of the tail. The rattle is not an indication of the age of the snake. The rings are parts of incompletely shed skins and the snake may be many years older than it has rings. Also, it seems unlikely that it is aware of rattling its rattle; but it vibrates the tail in its excitement and thus inadvertently warns a person. I was going away when a small boy showed me the button in front of the case which when pushed shakes the rattle and gives a buzzing replica of the true rattle. I had heard the rattling almost continuously while in the room but had not known what was causing it. At one end of the room is a large group of Komodo lizards with painted background and various logs and grasses to complete the picture, and a movie reel is run on request, showing the lizards at home, lumbering about the beach and tearing on a carcass. It was being started for five children seated on a bench in front of the screen, so I joined them—and then somewhat sheepishly, two boys of about Joe Nowak's age joined the party. It lasted about fifteen minutes. The big feature of the room is a king cobra among bamboos, with a rock at one end of the case, and a mongoose vigilantly curving round the rock and observing the snake. The card stated that mongooses usually do not attack quite so large a cobra and that this one is considering whether to retire or proceed. Also there is information about serums. First wash the bite with permanganate of potash solution—any of several percents; then tie the arm, leg or body to prevent circulation between that point and the heart; untying the ligature every twenty minutes and tying it again; and get as soon as possible the required serum. Alcohol will do no good and may do a great deal of harm. There were no jerboas; there were 2 American kangaroo rats and some pocket mice, and 2 opossums in a marsupium, but no jerboas.

I then visited the birds and after a terrible hunt, found in a special bequest, a "fawn-breast"; a bird about the size of a flicker—and very modest indeed in appearance. Bower-birds it seems are of the crow family, and from their cute ways, I am not surprised. The satin bower-birds are male, black like a crow; female, tea-leaf green with rust speckled front, a little bigger than a crow, not as big as a raven. I saw cursorily, the wood-peckers and owls. The finest of the owls I took to be the European barn-owl, little but wonderful with breast spangled with symmetrical groups of pin dots. The peacock pheasant (which I know pretty well) is mounted in the act of preening its feathers, and the peacock eyes bordering the tail and the wing edges on the dark bluish ground color are remarkable. The ostriches, cassowaries, and kiwi, are a fine exhibit. There are two penguins with a group of black pebbles found in the stomach of one—not as grinders but eaten at a venture; the penguin has not a gizzard but a stomach (like yours).

En route to the library to get some information about the jerboa of which I was now in desperate need, I got by mistake into the Costa Rican section and looked at the gold pumas, bats, and tapirs, parrot-bill dagger handles, gold and silver llamas, and so on; and the largest jade axe-head that has ever been found.

In the library you ring a bell and an assistant comes out and hunts books for you and brings them. I had a very "lovely" one but the information about the jerboa was not from personal experience but hearsay I regret to find. They do not live "in troops" and do not live among woods; as pictured in the book brought me. It did state, however, that natives rob their mounds, getting several bushels of wheat within a small area.

On the way down-stairs I paused among the Audubon souvenirs and original drawings. They are tiered on a three-story wall surrounding the stairs; some were under yellow glass, and all shades were drawn down, so seeing was to some extent, a matter of belief. The prairie dogs fared the worst, being the highest. But a flock of birds among what seemed to [be] peach-leaves, was a very notable piece of detail; also a small spotted bird, standing a little pigeon-toed with a waiting expression, and a raccoon on a branch, against an unfinished squared white background—a masterpiece of liveliness and texture, every guard hair and claw depicted, and the body color suggested by grayish brown water-color. Also there was a pink-footed tern of some kind, and some handwriting. I hastened home; but of course had telephoned Mouse that I was "delayed."

Mary Watson spoke with great appreciation of her visit to Crestwood, of Constance, and how she enjoyed being with the children; said Johnnie was in certain ways a little like Sue's Johnnie. Also, I meant to say that May when here last month, seemed very much delighted with the house, surprised to find it so roomy and very much liked the furniture and the way it looks against light walls. She said Leo would be working at the detail of the house when we were at Woodbury and doesn't like to be interrupted, but "he is not to cut off his service to you; and if you want to go any where in the car or take some drives, just tell him and don't spoil him or make a fuss over his work on the house for he revels in praise."[13]

The radio at times has remarkable things on it and we have it as loud as we like—and "make them suffer like they make us suffer"; then again it is ludicrous indeed. I'll be tweezing gravely for some reasonable thing and it'll say, "now I'm goin to ask you a shivery question and you can't help but agree. What makes you so sweet." Or "These are the songs you love best; sung the way you love to hear them. First on tonight's program will be 'I've a date with an Angel' by the sun-burned boys in the balloon-ball-room at Luna Park, Coney Island—accompanied by our Fourth of Juliars." Ed Wynn's band is the Voorhees Orchestra and they give us last week, "Oh Gee, Oh Joy" and "Roar, Lion, Roar." I don't know whether Mouse likes it or not; anyhow she bears it; said, I think, it was no great strain on the emotions; whereas during one of the pieces up at the Stadium she nearly bit me for rattling a paper and thinking of reading during it.

Tremendous lopings. Wall Street; Wanamaker's; Schulte's, yesterday and day before. Outside Schulte's we were joined by David Lawson, Lola Ridge's husband. He was very kind, said he would urge us to come to his

13. MM and MWM spent part of this summer in May Eustis's house in Woodbury, Ct.

rooms to tea but he didn't want to have us climb the stairs on a hot day, and so on. He said Lola had been in Mesopotamia but was now visiting Mrs. Floyd and, was going later to Yaddo. He said he had had a letter from "Lore-a" [Laura] Benét. That Mrs. Benét had had an illness and I think an operation on her eyes; she needed the operation before leaving but they had waited so long to go abroad—had never been abroad—they feared if they didn't go they might never go. Lore-a had seen [Walter] de la Mare. Mr. Lawson smiled. "That's Lore-a; that's the only thing to say about it," he added. "She was surprised to find him selling petroleum or petrol—a man like that." Again he smiled; but he said they were delighted with the trip in spite of backsets.

I was greatly intrigued by Mr. Pesky in Schulte's "P. Pesky, Sec'y." I asked him where reptiles were. "Rep-tiles?" he said briskly. "Right here, Miss Moore. Rep-tiles and lizzeds in this alcove." But I didn't find any; at least no basilisks. I find from the library that newts are moist-skinned flat-tailed animals whereas lizzeds have dry scales and a cylindrical tail.

Today we got Mouse's glasses adjusted, bought her a pair of shoes—brown with lowish heels and a strap and buckle—at Hanan's, next Merowitz's; got her a pongee kimono with blue hem and an ice-cream festival chrysanthemum-and-lantern pattern across the shoulders—wondrous flimsy; but its lightness is good, it will wash, and she is wearing it *right away*. We got for me a tiny blouse—white muslin with pink polka dots, sleeves half-way to the elbow—69¢—that fits me better and looks better on me than anything I've had for several years; and a large baku dark blue hat for 5 dollars reduced from $12.95 which Mouse had been pining to get me at the regular price, but left me go. This is a big deal. I haven't gone anywhere but to church that Mouse hasn't urged me to get a hat, and told me how puny I looked.

I got Mouse from the library Lord Kilbracken's Memoirs [*Reminiscences of Lord Kilbracken*] and it is a very impressive book, modest, tolerant, and vivid. I had a letter from Ezra today—very, very considerate and attentive—urging also that we have Louis Zukofsky to the house. This is the third approach on the subject and we think in the fall we will let him over. Ezra says he feels that Ford M. Ford and I had been underestimated by him in his previous summaries and he was glad to put in this anthology all of my poems that he had; but that mere oversight was not his reason. And I appreciate this very much; though I never felt he slighted me. [Superimposed on this final paragraph is MM's sketch of a cobra in a tree; see page 147.]

Af'n'ly,   R   Rusty Mongoose

To John Warner Moore   *July 24, 1932*

Dear Pago,

I can't write you on the typewriter on Sunday lest people think we had backslid and got worldly during your absence. (I am writing on my lucky alligator-skin board which benefits you as well as me.)

We had some fine music last night from Mr. von Hoogstraten, Schubert's Symphony in G major complete. Mouse was so affected that when I went to the kitchen to get the beetle to mash the currants for jelly for her, she pounced on me with, "We aren't leaving town tonight, are we? Are you coming, or shall I shut this off?" And off snaps the radio! And on Mouse's desk I see a card saying "WOR Newark New Jersey: 61" which tells its own story. And how Mouse glared and lowered on me.

(I should have told you that Mr Pesky said "rep-tile" with a long i right after me saying reptile; also that when we deprecated taking his time when he was adding etc., he said, "Not at all, not at all. I rather enjoy it." "Rather"!)

My Jerboa is accepted; and I am now proceeding with my feather basilisk. You don't remember, do you, where you first saw the term? Mouse says you made it up; but I think some traveller alluded to it—or historian. And plumifrous or plumet basilisk is the regular term.

We came on a rather droll anecdote in Lord Kilbracken's memoirs. Dr. [Benjamin] Jowett of Balliol had rasped a student who was a fanatical Roman Catholic & in answering an examination paper, the student framed the answers in such a way as to imply that Dr. Jowett denied the divinity of Christ and was a Christian detractor generally,—hoping to arouse controversy. Dr. Jowett after reading the paper said to him, "Mr._____, are you a Quaker?" and with that dismissed him.

As we came in last night, from getting the currants, we met Mr. Jordan at the door. After letting us in, he told us he has to have another operation; tomorrow—a rupture as the result of moving a couple of gas-stoves & washing the hall windows. He was very game, even joked about the matter and said, "I think the wife'll get suspicious if I do this every year, & think I am planning a nice vacation for myself, so I can pull up on my reading." He'll be in the hospital about 2 weeks, and Mrs. Jordan will run the hot water heater. I hope "Harry" will not oppress them or threaten Mr. Jordan because he is "weak."

We are just home from public worship at the Lafayette Ave. Church. Dr. Mahairy is in Eng. & France for 2 months travelling with his son. Dr. Clarence H. Barbour (Pres. of Brown Univ.) preached & Mouse is so roused against him for praising Borah[14] & not mentioning Mr. Hoover that after

14. William Borah (1865–1940), senator from Idaho, leader of isolationist faction in the 1930s.

the election she is going to write him & tell him that he has got what he was looking for "beyond the horizon" but did not mention. *However*, Mouse said to me when I endeavored to tame & pacify her & pass my hand over the back, "I am not affected by him except as I would pray for the defeat of that wicked boar-pig & for the continuance of one *so* different." (Not affected by him. Also he defamed the radio which Mouse is now ardent for.)

In speaking of the radio I forgot to say, we heard yesterday for 20 minutes the German Saengerfest at Frankfurt on the Main, singing in honor of Goethe's senteenery [centenary] 2 of Goethe's Songs, "Rest on the Mountaintops" & "In the Moonlight." 20,000 male mice. They hold these fests once in 4 years & the quality of the singing was remarkable—such volume & carefully timed conclusions, & easy crescendos. When the American who described the proceedings (the immense gathering in a hall flying the red, black & gold and the stars and stripes as the only other national flag,) said "and now I am sorry not to let you hear the rest of this ballad (the implacable Captain) but I must switch you back to America," Mouse stuck her tongue out and made a fierce ugly face—beating downwards with the paws.

Yr. affec.t.n.e.   Basilisk

I am now a basilisk—(harmless however). And my hat was 5 dollars & had been 15. not 12.95.

To Ezra Pound   *July 29, 1932*

~~Dear Mr. Pound:~~Dear E. P.,

It is a pleasure to know something of the literary and moral currents influencing the *Anthology*.[15] The result, collectively, is a triumph, there is no doubt of that. And no one in it could agree with you about your ever having underestimated him. I feel sure I did not offer elsewhere, poems I had submitted to you, but can also say I had forgotten not getting them back. You did, I recall, write me very helpfully about that Tiger poem.[16] You are even over-magnanimous, I feel, in "passing" blunders and marking the virtues a hundred plus. I have not that catholic grace. Yeats is the only person, for me, whose deficiencies do not impair the marrow. In your own case I take a liberty, and like to imagine how immense the wave would seem without certain small posts and breaks to the main purport.

I don't quite understand your omitting Wallace Stevens. His "Academic Discourse in Havana" equals any of his earlier things I should say;

15. In May 1932 EP published *Profile: An Anthology Collected in* MCMXXXI.

16. MM had sent "Old Tiger" to EP in 1918 (he commented on it in a letter to her dated December 16, 1918), but its first and only publication was in the *Profile* anthology.

and after what was said in *The Times* about the reissue of *Harmonium*, I feel as if one could not do too much for him. Dr. Hutchison and Dr. Eda Lou Walton as judges of verse are perfect examples of the ape-man with tail removed to fit the requirements of the archaeological party.[17]

Your vim in supposing I might guide or correlate the younger generation, is engaging; "it is pretty that you say." But I am without legs or wings in that matter. A magazine can be a nightmare of seeming ingratitude to friends by whom one has been lastingly obliged; offset of course by many zests; by good manuscripts, good printing, etc. The unresentment of my colleagues, S. W. [Sibley Watson] and S. T. [Scofield Thayer] toward the unkempt, their unwillingness to be hoodwinked, and their editorial unanimity, I was and am all for. But they will never have replicas.

The imperviousness of the people with power, to ability, is a dastardly thing. Nevertheless, talent can not be exterminated by uncordiality. When I look at Audubon's studies and feel the passion with which he worked, and recall that he kept a general store, was an itinerant portrait-painter of the dead, and could not get subscriptions for his folio, the inference concerning gusto is plain.

The majority of our practitioners I do not know. I do not listen to every word that is said and do not like to take time to study what has escaped me. Therefore I am not in a position to damn or encourage; and I shrink from misjudging. To be underestimated can be a benefit, but to one in earnest, everything is either a pain or a pleasure, and I don't want responsibility, except in the case of rather large talent. Courage against the bad is, as you say, a serious duty. The way to deal with caterpillars in a hive, however, is to wax them over. It is a temptation to rag them but the best way of annoying them is not to know that they exist. There are several semi-prominent writers that—to understate the matter—I do not like; but I don't wear myself out hating them.

One thing I am convinced of: the very greatest aid to the palpitant striver is the secure performance of an initiate.

As for myself, I feel that I have never been underestimated, in the right quarters. My product has been of no great account and my concern is to get expressed. I am under obligation to Lincoln Kirstein for his heartiness about my contributions to *The Hound & Horn,* and to Mr. Eliot for making me party to the subterranean processes of *The Criterion,* and to your commendations of course.

Conversation is a pleasure and I see no harm in it. On the other hand,

17. *Harmonium* was reissued in 1931. Percy Hutchison, in "Pure Poetry and Mr. Wallace Stevens" (*New York Times Book Review,* August 9, 1931), called the book a "stunt" and attacked pure poetry as "a glittering edifice of icicles." Eda Lou Walton, in "Beyond the Wasteland" (*Nation,* September 9, 1931), called Stevens a sensuous poet in "death valley" who practices a "deliberate deflation of the emotions."

I am conscious of the value of others' time and health, and am growing hard toward callers of the kind that ask you as you are being carried on a stretcher from your house to an ambulance, which you think is the greatest— William Faulkner, Robinson Jeffers, or Josephine Baker.[18] I am cautious, that is to say, about encouraging visitors who might stay too long or might bore my mother. She is over the heads of most of them, though at pains to conceal the fact and is over-solicitous about them as animals—their needs and feelings. I said recently, "The visitor couldn't have felt hurt, for you delayed him after he had said he must go." "Yes, but he knew that I delayed him out of contrition for not wanting him."! I see no reason why I should see Louis Zukofsky, but there is no reason why I should not, when we return from a two or three weeks' stay in the country. Your friendliness judiciously hazarded, I respect.[19] I much approve the saying a word while the person is alive to get the benefit. Also, I welcomed what you say of Harold Monro in *The Criterion*. It has never been an effort for me to be just to Harold Monro. I feel regret for him as a person, and an emotional debt to him if one can use the word. I did sigh over that absent-minded allusion to him in *Poetry*. And *Poetry* is usually, almost too brave.

In a number of the *Fifth Floor Window* that I have seen, a page by Harold Rosenberg[20] interested me, and two poems by W. W. E. Ross. But the name—*Fifth Floor Window*. One doesn't call oneself the fire-escape or the pollard rubber-tree.

As you surmise, anything you or William Carlos Williams have written, I should like to see; I have just bought his *Novelette* [*and Other Prose (1921–1931)*] and your Vol. I [*A Draft of XXX Cantos*] and am glad to infer a rush on them. (The price has been moved up from 50¢ to 75.) Whatever the struggle, the right things should be appearing and should be bought; and I feel low when buying second-hand. It is not mere formula, however, in the matter of your out-of-print books, and despite Miss Monroe's sympathetic regret at not being able to reward me highly in the matter of your *Cantos*— and regret at not being able to give me the review copy—I was so crude as to tell her when I saw her what I spent on *Pavannes and Divisions* (a John Quinn copy with a Jack Yeats drawing) and on the *Antheil*. I am delighted that *Romance* is reappearing, and to have the *How to Read* bound—for Mr. Strange could hardly pretend it's not the identical newspaper; the pages unbound, however, were so difficult to refer to, I find the volume very handy.[21] I could never take back anything I've said in praise of William Carlos

---

18. Josephine Baker (1906–1975), American-born Parisian singer and entertainer.

19. EP had encouraged Zukofsky to visit MM.

20. American art and literary critic (1906–1978).

21. EP's *Pavannes and Divisions* appeared in 1918; *Antheil and the Treatise on Harmony* in 1924. Five chapters of EP's *The Spirit of Romance* (1910) were reissued in

Williams; but his prose is not quite his verse; or is it that he is not infallible as a thinker? It is true, as he says, that "excellence defeats sales." Our publishers are a sorrow. But I disagree with William Carlos' every word on page 100; e.g. If you have not time for a library, learn to be a bartender.

I hope this will find you well; also your aides-de-camp, Mr. and Mrs. H. [Homer] P. [Pound].

Yours sincerely,   Marianne Moore

To Bryher   *October 3, 1932*

Dear Bryher,

Your letter has just come, and the account of [Sir Leonard] Woolley;[22] and a few days ago, *Close-Up*. It is a pleasure to know you have been seeing your family and that London is so gay. I wonder if you had time to go to the Zoo and if the little plumet basilisk they received a year or so ago is living. We shall be glad to see Dr. [Hanns] Sachs[23] if he should call on us. We liked his statement on Capital Punishment. Our telephone number is Sterling 3-1123.

I don't see as many movies as I should like to, and we don't go to the theatre at all, but I saw *Bring 'Em Back Alive* three times. Frank Buck was there "in person" and though nearly everything he said was, from an oratorical point of view, unfortunate, I had confidence in him; he seemed modest, sincere, and possessed of so much more than he was exhibiting. And didn't you think, in the film, that he dealt with the animals rather kindly and respectfully? At least I did not see him sitting on dead animals as Osa and Martin Johnson sometimes do. It is unnerving to see an agitated, passive creature like the monitor lizard tied down so it can't move and rushed awkwardly to a pen; the taste of the commentary, and the unauthentic interpretation put on the mannerisms of the silvery gibbon, reached a high level of asininity, but one has to bear in mind that scenario writing shows man and beast at their worst.

I enjoyed in *Close-Up*, your paragraphs on *Nippon*—"it is the way the grasses bend as they walk that is important." "The shadows of deer in a park become those of mediaeval beasts." And the comment on *Das keimende Leben*—"the 50 young babies lying in their baskets, the camera wandering from one basket to the other, taking close-ups of the little beings who seem to look all alike." The puppy and camel are priceless. I have never before

---

1932 in *Prolegomena 1–2*, which also included his *How to Read* (originally a series of articles in the New York *Herald Tribune* in 1929).

22. English archaeologist (1880–1960), who directed the excavations at Ur in Mesopotamia between 1922 and 1934.

23. Bryher's psychiatrist in Berlin, who published articles in *Close-Up*.

seen so graphic a view of a camel's hind legs folded, and I like the picture of Brigitte Helm. The Bumpus advertisement also is a pleasure—a remarkable sample of verbiage.

We are much interested in this abstract of the Woolley lecture. I once met Mr. Woolley at a reception given for him by the Oxford Press and was delighted with him.

During August we were in Connecticut, about a hundred miles away, in a friend's house while she and her husband were in the Adirondacks. She sent for us with her car and returned us in it. I wish you could see some of this New England country with its old trees, austerely kept, original houses, and Charles Demuth churches. To be there in the country, at leisure, was a greater pleasure than I can suggest in mentioning it, with giant petunias and pink lilies in bloom, woodpeckers, chipmunks and katydids to watch, and a tree-toad about the size of a cherry-stone—with silver-brown legs, green back, and gold line above each eye; but far from round. It was a miniature frog in every detail. I should not have been at leisure, for I had a review to write, of the Mabel Loomis Todd Emily Dickinson *Letters* published last fall. After coming home, I finished it and it is not as keen as it might be, but each try helps the next—I hope.

America is pestered at present by a man named Franklin D. Roosevelt, as Germany has been with Hitler, but I think Mr. Hoover will "win," as our neo-Hitler would put it.

I can't tell you how sorry I am to have you say your family seemed only "fairly" well; I hope the weather this winter will not be trying. Mother sends you her love.

Affectionately,   M. M.

P.S. We haven't yet settled on the present; as soon as we have, I shall tell you what it is.

To Alyse Gregory   *October 17, 1932*

Dear Alyse,

After our visit in Connecticut this summer, the flowers you mention and the walks you speak of taking, and the mushrooms, seem so real and delightful I ought not to wish you away from East Chaldon, but I do wish you were here to vote. Such an untutored clamor as is going up rouses the blood of even so schizoid a lizard as I.

Sir Oliver Lodge[24] has been a great inspiration to me—his way of saying things; also his attitude to life. I shall have in mind his son's book. Your chivalry to my monkey-puzzler stirs me to the soul. I can scarcely trust the

24. English physicist, philosopher, and student of psychic phenomena, particularly communication with the dead (1851–1940).

news that somebody likes my "poems," but your kindness to them and your suggesting that I go on has had a part in keeping me alert and in my dashing into print again. I had a few lines—rather weak—in the October *Poetry;* a better thing and two not very good ones in the June *Poetry,* and just now "The Jerboa" in *The Hound & Horn.* It may be that I should try to keep to prose, but if I should ever hazard another book you shall have it.

I had a letter from Ellen Thayer not long ago. She says Mrs. Thayer sees Scofield from time to time and I infer that he is intermittently reciprocal and not more unhappy than he has been. But Ellen wishes his mother had a counter distraction and were not so concentrated upon Scofield. Ellen did not mention the Watsons of whom I have not heard anything, nor Mr. McBride nor any of *The Dial* staff but spoke of her cousin Marjorie Clary and her new baby, and of Mrs. McDermot's having a baby, a son.

Like you, I don't feel sympathetic with the 18th century and do feel sympathetic with Swift. Last winter I was reading Thackeray's essay on him and glanced into a book of miscellaneous pieces by Swift—a stray volume from a set that we had once got second hand and had not read—letters and jottings. I was so charmed and stirred, I did not see how it is that I waste time as I do on newspapers and ephemera in the library. It takes as long to read an upstart letter to a young author by Virginia Woolf in *The Yale Review* as it takes to read a genuinely mordant letter by Swift or ten pages by Bacon. I am sure I should agree with you about Carl Van Doren's Swift and his straining to be clever. There is something lovable about Mark Van Doren and real ability in both the Van Dorens, I think, but they require a kind of conscientious good behavior on the part of the reader that is not a good omen. It's like the "admirable" and "symptomatic" and "well documented" of Babette Deutsch and Gorham Munson. We are not very enterprising and come on either blunders or hits, largely by accident.

Machiavelli is another real magician, to me, though all I know is *The History of Florence.* I am sure those letters are gems and that Llewelyn lets nothing escape him.

I am glad of that cook who comes to you three times a week. I had never seen anything that even approached the charm and snugness of your house on the White Nose and to have you say this one you now have is snugger, indeed paints a picture.

We receive mail from Samoa once a month and are in a great flurry of excitement always over that but nothing else seems to happen [to] us. I see that Yeats is to lecture in Brooklyn sometime during the winter.

I hope you both are well and that you did go to London, for the play and for other things. We think of you in so many ways; when taking walks which I do obediently to an oculist's recommendation, and in ways you might not even guess. I feel so strongly that your writing should be fostered.

Affectionate wishes to you and Llewelyn from us both.

Did you ever get a fountain pen that you like as well as the one you were going to replace?

I noticed in something that Gilbert Seldes & Georg Grosz are inaugurating an art magazine of some kind;—better news perhaps—that Albert Einstein is coming to America to teach. He is one of the over-photographed persons that is, I think possessed of real life & originality.

To Monroe Wheeler   *November 20, 1932*

Dear Monroe,

What a surprise! One of a thousand good ones for you, I hope. Japan I am sometimes interested in, but China is the magic place. I have just recently been trying to write something about dragons, "true" dragons and the malign variety.

It is impressive to us that with all your multitude of goings and obligations you can bear us in mind and be at trouble for us in these many ways—sending the chapel miniatures and the animal portraits, and just now, the Christie catalogue. It may be a coincidence of which you were not aware—but the Dresden candelabrum swan is the kind of which I was thinking, in a small thing of mine which *Poetry* published this fall; indeed better I think than the Lord Balfour swan which I had in mind—and the bulrushes are capital. I look on the Chippendale tripod stands as acquaintances also, and could not say how I prize the hound's mask, the Tigerware jug, the needlework, the many expert descriptions, the official statement on the title-page, and so on.

Among the animal portraits, I set particular store by the macaw, having always wanted a picture of those feather stripes that surround the eye, and the iguana is another favorite.

I seem to be writing this letter by commas, so many interruptions, pleasant and others, occur. We have had [Arturo] Toscanini and [Leopold] Stokowski alternately, vying with each other, to be modern—Bernard Brooks [?] vs. Bernard Wagenaar—; Mildred Dilling and a quartet playing Mozart and some contemporary pieces for horn and flute, a lecture on the brain and learning processes of the ant, and a heartrending account of the people in the Colca-Valley in Peru—with their bare feet and drunken speeches, llamas and mules, grass bridges and borrowed saints on white horses with scintillating draperies and gold-leaf trees.

Miss Monroe read at the Institute and spent an evening with us. She seems to be encouraged about *Poetry*'s continuing, but I am sure would be happier if poets were as eager subscribers as they are contributors.

To return to that incident of the corner table at the Café de la Paix which Burton Holmes took to New York with him, I have been meaning to add that the really entertaining feature, I thought, was the dismay of two writers conferring unobserved, as they thought, in the very rear of the tables. Their disgust was dramatic beyond any sleights of hand over a table.

This will not get to you in time to take our Christmas wishes but they last far beyond a day, or dates, and we are hoping your trip will have all the glamor and none of the deprivations of "the Oriental adventure."

Warner unfortunately is not near enough your ports, to see you. His address, in case you should extend your itinerary, is Pago-Pago, Tutuila, American Samoa.

Yours affectionately,   Marianne M.

To Kenneth Burke   *November 30, 1932*

Dear Mr. Burke:

This is salient; what you say in "The Poet and the Passwords"—in key and as a piece of writing, and it does me a world of good, for I am tired of rough writing. I hope you can let me keep both enclosures; though I shall not backfire if you had not meant to. The Stoic is a fascinating touch and extremely characteristic of yourself. Glenway Wescott's aesthetic proficiencies are remarkable, I think, and in some ways unique but his deficiencies in the matter of philosophy and economics render him useless in those fields.

As for capital and labor, I agree with every word[25]—or nearly, as follows: capitalism leads to revolution and the remedies are increased taxation, nationalization of industries, and compulsory national service, civil and military. But "the people," you and I, and always the artist, elude responsibility and the result is likely to be a dictatorship such as they have in Russia or in Spain or in Italy.

It is trying, to have people who think well in one direction, dodge thinking about the whole; but we are subject to illusions about labor as well as about capital. "Trade unionism is itself a phase of capitalism for it applies to labor as a commodity, capital's principle of selling in the dearest market and giving as little as possible for the price." Furthermore, "labor will not surrender its right to be idle, and it repudiates national service." So whether capital or labor has the power, there is a deadlock.

Ezra Pound disapproves so strongly of Washington that he writes it a pamphlet of instructions but he has not been voting and does not expect to vote. Glenway Wescott asks the world to give him the necessary hours in which to write a book about its troubles and when we have the book, it is about him and not about the world:—(e.g. it is inexcusable of the throne of

25. KB's letter included a three-page discussion of labor economics.

the copper king to shake so much for when it shakes, writers can't write. All parents are asked to eat their third baby, for to see so many hungry mouths about us is agitating and a menace to art). I am not prepossessed by patriotism in absentia, but hypocrisy is equally abhorrent and at the risk of making myself look worse than I am, I confess to buying butter and potatoes at the A. & P. though my small grocer whom I occasionally patronize, goes out of business; and to writing a poem on a persimmon let us say instead of joining with our capitalist friends in handing out the local dole; and I should hate to see you interrupt your remarkable writing, for it is that, to make speeches for Norman Thomas[26] or organize such emergency unemployment for labor as you yourself approve. For you to take time to write to me so carefully is an unusual thing for anyone to do; and I look on Mahatma Gandhi as unusual; we, most of us, abhor public service and so long as we do, there will always be a Senator [Hiram W.] Johnson or Britten [Sam G. Bratten?] who rejoices to pinch-hit for us.

As for prospective political salvation Governor Roosevelt, when he speaks, always says just the unsuitable thing and I don't know how we are to expect him henceforth to be wise. His grateful co-operation, since election, with Hearst, with the anti-Negro south, and the Cermak-Farley north, does not ease my sense of insecurity. And the bargaining tariff which he still speaks of operating means that he would befriend some of his "people" and some, not.[27]

Mr. Thomas is for something that will work, and alludes sourly to his resting rival's Gallically divided party; but both Norman Thomas and Mr. Roosevelt, however enlightened the aim they profess, are, to me,—like the spotily pigmented offspring of a Negro and a white parent, biologically inept, and we don't want them—or rather, need not want them, for we said at the polls that we wanted one of them. Thomas Mann would not, I know, employ Fannie Hurst[28] as an amanuensis, however much Fannie H. wanted him to. That is to say, the inward characteristic of either Thomas or Roosevelt is an inharmony which nothing but death will cure. I talk as if I thought I were Plato; whereas it is as a poor Hopi that I speak. But let me add, I feel so much your kindness—another rare commodity—in writing out for me this genealogy of our condition that I don't know how to seem as grateful as I am. Your "faith" in a program also, is intrinsically a benefit;

26. Norman Mattoon Thomas (1884–1968) had been Socialist candidate for president in 1928 and 1932.

27. Refers to the political ties between (Boss) Anton J. Cermak, mayor of Chicago, and James A. Farley, FDR's manager. In 1931 Farley collaborated with Cermak to hold the Democratic National Convention in Chicago. Cermak headed the third-largest delegation.

28. American novelist known for her sentimental and morally didactic fiction (1889–1968).

but until we get someone who is a better target than Norman Thomas, I am subterranean.

M. M.

To John Warner Moore, Jr.   *December 9, 1932*

Dear Johnnie, I guess you know what this is. There was a picture of an ant-eater like this in the book about strange animals, that you gave me; and it is

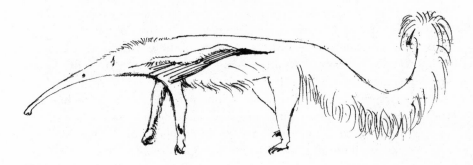

walking on the backs of its hands and has a large plumy tail. This one is stuffed and the kind of alligator I have made on the side is a jet black mark and there are several cowlicks on him—one on the neck, one under the chin, and one back of the ear. What wouldn't I give if you had all been with me today at the Museum. In the Nature Room, there are live white rats, a kangaroo-rat, a flying squirrel, a gray squirrel and several other live animals. The kangaroo-rat has the softest fur I ever felt and I wish you could have seen it fill its cheeks with bird-seed and hop to a corner of the cage and bury it in the sand and then go to sleep in a ball not much bigger than a walnut. It has been in the Museum two years and has never taken a drop of water although there was some where it could get it; for the grain it eats is turned to water in its body. It has a little house the size of a strawberry box.

I was allowed to pick up the tiger salamander but did not hold it long for it loves to cover itself up with black moss and not let a soul see it. It was about five inches long, with black islands and circles on a pale gray background, and rests in curves that are more graceful than anything anybody could draw. Please tell Bee and Sallie about him and tell them I was allowed to feed the red efts little white worms—about a quarter of an inch long and small as a hair, these worms were.

Please tell your mother and Mary that the scout exhibits of oak-leaves and oak bark, and pig-hickory, and birch buds made me wish I had been with them in the Westchester woods last year. There was too, a perfect model of beavers building a dam and stocking their lake-side with twigs for the winter, and among the insects was a moth bigger than my hand with lavender stripes, one on each wing, and moon-like peacock eyes made of a black line, a pale green line, and a round yellow centre. I passed it and then went back to make a hurried picture. Two boys came up close to see the picture, and one said as if he were not very serious, "the *ar*-tist!" But I did not take offense and we talked for several minutes about the bird pictures and the mosses that were exhibited and labeled near-by.

Your daddy might have been interested in the many sun-dials and compasses showing the history of such things from the very beginning. Many were pocket dials with a compass about as big as a quarter at the bottom. And the fin of the sun-dial which stands out from the face, folded down flat so as to take no room. One of these fins was in the shape of a bird with the eye of the bird made by a nail-head that fastened two sheets of brass together. And the numbers were beautifully engraved in the brass.

The ant-eater does not seem to want me to type-write all over his Pomeranian tail, so good-bye, and give my love to each one.

Affectionately,   Rat

The ant-eater I saw and made this picture of, is about as long as your dining-room table.

To John Warner Moore   *Dec[ember] 18, 1932*

Dear Pago,

I requested the Sergeants to protest and I told the S.P.C.A. [Society for the Prevention of Cruelty to Animals] they might ask Prof. W. L. Phelps, the Department of English, etc., to protest; that his opinion has great weight and that he had spoken against Ernest Hemingway's *Death in the Afternoon*, in his talks on books at the Brooklyn Institute. Having thrashed about in the bamboos till I was tired I went to bed and had a good sleep and yesterday morning I got a letter from Carl Laemmle of the U.P. [Universal Pictures] Corporation saying their only wish was to entertain & not to be gory but I would probably be glad to know that they were not making the film—at least not yet. (Yes, I also wrote Mr. Barrett of the Nat'nl Board of Review which sends me invitations to previews, urging that the Board not pass the film if the Universal P. Corp. persisted in making it.) *Now* if they start making it, I am going to get Bryher of *Close-Up* to protest, and give them no comfort. This film is being promoted to prepare sentiment on the part of people for bull-fighting in America. (Unless Ernest Hemingway has delivered an estocada to the gizzard beforehand.)[29]

29. The whole first paragraph and several later words and phrases were crossed out in blue pencil, but not, apparently, by MM. Some crossed-out words, for example, are needed in order to make sense of a sentence, or their context.

Park Pressey of ——————, was excellent on Longfellow, Emerson, Lowell, Holmes, and Whittier, with wonderful pictures of the L. house in Portland, of the habber [harbor], of the Wayside Inn (now owned by Mr. Ford) and the insides of the respective houses. The North and South Churches in Boston inside and out were perfect; and all his views illustrating places mentioned in the poems; the "meccars" of all who love our New England authors and their lit.

I forgot to mention that Mark Haight who lectured on English Inns showed photographs of the *Victory* which is not allowed to be photographed but the Admiral was so kind as to say he would go over the ship and if the pictures were taken in his presence no objections could be made. It is rather ornate at the stern but a fine-looking thing and certainly a thought provoking one.

Yeats made a very great hit with me, and the audience behaved better than for any other unadulteratedly literary person so I suppose he has a lure for all; they rustle and get up and go out, and yawn, and play hippopotamus under the slightest sense of ennui. He spoke on The New Ireland—introduced by Mark Van Doren—author of *Jonathan Gentry*. He has white hair and instead of being retired and rasped by ague as Padraic Colum had given me the impression he was, he is hearty, smiling, benevolent, and elegant with a springiness and vigor that no invalid could very well counterfeit. He traced the ills of Ireland, the inevitableness of the revolution, and the sentiment which insists on Gaelic for all, and the literary element as part of the political. You could never hear more finished speaking or see a finer manner; he has the hands of a hereditary royalist who never picked up a stone or touched his own shoes; (but the evening clothes could have been given a few lessons on repose by Tripler or Gieves). However nothing was actually not right. Dr. Van Doren sat in his chair like a post-boy sleeping by the harness, not that his attention wandered but he seemed far from the picture in which the experienced impresario was figuring. He has the very instructive gift— for a writer—of mingling lowly words with the aristocratic so that there is never the effect of stiffness or "side," and is witty in addition—though also unsatisfactory where boors are concerned; as when a woman asked, something about "Shaw Desmond," a quack Irish lecturer of whom the snobbish Mrs. Colum said "It sounds as if you called yourself Mr. Uncle-Sam-Vanderbilt." Mr. Yeats looked very amused but said cordially, "Since coming to America, I have heard a number of Irish names that are new to me, and this is one about which I shall have to inform myself when I get back to Ireland." As a sample of his "prose" he was talking about Lady Gregory and he said, "She had a quality praised by Aristotle. If you are buying a ball and that ball costs only sixpence and is the best ball, it has the virtue of magnificence. Sir T. Malory gave that quality to King Arthur. It is a quality that means in a writer you will never give the people less than your best—if that best has to wait a century to be accepted by them . . . Passion delights in extreme courses and despite our loyalty to the ideal which united us, we never could have kept to it if we had not been kept to it by Lady Gregory's fortitude and her patience." A classic of the street that he quoted amused Mouse. It is as follows: after the war, 1340:

> *You haven't an eye and you haven't a leg*
> " " " " " " " " "
> *You're an eyeless noseless chickenless egg*
> *And you'll have to be put in a bowl to beg.*
> *Johnnie, I hardly knew you.*

I have never seen greater ease, and after the lecture, he said, "If there are any questions you'd like to ask, I can perhaps throw light on some things that in my address I was not able to touch on." Quite a pause. "It's a bold man that will ask the first question," he said, and then there were one or two. Much and too much was said about Liam O'Flaherty and others and I therefore asked if Daniel Corkery was not very accurate in descriptions of his locality. "Yes," he said he was; and that he occupied a very interesting position he stood for a Gaelic Catholic Ireland and could not accept the position of the protestant literary men "and for this reason," he said "he refused our invitation to be a member of the Irish Academy. It's an interesting position and perhaps a useful one, in providing something against which to protest."

Afterward, I decided I would go round and speak to him and to Mark Van Doren. The lecture was in the opera house and generously on the part of the Institute, free to members and the second-tier boxes were free, so having gone a little early, I sat in one of those boxes. I could not find a rathole leading to the stage so went out and around and was waiting by the lost and found cage when Mark and a lady came out. Much blinking and swallering; I don't know just why; I now think because of the lady; for it was not Mrs. V. D. and although I should see nothing wrong with that; if Mark did, then I would. He was all courtesy, had been meaning to thank me for my review; in fact it was the one he cared about most, it was the only one that really dealt with the book. We discussed the book and he asked me about the Powyses and I tried to urge him to suggest reviews for them in *The Nation* or *Tribune* though I did not mention those names. A chief usher who always favors Mole and me had been hanging around to take me to the reception-room as he was the chamberlain, but before we finished with *Jonathan Gentry* Mr. Yeats came out with the lecture-bureau man and nothing could be more gracious; he made a stately bow and made some remark about my writing, in the form of a question but in my excitement I missed it and I said something about his brother, Mr. Jack Yeats who gave me the photograph of his painting *The Spotted Pony*—having said in the beginning, "Your being here is a great blessing to America and I hope it's not too paining an experience for you" (tastefully received). He went out; I having said he mustn't be kept, tired as he would be after speaking, and Mark and the lady, a Mrs. Jameson I think, lingered a few minutes to praise Mr. Yeats and taper off.

Not having expected to speak to Mr. Yeats till Mole said she thought it might be well I had on my house-dress which has on the light blue trimming the ineradicable vestiges of a cod-liver oil spot I got on it before I went to *The Dial*—so Mr. Yeats is more than quits on the score of the evening clothes. But naturally, I had on my coat with the raccoon fur, and my caterpillar derby and a tolerable pair of yellow chamois gloves. And there were ten or 11 people creating a woods. Somewhat meditative on the subject, however, when I got home, I said to Mole, "I look a little insignificant, don't I, in this short Tyrolean petticoat of a dress?" and Mole said, "Yes, you do."

I had your mouse in Baffin Land today—Fort Greene Park. The snow is light and clean and most of the paths were shoveled; the park was full of flexible flyers, colored children, white children, poppas, sparrows, and so on. Yesterday we had an all-day snowing—steady diagonal blizzard-snow with fishes and mountains forming on the windows such as I haven't seen since I was a baby. Mr. Jordan and others had to go out every little while and shovel, and the wheels of cars spun helplessly and to no purpose. Now things are pretty well cleared, but it is still a pretty scene. I wish you could get a little of it.

Joe and Mrs. Nowack & Miss Esther Knable, Joe's "girl," came in this morning. She is a lovely girl, exceedingly pretty; also serious with large eyes which she fixes on you as if anticipating some great excitement; very slight; with cold, claw-like hands and dainty but judicious clothes and she is very "bright"; in her fourth year at Cooper Union. You would have thought Joe has shown his ability once again. She obtained for him through a friend the position of time-keeper at the new Cornell Medical Center and he has been there since September. Hours 7 to 4 or 2 to 12; but he doesn't complain and I think with so fine and helpful a girl, his patience should be augmented. He spied the tapa cloth and said, "Did your brother send you that skin?" They pored over the symbols on it and Joe pointed out the other things he wanted *Esther* to "see."

To Ezra Pound　　　*January 18, 1933*

Dear E.P.,

I see the point. The workshop, moreover, would be a much more useful place if all were frank as well as prompt.

Mr. Burke is an expert, literarily, in several ways and has important essays in his book, *Counter-Statement*, and I bring down the knobbed club of a cannibal on the head of anyone who says he isn't or hasn't—though I don't agree with him in matters pertaining to religion and politics. I should stop here but honesty gets the better of me and I will say that it was careless and unsophisticated to propose as a substitute a man who was—with his work—in plain sight for all to see. Nevertheless, when each searches his conscience, is any guiltless.

The James does not require a notice, I suspect; my suspicion being corroborated by Mr. Zabel who said when here shortly ago, "I should think you would need to supplement it with other writing of James's on the theatre." E. E. Cummings still seems promising, but I do not ask authors for their books, and some authors aren't in libraries.

I like *Il Mare*[30] very much—and those excellent pictures—and of course don't object to being the object of selectly exaggerated encomiastik criticism—much more suited shall we say to Mary Butts of *Seed*. What is a subscription to *Il Mare* in dollars?

I have not turned down Mr. Leippert, and indeed honored him with an explanation:—that I cannot enter upon an official program of any sort with anyone. You got *The Criterion* to let me write for it and I should like to contribute twice—three times perhaps—before apprenticing myself to another magazine. There is *The New Act* though *Act III* would sound better. I am weakening in the direction of *Contempo* which came before Mr. Leippert.

January 26. I had got so far when it was necessary for me to write a review of *The Warden* by Anthony Trollope. I shall, of course, sign.[31] It's what I've been doing for years in anything I wrote. As for launching something, you force from me again the discreditable statement that I am glad of hospitality but will not work. The donkeys that turn windlasses to raise water from stage to stage of the river-bank, are not the best specimens of the country's fauna. I am, as you know, against toadying to intellect; and am against social mercy i.e. helping the book of a somebody who is nobody; against helping the book of one's patron or protégé if his book is inferior. Bickering is in general, wasteful. With regard to the upstart, denunciation is praise. And centipedes should be avoided, not portrayed by Boutet de Monvel,[32] *fils*, for the magazine with coated paper.

As for signers. I don't see how even the best of cowboys can round the animals up without being among them; the sorts that we have, being for the zoo, besides, rather than for the corral.

Joe Gould and Mr. Cummings are bright but unbenevolent. I have,

30. EP had arranged for MM to receive the Rapallo newspaper (EP to MM, November 27, 1932).

31. In 1933 EP was circulating a manifesto concerning standards for criticism.

32. Boutet de Monvel (1850–1913), French artist who illustrated books for children, including books by Anatole France and Jean de La Fontaine.

once or twice, thought well of Francis Fergusson but he may not be a joiner.
I think I have seen an article by Stanley Kunitz that I thought well of. Morris U. Schappes wrote a better review of Mabel Loomis Todd's *Emily Dickinson (Symposium)* than I wrote of it. That is all I know of him. I think I
recall in the same magazine a good review by Philip Rice. John Chamberlain of *The Times* is as good as anyone we have, and does not wear the
frogged livery of a doorman. I don't know him but infer that he is young.
Herbert Gorman was quite remarkable a little while ago, on Hawthorne
and the Sophia Hawthorne scandal and a long while ago reviewed my book
in a way not by any means crude. Sherry Mangan's poem on a seagull is one
of the best on this bird that I know, and as editor of *Larus* he did the printing himself, so I am for him.[33] But such evaluations are folly, being subject
to revision and certain ones as you would know are confidential. To include
Carl Rakosi and leave out Kenneth Burke is humorous to me who have
ranged this part of the world. Such confusions lay one open to the charge of
bigotry. Louis Zukofsky does not write very well in prose and his verse is
fluttered; but he has a heart for the thing and in a measure profits by the experience of others, so I would think it right for him to sign. (I have not yet
asked him to come to see us, being engrossed with my distant family—and
letters now and then on unpugnacious essays or poems by a beginner. I
staked all for some weeks on a poem about the plumet basilisk; am hampered by a love for music and certain little lectures at the Brooklyn Academy of Arts and Sciences. Thus a week—perhaps three weeks—will pass
without my getting to the work in hand.)

Basil Bunting's I-said-the-fly manner in the August *Poetry* was so acceptable that I can pardon a great deal but there is a great deal to pardon.
He broke Rule I in the Jan. *Hound & Horn*, ignoring the rudimentary
axiom that nowadays the man who hates you is the man who loves you.
The decencies of speech, moreover, are not negligible—even supposing
a-spade-a-spade means nothing by the terms he uses which I would not use
at all.

Hyatt Mayor and James Farrell I don't know. H[enry] B[amford]
Parkes I shall examine in the current *Hound & Horn*.

The housemaid's chorus does not clean the house but if there is to be
a manifesto I am sure all appropriate editors and ex-editors, if I may say
so, should be signers. In stressing principles I do not see how they could

33. Francis Fergusson (1904–1986), American educator, author, and poet; Stanley Kunitz (1905–), American poet; Philip Rice (1904–1956), American philosopher
and editor of the *Kenyon Review* (1938–44); John Chamberlain (1903–1995), American editor, critic, and author of *Farewell to Reform* (1932); Herbert Gorman
(1893–1954), American biographer and poet; Sherry Mangan (1904–1961), American
fiction writer, poet, book designer, editor, and assistant editor of *Pagany: A Native
Quarterly* (1930–33).

be thought to be praising themselves. Or perhaps the objection was a subtler one.

Mr. Foster and Mr. [George] Hays, of whom I hear good things.

T. S. Eliot before he leaves us.

Mr. and Mrs. Abernethy.

Lincoln Kirstein

Wm. Carlos Williams and Dr. Zabel.

Miss Monroe is in constant contact with the callow, and is unfluctuatingly kind and should, I think, as opportunity offers, be cited for bravery.

H.D. (address: Case Postale 72 La Tour Vaud-Suisse)

Yours sincerely, Marianne Moore

To John Warner Moore *Feb[ruary] 12, 1933*

Dear Pen-viper,

I am glad you were considered to have been reared enough, literally—to take charge of the paper, and you certainly would have been in clover with Willow and me as legs for the project. I am always glad to make changes that are *good;* in fact would pay any possum for describing with his tail any diagrams that are helpful and *artistic*. But the work of editing don't seem requited properly by the bananas they give you, so *don't* accept. They'll ask you again presently; and you say your paws are full.

As for those alligator-pots, there is a place on the Upper Nile, I think, where alligators—nay crocodiles—abound, and the pots should be first tried there—running far into the bush and not going back to see how many alligators were potted, for an alligator is one of those fish that is very ambitious to be its own satchel. They become very readily entangled in their own osiers, however. Just now, I have looked about 2 hours for a quotation by Pliny or Fuller or someone in Alice Morse Earle's *Sun-dials and Roses of Yesterday*—in vain; about the bee as an animal that ever loves to return to its home and is eminently busie and sober.

I am very nearly like an imprisoned blue-bottle with my reading and potential engagements. I went to hear Mrs. Leonora Speyer and Joseph Auslander[34] read the other night and was much impressed. Mrs. Speyer was beautifully dressed—in black with fringed over-wings, black slippers with onyx-and-diamond-buckles, a gray pearl on the right pad—as big as a small grape—and a white one the same size on the left paw. She read as an encore, a reply to an editor who said a poem was too long. She said:

> *"You gave me sky:*
> *Then clipped my wings and said I should not fly."*

---

34. Leonora Speyer (1872–1956), American poet who won a Pulitzer Prize in 1927 for *Fiddler's Farewell;* Joseph Auslander (1897–1965), American poet.

Joseph is talented and over-worked—not dressed like he should be but a re-markable person I would say—and grateful. He urged me to have lunch with him in memory of his offerings to *The Dial* and I value that, though I said I didn't live in New York no more and must not accept but that I might call on him for advice sometime—by letter—for some beginner I was help-ing. "That's bully of you," he said. Mrs. S. ast me if I would come to see her sometime—phone her soon—tomorrow at one; and Miss Bonner said she was going to take advantage of my suggestion that she come to see my mother and me and phone me maybe Friday—but didn't. Thursday I called on Mrs. Speyer. She used to live on Wash. Sq.; now at 60 Gramercy Park North—in a building like 101 Lafayette Ave.—on the 6th floor at the very point on the Park where the street that bounds the west side runs, and a tall tree with a white bird-house with about 100 holes in it stands on that edge of the park. The apt. has 3 doors—2 front, one at rt. angles—each with a cocoa-fibre mat in front of it—tan with red letters—L.S.—and I take it two daughters live with Mrs. S. I was shown into a longish narrow drawing-room with 2 windows—full to the picture-moulding with madonnas in im-mense gold filigree frames—triptychs of saints and haloes on *vargueños*, high-backed chairs with *scutari* red or dark blue velvet gold-braided uphol-stery and sundry Italian and Persian and Spanish potteries. I was then led to the hall and into door 2. There I entered into Elizabethan congeries of petit-point James I chairs, foot-stools, miniature arm-chairs, love-seats, gate-legged tables with a vase of yellow tulips—antique refectory table used as a desk with iron snake paper-weight—French phone—many let-ters with black borders addressed to ladies (I ween). Mrs. Speyer came in immediately but had no sooner sat down than the phone rang and she said, "I'm going to take this in another room; I don't want to bother you with this rather tiresome committee-business—and I'll make it short. It's too annoy-ing to be broken in on this way. It'll be *one* moment." I examined the ani-mals on the needle-point chair and they certainly are droll—a kind of kangaroo antelope, and six or 7 birds—no two alike with very sly foolish at-titudes. Well I had no sooner examined one when Mrs. Speyer sped back into the room and we discussed the arts for some time. Finally it appeared that "Harriet" [Monroe] had been trying to get Mrs. Speyer to patronize her despite three "insults." Mrs. Speyer always gave $100 a year to *Poetry*—asked Miss Monroe to dinner—Hen. 8 to Cardinal Wolsey as it were—and is Vice-Pres. of the Poetry Society. A few years ago, Miss Monroe got (through Mrs. McCormick who died recently,) a pension for Ernest Walsh—a poet and ex-flier—and $2000 in cash. He squandered the money and was robbed in New York and was sailing for France and Miss Monroe got Miss Speyer to lend the money and it resulted in Mrs. Speyer eventually giving most of it though Miss Monroe supplied some of it. Since then Mrs. S. received a Pulitzer Prize, a Blindman Prize and I think 2 others—and had had a prize from *Poetry*. But Miss Monroe, incensed that certain of her protégés were overlooked and that the prize was awarded by Dr. Cross, John Erskine and someone else, none of whom writes poetry, wrote a 3 or 4 page editorial lampooning the award as a Wall Street Columbia connivance and ended by saying she hoped other prizes would be awarded by a committee of *poets*—to someone "of worth and incidentally not a person of wealth." In the course of the lampoon she said "Mrs. Speyer is a poet of fine quality" but this was contradicted almost throughout. She said better poets should have got the Blindman prize and that the committee of award meant nothing unless it was made up of poets. Also she quoted a protest from an indignant reader—not giving the name—a very rough, tousled letter by an obvious nobody. *Mr.* Speyer said Miss Monroe should never enter their house again. Since that he has died, so Mrs. Speyer feels a kind of sacred obligation to ban Harriet. But Harriet wrote her, saying, "Dear Leonora, be an angel and send me the $100 you have been giving as a guarantor. And by the way, congratulations on the Pulitzer Prize." Mrs. S. replied, "My dear Harriet, I am always glad to be a friend of *Poetry* and enclose my cheque for $100, but are not your congratulations, Dear Harriet, a little belated—as adding to the happiness of that for me really joyous event? And was not the unsigned letter something quite apart from your individual opinion of the award? Was not that irrelevant—and should I be made a stick for beating the invulnerable back of John Erskine?" I don't quote it exactly. Then Mrs. Speyer's last book, *Naked Heel* was reviewed by Stanley Kunitz in *Poetry* and she was made a fringe worsted monkey of; and in the February issue, "Dr. Zabel" says David Morton's anthology containing Leonora Speyer, V. Sackville-West, Margaret Emerson Bailey, etc., is foolish to have such inclusions if Eliot, Marianne Moore, etc. are omitted. These odors having been just loosed, Miss Monroe comes to town en route to Mexico and the Poetry Society meeting comes the same week. "The girls telephoned me in a flutter of embarrassment and despair," Mrs. Speyer said & asked "*What shall we do?*" I said, "*She is invited to the dinner—of course—and she has the place of honor, at the speakers' table.*" Then when Miss Monroe arrived, Mrs. S. greeted her handsomely and led her to the speakers' table; and saw nothing of her the rest of the evening.

I was sorry to see that the disparagement of the prize and Mr. Speyer's wounds have half spoiled Mrs. S's joy in her work—and I know Miss Monroe so well psychologically as the cat that upsets the flower-pot in its hurry to go somewhere, that I dethorned the harm as best I could—but when Mrs. Speyer mailed me the Pulitzer Comment by Miss Monroe I felt and Mouse feels that it ought to be atoned for, because of its laidliness—almost coarseness. And I wrote her so. She said as I was leaving her house, "Harriet is an envious self-centred egomaniac without any sense of humor, and if that isn't the worst combination of qualities you could have, I'd like to know what they are." But Harriet does like her poetry, and her—and of course the dinners and the money. But I hope they can neutralize the hatiness and each succeed—for Mr. Speyer is dead and Miss Monroe never had a husband, and nothing but bitterness to nourish is a sad fate. Mrs. Speyer is a fascinating creature, a wonderful giver, and desiring to have no hard feeling and her "work" is her harp carried by an orphan boy. I told her it was enough to me to like what I write myself and know that 2 or 3 others like it—that logic tells me it is better than Kathleen Millay or the flock of imposters; yet that I *don't* like it as well as I like Chaucer and Shakespeare—so carpers don't figure in my activities. Still she fleas herself furiously and begs aid. She said, "*You* are a very powerful person, but when John Erskine says I am a poet, they think, 'that fool, what does *he* know!'" She said, "Harriet is all smiles and comes up, *dear Leonora,* just as if nothing had happened, and telephones me, and wants to come to lunch; but I *don't feel* that way, though I always greet her just as if nothing was the matter." She kept saying, "I *must* meet your mother sometime, I *must;* now that I've found you, you know, you're not going to escape me." She gave me *Naked Heel* and inscribed it enthusiastically, and you may remember, put me in an anthology one time published by Kurt Wolff—giving me two leather-backed special copies, about 8 years ago.

To Morton Dauwen Zabel   *February 15, 1933*

Dear Mr. Zabel,

I have been wanting all my life to write about Yeats and now seem to be taking a lifetime to write about him. I plan to send you 1000 words by air mail as soon as the paper is done, but am writing you now that you may tell me to defer it till the May issue in case more manuscript has arrived than you can use and you are wondering whom to defer. To write even a few lines about Mr. Yeats, one needs, I find,—despite Edmund Wilson—to have read *A Vision,* enthralling but long. And in reading the recent *Words for Music Perhaps & Other Poems* which I haven't received but got in the library rare book-room, with *A Vision,* I saw that it is more important perhaps than *The Winding Stair* and *The Tower.* I have four or five of the books but had no idea it would be so difficult to find the others—and there are a good many, besides an author or two that should be consulted on alchemy and the Rosicrucians. You have not been "haggling" but very generous and I am almost in despair to find myself so cluttered as I am.

I called on Miss Monroe at The Bristol and heard her read some of her poems over the radio, the next morning. She seemed happy in the prospect of her trip and of going with friends—and of leaving the paper in your hands. I hope you won't find the last ironic.

It is most interesting news you give of the music you have been hearing, of the magazines, and of T. S. Eliot; and it is good of you to tell me with whom I shall appear. We have heard Prokofiev over the radio, and Ellen Thayer tells me that T. S. Eliot is to lecture at the New School April 17th and 20th. If there was no furor over him at Harvard I am not surprised but I am sorry. What is quiet and serious is what one expects from him and I am disappointed if Harvard was not responsive. But real mental attainment is a barrier to popularity. As a bookseller said to me the other day when I was enquiring about Yeats, "I don't want him; he's a very poor seller."

I am afraid I agree with you about Louis Zukofsky, Carl Rakosi, and Basil Bunting, though Basil Bunting was very entertaining in the August *Poetry*. As for myself, while Ezra Pound is teaching me to play puss-in-the-corner with rejection slips, your exaggerated praise is timely aid. I do feel a very great debt to you for this article in the *Journal des Poètes*—and for your missing me from the David Morton anthology.

I have been so buried in Yeats reading, I know nothing about any sporting event except that I saw a line in *The Times* about the whisker-weight crown contended for by Corporal Jubb, 92 years old; and George Washington Brown, 80 years old. Burton Rascoe's *Titans of Literature*— including Milton and Dante,—are not luring me away from the Yeats.

I gave Miss Monroe a copy of some published poems by Mary Hoxie Jones, daughter of Mr. Rufus Jones, the Quaker, and suggested to Miss Monroe that she show them to you. Since that I hear that Miss Jones submitted something to *Poetry*; but what, I don't know.

Sincerely yours,   Marianne Moore

P.S. Speaking of Ezra Pound, a favor that for a long time I have been meaning to ask of you, I think I will ask even in a postscript. Would you give me back—or destroy—a letter from me to *Poetry* about my *Cantos* review— soon after it came out—in which I said that Ezra Pound was likely to be abominable or astonishing—I don't remember just what? I was not satisfied to say it at the time I wrote it and should have obeyed my instinct, instead of saving my time then and wasting yours now. Not only did Ezra Pound not receive the review unkindly but since that has exerted himself in my behalf; and even before that, though undecorous to my friends at *The Dial*, he never was so to me.

To Bryher   *February 22, 1933*

Dear Bryher,

What matchless friendship, for you to think toward us and invite us to open our hearts in distress. And better even than having you give to us if we were in perplexity, is knowing that we have a friend that we could turn to without shame or the sense of desperation. We did lose most of my earnings, but have the greater part of the income we had before I went to *The Dial*, and Warner was so outraged at the thought of our losses that he is almost unbalanced in his determination to make it up to us; giving us, for instance, a Navy allotment that more than covers our rent, paying our telephone-bill, and subscribing to *The Times* for us—(and to *The Landmark!*[35] I suppose you know what that is). The situation throughout the country is unbelievably sad; a widower getting himself arrested—a ten months' prison sentence—for having abandoned his children, so the grandparents would receive aid from a welfare committee; an etcher with a wife and small child being dispossessed because the pictures he had sold were not paid for; and miners in almost unconceivably desperate circumstances. I shall never cease to respect Mr. Wrigley of the chewing-gum we despise, for raising the wages of all his employees so they will have a little more than they spend for mere existence. And you could not know—whatever I might say—what I feel about your principle of philanthropy. It inspires me to do my very best—not only for the worthy but for the unworthy. As my Uncle said, "I hear too much about helping God's poor, let me help the devil's poor." (I may have spoken of him to you before.) I have been glad this winter to help various young writers with criticism which, when one has work pressing, one tends to evade. It is unbearable, however, to feel that one is doing nothing for anyone.

Under such circumstances, to be buying jewelry seemed to me dastardly, but Mother was determined your gift should be brought before us constantly by something we delight in, so you will know how much I must have said about elephant-hairs—though unwittingly.

I am delighted to try an article for *Close-Up*, and if it should be a disappointment to you or is not what combines well with other content, or if Mr. Macpherson does not fancy it, don't shrink from saying so for I shall have enjoyed writing it. I doubt that there is anyone living who is more enthusiastic about movies than I am. *Close-Up* has discussed *Maedchen in Uniform*[36] which is the best thing I've seen this winter, but our museum men are remarkable, and perhaps allusion to them would not be too irrelevant; and the world-travellers sometimes do things better than the studio men, I think.

I am glad you suggest writing to Violet Hunt.[37] It would be a pleasure to do that. We feel genuinely indebted to her—with the added reactive impetus from scepticism of Ford M. Ford. Our Christmas reading has been completely stopped, and while far from resting, and for many and opposite reasons, we have not had volition for the recent crowded days of the new

35. *The Landmark* (1919–38), English monthly periodical.
36. German film (1931) directed by Leontine Sagan.
37. English writer and active feminist (1866–1942).

year but life can't last that way and we shall begin thinking and reading again. At Christmas I went a little way in *The Lost Glen,* like it exceedingly, and am eager to go on with it. For a hardened despiser of current fiction that is saying a good deal. Before Christmas I submitted to *The Criterion* a long piece of verse called "The Plumet Basilisk." Mr. Leippert of *The Lion & Crown* has not seen it but proposes to reprint it and "The Jerboa" and "The Steeple-Jack" next fall, as a pamphlet—which trio I shall send you in case the eggs are not broken. I am delighted with *Seed,* which I think you sent me. Mary Butts is strange but her poem is something to be treasured, and H.D. I have always treasured.

I think you should come over here; for a long or short visit, the longer the better. Warner is in Samoa, as you know, and if you were alone, we have a small room of his which perhaps you would be willing to occupy, though Brooklyn is not ideally convenient to New York. If you felt you must be in New York at any time overnight, there is The Ambassador where Osbert Sitwell stayed, and (my own choice) The Bristol at 48th Street and Broadway—$16 to $25 a week with bath and with meals. Miss Monroe stays there when she comes to New York, and I have cousins in Albany who have been exceedingly well cared for there. Our summer months are very hot, so I would suggest your coming now rather than waiting till autumn though we should be equally glad to see you then. Perhaps I should say that I am not in things,—professionally, socially, or any other way, and should merely be headquarters, I fear; but I do think you might have a good time.

I hope all is well with your mother and father and that they would not feel anxious about your coming.

Love from us both.   a dactyl

[MM sketches four times, in increasing fineness of detail, the elephant-hair-and-gold-wire bracelet she has bought, with notes about the shape, size, and colors of the original.]

To Morton Dauwen Zabel   *February 22, 1933*

Dear Mr. Zabel,

We are sorry to know that you have been ill and well know that a week in bed means a week before and a week after that one should have been there. I wish I need not have given you letters to write, and worry.

I am hoping the Yeats will do. I fear it may seem to you naively unscientific in view of that difficult aspect which you yourself characterize and which in the review is not touched on. The central third of what I wrote is taken up with this, but I realized that you must not be burdened with more than was specifically suited to *Poetry.* (I began with the associations which determine the colour of the work—prose and verse; then named as well as I could, the doctrines; spoke of drama; the prose as style; and finally, the verse—which portion of the article I sent you. This needless writing was not so to speak intentional; I expected originally to write 900 words on the recent verse, but having been puzzled by such phrases as "the crime of dying and being born" and the thought of an egg perpetually turning inside out without breaking the shell, I feel unable to disregard, without knowing what I was disregarding. I did not feel sound, that is to say, regarding the verse without defining to myself the prose, and the extra work reinforces my own hope of writing well. Also, it might be that the first part of the article could be adapted to a prose magazine.)

I do thank you for extenuating my letter about Ezra Pound, and for saying that you will withdraw it.

I was glad to see your poem in the *Journal des Poètes* and enjoy especially the foreign effect in the second stanza. (I still feel a little too far from leisure to write anything myself. I think I told you that I sent T. S. Eliot before Christmas a rather long piece called "The Plumet-Basilisk." I have not heard if it is to be used, but even if it should not be, it is, I think, too long for *Poetry*. Besides, Miss Monroe is seriously against long lines.)

I am pleased to know of *Scrutiny*. That first issue of *Seed* was sent me and Mary Butts is certainly the frog that jumps twenty times his own length. No wonder *Poetry* is regarded as an individuality in the world of letters when your reading and awareness are so unmistakably reflected in it.

With regard to the President, your opinion surely belongs in the magazine that you are so generously giving your mind to, and that you should consider my possible feeling of estrangement from the February issue, I value,—more even than I value the help you have given me with my work; and you know somewhat, I hope, how large gratitude for that, is.

When a man cares for another man's good as much as for his own and is a deep thinker, as Mr. Hoover is, I respect him; and there are men whom I respect, in the Democratic Party. The women who are prominent in the party, I highly disrespect. The serpent, the tiger, and the cockatoo, are fit emblems for the greater number of the New York constituency of this party, and when one reads in the paper of the proposed representation from New York in the Inauguration, one realizes that some gangsters are in jail, some are being searched for, and some parade. Al Smith is possessed of all his faculties and when Mr. Morgenthau, Sr., Owen Young, and some few others, argue in favor of certain policies I defer to their mentality. When Mr. Root or Mr. Hoover, Mr. Edison, Mr. Taft, or Colonel Lindbergh,[38] have spoken contrarily, I agreed and am in that sense a Republican; so, with me you see,

38. Elihu Root (1845–1937), American cabinet member, diplomat, and lawyer prominent in Republican politics; Thomas Alva Edison, Jr. (1876–1935), son of the inventor Thomas Edison and an engineer and prominent Republican; Robert A. Taft

it becomes a moral issue. Mr. Hoover is one of our great men, I feel. Whether his political economy is the best, I am not wise enough to say. He has worked for the good of the country, to the point of martyrdom. He does the work that is there for him to do—and the amount of it is an infamy—without being aware that he is a prominent man who occupies the White House, any more than I am aware while writing this letter, of my good clothes that hang in the cupboard. It would be more to the point if instead of this, I sent you a poem—and if I were ready writer enough to do this, it would be as a patriot and not as a traitor that I spoke. That is to say, the dedication of the piece would be implicit and not a partisan label that made nonsense of Mr. Hoover's call for a poem and discredited by its tottering impropriety, any seemingly decent thing I had already produced.

If the allusion is not clear, no matter.

I shall drop a note to Mary Hoxie Jones. Enclosed is a copy of the poems I gave Miss Monroe. When I was at *The Dial* I was very used to suggestions from my friends and from other people's friends that we publish something we ought not to publish, and there is nothing I should take more unkindly than favor shown protégés of mine that would not be shown in a different connection. I could not, if I thought a mind worthless, suggest that the person offer work to a magazine. At the same time, I think you know that I would wish the work looked at from the point of view of editorial self-interest and always would expect to support the point of view of the magazine. In advice given, I am careful to stress the importance of an intelligent attitude to rejections, referring to myself as an illustration of one who will never have a market and who accepts peaceably the justice of the indifferent.

When I look at the length of this letter, I fear you will never wish me to be ill again.

Sincerely yours,   Marianne Moore

Miss Jones' book—the work of 12 years—was published by Macmillan[39] but she has never had work in a magazine and has received from magazines only the formal rejection so was resolved never to try again. All this I learned when a friend sent me her book, and it is from what you say that I suspect work of hers was returned by *Poetry*. She has shown no disposition to cling to me.

The Eliot will probably come shortly.[40]

(1889–1953), outspoken Republican critic of Roosevelt and New Deal welfare legislation, elected to the U.S. Senate in 1938; Charles Augustus Lindbergh (1902–1974), American aviator who made the first solo, nonstop transatlantic flight in 1927, and whose politics were conservative.

39. *Arrows of Desire* (1931).

40. *Sweeney Agonistes,* which MM reviewed for *Poetry* in May 1933.

To Ezra Pound   *March 2, 1933*

Dear E.P.,

The height and extent which selfishness can leap is always an aston-
ishment and I *may* be able to offer you "Camellia Sabina." Nothing tempts
me so much as a poem but this unwritten one is so to speak all I have. If you
did use it, by when would you have to see it? Shortly before Christmas I
offered "The Plumet Basilisk" to T. S. Eliot for *The Criterion*—sent it to
him to Cambridge with a letter, and enclosed a stamped envelope. The fact
that I haven't heard from it may mean that it is to be used. If it is not to be
used, or if it was lost, I still have it, so please entrust me with a date. However—it may be longer than you could use. It is 3½ pages of typing; and if
T. S. Eliot does not like it, you might not either.

With regard to Mr. [George] Hays.

Robert Frost was at the Brooklyn Institute this winter and is one of the
best speakers I ever listened to. Afterward when I was saying a few words to
him about the evening he asked how I was coming on and was not my book
out of print. I said it was and he said "I'm going to *do* something about that."
I said I wanted first to prepare some other things. But his helping me in this
way, and the help you and Mr. Kirstein, T. S. Eliot and Mr. Zabel, have given
me has made me feel that I ought to give some help to others. So, when ap-
pealed to for advice this winter, I have been rather diligent, besides working
in other directions—and if I do one thing more or write one more letter it
will not be said that I am, but that I was, a tireless worker.

By the decencies of speech I do not mean something pretty.

For F. M. Ford the editor, too much could not be said. As a philosopher,
he is a striking example of how when a man despises himself and multiplies
words to convince you that he does not, charm departs.

The sportiveness and energy of the *Almanacco Letterario*[41] are
supreme and I am pleased to be included.

I am writing a word or two on the movies for Bryher—having just
been left for dead by an article on Yeats which is the result of a suggestion
from Mr. Zabel a year or two ago that I review *The Winding Stair* for *Poetry*. The closing paragraphs of this article I have now sent *Poetry*. The
other part, I think of submitting—when emended—to *The Yale Review*
which was once a dodo of politeness to me but has never taken anything. (I
seemed to have to overdo the thing in order to come at the few pages I was
asked for, and am in arrears in several directions, but shall see what I can do
about the poem.) I should also like to review the Bompiani.

> *Sincerely yours,*   Marianne Moore

41. *Dizionario delle opere e dei personaggi di tutti i tempi e di tutte le letterature.*
An Italian cultural dictionary or encyclopedia of "opera and all the characters of literature of all ages." Bompiani is the name of the publisher/compiler.

Mar. 4

I have now, your letter of February 21.

I feel cooperative if one has anything to present toward making art great, or keeping it unmuddied, but I cannot see that I am unique in this. Every clear thinker and sound worker that we have, is committed to the procedure. You, for instance, have been untiring in producing best work. So has Mr. Zabel, and though I should never have thought to say so independently, I have myself—by intention at least; and it seems wasteful to let production be hindered by taking time to analyze the negative aspect of progress. I think I asked you before, why lend conspicuousness to writers whom we regard as silly or corrupt? If we leave off work to exterminate what some call "their" work, might we not find ourselves in internal disagreement as to who *are* vermin? Can a litterateur create works of art with one hand and be hailing people to justice with the other? As you said yourself, I think?, it is now time to copy the East and live deliberately. I suppose you are sufficiently familiar with Scripture to recall the value of not rooting out the wheat in a mad desire to destroy the tares. In these days of torrentially piled on obligations, I find myself steeled against bickering. No one is worth it.

Moreover, a dilemma that I am very conscious of is our dependence on publications that are less than perfect. An absolute chivalrous necessity compels the continuing to keep faith with a publication to the degree one showed it by consenting to appear in it.

I feel also that in giving us hospitality, a magazine does not give us jurisdiction over its pages. (In assuming the contrary one appears green—and jeopardizes one's own eggs.)

With regard to the manifesto itself, you will agree that exactness is essential. I see no fault with 1 and 2 (present form). 3 lacks your characteristic economy and precision. Perhaps a word has been left out.

I abhor the person who can't adventure but it is a greatly imprisoned Jerusalem which justifies crusade after crusade. And lacking Jerusalem, it is not everyone, can be an endearing Don Quixote.

To Monroe Wheeler   *March 3, 1933*

[Typed around flower and leaf design.]

Dear Monroe,

The word of China's glories—that is to say of your having them—rejoices us. It is so possible to go to a country and see the proffered wonders, missing the true ones; not to mention being swallowed up in population and seeing nothing of the people who are wonders. You epitomize China—for us in your comparison of it with Japan; not that one doesn't admire the special proficiencies of Japan, the dexterity, sense of scenery, concise imagination and so on, but for sagesse as Lachaise called it, one takes China; and of course at present our sympathies establish new loyalties.

The handkerchiefs almost frighten us by their perfection. Even a bungler must see that maintained rectangles in drawn-work so tenuous and complicated, required genius and many years' apprenticeship; and the fineness of the material is to begin with a constant wonder.

This paper was a piquant sight to western eyes—the etched red dog on the green cover sheet not being the least feature. I think the two red gum leaves are perhaps the masterpiece, though one has leanings toward the frog—& toward both envelopes. To think of hazarding two such birds near P. Office cancellation marks seems blasphemy. Accuracy and liveness so remarkable—presented freely in this way as if it were an everyday affair, make one breathe easier having set up for a writer rather than as a painter. (If I could read Chinese I might be in deeper trouble.) Speaking of trades, I was interested to see the other day—apropos his *The Cabinet Maker's & Upholsterer's Drawing Book*—that [James Paterson] Sheraton was registered as an author, bookseller, scholar, & preacher.

To have seen Mei Lan Fang would in itself be enough reward for going to China—let alone several times, and personally, as you have. I liked him so much the one time I saw him in New York, that I was well satisfied not to go to anything else at the theatre afterward that season.

W. B. Yeats and the Abbey Players have been here, and John Masefield and Robert Frost. Mr. Yeats in his effect of native aristocracy and perceptiveness, I shall never forget. He spoke here in Brooklyn and I had a few words with him afterward but no conversation. John Masefield was a revelation to me of an exalted, aspiring, and delicate mind. And I feel an equal debt to Robert Frost.

We have heard Nathan Milstein and [Walter] Gieseking, over the radio; and Brahms' 2nd Symphony with [Ossip] Gabrilowitsch. And to offset these, we have been ill; I for ten days and Mother just at present but she is already much recovered. About a year and a half ago *Poetry* suggested that I review *The Winding Stair*. This winter when *Words for Music Perhaps & Other Poems* came out and Mr. Yeats had just been here, it seemed propitious to write on both books together. Finding, however, that ignorance of Zoroastrianism, Rosicrucianism, and Yoga, were hampering me, I read a little about such things and various books by Mr. Yeats himself, until I found myself presently, writing a book. Coinciding with this excess, I was lured to New York to make a call, and of my own accord went to the Institute to a lecture on American, Spanish, and Chinese alpine flora and to a series of bird and animal motion pictures by Drs. Bailey and Niedbrock of Chicago—one of the rarest presentations I have ever seen. I do not feel that all's well that ends well but that jail is jail; and am much ashamed, so you must not remember to mention or even think about the double quag that has been honored by our feet. I hope that heat, cold, late hours and other oppressions have not hurt your own health and that you are able to eat as you please—even the "little rolls of burnt carpet" you once accused Chinese restaurateurs of trying to feed one.

Miss Monroe was in town prior to a trip to Yucatán and the Monte Alban ruins and seemed full of delight in the prospect of her adventure.

[Pavel] Tchelitchew, and Kurt Baasch's photographs, at the Julien Levy Gallery are being mentioned but I don't hear anything of the promised exhibition of Pierre Roy; and of course it has been impossible for me to go over. I missed also the opening of George Lynes' studio which he was so kind as to invite me to.

Mother has been scorning me for writing a letter to a child in Samoa, on Chinese paper, when I might have been writing to you, and she says to tell you she has been most unhappy not to be in at least as close communication with you as when you were in Paris, and is glad to think this letter will be going there. She says to say also that she is, nevertheless, proud and thankful for you to have had the tremendous advantage of the long trip.

Your mention of the family in Samoa will be greatly valued there.

Affectionately,   Marianne M.

To Morton Dauwen Zabel   *March 14, 1933*

Dear Mr. Zabel,

My record for tentativeness and for falling through the cracks in the boardwalk being what it is, I submit a review of the *Sweeney Agonistes* upon what is for me the instant of receiving it and if it is not what you need, please don't feel a delicacy about saying so.

When I alluded casually to the book, I did not realize that you were sending it to me as a gift and I do thank you. One always finds substance in T. S. Eliot, and though I resisted this struggle of his—perhaps resented is better—in *The Criterion*, I dislike it less as a book; perhaps because I'm older. The fastidiousness of manufacture—the definiteness of the printing, the margins, and vermilion lettering on the blue—are surely a delight.

I told Ezra Pound that I saw no need of a manifesto but that I would sign a protest against corrupt and influenced criticism if he wished me to. I was appalled accordingly by the not very happily worded sentences I received a few days ago—signed conspicuously by myself, my benefactor, and his other incorruptible critical beneficiaries. He had asked me if I signed, what other American critics I thought should be invited to sign. I mentioned you and Miss Monroe, T. S. Eliot, William Carlos Williams, Mr.

Schappes, Francis Fergusson, Kenneth Burke, Herbert Gorman, John Chamberlain, and various others. When I next write, I shall say that from my point of view it would be a vagary for a manifesto arising from America to appear without Mr. Schappes, and *yourself* as author of the article on critics in the March *Poetry*. I relish each of the points you make, nor were the [Ben] Jonson Wrastlers lost on me. I shall also say that while Louis Zukofsky has talent, he has been forcing production, and that his term objectivism is forced. As I have said to Ezra Pound various times, one may be unable to support a position yet avoid attacking a man lest he mistake critical disapproval for personal dislike. Your article has compassed this housecleaning which has been so much on Mr. Pound's mind and I hope he will elect to be modest and reprint the article and not press on with thirst for blood.

I greatly like the poem by May Lewis in this issue of *Poetry*.

Your so unselfishly devoting careful thought to Miss Jones is indeed a help to me and to write to her will be one of my first cares when these selfish concerns of my own are dispatched. I have struggled and delved to get an emphasizing title for the Eliot in case it is used, but anything that comes to the mind—apart from *Sweeney Agonistes*—weakens rather than enhances.

I am exceedingly thankful that you don't find the Yeats an embarrassment. I ordered *Words for Music* [*Perhaps*] from Miss Yeats in order to have it for the review but in being referred on to London had to read it at the library as I think I mentioned. I now hear from Mr. E. Joiner, of William Jackson, Ltd., 18 Took's Court, Cursitor Street, Chancery Lane, E.C. 4 (London) that he got me a copy somewhere and is sending it. I am sure this and *Stories of Michael Robartes and His Friends* [1931] can be got here though I was unfortunate in my enquiries. Mr. Joiner is charging me 15 shillings.

I am not able to speak of Hart Crane's work, not knowing it very well, but your chivalry to it does me good, and your taking trouble for him as you do.

My mother has been very ill for two weeks but is up today. Her promoting the *Sweeney* for the past week is responsible for your having it—whether it is worthless or something you want. (I have not heard from *The Criterion* about the poem. It cheers me that you would care to look at it for *Poetry*.)

Sincerely yours,   Marianne Moore

Pierre Roy is being exhibited at the Brummer Gallery but I have not yet seen the things.

To Bryher   *May 16, 1933*

Dear Bryher,

I enclose some clippings, though you may see our newspapers. The situation is surely beyond bearing. The people here are roused more than I have ever known them to be; the purposes and activity noted in the papers do not suggest the strength of indignation and pity that is general among people of all interests. I was asked to review something for the July *Criterion* and though I told the Secretary not to use it if it is not needed, I sent a short notice of the Bompiani *Almanacco Letterario 1933* and mentioned in it Heinrich Mann[42] and the persecution of "that ancient and valuable race, the Jews." (It sounds as if I thought the Manns Jews—and I did—but I believe they are not?) At the circus I was standing by one of the cages when Governor Smith came by and though I am not acquainted with him, I ventured to tell him that we are all grateful for what he has been doing on behalf of the Jews. I am willing to sign or have you put my name to any paper in any country protesting against this persecution.

I have not written to Heinrich Mann himself—nor to Violet Hunt—nor have I been able to mention the Secret International about which a pamphlet came—perhaps from you? It seems odd but every week has been a problem, the sense of pressure has been so great. I deplored it for Mother and now have reason to; she has had a swelling around the eye about which I have been a good deal alarmed. They tell us it is the result of nervous strain, but by the time you get this we shall have learned our lesson and be well, so do not carry the thought of it in your mind.

Of your writing the poem for me, nothing I say could suggest what I feel; how honored and benefitted I am in your thinking about me, and how struck I immediately was by the skill of the thing and the discipline of this whole group of yours. I wish that you would mobilize in your own right, neglecting others' work for a time if necessary.

The length of my movie-digest looks as if I had had too *much* leisure and you must not use it if it is not what you wanted or if Mr. Macpherson dislikes it. If you do use it, please feel free to cut or take only a small part; space in a quarterly is valuable.

Speaking of the circus, I had said at the box-office I wanted a seat on any corner—*not* over the band and the man misunderstood me or else did not waste words telling me that the band only was available and when the performance got started nothing could have persuaded me to sit anywhere else. The leader faced the ring and conducted by means of wavings toward the back with a minute whalebone and the motions of a traffic policeman;

42. German novelist (1871–1950) and older brother of Thomas Mann.

the calliope-operator had no score and played with a limber wrist-action but otherwise without motions or effort, and the expression of the "musicians" was more than droll while everything was silenced and two sea-lions in turn stumbled—with their noses—through "My Country, 'Tis of Thee."

I hope you keep well despite all that is on your mind and that things go well with the family in London. Your garden sounds irresistible whatever the stubbornness of the soil.

Mother sends you her love and has been wishing to write to you.

Affectionately,   a dactyl

To Morton Dauwen Zabel   *May 23, 1933*

Dear Dr. Zabel,

By telephoning I find that [Pascal] Covici, [Donald] Friede, wish the bill for the Cummings paid by *Poetry* rather than by me, so I enclose it and am putting you to the trouble of writing them again. I enclose six cents (postage) but shall let my debt to *Poetry* be deducted from the honorarium for this review, guessing that it would be covered.[43]

him, I saw acted by Erin O'Brien-Moore and William S. Johnston. The staging—especially a winter street with filtering snow, I liked; the presenting of "him" as a something outside the play; and various other effects.

Thank you for speaking of the Gertrude Stein. By the merest accident I had come on it at my dentist's, but that does not hinder my feeling that I owe the discovery of it to you. And I saw there, Cecil Beaton's account of his sister Nancy's wedding (*Vogue*–May 1)—very able.

With regard to the Pound "Canto," I have scores of reasons technical and other for liking it but in this am indebted to *Poetry*, for having asked me to review *The XXX Cantos*. More and more I am aware that however well one knows the work of Ezra Pound, it is a re-reading of him chronologically, prose and verse, that unlocks the recent work and seals the uniqueness. I don't know about the wisdom of compressing to the point of concealment but evidently it is his instinct to muse Chinesely.

Speaking of Ezra Pound reminds me that you did not send me, or tell me you had destroyed, my letter of October 1, 1931. One ought not to speak to an organization as one does in confidence—friend to friend—and I was so heedless as to forget the dignity of incorporated personality.

Sincerely yours,   Marianne Moore

Of course I like Lewis Carroll but always there is pressure: and one relinquishes domestic obligation or the other.

43. MM reviewed Cummings's *Eimi* for *Poetry*.

To Hildegarde Watson   *May 25, 1933*

Dear Hildegarde,

With regard to the play[44]—to be thwarted by bozos in matters about which one knows a great deal is a distress but if things do not go as they could, I hope you will feel as the indelicate Rivera felt about the Detroit murals: "If they are destroyed I shall be distressed for I put into them my life and the best of my talent but tomorrow I shall be busy making others,—as a tree produces flowers and fruit nor mourns their loss each year."[45] From what you say, I know the photography is expert, and from what you don't say about your own music I am sure it is also that, and I owe more to you than you know for setting me an unmixed example of philosophical independence. My brother feels that suffering—if one takes it—is like a raft which is able to carry one further than one would have been able to go without it. I said to my mother not long ago, "He has had that idea for years." She said, "And it does him a great deal of good, but I don't feel that he explains it fully." About my own work, I may not succeed, but I have come to the conclusion that I am at least going to try. William Carlos Williams says excellence restricts sales; and I was slightly encouraged last week by the moroseness of Edmund Wilson who has written a play which he can't get produced. "Intrinsic merit of the things has nothing to do with it; that's of no interest to producers; you might be Homer and it would mean nothing to them," etc.

The little set of Joyce poems I wanted to send you is out of print and I have been making a copy which I shall send to Rochester in a day or two; small interruptions have delayed me though there is not much to copy; I'm sorry however not to be able to get the thing itself, which is interesting partly because of its smallness and form.

Your letter to my mother gives her much, and she is hoping for you and "Mr. Watson" to "come to see her some afternoon, and to supper next winter." She feels about Anne[46] that one could help her only by seeming to think something that has no connection with her and that my idea of infusing her definitely with an ideal is naive. Anne's enthusiasm about chatter of mine merely reiterates what my mother said while doing something to my costume—"let me attend to this, and you go on talking and entertaining yourself."

44. *Lot in Sodom*, an experimental film produced in Rochester in 1933 by Sibley Watson and Melville Webber.

45. Diego Rivera (1886–1957), the Mexican artist, painted murals over the Italian baroque architecture in the court of the Detroit Institute of Arts. A controversy ensued and many critics advocated destruction of the murals.

46. Anne Holahan, a Rochester acquaintance of the Watsons', was in New York to pursue a stage career.

I am putting an "e" in Hildegarde, for though I don't see one I think I remember it has one.

Marianne M.

To John Warner Moore   *June 11, 1933*

Dear Pago,

The *Mid-Pacific Magazine* is a world of entertainment—very nutritive; picked you out among the white-pants, and hut-hats.

Mouse has just asked me delicately if her letter is all right. (I: "Very nice.") Mouse: I couldn't help saying something about those—matters. (Laughter) Mouse: I don't like alligators.

Her remark that my lavender dress is again in commission also makes me smile. It took one week of the front legs between loping hind legs, to get it so but I guess it will be a help to us.

At the tea-party when Gilbert [Seldes] said, "Miss Moore, I have every letter you ever wrote me." And then patronizingly to T. S. Eliot, "Miss Moore's letters are very remarkable," T. S. said, "Your letters to editors are very terse." & I said, "So are yours," whereat there was loud laughter as if I was Ed Wynn. And also when Ed. Wilson offered me milk—T. S. Eliot having poured a portion of it into his tea, I said—after refusing—"You're very humane." The conversation was trivial and discreditable but I don't know how a fellow was to talk to T. S. E. about [George] Herbert and Bishop [Lancelot] Andrewes (Gilbert and Mrs. Seldes and Mr. Wilson and a timid stranger sitting by, with much news of Shankar the Hindoo dancer and a drummer whose drums were disguised about the room as cocoanuts and cockatoos, etc.). The stranger said not a word but would smile faintly now and then.

About the money: the idea originated with Mrs. Watson but I am sure was joined in by Doc. and it is remarkable, I think, that after all they spent on *The Dial* and me in particular, they would feel like giving it to us.[47] She said they hoped I would accept it—perhaps for a vacation, so I wrote her of your plan—yours and C's for us to go to Black Lake and that in September we would try to do that. She also sent me a pencil drawing of an elephant galloping and making little curls of dust—by E. E. Cummings—since I think so much of elephants.

Without being near the Institute nor a movie-theatre, I have been busier than a bumble-bee. A man, a M. Maria Manent, is getting up an anthology of English and American poems and wanted one of my books from

47. Hildegarde and Sibley Watson had sent MM $300.

which to pick something to translate. Not having a book to send, I copied out about 30 things for him to choose from and got them mailed. He is in Barcelona, S. G. I don't know what S. G. means but that's where he is. He also sent me a book of poems he has translated from the Chinese with head and tail pieces printed in brown from wood blocks and it is a very handsome thing.

Then a Matthew Satra sent me a leaflet in English and in Hebrew as an attention in acknowledgement of something I had written that he liked; he didn't say what; I thanked him and he thanked me for thanking him. He lives at 764 DeKalb Avenue but didn't say he would drop in!

Then a Mr. Martin Jay proposes starting a quarterly in October, wants me to contribute but mainly that I would let him reissue my *Observations* with additions. This I said no to, but we have decided to let him do it. He lives in New York, says that Wallace Stevens is contributing to his first number and that he (Mr. Jay) is violently opposed to proletarian literature. I am myself but the favorable feature of his plan is that if he can't get the right kind of material for his paper, he won't continue through thick and thin; but he thinks he can—like the small engine. I have the copyright to the book and the recent things I have would give some face to the proceeding I guess.

I revised my longer review of Mr. [W. W. E.] Ross that I had written and sent it to *Scrutiny*, a quarterly published in Cambridge and a couple of days' work will be enough for the finishing of my Yeats article that was the body for the tail-hairs I gave *Poetry*. They vigorously objected to more than say, 4¼ hairs—so I am not to blame that this is the really interesting part of the essay; and I am quite pleased with it. It seems to me unhackneyed and written in a natural vein. I am going to send it to *The Yale Review* and if I get it back, I will still think it A-1 and far more succulent than the much snake-plant they offer for sale. (Mouse said this morning, looking at the opposite apartment-house, "That snake-weed must be a terrible thing in its native country, when it is the affliction it is where it is a luxury.")

Forgot to mention that in the *Herald Tribune* for March 19, 1933, among the pictures there was a page called Exploring Little Known Islands of the Pacific, showing the Yacht Zaca and a vast number of Galápagos iguanas; and some animals obtained by Templeton Crocker for the San Francisco Academy of Sciences. I think I did tell you however, of a young frigate-bird and beside it "the grown bird"—which was by no means a frigate-bird but a penguin. They were on this page. I believe it was called the Templeton Crocker Scientific Expedition.

The present exhibition of American Sources at the Museum of Modern Art is a most impressive one—and a masterpiece of arrangement, with things of a kind from 6 or 7 different museums or owners grouped together. I saw a number of things I know well, from seeing them at the Amer. Museum of Nat. History: a little silver figure of a man with transverse gold bands; a large silver llama with drooping eyelid, and a lot of gold pickanin-nies of various breeds. One of the most original things was a pottery vase with orange designs on it—of a noble carried in a litter like a sedan-chair; and *under* the litter travelled a little dog with tail curling up in a sickle and a purple saddle-cloth on him rounded like a tongue, edged with yellow, or maybe gold. Another thing was a large pot or dish like the one in which the 4 and 20 blackbirds were baked, of black pottery and the lid was a yawning jaguar-mouth with strong teeth at either side; the ears were round bat-ears and on the neck were rudely crosshatched spots about the size of dimes—a very quaint thing. I believe the objects of which they are proudest are wall reliefs like the Egyptian with strange hieroglyphics on them, in very fine carving, and there are various carvings in white stone of maize goddesses and one of a dragon or serpent. The weavings with pelicans, cats, dancers, and zigzags of geometric design were rare, moreover.

On the first floor they had some specimens of modern American work which shows the influence of these old things, the best of these without a doubt being a rattler by John Flannagan—carved out of naturally tinted rough brown stone, in a curl, browner on the top coils like a loaf of bread, but the good thing was the slight amount of detail and the exactness of the "features"—mean little eyes and cold smile. "The better the worse," said Mouse when told about it.

You have heard of Ruffina;[48] well, since Wednesday—and this is Sun-day—Mouse's Grevy's Zebra summer dress, which she wears for best and for which she has no substitute, has been missing. At no summer tea has she been without it. Whenever there was a moment's pause from doing other things, claws were extended into packages of underwear or winter-clothes or stockings, or among hats, hunting for this cover; Mouse saying testily at times, "yes, I was going to look there but I *don't* want to do it now." Yester-day afternoon about 3 o'clock, after disembowling for the second time everything in the mahogany chest of drawers in the dining-room, from the lowest up, it was found—by me—among my clippings and some table sup-plies in the *top* narrow drawer, at the left side. (However, two living moth-worms had been found.) The "stripes," so white and clean, nicely ironed and flat as a lily-pad, are not where Mouse had *thought* they were—in the wal-nut chest in our bed-room.

I have now lost among those papers I upsnouted, the piece I was so in-terested in about the fog-detector by infra-red rays—for ships, so you will hear of that maybe toward August.

I am much pleased by that chain Mouse got me, and shall be taking it to S. [Sedgwick] Island in September as well as wearing it meantime. It has got clear and windy here with a bright sun; I hope you are not having

48. During the 1930s the Moores used "ruffina" or "ruffinoed" to indicate a wild search for some object or any extremely disruptive activity.

teasers such as you had when May was there. And it has been 100 in Albany. We gave Cousin Mary my Mr. Messina interest[49]—for her need was very desperate—not knowing of course about the Watsons—and I am surely glad we did. It is a desperate thing not to know where to turn for money to pay bills that are cold and urgent and since we have been spared that agony when we might have suffered, I feel it is all too little to give her. Weak as she was, she wrote out a promissory note for the amount, to be paid in July but we told [her] we *could* not take the money back. Mary Watson telephoned a week ago to say she had left her practically well—but unwilling to come to N.Y. for a visit.

Yakappy

Sallie certainly has a very remarkable talent for drawing—is very accurate and interpretative.

To Hildegarde Watson   *July 22, 1933*

Dear Hildegarde,

What an El Greco! I have never seen anything by him to which I was indifferent and this is a maximum peak of sensibility. What magical mixing up and differentiating of major minutiae. And unless I'm too knowing, there is a standing seagull on one of the rocks. Those rooms at the Fair make me think of the Louvre; and on the racetrack I think the Fair, from what you say, would win "by the soft part of the nose."

Jeanne's struggle on behalf of Rembrandt is joyfully noted. I don't long to own Rembrandts and might say to her as Anne said to me about the movies, "I think you and I like the same things." I like Palestrina.[50] And we do *so* like the portrait, though again I say you should give me *nothing*, and I should tell you nothing of my difficulties. But one I was in the middle of, on Wednesday, the day I received your letter with the El Greco, I must tell you of because of its good ending—that is, its ending as we hope. And as you would know, I do not expect to tell anyone else; that is any others.

We asked Dr. Pack (of Memorial Hospital) that day if he could look at something for me. Wednesday is not one of his days for office hours I found afterward, but he said to come and found that I had an infected cyst on the left side, in the breast, but not cancer! He aspirated? *it,* has had me keep compresses and heat on it, and from that on, I was a different being; and he is watching it.

49. The Moores received around $150 a year in interest on investments handled by Mr. Messina, according to JWM in 1940. Cousin Mary was recovering from a gallbladder attack. MM sent an additional $15 of her own that she had just received for an essay published in *Motion Pictures.*

50. Sixteenth-century Italian composer of contrapuntal choral music (1525–1594).

Last night we had a pompano for supper—for me, I was told. While Mr. Di Palma the fishman, was unburying it from the ice, I said I had only heard of the pompano recently, in New York; that my mother had planned to get a mackerel. "Was your mother with you when you had the pompano?" he said. I said no. "Well," he said, she'll like this much better; people *rave* about these fish! And, despite scepticism while it was broiling, she did. I proprietorially drawing attention to the scaleless skin and palm-leaf fan back-bone. One time I got a bone bead in the shape of a pompano at the Nippon Garden on Fifth Avenue and now, having seen the fish, realize what in my ignorance I was discerning enough to select. About that time I also selected Louis Bouché[51] for his fresco pinks that you speak of, and serpent blues; and the square person among square things is a pun that should be repeated, and is a portrait that might well be craved.

I am very much impressed with the importance of your recommendation—looking at the black silk hat and through rather than with the eyes.

Yours affectionately,   Marianne

To William Rose Benét   *July 28, 1933*

Dear William,

I thank you for the Anthology[52] and can't but say—that is I do say—that it would be difficult for you to arrive at an autobiographic statement more desirable than you give in your critical notes concerning other people.

You have not been soured; nor have Messrs. Williams and Frost. Indeed the news evoked from the more mythical beings among us is valuable and fascinating to a degree that our uncritical critical newspaper boys had not led me to anticipate. All the included should chip in and send William Carlos Williams a gold trout or rooster for being so game.

On hearing from you that you wanted Ezra Pound in the book I was so public-spirited as to write to him and tell him to stop growling and contribute his bone, saying that if he knew you personally he would recall that you were singularly without acridity; and mentioning your reading at the Brooklyn Institute—your having given without proffering it as doctrine, the best explanation of how and why one writes poetry of any analyst of retrospect I had heard. He ought to be in the book; he certainly is greater than his grouches.

Yours sincerely,   Marianne Moore

PS   Here is the pegasus giraffe by Munari. I specialize in giraffes; is the paddock ever over-crowded?

51. American painter (1896–1969).
52. *Fifty Poets.*

To William Rose Benét   *August 21, 1933*

Dear William,

I am not going to praise your letter till I have made myself obnoxious in the way well known to an editor. I was born pro-Chinese and bombs busting in air from Japan have not reversed my allegiance; but I feel that the shrinking Noguchi was a song-bird nurtured by Cuckoos. At any rate I am hell bent on helping him if I can, and wonder if *The* [*Saturday*] *Review* could compass an autumn letter—here enclosed? He wants me to get the Viking Press to sponsor for England and America, a set of essays he is having published in Tokyo and I thought it would help if I offered one or two to magazines.

I am quite enthusiastic about Dickinson [College]; and a little more since reading of Priestley's astronomical paraphernalia now housed there (the older Priestley's; the younger's product is perhaps terrestrial)[53] and when I remember the mermaid weathervane and hear that they have a portrait of Mr. John Hays that looks like him. I wish I could see you and Stephen get your degrees. I should have a spontaneously straight face, I assure you. I noticed the Yale Younger Poets "under the command" of Stephen Benét, the advance note of the play Mrs. L. B.[54] is to act in this autumn, and the enclosed poem by Miss L. B. [Laura Benét]; you probably have it; don't bother to acknowledge.

About the decay of manners and spread of communism I loudly agree. And Ezra Pound does wrong in the fullest sense of the word in a thousand ways. But I owe a great deal, scholastically, to his *The Spirit of Romance;* and to his Guido by which I was propelled toward the precursors of Dante that I would now not part with for the world. I don't know what to make of Babette Deutsch and others who say *The Cantos* are too expanded to be prepossessing; they are too condensed; if the very seemly amateurism that underlies them had not been reduced with a Hitlerlike fanaticism, everybody would be seeing the point. But one speaks up for a person who helps one.

Don't take time for me in fending off the essay if they don't want it; I mean make no bones about returning it without a letter. Sorry on a form will answer the purpose, though I weaken in so far as to say your letter was a pleasure.

                                        Marianne Moore

53. Joseph Priestley (1733–1804), English physicist and educator who immigrated to Philadelphia in 1794, where he continued his scientific experimentation and religious and political liberalism. "The younger Priestley" is probably J. B. Priestley.

54. Lora Baxter, an actress, who was William Benét's third wife.

To Hildegarde Watson   *September 3, 1933*

Dear Hildegarde,

We are overwhelmed by the film—by the strength of it and the inter-related beauty of the various high points; by the rapt listening effect and premonitoriness of your face and attitudes throughout; and one notices of course the harmoniousness with you—of the daughter.[55] The painting-and-poetry is very nearly too exciting for a patron of old newsreel, and the general power and aesthetic correlation of the various influences literally overwhelmed us. As Mother remarked earnestly to Mr. Gale[56] afterward, "It should be seen by a conventicle of scholars." He said, "conventicle sounds Scotch but then Dr. Watson *is* Scotch, I imagine." She had said previously to me, "I was careful not to intimate to him that I hadn't been invited for fear he wouldn't let me in." But she *had* been invited; I reminded her of Anne's consternation at the word she (mother) was not going with me the time it was finishing as I entered the door! I don't know how to say what we feel about your giving us the chance to see it. I am in a frenzy to write something about it, and have been dashing things out of the way since Thursday. (A young man who was as Anne put it "let come in," and Yoné Noguchi, and the anti-Nazi testimony I spoke to you about.) (I told *Close-Up* I would not be offering anything again till after the winter, so they may decline me; and what I say will not be long; nor good by comparison with the subject.) The angel surely realized the requirements of illusion; Lot was astonishingly real, and "Hebrew." The symbol of iniquity with beady eyes, and the spots on the lily are dazzling; a chill passed over me as the blood wandered down the torso of the prostrate body, and I thought the use of slow motion and distortion, the Blake designs in the fire, and the Pascin, Giotto and El Greco effects, wonderful. Would you give me some help? That is, would you give me these sequences?

> *the city*
> *the tree of life*
> *Lot's house*
> *his dream*
> *his wife and daughter—first appearance*
> *his prayer*
> *the angel, first appearance*
> *the angel at meat*
> *Lot's house—morning*

55. HW appeared as Lot's wife; Dorothea Haus (Mrs. Paul Paine) was the daughter.

56. Manager of the Little Picture Theatre and head of an amateur filmmakers' society in New York.

the man thrown into the pit, the knees running, the triangles of fire growing out the horizontals of fire, the roots, the lily, the lily in bloom, the snake,
the doves, the body with the blood on it, the stones being picked up. And if
it is not too trying, I should like to know the lines—or verse and chapter!
from Ecclesiastes & the Song of Solomon, and the words that come just before Mulier.

I can't tell you how excited we are, and in retrospect how peculiarly detached and judicial you & Sibley seemed about the film. I firmly believe that
anyone who has not been seeing it and feels indifferent on first seeing it is
crazy or not really interested in art. The music[57] is very nearly up to the film
I think, with some startling intuitivenesses—but tends perhaps to
overdo—through loyalty. Maybe you would give me a hint there?

M.

P.S. I hope the little dog is growing up to his growl.

To Hildegarde Watson   *October 25, 1933*

Dear Higgie,

I don't know how you can say such things—or wish to say them.[58] I go
thrashing along like a farm tractor of the oldfashioned kind, determined not
to come to a halt; that is the most that can be said of me. And my wares
nearly fall to pieces from being peddled before someone gets a handful of
patrons for them. Gardie's praise of the water-bugs is a great consolation.[59]
There was a fleet of them spraddled over the smooth part of our trout-brook
below a weir, at Woodbury, summer before last, and I also "watched them
for hours." Mention of me in connection with [Henri] Rousseau is making
a silk purse, I'm afraid. But a help to me. I can't wait to see the morning-
glory. I wanted to draw the lily the other day—the browallia (our flower in
a flower-pot) and wasn't succeeding. Mother said, "Well—you can at least
put the teeth on the leaves." When it came, that night, after we had been at
Anne's, I was looking for it in the dictionary: "a small genus of tropical or-
namental annual herbs or shrubs of the figwort family with showy blue or
white flowers." How's that! "It's all wrong," Mother said; and nearly anything would be by comparison with such a dazzle of gems, with those alternately folding serpentine scrolls getting pale toward the top. The blue buds
alternating with the cerise are now slightly higher on the pyramid than
they were, and like those other tropical buds we were speaking of, outlined
in stronger color on the edge of the petal as they come together at the top;
(the gardenia buds, and the bouvardia buds). A better than Claude Bragdon

57. Louis Siegel (1886–1955), a concert violinist, composed the music for *Lot*.
58. HW's letter had referred to "marvellous poems" by MM.
59. In "The Plumet Basilisk." Gardie is Hildegarde Verdi, HW's niece.

Babylonian truncheon that does not need to be looked at with a microscope, marplot Higgie. The okapi gray cross stripes on the blue green leaves, with the tennis-ball felt on the stem of the flower proper, would throw [André] Derain into a delirium; and there is somewhere from it, a rather scary odor of the beehive or grapes in bloom. But more about it than the definition is all wrong; and strike me dead if I ever admire anything curious in your presence again!

When I sent Mr. Kirstein the poems, I said I might have fitted them to some other magazine; but the fact that Dr. Watson didn't know he was being exposed should make editorial self-interest easy; Mrs. Watson had shown the things to me. I enclose a copy of what I sent him for probably the line arrangements aren't just right. I said the commentary on Harry Alan Potamkin[60] was a gallant tribute, notwithstanding the fact that since seeing *Lot in Sodom,* "I am out to prove that Dr. Watson 'knows more about the art of film than anyone else in America.'"

If Anne [Holahan] will attend to the showing, I can provide audiences—not worked up ones but some of both. I infected the hospital with some curiosity it seems and I talked with a Graham McNamee[61] intensity at dinner the other night; the workers-in-industry one given for Miss M. Carey Thomas at the Park Lane. I was sitting with the Flexners—Dr. and Mrs. Simon F.; Mr. Thomas (Mrs. Flexner's brother); and James Flexner. Mr. Thomas whose wife is always trying—without success—to get him to go to the movies; says he would like very much to see the *Lot*—will surely go if it's given.

Close-Up is using my notice after all, and like Paul Rosenfeld, continuing to write the thing after it has gone to press, I am inserting the chanted lines. Mother finds, "And the glorious beauty, which is on the head of the fat valley, shall be a fading flower," in Isaiah 28.4 and a similar passage about the drunkards of Ephraim in Isaiah 28.1 whose, "glorious beauty is a fading flower, which are on the head of the fat valleys of them that are overcome with wine!" and Isaiah 34.10 "from generation to generation it shall be waste; none shall pass through it for ever and ever." We were interested also in the summary of Sodom in the 17th chapter of Ezekiel.

I would like the pictures, though I would be happy enough if you gave me the one large portrait head of yourself from the House of Usher and beg that you will not let any searching for anything be done till S. W. *is rid of the cold he has.* Mother thought he looked as if he has been under strain, and he should go about a recovery of vitality—before like Mr. Siegel and me—being committed to the hands of physicians. We are so glad that Mr. Siegel is better.

60. Film critic for *The Hound & Horn* (1900–1933).
61. Radio announcer noted for his enthusiastic coverage of live sports and political events.

Nov. 4 at 12:30 unless the *Lot* is being shown Anne & Evelyn Holahan are coming to lunch here & then going with me to the Brooklyn Institute to see Dr. H. C. Raven of the Amer. Museum show slides & movies of chimpanzees & gorillas & show his chimpanzee Meshie. I won't mention *Lot* prematurely.

LOVE, M. M.

P.S. Since the review is being used, I am telling Anne who has borrowed it to show the theatre—that it mustn't be quoted from till the Dec. *Close-Up* is out. M.

To T. S. Eliot *January 18, 1934*

Dear Mr. Eliot,

With regard to your suggestion, I am in a dilemma. I have not yet quite enough for a book, nor do I forget that you might not care to sponsor the pieces when you saw them. Perhaps no one would.

I was asked last fall by the Macmillan Company (New York) if I had something they could publish and said that when I had accumulated enough for a book I would submit it.

I think it goes without saying that if something by me were to come out, I should like to have your hand in it. Taking an interest as I do, in many of the Faber & Faber books, and having as it were since we discontinued *The Dial*, no associates, I feel it a calamity to forego the congenial atmosphere of these publishers. But you might not, as I said, after seeing the material, care to bring it out. In any case I must observe my promise to Macmillan.

I am sure it is true there is not money in poetry for anybody and to say that I dislike the thought of being a loss to a publisher is far more than a mere understatement. I have known for a long time that I ought not to plan to live on money derived from authorship. The writing in itself pays one or something is wrong with it; yet the commercial superstition is such that one does need a certain financial recognition and I should be entirely pleased with the royalty you mention.

I should be grateful if you could make Faber & Faber aware of the benefit their thought of me is to me; there is no house where I should like more to be allowed to feel at home.

I am trying to prepare something on Henry James for *The Hound & Horn*; we are just back, my mother and I, from Pennsylvania, and after finishing the James I should like to see what I can do with a poem I have been working on; verse is the work I like best.

An array of appreciators is so unessential if one is valued by five or even two, that I cannot see why Ezra Pound exhausts himself trying to engender intelligence in the whole world. But a dearth of backers emphasizes the magnanimity of the fearless and I hesitate to attempt to tell you the good your letter confers.

Sincerely yours,   Marianne Moore

To William Carlos Williams   *January 26, 1934*

Dear William,

The catnip that art is, or *ignis fatuus*, or drop on the cactus, does seem worth the martyrdom of pursuit, I feel. If the value is valuable enough to one, one achieves it. So bless the collective wheelbarrow; with Wallace Stevens beside it like a Chinese beside a huge pair of oxen; also "Birds and Flowers"—the one instance, to my mind, of a love poem where the message would stand some chance of advancing the motive.

"His writing has been about evenly divided between prose and verse." I wish I had said it.

Yours much in debt,

I shall ponder the [Charles] Reznikoffs.

To John Warner Moore   *March 1, 1934*

Dear Badger Volcanologist (you wouldn't like me to call you pit-viper),

Your account from at sea stiffened our sinews exceedingly—except that that round of parties for and from polite people is from one of the accursed things of the earth, of which like the serpent's tooth, the effects are lasting.

Don't think you won't be ast what you saw in the winter home and the summer home of the Frears; nor about the tour of the museum, you knowing little but knowing more than you seemed to know and Pomposity-paws knowing something but divining nothing of what was going on under his palanquin.

We are delighted about the private cabin and the steward; and crushed and shivered by the faithfulness and attentions of the Islanders on leaving P-P [Pago-Pago]. Perhaps you will get a little sense of respite and leisure on *The Republic*. It seems odd you didn't get our letters sent care of the Pynes.

We are "well off"; despite the anxieties about Cousin Henry. Mole has just been referring to Aunt Annie Armstrong's kindness in Pittsburgh, and making hot biscuits and the soul-saving festivity of such visits with Cousin Annie and Henry in childhood—Mole aged 6, and Cousin Henry's affection and spindling health. I had just said the sum total of his earthly happiness has been so infinitesimal and so adulterated that his robbing us—of almost any amount—seems forgettable in view of that meagerness. Atlantic City and the sense that he was going somewhere or had been somewhere is about the nearest approach to exhilaration I suppose, that he ever had. Mole is now restraining and quieting the Safe Deposit and Trust Company that they refrain from setting on him, Keeper-like, and tearing his apparel. I marvel at the decent and reasonable way in which things have progressed and hope he can be saved agonies of the kind that pierce him the most.[62]

Mr. Morley's visit was a great pleasure to us. *There* is "a man." He and T. S. Eliot and Mr. Latham are, so far, my first experience of real publishers. Ask me about this, and you shall hear; and of Paul Revere at Macmillan's also. It is my poems they are asking me about, and I had demurred; whereon I had a terrific shove from the rear from Ezra Pound. Mr. Morley was wearing a shepherd's plaid raglan coat made of wool sheared from his own sheep and did a most amusing thing. As he sat and conversed, his right foot rested about in a straight line out from the body, and he planted his left foot crosswise on it, so it resembled a most Tweedle-dee like effect. Another thing I value—and very rare, he said in his letter received today, to send Miss Jones to him if I thought he could do anything for her in London. (Mary Hoxie Jones, daughter of Mr. Rufus Jones, whom I have been helping with her writing.) I had mentioned her, in case he should meet her or happen to hear of her, so he would have an interest. But I am not sure I *will* send her to him.

Monroe invited us to Gertrude Stein's opera, *Four Saints in Three Acts,* a blasphemous but talented thing, with music by Virgil Thomson which is very fine and well worth the hearing. The cast is all negroes and the singing is superb. The only bearable soprano voice I ever heard was Saint Teresa's, and I could not detect the touch of the comb in any of the others. Ellen and Miss Nagel had also invited me—to occupy a seat they had got for Lucy Thayer who could not go. Naturally I suggested to Ellen that we have a word afterward. Monroe knows Virgil Thomson and there was a great tail-wagging; Ellen told Monroe how unique he was to have got me to New York, that it is four years since she has seen me, etc.; so Mole suggested I write Ellen that if she has time we'd like her to make us a visit this week! Miss Nagel is going to St. Louis and Ellen, expecting to be lonely. Monroe much regrets that Lincoln Kirstein who knew he and I would be there, could not find us though he searched diligently. That would have been quite a heap of dogs and I would as soon see him where it is quiet.

While I think of it, Mr. Morley said a great many notable things—among them, that a publisher is almost like a person who loves animals being in a slaughter-yard; and that what one needs to feel in a person's work is

62. As early as the mid-twenties, the family feared that MWM's cousin Henry had been misusing funds and tampering with deeds in the family trust.

a sense of seriousness and weight back of it, of consolidated feeling, rather than any special one good quality. That is not what he said, but something like it.

I may get writing to you again, but it is very nearly the last letter going. We have cash—too much, no doubt—and I am encouraged to have Mole's eyes examined and new lenses ordered, and to have obligations discharged. I now have no review waiting to be finished; be thankful you weren't here to usher in the James article!

Rat

To Samuel French Morse   *March 7, 1934*

Dear Mr. Morse,

With regard to form, I value an effect of naturalness and feel that the motion of the composition should reinforce the meaning and make it cumulatively impressive. I have an objection to the reversed order of words and to using words for the sake of the rhythm that would be omitted if one were writing prose.

With regard to color and image, the arts are so closely interrelated it seems to me, that descriptiveness in any one of them can achieve itself in the terms of another. Exact representation is, is it not, a major objective in each?

As for my attitude to my work, the worker is so near his work that appraisal from him lacks perspective. A number of persons have told me, however, that in my verse the contrapuntal effects are the distinguishing value.

I hope the perplexity of dealing with these matters will bring reward to you in the pleasure you will have from your own work.

Sincerely yours,   Marianne Moore

To Ann Borden   *March 8, 1934*

Dear Aunt Ann,

If you will write to me again permitting me to meet Miss Bishop, and let me write to you again when I have been able to shake or fulfill present obligations, I should like to meet the pilgrim half-way; that is, in New York, and have the word on poetry that you propose and perhaps that same afternoon—or morning if morning would suit Miss Bishop better—I could attend to a matter that I have been evilly postponing. For professional Rip Van Winkles, we have had a very alert year. Three friends from London and a friend from Paris, separately from one another have been in New York and their powerful management of their programs has filled me with envy and maddened me into saying "Of course I can," so often that I have been twice sick-a-bed, hiding the truth when I could, but at last confessing that I *was* in bed.

I cannot bear people who refuse, and besides I am interested in college boys and girls who are interested in poetry—that is one reason I keep so busy—so do not "powerfully" withdraw your protégé[e], but let me plod a space further and then make an appointment. We could meet at the 42nd Street Library or at the Museum of Modern Art or a store—any spot that would be convenient. Seniors are busier than anybody else in the world and I know Miss Bishop will thank me for needing to come to New York.

I have been negotiating for a copy of Mr. John Johnson's Dent lecture on printing for you, ("The Printer to his Customers and his Men") ever since we saw you. Perhaps however, you already have it or have read it. I sent for it to Dutton's who are Dent's American partners, I thought. After a long time they said they had no jurisdiction over the Dent publications; so now you will receive it from G. E. Stechert a little later—and when Mother can order her literary affairs as she eventually will if I don't need to be taken care of as a patient continually, you will receive the Edwin Howard pamphlet.

I hope your own pilgrimage here did you no harm and that you kept warm at Vassar despite the freezing weather.

Yours affectionately, Marianne

To Morton Dauwen Zabel *March 31, 1934*

Dear Dr. Zabel,

Each time in looking at your letter of February 28th, I feel anew, your generosity; also the mountainous structure of your work, and your achievement in commanding, despite herculean labor, the respite of reading. That joyous recreation I seem unable to attain. And how is it possible in the midst of all this for you to be slaving at your own fiction!

Poetry's Pound warfare would be enjoyable to the world in proportion as it is inexplicable. The healing efficacy of the delayed "Canto" has found the world boasting stoutly that it cannot be cured, so the "Canto" still has ample scope for therapy. I gave the March issue to Mr. Frank Morley who was saying he liked very much your "Cows in the Garden," and think I must have given both copies received, so I haven't the "Canto" here to look at, but my recollection is favorable. I noticed that the wording of certain documents quoted, so fascinated E.P. he cannot resist exact quotation, and the quoted words are not always precisely in unison with his own lyrical effects. But since that is my quagmire too, I must ponder rather than object. I do feel the brio and memorableness of the "Canto."

In your summary of magazines I was interested not only in the information about myself but in the literary outlook which the itemizing and discussing represent, and I should be greatly obliged if you would give me another copy of this issue. A plebeian suggestion is that you give me instead of two April issues, a March copy and but one April.

I suppose you noticed my aberration in sending you the Williams review with a title but no data of format and so on. I did not mean to be lazy; it is strange that such omissions occur to one too late.

The piece of verse I enclose, you may not care for and even if you should, Miss Monroe may not.[63] But whether or not you can use it, it is for me the gratification of a wish I have long had, to send you something.

I have been approached by various little enterprises. The handwriting-in-facsimile one vanished without leaving a trace. The proposal that has just come—for an anthology to appear in June—offers to include anything of mine that has not come out in book form, and if you decided to publish this piece, I would let them have it. But not if doing so would put you to inconvenience. Parker Tyler, who is assembling the material, was so kind as to say the book could be delayed a few weeks, and I suppose that would mean July. But what I really wish is to submit something to *Poetry* and I refuse to invalidate with suggestions what I do submit. If the stanzas enclosed will not do, I shall have it in mind to offer you something else.

My mother sends her hearty regards and begs that you will grant yourself all the enjoyment that is within reach.

Sincerely yours,   Marianne Moore

To T. S. Eliot   *May 16, 1934*

Dear Mr. Eliot,

Here are the notes which pertain to the material recently sent you. They could be reduced further, or omitted if that would be best, and I would say this with respect to the notes on recent work given Mr. Morley. Despite the extreme amount of conscience I seem to have shown, in preparing the 1924 book I think I was erratic, or somnambulistic; it looks to me, that is to say, as if I had "quoted" things that were my own, and as if I had taken from you the titles, *Observations*, and "Picking and Choosing."

If you would be willing to introduce the book, or preface it with comment, I should be grateful.[64] That the things would profit by being sponsored is perhaps a reason against your undertaking them, so I leave it to you; you must safeguard yourself in any way that seems best, against permitting

---

63. MM sent "The Buffalo."

64. In a letter to MM (April 12, 1934), TSE had indicated his willingness to write a preface to *Selected Poems*.

this venture to be a bugbear. I have not seen the Pound, and though I have been intending to buy it, surely would not need to see it in connection with what you might do for me.

Sincerely yours,

P.S. If notes are included, it would necessitate with each note a corresponding page number, though line numbers I think could be omitted.

To Hildegarde Watson   *May 23, 1934*

Dear Higgie,

You are very consoling and as I am beginning to realize, self-stabilizing; though the phrase "series of concerts" makes me tremble like a leaf. You said gamut, however, not series. You will be coming back soon, won't you? and will remember to lend us the concert notice we did not see? I saw a notice of a novel by Eric Knight[65] just after you were here but have a notion that his field is criticism.

That is fine news of Sweden about *Lot.* As William Carlos Williams has his hero say about the cat, in *The White Mule*—that was disappointing as a mouser—"Give him time, give him time; he isn't a year old yet."

We like too, the pictures of Henry James by Miss [Alice] Boughton—and the uneven enlarged snapshot taken by a gamekeeper, in Mrs. [Edith] Wharton's *A Backward Glance.* (I curse without shame or fear, a review like the one by Isabel Paterson of Mrs. Wharton, in *The Herald Tribune.*) I am grateful to you both for taking me seriously in *The Hound & Horn*, and to Mr. Cummings for noticing the quotations. I very nearly can't eat when I think of the good ones I had to omit.

Appalled by the hairy legs of the monsters in the English *Active Anthology*, I had thought I would never contribute to the American *Active Anthology* and finally wrote the editor a ferocious letter saying "My Mother and I have been annihilated by illness and I must ask you to regard this statement as final," but he kept egging me on by news of his progress! "E. E. Cummings is going to contribute," "E. E. Cummings has given us five interesting new poems," etc.

I can understand your feeling strange in the north after being among pelicans and mocking-birds; but you found no little fossil clam-shells in Florida, did you! There is a thrilling double page of pelicans in *The Illustrated London News* for Mar. 24th showing how a pelican lights on the ground, and how capacious the pouch is.

65. Drama critic, novelist, and author of *Lassie Come Home* (1897–1943); his 1934 book was *Invitation to Life.*

However hatchet-hearted I feel, the Andrew Lang *Aucassin and Nico-lette* makes me feel like a dog in a harness of roses. Is it the little Mosher edition that you were reading!

I enjoyed very much in the paper this morning—yesterday morning I should say—a paragraph on Dr. Sherman Bishop of the University of Rochester—*Salamanders of New York State.*

I do not feel as stoical as when last writing to you, but I'm afraid it is irresponsibleness not courage, that helps me out from time to time. If you should need to stay near New York this summer for your work, we would not be sorry! I am still convinced that it is the place where an artist thrives best. Mother had a terrible letter from Alyse recently which makes me realize that I am a kind of bonus marcher as far as heroism is concerned.

Love to you, and encourage Jeanne to have more dreams.

M.

("Marianna of the Moated etc." as Ezra Pound remarked, misprinting every word in the phrase but "of.")

To T. S. Eliot   *June 16, 1934*

Dear Mr. Eliot,

It is good of you to send me *The Rock.* The effect of repose and meditation despite the various kinds of effort that must have gone to it, is really a marvel. I have been exceedingly anxious to see it but sentience was not able to prefigure for me what it is. Two friends of a friend of mine were to be in London in June; and I wished so much to read *The Rock,* that I even thought of asking my friend to burden hers with a commission. In their bringing it to me, however, had I been so bold, I should have lost the pleasure of having it from your own hand.

A staged play is a consummation but however right the music may be and the other effects, I feel it all here on the page. How happy a person is in having been entrusted with a message to man, of permanent significance. When taken to task for going to church, I have sometimes answered that we do not refuse to have money because there are counterfeits, but the reply seems to need reiterating. *The Rock* is unanswerable.

The alternating of effects—the careful and the free—is so pleasurable and invigorating, the litterer of Sunday newspapers does not deserve to be reformed so graciously; does not deserve Bert's song, nor Mrs. Poultridge versus Mrs. Ethelbert; nor page 84 at all; but it is not he primarily who is addressed.

I have received the Pound *Selected Poems* and am much interested in your carefully unequivocal analysis and in the choice of poems. I wish I had had this by me when writing on *The Cantos.*

I like a book to open flat as this does, the clear type, and the unsnobbish price. I question the color and certain details perhaps. But I think you were not asking me about format?

With regard to errata and addenda sent you for my approaching book, I may seem like one of the staff of the Macmillan Company who some years ago, when connected by telephone with a professor at Columbia said, "This is Callahan speaking. I've forgotten what it was I wanted to say to you; I may think of it later."

Present laters I enclose on a separate sheet, together with a final new poem—and notes to it. *Poetry* asked if I could send something to be published with "The Buffalo" and I am offering this.

Speaking of a friend of a friend, and knowing that you have the protection of being a friend one count further away, I am enclosing work of a *Dial* contributor in whose talent we were interested. I have not met him but know that he is a chemist for the Canadian government and that he writes music. Mary Lowry Ross whose fiction you may have seen, is his wife. If I did not like the work I would not be sending it but an almost chief reason for my sending it is that it would do the Rosses good to receive recognition which they would value. I am, that is, submitting the poems to *The Criterion* but hasten to add a word of protection for the friend of a friend once removed; viz. that Mr. Ross is unaware of my submitting the poems. I merely asked permission not to return them immediately when he allowed me to see them.

I cannot say too earnestly that I am much aware of the contrast compelled upon you by those who rush in at this notable time.

Sincerely yours,   Marianne Moore

To Bryher   *July 24, 1934*

Dear Bryher,

I hope you can condone something I have done. I submitted to Dr. Zabel "Wish," ending it with the word, "seals." I inquired your judgment on that point, to Switzerland, and when you didn't reprove me, guiltily risked typing the poem without the final words. Please tell me if I must tell Dr. Zabel that I did wrong. "Before Revolution" he returns. There is time, I feel, for you to punish me if you must. Publication of two poems of mine, for instance, has been deferred from spring till November.

That you found things to like in the art selections, does me a great deal of good; I shall have in mind for you other things as I come on them. I too like Mrs. Quash for such reasons as you mention—also little Miss Hone, and take courage from the fact that Morse was hampered and at times discouraged about his work to the point of suppressing it. I agree with nearly all your uncertainties. Charles Demuth has been an invalid since 1915, per-haps longer, and his mind for me is tinged with disability; perhaps I should say eccentricity, but his flower water-colors at their best are marvels of in-terpreted accuracy I think. His imitator, Elsie Driggs, I like exceedingly when she is not imitating. Her studies—really scientific portraits—of the mullein weed are remarkable but I had no example to send you. One of the best water-colors I have ever seen is a Maine landscape by William Zorach, the sculptor. It belongs to the Museum of Modern Art and as design, color, and method is a triumph—definite, and characteristic of Maine, in its fir, cloud, and peacock-eye marine richness. As a rule, I like Marguerite Zorach better than William; a something more aware and feminine in the selection of theme. Ernest Fiene's lithographs of the New England farm, Christopher Wren steeple, elm avenue, and river-craft, are strictly America; also very delicate; and his circus studies are favorites of mine. I wish I could have sent you Charles Sheeler's *Yachts and Yachting;* his pencil drawing of a wooden stair from the under side, and some more recent studies of grain elevators and silos. His oils, that resemble a postage-stamp-album under a magnify-ing-glass I don't care for, but anything he does I respect; he works from in-ner necessity, without tricks, regardless of inducement and favor. Reginald Marsh has force. I like *Why Not Take the L* and accept him, though some-what against inclination. Benjamin Kopman is just a little phobia of mine. Winslow Homer, as Mr. McBride said this year, reviewing one of our large all-American exhibitions, was "the glory of the exhibition." Adolf Dehn is officially "out" for me but if I manage to arrest reason, I admire the method of such lithographs as *The Sunset* and *Central Park* I sent you. I *hope* I sent them (two small Weyhe Gallery exhibition notices). If they were not with the other things, please tell me.

Naomi Mitchison's *Vienna Diary* was forwarded to us from Brooklyn and I do thank you for it. I am in no veneration-of-Pabst[66] mood about it but I need to know these things, and I have also been glad to see other behind-scenes documents that you have given me. I look forward eagerly to the Jane Williams.

Your letter, Lady Ellerman's and Mr. Plank's, was a delightful surprise. I hope you let Mr. Plank know of the recent verse you have been writing, and of certain articles in *Close-Up; The Light-hearted Student*[67] too, I find myself consulting and liking better and better as time goes on. I did not know about Mr. Plank's Jameses, and am delighted that you thought my *Hound & Horn* article worth giving him; but am not at all delighted to have had you buy it.

Your welcome to my poems is indeed a comfort to me. There will be both old and newer things but the book will be small. Better not recom-

66. Georg Wilhelm Pabst (1885–1967), Austrian film director.
67. German textbook published by Bryher and Trude Weiss in 1930.

mend it, let alone buy it until you have seen it. Your thought that there will be a kind reception for it from others beside yourself is your Mei Lan Fang touch of magnificence, I'm afraid.

I hope Eileen escaped illness and after-shock from those dangers she was in, in Vienna. We were much drawn to her and should like to have been able to say before she left America how much we felt her, in the goodbye letter she wrote Mother.

Your allusion to financial cares is really frightening, even when one knows none of the detail. I am so glad you and Lady Ellerman have each other in these trials, and have for each other the sensibility that official administrators are so laceratingly devoid of.

Horace Gregory had a thoughtful review of [André] Malraux in *The Herald Tribune* not long ago. He surely can be trusted to have laughed with you at the *Richard III;* not at England.

Yours affectionately,   M. M.

To Bryher   *August 27, 1934*

Dear Bryher,

This is grieving word of Hilda; I don't know which is worse, the distress of the suffering in illness or the distress of mind in being forced to be helpless. I am glad you could say before mailing the letter that she was better, and that you had a doctor you thought good.

You don't say from where Lady Ellerman is just returning but we are so very glad she was benefitted; and know that it will be consoling to her to be at home, hard though that is too.

I am delighted about the gift to yourself though once again it is wrong. Couldn't you change your mind? You ought to have a book exclusively your own. Of poems I would say; but one of prose also, descriptive and autobiographic perhaps? I don't feel that I can advise about prose except that the letter-conversational style is what pictures itself to my mind. But with regard to the verse I *would* have something to say if you would allow me to do the not-done and tell you in detail what I think of the work—all there is. I am sure it is a mistake for you to leave matters to chance. If left to myself I would be likely to throw away everything I have done, except what I might be working on at the moment. One feels a certain repugnance toward one's past; but profits by others' identity of experience and I think it is selfish to insulate oneself too well. Even for oneself it is a duty to be definite. We do better by working deeper and how are we to do that without a sense of the comparative, and standing one's attempt up and looking at it? I would not labor the matter if you did not do all you can to bring others' talent to life.

In doing that you must know that the most of those you help, don't do as well as you can do yourself.

If you disregard me and *will* bring out a miscellany, I should like to be in it and have been thinking about the matter. I could not write on American painting (I am not to be relied on about it) but for some time I have had in mind saying something about the technique of writing—about verbal precision but I am not ready with either the material or the writing—supposing such an article were what you wanted. The bungling I have done when I have tried to force things, has made me resolve that at all cost, despite every temptation, I must take more time to [do] things. About my *Selected Poems* I am prepared to learn once more that the beatings one brings down on one's own head are the most drastic.

Faber & Faber tell me that for copyright reasons Macmillan's stipulate that I be postponed in England till January.

Your allusion to "many places where" I "have appreciation for" my "work" is a little humorous, the many places being *The Hound & Horn* (now discontinued) and *Poetry*. *The Criterion* made room, I see, for my "Frigate Pelican," a premature attempt; but *The Criterion* is evidently crowded. English writers are the ones to occupy an English magazine, I feel very strongly. Having had to do with a magazine I do not feel that one should try to wring a living from editors who fear the sight of one's signature and I never think a magazine purblind for wishing to stick to the plan of publication it has set for itself; I have no sympathy with people who find unpopularity embittering. I am literal when I say that I am Bob Acres[68] attempting the minuet any time that I intimate to the editor of any magazine or newspaper in America that I might contribute a word—of criticism, comment, or verse.

We three are charmed and delighted with the [guidebook about] Cornwall and are especially interested in the part about the Scillies. The photographs are wonders, and I think I have never seen bird notes that I like so well as the page describing the appearance and characteristic walk of the birds pictured. The legends too, are to us fascinating.

I shrink from believing the cruelties you speak of. It will be a long time, I'm afraid, before either Eileen or your friend Alice [Modern-Alt] will recover from the shock, to nature as well as to the mind, that such things are.[69]

Warner is to be here at Portsmouth for about three years and then be back to sea duty. September 6th he expects to drive to Black Lake to the camp the family have there near the Canadian border, taking us with him

68. Character in Richard Brinsley Sheridan's *The Rivals*. Acres is a country buffoon trying to impress Bath society.

69. This appears to be a reference to Nazi persecution; see MM to Bryher, June 10, 1938.

as far as Brooklyn. Last week he drove us to Williamsburg to see the Rockefeller restorations—the Capitol and Governor's Palace. These colonial grandeurs and simplicities would not have excited you so much as they did us, but it was valuable and romantic in our eyes; the "strong sweet prison" with a shingle roof, and immense mulberry trees for colonial silk-worms, etc., in rebellious Yorktown! by way of which we came home. We had visited Warner at Yorktown in 1927 and had then also gone to Williamsburg but some things keep on improving. Though if anyone could be inclined to think so, we are the ones to think that Yorktown was a mistake.

Love to you always,   M. M.

To T. S. Eliot   *October 23, 1934*

Dear Mr. Eliot,

What could you think I think I am, if I were able to appropriate easily the comments you are granting my book? I want to, badly enough. One could scarcely be human and not wish your "Introduction" might have the effect of a tidal wave, on the public, that it has had on me. The energy of thought that you bring to bear in behalf of this venture is the kind one summons in a case of fire or flood, and is a generosity the most self-ministering could not hope or pray for. And you do it with such sobriety and fine dignity. A test "of anything really new and genuine, seems to be its capacity for exciting aversion among 'lovers of poetry'" is one of your tallest strokes and "if you aim only at the poetry in poetry there is no poetry either" is another.

To be elucidated is a spur both as regards rectitude and abandon and I begin to find myself on a better level by being even in the Barrie Dear Brutus[70] sense, *understood*. I might tell you with regard to my froward rhymes that my mother acknowledges being converted from what for years has been an aggrieved sense of the family gone astray. When a friend recently, noted my "using no rhymes," she said, "Don't enlighten him." Even now she thinks she ought to read the "Introduction" at least once a week.

It shocks one to see people confidently paying debts of the kind that cannot be paid; but aware of the inevitable actualities, I am venturing to hope there will be returns that can be shared with you. I think of *Dial* days when it did not at all put the blight of contamination on beauty to say "At such and such a time we shall be sending you a cheque for —— dollars." Persons seemed apart from the organization; but we know that individual debts are honorable too. If not neglected.

I do not like to see pruned away, "We have our professional secrets," but I am following your corrections for Macmillan's, exactly. I wonder if you

70. J. M. Barrie's *Dear Brutus*, a British comedy first published in 1922. A character named Purdie complains that his wife does not understand his finer points.

know that it was by *The Egoist* I was first published, not *Poetry;* it is only loyalty however that leads me to mention this. I cannot speak fitly—in fact at all—of the coolness with which you spike the guns of the critic before he attacks. The summit of persuasiveness is in making a claim that seems not to be claiming more than could be claimed; and there is plenty of charm for those with the right kind of humour, in what you say about prejudice and about liking for the wrong reasons; and for myself especially in your logic about the coral feet and in your sympathetic allusion to my animals. Unless I compel myself however to have done with my appreciations, you will feel that authors are more dangerous than the public.

As you would know, my letter requesting changes was mailed before I had received the proof. Thank you for deciding for me to keep the lines I had removed.

Sincerely yours,   Marianne Moore

P.S. I like the choice of type *very* much.

To T. C. Wilson   *November 8, 1934*

Dear Mr. Wilson,

I share your feeling of embarrassment before effrontery; but what a pleasure, really what a delight, it is to help those who are fit to be helped. Miss Bishop probably was assisted by your invitation to send other work, to reach this better statement of herself, in "The Map." If *College Verse* should send me work by her to comment on, and this poem is not included, perhaps you would allow me to speak of it? I have not seen it, nor other verse of hers. I was willing to suggest her offering you something because in comments which she had made to me on Gerard Hopkins and others, I felt her ability and technical interest, and felt that in taste she was concentrated and selective.

William Justema's brief poem which you quote, I like—for the power of suggestion that he achieves in the two words "In water," and the precision through not specifying sea or ocean. I like too, "Somehow my mind." I have not seen "A Man Remembers the World" but am glad that you feel ability in it. He seems a-quiver to find technical justification and does verge on it perhaps in some of his prose remarks, such as "How one is turned by one's sentences—until indecision ties the hands." The lightness could easily be too much, but the proffering of confidence has a sobering effect; your helpfulness for each of the persons I know about, is of large significance; for none possibly, more than for Mr. Ross. I have not heard from him but his offering you work is an acknowledgement. I have encouraged Mr. [Melville] Webber to send you a poem of his called "Lake Canandaigua: The Echo."

Thank you for telling me of Bonamy Dobrée's *Modern Prose Style.* A travel article by Bonamy Dobrée a year or so ago in *The Spectator* (London) interested me. His articles on the drama were less interesting but I was reading hurriedly. I once bought, for the pictures, Eric Parker's *A Book of the Zoo* (Methuen 7/6) and came to be equally attached to the text. A cold eye might scorn the humaneness of attitude but the book is full of spurs to the imagination. *English Wild Life* I shall certainly try to read; also Sir Thomas Wyatt whom I do not know except in anthologies. My mother and I are "rushed from this to that" so as almost to make it an affectation to speak of our reading but are trying to make it possible for reading once more to seem natural; even to hear of your present mode of life is a pleasure and an assistance. You no doubt included Robert Henryson[71] in your college reading. I get unimaginable good from him and though I buy few books, deciding I must have the Harvey Wood edition of him, I asked *The Criterion* to do me the favor of paying me for a certain review by purchasing this book for me, and if you would care to borrow it to read at your convenience—for the winter if you liked—and *A Book of the Zoo* as well, it would by no means be a burden to me to send them to you.

The word you give me of the kindness of Macmillan and of *The Westminster Magazine* and of their reciprocity is most cheering. The present arrangement would I should think please Mr. Latham as much as it does either you or me.

I am again bothering you with a change in punctuation. I have let *The Criterion* version of this stanza (which I enclose separately) stand in my book and since the *Anthology* has not yet been printed, suppose it best to have the versions identical.[72] I hope this need not give you a letter to write.

Sincerely yours,   Marianne Moore

I suppose and hope, you and Ezra Pound are including yourselves in the *Anthology.* Also, might I say, after asking you if you had contributed to *Poetry* anything but the recent reviews we were speaking of the day you called, I remembered having mentioned to Dr. Zabel in a letter, liking criticism of yours that he had published. When I spoke to him about it, it was the article rather than the name that remained in my recollection.

To John Warner Moore   *November 27, 1934*

Dear Badger-cat, we are excited beyond bearance by the account of Professor Loram's visit (the two-headed snake, etc.). Mouse said shyly "if Badger

71. Scottish poet (1424?–1506) of the school of Chaucer.
72. *The Westminster Anthology* (1935), edited by Pound and Wilson, included MM's "The Frigate Pelican."

had known how great a man he was he would have been afeered to rub against his leg."

When I want to discipline the beast I threaten to cut off "Badger's other leg" on the snapshot that Mouse keeps in the Bible—the one she said she had never been able to see the leg on. Then she said, "And now I do see it."

We are having a *terrible* time with a poem on three mocking-birds that I am writing for [Malcolm] "Cowley." It is one of my worst o'er leapings of myself. Mouse blinks and blinks and reflects and bleats and then with doubting conjecture returns it for improvements!! And the pattern is such as not to admit of *any* change whatever. Ant-bears alive! antbears at Williamsburg. Antbears of the [Alexis Everett] Frye's Geography [*Complete Geography*]!

Hildegarde has sent us—this PM—a box of roses and a large important gardenia apiece, as a Thanksgiving present. The leaves are wonderful—like yours on your little bush by the side road, only larger.

I hope the dawgs do sleep at night. I could half kill them dawgs if they get you awake nights. Their obligation to go out mornings is beat-worthy enough. I would give somebody something who could train them beasts to jump up in the bathroom and tree like Trix Ferris.

Yesterday I went to Macmillan's with my galley proof and then got Mouse's black pen repaired, that you give me for my birthday before you went to Samoa, and then when I got home your letter enclosing "Percy's" was on the table. Mouse read it appreciatively—and I—and then we took it to Pratt Station to be cancelled indistinctly but the sewer-rats there glared at Mouse reprovingly and said, "lady we wouldn't be allowed to do any such thing." Mouse said pertly, "very well, but I would like to say that this is the *second* time I have been refused a favor at this office that was a mere *nothing*." It then led me to the branch office at Myrtle and Cumberland. They could do nothing for the beast, it then led me to De Kalb Avenue and we took the car to the big post-office—a Park Row car that let us off *at* the door of the P.O. and a very leisurely postofficer obliged the Mouse, saying benignly, "but when it gets upstairs, they may put a mark on it that's going to show." Oh yes, one fellow said, "Now if you just knew someone in Norfolk, you could send it there and get it postmarked Norfolk."

This is my new paper. And we got a box of envelopes at less than half a cent a piece at Lerman Bros. on East 14th Street. Mr. Lerman was saying as he tied the box up, "No, I gotta take in some money before I run up any more bills."

A much pursued ha-cat.

P.S. I have just passed the poem through my paws for the last time & mailed it. Mouse said with regard [to] the struggle—"Yes you were riding with every tire punctured."! If Cowley returns it, I have other homes for my cats.

Space for Blackie[73]

See enclosure. Sent in appreciation of the blackie bear black record for my typewriter.

73. MWM wrote the final two pages of the letter; no evidence remains of the enclosure MM mentions.

May 2, 1940

260 CUMBERLAND STREET
BROOKLYN, NEW YORK

Dear Louise,

Nothing to be answered, but something for you to think about. (This is a very close pansy.) Elizabeth said you had been sick the time I went to speak at the Young Men's Hebrew Association. Otherwise I might have seen you there! Thinking you had just been sensible, not really sick in bed, I didn't bother you to tell me. Lester Littlefield has just telephoned saying, among other things, you were in bed about a week. I don't know what I could have done but be in the way. But we just can't stand it to know you've had a real illness, nor to feel that you may not be entirely over the effects yet, though it sounds brave and natural, that you had some acquaintances to dinner with you last evening. You don't know how consoling it is to us, Louise, that you made room for Lester, and that you have at other times. I doubt that you ever added anyone to the group you were having, who got more intensive good of the pleasure. His appreciation of things has the least alloy of extraneousness, of anyones I think I ever knew and your effort for people and himself, is so real to him, and his concern for others is so unperfunctory. He spoke with a kind of dismay (though

Printed version on page 399

1935-1941
New Friends, New Forms

SELECTED POEMS (1935) and *The Pangolin and Other Verse* (1936) signaled success for Moore, adding to her stature as a major poet. A letter from Warner captured the importance of the publication of her *Selected Poems*, underscoring the collective pride the family continued to take in her creative enterprise: "'The Postscript' [to the volume] is the supreme touch to me. It is a beautiful thing from any point of view; and a poem in itself; but from the point of view of our family knowledge it is like the intimate fire of a diamond. It lights the present moment with divine fire, and at the same time, speaks of our entire history, or our Life hid in each other. In it there is the witness to our origin, to our period of growth, to what we ever shall be" (April 16, 1935). In the "postscript" to the volume, Moore had, without naming her mother directly, acknowledged her mother's presence in the language of the poems and the thinking behind them.

Selected Poems elicited supportive reviews from Wallace Stevens in *Life and Letters Today* and from Morton Dauwen Zabel in *Poetry*. The correspondence reveals that Moore was instrumental in helping place Stevens's review, "A Poet That Matters," in Bryher's *Life and Letters Today*. Moore was delighted by Stevens's praise, having long admired him. (She had written to Sibley Watson at *The Dial* in 1921, suggesting Stevens as a reviewer for *Poems*.) Writing to Bryher in 1935, Moore confided that "all [her] efforts in writing criticism and in writing verse [had] been for years, a chameleon attempt to bring [her] product into some sort of compatibility with Wallace Stevens" (see August 9, 1935). Moore and Stevens had begun corresponding in the twenties, when Moore, while editor of *The Dial*, had solicited both poetry and prose from him. Although Moore and Stevens remained on rather formal terms, never addressing each other by first name, they corresponded regularly until Stevens's death in 1955 and their letters reveal their unfailing loyalty to each other's work.

This period was not without its inner conflicts and frustrations. Moore seemed to be taking stock of the destruction and despair around her, particularly in Europe, and struggling with her own sense of powerlessness. Writing to Bryher in 1937, she asserted: "All of political or civic nature is disturbing, but I try to take revenge on Confusion by refusing to be darkened or embittered. Do not, however, withhold what it is for one's good to know; and do not conceive such a dislike for America that you will not care to visit it" (July 4, 1937). Moore's sense of the poet's role and responsibility at such a time of crisis was called into question by what she witnessed; by 1940, when she wrote to Warner that "technical virtuosity is not the essential nourishment we need at this time" (March 20, 1940), she no longer seemed to feel she could or should take private refuge in her art. A few weeks later, she wrote again: "These are not times for self-consciousness & agitation about one's self or poetry or any other thing" (April 3, 1940).

When Moore did make time for writing, she turned seriously toward the genre of fiction, which had been an interest of hers since her college years. She struggled privately with the writing of a novel, which in its early stages she called "Job's Protestations of Integrity," and then titled "The Way We Live Now." Throughout the late thirties Moore frequently wrote to Warner about her progress with her "story." These letters convey just how important this venture was to her and the extent of her swings of mood about it. In 1936 she wrote Warner: "Last night it (yr Bear) was going over my story and says it holds the attention; I have typed about 16 pages representing what I have written since coming home. I am belly deep in the detail and general significance and am determined to keep my paws right on the bone" (January 30, 1936). A year later, she expressed some of her frustration, noting, "My story is tedjus; unbelievably far from 'correct.' I've worked all afternoon on a few sentences..." (November, undated, 1937). By 1939 Moore had submitted the manuscript to Macmillan; again, Warner's response gives us an insight into Moore's own feelings: "Rat's observations as to whether or not his story is well received by Macmillan convince me that his story is exactly what will appeal to the thoughtful readers to whom Macmillan caters; and as he says in any case, nothing can mar the effort as a record of our PHILOSOPHY; in our pleasure in recording it together!" (February 28, 1939). When Macmillan rejected the novel, Moore turned elsewhere, but nothing came of this effort and the novel remains unpublished. Moore also encountered difficulties when she began to send her poems out again. In 1940 "What Are Years?" was rejected by the *Atlantic Monthly*, although later that year it would be published by the *Kenyon Review*, becoming the title poem of the book she published in 1941, *What Are Years*.

Moore's troubles were not just confined to the realm of publishing; she and especially her mother were frequently ill during these years. Moore became increasingly aware of her mother's frailty and spent more and more of her time nursing or watching out for her. The seclusion and quiet they had welcomed in Brooklyn when they first arrived had become a necessity, as Mrs. Moore entered the last decade of her life. In 1935 Moore and her mother moved to a smaller and less noisy apartment in the same building. Writing to Zabel, Moore remarked: "I have been rather severely ill for three or four days this winter and now we are in the midst of what is psychological illness. We are removing from our present apartment to another in this same house" (April 23, 1935).

Despite these troubles, Moore expended great energy critiquing her friends' and acquaintances' work. A letter to Bryher, thanking her for gifts and telling her how ill she and her mother had been, is typical of this period, combining as it does references to the quotidian and literary matters: "This may be a letter of several sorts—business, literary, and personal. I wish first to say how much more than I can tell you, your taking care of us in this depth of illness has helped us. I felt immediate improvement from the calf-foot jelly; and the Port although we administer it almost with a dropper, has helped us both, and it is a kind of consolation and reassurance that we have it." A paragraph later, she commented on Zabel's "fearless article on [her] *Selected Poems*." Then she switched to a description of an Esquimaux needle-case that she was sending to Bryher as a gift (March 14, 1936).

Many of the letters written at this time deal extensively with what Moore was reading and reviewing; despite her private disappointments, she continued to make critical pronouncements about her own generation (particularly Stevens, whom she always admired, and Pound, who often behaved unacceptably) and to mentor younger poets and writers, such as Elizabeth Bishop, T. C. Wilson, Mary Hoxie Jones, and others. Moore often commented on Pound's unpredictable and irrational behavior. In a letter to Wilson, who was editing *The Westminster Anthology* with Pound, she asserted that Pound "has the mechanics of a somewhat rare firearm and is no two times alike" (see September 29, 1935). And when she sent Pound a review of Stevens's *Ideas of Order*, she wrote to Wilson: "Ezra Pound's tendency or perhaps I should say determination to be indifferent to Wallace Stevens may operate to punish me" (September, undated, 1935). Although no longer editor of *The Dial*, Moore continued to exert her influence with various journals, recommending her protégés and her contemporaries to Bryher for *Life and Letters Today* and to Zabel for *Poetry*.

The highlight of this period is Moore's correspondence with Bishop. Between 1934 and 1940 Moore and her mother, who continued to advise those around her, suggested countless revisions for Bishop's poems and stories. Many of these exchanges are by now well known. It is clear from the correspondence that Bishop both relied on Moore's good eye and resisted some of her recommendations. Moore's letters to Wilson also contain advice and recommendations; but the correspondence is most compelling for the insights it gives us into Moore's thoughts concerning whether poetics could be divorced from politics. Once, for example, in a letter to Wilson, she disparaged her friend Kenneth Burke: "Kenneth Burke in his *Frontiers of Credulity*, says some shrewd things, but like various other writers whom I like, whenever he becomes political, he puts great strain on my loyalty to his specifically literary shrewdness. Even a touch of vindictiveness makes logic suspect" (January 3, 1938). By the end of the decade, Moore's sense of the poet's need to take public stock of what was happening in the world at large had shifted, leading in the years to come to poems like "In Distrust of Merits" (1943). By the early forties Moore had begun publishing poems again: "Four Quartz Crystal Clocks," "What Are Years?," "The Paper Nautilus," and "Rigorists" all appeared in 1940. The period ends with Moore receiving the Shelley Memorial Award (1940) and with the publication of her fifth volume of poetry, *What Are Years*, which was dedicated to Warner.

To Ezra Pound   *260 Cumberland Street   Brooklyn, New York*
January 5, 1934 [1935]

Dear Ezra,

I can do nothing about J. S. W. Impropriety is a part of courage, I suppose, and I have benefitted by your boldness on my behalf, but I cannot conceive of putting the handcuffs of advice on J. S. Watson or on an active philanthropist like Bryher.

Lines quoted by a reviewer, from *The Trumpeting Crane* (Helene Margaret) I liked so much I was sorry not to be doing something for the book. Other lines in another review aroused doubts. It is hard work trying to keep from being disappointed in people.

Miss Bishop is not one who takes encouragement crassly or is easy on herself. She is but just out of college and naturally is under academic handicap—the tin cuirass of lightness—but for this very reason I feel that there is on us a certain obligation. Her letters and T. C. Wilson's are the best letters from young people that I have ever seen. If I had only letters to go by, I would take a long leap away from Miss Barnard.

As for snobbery about anybody, Jew or Gentile, I have exerted myself for too large a number of the indiscriminately mixed two you would say;— of the I-am-Blind or the I-Believed-in-Beer, who will never get help from anybody else. A waste no doubt, but I don't forget the help I have received myself. From those who need no such hidden effort, I feel free to take a moment's leisure for what I very much need to do. Anyone who has had assistance from yourself, W. C. Williams, and T. S. Eliot, and is inclined to pine, should be exposed to die. The pestilence of illness and of private obligation don't invade some lives. But perhaps if I had all the time there is, I should write too much and have too congenial a time. I know how it would be, when once in a while we see people that are to our taste.

As for Dr. Zabel, I think Chicago is further away from New York than it is from Rapallo. His vacations seem to take him west instead of east, and the inside workings of the magazine are completely unknown to me. I think Miss Monroe still considers it her magazine but even without knowing, I am sure that most of the work done, is done by M.Z. My mother says you and I are too much alike, except that you know a great deal more than I do—too bellicose—to be useful to the misguided. But even I can't think it good for anyone to drudge incessantly and I wish you could show Dr. Zabel some of the master features of Italy. I was under obligation to him for giving us your political ditty in the last *Poetry* and there will be more than I to welcome it. *Poetry* wants to publish work by Yeats, T. S. Eliot, yourself, W. C. Williams, T. C. Wilson—anybody who is interesting. But no magazine hires its contributors to make up the issues, arrange for future material, or censor the work of fellow contributors. As for crushing a paper into compliance with one's personal wisdom by threats of starting a magazine, the more magazines there are, the more energy is bred. The situation is not jeopardized but relieved by having a dissatisfied author take off independently. Another target for practice shots is put up, and every aspect of the matter should be welcome to a resolute editor. The reformer's task is one not of laming, but of luring into compliance.

There is something in the idea that the talented should have unlimited voice and that the average man should assume the drudgery and expense. But I feel very strongly that the man who puts his time into a publication has a right to have the thing the way he wants it. A magazine is like the shape of a nose or the set of the teeth. Nothing is altered for you by saying they could be re-designed better. You can withhold subsistence—contributions and awareness, so the magazine will droop—and hope that something better will spring up. Or you could undertake someone's drudgery and thus undertake him; but you can't ask him to run the errands, telling him that you will provide the intelligence.

As for T. S. Eliot, I am not firm with anyone and by no means with him. One can't have sufficient momentum, do you think, to create an organ which seems worth making better, and not be inconveniently impervious to gratuitous influence? I mean T. S. Eliot's peculiarities are part of the special aptitudes which tempt you to interfere with him.

Your *à volonté* way of disseminating your views on economics by side-columns on stationery is good. I wish I knew more about economics than I do.

Yours respectfully; or as your abbreviating forerunner "the dear Queen" used to write,

Yours aff'ly,   M. M.

I shall be very glad to see that Cummings-Cocteau pronouncement.

To H.D.   *January 6, 1935*

Dear H,

There, in a way of which I was not conscious perhaps; but in these books in a way I *am* conscious of. The sense of impassioned triumph, the torture, if you don't mind the word, is transmuted into accuracy. I haven't felt it in this way for a long time. I was going to say when writing you before, that I worried about you lest you were being intruded on. I don't know that it matters, so long as the zest for continuing is alive in one. But I do want you to be happy. I shall die without having learned to transfer vitally felt acuteness; but you help one to feel that the battering we endure need not be the last word.

And now you send us the strange golden tree to make us happy at Christmas—besides what you said of the clock. (And your ineffable beaver water-mark!)

I am so touched that you would care to have me with you in Bryher's series. I hope you will not resent T. S. Eliot's having me imitate you—in the preface to Faber & Faber's reissue of my book. I enclose the line though I should not, since the book is delayed.

I abhor the thought of trying to equalize obligation; one must be indebted. But you have done so much for me, at times when it was crucial—and intrinsically unbelievable—that I do not know why it is I never should be able to benefit you.

MM

To T. C. Wilson   *January 18, 1934 [1935]*

Dear Mr. Wilson,

Miss Winslow's attack is astonishing beyond normal accounting for.[1] One who understands Ezra Pound's idiosyncrasies can take or leave what one hasn't at the moment elasticity or verve sufficient to return—as in an athletic rally; but this lady is merely to be left in quiet if quiet were not a fiction in any place where she is;—and seek quiet as quickly and in as safe a place as it is to be found. A letter came to me yesterday from her, of abuse and demand, that is not even curious enough in interest to justify your reading or my rereading. Fortunately she does not refer to writing or to you. I could not very well bear to be silent if friends were maligned. She wants monetary support for *College Verse,* but scarcely expects to hear from me.

Ezra Pound of course is highly disappointing; but it is not philosophical to be wishing him to be something he has not been before.

I am greatly pleased that the writers I am interested in have had your help—costly though it is to give such help—and that you think of issuing some [of] their work later. That is a good title of Miss Bishop's, and I shall ask her to let me see the poem.

1. Ann Winslow, who edited *Trial Balances,* had invited Wilson to contribute as a critic to her anthology rather than as a poet. Wilson wrote back that he would rather be represented by his poetry. He then indicated which poems he would have liked to see included. Winslow responded by saying she thought more highly of his criticism than of his poetry.

T. S. Eliot's *The Rock* is one of the few current writings from which ideas seem to spring at one. But anything churchly, devout, or divine, seems to engender in Ezra Pound a kind of madness.

I am easily upset by the unexpected when it is adverse but Miss Winslow's choler toward you and toward me seems to have meaning only in its reflex toward her.

I have been thinking about what you say of "Modern Prose Style" in *The Criterion*, and agree with you. I can't admit the distinction between innate personality and specious personality.

Thank you for wishing us to be well. We are, and surely hope that you are.

Sincerely yours,   Marianne Moore

To Ezra Pound   *March 4, 1935*

Dear Ezra,

I had not mustered an animal for you, so that is all right.[2]

If I go to Norfolk this summer, as I may, I shall write you regarding the Confederacy. There is a fine nest of southern politico-economic and colonial material in a small library at Fort Monroe across the river from Norfolk. My Brooklyn-Oxford surroundings do not yield much; though if anyone at Pratt Library should "push the bashful stranger to his food"[3] your queries will not be deferred.

I had partly answered previous letters on a rather large scale, regarding Miss Bishop and her clavichord, Ralph Kirkpatrick and his pedagogy, problems of advanced mathematics, Mr. Wilson, etc.: "freshness of perception and technical certitude, every detail giving meaning to every other detail"; but none of this is very essential as regards *The New English Weekly* or economics.[4] I do think she says what she says very well, about the way in which the rhythm in a poem keeps up with itself like an acrobat catching his partner's ankles while affording, in safety, an extra turn and flourish within the fall; and the problem of depicting a mind thinking, so that the idea is not separated from the act of experiencing it; how in writing a poem it seems impossible to get the material into motion in its chaotic state and the poem, unique and perfect, seems to be separate from the conscious mind, avoiding it while the conscious mind takes deliberate steps toward it.

2. EP had asked MM to contribute to Alfred Orage's *The New English Weekly*, to which he was a regular contributor; most of MM's poems at this time were based on animal descriptions. His letter of July 11, 1934, advised her to read up on economics.

3. "Or press the bashful stranger to his food, / Or learn the luxury of doing good." Oliver Goldsmith, "The Traveller." See also MM to TSE, March 12, 1935.

4. MM is referring to Elizabeth Bishop's "Gerard Manley Hopkins: Notes on Timing in His Poetry" (*Vassar Review*, February 1934). EB had bought a clavichord and was learning to play it under the direction of Ralph Kirkpatrick.

I give strict attention to anything that is said about the economic foundation on which or in spite of which we live, but in art some things which seem inevitable ought to be concealed, like the working of the gastric juice. A glass stomach might not kill *one*, and is interesting to inspect—compulsory for all, under a Hanfstaengl[5]-Hitler-Russo-Japanese-General edict, not good.

> *Yours cheerfully,*   Marianne Moore

P.S. You said something about building a fire under a mule but confused T. S. Eliot with me I think. Certainly in the matter of ready judgments on rich people, I am as much against scattering mud on near objects as you once were yourself and I consider impersonal terms of abuse as an affront to me.

I am sending for *The New English Weekly* on Cummings.[6]
I have received from Italy a notice of shortwave wireless activities.

To T. S. Eliot   *March 12, 1935*

Dear Mr. Eliot,
Your "New Hampshire" and "Virginia" are surely poems, and in very fine dress. As for me I was almost in Nero's plight when he lost the 8-cornered tent which could not be replaced, the envelope conveying the poems being addressed to 3 instead of 2 sixty Cumberland Street. 260 seems to be a hard number to remember; various things addressed 160 have been lost, though possibly not always lost; there [are] four or five more Moores nearby who seem prominent and less conscienceful than the two at 260. But this time fortune was kind.
The accurate

> *". . . gates wait. Purple trees,*
> *White trees"*

brings back to me last summer and my brother's lawn bordered by crepe myrtle trees, and visited by the mocking-bird. You seem to have been able by deciding carefully from what point to speak to say it all; and the originality in tempo (especially of the "New Hampshire") and your indigenous rhythm ought to be a great pleasure to you.
In real poems as here, one perceives something one had not seen before, each time one reads them. Having too, a cover that is fitting in "being intrinsically a piece of artistry is something for congratulation." It seems almost foolish to say—I do thank you.

> *Sincerely yours,*   Marianne Moore

5. Ernst Hanfstaengl (1887–1975), chief of the Foreign Press Department of the Nazi party.
6. Pound had reviewed *Eimi* for *The New English Weekly*.

N.B. This is to warn you of something as the English say, overleaf.

I fear I shall shortly be sending you two things more burdensome than peacock feathers and not so fine as what they cover—one of my own productions called "The Pangolin"; and some sonnets by a Miss Elizabeth Bishop if she will hazard herself in my company. I have been impressed by some remarks of hers about Gerard Hopkins, in a Vassar undergraduate paper. She speaks of the rhythm running under superimposed rhythm like an acrobat who in catching his partner's ankles, is able within the fall to afford an extra turn and flourish without spoiling the form of his flight, and how in writing a poem it seems impossible to get the material into motion in its chaotic state, the poem, unique and perfect, seeming to be separate from the conscious mind, avoiding it while the conscious mind takes deliberate steps toward it.

One can't lay a burden without laying it, yet I have not forgotten that it is often an adventure to read the manuscript of strangers "and learn the luxury of doing good"; sometimes less an adventure, to be regarded as the proper custodian of the work of an acquaintance. However, with entire sincerity I would suggest that you save yourself particular concern in the matter of these offerings and have them returned to me by someone if *The Criterion* could not use them, that they may be "offered elsewhere."

M. M.

To T. C. Wilson   *April 15, 1935*

Dear Mr. Wilson,

Ezra Pound's abuse of America and American cities has a connection it would seem to me with the psychologists' interpretation of love and hate as not precise opposites. His advocating that you use money so arbitrarily as he suggests—money that could be used more directly in furthering the work that brought it to you, is—though he does not mean it so—unscrupulous; also an ignoring the sincerity of one's replies, seems to be a settled tendency of his. I think it should be met with similar ignorings.

None of this worries me, but I regret what seems to be a willingness on his part to interfere with individuality. The fact that he is discerning of ability makes one doubtful of what he finds fault with, but I feel—especially at this epoch of his own thinking—that one must muster one's own nature and justify it. No doubt what he does not like about your preface, and the same is true doubtless of the poem, is the very characteristic he should value in it. I am keeping the poem to add it to those in the magazine.

I should very much like to see what Miss Bishop would write on Ben

Jonson and hope she will, as you suggest, do some work of this kind. A thing that I think promising is that she is deliberate and does not force production.

What Wallace Stevens says is surely very nice, and if you feel that he would not be disturbed by being anticipated—or as it were kept to a promise—I should of course be glad to have it included.

Instead of feeling ourselves wrongfully arraigned by E.P. it seems to me there is much cause for patience—but not for a patient attitude; for that would incense him, but it is well to understand his private predicament. Things are going on in London and here, that interest him and he is not there, or here. I would only beg that you do not alter your writing procedure and I think the self-justification of having nothing to say in reply to the un-permissible has a chastening effect on him.

When, as you will presently, receive a copy of my book, do not take the time that you are so much needing for other things, to send me word of receiving it.

Sincerely yours,   Marianne Moore

To William Carlos Williams   *June 22, 1935*

Dear William,

I was at Bryn Mawr a few days ago to read my poems. I recited "The Red Wheelbarrow" and referred to what you said about unquenchable exaltation as coming very near to a definition of poetry; the first stanza of [Stevens's] "Sailing after Lunch," and

> *and this be my fame*
> *the harder the wind blows*
> *the taller I am*

Before reading, however, there was time during supper on the porch, to talk to various students and instructors and one of the instructors said "William Carlos Williams is the only person I read that makes *me* feel parochial." Certainly your remark about similarity would make up to one for a great deal of thwarting and imperfection; I say *would* because I suppose the most that we suffer is trifling compared with battles with conscience on the part of martyrs in England, Germany, Italy, Spain, and elsewhere. Every time I see a newspaper that mentions Hitler or Abyssinia I wonder why I do not walk up and down the street like a sandwich-man wearing as broadside your "Item," for good though certain other things are this says it all.

I am sorry to have missed the game at the polo grounds but I miss so much, nearly everything, that I am hardened to loss.

The remarks of "The Rocking Horse" are too good for me; but served at the same time, to make me wonder why I did not send you a copy of my book. I got one with you in mind, in case I saw you—this is to make you feel sorry for your obduracy about not coming over—but also I felt you may have all you care to have that is in my book. I am now going to get the copy out of the old cherry bureau in which it is, and send it to you, solving the problem by not writing in it so that you can transfer it to someone as occasion offers, and you are not to be bothered thanking me.

You and Florence and the boys must come over here in the fall when we get back from Virginia. Or journey in a body to the Metropolitan Museum to see the animal-rugs? Or to a good cheap restaurant to eat some tough bread? The idea of foregoing visits as one becomes an older and older musketeer and needs them the more, is the apex of folly.

Yours affectionately,   Marianne M.

To George Plank   *June 25, 1935*

Dear George,

Thank you for thinking of me when you see dragons, and for being as willing to encourage me about my book now that it is out, as you were before. If I could get over the feeling that it inconveniences my friends you would have had a lizard green copy sent you to England.

I am sceptical too, of Bryher's need for me in her series. If *Life and Letters*, however, has not altered her plan and I am to be allowed to have the drawings, what would you think of drawing something for "The Pangolin," the butterfly piece, and "Pigeons" perhaps, but not for the mocking-bird-and-the-three-fledglings? since the concept borders on the comic—on the thought of [George Cooper's] twenty froggies or the nine lizards: "Bask said the mother, bask said the eight," and so on. I wish you could plagiarize your swallowtail butterfly, but anything you liked or did would be liked by me.

I am enclosing the ruffles and the diamond eclipsing the world, the detail of which did not seem quite fresh in your mind when I spoke of it. But please let me have it back—when you would be writing otherwise; because I set great store by this midget medallion.

We hope Switzerland is being to you what it sounds to us; for that matter, what Sussex sounds to us. We are to be with my brother in Norfolk from now until September, but we shall not mind the unSwiss climate since we can be with him. I wrote him last winter about my afternoon at the theatre, and your tea-party at the hotel, which shows what a ruffian one becomes, living in the city—boasting to those at a distance of the pleasures of town life.

With grateful thoughts from us both—from us all.   Marianne M.

The poems are not ready but I shall send them as soon as I can.

To T. S. Eliot *June 27, 1935*

Dear Mr. Eliot,

I received a few days ago your play, *Murder in the Cathedral*, and you are truly to be thanked; also to be envied, because the triumph of living is to influence others; sorry as one is that there should be knowledge that would make the writing of some parts of it possible. Suffering, however, is known to everyone.

This is great writing; with remarkable insets of music, or as it were, chords of rhythm; not to mention a formed conclusiveness that manages beyond misunderstanding to be firm and lucid, dangerously so. "Personally I had a great admiration for him," "*we* are not getting a penny out of this," and your recognition of the collector mania (page 13), will be congenial to more than one or two. The principle of complementariness as diction and meaning, throughout,

> ... *acting is suffering*
> *And suffering action.* ...
> ... *turn and still*
> *Be forever still.*

one could never get by rules or formulas; or the closeness of the climax beginning "Clear the air! Clean the sky!"

Sincerely yours, Marianne Moore

P.S. You will be amused to note—whereas I am profoundly grateful for— the armor afforded me by your introduction to my book. Reviewers bow to the defense; though a few admonish; and one, Mrs. Padraic Colum, would destroy armor and all, but the writers whose opinion one truly values seem minded to conform and say "this is what he says."

There is human interest of course in such things as the enclosed, but you must not take time to acknowledge them. I would not be sending them if I thought you would be tempted to do so.[7]

To T. C. Wilson *c/o J. W. Moore, USN* *Building 32, Norfolk Navy Yard*
Portsmouth, Virginia *July 5, 1935*

Dear Mr. Wilson,

I can hardly credit it that one so finished in his work as Wallace Stevens, should say these things about my book. I can't conceive of generosity so great, as his going out of his way to do me this great kindness; and I thank you for allowing me to see the article and know besides, what he said to you about it. Since he seems willing, do send it to Mrs. Macpherson with

---

7. MM enclosed a transcription and clippings of reviews of *Selected Poems*.

such explanation as you have suggested. I wrote to her after talking with you and said I thought you might be sending it.

Since Mr. Stevens suggested "scrupulous" instead of "fastidious," I should like to have it, and think it worth the "fussing"—keeping fastidious of course in the two middle phrases—(?): "fastidious a la mode" and "communicated in the fastidious."

Your letter in which you spoke of Mr. Bird,[8] E. E. Cummings, and Wallace Stevens, I received as I was leaving home. *No Thanks* has not yet been returned to me and I had only glanced into it, so I cannot say how it impressed me, but *Eimi* seemed to me intensified over previous books. Mr. Cummings is always a shock to me in two ways—in his virtuosity and in the fact of his existing like a mote in the air without response to what as it seems to me is the import of life; but his replacing of life with art may have life and in that case I am contradicting myself.

Wallace Stevens I interpret somewhat as he expresses things in this article, by the contrary of appearance. His great accuracy and refracted images and averted manner indicate to me a certain interior reconcentration of being. One who has borne heat and burden as well as he has, and as long as he has, is very deeplaid. I feel sure that the support he needs would not come from general society but from men—men whom he likes, who are aware of his mental strife and are not on the surface with regard to his interior debts and insufficiencies. A man like Bernard Shaw does not consider dying by inches permissible. Men of compulsions and poetic respects, like Donne and Gerard Hopkins, or Dante, would undoubtedly have been swine if they had not been able to assert that life that amounts to anything is a matter of being colossally inconvenienced—is a kind of supernatural salamander.

If Schulte does not send me the William Empson[9] that I ordered (in exchange for something I sold) I should certainly like to borrow yours and shall ask you for it. I read the first few pages when at Bryn Mawr and am grateful that you should think of letting me see yours.

Sincerely yours,   Marianne Moore

To Wallace Stevens   *John Warner Moore, my brother's home*
                              19 Western Branch Boulevard
                              Waterview Portsmouth, Virginia   July 11, 1935

Dear Mr. Stevens,

It is easy to say something when there is nothing to say, but not when there is too much to say. Whatever the coarseness of statement however, I

---

8. Otto Bird (1914–), American poet.

9. English poet and critic (1906–1984); MM is probably referring to *Seven Types of Ambiguity*, 1930.

am not willing to leave to conjecture the sense of benefit I feel from what you said in the article just now lent me by Mr. Wilson. (I returned it to him the day I received it.)

In writing for oneself as one is obliged to be doing, there is mercurial exhilaration but even so one lapses into patience that at times is nearly morbid. Therefore encouragement takes on an air of mirage-like illusion; though your matter-of-factness in counterfeiting the essential mirage is so actual one finds oneself perhaps permanently cheered. It is a delight to feel that this legerdemain is the usual for yourself; that is to say, that you never find the gossamer assuming the texture of carpet.

Your allusion to T. S. Eliot will do him good, and that again benefits me, in my sense of obligation to *him*. For in consenting to let Faber & Faber publish my collection I had no thought of involving any one person in a defense of me. (I should add however, since this sounds as if T. S. Eliot had unanticipatedly contributed an introduction that I had discussed with Mr. Frank Morley who came to see me when in New York, the reprinting of some things T. S. Eliot had said about me in *The Dial*.)

It is like one of Strindberg's exasperations that since you wrote it, *The Dial* could not have this article; also that calamity should have fallen on *The Westminster Magazine* at this time. But we will hope that Mrs. Macpherson will want your article as much as she wanted some of your verse.

Sincerely yours,   Marianne Moore

To Hildegarde Watson   *August 8, 1935*

Dear Hildegarde,

If it had to be one or the other, Sibley would not be long in choosing between the writing and any picture; and neither would I. When I see a drawing of leaves among leaves and seeds, I don't wonder that you make drawings but do wonder that you part with them.

With regard to the concerts, you have thought it out I am sure. Your muddled soul is the only one that could do the violently complex singing, travelling, studying, postponing and, behaving, in the midst of our misbehaved, mixed-up unmusical inopportune public.

I am sorry you couldn't get [Enid Bagnold's] *Alice and Thomas and Jane,* but the anxious thing is that Evelyn [Holahan] had to rush abroad like this. I was joking when I pretended to be scandalized about Anne's ingratitude for my book; I had had no thought she would write me. I don't like the possibilities in connection with this going abroad. Anne's paper on Hitler, her energy, and ideals of rashness, surely are for her danger-signals. Llewelyn would be diverted and entertained by her but why she would descend on an invalid-hostel by the foodless seacoast, or anyone so heartrendingly hospitable as Alyse, I don't know. I also can't help wondering why the help-less put themselves so criminally out of reach of human help.

If you find that you have at home two copies of [Cummings's] *No Thanks,* then sometime when you are there, and I am home, I would be willing to have you return me the one I sent you. But *NOTHING* would please me so much as to give you the book, in case it isn't an extra.

Pride and Prejudice has been luring me too—is not that odd; but I am not yet really reading it. The prides of Virginia, as found on my bookshelf—for Warner has been so busy he couldn't take us to many of the actual places,—have been eating up my time;—both the matter and the warmly self-sympathizing Southern manner. To hear so much about "the States" makes me feel as if I were in old England itself; and as if the first four presidents must have been under a misapprehension when they did anything about or for "Northern Virginia"—(the New England states). Union and Rebel are words on which the ink wouldn't take if anybody set them up down here. But I admit that "Northern Virginia" is a detail in a Captain John Smith book, not got from amongst these neighbors. And I also admit that these nice and fearsomely generous people, like so much our liking everything down here, that I feel as if I were John Calvin in the process of being made a Roman Catholic.

I hope you have no anxieties in addition to all you are doing and planning.

Love from us—   M.M.

To Bryher   *August 9, 1935*

Dear Bryher,

Your letter with enclosed messages from Cornwall has just arrived and I am much excited. I can believe George Plank *has* done a beautiful drawing and am glad you would not jeopardize it in the mail. Don't let *any* original be risked in the paws of the United States postal department.

I am a-tremble, in the other sense, about the Stevens article. I don't see how I can hold my head up, indeed remain in America, if the article should not appear; the whole matter being the result of overzealousness on my part. Enthusiasts do come to grief. Here I am—with the naiveté and pigheadedness of a sub-beginner, sending a review of Wallace Stevens' *Ideas of Order* to *The New English Weekly* to which Ezra Pound has been urging me to send something, Ezra Pound having set himself some while back as I think I told you, to exclude Wallace Stevens, and I shall no doubt get it back. And Mr. Herring of course must return the article if he must, and I realize that if he does not care for the article, he would not care for the Old Dominion poem I submitted to you, all my efforts in writing criticism and in writing verse having been for years, a chameleon attempt to bring my product into some sort of compatibility with Wallace Stevens. In *this* matter, however, I should not pray the staff not to blackball me; am very desirous in fact that I should not incommode or bore an editor. Do see to this for me and have the poem returned to me if there is dissatisfaction with it. I made up my mind—you are so suicidally generous—that I *would* offer you something for *Life & Letters*, since you declared you wished me to; and since you said verse, I decided it should be verse. However checkered the going moreover, this is not my last piece of verse and I would try to offer something different if you could not use the Virginia piece. I cannot tell you how glad I am that anyone here has said anything good to you about me.

I have had a letter from Miss Bishop from Brittany. She thinks of studying at a university in Europe this winter; or finding a place with a milder climate than New York and not studying. Perhaps, if you have received manuscript from her, you know this.

To return to myself, George Plank knows a fearsome amount about books and a book he planned would be just right. Fifteen dollars appals me, but I know that whereas the Darantière format is sufficient for poems, it is not ideal for drawings.

I got Mr. Latham's consent to my having the Darantière pamphlet; but to be sure of respecting my contract which promised Macmillan an option on the next thing I had for publication, I shall write to Mr. Latham of your present suggestion. (Our duty on books is so high that I might not be able to have the book myself; I paid duty on the copies given me of my Faber & Faber book. But perhaps there would be a way out.)

We are charmed with the picture of Cornwall and with Perdita's message and the news of the kitten and I thank you and George Plank, as you know, for thinking of me. I interpret the signature Dean as that of the friend you are visiting. Please thank her.

I shall write as soon as I hear from Macmillan. We expect to be in Virginia till the 22nd of September.

Love to you from us. M.M.

To George Plank *August 14, 1935*

Dear George,

That you feel that what I write is not unnecessary helps and encourages me more than merely thanking, can say. Interior and exterior barriers when one is attempting what has to do with art, are at times very grave. I shudder at the word of your having gone to such immense trouble about the mocking-birds. I was serious when I suggested to you drawing an illustration to something in your mind rather than to the literal reference—which might just as well have been something else. If we continue with the project, please remember this.

I have been follied into another effort—a kind of commentary on Virginia, having told Bryher I hoped to send her something for the December *Life and Letters;* and in that case since pages are needed for the separate group, the publishing of the group would be delayed. So save yourself as regards the material of mine you have now, till you see this piece. It deals with Jamestown church-tower ruin and table tombstones, and Captain John Smith's coat of arms, (a Turk's head and an ostrich with a horseshoe in its beak), dwarf box-edged flower beds, ivy arbors and lead statuary, saddle horses, hounds, raccoons, owls, French furniture, and so on; the pomegranate and African violet also. The violet as you may know is begonia like and scentless but a complete small thing like the cowslip or the oriental sprouting arabesques of grass that you see in Persian miniatures.

As for not being Persian or Chinese; you spoke the truth—if not in the sense in which you meant it—when you said you would never add to the bad prose which is being written. Bryher was right; you *should* be writing, though it abashes me to think you were nearly made to undertake an apologia for me.

I can realize the change in your retreat at Marvells made by attempted conversations such as you speak of. And I also know how when one is fond of people one has to be with them. We, liking cool weather, are liking it better than anything in the world, to be here with my brother—in torrid heat. My mother has been well.

We expect to return sometime before October. If you come to New York, please do try to make time to come to see us. The telephone number, as you may have forgotten is Sterling 3-1123.

Sincerely yours,   *Marianne Moore*

To Elizabeth Bishop   *September 8, 1935*

Dear Miss Bishop,

I was much surprised though of course pleased to see the French postmark on your letter, but am much *dis*pleased by the way one is treated by our post-office, and hope you can still send me the letter that was returned to you after we left home to come to Virginia.

If you can find a place in France that would benefit asthma and save you such a winter as last one, what a blessing that would be. How like magic if it were also a place in which there is a university since you say you have a thought of studying at one.

What you say of Brittany and the blue nets and the circus seems like pure fairytale; I can't imagine anything more delightful than the experiences you tell of; or more instructive if one can be objective about it than the uninfatuation with Americans, you mentioned. My mother and I have been entertained the last few days by a book we found here in my brother's house—*A Vacation in Brittany* by Donald Moffat—dated 1931. It is about St. Amélie and speaks of how the French play tennis and of an elephant from a circus that was allowed in the water and was so delighted with the sea that the keeper was obliged to wade to it and ride it back to shore.

I hope you will do as you thought of doing and offer something to Mrs. Macpherson for *Life & Letters*. Robert Herring is the editor but I feel like being ignorant and sending anything I have to offer, to her. I hope I shall see what you have done whether or not you arrange to let it be published. Ezra Pound urges me from Venice to send prose or verse to *The New English Weekly*, regretting that contributions are not paid for. Might you consider sending something to it? I can give you the address when I reach home, though you probably know it yourself.

Mrs. Macpherson still plans to issue for me, the poems I have written since my book came out but to wait till December in order to give *The New Republic* time to publish my piece about mocking-birds which it has had since last November. My timidities are not being rapidly metamorphosed into conceitedness.

In the Gerard Hopkins, I was impressed more than by anything with the unhumility, the thirst for reciprocity,—and against my will,—with the inclemency so to speak of Gerard Hopkins' faith; his intestinal disorders and the wan cheerlessness of his duties. The first letter—the one to Canon Dixon of self introduction has as much charm I think as anything I ever read, and I am greatly struck by the poetry of wording, the inventive compactness of vocabulary. The passages about mathematics and the allusions to music interest me too—and confirm a great deal that I have always tried myself to think was so.

I regard a vacation abroad as a kind of sacrosanctity and although anything you might tell of it would be a pleasure to hear, do let yourself feel your freedom and forget, if it would be best, your stodgily employed friends on this side of the water. But not of course, forever.

We are still in Virginia in order to have a visit with my sister-in-law and the children when they return from Black Lake with my brother next week, but we expect to be home after September 21. It has been a great pleasure this summer to watch the birds—their idiosyncrasies and their treatment of one another. A crepe myrtle tree last evening with a cardinal bird and a gold finch perched on it at the same time were just like a Chinese flower and insect painting; and the immense crickets and their immense chirping has also been impressive.

My mother feels deeply, your transferring to us the enchantment of your surroundings and asks me to send you her love and tell you what it is

perfectly unnecessary to tell you—that we shall miss you. With affectionate wishes from us both for all good to you, especially in health,

Marianne Moore

We'll be grateful for the postcards.

To T. C. Wilson   *260 Cumberland Street   Brooklyn, N.Y.*
                        September 29, 1935

Dear Mr. Wilson,

After writing to you of Mrs. Macpherson's pleasure in receiving poems
from you and the Wallace Stevens article, I had another letter from her
which alluded to the article hesitatingly;—which said that Robert Herring
who had been appointed editor of *Life & Letters* was not quite sure of wishing to review me in that way. She also said that poems which Miss Bishop
had sent, she herself liked but feared Robert Herring did not. I replied that
my efforts in writing, could be but an attempt to approximate consanguin-
ity with Wallace Stevens, either his prose or verse; that one must not cavil,
however, at an editor's ultimatums.

With regard to *The Westminster Anthology*, a copy was sent me. You
are in your verse contribution so guarded, so spare indeed, that one feels de-
frauded; the more, that one has the great largesse of reiteration elsewhere.
Your introduction I suppose does lack the spontaneous happiness of un-
hampered critical zeal; but it achieves a great thing in making it evident
that you were permitted to sponsor what had been forcibly not to say violently reconstructed. One benefits by this courage you show and I am sure
no one will attribute to you the bizarre printing and thinking of the anthology as a whole. Misassociation is indeed a hardship and I hope the editing you are doing will not be that—so fully at any rate as you fear. Editing
is toil and exacts the whole of one's self, so it is not easy to accept disappointments in it impersonally.

If you will let me see the poems you have written, it will be not a favor
to you but to me. I am by no means sure that one can know that Ezra Pound
feels that you have been a means of his wasting his time. It is very seldom I
think, that inferences concerning Ezra Pound can be literal ones. He has the
mechanics of a somewhat rare firearm and is no two times alike. Furthermore, like the parent who beats a child that has run away, out of relief at
seeing it safe home, he likes to bear down on anyone in whom he has confidence.

I hope you can pardon subserviently prosaic philosophizing such as
this. But I do feel greatly roused against the possibility of your being worried or handicapped by what will seem to you retrospectively no more than
an incommoding handful of dust.

Mrs. Macpherson gave me the office address of *Life & Letters* 26 Maiden Lane, Strand, W.C. 2, London, and suggested that anything for the magazine be sent there. She did not refer again to your poems but I hope you have had some direct word by this time.

I have heard from *The Criterion* that my *Ideas of Order* review is to be used; in the next issue; I suppose that will be December. To have Wallace Stevens' own work questioned or hesitated over by the new editor of *Life & Letters* seems unbelievable. But I have the feeling that Mrs. Macpherson's wish to have the article may overrule.

Sincerely yours, Marianne Moore

Do not be hurried in returning *Ideas of Order*.

To Ronald Lane Latimer   *October 3, 1935*

Dear Mr. Latimer,

I understand your allusion to personal sacrifice, and cannot say how impressive to me it is that there could ever be those who instead of publishing their own work, publish the work of others; and one does not have to be an expert of finance to know that the kind of publishing you do is not an exploiting of the author.

When I see Mr. Latham of The Macmillan Company, I think I shall speak of what you have suggested to me though he has been so kind in overlooking irregularities, and condoning what might be regarded as encroachments by me, that I feel uneasy at thought of seeming willing to be continuously counter to my publishers' original expectation.

I feel about "an aesthetic credo"—and about "decoration"—as I do about the sense of humor, that it is an outgrowth of the deepest part of one's nature.

I am not sure that I understand the second question—with regard to "the mastery of facts as associated with the possibility of more effective action in the historical sphere." But I would say that aesthetic expression is, with me at any rate, a kind of transposed and protected doctrine of existence, resting on the attitude to behavior and concept of history; and that those two perhaps are the impulsion underneath it.

Sincerely yours, Marianne Moore

To Ronald Lane Latimer   *October 7, 1935*

Dear Mr. Latimer,

I am thanking you again for a great deal; the more, that the persistent readers of an author should not be parasites.

You and Dr. Williams are surely to be congratulated on the title of this book—*An Early Martyr.* William Carlos Williams in himself is one who makes one not ashamed of being an American. I wish in his desperation against the unchangeable and the abominable he need not come so near ruining his thrust. There is nothing like it when it comes straight. One is maddened sometimes into taking the wrong revenge. Perhaps we are all maddened, and not steadied enough to say what is wrong or what right. In any case one must respect a man's compulsions.

Sincerely yours,   Marianne Moore

To T. C. Wilson   *November 29, 1935*

Dear Mr. Wilson,

I was surprised to hear, from your letter of October 27th, that you had had no word from the editors about your poems and the Stevens essay, and about a week ago (longer than a week ago; perhaps November 10th) when writing to Mrs. Macpherson asked if she would not find out for me whether they could be offered elsewhere—but was careful she should know you had in no way suggested that I speak of the matter—that you had merely permitted me to know that you were in doubt. I hope your surmise is correct about the publishing of the Stevens article. Purblindness regarding Wallace Stevens ought not to be one of our current misfortunes in letters and I wish I had succeeded in saying in my notice of *Ideas of Order* what you say clearly and so impressively in your letter—about looking things in the face and about Wallace Stevens' composure as the result of struggle. I hope you will be presenting these thoughts yourself. And I hope too, that you will be able to let me see the poems of yours you had thought of sending me. But might I suggest that you be cautious in demanding of yourself that you compass ends that are desirable; it is a strain on one perhaps to protract what could be accomplished by over-exertion but one must be humble, I think, and make sure that one stays well. I owe a great deal to you for the word you give me of your reading, for speaking of the [Sir Philip] Sidney, which is not in anything that I own—"You Gote-heard Gods," and which I look forward to finding in the library; and for sending me this article of T. S. Eliot's, which I think you meant me to keep? But if not, do tell me. It is a long time since I have got so much good from anything as from this—from the manner and subdued force of the article.

I am not sorry so much as aghast at the thought of your having fallen into hands so ill fitted to help you or get from you as these you are now in, and feel, with you, that adaptation does not seem the remedy so much as escape; but escaping or staying, one is grievously hampered and affronted by such conditions of existence. There is consolation, however, to be had from the belief that one's friends have in one, and in books. I have, I think, spoken of the good I have got from Marcus Aurelius's view of misfortune, and again and again I think of that unqualified, even desperate assertion of [Giordano] Bruno's—difficulty is ordained to check poltroons; for we can demand the assurance of ourselves that we are not going to be downed.

I am sending my notice of Wallace Stevens which should encourage you, I think, as showing you how far others fall short; I had promised to show it to Mr. Latimer and he says he sent it on to Wallace Stevens, so having no copy for reference, I shall let you return it to me; but if I am able to subscribe to *The Criterion* and there are articles that I think you would be interested in, I shall be sending you the magazine. Perhaps as you say, there will be a way for you to exchange your present work for other. I do hope so, and in any case that you will keep well, and at peace enough to make these experiences a mere stiffening of the muscles and not a scar on your progress. I hope too that you can pardon advice which may merely emphasize to you your difficulties.

To be studying Greek would compensate me for a great deal. I try to work at it but do so feebly, and am always being frustrated.

In *The Westminster Anthology* my mother and I liked greatly the woodcut used as tail-piece and wondered if the using of it was your suggestion.

Sincerely yours,   Marianne Moore

To Elizabeth Bishop   *December 20, 1935*

Dear Miss Bishop,

How kind you are, I cannot say what I feel in having you and Miss Crane willing to share your pleasures with me. And how much pleasure you have transferred by what you tell in these letters of November 10th and November 20th;[10] it has been a rich enjoyment to us. I should not be able to come to Spain, or even to France, but not for want of desire. My interest in Spain is, I fear, discreditably unstudious. I have always wanted to see corktrees like those under which Sancho Panza and Don Quixote rested; the Hispanic Museum catalogue of flocks, grilles, and weapons, made me imagine that wrought iron is one of my hobbies, and I have as the result of a letter or two from Mario Manént, been interested in Barcelona and some of the printing done there.

Your word of the pigeons in the blue cage, and of the Chinese collection of Mr. Loo—his dragons with movable eyes and ears especially—delighted me beyond measure; and how glad I am that you have the

10. EB and Louise Crane were staying in an apartment on Rue de Vaugirard in Paris.

clavichord at last, and can take the lessons you speak of with a teacher who harmonizes with the instrument. We heard Monday afternoon, over the radio, a sextet from the Library of Congress—Ralph Kirkpatrick playing the harpsichord, Georges Barrére the flute, W. Gordon, the cello, in Bach's *Little Offering,* violin sonata in e major; fugue for harpsichord, for flute, the canonical fugue, and fugue perpetua. And Tuesday there was a recital by the Society of Ancient Instruments, a Frescobaldi toccata, and various jigs. The gossamer precision of Ralph Kirkpatrick however, was a thing like nothing else, and seemed to have a kind of physical therapy even. My mother has been very ill but was able to listen to the music and the fact that she is recovering made the two concerts completely a pleasure. I had undertaken too much and fallen ill and she then caught the fever and rheumatism—if it was rheumatism—that I had had. Please do not let the thought of it stay in your mind.

Speaking of the pigeon-cage. I meant to show you the afternoon that you and Miss Crane were here, the cricket-cage you had given me, in which I had a seated Swiss bear. I have since put a velvet one in it and the Swiss one outside, under the door.

It was not a trouble but a pleasure to answer the letter from Mr. [Edward] Aswell. My only hesitation in such matters is that you may be interrupted with letters to answer. However, I have given your address to James Laughlin who has asked for it, hoping you could give him something for *New Democracy* of which he is literary editor. He was at Harvard two years, then abroad for a year or two, and is now going on with work at Harvard. He said in contributing to the paper you (a poet) might feel as if you were contributing to a feed-store bulletin but that verse is paid for, prose not.

You spoke of letting me see verse you have been writing and I hope that you will. Even if you should have a typewriter, do not take time to type the poems. For myself I should prefer handwriting. But it has occurred to me in this connection that if you were offering something to a magazine, to let me type it for you might be a convenience to you and would surely be no burden.

I seem to have fallen into the depraved habit of writing a thing after it has begun to be printed, so feel a certain resentment toward "Pigeons" which there was not time to alter in accordance with my belated abridgement; and certain divided words in a piece called "Virginia Britannia" which is to be in *Life & Letters To-Day,* I have rearranged; so I have a stoical feeling about that prematureness also.

As for the books, the Marjory Fleming and the Pound, I had forgotten that you had them, but shall feel free to ask Miss Miller[11] for either if I should need it. I feel very much your willingness to spend time in looking

---

11. Margaret Miller (1912–), a friend of EB and Louise Crane's; painter, art critic, and later assistant curator at the Museum of Modern Art.

up or procuring things for me but at present I think of nothing I want. Unless it might be to know to whom the lion watermark belongs of the paper on which you wrote me—just that I have a perhaps idle curiosity about watermarks.

I have been looking into the [H.] J.C. Grierson and G. Bullough *Oxford Book of 17th Century Verse*, and the Thomas Randolph selections please me greatly, particularly "A Gratulatory to Mr. Ben Jonson;" likely you remember it; Mary Butts' story "The Guest" in *Life & Letters Today* seems to me remarkable, and I have been reading to my mother during her illness, [Thomas] Hardy's *Under the Greenwood Tree* and George Moore's *Avowals*.

You say much too little about your health, knowing as I think you do, how concerned we are about it. One is always hearing of people who found just what they needed in climate, in the Pyrenees or Portugal or the Tyrol, and perhaps you will be having what you ought to have had here.

I am yours affectionately, and please remember us to Miss Crane,

Marianne Moore

To Bryher   *January 18, 1936*

Dear Bryher,

I have your letter of January 9th and unable as I am to find words in which to answer,—I am glad that I am not unable to grasp the significance of an attitude such as yours, and of certain small things in connection with it, in the way of expressing things.

The tendency of some people to prey on others creates in one a kind of hostility to money, and on my part a perhaps misleading attitude of disdain; whereas no one better than I, I think, is in a position to feel money an actual phase of the supernatural, as an agent of solicitude and unselfishness. As one comes to understand life better, one says that one does not wish to have more than is necessary. But a frenzied miser could not have been more desperate than I have been at times, in thinking of lost savings which I am now incapable of re-earning. No one could be more difficult to assist than I am, under any principle of stipulated proof that production would justify the confidence and assistance extended. No one could understand better than I, the demoralizing effect of a sense of insecurity or need more than I do for those I care about, the freedom of being self-dependent. So I should like you to know that for the accumulated "certain small sums" you refer to—with additions saved from a monthly amount from my brother—a protected investment which he has found for us, will now be paying $26.25 a quarter and itself be growing more valuable. Nor does it represent those entire savings, nor is it the result of disregarding your wish that a little life should be introduced into our routine. Illness and my great desire to get some writing done keep us from appearing to be very active, but we heed with literalness your wish and my brother's (in his phrasing) that we "deny" ourselves "nothing."

The addition you speak of makes me realise more than ever, that one's debts of gratitude must needs be paid to someone other than the one from whom one receives; and shows me once again that however great the gift, and extreme one's need, might be, nothing of the benefit could be so great as the sense of support conveyed by the feeling which actuated the giving.

This is all very clumsy, but I am better able to annoy you with it than to suppress it. Yet there is so much to say regarding specific good you have been doing us—especially during this illness, in keeping us warm and appropriately habited, that I am almost compelled to reticence, no emphasis being sufficient.

So far as the draft for five pounds is concerned, it seems to me that *Life & Letters To-Day* is like the baby Solomon was about to divide with the sword. I do not see that your half of the paper could fail to benefit by anything by which Mr. Herring's half benefits; and if you feel in any way thwarted, let it be a warning to you not to overpower those who are weak.

We are sorry it seems best Lady Ellerman should not take the trip she needs, and sorry for the word of King George's illness. Weather here has been violent and raw with a day of sun occasionally. One wishes the artificial atmospheres they are using now in California, for bronchitis, or asthma, or sinus trouble, could be transferred to England. Eventually nothing will be local, but one wishes the thing at the moment it is needed.

Love to you, and you no doubt will be hearing from me again; perhaps not, but I feel as if the matters here touched on would need a letter every day.

M.M.

I am much pleased to have the clipping, and interested to hear that you liked *Salamina.*[12]

To Wallace Stevens   *March 10, 1936*

Dear Mr. Stevens,

I have not seen the Grigson review,[13] but how you can think as you do, and "think" that Geoffrey Grigson "is justified in what he says" I don't know. Our good minds, Paul Rosenfeld, Mr. W. W. E. Ross, T. S. Eliot, Dr. Watson of *The Dial* and others associated with *The Dial*—William Carlos

12. Book about Greenland, authored and illustrated by Rockwell Kent.
13. Grigson had written a negative review of WS's *Ideas of Order* for *New Verse* in 1936.

Williams, E. E. Cummings, a cohort of exacting fanaticals, hesitate to say the obvious to you or even about you for fear of seeming "wholehearted" and crass, they regarding the pinnacle of deserved triumph which a fortified author enjoys, as imperialists do the regalia in the Tower. I could scarcely feel that it was not irony when you wrote me to *The Dial àpropos* the Award to William Carlos Williams, "lucky Carlos" or some such word of apparent humility. You must not honor even so much as to be aware of them, the critical shadows that darken lines and pages they cannot produce. T. S. Eliot wrote me of being delighted to be able to include in *The Criterion* a review of you. I recall hearing, through a protracted dinner, no topic discussed but your verse, and am sceptical of your not being surfeited and impeded with initiate compliments of the delicate sort. *Ideas of Order* is an enviable unity—a kind of volume-progression on certain individual poems of previous years, and were it not that one feels a fool in saying what is no secret, it would be a temptation to particularize.

Roger Roughton[14] whom my penmanship misnamed Roger Boughton, is somewhat of a curiosity and responsibility;—about 20 years old, an orphan whose father was killed in the war—who says much that sounds didactic, that is touching when reflected on, as being a phase of purposefulness, I think, and self-pardon.

Sincerely yours,   Marianne Moore

To Elizabeth Bishop   *March 14, 1936*

Dear Miss Bishop,

It is distressing that you should know so much about illness. You cannot think what we felt on seeing the photograph of you that fell from the letter into my hand as I opened the envelope. How good, that you were in Paris, not Morocco, when this operation became necessary, and that Miss Crane was with you. Perhaps other illness you might have been subject to will now be avoided. We are glad to have the picture—apart from the fact that it looks like [Alexander] Pope, and it does[15]—and to have the other ones, are amazed indeed by the beautifully precise detail, the Vichy bottle, and the feet of the dove curving over the edge of the cage, and the shadows of the two heads and beaks. We have enjoyed too, the Gothic sculpture you sent me and the door of your Paris apartment. I had meant to speak of these

14. Roger Roughton had invited MM to contribute to *Contemporary Poetry and Prose,* a new monthly; he had also asked her to invite Stevens to contribute something.

15. MM is referring to a picture EB sent of herself in the hospital with a bandaged head which EB said made her look like Alexander Pope. She was there for a mastoid operation.

cards when writing before. I resist certain Gothic literalisms—certain interpretations of Bible stories for instance—yet always admire the helpless artist in them and feel the art as a whole, a treasure.

I have wished I might know something of the Chinese exhibition and should surely like when you come home, to see the Ashton and Gray you speak of, and the Hugh Porteus. I have read only a page or two of [William Empson's] *Seven Types of Ambiguity;* it was somewhat minute and vermicular to my eyes but I should like to go on with it, and to see [his] *Some Versions of Pastoral.*

Wallace Stevens much over-praised me but I am glad you and Miss Crane condone him and also my somewhat "wholehearted" review of him.

I have heard nothing more from Mr. Aswell but am glad you let him see some of your work. The poem by you in *Life & Letters To-Day* takes me by surprise. It is difficult to sustain atmosphere such as you have there. But you do sustain it and one's feeling that the treatment is right is corroborated by one's sense of indigenousness, and of moderate key. I had a note from Mr. Laughlin a few days ago saying he was sending poems of yours to the printer, and thanking me for having helped him to get for *New Democracy* "this interesting work."

The winter for us has been a series of frights and disappointments and I have not till now been writing letters, my mother having had a sacro-iliac difficulty that was acute, and I bronchitis; and then last week after I was as I thought recovered, having a return of it. I had let myself be tempted to accept an invitation to Bryn Mawr to meet Mr. I. A. Richards who is giving a course of lectures there on prose style, to hear him speak, and make some remarks myself. After going downtown to get certain trifles connected with my going, I was ill once more—iller than I ever remember to have been and we sent word I must not go. We are now beginning to feel as if life for us would sometime seem natural again. To be snakes in alcohol is abhorrent to us and you must efface this image of us; and when you have come back, help us by example, to have leisurely habits and better health. And perhaps you will tell us about camels and date-trees; several months ago we saw a remarkable film of Morocco, of horses of various types in a race, of high Moroccan ladies doing fancy-work and having tea.

> *Affectionately yours,*   Marianne Moore

To Elizabeth Bishop   *446 Oak Grove Road   Norfolk, Virginia*
August 28, 1936

Dear Miss Bishop, or if you meant to say so, Elizabeth,

I am sorry you have had ivy poisoning. Sorry does not express it, for I have had it and can think of nothing I fear more unless it is a cobra. Carbolic acid diluted, had effect as I remember, but nothing milder.

What you say about studying medicine does not disturb me at all; for interesting as medicine is, I feel you would not be able to give up writing, with the ability for it that you have; but it does disturb me that you should have the *feeling* that it might be well to give it up. To have produced what you have—either verse or prose is enviable, and you certainly could not suppose that such method as goes with a precise and proportioning ear is "contemporary" or usual. I hope you will have reason to be glad you allowed *The Southern Review* and Roger Roughton to have something. Soon after writing you, I received an urgent plea from Mr. Zabel, that I ask you to offer *Poetry* something, and wish now I had written to you at once but I didn't want you to be like the Hudson Day Line ticket agent to whom my brother wrote one year, reserving and unreserving rooms in accordance with his family's altering plans. (My brother said the man would think something was wrong if he didn't hear from him "everyday.")

The kitten is a masterpiece of a little creature; and what a picture! How kind it is of you to give us the picture. I much prefer the name Minnow to the other;[16] in fact we gave it to a silver gray kitten we borrowed several years ago, to guard the pantry in the house my brother's family have at Black Lake.

As for the Sapolio album, it is so superb, I certainly shall take care of it for you and not let you take it from yourself. It's rococo unbelievableness at its peak.

I did not know Miss Miller is a painter, but can well believe it.

With regard to Virginia, although I think I tend to overdraw beauty that my friends are not present to verify, the Cape Henry sand-dunes, the beach and its follies, the Chinese strangeness of the waterbirds, would be hard to exaggerate. One evening as I may have told you, we saw two large slender birds skimming the water side by side. The wings were black with a gray edge—white underneath, and there was a large piercing scarlet disc around each eye.

I wish I could see Miss Crane's boat. My brother's children have a boat—a "snipe" which we tend as if it were a priceless insect that had to be fed and sheltered by special Hindoos. Its wardrobe received a sailbag today, and an unbleached muslin starfish is to go on the nose of the rowboat as a bumper to keep the snipe from being battered.

Maybe you would care to show me what you have been writing? We expect to be back in Brooklyn the end of next week. I think I recall complaining of having to look at things which were sent me for advice, but I never have complained of writing that I *asked* to see. In fact I have rather serious cause of complaint against you for stinginess in this matter.

Affectionately yours, Marianne M.

16. EB had written to say she was sorry she had not named the kitten Pterry.

To Elizabeth Bishop   *260 Cumberland Street   Brooklyn, New York*
                               September 20, 1936

Dear Elizabeth, if that is not tedious,

The kitten is a masterpiece. Its natural lynx stomach and limp paws would make any elaborate camera envious. And the poems are so fine, and dart-proof in every way,—especially "The Weed" and "Paris, 7 A.M."—that they shiver my impulsive offers of helpfulness. This exteriorizing of the interior, and the aliveness all through, it seems to me are the essential sincerity that unsatisfactory surrealism struggles toward. Yet the sobriety and weight and impact of the past are also there. The great amount of care, the reach of imagination, and the pleasure conveyed, make it hard for me not to say a great deal; but I fear to make suggestions lest I hamper you. Specific comment is bound to be hapless. Still, I venture, in the way of soliloquy—not request—and should be very glad to have you keep everything just as you have it. But I do wish you would send, or allow me to send, "The Weed" and "Paris, 7 A.M." to *Poetry*. Mr. Zabel was urgent about securing something from you.

As for Coney Island, I not only should be willing to go but have been anxious to go, and wondering how I could persuade my mother to the thought for I think it would do her good. She says she ought not to go but feels very greatly yours and Miss Crane's thought of her.

                                                                    M.M.

I have an appointment at Dr. Baldwin's, my dentist's, for Tuesday but otherwise have no plans.

To Elizabeth Bishop   *October 1, 1936*

Dear Elizabeth,

Your doubt respecting Coney Island helps me to be bold in telling you of my childish enjoyment of it all, and to tell you another thing under the same head—childish—that it was as much as my natural capacity would permit of my having without adding even the theatre as you would have wished it to be.

The "carousell," the pony-stands, the shooting-gallery with you sighting the gun, the swimmers, the red Indians on the hand-ball court, and the empty streets,—were far beyond my expectations. The dinner was notable, and I am not likely to forget ever, that night blue of the sea or Miss Crane's driving, which certainly were heights.

I am sending "Paris, 7 A.M.," to Mr. Zabel—not only satisfied that you should keep "apartment" but very grateful that you do, for otherwise I would be deterred from saying exactly what I feel about a word or connotation. I have been thinking about the word "Revelations" for instance. I realize that the "s" is used intentionally and why; but I wonder if it is best to ignore the first impression of it, as an error by reason of the title of the book in the Bible.

Respecting your theatre-engagement, without knowing about it, the impression left on me was that you did just right, sorry as I was not to see more of you and have Mother see you both. It is a pleasure to have the Chinese art longer.

I wish I could feel that there is reason for your statement in connection with Mr. Zabel's article, about my work, as affecting one's interpretation of other poetry, for that is surely the very summit it seems to me of what one would wish to achieve—to subterraneously change the observer so that afterward his critical apparatus seemed different. But the generous basis of your comment does alarm me.

I intended on Saturday, to give you the copy (enclosed) of what I said to Roger Roughton about "The Weed," and these pages, about watermarks. There are some dire mothholes in these last and if a remedy or remedies should be self-evident to you, without your expending time, it would be a great help to me to be told. But do not take time from yourself for writing a letter.

I did not wish the magazine's return or need the poem, unless you have no place for them.

Affectionately yours,   Marianne M.

You will tell Louise Crane will you not how *much* I enjoyed her, and the going to Coney Island?

To Morton Dauwen Zabel   *October 1, 1936*

Dear Mr. Zabel,

In mailing my letter to you on Friday I thought of Miss Monroe as returning shortly from Peru, and telling us presently in an editorial, of her experiences and her impressions of writers at the conference. You would know I think, what I feel in hearing of her death. We are not prompt in reading *The Times* for Sunday, but on seeing the editorial page Tuesday, I looked for an earlier notice, unable to believe that Miss Monroe could have died, and at length found in the Sunday pages the account of her death. Her goodness to us all, her imperviousness to plebeian behavior, and her fearless battle for art—and in art—I have always revered and marvelled at. And her auspiciously contemporary, somewhat sceptical proffer of writing experience and opinion, when she spoke at the Brooklyn Institute a year or two ago, were so very congenial to me. I was glad, in *The Times* headline, of the word Poet, for Miss Monroe would have liked that.

The enclosed stanzas, one of the poems I hoped to send you, I am submitting alone; Miss Bishop says she had submitted the other one, "The Weed," elsewhere but will surely let me offer it if it is returned. Now if because of my seeming urgency, you try to use this against feeling of your own, it would disturb me very much and Miss Bishop no less. I should like also to save you the trouble of a letter. In case the poem is not to be used, in simply being returned to me in the enclosed envelope, it would be its own explanation. Miss Bishop's address, however, in case you did wish to write to her—either in accepting it or saying something regarding it—is for the present, c/o Miss Louise Crane, 820 Fifth Avenue, New York City.

Sincerely yours,   Marianne Moore

P.S. This is scarcely the time to speak of what I had expected to quote to you from a letter of Miss Bishop's regarding your *Poetry* editorial on my book; but I thought it would interest you and it seems unnatural to not speak of it: "It seems to me that he has attempted and managed to express a great deal that has never been touched on before. I like very much the part at the first: '—and other sleights of hand demanded by public success or moral insecurity,' and, 'the banalities of allegory.' And 'when they present a thought, they do so in terms of all the accidents, analogies and inhibitory influences that went into its formulation.'"

To Elizabeth Bishop   *October 19 [1936]*

Dear Elizabeth,

Something may have attacked my nerves and I hope you will not take fright at this over-intent analyzing of your work, but just as I was sealing my letter to Mr. Zabel, it seemed to me that in two lines, the rhythm did not seem continuous with what went before. If I am trying to disturb an intentional balance of inequalities, or mishearing indubitable equalities, please pay no attention. And I *beg* that you will in any case send Mr. Zabel a version of "The Weed," the one you typed and signed, or one changed a little, tomorrow or Wednesday.

As for "The Baptism," you have the mechanics of fiction—the verisimilitude is a marvel—in particular in the conveying of implacable cold; and do send this to *L. & L.* I am querying certain phrases.

M.M.

P.S. I had already sent Mr. Zabel a return envelope.

To John Warner Moore   *Oct[ober] 20 [1936]*

Dear Nigger-Demus (ruler of the Jews),[17]

Bear has stopped working like she was working on a boat but I have been working like I was working on a boat and like I was working on an In-vocation—at this letter to *Poetry*—in tribute to Miss Monroe. Bear help-ing with one claw.

The young Bear and the young but tentative Plato [a cat]. (Bear is not tentative.) It would "get" you to see Bear in the second row, right under the sloping lecture-desk, looking up at Dr. Griggs, not nodding the entire evening till 9:45—hearing differing equivalents for s-o-f-r-a-s-u-n-e (par-don the English instead of Greek)! and laughing at Socrates' ironies con-cerning the generals Laches and Nicias, and the armor. Pardon me also for not telling you that *sofrasune* means temperance.

We are glad about your good preaching in the afternoon and then in the evening. That is very significant that the Admiral was so deep in cogi-tation over the Barracks presentation that he wrote you at length.

Glad your drake "et cet." are on the grass.[18] I guess the Talbots could take the three in with theirs if they get irksome to 446.

I'm reviewing Wallace Stevens now for *Poetry*, having been indefati-gable about Miss Bishop's poem "The Weed" for *Poetry* and a story "The Baptism" which describes three sisters in Nova Scotia. We think it a very fine story. Mr. Zabel has accepted *one* poem, much to Miss B's joy and is being sent "The Weed" which Roger Roughton returned, causing Miss Bishop to roll and tear the grass up with chagrin. I said Roger Roughton was a curiosity—a Postal Telegraph boy who should and would be de-frocked, but it did not console her. She went into ground-hog retirement over it. My triumph over Roger causes me to pass my hand over my whiskers, inconse-quently.

As for Kitty beer and bear-brand Brandy, don't you say *nothing*, water-fly. I half obtained the brandy with you in mind. I wouldn't want to be with-out it. Bay-rum *truly* is not the same thing. B-rum is for cake-walking, immersings, and the like—not for Old Rough when drained of blood by a weasel.

Dearest love,

17. Here MM repeats JWM's earlier use of this name for himself, itself perhaps a response to MWM's description of a sermon referring to the "excitability" of "the Jews + the Negroes + the Irish" as a prelude to the story of Jesus driving moneychangers from the temple (to JWM, October 15, 1936). Nicodemus is also referred to in early family letters, perhaps appealing to the Moores as a secret follower of Jesus, hence anal-ogous to each of them in their intensely shared private life.

18. The Moore family had two domestic fowls: Barnacle Bill, a drake, and his mate, Queeta. Talbot Park was a neighbor's estate, home to countless guinea fowl.

To Wallace Stevens   *October 29, 1936*

Dear Mr. Stevens,

Owl's Clover received from you this morning, I had been reading, having been sent the pages by *Poetry*—I would not say for review, no review of
such precipitates and beauties being possible—but for comment; and it
made me hope for you that in giving to the world one gives to oneself. The
world probably is not owl enough to thank you for troubling about it; but an
unkilled and tough-lived fortitude is a great help to us, conveyed as it is by
your disguises, and may I say as the tenantry say to still persisting members
of an aristocracy, "long life to it," to this hero which you exemplify.

Sincerely yours,   Marianne Moore

To Bryher   *November 7, 1936*

Dear Bryher,

I received some days ago your letter of October 16th and hope it will
not be bad for you to be in London for a time, because I cannot help feeling
glad that you are there and that things are going so well with *Life & Letters*.
That you have a stall at the Book Exhibition should not surprise me, or that
you are managing to show *The Pangolin*, but the doughtiness of the proceeding dwarfs Excalibur. I am very sure no one is showing my *Selected Poems* at the New York Book Fair which opened just now at Rockefeller
Centre.

I have been observing your rearing of Perdita and can't tell you how it
inspires me. I took ten driving lessons here in Brooklyn and had two or three
in Norfolk summer before last from Warner, but have taken no tests.

It is good news about the Swiss Prize to Ramuz.[19] The word from Spain
is very dark and one hates to feel that what you say of Germany and Italy is

---

19. Charles Ferdinand Ramuz (1878–1947), Swiss author who wrote in French.

true. A firm article by Sir Herbert Samuel sent us by Warner entertains and pleases us. It is condensed information about the Cabinet but includes various remarks of this sort: "The United Kingdom is illogical. No constitutional lawyer could have designed it; the system has every defect, is open to every criticism, and has only one virtue. It works."

We feel, and many who did not vote as we did, feel that our recent election shows that the majority of the people are willing to profit at the expense of others,—are in favor of spoils, that is to say. We have such an appetite for Relief that we are like the frogs who would have a king. But if Mr. Landon[20] had been elected, his ideal of sacrifice on the part of those who have something, so that those who have nothing might live, would not have been popular; and instead of a sound country at last, we might have had a dead patriot.

I am hardly the one to be satirizing relief, having received word in October from The Peoples Trust Company of an addition to my account. As I told you last summer, the exigencies of travel between Warner's office and home are tedious but the consolation it is to us, especially in this almost constant rain, to know that he has the convenience of taking his car to the ferry, is beyond any form of luxury, and he speaks of it frequently. I think I should tell you too that I gave a theatre party, inviting five friends to the Negro *Macbeth* at a little theatre here;—Landonlike, occupying the 35-cent gallery seats but at the same time the best in the house. And I also prevailed on Sylvia Beach to see it. I would have gone with her but was struggling with a too recently requested review of Gertrude Stein for *The Nation*.

I could not say how fine I thought Sylvia Beach, or how much good it did me to meet her. I was not sorry to have her say that she thinks your *Manchester* has "a future." Indeed I *know* it has. I was much impressed with her cautious honesty of opinion and gracile youthfulness; and of course with her generosity. It was all I could do to wriggle out of being her guest at supper and could hardly entice her to the theatre although she had been trying to get to see the play.

I had a very kind letter from Mr. Herring this week and immediately wrote to him, and succeeded in a day or two to get ready something which I submitted. All summer I have thought I would ask him if he would care to publish simultaneously with *Poetry* a poem that for nearly a year I had promised Mr. Zabel I would finish and when I showed it to him as a kind of pledge of my good faith in producing it, he spoke of publishing it after Christmas. So I was much surprised when he wrote me he would like to use it in the November issue if I thought it could stand, without alterations. I wished so much to submit something special to *Life & Letters* that I offered Mr. Herring several pages of prose; and sent also the poem, in case so long a

20. Alf[red] Mossman Landon (1887–1987), American politician who ran, as a Republican, in the presidential election of 1936 against Franklin D. Roosevelt.

thing could be used, and thinking that perhaps *Poetry* has few subscribers in England. I had mentioned in it—somewhat for your eye—Original Old Turkey Mill, the watermark in the Coutts Bank blue stationery, and the anvil in English handmade paper; but perhaps for all my faults in connection with the piece I deserve retribution.

We send you our love and hope that in all your exertion and giving of pleasures there may be something for you to receive that you really want.

M.M.

To Ezra Pound *November 24, 1936*

Dear Ezra,

The freshest advices from America concern some Max Ernst paintings at the Julien Levy Gallery but I did not see Max Ernst. I arrived early and could not stay to meet him. Some Hans Mardersteig Officina Bodoni books at the Institute of Graphic Arts; and the book fair with such speakers as Frederic Goudy[21] and Dr. Rosenbach.

I am to see Mr. [T. C.] Wilson when through with some reviewing and able to discuss a poem with him and look at the paintings of a Mr. Powell who lives with him. Otto Bird whom he brought to call a while ago, was too agile to judge of. I think well of Mr. Laughlin and he has my support though he may not think so (as reviewed by me in *The Nation* Christmas book number together with *New Writing II* and *The New Caravan*).

I read your *Jefferson and/or Mussolini*, a page a day as a kind of "daily light."

Mr. Zabel takes pains with writing and with writers, shows courage in the matter of my work, and has published every unknown person I have urged on him. Besides—I believe in chivalry to the living as well as to the dead; especially when one is on trial so to speak and wolves rush to invade an undefended citadel. Nothing would induce me to molest him. I am anxious to see your comment on Miss Monroe.

H.D. has a native literariness which is strange and delightful and I groan to see it misrepresented at times by a wrongly reclusive abandon.

Mary Barnard was in the East last spring and I saw her at an Alcestis Press party, again when I called on her, and again when she came to see me during a spare hour at my dentist's. I think she has talent and surely was shepherded by various interested persons toward the metropolitan experiences that young people like. The desire to be correct and the sense of deprivation—even more than phases of it—make real helpfulness diffi-

21. Hans Mardersteig (a.k.a. Giovanni Mardersteig, 1892–1977) established the Bodoni handpress in 1922; Frederic Goudy (1865–1947), designer, printer, and proprietor of the Village Press.

cult, but she is pleasing personally,—trim, pale, and spare. Though she says she will never be able to write prose, she needs to make the effort. She has not had a chance to read many modern authors and ought to "read the papers" and be not wholly in the dark about politics and interests of others.

William Carlos Williams has always been valuable but if you have not seen him in recent years, he should be seen. You would be astonished at his growth. The way in which he augments is a marvel. His "Crimson Cyclamen" and some of his prose—(not the Gen. Washington play in *The* [*New*] *Caravan*) show a compacted weight that is very rare, I think.

Ruth Lechlitner[22] is our hope—or to be exact—*my* hope at present; very talented in verse and as a critic; with the faculty of making you satisfied as you read, that her analysis is reliable, for when bothered by an uncertainty, she admits that she is. (Businesslike, young, unspoiled, friendly and prepossessing.) She does not feel that she has done anything special and is pleased to hear what others have to say.

I have been learning Italian from your short-wave authorities; also manners, e.g. from the uncouth-er *Julietta e Romeo.*

Sincerely yours,   Marianne Moore

My Faber book was published by Macmillan and prospers mildly.

To William Carlos Williams   *December 7, 1936*

Dear William,

Your air of joy and hope is more than equalled by those elder and younger, on this side the river. Blessings on you for keeping your hawk eye on my helpless mother. I was partially but not wholly thwarted in watching Florence; she lurked in the dimness too skillfully.

The untainted finality of your reading, and things that you said, exhilarated me so that I lost all sense of mulish resistance to my position of candy-box that plays when you pick it up, and Mother and I came home in high spirits. Miss Bishop said she felt she must now "read all" you "have written," and has been giving much thought to your anti-sonnet theory of form; as I have also; we being, however, animals with a little different markings from yours.

Florence was, and always has been to me, an ideal—an incentive— and we want you both to have in mind the original visit of the four—I wish your mother were able to take such trips—here to Cumberland Street sometime. That visit last spring was too good not to have a sequel.

I cannot so much as touch on *Adam & Eve & the City;* it sets me off toward so much that needs italics. In some ways it is your hardest and finest

22. American poet (1901–?).

product and as I said to Ezra P. last month on hearing from him for the first time in a year or so, what a wonderful thing it is to augment as you (W. C. Williams) do, rather than parch. Gray hairs are execrable, were it not that without them the brain might be failing to mature sufficiently.

Would you lend me your poem, "The Sun"? I have a tentative home for it, unless it's already promised. I enclose an envelope to save you time.

Yours both, gratefully,

To William Carlos Williams   *December 15, 1936*

Dear William,

The poems have a life, a style, that should not surprise me, but does; like dew-drops on the coat of a raccoon that was a fortunate animal to begin with. Nothing you have written has anything better in it as sound than the placing of the words in "A Coronal"—

> *and cresses*
> *stood green in the slender source*

and "Weasel Snout" from whisker to tail-tip is too good to be true. Any complaints you have against life should be like the dog's proverbial one flea for health.

I don't want to be the kind of person who betrays people's indulgence but *would* you let me offer "Advent of Today" to *The Brooklyn Eagle*? I have not met William Gilmore but have had some dealings with him and he is bed-rock.

Already yours gratefully,

To Elizabeth Bishop   *December 17, 1936*

Dear Elizabeth,

It wouldn't be possible for anyone's interest in a certain kind of writing to be more lasting than mine, and I hope you will not be "judicious" about holding back work if suggestions might be of use; for although a person is likely incompetent to aid the essential value of a thing, drudging meticulousness is often, I think, a help in overcoming hesitations on the part of the cursory reader. On the other hand, zeal for improving things tends to run away with me and I do not wish, even inconsequentially, to menace your freedom.

I should say, in candor, that most of the pencilled interpolations on these two pages of suggestions were "contributed," and that Mother is a rabid advocate of the power of suggestion versus statement, and wishes you need not say just at the end that he was drunk. She thinks the study a marvellous satire on life; let alone writing.

I hope you will be surer of keeping well in Florida. You minimize everything and keep everything so dark. Please know that it is not being kind to me to be as over-brave as I have had occasion to know you were, at times.

The party yesterday will be a lasting satisfaction to me unless it was over-wearying for you; it was plain to me that it was not the food but the conversation with you,—and with Mr. Wilson,—of which the luncheon consisted for Bryher.

Affectionately yours,   Marianne M.

To Hildegarde Watson   *December 19, 1936*

Dear Hildegarde,

How can it be that of some who love one another it is yet true that giving comes only from one and always the same one? And such giving! What can dispel the fright of being faced, always by one's desire to do for you, and seeing you instead, making the lap not full;—*over* full? Dear Hildegarde, why does love not devise for us ways of fending for you? There could, if I just knew it, be a means of making this mountain of money be a servant to some of the subordinate needs of your work. As things are, no one would ever know that Mother and I feel that your need is our need. Should it serve only the direct interests you have devoted it to, I pray Heaven will save it from mere ordinary sordid use.

I look with admiration on the beauty of your Christmas party. May you be made happy by seeing goodness and joy be the outcome, and yourself have that chance of disappearing that you hint at. We have been kindly urged to Norfolk but are staying here.

I went last night, out of respect as I thought to the hospitality *The Hound & Horn* used to offer me, to hear a lecture by Lincoln Kirstein on *The Dance;* but instead of being able to feel courteous I came home under a deeper debt than ever. I have never seen such pictures, so learned and so beautiful of dancing steps and hand-shaking movements, and savage formalities concerning the "round of the seasons." I wish you might have seen it. We did have you with us one evening however when after I had tried mechanically to lighten our spirits by a little quaint reading in Queen Victoria's diary of her stay in the Highlands, Mother asked me to read in the [Mary Baker Eddy] *Science and Health* you gave us; as you thought, she finds yet more in it than in the [Eddy] *Miscellaneous Writings*. I read the part on the atonement and the one on Prayer, and again felt the goodness of your giving.

The word of your radio practice excites us. It does seem to me—I have felt all along—that since there is a real thirst for a finer kind of radio singing than we have, that you are needed in such work if you would be willing to do it. Concerts have a glamor that needn't of course be shunned by you whatever you were doing most of; but a concert public requires a certain fostering that it irks me to think of in connection with *you;* and a compulsory agreeableness that could amount to servitude. And the radio seems free by comparison, despite the rigid timing and punctuality. Already I all but feel your voice. The light of the Star of Bethlehem from your letter will shed its rays long after this Christmas time: "God without the image and likeness of Himself would be a nonentity, or Mind unexpressed. He would be without a witness or proof of his own nature."[23] That is a radiance.

We send you love. Can those words say anything of the feeling that travels to you from us both?

M.

To Ezra Pound   *December 26, 1936*

Dear Ezra,

In the Williams poem at head of column, in a December 20th *Brooklyn Eagle* sent you, please insert a two-word line:—"the leaves"—

> *the rain against*
> *the storm's slow majesty—*
> *the leaves*

; "the leaves" having through oversight been omitted by me in typing the poem!

And on page 5 of *The Pangolin*—to be sent you from London—please delete "muses" and substitute for me, in left hand margin, "musing."

I am always optimistic, but I consider that Mr. Zabel will do well as *Poetry's* Achates[24]—if not mistreated. Do not sour the man. I have borrowed the Manifesto—or is it The Manifesto?—and if I had received it, embittered by the psychic myopia of someone's asking me to say what I could not believe about myself, I would have written a most nasty letter, not for publication. As policy and as a reader of you myself, I probably would have printed the manuscript as correspondence; as accepted doctrine and *mea culpa,* No.

23. HW had quoted these words without attribution in her letter of December 14, 1936.
24. In Virgil's *Aeneid,* Achates was a faithful friend and lieutenant to Aeneas.
25. This was one of the labors of Hercules.

You cannot cleanse the Augean stables[25] from a select retreat; the only answer to need for violent housecleaning is a magazine written by and edited by oneself, on the spot. In producing a magazine with even a shadow of miscellaneous popular support, there has to be adjustment; we might as well face it.

With regard to T. S. Eliot, I value his verse, also his prose. But since he has not noticed my asking him to come to see us when he would be in America, and I have not heard from him individually in several official dealings in which it would not have been unfitting for him to write,—although I am not touchy and am in favor of people's doing what is expedient, without explanation—I don't see how I can very well propagandize him.

I dislike Anthony Eden and Stanley Baldwin[26] as much as if I knew them personally, and am for King Edward as for a brother.

Yours sincerely, Marianne Moore

To John Warner Moore *Monday Jan[uary] 4 [1937]*

Dear fellow,

We are much impressed by your Salutatory to Peep [Mary]. You have covered everything, I think, in saying the great dreams of youth for worldly success are realized through unselfishness and service. I would add specifically that EASE and a DEMANDINGNESS that does not put you in the exact place of the person who furnishes the required thing, and "SELECTNESS" (i.e. disdain) for the repellent UNadvantaged human being, are the great foes of tenderly reared children. You've got to think, when you want your dress-ruffles pleated and your nightgown ironed, how tired it makes the servant. Irritating people, "fat" people, (as Johnny so delicately reasoned out), smelly people, deaf people, "fresh" people suffering from inferiority, are not to be sneered at as denizens of another world—as just ephemera to avoid—(are to be respected for *your* sake, not theirs).

On the other side, Bernard Shaw's remark in an *Unsocial Socialist* is good psychology. People all tend to think themselves "an exception." Great comfort is to be got (in hurts to vanity & in being bossed) from realizing that almost every mortal has the same sense of thwarting, of desolation, of not being appreciated. As Dr. Cabot said, "when you have lost someone dear to you & are walking alone by the sea or on a street, you are embittered perhaps thinking, Nature doesn't care. Why should it? God is the centre of another world." And here your remark about relating things to God comes in.

26. Anthony Eden (1897–1977) and Stanley Baldwin (1867–1947) were British Conservative ministers. Baldwin was prime minister during the crisis over Edward VII's abdication.

FINALLY, there is a spur to renewed effort & an aid to fortitude, in the sense of your gifts; & in Louis Bisch's (*Reader's Digest*)[27] findings & convictions: that you cannot have a neurotic moron—that it is the person with an imagination which makes hurts & menaces sink in, who has the talent to soar to dizzy heights. You could not be so sensitive if you weren't correspondingly able.

Yes, and as Dr. Link (*Reader's Digest*)[28] says, a fine personality is not just the result of clear vision & a sudden resolve; it is the result of HABITS decided upon and deepened by purpose.

David Seabury said one of his best things last month, when he said, getting over nervousness, depression, or any bad fault, is ONLY possible through *Sincerity of Purpose.*

What you say of punctuality is fine. We all assent to our not being perfect but hate to have the actual fault specified.

I like Miss Bishop better than any of our friends—of the friends we have adopted, & are not beating off. But my whole feeling of enthusiasm is tempered by her tendency to be late—10 minutes, 20, 5. And my whole respect for Mary Watson [Craig] Heindel is diminished by her wearing insignificant shoes or unshined shoes; and for myself, by the fact that I consent to economize by using grubby handkerchiefs & tattered Kleenex handkerchiefs. I would rather die than use one when certain people are present, but I had better not use one at all. I hate waste so much that I do these things but it is not good.

(Our children however need to methodize their *fastidiousness.* They are too autocratic, I think, in not tolerating the second-rate.)

You may not want these comments; but lest you intended to see what we think too of life, as you envisaged it in the commentary, I speak out. Surely it will be a talisman that Mary will prize as her veritable blood— that substance & the way you have presented it.

I can hardly sustain the thought of that children's Christmas present rattle but it was your privilege to do things that others say are "impossible."

Regarding Mary, I suppose, other things will keep occurring to me. But this is, I think, important. In college, the lack of intimate consultation with parents & certain teachers, and the lack of *Praise*, is a terrible contrast to the years just before. At Wellesley they are more personal & informal, I think, than at B.M. But the witheringly impersonal roll call or reproof was a world wonder to me—together with an academic "*hauteur*" which I shall never forget. We weren't precisely ridiculed, but the reprehensions were

27. Louis Edward Bisch first published "Wanted: More Neurotics" in the *American Mercury* in December 1936.

28. Henry Charles Link published "Personality Can Be Acquired" in the December 1936 *Reader's Digest*.

merciless. When I see Dr. Frank's ordinary, not too impeccably worded reviews of books sometimes, I can't connect them with the astute whimsicality of his ironies in the class-room.

I think if one is warned of the profound sense of isolation & of the good effort that misses fire half the time in college work, one's equipoise would be protected.

I also think Mary should be cautioned against friends—against lending, borrowing, telling her income, or too much about the Turnbull school & the boat and driving the car, & your prowess. Others are adders of inquisitiveness & calculate or infer usefulness through innocent remarks dropped; & it is a sad experience to "accept" so to speak, a genteel B.T., or leech-like admirer & then later have to detach the menace. Such advice is no doubt beside the point. She is naturally delicate, modest, & exacting so I 'don't fear' that she will be exploited; but her generosity & sense of humor might easily lead her to give or lend a dress or tell a droll incident (as she gave the sewing machine to Roger Ascham).

And IF there is any thought of working in sociabilities at Harvard or Boston, I would privately do some strong undermining of it. 4 years are short; the lack of dignity (despite superficial prestige) of maintaining fellows & beaus at college is pitiable, and the lack of saturation and "quality" to the studying caused by negotiating get-togethers exactly defeats the purpose of going to college. I remember two girls at BM who always passed well without preparation, who were always "on the train" with patent leather hat boxes, & orchids on the coat, and their place in college was picturesque (at best), but without realness. (It is early to be doing Society even after graduating.)

We got the writing paper after this morning (that is, I did,) at Loeser's, $22.50. And the clerk who suffered me, earned her pay. I could have *got* some at $15 but it was not *right*; and after severe thought & positively disemboweling the store for varieties & shapes & weights of paper, I found only this paper & shape of envelopes that I dared risk. I tried to get plain second sheets to accompany the stamped sheets but no regular paper-company sells by quantity the woman said—only envelope-&-sheet. I hate using any but a plain sheet, after the first lettered piece. It is wasteful & bad form; but I relinquished that intention of plain sheets.

Each dye was $1.59 SEM (about like that).[29] I do hope this will be right, and we'll know that your one thought is to have us done justice to. (I guess you nigh mad did go with the books, bats, baby dolls etc. from Florida, Philadelphia, Woodbury, Crestwood & parts unknown.)

I quit.

29. MM ordered initialed stationery for her three nieces: Sarah Eustis Moore, Mary Markwick Moore, and Marianne Craig Moore.

We are full of business. I'm trying a short article for a paper called *Globe* & another review perhaps for *The Nation*.

I got 100 sheets for each MMM, MCM, SEM (navy blue).

To Elizabeth Bishop   *January 24, 1937*

Dear Master of Minnow,

You would compare bushmasters and elephants with your gifted pet! Any misprints that could be charged to her are well compensated for. The incident of the clams should be in "Minnow's Book." Her tuft-like ears and large translucent eyes like topazes or olivines, and the butterfly-silk on the insides of her forepaws, make me think so much of a great horned owl, that I got into the way of referring to her as that, so that afterwhile if she heard anything about "a great horned owl" she would move her tail-tip or close her eyes, showing that she knew she was being talked about.[30] The evening of the impromptu second supper, however, as we came in from Burton Holmes' lecture on England and Scotland, she excited compassion, she looked so helpless and diminutive. She loyally came running out to meet us, her bell tinkling faintly, her paws interfering with each other, her head nodding and eyes mere insignificant slits. I picked her up and began to sympathize with her for having had to stay alone and sleep all evening. But the litter of clam-shells in the kitchen quieted my great solicitude. The first time she was given a clam, she growled and wouldn't let anyone come near her, then trotted about the house with it as if it were a rat. That is one of her most endearing savageries, I think,— her habit of carrying things with her and keeping guard over them.

"In the bitter cold" does not yet seem to me to have the protected and confirmed simplicity that you excel in, but it does seem better. Your patience with my incompletenesses, I do feel; I regretted having omitted to enclose the copy you had let me have, of "A Miracle [for Breakfast]." I am returning it now.

The grooved cockles and faint differentiations of color on them in contrast with the smooth heart and foot-marked sand, are themselves a poem. The bayonet points of the palms above the confident little rooster, have greatly the sense of the place, and the boat scene defies comment. You certainly must let it be returned to you some time. Is it anonymous? The postures, the surgically sharp skiffs with the corals in them, the joined braids, the distant party, and the actuality of the distant roofs, have a great skill beneath them. The *real* shells, in the large shell, tied with the pink ribbon exactly the color of the pinkest rainbow-shell, have been a pleasure to see, and

30. MM was caring for a cat owned by Louise Crane and EB.

in thought, ever since Louise Crane gave them to us. The plaster white one with little claws turning back from the edge, I have never seen even in a shell book, and the semi-transparent dullness and spiral precision of the lady's ear, seem stranger the longer one studies them.

The cocoa-nut is, I think, about to be opened. Like Friar Tuck's leather bottle, when shaken it gurgles in a way that makes me impatient to get to the milk; I removed the last fragment of husk today, but a neighbor said on no account to open the inner nut until it had ripened.

I am sending you [Jean Cocteau's] *The Infernal Machine* which you may return eventually *unless* it is something you had it in mind to buy. In that case, I do beg you not to return it. *The Criterion* is not to be returned. The Frank O'Connor story gives me a great deal to think about—perhaps *too* much. Please ignore the review of Karl Barth which seems to me exactly like the fibres that surrounded the cocoa-nut.

I fear you have not heard from your story, and am tempted to quote an anatomy of inertia just received from Ezra Pound but must not be tempted.

The enclosed review of *The Infernal Machine*[31] I made an extra copy of in case you might like to have it, but I don't see what use it could be to you, and if you have a feeling against destroying things, then it could be returned to me, but I don't need it.

The weather is not formidable but we are glad you are giving yourself protection in the way of climate, and do hope you have not had anything to fight. (We are well, and have to keep our minds off Minnow, to avoid melancholia.)

Yours affectionately,   Marianne M.

My surrealist article was returned by *Globe,* and I think of revising it and offering it to *The Southern Review.*

I have great confidence in Miss Mack and must tell you sometime about Rusty, her prize Manchester terrier. She is at 8 Perry Street, but I enquired before starting, the day I got Minnow. (As for *carrying* Minnow, I would transport her little self and baggage miles, on the smallest pretext. Her pink nose was at the airhole of the valise most of the way.) I do wish you could have seen his inventory of the house.

I sent a "coupon" to the American Museum, to have sent you an article, "The Bridge That Walks."

To John Warner Moore   *Friday, Jan[uary] 30 [1937]*

Dear Habby,

I had just got the date and half of Dear Habby written when the bell

31. MM had reviewed *The Infernal Machine* for *The Nation.*

rang and Marsden Hartley appeared—, dear dear! I thought my bear might depart the sanctuary—I mean die. It was so serious & protracted a considering of the literary situation and the painting situation and the health situation. And it is very hard for me not to hate anyone who looks at Bear & sees how delicate she is, & yet muskoxes the horns out and remains as if continuous with the frame of the furniture. But we both think *once* was not wrong; in fact Christian, and if I can push Marsden towards any manager or publisher or patron, I won't refuse. He has lost his sense of humor somewhat, through seeing others succeed, be praised, and raise up much seed to themselves. And since *we* prosper, it would be loathsome to turn away from him with a rhinoceros kick up of dust. Bear did *not* invite him to come again—a thing which surprised & reassured me greatly; & Mr. Stieglitz, who keeps the breath of life in him by showing his paintings at 509 Madison Ave, was exceedingly kind over the phone, saying, "Now when Marsden Hartley comes to see you, tell him what he should do but let *him* do it. Don't do any work yourself. He can write to publishers and editors and anyone who might help him. But he does need the advice."

The pomologist last night was a very fine young man from Geneva, N.Y. He showed a picture of that scoundrel, the "Kieffer pear" & said they were trying to produce Bartletts that would bear each in a different month of the year so we would have them all the year round, and he showed various peaches, saying, "if every Elberta pear tree were rooted up & destroyed the peach industry would be way ahead." I liked the fellow extremely. I attended in order to get a point or two for my story, and I was much tempted to stop off in the music hall where they had a parlor magician but continued up to the lecture room. There, there was a choice body of some 16 persons straggled out towards the back of the room, but the lecture was all I had hoped.

I must tell you about Tyrranus Tiny. One day last week I was *very* busy in the midst of my Cocteau article & Bear kept reading and reading, at worship, till finally it got to be half past, and very near a quarter to ten. I said "Come on, Bear; come on," very timidly. Bear laid the Bible down & came at me hostile-ly, belaboring & accusing me, and saying we needn't read at all, etc. I thought no more of it till the following day, when Bear started, & I said, "You *read* that." Bear then went for me right. She said "*You'd* stop a person in the middle of a sentence. I was *beginning* to read it when you STOPPED me." !! etc. It fulminated & glared at me and kept showing the whites of its eyes & its bead teeth, till I had to flea myself for variety.

Well, the weather is splendid, clear, sunny, & fresh. And we are going out.

Tonight at 9. PM I am going to *Dr. Faustus* with Louise Crane. It lasts only an hour.

Yr loving Brother

To Louise Crane   *February 21, 1937*

Dear Miss Crane,

It is well I did not know when I received the mysterious box, that a nautilus was inside, or my hand might have shaken so as to injure it. A nautilus has always seemed to me something supernatural. The more I look at it the less I can credit it,—this large yet weightless thing, with a glaze like ivory on the entrance and even on the sides. How curious the sudden change of direction in the corrugations, and the transparent oyster white dullness of the "paper." The wings are so symmetrical I should not know any part had been broken if you had not said so.

The clipping you enclose makes me need a house by no means transparent.[32] But I protect myself by a ruse. There is another Marianne Moore, I have heard,—the daughter of a professor in the west; and there are two other Marianne Moores in Brooklyn. Nevertheless I am dismayed.

Since you took time to go to see the retables,[33] I am gratified that you found them as interesting as I did. I liked the one with the kite especially; also the cluster of brown devils.

You are very good to say it would not be an interruption to you and your mother to have me come in some day. And it is good news that Elizabeth is coming back by March; the cold weather will surely be over by that time.

Mother takes as much pleasure in the nautilus as I do, and was so impressed with the beauty of the wrappings, my opening of the box and the envelope, was considerably delayed.

Affectionately yours,   Marianne M.

The marplot Toby [a cat], did the treasure no harm.

To Elizabeth Bishop   *March 1, 1937*

Dear Elizabeth,

Presentiments are not very mysterious when one has been thinking about a definite cause for apprehension, and your mention of rain made us

32. Besides the paper nautilus, Crane had sent a clipping from *Town and Country* which listed celebrities and socialites who "can hold their own with either intellectuals or Bohemians." MM was listed under "intellectual": "Here is a classification that includes blue-stockings, women belonging to a vaguely Bohemian group, women either active in or allied with the arts, and women with INTERESTS. You'll have to work out which one is which—we'll stick our necks out just so far and no farther. In any event, these are the girls to ask in to dinner at your own house."

33. MM had recommended an exhibition at the Georgette Passedoit Gallery, of Mexican retables (votive paintings) by Harry Watrous.

anxious. We can hardly bear it that you have been in bed, forced to stay there and wait until you got better,—with no one to help you but strangers. They would strongly wish to do anything outside persons could; one's confidence in that is certain, and a consolation; but with special friends or without, illness seems so unjust, so apart from one; and you dismiss it so triumphantly, it is grieving to realize that you have, after all, not banished it. Ignorance keeps me from suggesting, asking, and wondering. You know to do and of course do, everything you ought to be doing, and as Bacon said, "The physician commands so over the patient that the medicine cannot command over the disease." Yet one can't but repudiate and turn with aversion from science that does not know anything specific and infallible to do for whatever it is that has worked against you. The weather here just now, is cool, dry, and sunny, and it is hard not to hope you will soon be coming back.

Having things returned is very "hatey," to use my nephew's word. My surrealist article was returned by *Globe,* was revised and has just been returned by *Transition*, and nothing daunted I am sending it to *The Southern Review.* I have been writing (briefly) for *The [Brooklyn] Eagle,* on a book called *How Writers Write.* The two rejection slips you received from *The Criterion* seem to me a point for a book to be entitled *How Editors Edit;* but T. S. Eliot's kind and generous remarks in introducing Djuna Barnes' *Nightwood* which I have just been looking at, make me feel patient with him and, in a broad way, much indebted.

I tremble to advise you about the Laughlin series. I feel in Mr. Laughlin real respect for the "author," and his spontaneous catching of the spirit of your own *New Democracy* contribution impressed me greatly, so I am inclined to say Yes. But please be uninfluenced if possible. I do not know how wise this is, either: but I should like to see your poems, "The Baptism," your Hopkins article, and one about abstract art and Gertrude Stein, which Miss Miller spoke of to me Friday in a way which showed me how good it is, come out all together. The things seem to support and as it were necessitate one another in a way that is intrinsically of the greatest interest, and of interest for writing in general. I cannot see that special or somewhat restricted publishing would prevent more formal publishing later. On the other hand, one might be hampered by a persisting sense of personal obligation in connection with special publishing.

In the same mail with your letter this morning, the snake-fangs, the rattle, the alligator-teeth, and the shells, came,—each of them safe; and I have just now (in opening *The Criterion*) come on the beautiful fan shell with the heliotrope and blue tints at the apex. The ribbed replica of it in the soft white paper you had folded round it, is almost as beautiful as the shell itself.

I have always wanted to see the hypodermic opening in a snake-fang, but could not have anticipated what a treatise on specialization the entire implement is,—with that swirling taper and high polish. To think of your sending two fangs and two alligator-teeth. The rattle in nine or ten ways is a mechanism of inexhaustible interest. I foolishly used to imagine that it was a series of pockets with little "nasturtium-seeds" in them, and am amazed to see this nesting of a chained membrane in another membrane. Also the varied tones of the brown when the rattle is held up to the light, suggest a great many things. I felt a slight shudder of superstition as I first held it up, as if I were touching the bones of Osiris.

The pelicans you describe, make me think of one of the most beautiful things I ever saw in the movies,—a view of an alligator-farm in Alabama, of alligators (some, of the large thousand dollar size referred to in the folder) ascending an artificial bluff, to a shute-the-shute, and sliding down at great speed, only to toil up the rock and do it again.

But do not let my intense gratitude for what you tell and find, go on subtracting time from your writing which it is imperative you be doing ("you be doing" sounds like an unsuccessful colloquial touch in an Irish tale). I could keep you from it indefinitely, saying what I feel about the raccoon, and the fish, and that dear good little dog. Your raccoon-toes (not only front feet but a hind foot!) are a miracle of delineation. And the "found" sirens of the Hardware Shop are supreme. I regard them as part of your equipment, and you must have them by you shortly.

I had passed over the [Reinhold] Niebuhr review and find it of the greatest interest.

When you come home, I shall give you any of these things that I have been writing or reading that you may wish to see. The Cocteau translation deserves the sourest comment; I kept changing it in the book as I went along, and am disgraced that I evaded mention of it. The unintentional rhymes I had noted for mention, originally; and thought of using as illustrations of over-wonderfulness, "I was woken up by my head hitting on my chest," and "the horses who screamed as they rolled over."

The letter Mr. [James] Sweeney (art editor of *Transition*) [sent] in returning my "Concerning the Marvelous" was very hearty and nice. Perhaps you would be willing to let me offer him a poem of yours? if you have one, or will have one, not promised more auspiciously? Do when you can, let me see the story; and the Auden review,[34] if you would. Also, if there is something we could do in connection with your coming home, please tell us.

Affectionately yours,   Marianne M.

I am sending you the March *Poetry*,—disappointed to see you are not in it. I am much interested in the article from *Town & Country*, especially the opening paragraph.

---

34. EB began "The Mechanics of Pretense" but never completed it.

To Elizabeth Bishop   *March 7, 1937*

Dear Elizabeth,

I enclose the suggestions I spoke of, about "The Labors of Hannibal."[35] Your things have the insidiousness of creativeness, in that the after impression is stronger than the impression while reading, but you are menaced by the goodness of your mechanics. One should, of course, have the feeling,—this is ingeniously contrived;—but a thing should make one feel after reading it, that one's life has been altered or added to. When I set out to find fault with you, there are so many excellences in your mechanics that I seem to be commending you instead, and I wish to say, above all, that I am sure good treatment is a handicap unless along with it, significant values come out with an essential baldness. I hope the *un*essential baldness of this attack will not make it seem that I am against minutiae. Do let me have the Auden review, and a poem if you think best, to offer *Transition* with "The Sea and Its Shore."

M. M.

[The postscript refers to specific corrections in "The Labors of Hannibal."]

To Hildegarde Watson   *August 15, 1937*

Dear Hildegarde,

Are you there,—hiving away songs and wisdom for the autumn? But how like a tiger-on-fire for recklessness of you, to take time when you were in the midst of so much, to write me! And to draw that flower and leaf and star with rays. "Stars *look* so divine," Mother said the other evening, "if one had never heard of worship we would feel instinctively that we must pray to them." (To mention me in connection with a star is blasphemy, even for Sibley to.) That remark of his about Bach and Bach's building houses with separate rooms, and Handel's extensiveness, is very potent and causes me to pound my insensate head with my own hand for having so dully proposed his writing about photography; for it does seem like making a historical painting of putting on one's hat, that matter of the *means* being almost irrelevant compared with his talent for causes and significances. I do think, however, foolish as the novel seems when we pick up some insufficiently curtailed opus, that he should *some* time write a novel.

Your mention of Mr. Burke almost capsized me, it is so generous to think of anyone as a force. I see a carefulness and closeness of effort and continued progress in Mr. Burke too, however, and cannot ever forget his talented adaptability and almost uncanny loyalty to *The Dial* when he was

35. The story was never published and has not been found among EB's or MM's papers.

helping with it, nearly producing whole issues by himself at times,—and with a taking, insouciant jauntiness at bad moments. And his impassioned respect for Sibley has perhaps been his salvation; so it seems a kind of justice that S. does not abandon him.

With regards to rest, I realize that you can't rest unless you do "rest more deeply into music" and for that reason I exult in your word of the Bach *Erbarm' dich* with the violin obbligato;[36] and am wondering what those "other nice things" may be.

I used to lie in the grass under a spruce-tree at Monhegan looking at "the Camden Hills," little knowing how much nearer those harmonious shapes would seem to me later when I was further away from them! Don't get too powerful against yourself there in Maine—but more pardoning. Your ability to make yourself do what seems best and do without things if you think you're better without them, and mature decisions, and keep promises and combine rigors, is frightening; and yet you know your way amid the bracken so I shan't try to be there too, too much.

We are actively idle with the pen and the needle & reading, one or two things, that you like or would like, I feel.

Love to you from us;—to all if that is not offensive.

M.M.

I see that a new edition of Dr. Bates' book has been issued, and we have a booklet on breathing that says that no singers have high blood pressure—because singers breathe deeply and are by habit, expanded. I like the book Mother says "for the most puerile reasons" because of the pretty colored pictures of venous and arterial blood, but I also liked and "studied on" that remark about singers!

To Elizabeth Bishop   *[late August 1937]*

Elizabeth,

How thank you for knowing how to put things and for your brave way of suffering.[37] In such distress, even to think toward consolation is embittering one; love is all that can help; but human love being what it is, I think Heaven can not but be aware of and pity such sorrow. Your thinking to mention the good surgeon and the insurance and the fact that Mrs. Miller came immediately shows that you know what the mind is and what anxiety about each of those things rushed upon us. Since receiving your letter I have hardly known what I was doing, in a vice, resisting the fact that the good

36. Bach prelude "Erbarm' dich mein, O Herre Gott" (Psalm 51).
37. EB wrote to MM on August 9, 1937, describing the accident, in which Margaret Miller lost the lower part of her arm. Louise Crane was the driver.

and magical car that has so blessed you each should have taken from Margaret Miller so much—that *any*thing should touch her beauty—and that you should each have had the pain of these weeks. But that is wrong. One starts from today. If Louise Crane were not the person she is, your lives might each have been lost. What mercy in her quickness; how well you know to go on a step at a time toward what would be best; and what a coward one is to feel anything but the helpful greatness and force of such courage as you speak of, in Margaret MILLER. And *Mrs.* Miller! (that Mrs. Miller, still has her and that her quiveringly portentous endowment and wonderful mind are not hurt, helps one be quieter). We have thought with such joy of this trip for you each! And to have been with you and Louise Crane, in your thoughts of me, as a phantom in Ireland, does me good. Nothing could exceed the pleasure of getting that glimpse of you and Louise Crane, so recognizably yourselves, against the curving masonry; and what a world of romance the envelope of treasures, spread before us. The shamrock tied with blue ribbon, and the Swift tablet, and the lines about the potato on the picture of Myrtle Grove; the (modestly proffered) Irish poems which do, however, mention fuchsias and water, the Tara brooch and the animals;—that harmless little cub covered with puppy-spots even on the tail, and the bear and tiger,—so close to one's eye, in its terrible reflective melancholy. It may be a mistake to pore over minutiae as I do, but it makes such work as the carved capitals on the cards of the Madeleine, an active poem, the Saint Paul cocoon, and the position of Joseph in the Flight to Egypt. And what can I say to make you realize the enjoyment and even fear with which one looks on your "primitive art." It is on the bookcase with the rosy murex beside it, echoing the shell-whiteness of the antimacassars. I could write to you a long time about only that, and how the burdensome wardrobe is a constant fascination as you have used it to reflect the bed, and how your treatment of the carpet and the wall surprise one by their continuously harmonious satisfactoriness. How unselfish of you too, to enclose the orphanage policeman and mill.

If you detected disapproval in the way I addressed the copy of *Poetry,* it was disgust with the Murray Hill Hotel. I kept the envelope a week, thinking I would be near the hotel and could have your address confirmed there, and then when I telephoned was met with open terror lest I be asking to have a letter with domestic postage forwarded to a foreign country, and could elicit not a word about the address. (For anyone so apperceptive as you, to be impervious to teaching as you are, about destroying and withholding things, *could* excite disapproval, but I understand how in changed circumstances one repudiates any touch of what went before, and shall just say I wish you had let me have the letter that had been accidentally omitted from the envelope of souvenirs.

I fear you may have been ill, too, much more just now, under the weight of these grieving weeks, and when you can, do tell us how you are, and if Mrs. Miller & Louise Crane are well.

Bryher's wish to help always, and affectionate solicitude about your asthma, are characteristic, and I wish she had happened on some laboratory marvel of modern chemistry or treatment. For one who is not embarking upon Yoga or a program of hidden progresses like the carp's evolution toward the dragon, I mistrust psychoanalysis; but you are not a novice in evading what you don't need, so I hope Bryher can if necessary, just enjoy conferring with you about art, and meet Louise Crane perhaps, and consent to be helpless. She wrote me just after you sailed, urging me to persuade you to not be in London without letting Robert Herring see you, speaking so eagerly of your work, but I waited to forward [word] till I had your address. She also said *Life & Letters* is represented in the Exposition but did not say she herself expected to be in Paris.

With regard to *Poetry*, the strung tenseness and then the controlled naturalness of the lines, *We bring a message from the long black length of body:*

"Subside," it begs and begs

do me a great deal of good and the final stanza of the "Song" is one of your most valuable achievements, I think, in suggesting from its compactness, an immensity of atmosphere; and probity of process reassures one from every line of the group. Theodore Wilson, over the telephone soon after *Poetry* came out, spoke very eagerly of these poems, especially of "Song." The title, "Two Mornings and Two Evenings" is a real peak of individuality—of poetic carbon—to my mind. I hope you will send me the story you mention. *New Writing* might be a good destination for it; though the name *New Writing*, in its saneness is my chief reason for saying so, I'm afraid. A Mrs. Edward A. [Dorothy] Norman, 1160 Park Avenue, plans to issue a quarterly next autumn, to be called that, *A Quarterly;* Mr. Stieglitz has given her advice and I admire very much her intention to keep on or stop, according as she is able to find material, and as there is a proven need for such a magazine as she wants. I spoke of you and certain other persons and am taking the liberty of giving her your address, so that when she has an announcement ready, she could send it to you. Payment, she did not mention, but I think *would* pay for contributors; and she would like even now to see work if she could. (I fear to say more than just this, having urged you to various unjust frustrations, time after time.)

Pascal, as I think I said before you sailed, seems to me an eternal treasure; and I am more indebted to you than anything could say, for bringing the Auden—*Look Stranger*. It is a great while since the unreasoned effect of a book, for me, has been so incontrovertible and enticing.

It is presumptuous to want to console Margaret Miller, but to ourselves it is consolation to know that suffering endows one with beauties; a sense of that triumph keeps coming to me. And if it is wrong or if it is right, I can't help feeling that some great and miraculous thing—something definite— must come to her to overbalance all this woe.

You realize we send you love and loving demands for you each; and think too of Mrs. Crane in Salisbury [Connecticut] & her "happier" this summer, intermingled with all that you feel & do.

M.M.

P.S. I have deferred trying to write about the paper nautilus, but shall return to it. We have not minded heat and had a beautiful visit in Norfolk in June.

I have been struggling with myself about a matter,—I would so like to *give* Margaret Miller something, and fear to, for when one ventures an impulsiveness even, as one feels so that no trace of responsibility toward it remains, some arises sometime or somehow; but I *am* doing this, enclosing you five dollars, and wondering if you could and *would* for me, take the care of finding some little diversion for M. if possible, or a piece of underwear she might like to have or little French book to read. What I *feel* like doing, is asking to have sent her a copy of [William] Caxton's prologues and epilogues that I have heard of, but don't know what size it is. And what book is dear enough to compensate for having to travel with it! I could get this Caxton and keep it for her, or have it go from England, but what I want so much is that something unexpected could suddenly be entertainment for her. Perhaps Margaret has the Caxton or doesn't tend toward just that. And anything you get, I am thankful to you.

I am glad Minnow is to have her little wildcats and wish we could each see her with them.

We wrote Mme. Lucas Orseilly of the possibility of your coming and had the most warm and welcoming reply.

To Wallace Stevens   *October 20, 1937*

Dear Mr. Stevens,

As music is best described by performing it, poetry is best defined by writing it. And since so few do write it, what an experience to see someone put life and resonance into the distasteful thing, as you have done in your *Man with the Blue Guitar*. I am glad that of the many benefits I miss, I am so enviable as not to have to be without this one.

The view you take of misprints, and of Paul Elmer More's unvividness is very cheering and I must try to follow your example, but before I begin, might I ask that you insert for me the "is" omitted from your phrase

> *Always everything*
> *That is is dead*

in *Literary Opinion in America*, should you decide to get the book—which includes Paul Elmer More's "How to Read 'Lycidas'" and several other things. And "who" should be substituted for "was" (!) on another page. I note these matters on a separate sheet.

Bryher—Mrs. Kenneth Macpherson—of *Life & Letters To-Day*, has spoken or written to me several times, wishing the magazine could have some of your verse—as perhaps you know and I needn't reiterate for her. As a kind of souvenir from her, since the publishing was a present from her to me, I am sending you my little book, *The Pangolin*, which I lacked confidence to send at the time it appeared. And with it I enclose two things you may already have seen; Schulte's Paul Elmer More catalogue; and the Sibylla Merian booklet of worms and flowers,—easily given away if you or other members of the family have already been sent it.

Sincerely yours,   Marianne Moore

P.S. I'm afraid *Poetry* will gradually but surely settle to the bottom, without Mr. Zabel as editor; I had a note from him lately, saying he had resigned.

To Alfred Stieglitz   *January 28, 1938*

Dear Mr. Stieglitz,

I was sorry,—pained, I could more truly say—to hear from your letter that Miss [Georgia] O'Keeffe has been ill. I wanted to come over that very day to see her exhibition, but was not well myself. Since then, my brother's being here, a friend's being in a hospital, and yet other emergencies have kept me busy,—not as burdens but as responsibilities.—I know from what I've read in *The Times* and *Sun*, the exhibition was superlative.

In Dorothy Norman's poems, I feel a fiery loyalty, conscience, and great respect for art, and don't wonder the present number of *New Directions* is dedicated to her.[38] I hope she will find experience consoling, it is so dangerously intense for her. How kind you are, to give me the book. Apparently I take a valuable thing as easily as if I were not asserting every day with all my might that books produced by living persons should be bought, not given.

Yours gratefully,   Marianne Moore

To E. E. Cummings   *March 5, 1938*

Dear Mr. Cummings—blasphemous, inexorable, disrespectful, sinful author though you are—you received a cordial welcome at my door today. I remarked to my mother not long ago, "I wish I could write something that

---

38. Dorothy Norman's poems, *Dualities*, were privately printed in 1933.

people would regard with the anticipatory confidence with which I hear of any new book by E. E. Cummings." The "Introduction" to this one makes me blush for the moderateness of the above statement. The more I study the equivalences here of "mostpeople's" language, the formidable use of nursery lore, and the further unfortuities,—known to you as technique but never known to lookers-on,—the better, live-er, more undimmed and undiminished they seem. Those who are deaf to the sublime, have to be without it; that is their honorarium. So, *no thanks*,[39] in the sense that thanks are too trivial.

Sincerely yours,

To E. E. Cummings   *April 12, 1938*

Dear Mr. Cummings,

I marvel that one can give so much, and at your temerarious trust in our caterpillar-tractor post-office. After studying this very noble rose,—the turquoise under-leaf and touch of red reflected back even to the petals, I can surmise why botanical gardens and over-flowered shops do not abound in yellow roses. Yet they might, and still lack this one.

I try not to think of your loss in the fact of my having the painting. We say what a man has done, he can do again, but can he? An affect is got once. But another awaits him. At best or at worst, please know that in having the yellow rose, I study and enjoy it and am grateful.

Sincerely yours,   Marianne Moore

To Elizabeth Bishop   *May 1, 1938*

Dear Elizabeth,

You and Dr. Niebuhr are two abashing peaks in present experience for me. Never have I heard an abler man nor seen a more insidiously innocent and artless artifice of innuendo than in your prison meditations. The use of immediate experience and of reading is most remarkable,—the potent retiringness, the close observation and interassociating of the circumstantial with the exotic; your mention of the Turkey carpets and the air bubble of potential freedom; the leaves and the inoffensive striping of the uniforms. All this should be ever present consolation to you, I think, for any hard spots in progress; I am much hampered, in fact, in what I say, for fear of spoiling you.

39. *No Thanks* was the title of Cummings's 1935 volume.

On the other hand,—Dr. Niebuhr says Christianity is too much on the defensive, that it is more mysterious, more comprehensive, more lastingly deep and dependable than unsuccessfully simpler substitutes which objectors to it offer; and I feel that although large-scale "substance" runs the risk of inconsequence through aesthetic impotence, and am one of those who despise clamor about substance—to whom treatment really *is* substance—I can't help wishing you would sometime in some way, risk some unprotected profundity of experience; or since no one admits profundity of experience, some characteristic private defiance of the significantly detestable. Continuously fascinated as I am by the creativeness and uniqueness of these assemblings of yours—which are really poems—I feel responsibility against anything that might threaten you; yet fear to admit such anxiety, lest I influence you away from an essential necessity or particular strength. The golden eggs can't be dealt with theoretically, by presumptuous mass salvation formulae. But I do feel that tentativeness and interiorizing are your danger as well as your strength.

There are two or three sentences that could be re-worded a little, I think, without hurting the atmosphere of the part where they occur. Yet such complaints are so almost imaginary that only superstition makes me allude to them.

I am sending Louise Crane—to send you if she thinks worth while—some monkeys and parrots for your Edward Hicks Home in the Tropics.

The crabs and serpent star arrived safe and I can't bear to think you may not have got my letter saying so. Louise Crane wondered if I *had* received them.

With love,

The wrought excellence and infectious continuity of your thinkings—the abashingly as I said above—formidable demureness, disgust me with my own bald performances, and what I have said sounds preceptorial but such clumsiness perhaps is better than the conscientious timidity which kept me from writing.

I wish you'd been with us yesterday hearing Miss Nuvod's voice & rhythms. (Don't interrupt yourself to answer this deference & attack.)

To Bryher   *June 10, 1938*

Dear Bryher,

I am glad Alice Modern-Alt's husband was allowed to leave Vienna, and if I could help them in some way, here, I do hope I may. Uprooting is very sad, and persecution, worse than death. What you say of the friend who had earned so ably, provision for old age and is coming here not well or young to start new, where everything is strange, is heart-rending. We benefit—it is already perceptible—by the courage and magnificent minds of those driven here, but the destruction of our countries from within is a constant weight on one; it is difficult to be properly confident, and one's powerlessness is a desperation, but friends tell us that in the middle of the country and in New England there is not the tension, or the tendency to violence, that we feel so much here.

We are most sorry to hear of Perdita's having had measles; in having it when grown up one suffers greatly and the convalescence is almost as bad as the disease. I hope by now it has been effaced by work and exercise and all the things it interfered with. It is good of you to tell us about H.D. One worries and does not like to ask. I don't see how she has managed to keep well and hope that now she will have incentive and circumstances favorable to her writing.

We are encouraged by Douglas Hyde's election,[40] and by an occasional article or column in *The New York Times*—to be carefully distinguished from *The London Times* you tell me. And the way in which you take hold in *Life & Letters To-Day* of what needs to be done, is comforting to me beyond the power of words to express; in the matter of the Manns, Freud, and others; China, India, Spain, and the working people at home. Your own summary of the Goncourt *Journals* in its firmness and controlled fervor, says what we feel, and are so needing to have said. And I like Coomes.[41] With regard to myself I am too overwhelmed to even refer to it,—that you should not only help me directly but indirectly, with my struggle,—wondering how my story comes on. I still feel like a stranger to it, but am advancing a little, and shall, maybe, ask help of you once again later, with a page or two of the English part. Your presentment of *The Pangolin* and [H.D.'s] *The Hedgehog* make me feel as if I were watching a couple of humming-birds, I am so unable to connect myself with it. The spread of that advertisement is beautifully managed and a triumph for the printer, that the But is so perfectly aligned with the opposite page.

Regarding the Pub Survey, I am an easy prey for wits, having spoken enthusiastically of George List to a number of persons, and lent the Survey and planned to see if I couldn't prevail on you to publish other work by so able a man! So life is not all wormwood.

Since writing the above, I have received Marion R. Hart's *Who Called That Lady a Skipper?* and see an elephant in it and a native boat and some dragon tracks, and much vivid text. Noble Bryher. The interest you take in people and things makes me feel that it will *not* do to subside into the quick-

40. Douglas Hyde (1860–1949), Irish scholar and political leader who in 1938 became the president of Eire.

41. Bert Lewis Coomes (1893–1974), English novelist.

sand. I hope you can find a way to set down more work of the personal kind in Switzerland,—much as I like the reviews; and I hope Lady Ellerman is being benefitted by England, though Switzerland seems safer.

Much love, M.

Mother was happy to have the letter to her from you. Elizabeth Bishop is visiting Louise Crane for a little while, and I went with them to a movie yesterday,—*Generals Without Buttons.*

I have meant to tell you how interested I was in the catching of the pony that got into the seed field, and in what you told me of the bunching-machines in Cornwall.

M.

To Louise Crane and Elizabeth Bishop   *December 26th, 1938*

Dear Elizabeth/Louise [names are crossed together] and various Christmas angels, a little while ago a strong man, bent under the weight of it, carried into the pantry—as any room would seem in receiving it, a basket of grapefruit and oranges with kumquats lurking among them, and in comparison with ourselves Thackeray's "little boy of 2 trotting round the xmas tree crying out 'O Crissamy Tee Crissamy Tee'" was a Staffordshire image without eyes or feelings. How excited and amazed on this lowering day-after-Christmas we are, you can't imagine. Only to be thrice more incredulous on opening Alexander Selkirk's chest delivered a moment after, and finding within, the nest of minute paper-strips and within it, a family of sea-animals—or should I say the house of a family of sea-animals. I hope you have had this fairy abode in your White Street living-room, long enough to know it by heart. It is the most magic arrangement of fans and lanterns and shutters and reflectors ever made by the sea, I am sure, the light behaving through it in a thousand ways at once. And someone with proper respect for the miraculous surely chiselled it from the marble ledge on which it arose.

We have celebrated Christmas in a great many reprehensible ways, one only, that I can think of, being nearly suitable. Mother made temporary mittens over the hands of a mittenless child crying in a perambulator in front of a shoestore which had swallowed the mother. One mistake, was expecting too much of Mr. Pickwick—in the course of a fervently kind Christmas Eve celebration. How much more like the Alapitattitott ornament in our kitchen Thackeray (to return to him again) seems: "Mr. Bayard Taylor is here, '*der ein Hero ist.*'" A gallant bearded man with a handsome face. He is very like Francis I, so we think, and we like him even better. "Ah! America if your sons are all gallant gentlemen like this one, if your daughters simple ladies like his sisters I wonder, what profound remark shall I make now?"

My beloved  to quote Thackeray again,

please don't hold anything against me, if I did wrong in making it possible for *Vogue* to persecute you. A girl in the tiniest, most harmless voice I have ever heard, answered the telephone for Mr. Frank Rounds so well named, who was "out." Please keep well, and even though we are literally *hidden* under the greatness of our Christmas, don't forget us. A real gold angel, from Margaret Miller, adds to our smallness and disabling excitement. (Of china, with crimson "V" bodice and blue shirt and gold wings!)

Love to you both. M.

To John Warner Moore   *Sunday, Nov[ember] 19, [19]39*

Dearest Mongolian *gazelle,*

I daresay you have seen donkies like this, leading camels & cam*e*lopards. *I* have (in pictures).[42] Bear is ruined as it is, without adulations and pattings and honied messages,—and sets up the most piercing squeals of protest at the slightest opposition or absence of alacrity in complying with its "orders." I will say though, that under disappointment ye Bear is a tiny hero. We labored at our fiction yesterday and I filled out a questionnaire from a parasite British *Who's Who of Poets*—that demanded a poem for exhibition as well,—and then at 8:15 in the evening, we went to *Pygmalion* at the Institute. Or rather we went at 7:45 to be sure of a seat, & it's well we did, as the crowd was large. Bear dressed *very* carefully, like to go to a dinner or concert in its clean white blouse with a ruffle,—its black & white scarf you gave it money for, and its black gloves. We got some good of the play but it was preceded by a lot of newsreel of fighting-scenes past & present, and then a panorama of the motion-picture's progress that was not suited to little Bears. Bear is going to try again however, & go along to Mr. De Cou[43] on Wednesday in the *afternoon.* Matinees are the only thing for young bears.

42. Between the date and her salutation, MM pasted a cut-out picture of a donkey leading two camels.

43. Herbert De Cou, travel lecturer.

Bear likes Leslie Howard it says—but did not "understand" a good deal of the play it was so cryptically presented. (Says it didn't hear—).

Next week I hope to copy my story. I think all the patching has been done. I feel a little apprehensive about the parts we hurried over to concentrate on the plot, but we'll not evade nothing.

It is a little hard to find new material on old themes and maybe the familiar songs & poems are best; but on the church calendar this Thanksgiving excerpt from Wordsworth might be useful to you. Anyway we enclose it.

> *The towering headlands crowned with mist,*
> *Their feet among the billows, know*
> *That Ocean is a mighty harmonist*
> *Strains that support the Seasons in their round,*
> *Break forth into thanksgiving, etc.*

While waiting for the movie last night I read Bear a piece from *The Spectator* by Reinhold Niebuhr on Germany's condition as a race—in persecuting & being subject to Hitler, & though as Bear says we already know it, he reminds us that intolerance is at work in us all, *in all* countries;—that we ourselves "persecute" Jews & Negroes & submit to wrongful tyranny. Or at least feel "superior" in sundry ways.

Mr. Littlefield gave us a copy of *The Last Puritan*, & it is more practiced & more "interesting" to a seasoned reader than my little "juvenile" may be, I see; this is somewhat sobering. On the other hand, I knew in the first place that my story was not a thing to shake the world and render all other fiction needless. And [George] Santayana has—with all his skill and social lure and Harvard sophistication, a certain "BASENESS" as I regard it,—of word and ideal. Tha'ss all for now—

Dearest love,   Rat

Will I send my presidential suggestions to B.M. or wait till I hear from you and Constance? I'd suggest Dr. Simon Flexner, Reinhold Niebuhr, Margaret Bouticon Squidd (1909), Mr. Frank Morley!!!

To John Warner Moore   *Sat. Jan[uary] 20 [1940]*

Dear and treasured Snowflea: Bear and I are in an ecstasy over the reception of your yachting lecture. That a young fellow asked "what must I do to be a chaplain" is the supreme testimony to the power of the discourse,— your whole thesis being that moral attitude makes the worthy sportsman. I crave to see these presentations on paper.

My plucked slippers come this morning. Tanks. A Very beatworthy opossum I, but as you say, 'tis well to leave something, as an earnest of being back one of these days. I am very much pleased with the letter (enclosed) from Mr. Latham. Bear has the feeling he would like to have took the story. Anyhow, a doubt would kill our comfort in the matter. If the company had no hope of sales, they couldn't enjoin their salesmen to say "this is a big event." And we're safe and free. (How is my answer? psychologically.)

I'll pass the poem through my paws like you say to, and compose others and get a little air in the sails, and Macmillan's in the end are not going to use Flit perpetually towards me.[44]

Speaking of sails Constance give us several snapshots—among them one of yourself in the Snipe. She said, "John doesn't like this & wouldn't want me to give it to you. Something's wrong with the sail he says; but it shows *him* and Bee and the little snipe on the sail."

That intrigued me considerably. As for the image of me on your desk, the tail is UP, I'd have you remember.

We Bears have had our hair washed today; were tempted to have it done before "going," but were too pressed.

The snow helps the ground, but if big snows fall, you GOTTA hire a helper. The owners of the house can tell you of one.

I wisht we could be present the 28th but we'll be after all, and the more for having been in the chapel as we were. Percy is a glad thought to us always,—how much more that he can give you this re-inforcing at a time so crucial, & full of uses for power. Strange, but several times last Sunday, I thought about that previous Communion Service, and how it would have been observed & how suitable the setting and churchliness are.

I thirst to hear that the S. Base auditorium is finished. You didn't take us over Sunday night or into it when we were near, because you feared to have us see how ill protected from cold & how unequipped, you are. You planned again it from the first, crowbird, I know you. But the safer thing will come sometime.

T. S. Eliot, in his [*The*] *Idea of a Christian Society*, suffers from my trouble. He should have been persuaded to defer the book. But "there's interest in it." He says of pacifism, if we live under an authority in peace we live under it in war and to be a pacifist is a shirking of responsibilities. This seems sound. 'Bye Bulltoad. Write you further, later on.

Dearest love,   Rat

To Louise Crane   *February 14 [1940?]*

Dear Louise,

Lester Littlefield is speechless,—by which I mean the opposite,—at your kindness, and Mrs. Crane's. I have just had a letter from him saying

---

44. MM had submitted her novel to Macmillan, which turned it down. Flit is a brand of spray bug-killer.

Mrs. Crane had him read to her Monday night, and there was more pleasure in it for him than there could have been advantage to Mrs. Crane.

It had disheartened me to feel that an attack of egotism could prevent
anyone from accepting an invitation; but after receiving a second note
(from L.L.) hoping we could understand that the sacrifice had been "unavoidable" by reason of jacket and laundry, I trespassed on your prerogative
and ventured to tell him that our invitation had not been strictly social, that
Mrs. Crane needed a young man to read to her, and we had thought of him.
And when I mentioned what she paid, he said "Two dollars for an hour of
reading (which is a pleasure) would seem a great deal too much. I don't
know that I would like to take that; it's more than my day's pay now." He
wrote again saying he had not heard from you, but "perhaps this means that
too much good fortune is not to come to me." He said, besides, he was still
handicapped by the inappropriate jacket. I later offered to mend it. He says
he can't degrade me by permitting that, that he could replace it at once but
that under a doctor's advice, he is dieting and is tempted to wait till he
shrinks.! I burden you with this as explaining—if you *should* need him
again sometime,—a possible impression of indigenous destitution.

I had a letter from Elizabeth a day or two ago, which I am thinking of
having tattooed on me—in which she tells of Mrs. Almeyda's identifying
certain little dark specks in a white bowl, as "Them's lizard." And she enclosed a very valorous and concentrated poem about a fish. I thought of your
somewhat pensive statement, "Elizabeth is writing some poems; she is
working hard and will have more things;"—when we were pondering the
probability of enough to make a book; I wondered when the fish had begun
to be written and if I have missed any companion-piece to it. (What I myself sent *The New Yorker* was by no means that, and has been retired by me;
though Mr. Pearce asked in returning it if I would care to change a line. This
fraternal patience with me, I prize enough to make me not so sorry I was
precipitate. I can take more time and get the detail right I hope, in my
present consolation effort. At any rate, I've never been so kindly collaborated with.)

This is a rather devious and oblique valentine, Louise. But it *is* that, all
the same. I am stirred to the point of paralysis by your mighty yet secret ingenuities for birds with broken wings. I must find an expert to help me muzzle myself (I guess I should say, bind my beak)— (for nothing could induce
me to fly away myself,) so that you would not be in danger from me and my
uncurbed impulsiveness.

Affectionately,   Marianne

P.S. I am sorry I made things hard for Lester and consequently, difficult for
you by my sense of formality, in feeling you should be the one to mention
what you had in mind.

To Elizabeth Bishop   *March 17, 1940*

Dear Elizabeth,

I am glad the *Partisan Review* wants the article, and since the canoe trip gives a picture of Florida, you could surely send *it*. And if you ask if I "could bear" to see it again and if I "have time" to read it, I'll tell you a fib and say when I said I liked "The Fish," that I meant merely the title, not the poem itself. I don't feel that I am any real help to you and should so like to be. But in anxiety to protect the work I scrutinize every detail. Let me see the canoe trip when you have finished it, and don't change it much.

What you say of the first stanza of "What Are Years" (*The Kenyon Review* has taken "What Are Years") is a consolation to me as regards the clocks and so forth. I try to take my own advice about unfitness and a fondness for Maginot Lines of resistance. I mean failure usually has a clue in it for something better.

I take it very hard that Wallace Stevens was in Key West and didn't hunt you up. Anomalies of that kind are an unnecessary exasperation. Not to you, for you surely were crowded with goings and comings and "business" of a typewriting nature, but to me. Too crowded about your patience with certain social emergencies, I admire very much.

And I wish it were Robert Frost instead of *Furioso* that was coming to call. You have probably by this time seen the recent number (of *Furioso*) and are feeling uncomplimented by its being so sure you like toads and centipedes and caterpillars on all your chairs and vines. A thing has to be very clammy and scary indeed, to make me anything but obliged someone took the trouble to send it to me. (Very "weird" as Eda Lou Walton said yesterday of somebody.) I was at Newark at a poetry-reading contest and must tell you about it sometime.

I am delighted that Mr. Frankenberg is "with me" about Horatio Colony. The name *is* fortunate; but I keep on liking the poems despite much to efface them since a first reading. I hope Loren MacIver is painting the goats, or parts of them, and am envying you the hibiscus-flowers whether fallen or opening.

Affectionately,   Marianne

I am glad the *Partisan Review* is using "The Fish" though feeling thwarted personally because Robert Herring needs material he writes me and I thought "The Fish" would be a glorious bit of cheer if you could spare it.

To Louise Crane   *May 2, 1940*

Dear Louise,

Nothing to be answered, but something for you to think about. (This is a very cross pansy.) [See page 334.] Elizabeth said you had been sick the time I went to speak at the Young Men's Hebrew Association. Otherwise I might have seen you there! Thinking you had just been sensible, not really sick in bed, I didn't bother you to tell us. Lester Littlefield has just telephoned saying, among other things, you were in bed about a week. I don't know what I could have done but be in the way, but we can't *stand* it to know you've had a real illness, nor to feel that you may not be entirely over the effects yet, though it sounds brave and natural, that you had some acquaintances to dinner with you last evening. You don't know how consoling it is to us, Louise, that you made room for Lester, and that you have at other times. I doubt that you ever added anyone to the group you were having, who got more intensive good of the pleasure. His appreciation of things has the least alloy of extraneousness, of anyone's I think I ever knew and your effort for people, and himself, is so real to him, and his concern for others is so unperfunctory. He spoke with a kind of dismay (though unintrusively) of your not being [at] a party recently because you weren't yet over your illness.

I have been active as a fireman going to various lectures, to educate myself for a talk at Sarah Lawrence College last evening—George Dangerfield on "Books That Count," and Alfred Kreymborg on the "Radio, Movies & Television," at the Institute, & Julien Bryan on Mexico; and W. H. Auden on "The Lyric of Condensed Experience" at The New School. We had a scourge of ants that had to be eradicated, with "deadly poison" from Tuesday to Saturday (at intervals) and we thought we had to find a dress for me to wear yesterday that was not velvet because of the rain. And I flew to the Grand Central Station by mistake an hour ahead of the train-time, but all went well at Bronxville. Mr. Gregory, who had invited me to speak, and Mr. [James] Sweeney & his sister (guests of Mr. Gregory's,) and the faculty and students were friendliness itself and the grounds were more beautiful than I have ever seen the country, hyacinths and pansies in bloom, and the tennis-courts being used and a large orange cat bolting, like those Faust theatre flames we saw at the WPA play, from a secret passage way in a wall.

In my talk I mentioned Loren MacIver's *Lilac Time* & *Sand Dunes* as visual equivalents of poetry, & its language of related associations and quoted from *Madeline*—

> *In the middle of one night*
> *Miss Clavel turned on the light*
> *And said something is not right*

also more—but I hadn't the intrepidity to mention the scar; though I think that's the dynamic center of it all—apart from the sauciness in the drawings.

I have attempted some lines on the nautilus and though they are a weak expression of the most powerful incentive, I enclose them. Always speaking of the shell as Louise's nautilus, it would be morbid to suppress them.

We are troubled to know Elizabeth has been ill, and do hope that is past. It destroys my happiness in thinking of Florida, to know she *can* be ill there.

I am really trying to say, Louise, if there *might* be something I could do for you, I am strong & well and would be so exalted to be trusted with an errand or service of any kind you'd think me competent for. And you are not to trouble writing, if as my brother says, what you want is "quiet."

Our love and very sad thoughts that we are so irrelevant when danger threatens.

Marianne

To H.D.   *September 23, 1940*

Dear Hilda,

Two letters just now from Bryher,—one asking me to forward a letter to you and a picture; the other enclosing the picture and saying "I forgot the very important photograph of the house in all of yesterday's excitement. A lovely day to-day, silver lake with the trees heavy with plums and greengages along the side of it." How expressively Bryher—the quiet detail about the plums, offsetting the worry.

Our hearts are torn by the word each day of unpity for those persons and those things we love in London, and today word of the children lost in mid ocean. The fire of resolution kindled by these things, the valor and self control of everyone in England, make the wickedness seem the more intense. We wonder where, how, and what you are doing; but you must not, nor Perdita, be burdened writing; Bryher will give us word.

The paper (*Times*) reports every word Winston Churchill says, sometimes 3 or 4 times in various forms,—even remarks to homeless people, ("Don't worry; 'they'll' get it,"). One is thus fortified beyond expression. The martial spirit in *The Spectator,* our *Times, Life & L.,* are a medicine out of the suffering, and statements by persons like Rebecca West and J. B. Priestley, whom one has never idolized, show me for my betterment that animosities go, in hours of mortal stress. I refrain from saying what is told here about pilots and planes and ships and bundles for Britain since results perhaps, are the only sort of message you are allowed to receive. Our love to you, Hilda; and to Perdita, for whom we are hourly so grateful.

Marianne

James Angleton, Editor of *Furioso* (New Haven), in writing me about the magazine mentioned you as being deprivingly remote from America and in replying, I asked him to send you [the] summer number (that has in it something by Ezra P., E. E. Cummings, and others).

P.S. The enclosed word from Bryher, just as I was about to post the above. You may have her with you before this reaches you though she speaks of "months" perhaps. A note to her enclosed, which read if you have time. What excitement to be enclosing something for her to you after just reading, "I hope that perhaps I'll get away but it is dismally uncertain."

To John Warner Moore   *Sunday, Oct[ober] 6, [19]40*

Dearest Impala, *K.C.S.*,[45]

Yes it would have been a desperate thing to have led the Bear to think through 12 years, that you had seen impala deer if you had seen nothing but gazelles. Sometime I would not mind hearing again, of the antics of the antelopes about the park. Maybe those same impalas are exercising over them same bushes. I have spent a good part of my life at movies hoping to see the little creatures jump. Anybody who has seen real impalas doing a little real jumping, is pretty hard to please afterwards.

If your pad-marks had been a little closer together and *plainer,* it might have meant zebras but as it is, *nothing* but what I already told you— an animal animated by undue restlessness and ambition to get the good of something.

The Bear knows that story of the wedding-garment & it hasn't influenced it a whit. *Nevertheless* I aim to pick it out certain habiliments and put them on it like I got it that puss-in-boots very intriguing hat with the willow plume last year. I know a place where you get Knox Coats from the manufacturer & I am gonna attend to my cub *assiduously*.

Friday night on legs so short you would have mistook them for caterpillar legs, I went to Mr. Putnam's party.[46] "Mrs." was abed with bronchitis. A very anxious female in a maid's uniform let me in & via the living-room where Mr. Putnam welcomed me, I was taken to Mr. Putnam's bedroom— a somewhat routine little cubicle—and left my wraps. John Gould Fletcher whom I have never thought a very good writer (of prose or verse) was arrived, with his wife (a timid adjunct in a gray street dress). He regards himself as an oracle, is heavy & motionless like a basalt Buddha, wears a jade or

45. Knight Commander of the Sanctuary; the "Sanctuary" (sometimes "Bear's Sanctuary") is MM and MWM's apartment.
46. Probably Samuel Putnam (1892–1950), American biographer, translator, critic, and founder and editor of the *New Review*.

onyx ring the size of a small turtle, on each hand, & wears his eyes partly closed. I made it my business not to rasp him, in fact to draw his quills & I think succeeded, though it wasn't any too pleasing to him to have the company so favorable to me as they were, in fact over-praising me on various grounds,—Mrs. MacMaster insisting how I overcame her students at Sarah Lawrence & wrought upon them so they have been different ever since; Mr. Donald Adams, lit. ed. of the *Times,* leaving Mr. Fletcher & sitting for a year & a day on the divan by me, whilst I extolled Herbert Horwill of the *Times* & Peter Jack & spoke of some of Mr. Adams' recent reviews. A humorous thing in connection with Mr. Adams. Mrs. MacMaster said she never read newspaper literary sections any more, they were all identical & all accorded books length of review depending on the amount of advertising sold. Mr. Adams replied, "Oh no. You haven't really compared them & I *have.*" "Yes" said Mrs. M. "I wasn't in Scribner's advertising department 3 years for nothing. I *know.*" "But I *edit* the *Times Review*!!" said Mr. Adams with a solemn & menacing air. "Oh!" said Mrs. M. "How shall I cover my confusion. May I ask the name? Your *first* name." "*Donald,*" said Mr. Pearson beaming with satisfaction. "Call him Don if you like." Mr. Pearson is an intimate friend of Mrs. MacMaster & an amiable acquaintance of Mr. Adams, & a very intimate friend of the Putnams, as is Mr. Adams. So no great harm was done. But Donald is very stubborn. He was a classmate of Scofield's, a very austere Harvard man & I always disliked him, till last night. His review of Lewis Mumford was remarkable; also one of Thomas Wolfe recently & I have been busting to praise Herbert Horwill. Mr. Putnam told me in advance that he is very subdued because of being divorced & is not the Pharisee he used to be. At all events I got along excellent with him & he emerged from Mrs. Putnam's room as I was endeavoring to depart, to say goodbye.

Mr. Pearson is a great wag,—as offsetting his lameness & invalidness, I infer. At any rate his call him Don if you like was typical & he recited a limerick about the Van Dorens & the Morons to everyone's expected admiration. He said when he discovered my brother was a Yale man, that settled it, he was bound he was going to track me down & if he'd known I was in New London, he would have come over. He is wiry and thin, with a typical professor-writer alertness of eye & bookishness of bearing, rather short & lame of one leg. Looks like a dwarf tiger-cat & is always jesting. He is American editor of the Oxford Press it seems & rather babbles of his energies & activities there, though very pleasingly. He is not tiresome nor does he overrate himself.

The Gregorys were there—Mrs. Gregory, a very troubled self-propelled poet & would be social leader—and Horace, thin, white, crippled with infant paralysis & a bona fide litterateur. Mr. Putnam occupied himself in the vain task of converting John Gould Fletcher into an admirer of Mrs. Gregory; sat down by him & opened book after book of Mrs. G's poetry, turning the pages slowly as John Gould F. battened his shell down tighter & tighter, with the look of an underwater swimmer.

The other guest was a Mrs. Warren,[47] "a sculptor." She will be Mrs. Adams if some Pterodactyl of the literary swamp does not helpfully bear her away where she cannot set upon him. She looked like these too beautiful to be true mannequin figures in Bonwit Teller's or Revillon Frères, dressed in powderblue velvet with gold slippers & gold & blue earrings, with blue eyes, and golden hair rolled and arranged as for a court painting & she & Mr. Adams assisted Mr. Putnam with the food. Everything Mr. Adams thought, she thought & when Mr. Adams praised Elizabeth Roberts she said "I don't know that I would call her a *great* writer but she has one 'sweet pure note.'" She kindly said she wished she could entice me to *her* house sometime but we had no other conversation.

The shood[48] was (much liquor), baked ham, string beans, potato balls in bread crumbs, celery & Roquefort cheese, hot rolls, rye crisp, pecan ice cream, layer cake & coffee.

Doc Magary was very poor the Bear says. But he had a great theme,— lead me to the rock that is higher than I & he mentioned David, Job & Jonah as persons who had knowd *fear*, corking ignominious tedious duty, & humiliation. He said small humiliation or surfeits have even led people to take their own lives, that great feats & ordeals are not so disrupting as the inconspicuous ones.

Dearest love,   Rat

To Elizabeth Bishop   *October 16, 1940*

Dearest Elizabeth,

The Pope-ian sagacity, as I was just now saying to you, and your justice to "Peeter," and such a crucially enviable consummation as

> *From strained throats*
> *A senseless order floats,*

are like a din of churchbells in my ears, I am so excited.[49] (A little girl whom Mother had been teaching about the apostles, said in one of her answers to a little written examination, "And don't forget Peeter.")
"Flares begin to catch" is so precise and the rhyme with "patch," so perfect. I question as a desirable discord "v" and "s," and therefore suggest omitting "the many wives."!

47. Emily Warren, English artist and associate of the Women Artists Society.
48. In Moore parlance, this stands for food; see also January 21, 1941.
49. EB had given MM a draft of her poem "Roosters," which they had begun to discuss on the telephone.

> *The crown of red*
> *Set on your little head*

is a notable condensation of overtones and the sound is ideal. It strikes me that the "with" as in "with *'Gallus canit.'*" seems not quite explicit as prose; and as prose, to my ear, a "that" would be needed with "Even the Prince:" i.e. "that even the Prince." Then my "that" would conflict with the "that" in "That 'Deny, deny, deny.'"

Regarding the water-closet, Dylan Thomas, W. C. Williams, E. E. Cummings, and others, feel that they are avoiding a duty if they balk at anything like unprudishness, but I say to them, "I can't care about all things equally, I have a major effect to produce, and the heroisms of abstinence are as great as the heroisms of courage, and so are the rewards." I think it is to your credit, Elizabeth, that when I say you are not to say "water-closet," you go on saying it a little (like Donald in *National Velvet*),[50] and it is calculated to make me wonder if I haven't mistaken a cosmetic patch for a touch of lamp-black, but I think not. The trouble is, people are not depersonalized enough to accept the picture rather than the thought. You saw with what gusto I acclaimed "the mermaid's pap" in Christopher S[mart]. but few of us, it seems to me, are fundamentally rude enough to enrich our work in such ways without cost. If I tell Mother there is a feather on her dress and she says, "On my back?" I am likely to say, "No. On your rump," alluding to [William] Cowper's hare that "swung his rump around." But in my work, I daren't risk saying, "My mother had a feather on her rump."

I hope Dorothy Dix's[51] enclosure will not, as I said to you on the telephone, mean that I am never to hear from you or see you again.

Agitatedly, dearest Elizabeth,   Marianne

In the second line, I think if "blue" were omitted, it would come as an intensive and expander of the idea in the line about the blue window, but fear to try to leave it out. I attempted a slight variant of your "gun-metal blue window" because the unrelated thought came into my mind of those West Indian blue metal fittings, and I then saw that I had been evading the priceless concept of a blurry color filling the frame. "The blue blurr" is inimitable.

M.

---

50. The youth classic by Enid Bagnold was published in 1935. Donald Brown is a boy of four in the novel.

51. Dorothy Dix (Elizabeth Meriwether Gilmer, 1861–1951), well-known suffragist and journalist, and author of a widely syndicated advice column. The enclosure was a typescript of "The Cock," a version of Bishop's "Roosters" made by MM and MWM.

To John Warner Moore *Friday [November 22, 1940]*

Dearest Warble,

I resent that persiflage about the Cub as my substitute and I'll use her for my emergencies *just like I have* done. A Fine responsibility for her!

Very glad & thankful Johnny cares. That matter of the unintentional vacation is safe in your paws, I guess. I was of a tremble at first, for fear Mr. Underwood or someone would hear via Stephen or another person that Johnny was in New York. Better to tell them direct than have that happen. But you know what's what.

I have been jumping through the grass high and much today. Elizabeth Bishop has not been here since we got back from New London almost; & for one reason & another I have neither gone to see her nor let her come over here except once (she and Louise came then to Miss Monte's). So I journeyed over there today to the Murray Hill Hotel & am thankful I did. Louise came down to see me, we all had lunch there, & then Louise left us. Elizabeth wanted to say goodbye to Bear before going to Florida & I, fearing this was the best time or only time, said "could you come now?" "Why yes," she said and we came home together. I then walked to the subway with her & she said she had enjoyed being there *so* much. "I feel so much better," she said, sighing. (Bear says it was not seeing *her* made the difference but it was). These things are very affecting; most of all that Elizabeth watched the clock & was determined not to stay long; left very soon after getting here, in fact.

Louise was more pleasing & encouraging than I've ever seen her. So modest about the concerts she is managing, and gentle in her feeling about other people (Monroe, the [Alfred] Barrs, and others). She has a concert scheduled for next Wednesday evening—a Negro singer at Carnegie Hall in the chamber music salon, and I am hoping to go.

On the way to the subway here, Elizabeth and I passed a salOON with four pheasants in the window, among pumpkins and spruce twigs & bitter sweet berries. It was quite a sight. But no live animals for me. You are very game about Daniel; & I hope he will not desecrate your bed nor tear up your beret nor bark you up out of bed during the night. Those "small" exigencies are severe and of those you say nothing; the mistake at 2 a.m. & the barking fit at a quarter to 6, and so on.

Elizabeth is very heavy in soul, so weary & discouraged now & again that Louise took her to a psychiatrist. I told her that these impasses and unanswerable questions smite everyone; & that the quiet heroisms of faith are the big ones; that we are here for a purpose & have no right to disdain that purpose, & are never "alone," humanly speaking or in the greater sense.

MM folded the typescript, sealed it with a gold star, and wrote next to the seal: "Do not read at mealtime or on going to bed. D. D."

But the more highly organized people are, the harder they are to help. But she seemed grateful. She has just got $20 from *The New Republic* & various offers of reviewing so "all will be well."

Dearest love,   Rat

To Bryher   *December 8, 1940*

Dear Bryher,

It is a strain on me to have to permit a letter to take the place of an actual word with you. You and Hilda in your letters are so vivid,—"the sublime heroism of the masses," the extraordinary subway stairs you mention, lined with sleeping children, the unnatural danger of the blackout; and the obstacles to getting a job. When one is panting with desire to help the country win, and what is more rare—equipped at every point as you are, to do it—I know the white hot intensity of some of your wartime reflections. But there is a certain consolation, don't you think, in the sense that each of us is scourged with the very same sense of frustration,—an illusion after all, Bryher. What we *feel* is the sinews of war.

A magnificent little letter from Mrs. Hughes[52] asking about you. I told her you are with Hilda, and gave the Lowndes Square address. I hope Perdita got back safe from Cornwall. A letter from Hilda just now, suggests that you may move the office to "the environs of Cambridge." If this is possible, do be pleased about it, Bryher—even if it is not what you had in mind when you were trying to get back to England.

The books have just come, Marlowe and Roger Fry,—both so exciting. We have been wanting to see the Fry; certainly it is Mrs. Woolf at her best, a kind of testament of rightness, and nothing could tell you what I feel about the Marlowe, a veritable refuge, medicinal in the mere touch of it; any page that one turns to, casts a spell, suspending the shadow of care that follows each thought and act these days. What plates and printing and scholarship, and nutriment, on a page like that about Latin into English:

> *it is a worke of prayse to cause*
> *A Romaine borne to speake with English jawes.*

You are superhuman, Bryher, to be making it Christmas for us, this tense year. You don't know what feeling it evokes.

I rejoice to tell you we are well, having got past some "worries." Even I, who don't hide difficulties as you do, can't make myself name them to you seriatim. We both got to a color film of Guatemala about a week ago, and there saw an iguana market, innumerable pigs as spotted as jaguars; moun-

---

52. Molly Hughes, a writer and acquaintance of Bryher's whose work MM attempted to place.

tains, lakes, and handweaving at home by the door with chickens and pigs standing near.

Louise Crane has organized a series of folk concerts ("Four programs of un-concert music") that have been given at Pittsfield and Hartford, with Sofia Novoa, the gifted Spanish girl I may have mentioned, expositing Spanish songs and dancing, supplemented by Spanish bagpipes and Heronimo Villarina a guitarist. And she presented recently in New York a Negro singer, Ella Belle Davis whose sister accompanied her, in a concert of classical music and Negro spirituals.

Some pictures by Loren MacIver too, at the Pierre Matisse Gallery, I think you would like; restrained, unaggressively concealed almost, but unmistakable poems: Etruscan Vases, Case #42; Aran Island stone walls; Key West moonlight across a spool-post inconsequential lonely little bed distorted as by an earthquake or German bomb; a parallelogram of reeds in blue waters without any large object as a pretext for it, entitled *The Waters*. I go into detail because Lester Littlefield tells me certain press notices have not been very good. He lent us recently a picture of Adrienne Monnier[53] in her shop, because we had been so interested in the *Life & L.* articles.

Elizabeth Bishop was in town a month or two; but because of wrong health and its unholy submergements we saw her only hastily. She is now in Key West where she says all seemed whiteness and peace, with purple figs in the yard and a small green bird standing very still with a white moth in its beak.

Strange, isn't it, to be cheered by our not having rather than by having money come; but we have longed to give to England, and this way is very real. I can hardly breathe when I note in the paper with what judiciousness the country talks of *lending* money to England or Finland or Greece.

A few nuts have been finding their way into a box almost as by squirrel-paws, for you and Hilda and Perdita. If they are dominoes of hardness or archeological crumbs by the time they reach you, they could be ground up and used in cooking, I am told,—as flour. And we included a candy reindeer. If it comes broken, be sure to tell me. I said to Mother, "I think perhaps this is too childish to send," but she said, "*Send* him." When I was a child, we used to be given reindeer and churches and shepherds with crooks; and curious to say, I remember a little red locomotive.

Our love to you each. Please think of us as happy, indeed joyous, lost in our wonderful British books.

Marianne

(Once again, Bryher, about my *Dial* article. Unless you think I'd better wait, I'll infer that it would be all right for me to give it to *The Partisan Review*

53. Owner of the bookshop La Maison des Amies des Livres in Paris, known for her support of contemporary French writers.

without pestering Mr. Herring, further, because in any case, use here would not interfere with anything he might wish to do.)

To Marsden Hartley   *January 2, 1941*

Dear Mr. Hartley,

I have been pondering your book[54] and your kindness in giving it to me, and the fragrant balsam sprays; the scarlet papers under the silver and green bow; and the longer I think, the smaller any word of thanks looks, by comparison with what I am feeling.

"A Yankee Breughel," the "arbutus or, . . . may flowers," the violets "growing on little hillocks," "trailing evergreens and boxberry leaves," the sea bird "vegetarians," so absorbingly strange; the exciting subject matter of ["]The Family Album["]; "A Man—Going to Pieces"; you make one realize more than ever that true painting and poetry are almost indivisible.

And what perfection of beauty in the printing, paper, cover and outside cover of the book. To say dust-cover would be blasphemy.

You did wrong to destroy those poems of which you speak. I glanced eagerly into the pages here, to find them. Perhaps you will sometime revoke them.

Though not one by birth, my mother, like me, is a "Maine-iac" by choice and sends you intensest thanks for bringing before us Maine detail that we love.

Gratefully yours,   Marianne Moore

To William Carlos Williams   *January 7, 1941*

Dear William,

There is feeling in Sydney Salt: "Nature hath given me too great a struggle." "Once I dwelt in deep flowers and glory was a poor word." And how kind you are in both ways,—giving me this, and taking care of him.

Mr. Laughlin has sent me *The Broken Span.* Some of your "everyday" images, I would say, are too everyday to be condoned; and I become violently concerned about the punitive relentlessness of *In the Money.* Internal poison may require external poison to counteract it but there certainly must be a point at which the dose becomes dangerous.

"Against the Sky" has a tension as of held breath, that is beyond envy,—a finality so right it is like a suspended prism that doesn't move; and

54. His collection of poems, *Androscoggin* (1940); MM had earlier helped him by commenting on and typing his manuscript, *The Pressed Foot.*

I like almost as well, "The Predicter of Famine," "Sparrows Among Dry Leaves," and "Raleigh was Right."

I was grateful for your statement-without-veneer, on Wallace Stevens, in *The Harvard Advocate*. Anything you write, I want to see.

My love to Florence.   M.M.

I may be too shrewd, but I am wondering if James A. Decker is a possible reincarnation of James Leippert and J. Ronald Lane Latimer.

To James Laughlin   *January 7, 1941*

Dear Mr. Laughlin,

It is good that I am against the unprobity of any attempted equalizings of obligation; otherwise, in your debt as I am, I should be miserable.

I find in *The Broken Span* some examples of that William Carlos Williams intimidatingly perfect tension that others don't get. The effect of unlapsing Aeschylean threat, however, is almost too bitter; and some of the "everyday" images are, I would say, regrettably everyday.

This format is what I have wished for years to see realized; and I am much interested in the series for 1941; especially glad to see you have included John Wheelwright and Rilke.

Sincerely yours,   Marianne Moore

To Monroe Wheeler   *January 19, 1941*

Dear Monroe,

That you should give this careful thought to us in the midst of all with which you are beset, we feel so very much; have been treasuring your Christmas message and the calligraphic tree, knowing how pressed you are when you could snatch but one day for the wishful & devoted ones in Chicago.

I shall come to the Exhibition, and try to arrive at an hour when it would not be inhuman to ask for you; & shall try not [to] come as I undertook to see the shells you so watchfully told me of;—two days after the exhibition closed; (I telephoned however, did not go to Cooper Union itself). Since it doesn't seem possible to go to things in the evening, I shan't be at the reception but am delighted to have the invitation. The treatment of the beaver motive is wonderful indeed, with the tail folded upward and ears added so helpfully.

It frightens us to know of your night work, and the additional National Defense effort. One suffers in being merely an observer; but to engage so dangerously deep in the necessities of the hour is not taking the best care of others either. Do think of this, Monroe. I could write you another and even *another* letter, about the wishes and gratitudes that little meeting with you and your father stirred in me. Our reverences and affection demand sacrifices that may seem to be selfish ones; I don't believe that they are. I so crave to see your father at peace about you as well as proud of you. You have accomplished so very much already—even in the lesser direction of getting people interested in useful objects that are worthy as objects of beauty. Do set your creativeness to self-conservation, now.

Warner, so far distant apparently, shares closely in our thoughts and we each send you love. Perhaps you may see me one day at the Exhibition, meanwhile much gratitude and apology for seeming to arraign you, as a person on his honor obliged to do so and so. I know you understand. Mother has kept on fulfilling her determination to be well. Has bad times, but no disappointing illness. Is eagerly expecting to be *all well* in the end.

Affectionately,   Marianne

I am glad to see Ernest Boyd's serious effort, in reviewing Glenway's book for *Decision.*

To John Warner Moore   *Tuesday, January 21 [1941]*

Dearest Winks,

It "quiets" us to know you use Teddy's car during her absence; & that Johnny is satisfied with his situation. I bet all is now ready for Brother Baptist,—a kind of water rat (Gospel Rat) I perceive.

We,—Bear & me—accept your overture concerning ye Estrich— "He digesteth hard yron." That's what he's gonna do.

I rekkonize my trouble, as being too oblique & obscure, as a result of hating Crudeness (& Alvin E. Magary condescension and insulting didacticism). Always what I learn to regret, I try to avoid in the next try, it is very hard to REarrange a thing that has fallen in to the mold already. And *I shall endeavor* to be CLEARER. Thanks for the suggestions about Marshal Pétain.[55] I see he has stood firm on NOT using the fleet against England. Maybe I can't mention him by name, but I can be influenced by the feeling. And maybe I *can* git him in. I feel kind o'active as the result of my Award! I investigate the gazette with a kind of pity not far removed from gratification. It is wonderful to see how *writing* is moral force, not a judicious matter of covering the ground appropriately. Your editorial fault was over-emphasis; a final phrase like "to bring about such action,"—action having already been dwelt on considerable. Yet above all, the material was ship-shape. Always had drive and life and imagination. These poor D.S.C. laborers haven't got the exciting pineapple juice within.

55. Philippe Pétain (1856–1951), marshal of France and premier of German-controlled (Vichy) France (1940–44).

Poor Lester is coming over to Miss Monte's for dinner & then here for a short visit. He is exercised to a degree over my book "remaindering." I tell him the book is in print, nothing to exert ourselves about. He says couldn't the copies be all bought & sold judiciously to libraries & students. Also he's all stirred up over taking a civil service exam. for editorial work. Prof. Demnig at Dartmouth has got the application blanks & pushed things to such a point Lester's got to co-operate. This is a wonderful act of brotherhood on Arthur Demnig's part; since if Lester passes, he doesn't have to accept work now. Yet he boggles at it!!

Well, Cub & me have had a long & refreshing rest. Wisht you had had it. I'm going to the Institute & then to the shood place & be here this evening along w. Lester. He just heard of the remaindering by accident!!

Dearest love,   Rat

To Hildegarde Watson   *May 23, 1941*

I wonder if you have been to Vassar, Hildegarde, besides being with me on Wednesday! It was all so nice,—despite premonitory agues of unconfidence. And as I journeyed away from New York, in my azure dress seated on a new piece of cheese cloth I had taken along—with the left side of the blue hem folded over the right side, and my arms stiffly extended like a puppet's to prevent wrinkles in the sleeves, a young woman next to me, said "I am so interested in your *dress.*" I explained that I was going to give a talk to some students and that my dress had been given to me,—as was evident possibly, for I was afraid to breathe for fear something would happen to it. The woman said, "You'll make an impression. You wouldn't need to *tell* them anything." She then said that she was going to give a talk herself, to some boys at Napatuck (?) about "The Chambered Nautilus." After a little she asked what I was going to talk about. I said originality as a by-product of sincerity, and said I was going to read E. E. Cummings' "little man in a hurry"; and then recited it. Nodding fervently, she said, "Would you mind if I wrote that down?" Not at all, I said, and I then produced the manuscript so she could copy it.

Then at Vassar, I mentioned (at supper) the enthusiastic teacher who was going to Napatuck and one of the members of the English department said, "Three of us once had a suite together, and a maid in partnership and this maid used to amuse us by saying, 'When I was to Napatuck'—and she always kept a poem pinned to the curtain over the sink in the kitchen and changed the poem from time to time." So you see it was a harmonious day, Hildegarde.

Helen Sandison, who had invited me to speak—whom I had known at Bryn Mawr—head of the English Department at Vassar—met me in her car and took me [on] a tour of the campus; showed me the archery field, (surrounded by dense trees so that {in earlier days}, the men of the faculty would not be outraged by feminine participation in a sport!) the pond, the outdoor theatre, the golf course, the swimming pool which is deep turquoise—in a new building edged by beds of juniper or ground cedar that sent up an aromatic scent in the early afternoon sun; then the "science of living" building, and finally the Library, where a friend who is a librarian took me about. It is a most intimidating, intricate, orderly, inebriating place with a magazine room, and a history corridor & a sculpture room in white, and an Italian room in pink, and some other room in blue, and hundreds of alcoves and, seminaries, and reserved book shelves and "new-book" shelves. My talk was in a room used for faculty meetings, in a building formerly the gymnasium. Beside the door was a slab of fossil limestone covered with what looked like moulded Georgian (?) ceiling, in a pattern of odd raised interacting Y's and equilateral triangles.

The walls of the room are brick, painted a dull turquoise, with a rather big landscape portrait (chiefly blue) at one end. The furniture is of light wood upholstered in pale blue or dull rose and there is a beige rug on the floor and a pale thing almost like it on the wall behind the dais. No artificial light was needed for there is a skylight; and the side and one end of the room have windows the height of the wall. The platform—a rather low dais—is almost the length of the room and a refectory table of whitish wood, had behind it a blue chair and 2 rose ones.

I began with the "fear of the already said" and quoted Mr. Updike's[56] statement that style depends, not on decoration but on simplicity and proportion; that originality is not within our volition and so on; read a little of Wilfred Owen's "Strange Meeting" and Vernon Watkins' "Ballad of Dundrum Bay," and mentioned W. H. Auden's statement that poetry has always in it a tempting doubleness, "the immediate meaning and a possible meaning" and spoke of his paradoxes.

> *Whichever way we turn we see*
> *Man captured by his liberty*
>
> *The feminine which bids us come*
> *To find what we're escaping from.*

Little man in a hurry. Shakespeare's line—"the urchin-snouted boar," and the first stanza of Burns' "To a Mouse" were liked best I think. There were some very nice questions afterward and talk of Vassar magazines.

I left home on the 1.30 and came back on the 6.59, and despite the speedy schedule, Helen S. had arranged that four or five members of the fac-

---

56. Daniel Berkeley Updike (1860–1941), printer and founder of Merrymount Press, and author of several books on printing.

ulty, and we, should have dinner at Alumnae House. *The Dial* was alluded to in as lively and natural a way as if it were going on now, and I was given some entertaining reminiscences of undergraduates: how when Elizabeth Bishop was chided for not producing a long overdue paper, and Miss P. said, "You are working on it, I suppose?" she was amazed to hear Elizabeth say, "No I'm not, I've been working on the Year Book." (But it was admitted that not all the students are so candid.)

We so hope, Hildegarde, that summer is doing you good, not burdening you, and that each of the others is so well that care is light upon you. We try to feel that it is true, as we've been told that Rochester has so many trees in it, it is not like a city at all.

Yesterday afternoon, since I had been specially notified—I went to Lola Ridge's funeral,—here in Brooklyn. A clergyman who seemed somewhat like a layman, conducted the service and nothing more real or exalted at a funeral,—have I known at all. Many passages of scripture that we don't associate with sadness were read, there was a prayer, and William Benét read three poems by Lola Ridge. The room was full of laurel and summer flowers and all present were somewhat acquainted—or if not, spoke together afterward without introduction,—Ridgely Torrence, Aaron Copland, Paul Strand, Mrs. Canby, Martin Lewis, Stephen, Laura and Rosemary Benét and certain others I had I think met, but could not place. I am perhaps mentioning this because I had so expected to write to you yesterday; I wanted you and Sibley to be feeling with me the friendly afterwave of the reciprocities at Vassar. Mr. McBride who came to see us a little while ago asked if we knew how "Dr. Watson is, and what is he doing? I mean is he happy? He's a person one feels that way about." That little succession of disconnected but unmistakable meanings, was so characteristic and so cheering to us. And Mr. McBride himself, in a dark blue suit and blue tie with his light blue eyes and Malacca-handled umbrella, looked like the nicest thing Raoul Dufy ever did.

Our love, and better thoughts than I manage to convey in these lame jottings.

Marianne

To Louise Crane *June 5 [1941?]*

Dear Louise,

Last night has given me something to think about for fifteen years! I hope the man was there who was bothered by the mildness of the first Coffee Concert swing music.[57]

57. Louise Crane was the producer of a series of concerts (at the Museum of Modern Art and elsewhere) emphasizing cultural and ethnic variety.

I was much impressed by Billie Holiday's "barcarole" opening number, (and of course by her flame colored skirt and Japanese Mei Lan Fang aestheticism). There were so many novelties and peaks of sophistication in rhythm and tone-contrasts, I was taxed by the wealth of what was scattering out; though I rather horrified Lester by my avidity; and betrayed my opportunity, I suppose, for influencing him against any pastime which savors of rolling the bones and cartwheeling the time away. Mother,—even on hearsay—remarked as I was telling her about it, "why is my child so hardened!" "Mr." [Chester] Page is a virtuoso, certainly, in the humor of his manner—"his happy starling posturings"—as well as with the trumpet. I thought, as he was playing, of the lecturer on Chinese music, Mr. Leavis, who said that a Chinese flute-player must practice rigorously—maybe months—with a reed and bowl of water, to learn how to keep taking air in without ever stopping the current of breath coming out. The pianist with that group too, was a picked man, I would say, with a kind of streamlined action of the whole body that interested me very much. The contour of that song, "I don't think I'm going to be here long" haunts me, also the "intimate" song of Billie Holiday's about the eyes. When I asked Lester to refresh my memory about the words,—which it pesters me not to be able to recall,—he spoke in so formal a way of undertaking to get them for me, I again worried about my imperviousness to degradation but my unsophisticatedness and thirst for humor, take charge of me on a "high evening" like Wednesday, and under your protection, I burst out laughing and wore my hands out "regardless."

The last half, I didn't hear,—it is so late by the time I get home from 53rd Street. I could hardly make myself leave, the evening of the South American Panorama. Of all I have heard, I liked the Incaicos best and Elsie Houston's accompanist. I don't know that (in my ignorance) I ever witnessed such intuitiveness and style as Alderson Mowbray's, and inferring that the fruit would not be less worthy than the stem, I concentrated on the technique of the songs and felt the refinement, but Elsie Houston is such a *person*, it was hard for me to really listen. The definition and quietness of the Incaicos with their fleeting almost parenthetic poetic features, were amazing to me, for the contrast they constitute with Hawaiian and Maori music. Lester tells me the Voodoo drumming was impressive and unique and that the whole later part that evening was especially novel. I hope perhaps it will be recorded sometime, so I can hear it, or that you will put them on again;—if you are yet alive. I can't imagine the equipoise you must have commanded, to manage *one* evening let alone these six programs.

Returning to the stampede of last night. The *Times* seems to be suffering from jealousy again, in that sentence ending "the concluding number of the concerts & of the successful series." It would have been almost impossible to keep from writing, "the concluding number of a strikingly"—or overwhelmingly—"successful series." Zutie Singleton,—a born drummer, would have done something for us if he hadn't done more than allow his name to appear.

Despite my talkativeness, Louise, I am constrained,—overwhelmed by the pleasure and benefit the concerts have been to me. My whole perspective is changed and your unsordidly generous eye for minutiae, and disregard of box-office totals,—in trailing so large a band of us along with you—has emphasized to me as I mingled with the audience each time, how personal and intentional your creative control of the enterprise has been.

I wish Elizabeth might have been here. I don't know whether to give her my unrestrained feeling about it all, or reduce it to cheerful animation, it was such a sacrifice for her to compel herself to stay away.

If there is something I might do besides gape at your ingenuity in these official matters, I'd like to help, and not be looked on as a chronic mental paralytic. Though being a beginner, I don't know just where I could come in.

We have been waylaid by dentistry and my book,—(a small thing of just a few pages) but are coming on well.

Our love—and satisfaction in your triumph; for although there must have been things to dismay you—it is that.

                                                                Marianne

I hope Mrs. Crane feels contented about these high evenings, as well as a certain natural thankfulness that they have been rounded off for the summer.

To John Warner Moore   *June 21, [19]41*

Dearest Bible Duck,

Your letters,—both at once this A.M.—are very cheering. Bear is overjoyed about the gown and is going to *work* on you, to get you to "choose." I had give it up, but of course interest revives like an oil gusher. It wouldn't *add* to you, but on the other hand it is worthy your office that you have it; is strange, for you not to have one. (It is like Bear & me wearing hairy cotton stockings like a policeman's gloves when every janitress is wearing silk.)

Anything that shows trust in us—on Constance's part—is worth rubies; even if it would be wiser to not *need* the hospitality. What you say to do, we will do. I am glad we did not tell Hildegarde we would go to the Farm in July because even if you CAN'T have us in New London, we are occupied here. Perhaps you could indirectly encourage Constance to think someone should be in the house to "watch" it (?) while you are away and we could perhaps make a 2-day trip over to the Farm to see Hildegarde and return to

35 to "watch" it. If this is too bold a thought, we could transfer over there for 2 weeks in August perhaps.

As for someone to feed us, we do the marketing & work here and ought to be able to tend to things in New London without anybody to help us; and suggested to Hildegarde that we do that at the Farm. Frances Hickey is having trouble with her back and couldn't tend to us but Hildegarde said she could, through Mr. [William] Justema, get a Dutch woman to cook for we. Of course it is a staggering expense to use the Farm & we'd like to spare Hildegarde.

We are saddened by this word of the o-9. It is an embittering economy to save on old submarines and put to death 30 men. The paper implies that the ship was not from New London, but Portsmouth. Have you anything to do about it? about the families? I saw the headline on the way to Paul Rosenfeld's but hoped the diving bell would save them, not realizing that the construction of the submarine was probably the cause of the destruction.[58]

The party was a pathetic one in some ways. Paul has not as large an income as he "use to have," and lives in a minute 2-room apartment with a cooking-cupboard in the wall. His guests (at the time I arrived) were enough to jeopardize any party & he was storm-trooping along with an apparently fluent French about nothing vital. The guest of honor, André Breton is a large figure in French poetry & is very impressive but was "persecuted" by the futilities till John [Peale] Bishop & W. C. Williams arrived—though I helped a *little*. The men spoke an appallingly voluble French. Edna Bryner meanwhile, (a partial friend of the Eliots) was like a cannonball on my right arm and improved only a little at the end when I had convinced her I was not "scary." She started off on William Carlos Williams, "What did you think of *Murder in the Cathedral?*" William said (with hesitation), "*Eliot* is my bête noir" and that had to have an emergency squad. Then presently "Pound" was mentioned, & he said, "Ezra is an *ass*. He knows nothing about music but wants to pose as a great musician!" Edna B. remarked that his "hair was very coarse," & Paul said "yes"; Ezra had said in Paris "once he had a melody [he] must hunt up so & so, to fill in the *notes*"! So I undertook to whitewash Ezra & partly succeeded.

I wrote Johnny yesterday, enclosing some envelopes & stamps & "overdues," etc. thinking he could favor his summer companions. (All that I sent he already has.) But I felt it might please him to get them.

Dearest love,   Rat

Cub is now onto the Cub Brand of paper I procured for her. How do you like it?

58. JWM had conducted the memorial service for the officers and crew of the submarine *o-9*, which sank on a test-dive.

1942–1951
The Personal and the Public

T H E 1940s were for Moore a time of expanding friendships and increasing public recognition. These supports helped her as she tried her strength, with mixed success, in prose and translation. They were also a counterpoint to personal difficulties, especially her mother's failing health and eventual death in 1947.

Moore's public life was a whirlwind of lectures, readings, fund-raisers, and teaching engagements, often recounted to her friends. In 1942 and for several summers thereafter, Moore taught in Cummington, Massachusetts, at a summer program for the arts and humanities, and often included her contemporaries on her reading list. In 1943 she participated in a ten-day conference at Mount Holyoke College, organized by Jean Wahl and modeled after the Pontigny conferences in France from 1910 to 1940. The purpose of the conference was to exchange political and cultural ideas; the mornings were devoted to poetry, the afternoons to politics. Among the participants were fifty or sixty refugee intellectuals, along with Wallace Stevens, John Peale Bishop, James Rorty, Edmund Wilson, and other eminent figures. Moore's publication of *Nevertheless* in 1944 brought her greater recognition, including the Harriet Monroe Poetry Award, and an invitation, which she declined, to serve as poet in residence at the Library of Congress. To Warner she remarked, modestly, that "on the whole, I take more interest in it than in any of my other books & though I hate small books of verse, it looks neat & business like to me." The *Quarterly Review of Literature* published a special issue on her work in 1948, which included high praise from such contemporaries as Bishop, John Crowe Ransom, Williams, Stevens, and Louise Bogan. In 1945 she won a Guggenheim award and in 1946 a grant from the American Academy of Arts and Letters and the National Institute of Arts and Letters. In 1949 she received her first of many honorary degrees (from Wilson College). Moore accepted these laurels with characteristic humility. She declined to attend the award ceremony in Chicago for the Monroe Award, wondering whether it wasn't unpatriotic to travel for such occasions in time of war, and she questioned whether the Guggenheim Fellowship wasn't a mistake, since she hadn't applied for one. Moore's new status as a public figure was perhaps best marked by the famous photograph taken at the Gotham Book Mart for *Life*. Moore had come to know Edith and Osbert Sitwell at about this time (a friendship that would continue through the 1950s), and she was especially proud to be in their company. She wrote of the occasion to Hildegarde Watson, who supplied many of the garments that would serve her in this new public dais: "I have been very sinful, it seems Hildegarde—in the eyes of E. E. C. and Allen Tate because I went to the Vanguard Press–Gotham Book Mart tea for the Sitwells where two peregrines from *Life* circled round, photographing, and descended on victims at will. But if the Sitwells could be there, so could we? They are our guests—(over-innocent or aware) one need not ask it seems to me and they are two courageous warriors and as human as The House That Jack Built. Apropos of the falcons, I wore your brown suit—the tweed and as Stephen Benét said of his success at school one day (when about 10) 'as much as any, more than most!'" (November 11, 1948).

Many of those in Moore's cultural and literary circle had also become close friends, people she relied on for personal and artistic support. Among Moore's new friends was W. H. Auden, whom she met shortly after he arrived in the States in 1939, and whose work she reviewed for *The Nation* in 1941. But their personal bond began in the spring of 1944, when he accompanied her on a trip from New York City to lecture at Bryn Mawr, where he had been teaching. She was so impressed by his gallantry in rushing to hold the Thirtieth Street train for her in Philadelphia that she repeated the story to many of her correspondents. Auden offered help of another kind when he learned that Moore's novel had been rejected by Macmillan and that the publisher had postponed a volume of her prose. He offered to find her another publisher, and indeed, when she began her translation of Jean de La Fontaine in 1943, he introduced her to an editor at Reynal & Hitchcock. Auden may also have introduced Moore to Elizabeth Mayer, who collaborated with her on a translation of *Rock Crystal*, a German fairy tale by Adalbert Stifter, published in 1945. (This project combined two long-term interests of Moore's: children's literature and translation.) Auden was a regular visitor to 260 Cumberland Street throughout the 1940s and 1950s.

Another visitor was the painter Joseph Cornell. Moore had applauded work of his that had appeared in *View* in 1943 by writing to the editor, Charles Henri Ford. Her letter was one of the few responses Cornell had received to this early publication of his work, and it sparked a lively correspondence between kindred spirits. Moore's friendship and occasional correspondence with the American graphic artist and illustrator Edward McKnight Kauffer, a friend of both T. S. Eliot's and Monroe Wheeler's, also began in the early 1940s. Kauffer had been living in London but returned in 1939 with the artist and textile designer Marion Dorn, and the two soon became Moore's intimates. Moore would be a spiritual support to Kauffer in his last, desolate years in the early 1950s. Other artist friends of this period included the painter and decorator Loren MacIver (a friend of Louise Crane's and Elizabeth Bishop's), and her husband, writer and literary critic Lloyd Frankenberg, who was doing compensatory service as a conscientious objector. In 1949 Moore met the sculptress Malvina Hoffman at a meeting of the Academy of Arts and Sciences. They became close friends in the fifties.

Moore formed a number of other close female friendships in the early 1940s that would fill her personal life in later years. In 1942 she began a correspondence with Kathrine Jones, an unpublished poet from Brookline, Massachusetts (who spent her summers in Ellsworth, Maine). Jones had written an admiring letter about Moore's work, and this initiated an exchange not only of poems but of food, clothes, and other gifts that soon became occasions for elaborate, witty description. Moore also became close friends with Jones's companion, Marcia Chamberlain, and would stay with them in Maine several times. In the late 1940s, after her mother's death, Moore also began to correspond with family on her father's side, and she would maintain these connections—particularly with her father's cousin Edith Moore Love—for the rest of her life.

Friendships from the 1920s and 1930s developed and deepened during this period. Her old family friend from Carlisle, the artist George Plank, had illustrated *The Pangolin and Other Verse* in 1936, and this connection renewed old ties. Moore's relationship with Monroe Wheeler, which began in 1922, long before he became a director of the Museum of Modern Art, continued with frequent letters and visits that not only engaged their mutual interest in the arts but also display the intimacy between them and their attention to the concerns of daily life. Letters to Bryher, Louise Crane, and Hildegarde Watson indicate the range of Moore's interests and affections, as well as the gratitude she felt toward these friends for their practical, and often financial, support. The background of war is present particularly in her letters to Bryher and Hildegarde Watson, with whom she shared many spiritual and political views. To Bryher she wrote: "We haven't seen anything on the war that we care so much about as your paragraph about power and growth, and need to give, not remove" (June 22, 1942). Continuing a theme recurrent since the 1930s in correspondence with her brother, Moore also wrote Watson of her concern about the audacity of poetry in time of war: "I feel almost numbed by the irretrievable deaths the war is causing,

am uncertain of permission to assert feelings in any direction." Moore's relationship with Elizabeth Bishop gradually changed from one of men-
tor/protégée to one of mutual affection and indebtedness. Moore continued
to help Bishop in her publishing efforts and in obtaining grants, but her letters often express her frustration about her own writing, and her appreciation for Bishop's responses to it. On July 20, 1943, for instance, she wrote to
Bishop: "Anything I write does not seem 'written'—I just persist. And you
can't think how it helps me to know you don't repudiate *The Nation* poem
I hazarded. I have another—about a strawberry that is not so long,—that
still contrives to include a great deal of awkwardness. If I enclose it, don't
feel you must strain a point to like it or forgive its defects." In writing to
Bishop, Moore evaluated what she had read in the spirit of a fellow practi-
tioner and observer of the art of her time. Of Eliot's *Four Quartets*, she remarked: "The quartets seem to me very sad; so unegoistic a precipitate,
there is something alarming about them. Technically, I am too inexperi-
enced to know how prose-like, transitions between lyrics should be; and
tend to think that every word of every poem should be as melodious as a
Handel allegro—but the intensified honesty of this writing of T. S. Eliot's
is resolute and helpful—I can't seem to dwell over-much on the form. (Not
that I would imply that some of his writing wasn't honest.) It is just that I
feel self-consciousness is in abeyance." During these years, Moore also kept
up a lively correspondence with Ezra Pound, who in 1946 was incarcerated
in the government psychiatric hospital at St. Elizabeths, in Anacostia,
Maryland. While their letters continue to reveal profound differences in
their political and social views, they remained close friends and literary allies. Wallace Stevens remained for Moore a touchstone of artistic value. Answering a young invalid writer named John Putnam, she wrote, defending
his practice: "Wallace Stevens is a philosopher and so concentrated in his
reasoning, that often it seems to me, the person interpreting him, takes too
strongly to heart, some facet of his thought. Always he is defining,—
saying—By 'sentiment' I mean so and so. And often I find I had inferred
some opposite meaning, from the one implied. So if I may say so, let the 'enjoyment' be your guide" (January 7, 1943).

A major theme in all of Moore's letters, but especially throughout the
forties and fifties, is gift exchange. Some of Moore's liveliest descriptive
writing was in response to tokens received from friends—of food, clothing,
exotica, cards. It is clear that Moore's lyric effusions motivated her friends
to further gift exchanges. Mangoes, sapodillas, alligator pears, limes, sugar
apples, lime-tangerine marmalade, and papaya concentrate were among
the "gargantuan luxuries" Bishop sent Moore from Key West. Exotic fruit
became a favorite gift from Moore's friends over the years, always rousing
her to metaphor. To Chester Page she wrote: "The lichi-nuts are curious and

beautiful amid the green leaves—so heavy;—almost like stones; yet armoured like some echidna or armadillo. And you nested them in a very beautiful box. And exotic *indeed* the inner nut! Such a precious contrast to the state of the world" (December 12, 1956). From E. E. Cummings and Marion Morehouse, with whom she was in frequent contact in the forties and after, Moore often received flowers, as on January 27, 1944, when she wrote: "What splendor! Each of these stately flowers, like some royal thing of Siam, in the days of yellow umbrellas and elephants! (Elephants? Should I not be saying yelophants?) Each with sepals streaming joyously like yacht pennants."

But if the forties brought Moore the pleasure of public applause and an expanded circle of friends, they were not untroubled years, professionally or personally. With the change of editors, Reynal & Hitchcock dropped Moore's project of translating La Fontaine, and Macmillan (which had earlier challenged her right to pursue the project with another publisher) refused to pick it up. Viking, under the editorship of Monroe Engel, did take on the project, though, and finally published *The Fables of La Fontaine* in 1954. But this translation would cause Moore anxiety for more than a decade. In July 1945, thanking Hildegarde and Sibley Watson for their "thought and time for the fables," she remarked: "Clumping about among the meanings, I am like the Galápagos tortoises Melville talks about,—battering against objects on the deck, all night, & determined to move them as if machinery and hatches were coils of rope."

Personal difficulties also mounted in this decade. The years 1944 and 1945 are the last to contain much family correspondence. The primary cause was that Moore and her brother agreed that he should destroy her letters because of tension between Warner and Constance. Both brother and sister believed that Constance's jealousy would be fired by knowledge of their exchange. There are, however, cordial letters between Moore and Constance in the next decade.

Both Moore and her mother experienced health problems in 1944, and the letters of this period are dominated by reports of their "struggles" and advocacy of various health and vitamin cures. Mrs. Moore became seriously ill in 1946, at which time Moore hired Gladys Berry as her housekeeper, her own health having suffered from the strain of caring for her mother. Mrs. Moore's health steadily declined and she died on July 9, 1947. Moore's religious beliefs, bolstered by her brother's ministry, served her in this difficult time. The support of friends and relatives was essential in helping Moore through this loss. She traveled to Hagerstown to visit her cousin Mary Shoemaker, then stayed with Louise Crane in Windsor, Massachusetts, finally joining Kathrine Jones and Marcia Chamberlain in Ellsworth, Maine. At the time of Mary Warner Moore's death, Warner was senior chaplain at the Potomac River Naval Command in Washington, D.C., where he served until his retirement from the Navy in 1948. While visiting him there, Moore stopped in to see Ezra Pound at St. Elizabeths.

Amid these clouds over the late forties, it is not surprising that Moore's literary output was meager, or that the gathering of her poems into *Collected Poems* gets little mention in the correspondence. As she remarked to Robert McAlmon on January 27, 1952: "I wish if you want my *Collected Poems*, I could have sent you the book and not let you buy it; diffident as I feel about it—got together in too great a hurry and a mass of errors, not to mention tedious content for long stretches all through! But as [Diego] Rivera said, we are like [the] fruit-tree, going on without reference to the crop of the previous season." This volume, however, marked a transition to a new publisher and, even as it gathered up the past, heralded a new season in Moore's career.

To Elizabeth Bishop   *260 Cumberland Street [Brooklyn]*
January 31, 1942

Dear Elizabeth,

Although the papaya is now eaten, all that you say is of absorbing interest. I could not get Mother to eat *more than a sliver*, so I divided (seeds), fruit and stem with the Padleys, our neighbors, and they were delighted, hastened back to inquire just what they were eating and said they were "not at all sorry" you had been so good to me. I was fascinated by the seeds; first of all by the distribution and amethyst color, and then by the necks, set so they stood up like seed-pearls on stiff silk. I got a magnifying glass to examine the seed proper, which reminded me of those little squares called "Sens-Sens" that the drug-stores used to sell in tiny colored envelopes like miniature seed-packets? It is most wonderful of you, Elizabeth, to offer to send us bottled juice, but we are still hoarding the special orange papaya elixir, for a worthy occasion and I am in very bad repute with Mother anyhow, for pursuing with childish curiosity as I do, every Robinson Crusoe–like thing the torrid zone can produce. There did not seem to be a card in the box; though there had been one with the orange papaya concentrate and the kumquats—on which you had written a little message about not knowing how pleasing the "papaya stuff" might be; you had never tried it.

I infer from what you say about *The Southern Review* that I needn't buy. I had thought of ordering a copy. I would be much "disappointed in you" if you COULD feel about Yeats, as some of his acolytes seem to feel. An "effect," an exhaustively great sensibility—(with insensibility)?—and genius for word-sounds and sentences. But after all, what is this enviable apparatus for! if not to change our mortal psychic structure. It makes me think of the Malay princes,—the horde of eunuchs and entertainers and "bearers" of this and that; then suddenly the umbrella over the prince lowered, because a greater prince was passing.

I am intensely interested in the cleaner. Even the hundred and fifteen dollars do not induce apathy. You are sure it is AIREX and not AIRWAYS? But of course;— for the Airways has a glass cylinder of some sort, and nothing like a pot of miraculous water. Dust is my supreme hobgoblin. I don't mind having my packages and my clothes and my good spirits spoiled, if only the rain will neutralize the dust; can hardly persuade myself that the ascending dust clouds at the circus improve the arena-like perspective or that I really do dare eat a Brooklyn Bridge pretzel, on which I dote.

Noah's flood was a little thing compared with what we've been having just now, such darkness (at three o'clock) that we have had to have electric light; and the rain blowing in such horizontal torrents that little whiffs of spray strike you as you approach the tightly fastened windows, but we need rain.

Warner (my brother) says the Hardins will be *good* tenants, that they were—also—much liked in New London; he told me by return mail and now it is February. But you prophesied a good report yourself, before I asked him anything.

We are happy that emergencies have subsided for you and that you now can WRITE; and don't fail + let us know WHAT you write. My skunk is still a phantasy. I can't even find my little notes and references and rhymings about which I was beginning to be hopeful when you were here, haven't thought of them since that evening we ate at Miss Monte's. You can't imagine the prosaic criminalities in which I've been engaged,—another attempt at recording, though the Harvard one was not a success; (nothing was processed). This time for the National Council of Teachers of English, at the Reeves Sound Studio 1600 Broadway. All futile perhaps, but I was goaded into improving a bad line in my *ostrich* which I found I couldn't read as first written. In the cubicle adjoining the recording-cell, was a sublime photograph or framed photomural of the temple—the Burobadour (?) of Java with those bone-like silk-cotton or sand-box? trees in the foreground,—the bark whitish and the roots like tall narrow tents converging into a trunk. There are some in Panama near Morgan's Castle.

Also present, was José García Villa the Filipino poet (a student of Professor Wells's; Professor W. conducted the recording). Mr. Villa has an intense gazelle-like sensibility—and I was wrung to the heart to learn afterward from Mr. Wells that the boy's father is a prisoner of the Japanese; can't send any more funds for his son's tuition at Columbia and that José (G. V.) has suddenly to do outside work of various kinds and perhaps give up his college program. He has sent me some poems to comment on, and I am greatly surprised by the originality and color-sense in them, and the shrewd technique. (His name is familiar to me but I don't recall reading anything of his before that I liked as I did these recent poems.)

Dentistry, semi-literary appointments, desperate mending of a large Navajo rug that you haven't seen, but henceforth will not be able to overlook, other manuscripts—and a lecture or two have supplanted possible writing.

As you will suspect from my treachery to W. B. Yeats, I've been to a lecture on Java, by Burton Holmes, and one on Malay by Mrs. Carvette [Carveth?] Wells. (I think I mentioned Mrs. W.)

My standards are so low as to be on the ground, by comparison with yours and I thought Randall Jarrell parodied me rather well, (aside from the timidly riské [*sic*] touches). I am timid enough but ferociously un-riské, am I not? You are very consoling about my *Dial* article which I haven't yet had the courage to read. F. W. Dupee did me the greatest service (about 2 years ago!) in reducing it and obviating the sense of amassed repetition.

Wallace Stevens (again a caterpillar) I accepted with some gratitude. There are one or two characteristics and wholesome surprises in the poem, somewhere I thought. But I, too, resist obliqueness just now, of any kind in anyone. (Am like the inconsiderate Arthur, I suppose.)

Mother sends you love and begs you not to and *forbids you* to use your hands or let your mind rest on anything more in the way of consoling marvels for us.

Affectionately,   Marianne

P.S. Lester seems to be still in East Lynn. I wrote him some time ago, enclosing the now dead Harvard talk but have not heard. I agree with all my heart about *fun*, Elizabeth. But I think it would have been heathenish of Lester not to share his holiday with Mr. & Mrs. L.; and if what he says is true about having been granted "leave of absence" from the "Y.," I don't know that he would dare take more holiday? And honestly, don't you think it would be positively *abandoned* of him to raise or beg money for the trip to Florida, Elizabeth, when he can barely afford his room at 53rd Street and sometimes saves on food? omits meals and eats unwholesome food (or leans on coffee instead of food)? He emphasizes the opposite, but his Mother has intimated the truth. I resolved I would get him a different sort of work from YMCA Desk work and made a start toward it. This may be the reason he "avoids" me.!

M.

To Kathrine Jones   *March 19, 1942*

Dear Kathrine,

What giving! What mountainous, what dainty giving! The lady with the arched eyebrows; her fingers on the keys; the foreshortened music, the mulberry curtain; the curious, minute swirled feather edge of the frame, the old time writing on the back; the very worm-holes! So round & personed.

We have been in Italy; perhaps for that reason, ponder the fountain & its consoling ellipse, the more deeply. The surrounding greenness, & the experienced vision that could give the sense of that special place where all was secluded and Italian.

Something to look at, something to make us suitable ones to *be* looking; something to eat! What discernments! At breakfast yesterday I said, we "need two things: eggs & *cheese*. And that's all." But apparently it was *not*. This masterly cheese—would any other word suit—is a thing of mystery to us—the thickening surface like the rind of a tropical fruit; the cheese solid, firm & with form yet more like something still in the creamery. Onion soup, mock turtle soup, baby mushrooms, cooked noodles, cherries, and nectarines; majestic sour prunes! cocoa & tea—as if we were Mr. Churchill on his American furlough; and café des Invalides. Mother drinks coffee, though I don't. Shall I ever be able to persuade her to open that big holly-berry red Christmas can!

The Indian chutney! It shall be an ornament for a *long* long time,— possibly till my brother is here. The bottle foremost an ornament forever, flaming sun, on the label, and bright brown ribbon make me think of the marigold-orange coats of the horses in a Caldecott picture-book. And what reading—Merwanjee Poon jia jets & sons, 96, Frere Road, Bombay, British East India—1 lb. 1 oz Nett. Gold medal London silver medal Franco-British Exhibition Silver medal St. Louis. Prize medal Paris, memorial [word], Glasglow: And the grayish green bottle w. 2 circles & made in England on the bottom.

And then the "equipment," these touch us so very deftly,—the waxed paper, the shelf—and drawer—paper, the twine, the bulbs, the silver polish (paste and powder) and the O-Cedar polish and O-Cedar fabric cleaner.

It is well I am writing, not speaking, dear Kathrine, for I falter to be *admitting* that we have—that we are even, hoarding *some* French soap. Could you really expect us to *use* Roger et Gallet almond soap and "green" soap? We still have from 1927 one such cake brought us by my brother from France in 1927! And perfume not only could, but *must* be hoarded. What a bottle, and shiny ribbed stopper, the first perfume that has seemed to have a fine & violet fitfulness.

And what romance, in the box of powder with cerise border and velvet puff white as the driven snow with gold letters on the ribbon. Violette!

That you may not feel we hoard everything, let me say that the magic skin cream performed a miracle this very morning, altering me so that I could appear civilized & needfully delicate at a little talk I gave to Brooklyn College Eng. Students today. If it had not been for the mental preliminaries & typings you would have received word this afternoon. I think of our having the treasures that came yesterday, these strangely perfect things, but I am inarticulately, as it were, thanking you. When we are "recovered" somewhat you will have to hear more of this.

Yours affectionately, Marianne

To Marianne Craig Moore   *CRAIG & CRAIG, Ltd.*
Specialists in Arcana, etc.
Massachusetts, N.Y., Connecticut
May 5, 1942

Dear Craig II,

The firm here, is so happy over your election to the office of Recorder o.p., the senior member repaired to the circus immediately in celebration, wishing fervently that you, as soul and cause of the rejoicing, were also present.

Christian Association, chemistry, music, and rowing, sound like the right thing; and ever since hearing from you in April, I have been happy as a grasshop to know you wished me to have the gloves that were given you. They haven't come, but I felt reluctant to subtract them from your equipment dear Craiglet; so deliberate on this matter of the transfer till you are *very sure* what would be best.

I am delighted you think the wood-weasel looks like such a creature, and there is nothing that interests me so much as curiosity about structure. The expected order is often the best, I think, as in G. [Gilbert] & Sullivan.

> *And yet when no one's near,*
> *We manage to appear*
> *As unsusceptible to fear*
> *As anybody here.*

But I think the title of a poem should emphasize or summarize what is being said, so an impression of repetition is avoided, and rather than begin mechanically, "The Wood-weasel: the wood-weasel emerges," I preferred to make the title an indivisible part of the poem, for the lines are after all not august but in the nature of conversation; or perhaps, an "observation." Nor do I object to having the line begin "weak," or to having what would naturally be the end of the line, come in the middle of the line, because I think of the stanza, rather than the line, as the unit. A man in Baltimore wrote me very politely recently, to say that a prisoner he knows likes my *What Are Years*; but "each stanza conforms to this pattern," he says, "and my ear does not catch a syllabic identity when accents are differently placed in corresponding lines:

6,6,7,9,7,6,6"

In Gerard Hopkins' correspondence with, I think, Robert Bridges, it was brought out that when one follows a ten-syllable line with a 9-syllable line, or in any alternation of odd with even, the main pause comes in the middle of the line, (not at the end); and the long pauses usually between stanzas, come in the middle (of each stanza). I do not try to make this kind of pattern, it is instinctive, and usually I would prefer not to divide words at the end of the lines but am willing to, for sake of the larger and more inclusive symmetry. Anything that it occurs to you to wonder about, that you have time to speak of, do ask me about, Craiglet, for nothing could be a greater help to me in what I might be writing later.

It is like you to take such good care of *The Advocate*. I thought you might like to give it to someone, or tear out the wood-weasel—for we have to write some music for it (!) do we not, when pressure abates? But if you put three cents on it and sent it here, I could easily stow it away.

You are a wonderful animal to have found time to write me, Craiglet. Maybe you could visit these animals overnight sometime? Bear it in mind.

Love from Grandmary and Craig[1]

To Carl Rakosi   *September 7, 1942*

Dear Mr. Rakosi,

I am reluctant to say as I think I ought to say, that I too would be a better character reference for you than literary reference. And I feel I should say also, that a study of inhibition based on your writing does not seem to me auspicious. One assumes a terrible risk in trying to bring major value out of negative procedure.

I say these things with anxiety, because I am, myself, subject to frustration and discouragement and it is against logic and expectation that help has sometimes come to my rescue; so I would urge that you provide if possible, an alternative or alternatives to any specific literary project you have been counting on. It is the unsurmised opening that mends laceration.

Poetry is in some sense a safer staff to lean on than prose. Your prose I think needs rigorizing if you will allow me to say so. If you could take time to get advice on it from someone who really cares, I think it would make a difference in your prospering as a writer. The persons who come to my mind, seem to be deeply engaged in work they could not interrupt, and besides, one hesitates to lay one's problems at another's door without invitation. All I know to suggest is that if you cannot find the enthusiast for this that you need, I shan't take it amiss if you feel like showing me a paper sometime and letting me try to say what in my judgment would make your prose firmer; though what we need is not a comment nor specific revise but

1. MM included a typescript of "Propriety" with detailed chord or melodic notation ("e f e," etc.) for the first stanza and a note in the margin with an alternative scheme: "or Bach's c below middle c/e flat, g. (The Solfeggio is 3 flats and starts, does it not, c e b g?)."

persistent effort under hardened pedagogy. (I need it myself, and might be the blind professing to show you a way that is not the way.)

Sincerely yours,   Marianne Moore

Your letter was forwarded to me to Cummington where I was teaching; but the routine left me no time to say what I have been thinking about here at home and have partly said in this letter.

To William Carlos Williams   *September 7, 1942*

Dear Bill and enviable Grandsire,

I have been thinking about this woman;—found your letter here on our arrival from Cummington where I have been teaching, and revere the way in which you tear essential tissue from your life and part with it to the multitude.[2] I thought at once of *The Nation* and *The New Republic*, so thank you for pre-economizing effort. That matter of the son goes home, and I shall keep the case before me; let me know if a sudden way out is found.

My instinct is to find something automatic and routine—away from aesthetics. Honesty—however dangerous—should be as valuable as radium it seems to me, and I shall make some inquiries; shall ask Miss [Frances] Steloff of the Gotham Book Mart if she can suggest anything, and shall (if you do not stop me on the score of the irritability)—ask the Children's Museum here in Brooklyn, if they need a docent or guide to exhibits. Might package-and-umbrella-checker at a museum be too lowly a possibility. Don't take time to answer if I should proceed with possibilities as suggested.

It surely is a kind of blasphemy as well as beggary, for anyone to live as I do like a squirrel in a squirrel-wheel, away from my natural associates but their books and other books—and the house-cleaning (don't laugh)—are miraculous, don't you think, in maintaining an illusion of vividness; like Dr. Carrell's salt-solution with the industrious dog-heart or is it chicken-heart thriving gratefully in it. We do hope Florence's visit "to the baby" though you expressed it properly, will be a joy and not too strenuous for her. An M.D. in the Navy, junior grade, has a crucial assignment these days; one feels more than one says of your part and Florence's in that chivalry.

You know us quite well I think.   Marianne

2. WCW had shared with MM one of Marcia Nardi's letters; Nardi was a poet whom WCW befriended and promoted, later quoting from her letters in *Paterson*. Her letter mentioned that her son had come to New York in search of work.

To Elizabeth Bishop   *September 8, 1942*

Dear Elizabeth,

How patient you are with us,—remembering to give me Dr. Horney's[3] name, and enlivening us with the upright lace on the bandstand, and trusting me with your exquisite blue manuscript—and distressing though it is because you are so unflinching, your condensed account of the illnesses. I hardly dare ask you,—did you STOP having asthma? and did Mrs. S. [Marjorie Stevens] really get well when you left the dismal atmosphere that was so dangerous?

And then the property battle. What so crushing as RElayed word of one's books, one's things, one's house, in jeopardy. If I had been *in* the house I could not feel more militant about it than I do, it is so dexterous and astute and encouraging, and romantic, and personal, as you changed and perfected it. The garden alone makes one feel as if an all day and all night care-taker should be there. We are happy your books were rescued. Margaret Miller in her glowing, contagious, inaudible way, said (when we actually saw her last July), "I miss Elizabeth's books. I can hardly make any headway with anything I am trying to write, I miss them so." We had been talking about Margaret Friedlander's article on medicine and painting. Do you know about it? If not, there is plenty to lure you home from Mexico. And it helped to make me feel at home at Cummington when you were envied profoundly by certain of my students. (*Without prompting* I might say,—for I do have a habit of talking in quotation-marks.)

Despite every ambition to practice restraint and not damage anything, I shall probably reason with you when we see you,—about the overwhelming effect of your story on me. It is wonderful that I am not too swallowed up by melancholy to be writing you a letter at all. On, I think, the first page, there is an "at least" that has a beautiful deepening effect; and "later appeared in the newspapers" is expertly premonitory. So is the "ocean tragedy so far inland." Your way of selecting unobvious though incontrovertible essential detail makes me feel always: "Now this is the way to write. Why can't others write this way!" But I am stubborn about my little crotchets too; such as "in back of" when "at the back of" seems to me as good.

Well,—you couldn't have studied "under" me at Cummington. My ant-like gatherings of platitude and impropriety would have seemed to you very elementary. But *if* you could have seen the scarlet Indian paintbrushes by the roadside! the blue hills & giant elms; the hooked rug from Nova Scotia! of barn-house-&-chickens,—(in our bedroom)! The chipmunks with reddish fur and the apple trees bending down in garlands under their Kate Greenaway fruit. And James Bridie's little play, *Tobias & the Angel* I liked

3. Karen Horney (1885–1952), psychologist and author of *The Expression of Personality*.

so very much.

The fruit-cake was eaten before we went to Cummington but will *never* be forgotten. It is the one exciting fruit-cake in my experience. And the "Tropaya" is beyond imagining, it was so delicate and invigorating. I haven't had the strength to ask Lester if he gained on what we divided with him; or if he *wasted* it. He hasn't said enough about it and I am suspicious. The Mexican stamps are like visiting Escorial or the National Gallery.

Our love and gratitude, Elizabeth,   Marianne

To Joseph Cornell   *March 26, 1943*

Dear Mr. Cornell,

"Detaining" was understatement.[4] The pleasure given me by work of yours at the Museum of Modern Art, and the Julien Levy Gallery when it was on Madison Avenue, are so great a gift it is scarcely just that these present gifts should be added. Like the powdered rhinoceros horn of the ancients, your pulverizings, recompoundings, and prescribings, are as curative as actual.[5] The self-curling live juggler's ball on the head of the pangolin, and the armadillo's octagonned damascened coat are not more of an armorer's dream than the way in which you have shaped the claws of the pangolin. And the whole when held to the light, with moon and stars added, forms a Bali shadow picture that Berenice might indeed have hesitated to part with.

In being able to conjure up such a scene, you yourself feel, better than I can express, the limitless fire in the eye of the bearded vulture, and the verity of the bouquet in portraits. What fervent text, and beautiful landscapes,—aided so helpfully by the markers you have put in.

Could anything be more appropriate to the Alps than a dedication to the Countess of Pembroke; or more in keeping with Berenice than the maroon label for Volume II with ovoid stars and gold garlands.

My pangolin is reincarnated beyond itself in your juggling scene, and in being placed by the Edmund Scott article, next the George Eliot flower piece. What texture the silk has, behind the bouquet, and how unobtrusive the scrolled ribbon.

It was I no doubt who corrected the *Close-Up* article.[6] It is an injustice to me that you should have had to buy it.

Yours sincerely and with ever grateful wonder,

4. In her note to Charles Henri Ford, MM had remarked, among other things, on Cornell's "detaining tower," *The Tower of Berenice.*

5. MM is describing images Cornell had pasted on his letter to her.

6. Cornell had recalled finding a copy of MM's article "Fiction or Nature" in a secondhand bookstore, with handwritten corrections that he thought might have been her own (to MM, March 23, 1943).

To Elizabeth Bishop   *August 20, 1943*

Dear Elizabeth,

> *like long strings of an instrument*
> *laid on the stream*

has your best touch. Indeed there is in this poem an inescapableness that I would be initiated into if I could. My lines are always "stated" and bald. We (Mother, as well) like the "redoublings," the click click and the two ticks.

I was enmeshed in Mount Holyoke when your letter arrived or I would have been speedier in returning the text. I wonder did you ever meet or know a Miss White at Vassar—in the French Department? She was a pleasure at Mt. H. and a great help to me in conveying meanings,—during the discussion period after my talk. We stayed only a day—arrived the 10th and came home the 12th.

You don't know how pleased and excited we are that you consider trying the lens-cutting work or is that what it is called? That kind of optical work has always attracted me and constantly in the papers a need for it, is stressed. You would be indispensable I know, if you undertook it.

What you say of F. O. Matthiessen's *American Renaissance* is of immense interest,—and instruction to me. I did notice certain reiteratings; and Melville, Whitman and others are almost new ground to me, so I am a weak judge, but I admired the subduing of minutiae and temerariousness of saying explicitly as to what year this or that critic is worth reading & where he lapsed into senility. I feel reprehensible in not owning the book & shall try to imitate you, and conjure up a copy.

If you succeed in finding the Wolff book, do tell me the name and what it is like.

Your portrait is a deep piece of work,—one of Loren [MacIver]'s best! I feel; and though I am superstitious about differing from you in any matter of taste, I instantaneously thought when you said you don't like the jewelry,—that you are wrong. The pin is so unobtrusively faint and does localize the neck line somewhat. The fixity of expression and effect of mentality, are what made such an impression on me.

The maids you have had, read like a Poe tale; and then you would think of sending us preserves! It would be a cruelty on your diligence, Elizabeth. We are too wayward & stumbling to deserve beautiful products or ever such delicacies as you specialize in. And the thought of your packing anything for us, most of all food, makes us sad, we should so like to "look after you,"—if only by being non-existent.

You are just a thought wicked about ushering the rabbit out of the yard backward, or should I say in reverse. It's good I am not there, for any rabbit overcomes me on sight.

You should see the tiny hemlock cones at Holyoke; and hear the bells, which clang sonorously every hour and half hour so you feel as if you were in Europe. The "Entretiens" de Pontigny were transferred to [written above: "inaugurated in"] America last year and economists, dramatists, writers, and musicians present their views & the chairman gives a résumé and protracted discussions follow. I am ashamed to say, Elizabeth, that we are so handicapped by solitude that we were laborious adjuncts, but everyone is kindness and gentleness itself. André Spire did not come. Jacques Maritain has a diet of carrots & vitamins that the "school" could not supply so he was not present and Wallace Stevens arrived just in time for his lecture & left soon after. He is a phenomenon of sensibility and said things that I eagerly look forward to seeing in print—if he can be persuaded to let the lecture be published,—such as "If we are sceptical of rational ideas it is because they do not satisfy reason." "Poetry is personal," "honors can only be for cretins, rogues, and rascals." Then he said something (in what connection I forget), about "a rock that sparkles, a blue sea that lashes, a hemlock in which the sun merely fumbles." He was much consulted and valued but does not seem at all spoiled.

I've been wanting to tell you, Elizabeth, how above myself I feel in your Mexican slippers. I preserved them,—in the Mexican aspect—for a long while but was not wearing them, so I decided to make mules of them! and did and though Mother says I now look like "an inconsequential Arab" I have for the first time, slippers that are perfection. The soles inside and out are so smooth,—more like ivory than leather. And the suede makes our suede seem like sharkskin. I am forgetting things but do not want to delay the poem any longer.

Affectionately,   Marianne

To Hildegarde Watson   *August 27, 1943*

Dear Hildegarde,

Your letter came yesterday—your *letters* I should say, for could anything be more poignant than that line or two about the "little gray thing"; and today the dress and little French thing itself.

When anyone speaks of a knit dress, I think of the cumbrous, knapsack-like rolls of hammock-like yarn that people stuff into knitting-bags in the subway, before hastily getting out, and this delicate zephyr of a thing stirs us to the soul. To think of your not saving it on, for a season or more, till your present blue dresses are not so new! How could you do this? It is so interesting in the shoulders and the diagonals crossing the wrist; and the thread-lace-like, little flat hand made edge of the blouse (or jacket). The very small bits of knitting I have done, that took maybe a summer or a winter, make it almost impossible for me to grasp the fact that the entire skirt is hand knit, and the petunia flare is so chic. Nothing will have to be altered but me; you just can't metamorphose a partial hippopotamus into a dragon fly by a light-beam, so I shall ardently produce my knitting-needles and knit a small triangle—(I guess a tall triangle) for each side of the skirt so the flare will be preserved. (I'll take the skirt along, to be sure to get a really matched kind of wool.) I notice though, that the cashmere feel is different from plain wool, (so I may have to persevere a little about that).

The firm lively elastic is like none I ever saw, and I shall feel very happy with "Aileen Rice" accompanying me about as a talisman.

The ingenious gray fichu-bow, Mother admires and reveres and will surely wear. How French it is. And it too—is a thing that would keep. How unsordid you are, Hildegarde.

I read, spellbound, of the chimpanzee.[7] What a present for soldier son to bestow! and to think of your and Sibley's seeing the creature perform! Someday you must tell it again to us, when we can see and talk with you. And the squirrels raining down pear-skins is so realistic and in its privacy, even more poetic. I can almost see your branches through the window, with now and then a bird there, and these proprietorial squirrels.

As I guess you know, I might not leave it to chance for you to see my elephants and other experiments if it weren't that I feel doubtful of them and inclined to be clandestine. It gives me hope and ambition for some other attempt, to have you imply that you aren't estranged by this piece; and that Sibley isn't. I am so conscious of the weak parts and overdone lines. I can't overcome a sense of restiveness about it all. I suppose you have seen Mr. Cummings' Gravenstein apples? over a wall, the red and the round, Gravensteins fall,

> *with a kind of a blind*
> *big sound*
>   *on the ground.*

I am murdering it, so forget that I quoted it.

Jean Wahl (Professor Jean Wahl I should say) is an elfin and most touching exile, escaped from prison; and just now at Holyoke—one time at lunch,—he said he had asked Mr. Cummings to take part (in the French discussions) but he (Mr. C.) couldn't come. Then he said musingly "He wrote me a letter that itself was like a poem." Nothing more unintrusive, yet tense and industrious could be imagined than this brave young man,— drudging over the executive part of his committee-work and prompt to guide visitors to buildings or to "see the lake"; and as John Bishop said, "despite his griefs and losses, almost gay." After each talk or address, he gave a

---

7. HW had told about a friend, whose soldier son had sent her a chimpanzee from Africa.

résumé and invited discussion, and I was entertained as you may imagine to hear him quote my quotation from Wither (George Wither's motto)—

> *I grow and wither*
> *Both together*
> *I grow and* wee-*zair,*—
> *bow-se to-gez-zair*—

Professor Gustave Cohen, (the medievalist) the Director of all the meetings, was also something to observe and remember. Every day I have wanted to write to you about various aspects of that "French School" as the taxi-man called it. Wallace Stevens, who appeared a few moments before his address and left soon after, made me think of Sibley more than almost anyone could, but Michael. He spoke on "The Poet and His Art" and although he looks nothing like Sibley, his way of launching innuendos in an innocent manner—with a kind of delayed-action fuse—as if some other topic were now in order, so that everybody was inadvertently capsized, made us think of Sibley at once. The sad part was he is so natural and dislikes loudness so much, that about three-fourths of his doctrine and innuendo were lost. He said "If we are sceptical of rational ideas it is because they do not satisfy reason. . . . If the philosopher comes to nothing because of veils, the poet comes to nothing because he succeeds." With regard to spoiling things by dissecting every mystery, he quoted someone's statement: "He that has only clear ideas is surely a fool." And said, "Honors can only be for cretins, rogues, and rascals."

One of the prettiest parts of his lecture was when he illustrated something (for which I have lost the connection) by "a rock that sparkles, a blue sea that lashes, a hemlock in which the sun merely fumbles."

This paper will surely have to be published. As for mine, Hildegarde, it is too childish to be mentioned in the same breath with these lectures for academicians. Jean Wahl and John Bishop "lectured" too.

We stayed only a day & half of 2 days—partly because uneasy on Warner's account; I mean afraid we might miss a chance of seeing or hearing from him (He has just left for Honolulu, is to be with Admiral Nimitz)—and partly because we are disabled by solitude and immediately begin to die when in the environs of any excitement at all,—let alone part of it. I vowed—on our arrival home on Thursday evening—that I would not go adventuring for Mother's "good" in any more Pussy wants a corner ways. Yet an unselfish experiment like that of the Pontigny Committee, leaves a certain memory of exaltation, and a great desire to be of service to those who have suffered, and fought so well. And always the country leaves a charm that brightens as vicissitudes are forgotten. The white pines and infinitesimal hemlock cones, and an occasional squirrel on the speaker's table before anyone human was stirring, we shall remember, and the New England flowers and a huge white birch on the way to the Library. But our dangers were phenomenal and certain backsets in preparation which I don't want even to burden you with vaguely.

To know you and Mrs. Lasell are reviving at camp and feeling the romance of the water and the fir branches, is a joy, if only this rain does not become a steady autumn pour, and makes everything as Llewelyn [Powys] would say "sodden."

We still don't know if your thought of the radio has gone farther than the suggestion fr. Virgil Thomson, and are palpitating with interest.—But one must be superstitiously leisured under certain circumstances. We know that you're badly needed, I would say, from the quality of what we keep hearing.

I should not send you such a letter, Hildegarde. Please rectify it in your mind. Our love and great wish that these days in the woods may be happy ones for you and Mrs. Lasell.

Marianne

We look and look at those enlargements of Mrs. Lasell with the fly-rod and you in Robin Hood costume.

I am not quite sure of the Kennebago address so am sending this to Rochester to be forwarded.

To Lloyd Frankenberg   *September 19, 1943*

Dear Lloyd,

The sense of our visit with you and Loren remained with us and made the debt ours; and we are again grateful to have all the thoughtful data you give us, in your letter setting at rest wrong fears and imaginings.[8] Now that radiant-heaters and wool scarves are being hunted up and used, we can't but wonder what *you* have, and hope you have blankets and warm clothes and that your mental atmosphere too will have in it something you can use, as you suggest, it does. It is so very reassuring to have the detail you give us. We felt much when you were here, that we did not say,—most of all, the fact that to do what everyone is doing and what the whole country says you must do, is easier than to refuse to do it. To be misunderstood and mis-regarded without violence or bitterness, is hardihood such as only the saints have known—and their master. But we realize that awarenesses are mutual and that surely what we were thinking, you felt.

Loren telephoned us soon after our return from Holyoke but we haven't seen her. I wonder if her Bergdorf Goodman windows were finished

8. Frankenberg was a conscientious objector. The letter is addressed to C. P. S. Cam #52, Powellsville, Maryland.

in time for you to see them before you left? I think the one with the horn and the kettledrum and the cello is as truly her exciting best as anything of hers I know—surpassing even the Museum Coffee Concert first curtain that I so urged upon her to "copy"! The colors were so true and unfrantic and the chains of kindergarten-paper fell so elately and free. I stood so long looking and re-looking (at all the windows) I thought I knew them by heart—but remember best the Beethoven-Shostakovitch and this orchestral one. Other people seemed interested too and did some art-criticing, but I was probably the most impassioned visitor that day. It was a study, I felt, how well the clothes were permitted to be seen and how Loren did not force, but created a connection. I hope the store knows enough to be grateful for that—as well as for the intrinsic beauty of the designs.

Our visit to Mount Holyoke was valuable experience. A Miss White, of the French Department at Vassar, was a pleasure, and several members of the Holyoke faculty asked and discussed technical questions after lectures—that were congenial and much to the point,—as, for instance, if a student hasn't a good ear but has imagination and a love of books,—how improve the lack of ear; and of what real good is Semantics? and what really makes a poem good,—a feeling for the read words—or the inward ear irrespective of what readers or listeners do with the result.

John Bishop said many striking things in his lecture of which he let us see the manuscript since we arrived the day after he had given it. He said "The poet is attracted to verse because of the resistance it offers him," and "there is a contest between the rhythm and the metre." And I liked his saying "someone has defined a writer as one to whom writing comes with more difficulty than to ordinary people."

Wallace Stevens was present for part of a day and his lecture was full of exciting things. He said what we are feeling for in poetry, is liberation and "justification," a "new kind of justice we have not known." He quoted someone as saying "He that has only clear ideas is surely a fool" and when asked at the close of his address if he thought the poet had a duty to humanity and should "express his time?" he said "It's as if a musician who is going to write music must introduce something from the daily paper. It simply isn't true." He was friendly and ready to talk with people but did not stay very long,— left with Mr. and Mrs. Church who had brought him with them in their car from Amherst. (I think someone said they had been staying in Amherst.)

The country there at Holyoke is beautiful and a gray squirrel came down from a pine-tree and explored the speakers' table and the lecture-audience chairs each morning before anyone was about. But my mother and I are such city-sparrows, we were back in Brooklyn before our neighbors here knew we had gone away.

We hope the "Friends" will seem to you these days, Lloyd, as they have always seemed to us, like their name and that things will go so well for

Loren. You won't have anxieties or sadness. She sounded as if her courage was at its best the day I talked with her on the telephone. My mother and I shall be thinking of you both and are as you know,

Yours sincerely,   Marianne, and MWM

To Monroe Wheeler   *Oct[ober] 9, 1943*

Dear Monroe,

Having not really looked at the Parke-Bernet catalogue, at your house, the evening of the reception, I was delighted to find ourselves *given* a copy a day or two after and I know you are the giver, & also have sent me the clipping received this morning with the auction book-section in red parenthesis. How you can turn a thought in the direction of the sale without becoming violent, I don't know. You were so wronged by that maneuver of extorting your books to add lustre to the conflagration.

How good it is of you to send the [Alexander] Calder pictures; and since you don't say "on loan," I think you perhaps mean that we may keep them? If only I could be safeguarded somehow from being a menace to the camera. These groups are miraculous if it weren't for me. You are good indeed to say you won't circulate the super-ferocious one. They "piece" or collage pictures so much, couldn't you *excise* me? or cut off me *and* the man at my right rather than suppress the wonderful likeness of Chagall? If only one of his angels had put my hat on, to save us the blemish of a farmer peering at an eclipse! And George Lynes' kindness & skill with lights are remarkable; something I shall ever think back to with wonder & gratitude; but if one can't smile with the mind, what is the most leger of legerdemain.

I have always been excited by pictures—the camera kind even more than the painted kind; and I so thank you for hazarding me *twice* that afternoon. May you be blessed for your faith.

My "support"—photographically speaking, was a presage of what was to come, apparently—though corporeally I suffered *no whit* of damage Tuesday. I have (since the present Tuesday), October fifth, had bursitis and laryngitis,—and *conscienitis* and am paralyzed in soul (on Mother's behalf). I don't see how I could do this to her. To exorcise the threat of bursitis, I treated my left shoulder in a way that intensified the trouble, and no heat in the house did the rest. Mother, surmounting the milk strike by carrying milk for me from a store, and "cheating" herself at meals when there was a shortage through oversight,—by doing my hair, washing my clothes, feeding & breathing for me, has got me started on recovery. We had hoarded your candy thinking we might somehow be eating it with you, but in abandon we have been devouring it—disgraced and chagrinned beyond the telling.

MM with Alexander Calder,
Marc Chagall, and Martha
Graham. Photograph by
George Platt Lynes

MM, photograph by
Lotte Jacobi, c. 1946

When I am competent, and you find an opening that is not merely ignoring some terrible consequence, do tell us of an evening or afternoon when you could come to see us. The long distance here and back makes a self-carefully short visit seem "cold"; but do be persuaded that we want what is best for you.

Of pride, we have none & it seems to me that your living selectly most of the time makes scrambled comfort the less menacing to you as an exception. So maybe you would "come over" some time for supper at "The Green Hedges" (just a door or two from us). The table linen is cotton and the silver is metal without a trace of silver in it or on it but the food is alright and you could give your housekeeper an evening off and not be dying of starvation meanwhile; and perhaps in that way—by coming at 4? eating at 5 or 5.30?, returning after eating—or soon after—not squander too much time away from home or the Museum.

At all events, don't weary of us or think us the "moth of time." It is sad & strange to think what hardships you surmount and battles of the brain, and compel results. The better things go for you the more anxious we are, but I shall muzzle myself regarding your official burdens. I am so ignorant, I am no real use, and I feel the impropriety of *confessing* worries that are probably illusory.

Mother was going to write to you but I circumvented her, and if I have not said anything of what she wanted to say, she will then be writing you herself someday when I am less like an incubus being raised on an eye-dropper.

Affectionately,   Marianne

P.S. We know your care-taking mind and hands. *Don't*, Monroe, let this pitiful story of Icarus suggest *doing* something for us. Refraining on behalf of yourself will be doing for us. Besides, I am emerging and all we need is to hibernate for a time.

To Elizabeth Bishop   *November 16, 1943*

Dear Elizabeth,

The croton leaves? and all your help about my infirmities! I can never lose the sense of excitement with which we saw and felt the magic leaves— but first, about the poems.

You are three-fourths painter always, in whatever you write and it is a triumph for you that in a few lines that great scene of the cliff painting is made vivid and indelible on the mind:—especially the "burnt match sticks" (and of course "sticks" is very able); most of us would mar the lines by saying burnt "matches."

> *Receding for miles on either side*
> *into a flushed, still sky*
> *are overhanging pale blue cliffs,*

Blue is the perfect word,—strangely giving an ice-gray effect, because of the other tones.

The *thought* in the sighing of the aquatic animal is just what is needed; and in prose, "sighing" seems high art. But here it seems not so expert as the rest. ?? Perhaps it is the rhyme, "air," that seems a little facile—(And perhaps I have been ill. Pay no attention to my technical suggestions.)

The term "my great uncle" has a strong fascination & exotic flavor— for me: "My great uncle painted a big picture." ? But I have no confidence— truly none—in my present "ideas."

I like Leroy—best of all the songs;—"but it's not mine" and the change of mood in "I sit and look at our backyard." I also like the chorus (used as a separate song perhaps)? The time has come to call a halt.

"Umbrella" with "Varella" is *enviable*, Elizabeth.

Did you think "And it will take me anywhere" seemed too hackneyed? I am obsessed to accelerate and simplify every phrase I set down.

The leaves and tears poem is really deep and haunting—the black *seeds* taking root like *weeds*. These natural rhymes do one a world of good. And the phantom increase: "Like an army in a dream // the faces seem." Had you thought, I'm sure you had—of using "They're too real to be a dream." ??

Poems are so important and so exciting, it was a hardship, Elizabeth, not to write you immediately; but another "disease" fell on me & Dr. Kramer was obliged to wear me down testing me for sinister things that he feels sure now, I haven't got. (I am about over the cough, but shall surely remember your two remedies.) I am so grateful. Most people say "Have you seen a doctor?" and are entirely without experience of killing off a trouble personally and I feel so much your rushing to my rescue. I had almost asked Mother to cook me a treacly cough mixture of bone-set and flax-seed that we used to take for coughs years ago, I was so desperate. And your papaya-concentrate in water and grape-juice helped at a most crucial time, is still doing us good and entertaining us at the same time, it has so novel a flavor. I have to nibble at my food somewhat timidly even yet, but the sense that I am not on a path of increasing difficulties will make me reliable in no time, I feel sure.

The leaves are beyond anything we have experienced, Elizabeth, as tropical wonders. The cranberry-pink on the alligator-pear green, and the vein-system whereby each vein has a fork of hair fine ends, amaze and amaze us. Strange, too, the underside contrast,—as of a double faced ribbon,—the definite-pattern of cerise and green, then underneath, a cut-leaf maple flush all over. I have seen (in a blur) a movie of croton leaves that came back to me as I thought a while—but the hedge in the movie was a dull magenta blur. I could not have imagined such zebra brilliance of piercing colors. The rose-pink & green leaf, too, seems wonderful—and how strange to find the same "principle" in the cock's feathers—the fine leather texture and hair fine touch of coral at the edge of an otherwise froglike green, the little yellow freckles and parchment yellow translucence of all these leaves are a study. I rather soon laid the special croton leaf between blotters under "John Curry" (which weighs about 6 pounds) to press it & am glad I did for the other one and the cock's feathers have dried considerably and dulled in color. But the day they came they were all alive & I'll never forget the feel & look of the Florentine "leather or antelope-skin" strips of green with the flaming colors.

Have you been well, yourself, Elizabeth? I have the feeling you have not. Your handwriting "rushes" a little (in this last letter) and we are afraid the good weather you had, may have been swallowed up in fog or wind such as we have had. Nothing is so inescapable as clammy cold.

And have the books come? A collector had just arrived and was taking packages the day I mailed [Wilson's] *The Shock of Recognition* & the *Personality* book [Horney's *The Expression of Personality*] back to you, & I was pressured into letting the box go without insuring it. I am a-tremble over this.

I have not seen the Kipling poems but read the Eliot introduction in *The Atlantic Monthly* was it? and have the Auden "mystification." I have read only a little of the Auden, finding it somewhat imbricated for my immature mind but must "cogitate" it out.

I heard Mr. Auden at the Library this week, Elizabeth—reading new poems. It sounds irresistible and I had thought, "if only Elizabeth were going!" But I needed to have heard him the time I first heard him on "The Lyric of Condensed Experience" (at The New School)—to pardon him for this. I am probably anaemic, but it seemed coarse. He conscientiously read work in progress or just finished—something on a baby's animality (or worm-like selfishness) and some troubled sonnets, & "Prospero to Ariel"—part of a commentary on *The Tempest,* or as he said "part of a long poem on *The Tempest* I am writing." I am bound to Mr. Auden by "hoops of steel" and can "understand" any misfortune,—in fact like him the better for his adversities; & for his indomitableness, despite the sadness to which I know he couldn't but be subject. But it was not an evening for you to have been listening.

I am also penalized for my wickedness (in going to things when I am not able) for several friends I saw, think I am playing possum & just don't want to see them! But one must recover from his disgraces as well as from his wounds.

We don't see Lester, he is so held down by the heavy hours at the plant, but he telephoned yesterday evening to say that his mother (who was here last week) is ill & had gone home ill, with an acute kind of indigestion. I was alarmed lest she had got it from me but Lester kindly said she was taken sick two or three days after being here (& going to the Green Hedges with me). I couldn't eat that night & had *rudely* tried to save Mrs. L. from risking her strength by a trip over here—but she seems worried about Lester & had come anyhow. These things do make one sad. Lester's parents have had nothing but illness year after year. Mother & I send you love, Elizabeth. Do tell us how you are. *Don't suppress things, because of the distance.* And forgive me for writing about the poem.

Please thank "*Marjorie*" [Stevens] for the word about the organdy. I am delighted. A great weight (in the realm of vanity) is off my mind,—about the dress.

To Lloyd Frankenberg   *December 26, 1943*

Dear Lloyd,

Surely you are right; these "things that are stated without being said" are the most valuable, and even if to me the outward war is part of the inner war, it is a help to me that you should find my stanzas sufficiently real for you to use them and dwell on them.[9] A poem is not a poem, surely, unless there is a margin of undidactic implication,—an area which the reader can make his own. Nor did you distort me. I believe that the invisible and the sword of the spirit could and *shall* make the bayonet and the machine-gun impossible.

(In my simplicity, I see no better way than to sin,—with the enemy;—that is, accept the blasphemy of murder, that holiness may not be left to the mercy of what is not mercy.) One's reasoning is a strange thing; is really *not* reason, is a mingling of resistances, unperceptiveness, un-coordination and helplessness. You will pardon my rudimentariness.

My mother and I are ever your debtors, for what you have written me. How thankful we are that you are *permitted* to write and to think. How glad we are, that you have an acquaintance there, in your regulation activities, such as Mario Collaci. I shall remember the name,—backward though I am in semantics.

9. LF had responded in a letter to MM's "In Distrust of Merits."

I gave my deepest concentration to Loren's project, but it is nothing compared with my wish for you both. I was not able to be at peace a few days ago, when Loren telephoned,—and did not really talk with her, because we were under stress at the time. Mother when out on an errand Saturday, a week ago, fell and hurt her head on the part of it where she had had shingles. But do not dwell on this, all is becoming right with us. Vigilance & prompt antidotes of the swelling & inflammation, delivered us from what threatened to be desperation. We have a most wonderful doctor, and as you know, I cannot feel that we are alone in our battles. A stronger presence endows us with a power that we would declare is impossible to us. I know you have the sense of this also. Mother is greatly improved & Christmas— against every auspice—was happy and vibrant with hope. We revere your quiet attitude to your "position," Lloyd. Only fortitude is content to be inglorious.

May these strange days be not without good in them for you, and gratitude despite hardships.

Sincerely yours,   Marianne Moore

P.S. A note from Jane Ward, one of my Cummington students, speaks of you and Loren—says what a pleasure it was to meet Loren recently—of how David Newton introduced her, (Jane) and how she has "long been an admirer of *The Red Kite.*"

I have been an admirer of Jane ever since being at Cummington and it does me good to know that in a sense she is a friend of yours and Loren's. (She wrote an unforgettable story of a young idealist, a Japanese she knew in college,—

M. M.

fictitiously entitled "Kenzo" but I do not know that it has been published.)

To John Warner Moore   *March 9, [1944]*

Dearest Bible,

I have been pointing you out on the map to Bear, to the best of my ability. Those religious sacred names of islands is very affecting. FOR,—we get mail!!! one airmail letter this morning.

We are happy that you can say you are being fed and given safe water and every courtesy.

Yesterday I was "to town" exchanging the two shirts I got Bear. The creature preferred two cottons (with long sleeves) like two I had got for myself and they are "army rejects" so it is not only a soldier of the sea but a soldier of the land. You know you give it "sea" shirts.

I got, to my joy, at Best's a rabbit-hair and wool little kind of Norfolk jacket for Bear $7.00; then I was afraid to bring it home but the animal is much taken with it and it looks good on her; malachite green, one of its favorite colors. (Her light blue ribbed sweater is too unfortunate looking even to give away and the black cashmere won't do for everything. She herself said we could replace it, so I got active.)

Kathrine [Jones] has just sent us $7.00 worth of airmail envelopes and $3 worth of postage, so you should hear from us! Also, a beautiful little pallet-knife, (we do not know what for).

I have been—when on the eggs—and it is all too little, working on Cummings' book *One Times One* (*1 × 1*) as he prints it and am about through with it. My Swedish poem came out today, in *The Nation,* with the change I had wanted. But Mr. Putnam of Macmillan thinks I changed it for the worse and I wish I knew what you think. At all events I ask you: if you think it seems like burlesque to name the Jews so abruptly after the folk-dance?[10]

> *green shelf*
> *on shelf fanning out by itself;*
> *mirth's false-mouthed jugs drunk from in vain, that*
> *pour enough to drown one; the four-*
>
> *mouthed jugs and hand-spun carriage-rugs,*

OR

> *green shelf*
> *on shelf fanning out by itself;*
> *The deft white-stockinged dance in thick-soled*
> *shoes! Denmark's sanctuaried Jews!*
>
> *The puzzle-jugs and hand-spun rugs,*

It seems to me that the abrupt style introduces a series of peremptorinesses that help the poem a good deal but am not sure. You have so much on you, it is not right to strain your mind so don't strive to decide. I'll let Macmillan have it the way they want it. One has to see the poem as a whole, to know.

Just now I get two manuscripts that aren't "good" to advise Macmillan about, but I do not fear them. Then I have the Pavlova article to do. It is bright sunny weather and Bear can eat regular food and her head looks natural (on the forehead) though slightly flushed. We are not writing you 3 times a week lest you be bewildered with mail you can't read when you get back, but shall write you twice a week at a peradventure.

Dearest love, Rat

10. MM wrote in the margin next to the poem: "Disregard it if there is no time for it."

To H.D.   *March 13, 1944*

Two letters from Hilda! dear H.; two from Bryher! This "just a line" about the Valentine party and the pineapple, the "huge armadillo thing" from Madrid have a world of meaning for us, crushed as we are that you should be bombed and in mortal danger on and on; with noises that in themselves are desperation. The crashes of an August storm make one cower, let alone this *intentional* inferno. *The Times* says, "a few more weeks" should mark the end of it. And one night is a lifetime! And well we know the tension you must have been under with an agéd, bereft guest whose sadness you couldn't cure, as it were begging that you do it, or at least be *there*. Perdita and her "Americans" sounds very nice; one day we shall be hearing something of [the] detail of it? I do think we shall.

I think, Hilda, I may be able to ferret out something about Central America. Travellers do not always know what to tell one but I have heard from several that there is a heaven of beauty and safety and climate and interest, in the mountains above Mexico City. I *think* this is so. I am suspicious of Yucatán; I feel as if Wallace Stevens may have imagined the region and that it would be all sunstroke and horned toads. Illness the winter long prevented me from seeing several movies of Mexico and S. America but I shall accost Raymond Whitcomb or some travel bureau and see what is recommended. I finally wrote Mr. Pell and he indeed reveres your writing—as well as the possession of it; I shall see how heavy the correspondence is, for you ought to have it. *I assume that you compare statements with results?* financially. I am a miserably poor bully.

And I was nothing at all, at the Library; I did not "read"; I discussed points of technique that had arrested my attention—in archaic examples—of verse mainly; and wore a white blouse, a rough-woven tan skirt made from an English coat, and the black velvet jacket I wore at the Brevoort at B's dinner-party if you remember? May Sarton is surely kindly, in her illusions and loyalties. And I do not *yet* know what you, yourself, read; I know it was good, that is all. Be sure to say when you are writing, or ask Bryher perhaps, to just give me the title. It is most beautiful of you and Bryher, to receive as if they had life in them, our little greetings, so late and so small, and to make it seem as if there were a kind of benefit in the laggard transmitting of our love and thought.

We do pray that when this comes, the air will be safe, and that you can truly come to America, North and South.

M.

To John Warner Moore   *Bear Sanctuary   April 21 [1944]*

Dearest Elephant-Ears,

Your brother is back from Bryn Mawr. You would have gazed with benign pussy-eyes on Mr. Auden who sprang out of the Bryn Mawr local with me at 30th St., dashed down through the tunnel, up the escalator, & held the New York train for me, which came in simultaneous with our local train. Otherwise I would have been an hour later reaching home & the Bear would have been sitting up worrying instead of me popping in at 10:30 right as a trivet. I of course was dashing after him, but he carried the brief case and kep' the train from starting. His having the briefcase, made it easy for me to manage my dress & cape.

Well, Bible, you know how these journeys to halls of learning tremble an animal & require forethought of a speaking & *dressing* variety. Everything was ideal; Miss Finch met me with the car. Mr. Auden and a number of the Swarthmore faculty, a Dr. Mandelbaum & his wife, joined me at 30th Street station & the Paoli local was so crowded there was a seat only for one. A commuter gave me his seat, then people got out, & we all sat facing. Mr. Auden's father is in charge of a hospital in Birmingham, England. His mother died in 1941. He is truly a "genius" & a shrewd one; & gave a wonderful course of lectures in N.Y. He teaches both at Bryn Mawr & Swarthmore. T.S. published him in England, & Random House publishes him here, & I wrote a recommendation for him to the Guggenheim Foundation. By coming on that early train which he & the Mandelbaums took, he had to put in an hour or so at Bryn Mawr & then stay for dinner till 7:39 but seemed very willing to. I was a little put out with Miss Finch for not bringing us *all* to the college in the car but she is a level-headed little animal, in her light gray goatskin jacket & raspberry wool dress to the knees, & *very firm* & I think is slightly "opposed" to Mr. Auden for edging away & not accepting her dinner invitation till the last minute. He meanwhile takes to Miss Donnelly but didn't address a remark to Miss Finch all through dinner. These little pussy-feelings, are amusing & unavoidable perhaps. A Miss Finch delivered me over to a Miss Henderson who wanted to "record" me in Pembroke East basement. They have laid a stone walk along the campus side of Pembroke East under the window of my old room & the campus looked very very pretty. Miss Henderson is much deplored by Miss Donnelly for being over self-determined in her chosen field & I "feel the same." My "Carriage from Sweden" sounded as if a drunken falsetto bullfrog had assayed to sing. So I swelled up my frog chest & vowed I would beat the devil at his own game & had a wonderful success in my 3rd attempt. I was hoping to mend 2 bad spots & read my Strawberry & kiwi when Miss Finch peered through the crack at the side of the shade. (Miss H. had turned a little chicken-coop button on the door so no one could come in.) We let Miss Finch in & she gathered my effects & took me away to the car saying she would bring me back but she must get Miss Donnelly to the tea at the deanery. Miss H. said "you could leave Miss Moore here." "But I want her to see Miss Donnelly. It's her only chance," said Miss Finch, meaning the HOUSE, & we never got back. I regard this as a deliverance, for Harvard is as better than Miss H. as day is than night. Well, the drive to "New Palace" was like something in a book, all very handsome, quiet, stone colonial quaker houses, with tall trees & grounds with rocks—like Manchester by the Sea in Massachusetts. Miss Finch built this house for Miss Donnelly. It is 2-stories high with a stone porch at the back & matchless forest trees (greatly thinned) sloping up hill at the back of the house, with some natural wild flowers (all in bloom) re-inforced by transplanted ones, hepaticas, grape hyacinths, violets, blood root, & so on. On the stone porch are wire chairs like Alison's—& the house inside is like his, except the beds had no testers with ball-fringe, & is more learned, with whole walls of bookcases & every chair & picture hand-picked. I'd give my eyes if Bee & Johnny & the others could see it. It is more Oxford & Harvard even than Mr. Spencer's house. Miss Donnelly had em-broidered a burlap rug for Miss Finch's bedside of an elephant I almost thought I should bring home with me. In the living room was a little an-cient table six inches wide with drop leaves, for tea, & pale yellow roses on a table & large pink azaleas on the window sill. BUT the house had the cold-ness of an English church & I was almost in fear of my life even to be led through it for a fleeting inspection. Each un 'em, Miss F. & Miss Donnelly, has a little study opening onto the stone porch. Stepping out, the sunshine & mild summer air were like a Medicine, after the house & as we reached the Deanery & went in Miss Donnelly said "this house is always *dread*fully overheated." How fortunate I thought. Miss Finch has a superb little car with 2 seats upholstered in fawn cloth with every kind of nickel & chrome on the dashboard & wheel, & drives most astutely, small & childlike though she is in build.

The Deanery was THRONGED with students & a pleasing bevy they are, in costly dresses of silk, and silver necklaces & French embroidered vests & collars & so on. Four or five (maybe 10) members of the Faculty were there & the immense drawing room was crowded. The tea was really good & the cakes & cookies home made. Miss Donnelly introduced my talk. You would have wept at such generosity. "Miss Moore has been called America's fore-most poet," she this & that. I remember Miss Thomas—with a copy of *The Lantern* in her hand—in that blue room—saying to me, "This is the most promising work by any of our English students" etc. She spoke for some time about how my choice of words & craftsmanship were perfect, how T.S. had said with "his fullest weight of authority, 'her work is part of the durable body of our literature.'"

After my talk, hordes & hordes of students were led up,—3 nuns from

Rosemont & their students, a party of girls from Swarthmore, older students, graduate students, President McBride just returned from Baltimore (was among the faculty), two of Miss Donnelly's classmates.

After the talk, a cocktail party in the "blue" room, & Mrs. de Laguna & friends of Dr. Saunders & George Lyne's sister-in-law from the Shipley Schools & various neighbors of the college were led forward.

Dinner followed, in the room where we had had tea [with] Miss Donnelly, Miss Woodruff of the English faculty, Mr. Auden & Miss [Laurence] Stapleton. Miss Stapleton is a Smith graduate—one of the "brilliant" members of the Faculty. She was wonderfully kind about my talk, said "All your statements are new & fresh and at the same time grains of common sense. You dwell just long enough on each topic & hold the attention all the time. It's a gift & that means you must use it."

Dinner was an apex on cookery—a strange & pleasing soup,—a kind of vegetable broth,—broiled chicken, large young lima beans, potatoes, ice cream with fresh strawberry sauce, & ginger snaps. I was then conveyed to the train with Mr. Auden, by Miss Finch—& we stood talking till our train came. Then as you know, Mr. Auden wafted me onto my NY train at 30th St. The trains are badly crowded but I had a good seat both going & coming, & such comfortable downy seats & so *clean* that if I were a bum & could afford it I would spend my time travelling & just live on the train.

I never saw the country so beautiful, all the willow trees like green silk hair, all the lawns green. At Bryn Mawr there were carpets of giant pansies on some of the grounds flanking the walks up to the door.

Say I was not HAPPY to see my Cub when I got here at 10:30—the creature running out to the door with an eager smile to meet me. The sun was brilliant all day yesterday. Today it rains & is *raw & cold*. I must be an Israelite, Bible, like you learn about in Exodus.

I was urged & begged to come again to stay overnight;—Mr. Auden earnestly invited me to come to Swarthmore. When, (knowing he is poor & seeing his brand new tweed coat & *very* old trousers & shoes,) I begged him to take money for his transportation as my guest,—he said, "It was a treat,—nothing could *induce* me to let you do it." So I did not thrust it on him.

On arriving home, I saw a strange dress on Bear's bed,—a handsome beige wool dress; & behold Renée has sent it (& an "ensemble" beige & brown reversible coat), "to wear on nasty days to save your good things"; Bear eyed them coldly & said "I don't like to be given to." But I am dang glad of the dress for it liberates my new navy blue dress from Hildegarde so I can give it to Bear who looks good in it & is kind of shabby in her equipment. Renée's daughter Constance has been divorced & has got so thin she can't wear the dress! Sad. Well Bible, by my elephant hairs—I must write & thank Renée.

Dearest love, Rat

Hildegarde's blue dress was much extolled by Miss F. & Miss Donnelly.

To W. H. Auden   *October 12, 1944*

Dear Mr. Auden,

What kindness—that you should have defended not only my repudiated manuscript but my present booklet. I look forward eagerly to this review, which you too unselfsparingly wrote, I am sure, despite many pressures.

Regarding my turned down material, last spring Cummington Press offered to publish certain prose of mine—reviews of Wallace Stevens, E. E. Cummings, Gertrude Stein, T. S. Eliot, my review of [Auden's] *The Double Man*, and one or two other papers. Macmillan's have priority in publishing work of mine and since they asked to see the prose, I submitted it, suggesting that it perhaps be issued together with this present verse of mine which the Company was about to publish. The prose was returned as not being a judicious companion piece for the verse; but also, I suspect, as not being of crucial interest. That Mr. [Herbert] Weinstock—for Alfred Knopf—suggested recently that I submit work, is undoubtedly the result of your valor. Mentioning to Mr. Putnam of Macmillan's, that I thought of submitting my rejected prose to Alfred Knopf, Mr. Putnam has persuaded me to submit it to Macmillan again and I plan to do this presently.

It is indeed wasting you to intrude market-gardening of this kind on you but can I ever say how acutely I feel your courage for me? and your not stopping with courage but doing hard work.

I have been re-pondering *For the Time Being*, which came to me some days ago from Random House, perhaps at your suggestion. The dilemma— the scourge if it is not blasphemous to speak so—of awareness, has never been better expressed than in these thoughts of yours about anxiety and "heaven" and the mortal stress of being obliged to do what one does, alone. Your work has strength and your art is safe so long as you are safe,—you are well, I mean, and can write. It does not need to be reviewed; but feeling impelled to say certain things, I asked *The New Republic* if I might review you and finding that you had been reviewed, asked if *The Nation* had reviewed this book and found that it is being reviewed by Mr. [F. W.] Dupee, so my urgencies must wait.

Your concern for her penetrates my mother deeply. I am tempted to tell you certain things about the artistry of your book, that she has said, and the privateness of the prose rhythm, but shall not delay you longer; nor try to say what both my mother and I feel about your having caught the train at 30th Street station for me last April.

Sincerely yours,

I deplore typed letters but in being one's talkative, spare you penmanship.

To John Warner Moore *Oct[ober] 31 [19]44*

My indomitable and touching Bible Drake, fawned upon incessantly and capsized by the tongue of a couple of doting bruins, you are very invigorating & strengthening in the matter of these "honors." We figure the U. of Chicago i.e. Pres. (Hutchins & Committee) are having some trouble over me and me not going to Chicago;—for we don't hear from them. Cub said very pluckily today, "I'm sorry you didn't say you would go." But I SAY the check for the [Harriet Monroe Memorial] award should have CAME in the letter of announcement. Any symbolic or spiritual bequest *should* NOT be a big, external hullaballoo—and occasion for egotistical emphasis on clothes and personalities. Furthermore it's unpatriotic & crass to travel unnecessarily & Harriet Monroe was intensely patriotic & conscientious.

The judges, Mr. Zabel, Allen Tate, & Louise Bogan will be good & sore if the Award is NOT given me but I feel calm about it. I'll "mind" if I am belted down & *refused* the Award. *Still*, it was offered. And I would hate to relinquish the "bones" when I earn nothing and have to be maintained like a hairless caterpillar, but a sense of the right and wrong in this, helps one bear the results.

The Library of Congress matter, Bible, is somewhat misleading. It SOUNDS good, and if Washington or Jefferson or Lincoln or John Hay and a "true," stalwart committee were there in Washington I would have offered to serve from a distance even without being considered officially of the Committee for I would be sure of the high motives of all concerned. As it is, Carl Sandburg, Mark Van Doren & I would perhaps be the only citizens without an axe to grind. "Archibald" is serviceable and not corrupt but his very eyes are conditioned by the sense of promotion and benefice. It's like getting to be Pope, you gotta tend to business for heaven *& earth simultaneous.* Allen Tate has been a starved dog so long, all he can think of is breathing freely in a financial way & being among the elect—T.S. & the Harvards. I am positive Archibald MacLeish signed his letter "Archie MacLeish" in gratitude to me for not growling at him as at a hireling & because he smells T.S. & Wallace Stevens on me. If I felt I could overset graft & clean house in Washington I'd "join," but I'd be too much thwarted, I'm afraid.

Well, Bible, in the meantime, my little literary affairs are prospering all too good. Four letters lay there on the dining room table awaiting my activity about a copy of my book or an autograph & these enthusiasts are not grafting, they are having copies sent or offering to pay. Yesterday I went to N.Y. to see a young fellow (José Rodriguez-Feo) of Havana who is starting a quarterly *Origenes*. He was a student of F. O. Matthiessen at Harvard a year or so ago & says the "O" in F. O. M. . . . is just added arbitrarily by him,

Matthiessen, & stands for nothing (like Felix Gygax's Xerxes).[11] Most amusing Mr. Rodriguez-Feo hearing of my liking for Mr. M.'s work & not being able to get *American Renaissance,*—sent me a copy from Brentano's and in the front is a quotation from *King Lear* I had forgotten was there:

> *Men must endure*
> *Their going hence even as their coming hither:*
> *Ripeness is all.*

Shakespeare is certainly hard to beat.

This young fellow is poor, and his mother is a widow & they were much hurt by the recent hurricane in Cuba,—(worse than the 1926 one even, Mr. R. F. says)—and since *American Renaissance* is $5.00 I am going to repay the boy—send him the cash when he gets home. He had said if he found a copy he would send it to me,—and perhaps I would send him *What Are Years?* in exchange! I was talking to him at the Museum of Modern Art—53rd St. next St. Thomas's church & Monroe came in as I was about leaving. Monroe was all kindness, sat down & talked, & then led us into the exhibition early—it doesn't open till 2 o'clock—and had the lights turned on—and was *most* hearty. He looks anything but strong,—thin and small and worn down but didn't admit to ailing. (Too much excitement on him, I guess.)

Also, yesterday, Kathrine [Jones] sent us a lot of things, a vast number of stockings which we can use (but not till 1948 I would say, she has already sent us so many). A rayon scarf black & white (too old for Bear) & a blue plush one for me, and a pair of very fine, soft, washable BLACK "peccary pigskin" gloves, 6¼ in size. YOU got Bear in 1927, a remarkable pair of black kid in London of super quality & texture. These, Bear has, & they have not become lavender at the tips, or worn at any point, or thin but they are so good, she won't wear them unless one puts the bite on her. So I was "happy" to get these "regular" gloves that she can wear more careless, & they fit her exactly. Nowadays a 6¼ seems large enough. Maybe the skins are more elastic.

If *you* "scratch around" for a present, Bible, I'll set a mechanical alligator tick tocking under your desk and scare the paws off you. You DID give me a present last summer, *early,* when my Cub dwindled and needed a few tender pigeons to revive it—& the bracelet,—which I show to everybody as sent by my brother, and then this $25.00 for my book plus the 125 per month. Oh yes, and the removal of the Bear's wart was a present that I am ever aware of. The wart is GONE.

11. Gygax was a friend of JWM's on the USS *Mississippi* and was flag secretary to Admiral Hughes when he was commander in chief of the U.S. fleet. MM was misinformed about Matthiessen, whose middle name was Otto.

Tell Porker if I hear the word "distinguished" outen his trap, I'll go for him like I saw a small crocodile go for crayfish & frogs in a river in Venezuela last night. I went to a wonderful movie. Here, this crocodile of a light fawn brown, was shown waking up in the morning among the arum lilies & giant foliage of a small river. He blinked, opened his eyes & hastened off over the mud for food, tail-dragging gracefully & his rather small legs manfully straining to take big steps on the ooze as he made for the current. I haven't ever seen more vivid pictures. They was 4 big blue & yellow macaws on a tree, & I saw a young ocelot & some beautiful little anteaters covered with pale wool, devouring termites & stinging ants. The ants can't penetrate the wool. Well, Bible—we are THANKFUL your nights are cooler. Have you been bothered by mosquitoes? I hope not, & that your net works.

Dearest love,   Rat

To William Carlos Williams   *November 12, 1944*

Dear William:

If I had known all that is in your book—immensities reduced to a word—I would have feared to send you mine, and you can call it "exchanging books"; which is characteristic.[12]

For your touching statement about your mother there are no words. And Florence! A household right at hand, "for the duration," and Paul on a destroyer, anywhere but at hand. It's colossal.

I think you are wrong about Robert Frost. I think the death of his son was like an earthquake that has left fissures his impulses can't bridge; that he might want badly to have your books, and lose heart before doing anything about it.

As for Kenneth Rexroth, "sticks and stones" sound right to me—they're what the bower-bird uses (?)—and I shall connect with *The Phoenix and the Tortoise* at the first opportunity. I respect Byron Vazakas and like him as a person; and feel too, in him, an auspicious hatred of what does not quiver and speak for him privately; but I saw his work in too negative a way. You electrify me by what you say of him as an inventor of form. Wallace Gould, I remember, yes; but Byron Vazakas seems to me more real; more rooted.[13]

Wallace Stevens is beyond fathoming, he is so strange; it is as if he had a morbid secret he would rather perish than disclose and just as he tells it

12. MM sent WCW *Nevertheless;* he had sent her *The Wedge.*

13. Rexroth (1905–1982), Vazakas (1905–), and Gould (1882–1940), American poets.

in a perambulator in front of a shoestore which had swallowed the mother. One mistake, was expecting too much of Mr. Pickwick — in the course of a fervently kind Christmas Eve celebration. How much more like the Alapitattitott ornament in our kitchen Thackeray (to return to him again) seems: "Mrs Bayard Taylor is here. Der ein Hero ist." A gallant bearded man with a handsome face. He is very like Francis I, so we think, and we like him even better. Ah! America if your sons are all gallant gentlemen like this one, if your daughters ample ladies like his sisters I wonder, — what profound remark shall I make now?"

My beloved, & quote Thackeray again,

please don't hold anything against me, if I did wrong in making it possible for Vogue to persecute you. A girl in the tiniest, most harmless voice I have ever heard, answered the telephone for Mrs Frank Ronalds so well named, who was "out." Please keep well, and even though we are literally hidden under the greatness of our Christmas, don't forget us. A real gold angel, from Margaret Miller, adds to our smallness and breathless excitement. (Of china, with crimson "V" bodice and blue skirt and gold wings!) Love to you both.
M.

Printed version on pages 393–4

MM, photograph by
Arthur Steiner, 1938

MM and Mary Warner
Moore,
by Cecil Beaton, 1946

out in his sleep, he changes into an uncontradictable judiciary with a gown and a gavel and you are embarrassed to have heard anything.

> *His firm stanzas hang like hives in hell*
> *Or what hell was, since now both heaven and hell*
> *Are one, and here, O terra infidel.*

(Piece III in his "Esthétique du Mal," *Kenyon Review*, Autumn issue). Whatever this is saying, it is impossible to gainsay.?

I became careless and subscribed to the Chapel Hill *Quarterly* [*Review of Literature*], so will see your group,—I am glad to say. You have given me so much, I would feel a certain despair at encouraging you to part with yet more. I have seen some of T. [Theodore] Weiss's criticism and liked it.

Your best to my mother is certainly the word and the deed. "*Never*," she said, "have you had such a letter," as I read her about "the emptiness that goes with all good," "the pseudo-rock" and "we convince only those who were of themselves disposed to be convinced." And the tenant farmers. And then, your helping me with the carriage from Sweden. I not only am ignorant but go to a great deal of trouble to publish my ignorance. I had thought of Norway and Sweden as somewhat synonymous!!! Wonderful indeed,—that about yourself and "a dandelion seed floating." But it *is* floating where it ought to be, in your work, every time. Your introduction and what you say of a Sperry[14] and an artist and the part about distortion, and the manner—"One doesn't seek beauty," "So be it." If this is not the penicillin for all quackeries, I don't know what is. "In Chains," and "Prelude to Winter" are as perfect as anything you ever did. "Burning the Christmas Greens," each time I read it, seems like the suspense of a fairytale. "It can't disappoint me after all this." And it doesn't. I stifle comment because everything is too good; comment seems an offense.

Our love to you and Florence.   Marianne

Oh yes and the "oyster without a shell" a "brain without a skull"!

To John Warner Moore   *Jan[uary] 8 Monday [1945]*

Well, Bible,

Big snow, all day yesterday—old-fashioned steady fine-flaked blizzard & very pretty.

We have been industriously answering letters & Xmas cards. Aunt Ann says she "overheard the head of the Vassar bookshop who likes a quick

---

14. Elmer Ambrose Sperry (1860–1930), American inventor known for his electrical devices. WCW implicitly compared an artist to an inventor, noting that all either "can do is to drive toward his purpose, in the nature of his materials."

turnover," say she couldn't get enough copies of *Nevertheless.* She asks where and how Warner is. Says she is to retire in June but go on living in her house (she built) at Vassar.

Elizabeth Bishop besought a recommendation from me of her to Houghton Mifflin, is trying for their $1000 Award in Poetry. And I had no trouble with the thing at all!

The war staggers belief and paralyzes pity. The stupendous acts of heroism of poor solitary men—"grease monkeys" & orderlies & nurses. As one of the Bastogne commanders said, "There are no heroes, they are all heroes."

We don't hear a word of Johnny but infer that his initial radar training is going on—is routine and not too hard. Being among boys of picked intelligence ought to do him incalculable good.

We are certainly moving closer to Japan in the Philippines. A good map in today's paper we are saving so you can comment presently & we can picture "the route" since you left Pearl as you call it.

Dearest love,   Fangs

To George Plank   *March 23, 1945*

Dear George,

Of the letter you wrote Mother, in which you spoke of coming to be with your sister, what can one say. It was to us like one of the Gospels. To think your being over-brave for England—as Bryher says was the case—and because of that giving, suffer and all but die. I have always known that suffering is able to bless us, if we will let it. But how stern the days in which we "let it." Patience, reverence, gratitude, faith; it seems as if we cannot have them easily.

Again you help us by your astonishing verdict that one place is not as good as another! A little dampness, a cruel V. bomb, a shortage of everything, these surely are something apart from moral atmosphere, from what in "a Throne of stars, Thunders above." ! And we do hope, George, that England will soon be "liberated" and that you will be there when you wish to be, amid your books and your cowslips and your ash trees and your devoted friends. Bryher, I feel, must be happy, if not in every way, in some ways,—for her unmeasured giving and her pride in others, and her unselfpitying courage, and her indomitable carefulness of others in small things. I think you feel this.

I am grateful that you can see good in my little book. Thinking we might have a word with you when you were in America, I had hoped to offer you a copy. To my mystification, there now are no copies and I so thank you for having one, and for reassuring me about the book. What can one see but faults when a piece of work is irremediably in print? Indeed, I can't trust myself to look into the book.

It is hard, indeed, that you should lose pounds and pounds, in beautiful Asheville. I haven't been there, have merely heard of the wholesome climate and scenic beauty. And what sorrow, that your sister's brave, idealistic, too-useful husband should have had to pay for his idealism by dying,—when needed so much by your sister & by you—for her—and by countless others.

It is March, and in February we looked to March as our benefactor. Now we look forward to April as our friend, for truly the winter has been a puzzle. I am ashamed to be saying so nearly the same thing, year after year. It is as if we are ill on purpose to be sympathized with but this time we were so ambitious as to follow minor illness with the real thing, and we now have a nurse. On the door is a surly notice in red crayon—"Do Not RING or *Knock*. Leave package or other thing *inside apartment door*." We let the telephone ring. (Could even Socrates have mustered equanimity to do that!) We pay no attention when a delegate from a charitable organization—or a bill-collecting milkman—does ring the bell. We are rationed as to letter-writing, and dark threats are concentrated on us when, say, three notes lie waiting in the hallway to be mailed. But I think, I hope, we shall become human and be natural and be able to have a visit from you in April. Could you perhaps write us where we could reach you by telephone or letter when you are in New York? In hopefulness I would say, the best way of getting here is by *8th Ave. Independent Subway Line:*—an "A" Express downtown to Lafayette Station Brooklyn. You might have to take an F train (downtown) to connect with the A train.

Our ever live gratitude to you, George.　　Marianne

To Elizabeth Mayer　　*April 30, 1945*

Dear Mrs. Mayer,

The Chinese book is an invitation to perfection, a constant poem, is it not,—the crescent moon "one stroke less than the moon," the three beats of the heart set down like the footsteps of some woodland creature, the moon added to the sun to represent "brilliant" and the inexpressible brush effects in the writing. I have admired Chinese writing all my life. It is a joy to have this book and to be able to study the precision and apparent simplicity of the English wording. I do thank you. The vermillion wrapper with flakes of gold on it is a treasure in itself. And the doubled paper with its strange texture so suits the preponderance of space on the pages. It makes me think of the mushroom texture, or rather it feels as a mushroom looks.

I am sad to know your children must all be away from you. How you can give your mind to translating or to writing such thoughtful and kind letters as you write, I do not know. But I too feel what you say,—"the quiet luminous little world, full of faith and tradition," in the story. When you first wrote me, your mention by accident of 2200 words led me to feel I could surely undertake the work, or try to give you my view of the English phrasing. Then when I saw it is 22000 words I was afraid I might not be able to do so much, and I was very slow with the first part,—could not seem to get that part about the festivals unnoticeable enough and reverent enough—and wonder still if those first pages will do,—especially the sentence about old age and the cheering afterglow of Christmas. Now I find these later pages very much simpler and quicker; although I again settle down to an insoluble problem where you render the "sky pattern" of the nails so poetically. "Constellation" is the equivalent I suppose but "starry sky-pattern" is much better and I think in such cases a little redundance to get the poetic effect, is unavoidable. That commentary on the Shoemaker's evolution and worldly triumph—where the coat and the grey hat are mentioned—, acute and fascinating reading,—as rare in its way as the renderings of nature are in theirs! The picturesque words freighted with meaning—such as "*Schlangen*" for the twisting dye-strips—and *Holländerbusch* for the elder-bush—I find most beneficial; so that little "error" (in the number of the words) has really been the means of bringing me intense good.

I have gone as far as the children's return from the first visit to Millsdorf; but shall wait to send you those pages till I have done these new ones you send. I am truly delighted to have the earlier pages of your version. My dictionary is Cassell's German-English and the copy of *Bunte Steine* that Mr. Wolff sent me is one of the year 1911 printed in Altenburg—"*Ein Festgeschenk von Adalbert Stifter*"—on the title page. And the edges are stained gray—all edges, front and lower edges as well as the top,—with no running of the color into the margin!! I do like that prim practical aspect of a real European book. And of course the script.

I am relieved to know I did no harm in letting it be known I was assisting you with the translation.

Nothing could say how inspiring I find your poetic verity in giving the innate soul of the text,—as where you use the word "fallow" for the pine-branches,—a special unique color that transfers the intensity of the original, and it is a question how "odd" one may dare to be,—without harming the inconspicuous ease of the story. My mother, as you say, is of untold help with words and errors.

I anticipate something wonderful in the drawings, but I think Mrs. Wolff should not trouble to mail me anything; I can wait—should wait—till the work is being actually used.

Affectionately,   Marianne Moore

We have various interruptions, such as visits to doctors, and letters that need a prompt answer, and I am irked to be slower than I otherwise could be. But I know you will be patient with me, and realize that I am wishing all the time to go on with the story.

To Elizabeth Bishop   *September 27, 1945*

Dear Elizabeth,

The hurricane filled us with apprehension. I know you have said Key West is not in the path of what threatens Miami but there are storms everywhere at this season and your house and self and brave Mrs. Stevens, what have you done, and are you well enough without Dr. Baldwin while the visitor has your apartment here? Do you know the pain it is to be a useless automaton, Elizabeth—full of vivid imaginings with neither a solution for anyone nor a deliverance nor a pretty distraction like these touching turtles weighing from 300 to 400 pounds, gazing with stoic calm "upon us monsters"? The text on this card, is a little volume.

My "difficult chore" is my salvation though every line I do convicts me of a penitentiary crime. Your feeling about the workmanship (of the original) has been a great help to me. I have decided I can learn, if I can't devise equivalents. Such inexhaustible originality of construction,—and music that is taste and sensibility,—with no lapses, dazzles me into the most vehement exertion, and I have stopped despairing and retiring into fits of nervous frustration. I am as dogged as the Armenian demolition company destroying fireplaces and moulded ceilings in the mansion not far from us. Am on Master Gaster, fable II in Book III (but I change everything previous from time to time so am illusorily advancing).

What about your progress? Even if you dislike every new poem, think of what you have, that's perfection and surprising. I am sure we should not feel pushed and impelled by someone's utilitarian need. I nearly disappeared trying to do a page a day of my French. Now I do what I can, & am no slower. If you have anything to send me, it is *more* than "all right with me." I vow and declare, Elizabeth, we are not going to be victims all the time, of weather and superannuating mishaps.

Warner has been returned to Washington to duty. We may not see him often but he's near and we saw him two weeks ago; he came for overnight. Don't conceal anything, Elizabeth, if you're struggling or in perplexity. One's things and one's self can be mountainous but "you know you're going to win," Warner says. I hope this is so.

Not a soul have I seen or been to see—all these months—but someday I shall be natural again. See if I'm not.

With our love, Elizabeth,   Marianne

To Monroe Wheeler   *April 24, 1946*

I am so glad, dear Monroe, I had the glimpse of you at the Museum for I can't come tomorrow. The doctor who is deciding about us—the busiest one,—can see us only tomorrow the nurse says, so we have to submit.

    The whole aspect of life seems changed to me since seeing those wonders at the Museum,—the serious & unsavage expressions of intensity and awe in those roof-spire figures, and the incised patterns and the lizards from Easter Island, and the boar tusks and indeed the whole collection seem to renovate me, hurried though I *was* in my visit. And the Chagall pictures are a triumph of affection and romance, with never a false or mundane note— such a consolation to me. The stork and the wolf, the parrot, and the *Sun & Frogs*, are more like themselves than they ever were in life. I particularly revere the obscurity of the *Sun & Frogs*—the interpretations are so shallow that count & delineate every frog. When it is all so winning, you can think how I would like to say so to Mr. Chagall, but you understand. And how much I feel your being willing to make room for me.

    Our love, and a hope that too much struggle does not threaten you, Monroe.

Marianne

To Ezra Pound   *July 31, 1946*

Dear Ezra:

    Some months ago I wrote to you to say what goes without saying— that misfortune does not alter friendship. The money I enclosed, I hoped might procure something you might like to read, or eat, or wear; but I was told to "contact the Department of Justice"; I didn't know how to do that. I have now sent you the ten dollars I didn't get to you before, and am trying to say again, that I hope you can procure with it something cheerful—that combats care.

    Last winter I heard again from Mr. Schweiller[15] who seems to be at work in Milan; from William Carlos Williams yesterday; and had a sight of T. S. Eliot when he was in New York; and of Edward Kauffer that same day.

    I sound dull because I *am* dull. You know our propensity for illness; the gloom of which you helped to dissipate by visiting our infirmary. This time it is hard. My mother is having a battle to eat; or rather swallow (because of an injury to the nerve controlling the palate). I have been telling people I cannot write letters or even receive them; but we think of you, Ezra, and wish you could be comfortable. Don't be embittered. Embitterment is a sin—a subject on which I am an authority. I wish you would let me tell you

15. Probably Vanni Scheiwiller, EP's Italian publisher, who took over for his father, John Scheiwiller.

something about a sermon that Reinhold Niebuhr preached in the church near us two or three weeks ago. In any case, we are yours solicitously.

Marianne Moore

To Bryher *October 29, 1946*

How touching, how touching, Bryher, how overwhelming of you to do this—helping us day by day as it is, and exchange making what you have been sending us, larger now. Costs are unreasonable, yet how compassionate an imagination you have. Literally it is salvation to us to have the young colored girl who comes in the afternoons—but you did not *know* we have her! And nearly half the nourishment Mother has is a specialty of some kind—dehydrated goat-milk, vegetable iron, brewers' yeast and so on, and you did not know *this*. And we? We are so intent, surviving, I don't see how it can matter much whether or not we do survive. I have thought many times about your *birthday*, Bryher, but there is nothing to make you realize that I have, whereas you effect so much and so promptly. It would seem that I might send one line, one word to brave Molly Hughes but I have not written, either to thank her for advice she gave me about speaking to students, or to thank her for the loving words received from her on hearing from you that we were struggling.

You spoke of leaving the villa about this time, and we hope the work of transferring will not be over-hard, Bryher, and that you can have enough of your things about you not to be hampered, and that you feel encouraged about Hilda. You surely have real food nowadays? and sun that was lacking these last years in England? We grieved to see in *The Times*, pictures of English grain standing in water, and to know that rationing had become more rigid and more Spartan.

George Plank wrote us so noble and beautiful and enheartening a letter I do feel I must write to him sometime. The routine I keep to, I think must be unreal, it so inhibits me, Bryher; a mysterious constant perseverance; but it does seem to effect something; Mother has again been able to examine things, to try to take a stitch or two, and forgive my continuing with our provisions and vigilances, I impulsively persuaded a young woman who has a hardware-shop! near us—who does expert knitting—to knit a shawl that could alternate with one Mother has about her head to equalize the temperature—a lightweight thing I could wash. I had not realized how unobtainably expensive wool is nowadays, and you suddenly do this thing you have done! Surely, it is a portent; if it but may be a symbol of help and rescue that find you out and contradict hardship and weight upon your spirit.

I think I shall be writing again; I have not said anything, just that we marvel, that we long to feel your path is easier, Bryher, and that we are not harming you.

Our love, how feeble a plea;/but you don't need words, you feel things.

Marianne

To Ezra Pound   *June 22, 1947*

ROMAROMAROMAAMOR, dear Ezra? So rare a *carta da visita* indeed deserves to have on it, the Asian Gate, but as you very well know, beauty should not be mitigated by impropriety.

Of the non sequitur as applying to religious belief, no better thing could be said of it than

"Take not cliff for morass and treacherous bramble."

As for elephants ("all elephants"), anything that has E in its name is not "undistinguished." The trunk drawing water from the bucket reminds me of *Zoo in Budapest*—about 10 years ago, in which the elephant, demurely passing the tiger's cage after storing up a supply of water, suddenly turned and deluged the tiger.

T. S. Eliot has been in New York, as you probably know—a hard tour of duty—expounding Milton; then, as I think, went to Cambridge, then returned here. His brother Henry has died. Distress is something to which one does not become accustomed, so do not labor the religious non sequitur. One cannot alter a person, anyhow?

Affectionately yours and Mrs. P's.   M. M.

To Louise Crane   *July 9, 1947*

Dear Louise,

You have been ever so much with us of late, though you may not know it. It seemed that where ever I turned, you had helped me. And although it would seem that we now need help more than ever, it is really the opposite. You'll realize that I am trying to say Mother died today—at Brooklyn Hospital—this morning about half past nine. Supernatural care, and surprise after surprise of practical aid (Warner got us by ambulance to the Hospital July 2nd) & her defeat have resulted in her transcending her battles at last.

We are going to Washington tomorrow, Louise; have, on Saturday morning in our grandfather's church, a service which Warner plans to conduct, then I'll visit a cousin in Hagerstown over Sunday, & come back Monday perhaps.

You may be at Woods Hole—I hope so if it's going to be so warm as today. If not when I come back, maybe you'd telephone me?

Warner & I are both managing to be glad for Mother. We couldn't see her fight her utmost, and not be glad to have her transcend her disabilities somewhat soon. Much love from us both. And my special love to Mrs. Crane,

Marianne

To Hildegarde Watson and James Sibley Watson

5304 Moorland Lane   Bethesda 14, Maryland   July 16, 1947

Hildegarde and Sibley—

Consolation? a word, just a word, I have always felt, but now? that dispensation of the spirit made manifest in compassion which verily defeats death, through your's and Sibley's loving desire to defeat it.

How dear to Mole would your voice over the telephone have been, Hildegarde, that morning of the tenth. How dear to us, your saying in these lines just now received, "I thank God to have known Mole & been lifted by her tenderness, wisdom and grace over so many places it did not seem possible to endure." "Warner's wonderful voice keeps coming to me as a balm." The Mozart sonata played in tears. Hildegarde? These are gifts to us dear *Hildegarde.* As Warner said to us once, when overtested, "If you hadn't pitied me, I'd have been all right." So it is with your letter,—with this check of unrealizable greatness, dwarfing even our succession of inexorable expenses,—for the Hospital, x-rays, blood transfusions and other aid. (Though not all has intimidated & perplexed us. Troubled not to have received a bill from one of our most needed doctors, {the laryngologist from another hospital,} I received today, a letter saying his work for Mother & sympathy to us, are "too simple a gift.") Surely, dear Hildegarde and Sibley, courage should equal gratitude.

Warner has been sublime. His voice shook as he pronounced the benedictory words of farewell to mortal flesh, beside what is now her grave. So much the better. A strange effect of resolution and power was imparted. As he said to me the evening of July ninth, "We are thankful her spirit may have wider range, pray that the beauty of her love may embrace us, that we may be blessed and be enabled to play the man."

Truly it is a help that you and Sibley should care to see us as we are, and think of our everyday; the apartment—for instance, about which I used to wonder. Warner has been my deepest question. But tears, as he says, she does not need. They could only be for ourselves—shed in self concern. We are obligated to do certain work, his here; and I mine, there in Brooklyn. I have an affection for 260, and our good little Gladys Berry is just such rescue, Hildegarde, as you once visualized for us. She was heart-rending—vibrant in her devotion to Mole, and is looking after me even from a distance.

Constance's, Bee's, & Warner's (need I say) goodness to me, has been a miracle & has made of me something natural and reliable—upon leaving, I may go to see Louise Crane a few days, at Windsor near Pittsfield; in between this and a visit to Kathrine Jones & Marcia Chamberlain in Maine— (in Lowvine near Bar Harbor) I think I will see to some painting in one or two rooms (kitchen, bathroom, & Warner's room) for Gladys to manage during my absence perhaps. I could take La Fontaine with me to Maine, & go on with it after my return.

This is tentative, but we think of it hopefully. I shall from time to time send you word, if I may, about where I am.

The supernatural is indeed not natural. Nothing can explain or could have persuaded me beforehand that circumstance after circumstance could befriend us amid the irreparable, that friendship could make indecisiveness, safety and be not the assurance of things hoped for, but confer upon us here & now, undeniable peace.

As ever; it is those needing comfort who give it,—a penetrating—an alarming thought. We were afforded incalculable momentum by the clipping you let us have, Hildegarde, of Sibley's mechanism, that now *works;* after patient and silent perfecting, with the utmost possibility of defeat as progress hesitated. A result? is emancipation, rescue! And we are helped by your own handmark in usefulness. May endurance of such things as are unendurable, too, have its victory. The "meek" whom I have never liked to think about, it seems are the "begging?" whose humility is not hallucinary [*sic*]! We have all (if I may say so) been humbled by hardship, and I feel, shall be comforted.

Nothing I can say is worthy to be said to you, but we trust ourselves with you and are lovingly yours,

Marianne and Warner[16]

To John Warner Moore   *[260 Cumberland Street, Brooklyn?]*
                              Wednesday [late summer 1947]

Here I am, dear Bible—*sweet* Bullfrog—so safe and warm—with your letter just delivered. Bible, it is a *disgrace,* an *outrage,* that you would talk of sending me $20.00. Now that I have Gladys less, the difference is *incredible.* Don't send the money or I'll have to RETURN it. I got $86.50 in checks today. Subtract $12.00 & you see I have plenty besides about $1500.00 in [the] bank. Mrs. Melvin was fixing a dress of Hildegarde's for Mole which she is going to sell for us for $10.00. I've paid the rent & will get more money presently, so I doubt I could even need to *draw* any. *Mind* me, dear fellow. I'll be giving to *you* presently.

Yes I feel Mole smiles upon us—really do—and if I had just been out

16. JWM's signature is in his own hand.

of *hearing* distance at May's, you would have had a different impression. It was really a problem to simulate impersonal conversation & yet convey anything to you on the instant. May shut the door, but still one can hear, so I was body-held.

I attended a party last evening—first a dinner for 6 given by Margaret Marshall (on Stuyvesant Square she lives). I was overwhelmed—crabmeat in alligator pears, each a half broiled chicken, delicate peas, salad, & real pears & cheese. I was put by Stephen Spender who is quite a treat; he knew Yeats, knows Mr. Auden & T. S. Eliot well, and then afterward Louise Bogan came in & others. She has reviewed me *twice* you know very boldly & ardently. She is the picture of martyrdom & triumph. Her father is 86— wandering in his mind & talking all the time. He wants to be in Portland where he was born & she has him there with two people he likes who take care of him. She said "I'm not 'religious' or wouldn't call myself so but certain sayings that are part of religion indeed are true; we prove them true and one that doesn't mean much to some, is a real statement to me: 'He that loseth his life shall find it.' We know it's so." We talked on in this way for some time. When I know Mole is safe, what joy fills my heart (not stumbling & struggling). Then I came home quite late,—11:15 & found a telegram from Barbara Howes & William Smith—he's a poet & Rhodes Scholar—they are being married today, before he goes to Oxford—& invite me to a small party at 8:30 & I b'lieve I'll go.

I still have one or 2 fables of Books I–VI to revise but am much encouraged; & that glorious help, Bible, from you in having them typed is IN-CREDIBLE, makes all so easy.

The painters haven't come today & that's all right—it gives Gladys a little more time for the living-room & me for the fables & certain reducing of papers.

Two beautiful letters from K & M [Kathrine Jones and Marcia Chamberlain]. They are very touching, Bible—Marcia & K. I pray, dear Bible, that you won't be snarled up in pressures & irritations because I wrote Constance yesterday. I enclosed the Dodson letter publicly because he said "we SHALL GIVE you an accounting of assets" and Constance would then know nothing was yet chalked up in dollars & cents.[17]

Well, dear fellow, may I be delivered from bringing trouble on you.

Dearest love,   Rat

This little room is *delightful.*

---

17. JWM and MM felt Constance was concerned that they were arranging the settlement of MWM's estate in a manner that was unfair to the JWM household.

To George Meals   *November 6, 1947*

Dear Mr. Meals:

My brother and I realize that the work you plan to do, in providing us my mother's headstone of Vermont marble, engraved as was decided when the matter was discussed with you, will take time. Meanwhile we wish the work not to be delayed by lack of remuneration from us, and enclose you a check for five hundred dollars ($500).

May I say, Mr. Meals that I do not expect to marry, but wish our "forethought" on behalf of my mother, not to be marred by miscalculation and feel it would be best to have my name engraved

MARIANNE CRAIG MOORE

THEIR DAUGHTER

below my mother's as planned, but to leave space for a line beneath it (*above my date of birth*) were a line ever to be inserted there, designating marriage.

You are indeed kind, and have our grateful confidence.

Sincerely yours,   John Warner Moore Marianne C. Moore

Accompanying this letter is what we feel should be the wording for the stone.

To Elizabeth Bishop   *c/o Mrs. Marcia K. Chamberlain Ellsworth,*
Maine RFD #2   August 24, 1948

Words fail me, Elizabeth,

Your magic poem—every word a living wonder—with an unfoldment that does not ever go back on itself, and the colors! beyond compare in the small blue drums and the mackerel sky and the jelly-colored epergnes. What of your unabashed "awash with morals"! What would Bernard De Voto say! (who hates preachers).

Then the suicidal courage of your treatise! as based on Shakespeare and Poe and G. M. Hopkins.! *Alarmingly accurate,* Elizabeth, in what you say of the logarithms of? apology and the "incredible effort of justifying an initial pattern." So many pretty and "sweet" things in the course of your interpretation. The trouble and strain of such effort as you put on me, and the scientific subtitles! I am overwhelmed. It all seems a phantasy—like one of the interludes in *A Midsummer Night's Dream.* I keep wondering how it should be related to *me.*

Kathrine has been ill again—deficiency of vitamins, perhaps, the doctor thought, but is once more up and able to eat. She and Marcia smile at your modesty—a glass of water—but I guess, Elizabeth, we'll concentrate on art & literature, *if* you will do us the favor to come over, (or up or down,—whatever it would be) instead of my coming to you.

Could you come next week, say Wednesday or Thursday? (Marcia suggests about 3? She and K. so like your picture in the Oscar W. [Williams] ant[hology]! & of course, these pages for me. I have prized Andrews Wanning all along; think his article on W. H. Auden in *Furioso* the best I have seen,—do persuade him on my behalf to transport you here; I'll enclose directions (separate).

The picture of Stonington, is just what would tempt me if I were hunting a room—and I am glad you did not need to hold out in Wiscasset. Severe, though, to change plans, on the instant.

I can't come over to you, Elizabeth, for various reasons but shall be leaving Sept. 9th. Perhaps you'll be in New York after leaving Stonington?

La Fontaine. Slower & slower, but more and more reliable, I hope. I don't tire of La F.'s temperament; but oh how I tire of my tentatively happy insights. Professor Levin is a marvel. His patience and intensive studiousness and fancy for the lively word are making me rather scholastic! and really enthusiastic at times. Mr. Du Boucher has gone back to France.

You say nothing about how you are. I hope you have suitable food and don't have to fight asthma as you sometimes do in New York, Elizabeth.

My ink diminishes—perhaps you can read this in the strong sun.!

Affectionately,   Marianne

I hope Robert Lowell is able to go on with things he wants to do & is not too trammeled by government and academic plans.

The card is such a pleasure.

To Wallace Stevens   260 Cumberland Street   Brooklyn, N.Y.
September 18, 1948

Dear Mr. Stevens,

I ponder what you have from time to time said about life, its largesse and its deprivations. There is the enchantment of accuracy, which seems more imperative than the personal—"heliotrope, inconstant hue. Be sure the audience beholds you not your gown."[18] All of which is to ask you to infer thanks for your thoughts in *The Quarterly Review of Literature.*

Sincerely yours,   Marianne Moore

18. MM is quoting inexactly from Stevens's "In a Bad Time."

To Monroe Wheeler   *January 7, 1949*

Dear Monroe,

I don't know when anything has so weighed me down helplessly, as to have you walk to the subway in the rain and then back, with no umbrella— not even convalescent yet. I hope you are surmounting it all. If we could just have spent the rest of the winter there in the safety of the movie-cell or pumpkin shell lined with velvet.

Jean Cocteau is like a prism or vein of mica he is so grave and earnest in his scintillations—really a shock to me; I thought he must by now be so burdened by pressures and ravening wolves.

As you will see, Monroe, the elusive rose is about to reach you from the Metropolitan Museum and my postage is returned in a special envelope.

Affectionately,   Marianne

To William Carlos Williams   *February 21, 1949*

Dear William:

I am, most of the time so far as I can see, a creature obedient to superior forces, like the Belgian work-dogs; but also a beneficiary of concurring mysteries which I don't understand but dare not question. You electrify me. Of course a poet "sees things others never notice," life being in the eye not the thing. I shall never cease to marvel and to thank you.

I have no victrola, so must and am glad to take your word for it that the thing is as you say and not flimsy; must also wait to hear your recordings. I saw somewhere that William Benét says they are good.

May you and Florence be blessed.

M. M.

A bullet. Who in the world would think it or take the trouble to write me![19]

To Ezra Pound   *June 10, 1949*

Dear Ezra:

When I next hear from Dudley Huppler,[20] I shall tell him I gave you the drawings and what you say and he will be in an ecstasy.[21] He thirsts to come to New York but has not the money. He is thirty—by now 31—"self-

19. WCW had written to MM on February 18, 1949, saying that the last line of her "Reindeer poem" ("Rigorists") "hit [him] between the eyes like a bullet from space."

20. Visual artist and teacher of English who befriended MM.

21. EP had written to MM (mailed June 8, 1949): "Dudley H. is of ———— well right I has found. The mot juste. Il est quel q'un & I shd. be glad to meet him."

taught," had a first show at the Art Institute, Chicago a year ago, and works (I infer from his stationery) in a florist's shop. He writes well too.

Have you, a French Brooks Adams *La Loi de la Civilisation et de la Décadence?* I am in communication with Adrienne Monnier (*La Maison des Amis des Livres, 7 rue de l'Odéon*) and shall try to get it for you if you still want it? It is trying to me to have people give me what is not what they hope, but a burden to me, so I ask. And I would get her to send you a Pléiades La Fontaine (fables) if you don't *object* to the small print. I dote on it and would like you to be able to discard that disaffecting Brentano copy I sent you. Mr. Schiffrin, the designer, is a captive of Pantheon Books at present; i.e. The Bollingen F. (a friend of Edward Kauffer's—*quelq'un* to talk to. This you may know.—disabled by asthma, however). (Edward Kauffer has just heard from you and said "I must see the dear man.")

Literally, you have got my goat; I can't deny it.[22]

> *But as you'd reach a ripe old age,*
> Judge no one *by his countenance.*

> BOOK VI: V *(I believe this is under the ban)*

> *Or circumstances by appearances.*

I don't know whether my lavender-cajeput-thymol spray repels or attracts insects but am sending you some. (I am as my brother says, impetuous, for on telephoning the druggist about this, he says "it repels them.") Am also getting you a dark blue fish-net bag about a foot by half-a-foot in size for carrying trifles to the yard. If it seems effeminate or as much trouble as the articles themselves, let Mrs. Pound find a recipient. It is scarcely august enough for her to use on trips to the Hospital. I wish I could be of some service to her. I have been thinking about this and don't get very far. You have scores of friends—not scores as good as your animal-friends, but scores who somewhat sweeten their environs. You must not be profane, Ezra, without cause; or penny wise (no pun intended). Not to be in context where one belongs is misleading. I hope you will let context be your deciding factor if implored for passages by M. D. Z. When *The Dial* was mentioned, I could have said a good deal that I didn't and for all I know, Mr. Z. was helpless at the time you suffered from his myopia. Impoverished by hospital bills and taking care of his sister (subject to a brain tumor as I told you) does not conduce to lavish remuneration.

M. M.

Although I enclose you grass for the goat, such pets are not immortal and can be buried under some tree with no loss to anyone. I got it at a little

22. MM and EP enjoyed much wordplay in their letters. In this case, MM had sent EP a small figurine of a goat.

Oriental pottery-shop in 1918 on a table with a placard in the middle: "formally 30 cents."

To Louise Crane   *June 27, 1949*

Dearest L:

The perfect Léphant except that he should not be walked on. You should not take your time for messages, Louise, and pictures but you know my helpless curiosity—and relief to have you and Mrs. Crane so enthusiastic about your tour. Sintra is celestial—that glaze of floor and the lofty ceiling covered with "scenes." Warner was here at the time the Sala dos Cisnes arrived (it could not mean swans?) and I said, "Have you ever seen Sintra?" He said pensively, "Sintra? Y..e..s in*deed*." I felt quite bleak, Louise, to see you hurried and badgered on the very eve of departure and I thought the most protecting thing was to subtract myself. It would have been wrong for you to struggle to say goodbye.

I am really very happy, since W. and Constance are moving into the campus house at the Gunnery School this week, in fact this moment. That condensed statement covers a multitude of vicissitudes.

I am just back from Wilson College and seeing my cousin Mary (Mrs. Shoemaker in Hagerstown) and Ezra Pound, and being given my credentials. I shall show them to you sometime, and clippings from the [*Brooklyn*] *Eagle* and *World-Telegram*. Ezra P. asked why I must do all the fables and I said usually the lesser ones are slighted in favor of the most attractive and he said, "If at your mature age you feel obliged to mould character by discipline, I suppose you must." Robert Hillyer has been to Washington to plead with Senator Saltonstall to revoke E. P.'s Bollingen grant and the *Saturday R[eview] of Literature* is ardently publishing countless pages about the "new poetic priesthood" "meretricious verbiage" and "oddments" in lieu of original afflatus.

I had a phone-call from Mary as she was about to set off for Connecticut with Sylvia and Leonid.[23] Saturday evening Marion and Edward Kauffer came to dinner; Monroe, last night. He has had shingles but says he is over it; asked me particularly if I had "a forwarding address for you" and I reminded him of Cook's and showed him a pink envelope Marcia had given me for writing her and K.; so you may hear from him.

My La Fontaine is in a desperate state; I make scarcely a hair's breadth of progress but believe if I can play I'm a badger under a hedge surrounded by poison-ivy as I said to Ezra P., from now on, I should get to the end sometime.

Don't believe what you hear about the heat, Louise. The paper says city-dwellers are "enveloped in a sweltering pall of humid heat" 92°. So far

23. Sylvia Marlow, harpsichordist; Leonid Berman, painter.

as I am concerned—who hate winter—I am happy as an alligator in a mangrove swamp, without a care or problem. I don't mind cooking and I sleep better than for years—all that is wrong, I have the ambition of a motorcycle contestant and don't move. Monroe kindly urged that I spend weekends in the country with him and Glenway but I said I am so unadaptable I am hopeless, so he acquiesced.

Marcia and Kathrine will be disappointed not to be seeing you and Mrs. Crane somewhere: but are having a good time—delighted with Italy and a life of adventure. "Istanbul" sounds magical—I can't conceive of actually viewing the minarets and solid alabaster of romance. I hope it won't be too stifling, beggar-ridden and peopled with non-prize cattle to be what I picture. Be good to yourself, Louise, thank you for telling me Mrs. Crane is none the worse of all you are doing. Somehow I dreaded it for you.

With love to you both, Marianne

Now don't bother with me, Louise. You're "away."

To John Warner Moore *Friday, July 1, 1949*

Dearest Bible,

Before I draw another breath, as I would run to Mole and you with the word, I must tell you, that on sourly opening "*another*" letter from Norman Pearson, as I thought, just now, I find a check for $2500—as the first award of "The Bryher Foundation, Inc." The committee being Prof. Willard Thorp of Princeton, Harry Levin of Harvard, & Dudley Fitts of Andover.

Amazing! Award "for encouragement of literary endeavor": for my achievements in poetry & criticism, encouragement to others, personally & by example, "the Foundation would express its gratitude."

This is not to be publicized Mr. P. says—though not a severe "secret."

I am *dumb*. Can you conceive of such "charity"? I really am aquiver. Mole's piercing verity of thought and realness, look me in the eye, and her practical honesty: "Where do we get this money, for doctors" she asked, "for melons and expensive vitamins? Where?" This consoles me for mistakes I've made in buying for her, *determined* to give her the crucial thing—$90 for the fox fur and undershirts she never wore and it again makes me glad you spent the terrible amount you did on her dresses & "lace collar" and buttons & gloves. Why go on? They were offerings, and not to do us despite. I said from you, from Mole's own 14 years work & my 3½ years work teaching & from gifts.

Now, Bible, shall I put this in Mass. I. Trust? I always have an instinct to keep gifts separate—put it, say, in the Loomis-Sales Corp. (like M.I.T.)

but consolidating is so very important. I've just transferred about $1100 to M.I.T. but suppose it's best to add it to our M.I.T.

I'll inquire if it really is too late to send it in if it's to yield a July 30 dividend.

What a "challenge" as you used to say till I attacked you for the word.

Think of this benevolence—with W. H. Auden, Cummings, Louise Bogan & scores of others really needing & deserving the money.

Well Bible can I do my fables, or not? I guess I CAN, my valiant argonaut.

To the Bank now & then to the P.O. to pay for your *Vision and Craftsmanship*.[24] Pardon the allusion—alligators were never noted for not being crude.

I've received Marion Dorn's *House & Garden* & can bear it better now! that I'm so financial! (slight fellow that I am).

To Ezra Pound   *July 30, 1949*

Dear Ezra—

I am quite shaken by so much kindness, sacrifice and risk taken for me[25]—speed, patience, definiteness. I am not worth all this trouble but I can be trusted. No one will see the pages. I won't show, quote, or be led by gratitude accidentally to bite the hand that fed me. You cannot trust people, it's literally true, as severities to which I needn't allude have taught me. I know the dynamite that an "interpretation" of an admonition may set off. No exceptions, no impulsive absent-minded retrospects. And don't think I'll forget.

Despite what you had said, I did not see till now how absolutely the subject, object, predicate principle applies. The pernicious relative clause has done me a world of harm. I can get the straight order of words and try for active verbs and forego "hard bestead," and "ceaseless" etc. As for the rest, one can't make a silk purse out of a sow's ear and timidity would perish incentive if I weren't so grateful (I never could have succeeded without the help) and if I did not like the thing so well—the unhackneyed La F. cadences and little intimacies, by contrast with what you tell me is formality.

It is not useful to you to have me talk about handicaps—strange thought; money in particular. I am very sad about these things.

If ignorance is crooked, I *am* a crook. I looked into George Orwell some time ago and found him repugnant—undergrown as a writer—so gave no

24. *Vision and Craftsmanship: Studies in Ends and Means in Education*, by F. Crossfield Happold (1949).

25. EP returned copies of some of MM's La Fontaine translations with his comments in the margins. He instructed her to keep these communications confidential (September 19, 1949).

more thought to him. Persons who express themselves well and hazardously because they care about what they are saying (Winston Churchill and General J. de L. de Tassigny[26] for instance) have a helpful effect on me and I don't like to see them go wrong; but at best am barely managing "to live and think" about antimacassars, as you know. Why annoy you by reiterating.

I have not got a Brooks Adams for you yet, or word of one from Adrienne Monnier.

Last night at the Kauffers', Marion K. and John Edmunds played some clavichord pieces—Giles Farnaby's *The Dreame* and *Fayne Would I Wedd,* [William] Byrd's *The Queen's Alman,* and two Bach preludes. I can't imagine an instrument so modest it could make no difference to a person studying or asleep. John Edmunds has managed to have 16 [Henry] Purcell songs transcribed by a Chinese and 15 produced, inaugurated a Campion library in the San Francisco public library and plays surprisingly though he had not tried a clavichord till last night. He has written some very choice songs (to 16c. poems and others,) talked about you with ardor, has done a great deal almost without help—a hard worker.

Remember me to Mrs. Pound, please. I wonder about her, and about this kind of air for you all the time—then send you a pestilent dose of work! (If I can think what I am doing and look at words newly I'll get on better) . . .

M. M.

To William Carlos Williams   *February 2, 1950*

Dear William:

The meat of the missel is that medicine (pharmaceutical medicine) can be made unimportant by comparison with matters or acts of more burning importance. For instance this rescue of the panting and disabled sojourner (reindeer or versifier or editor) is a continual shock to me. Just recently I perhaps too mechanically made a rejoinder to The University of Kansas City *Review* and have half given something to a foreign magazine. Whereas one should burgeon forth with largesse that would make the sun seem cool. Why am I a pinhead? in the verbiage of Ringling Brothers. Maybe you will have to contribute to *Imagi* for me. Or maybe my head will enlarge automatically and I can lend Mr. Cole some of my chaos. I accumulate clues and hints and ravellings day by day and feel like plying my trade but have to get my La Fontaine finished. *don't I?*

I have not seen the Klees and I hope they're not gone. I did not see the Persian objects, the Van Goghs; have not seen the Titian, had to mail back

26. General Jean de Lattre de Tassigny (1889–1952), French army officer; inspector general of the French army, 1945–48.

my *Cocktail Party* ticket for today; am toiling over *Daphnis & Alcimadure*[27] in bed. Feel better, however, in reading what you say of "the well-known Spaniard." (Somehow it is the uncertified accuracies that effect maximum damage.) The thing is far too good for him—able as he is. Dylan Thomas will be heard at the Museum, Lloyd Frankenberg says, & I asked if I could be let in, and let in for your program. Sorry Ogden N[ash] is not to perform.

My love to you and Florence. Have been watching in vain for the next installment of your Biography.

M. M.

I have "Paterson III"—"a rare visitation." The bulldozer at Iwo Jima flattens out some objections! also the alleged differences between man & woman (which we never did believe in, did we).

To Ezra Pound   *June 21, 1950*

Dear Ezra,

You fire my ambition to get this "little boy & girl" material to Mr. Engel and the Vikings[28]; and I am asking Eleanor Padley (the *ne plus ultra* of reliability & efficiency {my immediate neighbor}) to mail the package 1st cl. registered or insured from the P. office next her place of business tomorrow—with a letter from me. Anyone can infer that the medium must be done justice to in these drawings—so I should think I need merely stipulate that reproduction to scale is essential. (I shall appeal to Mr. Engel {*and* Mr. Covici who keeps an eye on my activities and may think I forget this}).

I did not know Sr. de Angulo is *dying*. Perhaps he won't, if aided to struggle? Anyhow I shall dispatch the material. Cannot type because of a giraffe bronchitis which I now have but I can jeopardize myself to the extent of finding strong cardboard etc.; & Louis Dudek[29] donated an envelope (& stamps though I told him to give no thought to these matters).

As for my agitation, I thought I must have done you capital harm. Since you padlocked my jaws earlier about another matter if you remember. In any quarter in which the right work is being published, your name would *aid* the enterprise. *The Saturday Review,* in making a fit of the Bollingen matter, has set in motion a reaction or superstition against timidity and the academic past, it would seem. However I shall "watch myself."

27. *Daphnis et Alcimadure* (1754), an opera in three acts, a pastoral *languedocienne,* by Jean Joseph Cassanéa de Mondonville.

28. EP had entrusted MM with the publication of drawings and poems by Jaime de Angulo (*Indian Tales*). She was corresponding with Monroe Engel and Pascal Covici of Viking Press about this work.

29. Canadian poet and professor of English at McGill University (1918–).

All efforts toward enlightenment are a tissue of imperfections and Harvard has sheltered some purblind "teachers"; but you are the last living sage, it seems to me, to outlaw the oak because a few of its acorns do not form (are not acorns, but oakgalls)! What does he write? is my own criterion. And if Harry Levin's Joyce, & Stendhal studies are mean pronouncements, may my fables be the object of "excruciating irony." (Mr. Levin's phrase in a recent *Times*.) I am emerging from kindergarten in the matter of form, & of diction that is "in keeping" (Robt. Bridges' phobia). A mixed metaphor is better to me than a right one. A sentence does not have to have a verb so far as I am concerned. Writing, to me, is entrapped conversation. But La Fontaine IS, as you suggested, better "formal" and unimpaired by the bizarre, I find; and the uncontemptuous patience of my tutors is something for Molière, no less. (Whether I am the object of jeers or not, on publication—I have had a good time.)

As Dr. F. M. Eliot[30] says; "we are, in making our decisions, to be aware of but one influence upon us, the eye [of] god in heaven."

M. M.

A Nocturnal and clandestine view of campuses is the only one possible for me; —still, I find myself here & there on occasion; & that is a story in itself. I must not detain you.

Don't be disappointed if Mr. Angel[31] cannot produce the de Angulo. Maybe "Mr. Mellon" & Pantheon Books would? or John Ciardi? though his interest died when he found it was not [a] ms. by you.

Thank you for the copies of *je l'ai surpris.*[32]

To Hildegarde Watson and James Sibley Watson

c/o Mrs. M. K. Chamberlain
Ellsworth, Maine RD#2   August 24, 1950

Dear Hildegarde and Sibley,

I thought of you constantly at Harvard—a place of unparalleled chivalries once again—though I set a record for incompatibility in some respects! In going to *your* university, Hildegarde, I thought I should do as you advised, so wore my taffeta & velvet hat—or I believe I've told you so already! —*over* my sailor hat and no one seemed to detect an outrage— separating them of course on arrival.

Every moment was studious. The sessions of this summer school were

30. Dr. Frederick May Eliot (1889–1958), theologian and president of the American Unitarian Association.

31. "Angel" may be EP's version of Monroe Engel; Paul Mellon created the Bollingen Foundation and its book series, distributed by Pantheon.

32. EP had suggested MM read "Ecrits de Paris."

held in Sanders Theatre and there was a discussion by speakers & audience after the discourses,—after the prefatory & summarizing commentaries by Harry Levin.

I went, largely because Mr. Burke was to speak; and I wanted to hear what Harry Levin would say—all of it far beyond expectation. Mr. Burke summed up "The Poem & the Public"—after being introduced as "the best disentangler in the business"—whereupon he said, "If there was ever a speaker saved by the bell last evening, it was I," for Pierre Emmanuel's[33] moral-humanitarian plea for unselfishness in a world of chaos, was shattering by comparison with our scholastic trivialities about subjects and predicates. (Mr. B. was to have commented after P. Emmanuel's address but had to be postponed.)

Mr. Burke recommended T. R. Glover on Vergil; said the Roman peace was a peace of pacification whereas we should do all in our power to turn the world away from a cult of ultimate destruction. He was contagious and earnest, and of course has an awareness that operates as humor—without the reflective onus of jest. Pierre Emmanuel amazed me by his combined "conscience" & eloquence—heightened unintentionally by his valiant English. He began with: "One of the worst mediocrities for a man, is to be a permanent 'adóll,ascent'." The poet has a message but the public honors his work with misinterpretation,—insensible to the most impeccable logical reasons. . . . Lyrical power even if diverted toward material aims, is a spiritual movement; yet we live under the menace of an implacable ideology which prevents breathing—like the miser *hán*-ted by the fear of thieves. . . . O messenger of humble news, the descent into hell is the essential part of the hero's life as the Christian faith is the essential part of the rise from the dead. I wonder if we run the risk of death to find the reason for living." (End)

A ragged reminiscence but you will not be disgusted, I know.

As for me, I was the merest filament of a feather—(if that), by comparison with others. I had fortified my paper with quotations, however, and applied principles of translation as deduced from Rossetti, Ezra P., Dudley Fitts and others, to writing that is original. (Three teachers from the west approached me quite affectionately at breakfast the next morning—in the Student Union—and said they liked what I had said—didn't I hear that applause? and so on.) The feature of the conference, as recreation, was an afternoon of recorded masterpieces played by Professor Packard.

Harvard is rather strong meat for me, and your sustaining presence,—Hildegarde—as embodied in the gardenias—and the magically timed surprise of them,—put me on my mettle and empowered me with a superstitious sense that I must not blunder, & would not.

33. Pseudonym of Noël Mathieu (1916–), French poet and essayist.

I said, didn't I? how stately my surroundings were?—blue velvet & walnut—looking out on a porch with white columns and an iron fence lined with lilacs—and flags embedded in a nice grass which a gardener was always freshening with a sprinkler. The root of one elm was patched with concrete by a surgeon so neatly & minutely, it ranks with the phenomena of the "college." (M[arcia] & K[athrine] have just taken me to a play—gangster play in which the foil to the hero, says to his ex-secretary of state accomplice: "Get that Harvard College expression off your face.") I expect to go home by the Bar H[arbor] Express September 12th. I hope you are both finding peace—whether at the Farm or Sibley Place. I keep thinking about you.

Marianne

To Hildegarde Watson   *September 11, 1950*

These crisp aromatic leaves —pointed the same at both ends. I saw a round bed of dense lavender heliotrope one day, and thought: is verbena a memory only? & of how we used to top it and it would wilt and revive, and it seemed a part of summer and happiness. Here it is—so surprising as you always are.

That was hard for you, going back again to Whitinsville. Consolation is out of the question. One must somehow have fortitude not to need it, but I can see that having Arthur Wilson come and the responsibility of a person to be sane for, was a good thing. I of course see him only as a perilous ornament of *The Dial,* ipso facto under the wing of Merlin, or Till Eulenspiegel, in Scofield's eyes. The Windward Islands are just what I would expect of him.

I shall be home, Hildegarde, about 8, Wednesday morning; am taking the 4:45 (Bar Harbor Express) Tuesday afternoon, the 12th.

Mr. Burke;—If I spoke tentatively it was diffidence on my part I suppose; since he said some very strong things about me and is not a praiser;— I have been humbly pondering that evaluating commentary. He was committed to a summary—a specific recapitulation of what those who had preceded him had presented; (so I was no cherished theme—chosen from possible thousands)! He is a thinker, certainly, freeing himself by degrees from irrelevance, and does make the arcane attractive. Where Bertrand Russell in his boasted imperviousness, is repugnant to us, Mr. Burke is contagious—? Sad to say, I felt about him, an atmosphere of desolation—of his being outside that magic circle which Scofield & Sibley invariably suggested—recalled Edgartown harbor so "beautifully captured" & Sibley "descending out of the clouds like Christ." . . . I hope I am mistaken and that he has no inward sense of defeat.

I feel better about the two hats, since *you* would wear two, Hildegarde. But the pairs were so unsimilar, I suppose, I gain nothing after all.

Your thinking of being in N. York means something good about your music, I hope. Ever since meeting Miss Moseley[34] I have felt happier.

Saturday evening I at last saw a skunk—a baby, named Fleur—fed in the dining room of La Domaine Restaurant, and bustling about it was a large brown pointer named Peter, and two Kate Greenaway children who informed me that the skunk was Peter's pet, & he sometimes gave it a "bahth," with his tongue. Marcia and Kathrine are pretty particular about their food and for the first time I detected a snobbish flavor about Marcia, who refused to even glance at me when I got the skunk to sit up like a prairie-dog and floated its tail out, on which it had been sitting. M. said finally, "Odd pet, to have in a *restaurant!*"

I so hope it won't be long till I see you, dear H.

This rudimentary memento is for Sibley—was given me at Harvard.

I have rather encouraging word from Warner! Have been so uneasy.

Love to you and Sibley,   Marianne

To E. E. Cummings and Marion Morehouse Cummings

260 Cumberland Street   Brooklyn 5, New York
November 15, 1950

Dear and electrifying friends. Flowers like persons—no two like any other. Anemones with other anemones at the center; and angelic snow-white daisies bigger than the moon! Leaves of the sharpest, most chiselled beauty, glowing like the fieriest orange-scarlet of the forge. I am tongue-tied. Why should I labor the irrelevant and beg you not to have dared to be so criminal? I should be put in the stocks for having been responsible for such lawlessness—and we know it. But that autumn fragrance is too potent for me—that aromatic never vended perfume!

Best cease these bat-like dartings in an emphasizing daylight. You are indeed sweet to care to recall me today.[35]

M. M.

If it's copyrighted I still can't be put in jail can I? Since I was christened something of the sort myself?[36]

---

34. Lois Moseley was a voice teacher and friend of HW's. She was in charge of recording at Decca.

35. November 15 was MM's birthday.

36. MM is referring to the coincidence of her initials and Marion's.

To John Warner Moore   *Nov[ember] 16, 1950, 4* PM

Dearest Bible,

Your letters came at nine, and just now the little carton. How touching, Bible. I feel as *Mole* did about the wool dresses & hand embroidered collar!—especially that perfume—i.e. Coty powder—"Origan naturelle" means "natural marjoram" and I never would DREAM of buying that expensive thing—have observed it for years among the luxurious toiletries. I certainly expect to use it—not wrap it, & lay it in a recess where it never could make a petunia bed of a common alligator.

The little wire rod with the bristles is undoubtedly a milkbottle brush & I certainly *need* it. As for the nail-brush I need it too. I don't think my plastic miniature one would stand much wear.

I shall write you & Constance tomorrow about the mattress, (answer the letter regarding it) & when my pressure subsides, shall see what foam rubber ones cost—& get one regardless. Then when you send the rent check for November, I *may* use that for the mattress & may not! Shall see, Bible. I received your $15 Pacific Lighting check today & will deposit it tomorrow in your account (and mine). That is *not* mine, Bible Duck & you know it.

Dec. 1st we each get $15 from West Penn Power & Lighting I think it is—anyhow $15.

Louise and I *might* drive up to Great Barrington a couple of days after Thanksgiving. Shall see how things go. Never have I gone at such a rapid pace—due to the Sitwells I believe, & this matter of Flair's article & the pictures.

Tuesday evening Louise's home movies of S. Africa were perfectly *beautiful*—ostriches, male ones hatching eggs under A-shaped shelters in field—Merino rams being clipped—the wool is about 5 or 6 inches deep & so compact it takes gorilla-like strength to push it apart. Then the grapes—white, and blue—wrapped & shipped to foreign countries—close-ups with the bloom on them of huge pyramidal bunches. There were penguins too quaint for words, toddling & sliding into the sea. Well bless my addled little mind, I wrote you after getting home, I believe. But I *didn't* tell you of yesterday—Edith Sitwell's, Glenway's & Mrs. Flynn's *Macbeth* at the museum. Monroe made the opening speech of introduction. Edith wore a mantle of blue & gold damask & a turban. Glenway in a dress suit & Mrs. Flynn was unforgettable—in a pale ecru chiffon with elbow sleeves, gold slippers w. silver heels & a diamond or two in her necklace. Her hair is pale straw yellow—worn in a marcelled pompadour. Two weeks ago her daughter of 14 her only companion was kicked unintentionally by a horse from whom she dismounted, and Mrs. F's stately sensibility & authority were far ahead of anything on the stage that I've seen.

Henrietta[37] was there as my guest, & Mrs. Jean Untermeyer, Louis's former wife & Babette Deutsch joined on & sat with us in the 2nd row. Then Mrs. John Simon Guggenheim came & sat next me (I was at the end) & asked if I'd come to dinner sometime. I really love the woman and said I would. She's the image of Aunt Mary Scully & about so.

The fuss & fanfare afterward were unparalleled—Leo Lerman declared he was going to call me up—had my telephone number—(Lit. ed. of M'mell [*Mademoiselle*]). William J. Smith & wife hung on me—Eudora Welty was there, & Carson McCullers—& nearly everyone you've ever heard of, John Gielgud the actor & several prominent painters—Perdita & John Schaffner who'd asked me to luncheon but I had promised to go to the Sitwells', John & P. invited Henrietta instead. She was a great credit to me—looked distinguished & was dignified & refined. Had sent me 3 roses to wear, which I forgot to put on but it can't be helped. She also sent me Elizabeth Bowen's short stories & a great bouquet of snapdragons. Cummings & Marion sent me a huge bouquet of autumn flowers & leaves. Mrs. Mayer, a raisin cake,—Mrs. Skelley bought me a *really* rare & tempting caramel cake—like one Mole made my 1st birthday at 343. (Mole making a *layer cake*. Can you think of it, Bible?) Gladys sent me a very penetrating card. And as I told you, Loren, a mechanical elephant, Louise the maroon clutch bag with leather handles—Marcia, 2 boxes airmail paper, Kathrine, a French embroidered, pale blue handkerchief & stockings. And of course this mink collared coat. Lester, a telegram.

"Brother" as Mrs. MacManus calls him ("the Reliable Fur Company" opposite our shoe shine place) put me $3-strip of mink on the lower edge of the collar & everyone exclaims over it, even Sadie who said *not* to put any on.

The *snake-eggs*, Bible, are very near my favorite candy & I'll pass them Sunday when Miss Bowen, Henrietta & Bee come. It just strikes me. I'll have BEE stay to supper. Happy thought.

The YMHA has outdone itself—sent me a free press ticket for T. S. Dec. 4th & a free one for Cyril Connolly in the Spring. And the whippet who answered for the ticket-secretary (Cynthia Colby) who sent me the tickets was really quite snobbish toward me, & threatening;— saying *no one* could be admitted at this late date—that it had been long over subscribed.

George Lynes has given me an *awful* lot of prints dull & glossy for friends & press. I'm very glad I sent *him* the $10.00. Of course everyone wants one! But George says that is all right & I've just sent M. & K. a couple. You can't see them Bible, till later—alas. And it was ambition to revenge you on the hideous ones that really spurred me to be taken & to get the big hat.

Louise is *carried away* with the watch—really seems spellbound she

37. Henrietta Ford Holland, journalist and Brooklyn friend of MM's.

is so taken with it. Odd but she is & absented herself from guests to spell out the maker and so on—on the movement. Only it is a TERRIBLE amount of money you spent.

This is a very happy fortuity Bible, for we can never honor or gratify her enough. However others tried to reinforce Mole, Louise did the most— even more than Hildegarde. She was indomitable & so tender & unintrusive about it. Well I leave off, dear Bible. A birthday if ever there was one.

Osbert & Edith [Sitwell]—especially *Osbert*—are getting very purposeful & intently crouched, like the cat watching the magpie as regards me & I will have to watch myself—Mr. Horner (O.'s secretary) by his aggressiveness & aplomb egging Osbert on—in various ways. But one always can deal with a situation if one has an indomitable rigor & sense of decorum. I must say, Osbert is reverence personified—that is what rather intimidates me.

I wish, Bible, I could bring you some persimmons but shall just have to bear my restrictions.

Now I must analyze a Canadian's ms. of poems, for Elizabeth Bowen. (Eye of newt & toe of frog!)

Dear Bible. Bye,   Rat

Mrs. Haines has been in a tailspin over my flowers & parcels. "What was that *fancy one?*" etc. But I don't care.

I *implore* you Bible, don't take letters home for careful reading. Leave them in the box if you can't destroy them right there.

This is *crucial.*

To Monroe Wheeler   *December 29, 1950*

Magnificent squirrels, Monroe, "by probably the greatest painter of the German school." I don't feel like quarreling with that! Such absent minded busy, wild-animal-eyes.

I am glad your father and mother are well, and hope all is well with Richard & your sister Doris? When you see Mrs. Crane do tell her about the family—a little anyhow. She seemed very interested at our last meeting.

The Metropolitan Museum has sent me a really unique vermilion and yellow angel, Monroe, announcing that you have renewed *The Bulletin* for me. You are the only one who seems to read my mind in these matters. I get many a joyous hour studying *The Bulletin*—almost journeyed up there to hear Edith Standen, as a result of the silks issue. Not that I should *have* that *Bulletin,* Monroe. You really must resign from your protectorate. Why are you to be sacrified to my parasitism. I am not feminized to the degree that my conscience doesn't work at all. But this I may say: Quite often I buy a duplicate, since Marcia asked me to let her see my copies. I didn't like to pester her to mail them back, and I am not for casting treasure to the winds either.

I know you are propelled by duties to humanity. I haven't advanced with my work more than a millimeter since Dec. 1 and began to faint at a luncheon yesterday and had to be secluded in my hostess' bedroom for 15 minutes. So be warned. Rushing is the unwisest of unwise expedients.

Affectionately,   Marianne

To Edith Love   *January 10, 1951*

A magician, Cousin Edith. Your attitude to distance, stirs me; and tremendous transcending of the attendant circumstances—car fare, plane fare, and hobgoblins of residential timidity. One thing I know "this quite special peninsula would enthrall me" all of us managing to tame the winged horse together. Either you overestimate me (am afraid you do)—or I am the most undifferentiated native & natural, simple "writer" the land has ever known.

I must tell you "at once," that I am forced to be stationary yet a year or so. I always fly two or three times in imagination ahead of my literal speed. So, although I thought December 1950 would see my fables completed, months of work remain; (and I can't carry them with me since supervised simultaneously by Professor Levin at Harvard & the publisher). (And I've resorted to help with the typing to hasten matters, *so must be nearby.*) Furthermore, I am entangled in a *Collected Poems* which Faber & Faber have initiated i.e. T. S. Eliot & Mr. Du Sautoy of F. & F. *And* I have to give two talks: to the YMHA in N. York April 19 & one at Wellesley a day or so later—& said last summer I'd return to the Harvard Summer School again!!!

Much ado about nothing you will say. This visit must be HERE, Cousin Edith. Can't you & Mary Louise surprise us again? *Do.* I am straining every nerve to persuade R. H. Macy to take away a too large foam rubber mattress & bring me a right size. They feign paralysis but should consent to complete the transaction *sometime* & then you could stay with me & suffer my eccentricities maybe? (I don't omit meals but they are rather crude by comparison with those to which you are accustomed.)

How thank you? I can't. Just let me say it is an inexpressible thrill for me to know you feel this way about me & would *care* to have me.

I shall enclose your letter to Warner & Constance (who are giving me the mattress for the guest room bed).

The John Edmunds—(Edmund Scott; pseudonym)—article, I enclose. John E. wrote another, truly delicate & discerning article for *The Monitor* last spring, am not sure of the date; (I believe, too, there is to be an article about me in the Feb. *Park East,* a magazine I haven't seen so far).

I ferreted out this earlier one only recently; but note that I don't let things fade from memory—have meant ever since you were here to undo my memorabilia & see if I had this.

My affectionate gratitude to you Cousin Edith and Mary Louise; and if you should see her, to Stella. What an angelic, *learnedly* angelic presence she is. She really does triumph over distance & physical deterrents—sometimes sends me counsel from *The Monitor,* and I value these insights & givings. And I perceive that Cousin Gartley is quite rare too.

Affectionately,   Marianne

To Elizabeth Bishop   *Jan[uary] 26, 1951*

Dear Elizabeth,

I do judge by your writing and you have certainly been right about mine. That you are getting along on the whole, so safely and able to work is a great comfort to me. Sulkies are a thrilling thought? day or night. Samuel Riddle (who owned Man O War) was a cousin of mine and I faithfully cut out his obituary when I came on it in *The Times* recently,—(having been a very unsatisfactory & unhelpful relative in life).

How is my writing *now?* erratic but I have some "power"! I thought I was about well yesterday though I hadn't been out. Still, I dressed and let Mrs. Henry Church send her car to take me to the Wallace Stevens reading at the YMHA. I felt "outraged" in that I had to miss the Museum lecture and the "gold medal" ceremony Wednesday, so indignation bore me up (and I truly felt "up,"—so uncontrollable and feather headed I could hardly sit erect at the reading & am hoarse now) but am *glad* I went. You "should have been there"; it was unique—an orderly series from *Harmonium* on (with periodic, terse punctuating numerals—"*three,*" "*four,*" "*five,*" "SIX," for each group) ending with a Manuscript poem and a translation from ————? Fargue, a friend of Paul Valéry's. The translation (whether from Fargue or a pronouncement of W.S.'s own I can't be sure) but it ended this way: "this talent composed of the durable, the classic, the incontestable." "Chieftain Iffucan of Afghan [*sic:* Azcan] in caftan of tan, with henna hackles, *halt,*"—Mr. Stevens read with the acme of pith. All through the series he did not glance out at the audience, change the position of his feet, or so much as smile;—read deliberately, slowly and with eloquent pauses, was in evening dress & very "neat." I could hear every word (but was in row 3, Frances Steloff's guest) some couldn't. James Sweeney said to him afterward, "Why didn't you *laugh* now & then?" "I thought that was for the audience to do," Mr. Stevens said. "Eulalia-and-the-Sunshade" ["Certain Phenomena of Sound" III] was a perfect pearl of persuasive effectiveness. All I could murmur afterward was, "I don't see how you can achieve an effect of tranquility—without monotony."

Mrs. Church "had us to supper" though I had thought I was to be brought home or found a taxi home right after the program. (Mr. Stevens had autographed books "with such bad pens" for half an hour)—then a "very small committee" as Mrs. C. called it went to Mrs. Church's to speak to him: Marcel Duchamp (an old friend & intimate apparently) James & Laura Sweeney, & I. He, (W. S.) was staying at the Drake—& the car that brought me back here, left him at the Drake & Mr. Duchamp on 14th Street, en route. I had a perfect time & sick or well was grateful I was in motion sufficiently to go.

There is nothing to "send me," how like you, Elizabeth, to wonder and care. Gladys is still quite diligent about me, looking in every day. Louise brought me some dried beef & nuts I wanted, & I can manage quick cooking now. All I lack is a mind. You understand, I was going to say, but you couldn't. I am almost without intelligence when worn down. Be good to yourself, Elizabeth.

With love & so gratefully. Marianne

Don't spoil me, Elizabeth. This scraggly thing deserves no answer.

To Glenway Wescott *February 3, 1951*

Dear Glenway,

Exerting yourself to beguile my captivity, and certainly I enter into that Maurice Baring bracketing of the ant with the python! Now a captive yourself.

One of my consolations as I relinquished the program of prose and poetry by Wallace Stevens at the Museum, was the sense that *you* would be there and at the party Monroe gave afterward. However, my mother had a way of interposing prophecy at such times, and saying "Don't repine. Expect, under more favorable circumstances." Then the gold medal ceremony under the auspices of Mr. A. M. Sullivan and Miss Emma Mills! relinquished. *However*, I did get to the YMHA because Mrs. Henry Church had me conveyed to and fro; and took me home for conversation and refreshments after the reading.

I am now *partially* an authority on Mr. Stevens' declamatory manner, having threatened my accuracy of attention by constant note-taking and I am at your service as circumstances favor comment. Chieftain Iffucan, the green vine angering for life, "Eulalia & the Sunshade;" the fixity in motion of the cataract (from "The Auroras of Autumn",) were the delicate peak of perfection and of *fire*. Mr. Stevens ("*le grand et timide* Wallace Stevens" as *Mesures* called him) is not a *meek* man.

This perhaps exasperating volubility, is just to say that I am grateful to you, Glenway, for caring whether I live or die. I hope you are mending. And

I hope I was of *some* use to you in my rather fanatical comments on Eliza-beth Bishop. You'll probably have to recast them.

Yours affectionately,   Marianne

To Hildegarde Watson   *March 7, 1951*

The face of an angel, Hildegarde, against a pleated halo; tell me sometime just where it stood. And how should *I* have it? What celestial things you do, Hildegarde. And Arnold Genthe's[38]—that touching portrait with turned back cuffs & the gardenias. Framed just now, I think? The most touching, pensively touching, study; with that knot of white flowers—that I do asso-ciate with you, though I associate other flowers too.

Was talking of you and Sibley to Wallace Stevens last evening, after he'd received The National Book Award medal for his *The Auroras of Au-tumn*, telling him about the Farm and the dwarf laurel in the rocky pastures on the way to the Devil's Den.

What years it seems since I have seen you. All is well I hope. Maybe you'll be collaborating with Miss Moseley sometime and telephone me. Though I don't want to seem plaintive. Am not, you know.

Sibley does not gravitate toward mobs and garrulity, but I wish you might both have heard the responses to the Awards yesterday. Wallace Stevens said we can't compare modern poetry with "The Lady of the Lake" any more than we can compare Eisenhower with Agamemnon. "A modern poet is nothing more than a person of the present, finding his own thought and feeling in the thought and feeling of other people—*through* his own thought and feeling. What he derives from people he returns to people." And Robert Sherwood quoted St. Paul: "Tribulation worketh experience and experience, hope." We can subscribe to that, can't we?

Dear H. "be *well*," as I've said before. I see you in my thoughts so often in that little beaver acorn-cup of a hat like puffin down—(down of a chick) speeding through the aqueduct-like arches of the Plaza in search of our unidentifiable guest! Am loth to part from you even in script. I wish that I could bring you a heavenly blessing.

Marianne

38. The photograph of HW is at the Rosenbach Museum and Library.

1951–1972
What Are Years?

IN THE 1950s Moore became a public figure and spent a great deal of her time responding to the "tons of irrelevant mail" now arriving at 260 Cumberland Street—from would-be-acquaintances, autograph seekers, and aspiring writers looking for a nod of approval and a little promotional help from an established poet. In one letter, she mentioned a volume of fifty or sixty letters a day. On July 26, 1958, she complained to Hildegarde Watson, "Yesterday . . . instead of being mesmerized to work on, foolhardily, I returned a weight of ms.—(invited to re-read and write a *foreword*!) My misguided appreciators always thank me for rebuffing them—always send me another memento, strange-looking ocelot or submarine wombat." Of her famous exchange with the Ford Motor Company concerning the naming of the Edsel, she wrote: "Now—for my crazy mail; each day outdoes the other. You couldn't believe it if you saw yesterday's. In addition, a telegram—a long one—from the Maryland Motorist—Richard Reese: 'Have permission of *N. Yorker* magazine and The Ford Motor Co. to republish in our publication your correspondence with Mr. David Wallace about naming the Edsel, and so on. May we have yours? Wire collect.' Isn't that odd?" (to HW, October 4, 1957). To a certain extent, of course, Moore cultivated this broader public image and relished the celebrity that each day's mail confirmed. Moore was increasingly a participant in, not just an observer of, popular culture. Her prose appeared in such occasional and commercial venues as the *Ladies' Home Journal, Harper's Bazaar, Women's Wear Daily*, and *Seventeen*. She gave full vent to her early interests in film, the circus, sports, fashion, entertainment, as well as politics and industry. Indeed, popular culture overtook nature and art as subject matter for poetry.

Moore never wrote form letters; her quick notes of thanks or inquiry are full of pith and insight. Some of her correspondence in the fifties reveals the depth of religious and philosophical resolve that guided her life and art and which she offered to friends in distress. But much of the correspondence of this period has the shorthand casualness (in the case of personal letters) and brisk formality (in the case of public correspondence) of a busy person with a very broad range of correspondents. There are fewer of the long, descriptive letters one finds to family and friends in earlier years. Moore continued a regular correspondence with Warner (evinced by his letters to her), but her letters to him have not been preserved. (As a precaution against what they discerned as Constance's jealousy, they had agreed in the late forties that he would destroy Moore's letters immediately after reading them.) Warner and other close friends in many ways filled the role of witness to Moore's career, left vacant after Mrs. Moore's death. Moore's letters to Watson, for example, provide a kind of diary of her constant comings and goings—to parties, readings, award ceremonies, and other social and cultural events. On May 6, 1956, for instance, she wrote:

> I am in quite a state, Hildegarde—would be if I did not try "not ever to hurry." A tea Friday at the Fosbergs' for Osbert Sitwell who commissioned Mr. Fosberg to paint a portrait of him for Renishaw. I made a mistake and went Thursday instead of Friday; was forbearingly, indeed beautifully, welcomed and saw the portrait undistracted. Then went again Friday! . . . after church today am to have luncheon with Mrs. Church and Holly Stevens; Monday with Osbert, Monday evening dinner with T. S. Eliot & Marion Kauffer and Wednesday, am going to Amherst—returning Friday. Am not ready but will be; and am taking a through train to Northampton, (however inconvenient I am making it for James Merrill who says he will meet me and take me to Amherst).

The poet's lifelong interest in stylish clothes and accessories was much indulged by her wealthy friends, and Moore went to many celebrity events outfitted in the dresses, jackets, hats, pearls, diamonds, boas, and fox furs that Hildegarde, Kathrine Jones, Marcia Chamberlain, Louise Crane, and others had given her. The cape Moore often wore with her tricorn hat was given to her by Hildegarde's mother, Mrs. Lasell, and the gardenias that became another Moore signature were a regular tribute from her friend. Again, these gifts were occasions for descriptive flourish. Thanking Monroe Wheeler for a fan he had brought her from Japan, she wrote: "An evocation of every fish, monkey, bamboo-leaf, poppy or gauze, Japan ever produced. The consummate art of understatement-with-precision. . . . The gauze-fish gray like the willow-frond; and the silver-edging of the gauze, silver, like the underbody of the fish are absolutely complete—like carving jade or amber so as to use the possibilities of the color contrasts in stone" (January 18, 1959).

Moore also revived a correspondence with her cousin Mary Shoe-maker (who died in 1955) and pursued a correspondence with relatives on her father's side. Mary Warner Moore had cut off all relations with this side of the family, but Warner had met one of his paternal relatives in the 1940s, while stationed in Hawaii, and in the 1950s Moore saw some of these paternal relatives (Edith Love and Mary-Louise Schneeberger in particular) when she was in California to read at Scripps College and UCLA.

The first half of the decade was marked by the loss of some other close friends. Kathrine Jones died of cancer in 1952, and her companion, Marcia Chamberlain, died just three years later, after an extended illness. (Moore stayed in Brookline, Massachusetts, with Chamberlain for several weeks during her decline, and kept busy by taking driving lessons.) Moore's letters to T. S. Eliot during the fifties are taken up partly with their mutual concern for Edward McKnight Kauffer, whose separation from Marion Dorn, and decline in health and spirits are the subject of several long letters between these old acquaintances. On August 5, 1954, for instance, she wrote to Eliot: "Edward lives in the sense of former incentives and will refer suddenly to having come on this or that certificate or letter of commendation. I used to feel he should write a memoir, and that would give him lustre and something humanly reflexive. But shrinking under a sense of indignity as now, would he write with the necessary freedom?" Kauffer died in 1954 of liver complications due to alcoholism, and Moore wrote to Eliot movingly of his last days and of his burial.

These losses were buffered by many public triumphs: six honorary degrees between 1950 and 1955 (sixteen by 1969), and the Triple Crown of poetry prizes between 1951 and 1953—the Pulitzer Prize, the National Book Award, and the Bollingen Prize. In 1951 she also won the Gold Medal of the National Institute of Arts and Letters. New friends were made, old friendships renewed. Moore traveled to Bermuda twice with Frances and Norvelle Browne, sisters she had known when Frances was her classmate at Bryn Mawr. Moore and sculptor Malvina Hoffman became close friends, sharing the griefs and joys of their daily lives. In an undated letter to Hoffman, Moore's pleasure in their mutual sensibility is clear: " I almost called you up last evening to ask if you can see the moon from 35th Street—now a thin crescent with a perfect little diamond of a star facing it fairly near. But I had enough conscience to halt myself." The two women spent several summers together in Maine between 1954 and 1959, when Hoffman rented a house that had belonged to F. O. Matthiessen. Her letter to Hildegarde Watson of September 8, 1954, indicates how she valued the peaceful atmosphere of these country visits.

As a prominent artist of the modernist era, Moore was involved inevitably in retrospection during the fifties, her own and others'. She read and responded, in letters, to Williams's *Autobiography*. Reservations about the moral and aesthetic propriety of the late books of *Paterson* led her to decline a request from James Laughlin for a jacket comment, but the two poets remained friends, agreeing to disagree. Moore praised Laughlin for his past courage in publishing unproven writers. The literary world also celebrated her past accomplishments. In addition to the major prizes of the early fifties, she received the M. Carey Thomas Award from Bryn Mawr (1953), the Gold Medal Award for Lifetime Achievement from the Poetry Society (1967), and the National Medal for Literature (1968). But Moore was also actively interested in contemporary writing, and was often asked to stand as judge or adviser to the new generation of poets. During this decade, Moore responded to manuscripts by Allen Ginsberg, Ted Hughes, Robert Lowell, Sylvia Plath, Kenneth Rexroth, James Merrill, Charles Reznikoff, John Ashbery, and many others.

Moore's own poetic production was steady. Her *Fables* appeared in 1954, and for all her ambivalence about this achievement, it was clearly a relief to put the project behind her. "I am grateful that they are in print," she wrote to Hildegarde Watson, "perturbed as I am about the errors and the tameness" (May 21, 1954). She marked their completion by attempting a new genre. Moore had always been drawn to the performing arts (even as a college student, she had participated in productions), and in the fifties she frequented the theater—as a guest of Monroe Wheeler to the production of Molière's *Le Bourgeois Gentilhomme* (newly translated by Richard Wilbur), the opening of Stravinsky's *The Rake's Progress* (with libretto by W. H. Auden and Chester Kallman), several new Balanchine ballets produced by Lincoln Kirstein, and Eliot's new verse plays, *The Cocktail Party* and *The Confidential Clerk*. These performances and others inspired her to try her hand at playwriting, and in 1954 Moore wrote *The Absentee: A Comedy in Four Acts Based on Maria Edgeworth's Novel of the Same Name*. She sent it to Martin Browne, Eliot's London theatrical producer, but the play was not published until 1962. Her successes as a poet continued, however. She published *Like a Bulwark* in 1956 and *O To Be a Dragon* in 1959. *The Arctic Ox* appeared in 1964, *Tell Me, Tell Me* in 1966.

Moore's health during the 1950s reflected her age and the pressures of her public life, but she began seeing a new doctor in 1955 and marveled to her friends at the efficacy of her treatments. To Elizabeth Bishop she wrote, in her usual mocking self-description (July 27, 1955): "She does not minister to my vanity. She regards me, I know, as a stiff-legged, stiff-necked dromedary. But she has cured me of catching cold from air-conditioned movies, trains, & restaurants; and counteracted a wheeze I had when I would catch cold." In 1961, however, Moore suffered a collapse that her friends called a mild "stroke," and Louise Crane obtained for her a regular nurse, Ethel Taylor. Moore's wit and mental vitality were unaffected by these setbacks, apparently. "Nearly every word I write lacks a final letter," she wrote to Hildegarde Watson on December 3, 1967. "When Dr. [Nagla] Laf Loofy took me to a neurologist who diagnoses the cause of strokes and I said Am I mentally defective? I never spell a word without dropping a final letter, he said Do you know you do? O yes, I said. Then it's all right, he said since you are aware of doing it." Moore nevertheless continued to lead a relatively active life through the first part of the 1960s, traveling again with Norvelle and Frances Browne to Italy and Greece in 1962 (when she visited Pound), to England and Ireland in 1964 (when she visited Edith Sitwell, T. S. Eliot, and Alyse Gregory), and to Florida in 1966. She moved back to Greenwich Village in 1965 (her Brooklyn neighborhood having become unsafe) and carried on in her role as the public's poet, reading the Phi Beta Kappa poem at Harvard ("In Lieu of the Lyre"), making her famous appearances to throw the ball out at Yankee Stadium, to dine with Cassius Clay, and to brighten the covers of *Sports Illustrated, Vogue,* and *Look.* She published her *Complete Poems* in 1967, close to her eightieth birthday (which was met with much fanfare and honor, including a festschrift). Moore continued to write until a major stroke in 1969 left her permanently disabled. She died in her sleep on February 5, 1972.

The letters in this volume give a sense of what is amply evident in the correspondence as a whole—the sense of a long life fully lived, rich in both private and public rewards. Moore's family ties and her extended friendships in the world of arts and letters, and even in the popular culture, sustained her throughout her life. Her correspondence displays, to the end, the gusto she so admired in others, that quality of wit, exuberance, and freshness of response that is the signature of a great writer.

To William Carlos Williams   *260 Cumberland Street   Brooklyn 5, N.Y.*
June 22, 1951

Dear William:

This is a case in which I might apply my own advice when taken to task for "giving" you the Academy's Loines Award. I said, look for major merit in others; and for any defect, however small, in ourselves. This *letter* from you, has my salute! and seems to me characteristic, moreover. *It*, for me, is something that does NOT miss the mark.

The trouble for me with your rough and ready girl, is that she does not seem to me part of something that is inescapably typical. That is to say, writing is not just virtuosity; but an interpretation of life—protest as you may in the style of our early arguments about the lily and the mud. (One as "lovely" technically speaking, as the other!)

And I take it hard that the technical achievement here, in "Paterson IV," *is* achievement in the early parts, and useful to me. (Ponder this, if you will.)

Another complaint, I can't see the necessity for any ineradicable grudge. I would be invisible for spots (speaking as a leopard) if I stalled on grudges and scepticism of others' "approach" to writing.

The fact is, I must admit, that we usually exemplify—in some measure—the faults against which we inveigh. I am prone to excess, in art as in life, so that I resist anything which implies that the line of least resistance is normal; and there, perhaps, you have your reprieve—(so far as I dare accuse you). Wallace Stevens' "Final Soliloquy of the Interior Paramour" goes too far in the other direction from you, perhaps; but he *has* made his point, and with maximum force. Edmund Wilson is deplored and commiserated on his "feeble" play, *The Little Blue Light*, and misunderstood in a way that is maddening—for the play is a bulwark against decadence if ever there was one—despite the grudge, the axe to grind, and the continuously enervated "My God's." (Probably introduced as satire.) The presentment dominates the debility, as I see it. And fire and tone are what we have to have. (What *I* have to have.)

Make allowance, William, and muster charity. But no charity is needed so far as friendship is concerned, for friendship is my phobia. It is after all, loyalty which makes one resistful?

Love to Florence.   Marianne

I nearly perished of the results of my folly this spring—must command a slower pace.

To William Carlos Williams   *September 23, 1951*

"But all I meant was that sour grapes are just the same shape as sweet ones."
Unique.
Dear William:

The Autobiography; some of your very best accuracies and clues to presentment. To say nothing of "the local assertion" and the fervor! "What became of me has never seemed to me important, but the fates of ideas living against the grain in a nondescript world has always held me breathless." This is the summary, but where did Selden Rodman get it? From *In the American Grain,* I suppose, or is it here and I don't see what I read?

I should like to see "The Old Apple Tree." I suppose, you can't write it again? And "The Dog and the Fever," something to look forward to.

The portraits. Marsden Hartley's elephant eyes. Ezra Pound and "time." Florence, I am grateful to see, comes out as the hero she is. What a father, and your own father, his silent resignation to events, never making difficulties for anyone. I remember Charles Demuth clearly, in the rather high enormous hospital room at Morristown, and his touching little objects, jade and something china, and I think a few flowers. I was awed by the fact that he made nothing of his disability and gave the impression of being normal. Then Joe who rode along with you because his wife's cousins were no good, and then walked back.

There are no words for these things; for some others, either. You know my attitude to what I consider uninvigorating.

As for me, you see me in too good a light. I never held up anything and nobody loved me!

Love to Florence and yourself.   Marianne

I am a little puzzled by the statement that Kenneth Burke "took over after I left [*The Dial*]." I thought he left and I stayed; and we all left, the others of us in July 1929. And that matter of "The Waste Land." It showed—me at least—that we don't have to be Austin Dobson;[1] but more important than that, that urgency is the point—urgency in the author, whoever may or may not like the result.

I hesitate to write you lest I rouse you to a letter and you ought to spare yourself. I know you ought. Don't take risks. You would have heard from me at

---

1. English poet and essayist (1840–1921) who was also known for his biographies of eighteenth-century figures.

once, on the other hand for I do not become less impetuous with time, but I couldn't write—because of an eye, an inflamed retina. I realise how it is that Bryher is Sir John Ellerman here—whereas "Sir John's money" would not have published Gertrude Stein or anyone or given big parties, if Sir John's money had not been Bryher's money—the sad fact being that when one is not wise, there is no end to the penalty!—of a piece to me, William, with "the poor defeated body and its gulf."

To Edward McKnight Kauffer   *December 11, 1951*

Dear Edward,

To speak is to blunder but I venture, for I know the bewilderment one experiences in being misapprehended. We must face it, as you said. When we do well—that is to say, *you*—in designs of yours which are a standard— the Ethyl horse-power, the Gilbey's port, the Devon downs, the girl in the helmet with the star and effect of velvet darkness, the tall hat on the Victorian table, the door with the keyhole made dramatic,—there is a flash of splendor apart from the pretext; and when a thing snares the imagination, it is because of a secret excitement which contributes something private— an incontrovertible to admire afresh at each sight, like the bloom and tones of a grape or the glitter of Orion as one emerges into the dark from the ordinariness of lamplight. If we must cart rags and even for lack of a horse, substitute for one and mechanically drag along a dull street, there is no transcendence about us. As I mentioned one day, I was half sitting on a subway guard-rail and a woman came up kindly and said, "Are you all right?" I remember at Harvard when I was trying to read something to be recorded, and my one thought was to get the midnight train home, Professor Packard said, "Try that again and say to yourself, 'This is the most beautiful thing that was ever written';" that is to say (though I have said it before so pardon it) it is only enchantment that does it—together with a sense of obligation to what made us sensitive to vicissitudes and to beauty.

Whatever the problem, we must elude the sense of being trapped— even if all one can say to one's self is, "if not now, later." Disgust with me is often (or not often; occasionally) a lever, as when my mother said, "You have a vivid and expanding imagination; see that you put it to the right use." Miserable or exalted—the will has something to do with it. The better one's apperceptions, the more susceptible one is to a sense of degradation; I shrink—as you do—from forlorn or exasperating objects on the street. "Society" is intolerable—so decadent and pleased to be decadent, that one's heart fails one. However, since our life depends on immunizing ourselves to externalities that are destructive, we can do it.

A reviewer in England, does not see in my book, one extenuating quality. This should not depress me—though it raises a question. Where discerning readers "shudder for my future if this or that tendency grows" on me, I can learn. This is a matter of craft. As for perspective on life and projected wisdom or beauty, there is a magic of attraction to what can save us, which is inviolable; nothing can hurt it. If nothing charms or sustains us (and we are getting food and fresh air) it is for us to say, "If not now, later," and not mope. I never fully succeed and am beginning to think I never shall; still, the automatic sense of participation, brings one along. I can not work when resentful, and realize that I must be exasperated with no one but myself. Then particles are magnetized to a centre—of themselves—and one does not tire. This is what you have been doing for years—have exemplified as I see it—and it baffles me that you are requited at times with what is beyond bearing. But it is incidental, Edward; believe me. Any sense of defeat. These are dead axioms which I have been uttering?—may seem to be, I should say—but be sure that all is well, for it is. If one lies in wait; if one is ready for the problem, that is sufficient.

Affectionately and, as you see, insistently that you be happier; not happier but *happy*. If as happened with the man I was speaking of one time, every acquired skill left you, one would feel sombre. Not now.

Marianne

It is a trial to be made to think about what one does not care to think about. In any case, this letter, Edward, needs no answer. I shall be sorry I wrote if you must put things aside to reply. (I so doubt that I should impose these awkward thoughts on you, help me by not making me sorry I mailed them.)

To Lincoln Kirstein   *January 11, 1952*

The spirit cannot submit to the body, Lincoln, or its identity is impaired.[2] How should that which has been the most powerful part of us, choose to be less than that which has mattered least? You feel this, I am sure. I pray you need not be confused but strengthened. I am sure the spirit is not hurt by its warfare—the spirit of those we love. Then I weaken and wonder if I may *dare* to believe what I have believed. But such desperate responsibility, we need not take. Kierkegaard says no one who has ever really wanted help to believe has failed to find it. All that is asked of us is to ask. Blessed are those with the begging spirit, the New Testament says and I find it so.

I once objected after hearing that we must "have more faith," "and *how*? Where are we to find it?" and the speaker said, "The grain of mustard-seed is enough, with as much power in it as it needs, to become more than

2. The letter refers to the death of Kirstein's father.

it seems." Or this was the meaning as I interpreted it to myself and it seems to me to lift the sense of injustice.

Pardon me for pressing my thoughts on you. This you know; it would pain me if you felt you need seem to notice what I say. I trust you to let it lay no care on you.

With love, Marianne

To Malvina Hoffman   *January 12, 1952*

It saddens me, Malvina, to have you ill. I know something about this too— the form of cold I hate most,—since there is no compromise, and nothing for a time can make one less uncomfortable. I also know why you have it. One doesn't get these things unless over-tired or over burdened. I can only help you by letting you have privacy, it seems. It does comfort me, to realize that you can stay continuously in bed and yet have enough food and have the telephone answered for you. (The relentlessness of the telephone has often retarded me because I lacked the force of character to place the receiver on the telephone irrespective of colloquy.)

I supposed yesterday when I saw the picture of it in the paper, that you had been at the unveiling of the bust, and I telephoned partly to say how pleased I was, that your undertakings *flower*, and appropriately. Also to say that I had received a letter from Alyse Gregory from Darien—regretting that she must adhere to her original plan and prospects. Her sense of the heart and exciting contagiousness symbolized by your inquiry, Malvina, is very evident. She is not dead to the chivalry of your imagination and of your performance. The impact of both combined is so great that for timid and more hampered persons it seems unreal—speaking for myself. And I felt therefore that I was a suitable promoter of your offer. But Alyse is determined. We might as well accept it. She says, "I was so dazzled by Miss Hoffman's bewilderingly kind offer that only now have I been able to contemplate it with clear wits—and I see alas! that I am too old and too faint hearted to rise to such a rare opportunity, am too wedded to my country existence and too, I could not support myself in New York without the most watchful economy—without strain & anxiety & self destruction . . . *la vie intérieure se renouvelle la vie extérieure se détruit.* The delight of being in such beautiful harmonious surroundings would be almost wholly offset by my sense of inadequacy. But do not think that Miss Hoffman's beautiful generosity has not 'opened doors.' I can't tell you what a special surprised excitement and privilege it was [to] see some of those marvellous creations of hers among which I longed to linger and of which the memory is vividly with me. Will you explain to her my gratitude, & my feeble, insufficiency and I will write to her too."

Even death in New York would seem to me, preferable to "exile." I would clamber aboard a child's yacht drawn by a string if it could bring me into close proximity to "art." But having striven to be instrumental in opening a door, be at peace Malvina. You do usually implement what you visualize. That must suffice. (I would have died long since if I did not excel in defaulting. I better than anyone else, should see the barrier to Alyse's accepting rescue. I suppose independence is at the root of it, for & against. It would be at the root of my "embracing" your offer! even if I migrated from 157 to a quonset hut.) We are blessed with sympathetic insight anyhow. I now hope you can find the right custodian of your giraffes, elephants, personages & household treasures. *My* elephant will have to be one of many till I can reclaim it.

> *Affectionately,*   Marianne

I feel very much like sending this Special Delivery but I might wake you up or puzzle you so, Monday will have to do. Monday morning I am going to hear Reinhold Niebuhr at Union. (Constance Rulison & her sister have invited me & for lunch.) Then I agreed to be present at my church at a gigantic meeting from which I would not be missed but I must go. (Tuesday I may or may not be in town.) Wednesday morning I am to be interviewed by a radio reporter—and have Gilda Serla fix my (now) black velveteen dress you gave me. Mrs. Serla is *good*; and is also putting a collar on the velvet coat—keeps saying—"That is good velvet. I think you should let me put the collar on & stiffen it—*that is good velvet*, etc!", (showing me some new modern horsehair collar material). She rapidly puts in pins, stands you off and gets the effect, writes down the hour for a fitting, in a large engagement book, handed me the five dollars I had laid on the cutting table as a guarantee that I was not treacherous—and said "*Take* that *back*!"

Have Miss Julie tell me, Malvina when you are able to talk.

> M.

To William Carlos Williams   *January 27, 1952*

Dear William:

I thank you and Florence for sticking to me when I get what I shouldn't have; my insufficiencies and unproficiencies stand out in high relief. (You should have heard me at the Voice of America the other day {at the French desk!}.) I feel, however, that the momentum and potential momentum of the hopefully panting animal, does signify. And his friends' ungrudging affection should certainly help him get further. My case—disregarding gender;—something I have always done! Nobody knew me and I knew nobody in college days, William. I dogged Professor Mahaffy when he visited Bryn Mawr and the University of Pennsylvania and he magnanimously paused to speak with me once; and I knew the Skinners slightly.

The picture is *not* recent—taken by Charlotte and Arthur Steiner—here at 260 and must have been nested in *The Tribune* file; it improves me certainly but not my temper. I have repeatedly promised Arthur and Charlotte Steiner I would attribute it to them if used and either they get no mention or the picture is credited to *Acme News* and United Press, giving me the status of a foreign visitor but also of a scoundrel.

At the Institute, William, you puzzled me by effacing [your] accent; but your impassioned earnestness was epic—effecting anything you wanted effected—regardless of what.

Another broken promise if I don't stop right here. I promised Ruthven Todd to write Mrs. Ames, asking if there would not be room for David Gascoyne[3] this summer. Please go on being for me, and if life is unimaginably prolonged, I may justify your trust—at least "write so I can be understood" as you once said.

With love to Florence and yourself,   Marianne

To Robert McAlmon   *February 23, 1952*

Dear Robert:

I have the elephants, the skunk, and the cards and do thank you; am especially impressed by the walking elephant and the action in it. What a care for you, to pack these animals so they would suffer no damage.

The regular placing of the thorns on the beaver-tail cactus is a marvel and the drifts of color, like a sunset of the cactus in bloom over stretches of the desert are hard to credit; no one has ever thought to tell me that the plants are not always in bloom! Instructive, the chart of varieties. And what a remarkable photograph of the single Joshua tree.

Yes, I sometimes hear from Ezra Pound or Mrs. Pound and I certainly agree about Ezra P's translations. I don't know how I could have given you the impression that I distrusted the Sitwells. Have always taken an interest in them and Edith Sitwell's urgency, eloquence, and sense of responsibility during and since the war, should stir anyone, I think. I don't know a more expert study than Sacheverell [Sitwell]'s book on Domenico Scarlatti nor do I know the equal for humor and irony of Osbert Sitwell's *Escape with Me!*, about China.

I seem determined to be perverse, but I must defend William Benét. He battled for me from the first, Robert—put me in his *Fifty Poets*, the *Ox-*

3. Elizabeth Ames (1926–1969), executive director of Yaddo; Ruthven Todd (1914–1978), Scottish poet who became an American citizen in 1959; David Gascoyne (1916–), English poet, translator, novelist, critic, and editor.

ford Book of American Verse, in various reference books, was constantly try-ing to help my standing and did help it. He stood out against the whole rest of *The Saturday Review of L.* in the attack on Ezra Pound, and quoted a page of best things from *The Cantos* and other work of E P's—though Ezra had written him a really insurmountable letter many years previous, brusquely declining to be in an anthology and was constantly disparaging William and his associates. (These poems of mine—if you can call them that—are published by Faber & Faber; it was Faber and Faber who got me to put them together {i.e. T. S. Eliot}.)

I am sorry you have had trouble with your lungs; *I hope you are past it.* In any case, they seem to be discovering what really combats the thing.

(Imprudence and overwork have effaced me for some weeks but I am recovering. Am trying to finish a translation of La Fontaine's fables as I may have said.)

M. M.

To Allen Ginsberg   *July 4, 1952*

Dear Mr. Ginsberg:

I have been thinking about this manuscript[4] which you left me. I am sad to find that it reflects hardship. You have ability, and that means responsi-bility, does it not? There are in writing, a few technicalities to think about; but the thing that matters is our sense of awareness; this comes first. What are we to do about it? I am not satisfied with your solution of the problem.

There should be page-numbers to help one when referring to parts of the work. In the opening piece—or rather as the climax—the last line, you say, "I wandered off in search of a toilet." And I go with you, remember. Do I have to? I do if you take me with you in your book. Am I so stiff that I do not see that this is a poetic device? a tool? supposedly. The preponderant im-pression is the answer.

"I feel as if I am at a dead end." This is well harmonized.

"I Dream And Dream" Should the And be capitalized?

"Song": "crownly creaminess." This is too juicy, I would say. Adjectives are dangerous.

"Paterson": slobs and dumbells hardly sustain the Crucifixion metaphor.

"The Trembling of the Veil": The suggestion of the moon makes this pen-etrating; brings it to life (though as with my own work, I am not so sure about taking others' words and titles)?

"This is about Death": "to whoever." One can not be too careful about ac-tual parts of speech.

"Madness is Irrelevance": The truth, Mr. Ginsberg; this has depth, for me.

---

4. *Empty Mirror*, published in 1961 as *Empty Mirror: Early Poems.*

"the prison of selfhood." It is death, (for one's self and one's writing).

"In Death": "We know all about death//that we will ever know." This holds the attention by its intensity and moderate tone.

"The notion of change is beautiful as well as forms." "is" has to go with both notion and forms and it can't be used with forms. (Or have I misunderstood the passage?) Be careful about such things.

"Holding the dog with a frayed rope." I like this.

"The Archetype Poem": Are you for this? Is there any "universal" principle to be deduced? "sweat, skin, feces, sperm, saliva, odor." My comment here is the same as for the first poem.

"The Night-Apple": "Last night I dreamed/of one I loved." Why could you not go on with this in the way in which it starts? You betray us with a taunt; with an I fooled you.

This is wit with nothing spoiling it:

> *I learned a world from each*
> *one whom I loved;*
> *so many worlds without*
> *a Zodiac.* (the "whom" is good)

The brick-layers' lunch hour is fine work, accurate, contagious—even if it is William C. Williams instead (or as well as) Allen Ginsberg.

This is grandiose—Gregory Corso's story as well as false "release," I would say.

"The Blue Angel": This is well contrived.

"Walking home. Oh God, how horrible." This is penetrating; it *is* horrible and I protest. Is it all the impact of too much; or partly a submitting to look at it? as horrible. I don't know. A hard problem. People say, a cake of soap costs five cents; why be dirty? Not being dirty is much more than a matter of five cents.

"A Ghost May Come": this has so much the tone of William Carlos W., one cannot think about anything but him.

"How Sick I Am": "Is it this strange?" this strange will pass but if you follow it with "metier," the disparity grates on the reader; is not "in keeping."

"Life without joy, passion, consummation." There is the clue. Do take it. Even if we are sold out by everything and everyone, we have to look hope in the face and admit that there was, is or could be such a thing.

"Fragmenta Monumenti": I like this title, and the poem begins well but is unjust to expectation.

"I dreamed I was dreaming again.": This interests one, is interestingly stated.

Now you see, Mr. Ginsberg, that I am speaking to myself as well as to you, in the above comments. Let me, though I seem topheavy in doing it, try to think why the book as a whole dejected me. Patient or impatient repudiat-

ing of life, just repudiates itself. There is no point to it. What can be exciting to others is one's struggle with what is too hard. Unless one is improved
by what hurts one, it can't be of interest to others. What makes us read a
gruesome thing like Tolstoi's "The Power of Darkness" or Gogol's "A Lodg-
ing for a Night" or the Book of Job? We read it and thank it because it puts
a weapon in our hands; we are the better able to deal with injustice and with
a sense of "God's injustice." An understanding eye penetrated the dispiriting and called it dispiriting. If we share in the conspiracy against ourselves
and call existence an insult, who cares what we write?

　　Your disgust worries me and I can't make clear what I mean without
being objectionable. You left your manuscript at Random House and will
get the kind of note or card we don't like: "We thank you for having allowed
us to see these poems and regret that they are not suited to our requirements" or some such statement. Why? *Empty Mirror* is too literal, you don't
get behind it. You don't see that it is? It is "treatment." It is your "taste."
Note, however, that you did not choose [the] title, "His heart was a bag of
shit"; or "Existence is a load of shit." Any line that occurs in the course of
the work as your pronouncement should be able to serve as a title. These interpretations in the manuscript really equal the title you do use: Here is the
proof that something is wrong. What is it? the old hackneyed truism; affirm
or die. If I feel negative, why can't I say I am? Why feign what I don't feel?
I am not grateful. What would make me grateful? (Self-pity is bad, friend.)
Soliloquize in this way over and over; people will not listen. What can you do
about it, I don't know. As D. H. Lawrence said: "To hold on or to let go?" You
see and feel with interest. Can't you be grateful for *that*? If not, not. *But try.*
                                                                   M. M.

Why do I say all this? Because your trials, your own realness, and capacity,
affect me. If I despised it all, you would not be annoyed by an inconsiderate
harangue. A compliment. But this does not mean that you must thank me.
I am real myself. I write too many letters, then am too tired to do my work.
I don't want to make *you* too tired to work. So be spared, Mr. Ginsberg. Perhaps you can use at least something that I say and that would thank me.
                                                                   M. M.

To Louis Ginsberg   *July 11, 1952*

I am grateful to you, Mr. Ginsberg, for your reassuring letter. It pained me
to run the risk of perhaps estranging your son from wholesome pertinacity
and humility by possibly ill-adjudged resistance to his manuscript. If I have
persuaded him even somewhat toward "gratitude"—toward confidence in
God or humanity—I am glad.

We cannot equivocate, it seems to me. Self-centeredness and negative writing in the name of realism are self-destruction, I feel. Yet, as older fighters against disillusion and "injustice," we must have compassion on the malaise of younger persons. Your son, from what you tell me, has reason for being tempted to melancholy. I had not known this. I have had experience, myself—have experienced the mystery of others' disability. As for William Carlos Williams, loyal though I feel to him personally, I wish he could perceive the folly of a doctrinaire attitude to degradation and unhope. We are here to transcend and help others transcend what impairs us. Your son is blessed in having you; I hope as the years pass, that he can be a strength to you. (We all need a strong dose of joy—and what's to be done about that? I don't know.)

You, if I am not mistaken, wrote *The Dial* advertisement, "Against the *faux bon*"—the one the staff liked best, and one I carry with me in thought.

My work is partial (and I readily concur with those who tell me that "In Distrust of Merits" is not poetry—mere sincerity). It helps me to know that you can find good in it. If I can be of use to you, tell me.

Sincerely yours,   Marianne Moore

To Dorothy Pound and Ezra Pound   *July 31, 1952*

Dear Mrs. Pound and Ezra,

B for boorishness, however adaptable the string bags may be. I was much aware of your hospitalities and thank you for your three letters. The chocolates were a stubbornness detached from intellect. (Scant and something of a menace without a fork but I may dispatch a sequel when the weather is less Carthaginian.) A pleasing thought, Mrs. Pound—the 300 elephants. I wish the Republican party had selected a less sublime animal.[5]

I ought not to answer you, fearsomely resilient Ezra, concerning the models of effectiveness with whom I have been associated, but am too pugnacious to just doze deafly when J. S. Watson is mentioned—with 2 essential scientific inventions (pertaining to surgery) to his credit and plenty else. I shudder at false witness against my neighbor and if I do not attack you, then I concur in it.

Profanity and the Jews are other quaky quicksands against which may I warn you? You have seen turtles or armadillos, possibly, when annoyed and I sometimes have to be one of them. I take an avid interest in Mommsen, in

5. MM had visited EP at St. Elizabeths in July 1952. On July 17, 1952, Dorothy Pound wrote to MM thanking her for the visit and for several gifts she had brought. MM and EP had, since 1918, shared a playful enthusiasm for elephants and their symbolic possibilities. Mrs. Pound mentioned having read in Theodor Mommsen that "in the casements of Carthage there were stalls for 300 elephants."

the zealous Achilles Fang[6]; could he be a relative of Mei Lan Fang? a masterpiece of whom I would be ignorant had it not been for *Gilbert Seldes*, who warned me not to miss him. And (an interest in) *The Great Digest*—one of the principal reasons for my coming to Washington (and in facsimiles of Vivaldi manuscripts). I was wishing to tell you how I find it and regretted my digressiveness—much as I liked the young people. They transported me (conveyed me, should I say) to my Bus Depot, Mr. [Alexander] Del Mar regretting that he was unable to park and offer us tea, which I took it on myself to dispense in the form of Coca-Cola and orange juice, while discussing palmistry with Miss ———.

Now that I write, you may ask me to desist.

M. M.

The bags came fastly as my stationer would say.

Thank you, Mrs. Pound, for your address. I like to have it re-verified. (So very unselfish—and I don't know what can be done about it.)

To Louise Crane   *August 2, 1952*

Dear Louise, I've been afraid *you* were sick—was on the point of writing to Mrs. Crane to ask and to ask how she is herself. I assume she is at Woods Hole and well, or you would not be headed for the ceremonials.

The card is beautiful, Louise; and not only the little figures but the spiral columns of the altar-rail and the reredos embroidery.

I am reluctant to tell you, but Kathrine died in July—the 9th—I went to the service for her in Forest Hills, Brookline. Marcia was brave and as I tell her, beyond words *charmed* us in her management and affectionate care of everyone. It is touching, Louise. Fortunately she has help—Pauline, the Norwegian she used to have, and then "Myrtle"—Myrtle Ross a friend and trained nurse who assisted her years ago in Maine when Mr. King, her brother, died (also of cancer). I was planning to stay here this summer but am going to Maine the 20th for a while, to be with Marcia. She is not gloomy; but I don't know what she is going to do—having given up her business, hoping to do various things with Kathrine. Myrtle will be coming to Maine when I leave; she is ideal—I loved her on sight; maybe I can stay a day or so after she comes—maybe September 10th.

The Fables? Of a piece with Pompeii. Malcolm Cowley has forsaken me while lecturing at schools and is now I think writing a book of his own; says he "feels terrible".......... ! (Me too.) My letters and little local activities keep me employed while waiting for the text I have to emend! I have

6. Achilles Fang, author of a 1958 Harvard Ph.D. thesis on Pound entitled *Materials for the Study of Pound's Cantos.*

written a page for *Poetry*'s 40th anniversary issue (entitled "Then the Ermine": "Rather dead than spotted") and have just finished a piece on jockeys for the *Flair Annual*. But am counting before it is hatched. (Mrs. Cowles is no martyr to consistency.) Mr. Robert Offergeld, Editor, enlisted my services. I was going to write this anyhow—on Ted Atkinson; Tom Fool, Tiger Skin, (greentree horses {pink black stripes on sleeve; black cap.}!); Fats Waller, Ozzie Smith and Eubie Blake, champions of harmonious speed—in case I seem irresponsible. I thought of Kelly's Stable, Louise. (Have never been to a race meet but I am an assiduous reader of the sports news.) If I get my lines back, I'll offer them to *The New Yorker* and if back from there, to *Mademoiselle*, and if from there, retire and start my Bryn Mawr work. (But am reviewed in the *N. Yorker* for Aug. 2 {favorably}.)

I haven't had a word from Loren [MacIver] and Lloyd [Frankenberg]; I hope they are well. July 15th I went to Washington, called on the Pounds, took a bus to Hagerstown to see my Cousin Mary, stayed two nights and came home by the dilapidated Pennsylvania Railroad.

Plymouth radios are being stolen out of cars, here, Louise! My perfect dressmaker, Gilda, and her husband had theirs stolen several nights ago. I am indignant. They live round the corner on Carleton Avenue and had me to dinner Thursday evening—after Gilda finished her day's sewing and Mr. Serla came home from the packing-room of A & S. Gilda had just cleaned house with two of her sister's 12 children to help her. It is beautiful. She has three mirror-whatnots (very small) of miniature animals and birds and made all her slip-covers (flowered sateen). There is a guitar on the piano tilted up diagonal, and tinted grasses in a vase on the coffee-table and a splendid television set in one corner. We looked at *Amos & Andy* a while and then I asked the Serlas to come home and I exhibited my oddities and treasures—including a photo-mural of myself from the Youth United for Tomorrow—6 feet by four; and your gourd from Istanbul. They were charmed by the gourd.

Much love, Louise; to Victoria Kent too.   Marianne

Maine address:
c/o Mrs. Marcia K. Chamberlain
RFD 2 Ellsworth Maine
if you have time. I am very ambitious not to be a ball and chain.

To Hildegarde Watson   *November 19, 1952*

What sensibility, Hildegarde! Look askance at any word you wrote, and you are not my friend. "Haunted to sing—like even the insects"—you know or should know that you speak as an angel—and write like one.

And rosemary! the only fragrance, I think, that I really care for. The

aromatic spring calms my cobra-like animosity toward some ten of the letter-writing cormorants whose debris of egomania lies around me—detaining me from writing to you before now, & impinging on me as I do write!

Well—inconsequential, as I think of your brave plans, that the house
in Whitinsville should be of "some spiritual benefit." How right Sibley is
about the "clergy's small mindedness," particularly in business matters. I
think, Hildegarde, that when I saw you, you had hopes that the house *would*
be the benefit you had wished it to be.

Gallant of you to fly to Cambridge to hear Estlin.[7] He scintillated, I am
sure, and the better in having you there. There is something scary about that
Turkish mosque like, half timbered hunting-lodge of Henry the VIIIth
Saunders Theatre. I am happy to think the lectures will be published. Have
just been looking at Estlin's smiling face in *Life* for this Friday; and how
commanding is Wallace Stevens with his frown.

How beautifully, Hildegarde, you speak of Paul Valéry. Would that
you had been with me Sunday when Pierre Schneider[8] called. (My hyper-
scientific Parisian man of letters) and after some generalities concerning
Leonardo da Vinci, M. & Mme. Teste ("An Evening with M. Teste"), he admitted that he thinks Pl. Valéry "vague"!

I have been obliterated, dear Hildegarde, and still am. It is despicable.
No fables, no reading, no responsible activity of any kind. I do nothing but
robot-drudge—: a man who knows me is in jail on a false charge; a girl in
Mexico can't attack "a publisher"; three pages of fine print about me submitted to me for me to revise—which *had* to be redone. Even laudanum
couldn't have persuaded me it would pass. Macmillan has part of a travelling exhibit to assemble—that will tour America like the Goodwill London
buses, and needs letters, proof-sheets, and items of interest pertaining to my
C. Poems. (Is the book itself of interest? If not, I shudder for my pale carbon
copies.) On & on, (I struggle in a marathon, punctuated by a tea & dinner tomorrow & a sailor Saturday, who visits me annually). Marcia is to be at the
St. Regis from the 27th for a while & I do want her to have a good time. It is
urgent that I deal with my transient tasks beforehand and not be trammel-
ing her with them.

If you were suddenly to sing a mediaeval French song with fiery ac-
companiment! such as I recall, fondly—what a thrill and deliverance. But
I must not grumble—am too corrupt to live, Hildegarde.

Think of me; condone me; surprise me; could you not before long—be
unexpectedly arriving at the Park Chambers? The rosemary stirs hope,
Hildegarde. An auspice!

Affectionately, Marianne

7. E. E. Cummings was giving the Charles Eliot Norton Lectures at Harvard.

8. American-born art historian; author of "Le Paradis et l'habitat," about La
Fontaine (1869–1954).

Please tear up this tantrum or Sibley won't let you associate with me.

To Glenway Wescott   *Dec[ember] 10, 1952*

Dear Glenway,

   I do not know what sociabilities may have been planned for Wystan [Auden], but suspect he will be a maypole amid autograph seekers,—who gather back stage with leaning towers of Pisa numbering the authors' complete works. So I had thought of going incognito. *If* Wystan should fix his eye on me & BOW, (as I am assiduously writing down what he says,) be sure I shall seek him out and give him your kindly invitation. His subject is "The Nature of Comedy."

   You lead me to feel that I should send to L.L. Bean for the bird-call listed in his fall catalogue.

Affectionately,   Marianne

This should be a blueprint that becomes readable if laid in the sun.
I hope you are right & that Edith & Osbert are not reluctant to be trailed by me.

To Edith Sitwell and Osbert Sitwell   *December 19, 1952*

"Dr. [Dm.] Edith does not answer; shall I call Sir Sitwell?" The St. Regis says; so I am doing what I should have done in the first place and saying by pen that you made us very happy last evening—with jewelled aspect, even like the verse!

> *No, I can never forget the nest*
> *In which the huge eggs rest*

> *The road I trod*
> *From chaos on to God*

That rhyming, Edith, of seas and Hercules; . . . and the *"Rain"*—which if I had to say,—perhaps matters to me the most of all—enwound as it is with associations of my own at the time you wrote it—or rather, at the time I received it from Bryher.

   What an evening—your voices so clear and resonant—your sublime courtesy—inquiring if we heard; and the courtesy of your apparel. The silver-azure of the curtain fading from but slightly affording a setting; Edith, for your gold and azure and jet black wrist of the gown as you raised your hand at one point. I *could* not forget it! (And associate it in my mind with the Isaac Oliver miniature of Sir Philip Sidney—the turquoise band at the head of his coat skirt, his serpentine black pencil stripes on gold, black vel-

vet breeches & gloves—against the faint emerald & blue of Windsor's formal garden.)

Well—if you could have heard yourselves! I hope, Osbert, you felt the
reverence with which the audience received the squirrel wearing a rose in
his mouth; the interacting dexterities of your mingling the color of the
flower with the creature's life blood—how impressive that even the light-
est of listeners grieved. A witty implicativeness is almost enough, but with
you both what a treat to have it surpassed specifically,—and never a descent
to the flat. The word "incurious" for instance, the golden "apricot" Mr.
Goodliere, and then, to the joy of the multitude,:—

                                                                    flies

              Believe in private enterprise.

Never have I seen people more pleased—at the moment and after.

When your brother Sacheverell read, I was impressed by the effect of
contour as shaped by interior force—defined by the voice, like a shadow
recording in a laboratory. Again it held me entranced—in your difficult
one, Osbert; and in the longer portions with which you concluded, Edith. All
through, but so notably and unforgettably at some points.

I trust you were not too tired afterward. How much is expected of
you—to think, to ornament the scene, and be invulnerable. That the spirit
can conquer matter, is our reprieve. Note my friend Marcia's involuntary
comment after meeting you, Osbert: "How handsome and youthful Sir Osbert seems." (I had to *scold* her for having said she was the "proud posses-
sor" of my duplicate set of your *Autobiography*. But perhaps *you* should
scold *me*, since I had said it was a loan as long as she felt a need for the books
and that they beguiled her loneliness. (Hers had no pictures.)

Perhaps I might add, Edith, that I was not legally present at the big
party for you and Osbert at Glenway's & Monroe's. Am so incurable a fool
that I couldn't either speak to you or absent myself—knowing beyond
doubt that I was the victim of a cold! True enough, I was in bed four days
rallying enough last evening to venture out and menace more people. It did
seem to me mysterious of me to seem to avoid you where the party was *for*
you and Osbert! One further proof that you have a somewhat dangerous
friend—doubly dangerous because undetachable!

However many died of me last night—I STILL am glad that I was
there.

              Your fond and grateful listener,   Marianne

To make sure, I have disinfected my letter, but I *promise* it can't harm you.
One just came anyhow (externally). A fanatic! I sent my ticket back Special

Delivery to the YMHA lest I be unable to go out; and then called for it, I'm happy to say.

To W. H. Auden   *February 16, 1953*

Dear Wystan,

It is masterly—even if you did tear one heart from the body without a qualm—the diction, the melodies, the humor. It has tone; a fable with a moral that *is* a moral. Tom's collapse this time was entirely realistic. I hope he didn't hurt himself. Perhaps it doesn't matter but the two showers of gold on Thursday seemed to me more natural than one—pictorially; and Tom was in no state to be prudent with sovereigns. (Nor were *you* quite prudent though possessed of your senses—thinking we should have sherry and champagne at luncheon.)

You know, of course, that it is good luck not to be liked by Olin Down(e)s; he creates in himself a false sense of conscience every time—mildewing (palpably mildewing) since 1930 and this particularly is a case in which to adapt Ezra Pound's pronunciamento about critics: Never trust a critic who has not himself written a good libretto.

Dog-taxes are $2 for male dogs and $6.50 for females if paid on time; otherwise a dollar is added, in Connecticut. I asked Warner when he telephoned to ask how I liked the opera. And I obtained absolution for seeing *Love's Labour's Lost* on a Sunday! Lincoln and Fidelma took me in the evening and we had little Oliver Andes as Moth—the sweeter of the two boys, and smaller (for grappling with the serpent) Lincoln said. I hope he is the one you heard. Mr. Marre said the 18th c. air to the cuckoo is by Arne.

Please feel that this note, itself an acknowledgment, needs no acknowledgment; or rather, the La Fontaine essay, deferentially dated February 21, received at last from Earle & Calhoun.

I had a delectable time, Wystan. A fussy woman in the next box, Mrs. Church says, said: "I don't know yet what I think of this thing but I'm dying to take the children."

I am pondering those pages at the rear of the program.

To Hildegarde Watson   *153 Summit Avenue   Brookline 46 [Mass.]*
                              August 14, 1953

Hildegarde, the impossible! I have felt again and again since the storm, "if I could just see that tree again!" and I *see* it, and by it see *you.*[9] And *Marcia* can see you . . .

Symbolic to me of miracles, you have ever been. How strange—our being there! As I look at the bark and the filigree of delicate leaves that

9. HW had sent photos of the farm, taken after a tornado struck.

swung so nobly in the wind, I think of it *all*—the moonvine, the arbor vitae(s) by the other side of the house, the paddock, the yellow lilies, and iris-spears, the rose-garden within the stone wall, the pear-tree by the paddock, the flowers by the front door hovered by humming-birds, the squirrel among the grape-leaves and the two bed-rooms! the little French fireplace; and that *elephant* "E. E. Cummings" affixed to the wall—or pincushion; the tree toad I captured in a glass, and after having wanted all my life to see one, carried from the lilac bush and liberated halfway up the lane! Turn the picture sidewise, cover the light spot and the house and it still has the illusion of life—the tree. We were speaking of "God's injustices" last night, Kenneth Jones and I—a friend of Marcia's and cousin of Marcia's & my friend Kathrine Jones—Kenneth J. said "I just don't think about it too much." Well, Hildegarde, I do. I rave, am wild (like George Herbert in "The Collar")—and have to know that mortality would not be mortality if mysteries of the supernatural were plain to the mind's eye. It seems to me, your enthusiasms and attachments are so unsordidly sublime—and enlarging to the spirit,—you should not have to suffer through them. (As continually I felt about Mother.) The tree since we are immortal, however, is immortal too, living in our minds.

How paltry one can be is demonstrated when excitement possesses me. I trust to your charity.

Marianne

How consoling your thought of the 4th—, how uncontradictable. "Love is boundless to heal and bless." Marcia is very alive the last week, however beyond help helpless, it seems, physically; a guide and example to me, since if any might "resign," it is she.

To Mary Shoemaker   *260 Cumberland Street   Brooklyn 5, N.Y.*
February 16, 1954

Dear Cousin Mary,

It seemed so long since I knew how you are and what is happening. I planned to write to you yesterday and then your letter came,—to my pleasure & relief.

First, I so thank you for reminding me that Baltimore is not too far from Hagerstown. I wanted to accept that invitation to Goucher so that perhaps *could* see you and Sue and Ralph. But I declined since I wasn't equal to the heavy program as I thought, an address, two informal scholastic meetings, a tea or reception, and a dinner—involving a 3-days' visit, I think. One main event is about all I can manage. So I am not going to Baltimore. I *am* going to Vassar, to speak in the afternoon March (24th and come home that evening). I am urged to stay and I *would* stay if I didn't have to speak at New

York University the 26th, (the N. York engagement was made a year ago & I couldn't change & Vassar could *only* have me the 24th) and I need a day to settle myself. I shall write Martha a note before I come exempting her from my discourse if business or pleasure interferes but I *do* want to see her. Jane Hays Jones ("Ellinor" Hays's niece) is wife of the art teacher—Wendell Jones & I made no promise—but Ellinor wants me to at least speak to Jane. "Wendy" painted an amazingly lifelike portrait of Mr. Hays that hangs in Dickinson Main College, & I remember Jane as a child—a little girl of 6 or 7.

I am sad not to see Miss Borden again. She was for many years good to Warner & me—parting with college text-books to us when we were in college and couldn't buy many books; & her patience with me and my manifold excuses why I couldn't write letters, visit her, or meet for visits in New York or Boston, always stirred my gratitude. I did write to her during December saying I was coming to Vassar & would be sure to visit her a little while after my talk.

I don't know that I *have* to mention this, but I have been sick—for a week with a fever & a sinus cold—got well when Dr. McCabe prescribed: Sharpe & Dohms 3 sulfa-penicillin tablets. I managed to make a trip to see Warner,—found him far worse off than I had been but he managed not to have to stay in bed. Constance had been ill about ten days (then recovered and was making an over-night trip to a relative's). I got home chastened and perturbed about Warner who was almost too congested to talk—now recovered (or rather, recovering). No sooner had I got home than a 4-day spurt of typing, a church dinner, 6:30–10:30 and annual meeting, followed the next day by a dinner & T. S. Eliot's play—threw me into bed again. I am now up and planning to go to N. York tomorrow to luncheon. Frances Browne (my classmate) and Mrs. Walter Bottomley have invited me to luncheon. Mrs. B. was at Frances's N. Canaan farmhouse when I stayed overnight there in July. She is a "flower-expert" & writing a book on gardens for small incomes. Her husband was an architect (much thought of on L. Island).

My typing struggle was another perhaps injudicious adventure. For years I have been entertained by Maria Edgeworth's *The Absentee*.[10] Gertrude Flynn, a friend of Louise Crane's, is a rare girl & actress though she has only appeared in small plays & home theatricals. Her daughter (14) was killed by a horse (kicked after dismounting). I long to see her with a good part to act. So I have adapted *The Absentee* (hurrying to show it to Martin Browne who is here directing T. S. Eliot's play. T. S. Eliot is in S. Africa, & I did not wish to show *him* the play). I feel pretty sure it will not

---

10. MM had mentioned this play to JWM on July 26, 1906: "I have started to read the Mouse Maria Edgeworth's *Absentees* and have stopped as it is the dullest most drivelling story which ever strained tongue."

succeed,—or be staged. Warner says "the dialogue is brilliant," but it's too complicated to produce, & Sheridan to whom Mr. Edgeworth submitted it (Maria's father) said there are too many Irish parts (to be taken by English actors).

It was first written by Maria as a play, then reconstructed as a novel in 1812.

I never tire of it & have had a good time arranging it even if nothing comes of it. I got it done just in time for Mr. Browne to take away with him. He leaves for London tomorrow! (Gertrude knows nothing of this. And no one else knows about it.)

I strain your eyes, taxing you with my P. S.'s and interpolations, thinking I will make the letter seem shorter if it does not take too many sheets!

I have said, no one but you & Warner know(s) of "the play" except that I had to confide in Robert Giroux of Harcourt Brace, who took me to the play (*The Confidential Clerk*) and is T. S. Eliot's editor here. He was going to introduce me to Martin Browne but circumstances were not propitious, so I explained about the "script" & Robert said he would gladly give Mr. B. the envelope. He telephoned last evening to say that when he gave Mr. B. the manuscript Mr. B said "Oh! 18th c. Ireland—fascinating!"

Still, I see the difficulties of staging the play & Warner is sure it would be too hard to do & take too many stars. So I shall be disappointed but not surprised if [it] can't be used.

T. S. Eliot's *Clerk* really *is* a play but seems not too well liked. I shall tell you about it later.

Now a question. I am out of note paper or nearly out of it? and the dealer says Montag's have given up this sheet & envelope I use. He sends me a sample—not expensive, because smaller. You like fairly small sheets. Let me get you 3 or four boxes printed at the top—I enclose the sample—(and envelopes with address on back).

As for envelopes, the Air Mail envelope to match the paper is too small so I am getting a big size in a white ribbed envelope & want to get you the same, if you approve.

With much love,   Marianne

To Hildegarde Watson   *March 6, 1954*

Dear Hildegarde,

Your *tremendous*, unqualified hospitality and untyrannical, Socratic modesty, are so affecting to me. One should be willing to speak in a little waiting-room of a local railway-station, or under an elevated R'way or anywhere. And what a disruption of breakfast-to-dinner privacy are hospitalities, civic or private.

I *know* Estlin and Marion throve on the visit—on 6 Sibley Place, at all events. It is a charmed place like the temple of Hera amid pines and similar trees—(*white* pines not scaly-barks.)

How quaint you are about the brother Moose's soft-coal![11] Hephaestian as that coal smoke is. We have an anti-pollution control board here but the board must fear bridges for palls and monsoons of yellow or black or platinum-blue smoke cloud the atmosphere day by day in Brooklyn.

When I think of the *dress*, Hildegarde I can hardly breathe—terrified that I sanctioned your doing this. You do nothing but give to me—*Christmas*, last summer (when I should have been indicted)—the pearls. Well, I am now able to *wear* the dress. (That too lay on my morbid conscience—that this is a formal dress;—whereas if I ever manage to emerge from my cave or den, it is world news.) I do think now I can control my domestic concerns so as to stay well. Wilfulness and so-called self-reliance have got me into speaking (to earn a little) and attending affairs that are 150% struggle—and I am NOT going to do it.

And instead of dim music-less libraries, I would like a little music in my life. (I may get a Liberty Music shop record-player next year when my fables debris is cleared away.) They (or it) fill nearly everything but the hall and the centre of the floor.

Reading *The Absentee*! I ardently altered it as you know, but got it back from Mr. Martin Browne yesterday who says it would be expensive to produce,—with so many changes of scene as it needs—that he would suggest readings, to determine how strong the dramatic interest is. Lincoln Kirstein is sending it to Robert Chapman at Harvard. Nothing may ever come of it but I had immense fun working on it; and I MAY test the pluck of an editor by submitting the parts I wrote myself to some magazine. But am trammeled now by my talks, and allowing the play to age.

The talk at my church is changed from the 18th to the 16th and by the 27th I shall be liberated, Hildegarde. In any case, (I am preparing now) so I won't have to give more than the 24th–27th to the programs. So do, I implore you, when you come, let me know when I could see you. The weather too is such a help now—blustery but mellow. Maybe we could once again have luncheon or supper at the Exchange which isn't too far from the Park Chambers?

Bee (my niece Marianne) paid me a visit night before last and she is a pleasure,—a rare young creature,—with venerating memories of the Farm when she and the others came by your permission, to see Mole and me when we were there. Perhaps you remember.

I shall be writing as soon as the dress comes—(I hope the dear little fellow who has labored over it, is not a wreck). And *you*, what vital force is

11. "The Loyal Order of Moose" occupied the building across the street from the Watson residence.

expended in such an enterprise. We must estimate me henceforth, Hilde-garde, as what I am—and no Thumbelina refusing to stir if the 14-yard train is not supported by porcupines!

Your loving, M.

To Mary Shoemaker *April 9, 1954*

Dear Cousin Mary,

I marvel at you, visualizing so perfectly as you do, my situation, my so-ciabilities and my dentistry.

No, not adroit, Cousin Mary. I tell you everything. Sometimes in read-ing over your letters, I think, "Did I mention *that* tedious incident?" Indeed I debated saying nothing about Bee's operation; but it was so large in my mind & she is so encouragingly brave, that I did mention it. And my col-leagues at the Viking Press about my fables & their binding, loom large to me at the moment but will all reduce to a very usual-looking book. I sup-pose I told you that T. S. Eliot plans to publish a selection of my fables and then if it seems to be liked, a second selection, later. I favor this plan, am grateful to Faber & Faber for venturing on it.

I am glad you had the joy of Martha's presence and that she and her friend could have the vacation with you and together. I can imagine how lovely Vassar is now, with the Circle and the various shrubs growing green. How much we owe to Matthew Vassar![12]

Last evening, I had dinner with Marion Kauffer, the Sitwells, and a young painter, Brian Connolly, at 40 Central Park South. I had not been there at Marion's for a year, a sad, disruptive situation between the Kauffers having made it impractical. Each confided in me and seemed so really at-tached to the other that I felt the rift was temporary. But I finally saw that I was mistaken. Edward now has a studio on East 57th Street and Marion continues by herself at 40 Central Park South and works at her studio on 54th Street. (Perhaps as resentments subside, they might become recon-ciled.)

Edith and Osbert are gallant, spirited, and entertaining, and touch-ingly devoted to each other. Edith was wearing an emerald satin Chinese brocade coat and large pale broach (jade perhaps) and very large square cut aquamarines (rings); she has just returned from Hollywood—from making a film about Queen Elizabeth. In her script she referred to Anne Boleyn as "rocking to and fro" in an agony of grief and was dismayed to hear the di-rector say "Get the Queen's rocker" and a rocking-chair was produced!

12. Founder of Vassar College (1792–1868). Established in 1865, Vassar was the first college to offer the full liberal arts curriculum to women. MM had originally planned to go to Vassar.

We talked of Montegufoni, Osbert's castle in Italy where he and Edith will be for a time. He will then go to London to Carlisle Square where he lives and Edith to her club (The Sesame, 49 Grosvenor Street). They plan to return here next year. Osbert is almost helpless by reason of his "tremble," I do not see how he has the courage to go anywhere—(Parkinson's disease).

You seem so blessed and safe by comparison, Cousin Mary, "tottering about with your cane" as you call it.

I look forward to the 24th when I shall see Martha and John and Sue and Ralph, and Warner and Constance. How glad I am that my 24 of March trip to Vassar was not to be April 24th.

Sunday will be Mother's birthday and anniversaries are a deep part of one. They should strengthen us and should not induce sadness. If I could live life over, Mother's life would be a more joyous one than it was, but mercifully Warner supplied the vivid, grateful attitude, and enterprise and gaiety that I did not. I see so clearly now, that the present, each day as it comes, is the time for happiness and gratitude; and that despondency is never fair to "the others." If the Apostle Paul could "rejoice" when distrusted, beaten and cast in prison, certainly WE can forgive sinners, bless the charitable, and try to be of good courage. (As Warner says, be confident!)

I pitied him not long ago for his never lifted burdens and he said "Not at all. I am like a bumble bee busily walking about a flower & zooming off to the next one."

I shall write again soon. Our paper is now being printed. I hope it will be right.

With much love,   Marianne

How can I send you this shabby letter!

To Edward McKnight Kauffer   *Easter Day, 1954*

Dear Edward,

I in my exaggerated way, have considered that I was "afflicted, persecuted, and struck down" the past week, could hardly meet enforced demands and did not feel that I could well "steel" myself to the Hosannas of church services but felt I *must* go anyhow; and am forever the better of taking that risk. I have feared you were not recruiting your forces unless by the radio (which seems detached by comparison with the spoken word) and I have had a letter from Tom,[13] (solely about you and Marion), that touches

13. T. S. Eliot met Kauffer in or before 1919. Both expatriate Midwesterners living in London, they became close friends and Kauffer illustrated a number of Eliot's poems. They kept in touch after Kauffer returned to America in 1940.

and penetrates me to such an extent by its solicitude—that I cannot bear to benefit—without sharing; so let me say to you what I heard that helped me yesterday. Dr. Magary reminded us that as these mortal bodies are wasting away, the inner spirit is renewed day by day; therefore we do not lose heart. Though afflicted, persecuted, and struck down, there are some things that do not pass away. (It is not a matter of "resurrection" but of ana-stasis—the going forward.) (Like John Fiske,)[14] "we believe as a supreme act of faith in the reasonableness of God's work;" falteringly even doubtingly believe that this corruptible *shall* put on the incorruptible. So let not your heart be troubled, neither let it be afraid.

I do not tax your patience, do I, Edward, by insisting that you be encouraged and resolute? do not intrude, I mean.

On no account feel that a letter means an answer. The servitude of letters has brought me close to foundering on occasion. I shall feel that you show confidence in me if you do not make yourself write to me.

Affectionately,   Marianne

To Hildegarde Watson   PM *Portsmouth, N.H.*   *September 8, 1954*

I have your letter, Hildegarde,—so happy not to have left before receiving it. And Warner is enthusiastic, charmed,—telephoned me of his letters from you and Sibley, dwelling on them; evidently captivated (which affects me likewise)!

The hurricane was a disaster for many but did us no individual harm. I thought of Northbridge Center and Mrs. Lasell's pines—the ash and the bald look of familiar ground with the landmarks missing. Your solicitude, Hildegarde! And sense of the danger. I am hardly responsible enough to suffer, at a time of danger. Now, in seeing houses cut through to the fireplaces and wallpaper,—elms of the toughest fibre twisted off or partly, like a roll of newspaper—I can see what it was we watched.

No, I had not known of the plaque by William Eric and its memorable wording, Hildegarde. How consoling that the house should be dedicated for this very purpose—a home for the helpful and the scholarly. Desecration would lacerate one. And how faithful and full of faith you have been.

I am not going to miss you in N. York—had thought of lingering in & near Boston but shall be home by Friday the 10th. Indeed dear Hildegarde I shall not try to do what is too difficult. Kind Malvina said last evening, "It seems to me you are paying a high price for being in Maine," referring to the Memoir (which is 800 pages in length). I would be Franco if I were not awake to the many heart rendingly significant pages of the Memoir and I

14. American philosopher and historian (1842–1901).

MM with elephant and with parakeet, by Esther Bubley, 1953

MM with 1921
sculpture of her by
Gaston Lachaise.
Photograph by
Esther Bubley

MM c. 1961,
a photograph from
The New York Times

have had one of the happiest vacations of my life. The seclusion of this
house, with sun everywhere, and a sense of "the mind" in every room, almost puzzles me, it is so rare. The hair fine precision of the Ingres 1818
group by my bureau,—of parents, children, & spinet the slightly smiling
daughter turning from the keyboard on which one hand is resting, the detail of the father's stock, vest & overcoat-buttons; and the University—not
to say Harvard—flavor of the bookcases upstairs & down. I went upstairs
yesterday. Mr. Matthiessen's study (a bed-room) at one end of the house has
little square windows on three sides, a shallow fireplace which looks not
more than six inches deep (used however) and over the mantel, Russell
Cheney's oil of the staircase in Sarah Orne Jewett's house,—a white bookcase meeting in the corner by the fire,—a large one along the wall facing
the sea & a captain's chair at the table in the dormer toward the lighthouse
& sea. And every book I might say, is one I have been impatiently waiting to
read:— *T. E. Hulme* by Michael Roberts, Thucydides, about 12 volumes of
Emerson, marbled with morocco corners & spine, steel & tissue covered engravings that quite outdo [Edward] Steichen—Valéry's *Reflections on the
World Today,* six or seven [George] Santayanas (which I have *not* been
breathless to read)—John Jay Chapman's letters with wonderful pictures,
the Florio Montaigne and many French books. Malvina brought some enticing books also, the [Francis] Jammes poems with pictures of J. and his
bird of paradise tail jet black beard, a "candid camera" of him in old age
with his arm around [François] Mauriac—and, it seems to me I may never
have read the poems or the critical statements about simplicity and naturalness & animals—their fixed look and example—the iniquity of making
bears dance & animals overwork. (Did I say all this before, if so pardon it.)

Well—I am not too coherent. Please telephone, Hildegarde,—soon
after arrival?

With love, Marianne

Went into the Harvard co-operative in Cambridge for scissors I had forgotten & saw an Excello orlon shirt which I scarcely need but instantly bought
for the [illegible word]. It has those cellophane stays in the collar and fits
me exactly—and though twice marked down—the clerk—a kind of civic-
leader-garden-club-efficient librarian-like lady waiting eagerly on three
people at once, said, "if it doesn't fit, we'll take it back—we are always willing to do that." I was dumbfounded.

Marianne

This part of the country, and Boston, are like Brittany or Dalmatia after
42nd street and Borough Hall—Jay Street. The ticket-agent at North Station courteously turned his attention from a conversing friend when I asked
how soon one could go aboard the train for Portsmouth and said "Hoff an
hour previous," like Horace Mitchell, the Kittery printer who used he says

to come and talk aht (airt rather, without the "r") and wait a great while to be let in if he saw the cah in the garage.

You know it all well, I know—all these touches.

M.

And as usual I ought not to be so careless as to send you and Sibley ephemera. Seem not able to help what is indigenous.

To T. S. Eliot   *October 27, 1954*

Dear Tom,

The service for Edward. Marion wishes you to know that she has your cablegram, and said: "Will you do one thing—write to Tom for me and tell him everything?" I can *not*, Tom; but can say this—I was aware above everything, of the love Edward had inspired—of the wondering reverence for him. Dr. Kinsolving, Rector of St. James' Church, indeed a servant of God, compassionate and real, pronounced the words with majesty as he entered, "I am the resurrection and the life"; and before the benediction— although he had not expected to, he says,—referred to Edward's gifts and greatness of mind; then lingered after the service. Mr. Stierwald, his assistant, went with us, to Woodlawn; and what I shall remember of the service there, is his slow intent way of turning the leaves as he read; his gentleness with Sabro Hasigawa and care of the folded bird—bearer of the soul—Mr. Hasigawa had brought; and Marion's delicate way of thanking him afterward for entering into Mr. Hasigawa's thought in bringing the birds—one for Edward and one for her. Mr. Hasigawa is a friend of Edward's who teaches at the New School; he had brought him to the Hospital, a large white square of paper with J. brush characters: "May the sun be in your heart."

Marion achieved dignity of procedure; and in each of those matters which in a sense do not matter; the multitude of red roses, she felt to be essential. The grave is bleak, she feels; but is better for being away from cut grass and horticultural formality, I tell her; it faces old varied woodland and a magnificent cliff.

The music was right—music Edward liked—chosen by Nancy Reid. Unselfassertive Nancy. Service so touchingly, so privately rendered Edward day by day. It hurts me to have been no more help to him than I was. Bernard Waldman[15] let nothing keep him from supplying certain necessities Edward would scarcely ask for; said, "I assure you, Miss Moore, he

15. Advertising executive and patron of the arts (1900–1981); a friend of Edward McKnight Kauffer's and through him a friend of MM's. Father of poet and critic Grace Schulman, who was also acquainted with MM.

lacked for nothing"; was with him daily—a silent man, self-effacing like Nancy. And the doctor, Dr. Kreps, could not have been kinder or more congenial to Edward; it pleased Edward that Dr. Kreps liked the studio and the work there—that he too does some painting. Perhaps the thought of these things can help us—and the fact that Edward was not taxed by having to be moved; was in a quiet alcove.

If John Hayward would not be intruded on by the above details, please share them. I never saw Edward—till just before his death, that he did not say, "I am writing to Tom and am going to write to John Hayward."

Affectionately,   Marianne

*The service was at 81st Street and Madison Avenue,—the Campbell chapel.

To Chester Page   *January 10, 1955*

Dear Mr. Page,

I realized just after you left on Saturday,—that I had not thanked you for the turquoise bird, and the currant clusters—like translucent jade; or for your encouragement regarding my Sycamore and other lines. I was much dissatisfied with "The Sycamore" on seeing it in print and have, as I hope, improved it at least simplified it for my next small collection. (I shall probably be dissatisfied with this too—seem unable ever to get things just right.)

These are remarkable statements by Emerson which you quote; doubly significant where isolated from the page. As for the beautiful resting on the foundation of the necessary, I like the thought but it is in a special sense that that is true, is it not? I do think "our art is an expression of our needs." Am quoting myself though I am sure I saw that somewhere. I by no means deserve to exemplify to you the statement about the spirit of a plant or animal endowing nature with a new thing. It should. We long to think so......

As for precision. It is a phobia with me. (And my essays, verse,—everything I write abounds in imprecision.)

Yes. I should like to hear Myra Hess on January 21st. If you would be going yourself, let me reimburse you for two tickets,—fairly good seats only—or rather, whatever might be available. I am not a tyrant in my recreations—(never sit in the orchestra for plays unless I can't help it).

Sincerely yours,   Marianne Moore

Let me say that the roses—the two that seemed to droop—revived immediately when the stems were cut. They are all very stiff and confident now. The stems—well—it is ignorant to shorten them, but the flowers matter most?

To Ezra Pound   *[undated—June 5–7, 1955?]*

EZRA, when a philosopher's speech is unsavory, indeed foul, of what use has philosophy been to him.

This needs no date—no question-mark. It is for all time.

M. M.

To Malvina Hoffman   *July 5, 1955*

Dear Malvina,

It seems quite bleak without you. And in proportion as I need to be efficient, I am incompetent; surrendered and became continuously social,—though I have not yet finished the book review of Kenneth Burke and have some routine dentistry interfering with me.

I "sat" for Marion Kauffer, 1–4, the afternoon of the Fourth—for a watercolor of *just* my features and hair. I knew she would find me without a characteristic feature to fasten on. Tense, concentrated, determined, committed to achieving a masterpiece (and indeed her portraits are good) she strove and studied me, then said. "Let me begin all over. It looks nothing like you. Better, but too high on the page." I said, "Start another. You can't force these things. Do the hair and pay no attention to the features." "Oh dear. I hope you can forgive me," Marion said. "You are being so patient. I always get a likeness sooner than this." (Her likenesses *are* likenesses,— startling.) "I am under no strain," I said. "Am getting a much needed rest. I know I'm a baffler—only have expression when suddenly excited." Thus goaded, Marion got a very plausible map of my features, and melancholy eyes! It has to be painted later and *I* hadn't counted on *that*, was told "two hours."

Sunday evening I had supper with the Chutes, Mrs. Chute, Marchette and Joy; charitable, compassionate, talented girls, and mother. Both write,—Marchette & Joy. Marchette's last book is *The Wonderful Winter* about Shakespeare and a *then* young boy—Sir Robert Wakefield (published by Dutton because declined by Macmillan). *Declined;* I marvel—I don't know when I have read so valuable and charming a book—a study really in selection and dramatic imagination. Shakespeare helps Robin find a piece of jewelry at the Royal Exchange, a present for Mrs. H. who has befriended him (R.) and housed him;—himself secretly buying for R. a dagger Robin admired but feared a lady might not need. Shakespeare bought the boy a dagger—for presentation later, (I can't write.) The only stylistic flaw I see is "a"; "kind of (a)" or "sort of (a)" perhaps twice in the course of the book. The *Innocent Wayfaring* is another novel by M. set in Chaucer's time.

[*Geoffrey*] *Chaucer of England* was refused by 7, 8, or 9 publishers—I forget which, and is a major performance! We may take heart. Marchette also writes verse and it is graphic, tuneful, and yet reserved. e.g. the last line of "Art":

> *"And no one can see it until it is done."*

Figuratively, that *is an epitome*, isn't it?

Marchette met you at a party at Mrs. [Peggy] Cresson's,[16] Malvina, and was interested in what you said about a party at 157.

I then walked slowly to 3rd Ave. & down to a 60th Street bus-stop—where I welcomed the surprise of a locked outside case of huge ocean sponges—among pictures of divers and tropic ketches and palms on the shore. I have been looking for one—(a big symmetrical sponge to replace one that Warner has been prolonging the life of, past all reason).

On my way to 113 West 57th Street I went to this place today—The Plaza Paint Supply Co. (1026 3rd Avenue) (3rd at 60th)—& they have a rather large assortment of artists' brushes! I got a no. 12 American red sable (quite large), a 7 WSB Sargent American red sable (small), and unintentionally to tell the truth, a "made in Germany, vulcanized in rubber 1½ inches camel-hair." (1½ tall, I guess; & certainly 2 inches wide.) Anyone ought to pay me a dollar just to be allowed to feel it. It is rather bushy but comes to an edge like a razor's. I may never paint a grassblade but I was bewitched by the sight of these intrinsic works of art. Besides,—the clerk I had been exhausting, said to the boss, "give her a good price, Abe," & each brush was reduced 38¢, I believe. The man called me "Hon" *twice*! I couldn't believe my ears.

July 6th

Then—just missing a bus—I took a taxi across 57th Street to 113 W. 57th to pass on my recordings of a year ago—patched at the time, re-patched a month or so ago, and yesterday after deadly struggles to mend a few bad spots, we discovered Reel III,—and repairs that sounded still better. I was humiliated to have been late 15 minutes; but Mr. Bartok had not been ready, was winding his reels and deploying, then plugging wires, and moving round like a somnambulist. A very talented fellow, indeed a genius (his name is Peter); but oh the tedium of those mumblings of mine!

Now—tell me—before I close, Do *you* need a sponge? or a couple of brushes? or *the* camel hair? I would be honored to have found it for you if you fancy it. And, of course, some will *lend* to the right borrower! if on the shores of Maine.

Remember me, please, to Mrs. Cresson.

> *With love,* undefeatable *Malvina,*   Marianne (Honeyball)!

---

16. Hoffman's traveling companion.

To Kenneth Burke   *July 7, 1955*

Dear Kenneth B.,—if you could earn the term, mutt, call me debris—
which I am. Since pondering your grammars, rhetorics, counter-
statements, and *Moments*, I regretted sending you my *Predilections* lest I
embarrass you; indeed you dumbfound me by your magnanimity. Upon seeing your envelope, I thought, "Well, we Diogeneses must stand up to our
'clutter of tiny insights' when we let them be printed!" Your liberality is
great.

I am reviewing your *Moments* for *Encounter* (T. [Thurairajah] Tam-
bimuttu). Tremble. Not because "the reader has categorical expectations
which the poet must meet"; lest the reviewer be conspicuous for incapacity.

In any case, your detractors by this time do not seem even to resemble
a foe—are like the skeleton cars on the way to California, hoisted up as a
warning.

M. M.

To Louise Bogan   *October 8, 1955*

The book! Dear Louise, I pant with anxiety at the very thought of a backset for the Noonday Press,—an injustice I could not take calmly. This
book,[17] nutritious and at the same time a source of pride, helps me to feel
that life is worth while—and that we matter, personally. That might well
be said with a flutter of egotism, as I recall my sensations in not being
damned when my little books would appear, and my dubious monster,
(translation). But I think I can detach myself sufficiently to scan the scene,
and women as writers, in America and give thanks for your work. Its asso-
ciative creative insights, unfrivolity and humor certainly fortify my
courage. I am—with understandable trepidation—expecting to write on
the book for *Poetry London & N. York*. Perhaps you know this. The fact that
I *am* writing does not lessen my excitement in receiving the book from you,
self-centered as this is of me. I should restrain you and protect you from my
too grasping acquiescence.

My foot. I hope kind Morton [Zabel] did not receive too gloomy an impression of it from me. Dr. Henry Lange slivered off a protrusion of bone—
and the result is perfection. He is a master foot-man! That is self-evident.
But recuperation is a little slow and any kind of captivity maddening. I
didn't forget Dr. McLaughlin?—in fact the name engraved itself on my
mind the moment you told me of him, but my other doctors who know Dr.
Lange overcame my hesitations and to be near home was tempting.

I should like to hop up to 169th Street to see you,—but *must* go to

17. Bogan's *Selected Criticism* (1955).

Washington next Friday. Then if I return intact and we get some N[*ew*] *Yorker* Birnbaum squirrel weather, I'm going to ask you about it.

The [Emily] Dickinson article almost inhibits any attempt at communication on my part. It is a commanding piece of work; is a kind of natural apex upon the book. I can not ponder it enough. No use envying. One can but admire.

With affectionate gratitude,   Marianne

To Monroe Wheeler   *November 5, 1955*

The play, Monroe! As hordes thronged the sidewalk and the entrance and the lobby, half an hour early, I had a premonitory sense of what I might see. Nothing like the reality. Louis XIV might have been sitting there. If *nothing* had taken place, I still could have studied the winding stair and the balustrade with the caryatids and the fern heads of the bass viols. I think the music; churchly, shadowy and sustained, during the enormities of the astrologers, as rare as anything I shall ever hear. I wonder if the compositions were chosen new from [Jean-Baptiste] Lully or were played at the performances originally.

They could never have had a better Bourgeois Gentilhomme than Louis Seigner or dancing master than Jacques Charon (Instructor I must say nothing casual) or Marquise than Marie Sabouret. And Mme. Jourdain was epic, Germaine Rouer. Not a glance at the Marquise; first or last. Her finesse (Madame's) and hands as unbourgeois as any Countess's.

The costumes, Monroe! The Marquise's curls at the back and the dancing-master's feathers (with which he performed an intermittent pirouette);—the limber ears of M. J.'s exercising-cap. The instructor in philosophy and his abandoned book. The enunciation was such that even I got the words, most of which—(or *some* of which) I understood. Molière has the most devilish art of actuality without being banal (and the robbery of credit for the diamonds—"Don't ask her if she likes them. One never mentions a present."!) and I admire as part of the performance yesterday, the comments in the program—on his death, and other. (Molière's)

A "present," Monroe, needing Frances and Pauline to describe it. Your readiness to rob yourself is really frightening. That plane-trip at night, "all the way"! and this play are part of Orion—of the heavens entire.

With love,   Marianne

To Lincoln Kirstein   *November 24, 1955*

Dear Lincoln:

The Samuel Barber. I hear good things of it. As for Master Cocteau, Puss in Boots, waving hat and tail? *L'on s'attarde et l'on allonge!* I thank you,

Lincoln, for trusting me with it (one thing I wanted to see)—and Mrs. Curtis; and for being willing to take so very much trouble about me to make it possible for me to see the *Jeux d'Enfants*.

Not yet.

Pleasure, Lincoln! You are a magician. It did *not* occur to me.

You, Wystan, M. Balanchine, and *The Magic Flute* will be one—one inimitable thing, like little Oliver Andes.[18] I liven up at the very thought of it. (I am one of Wystan's primary children in his adult Shakespeare class. I hobble there on Wednesdays but not much of anywhere else.)

With love to you and Fidelma,   Marianne

To Hildegarde Watson   The Lord Jeffrey Inn, Amherst, Masstts.
May 11, 1956 PM

Hildegarde, how you help me! My blue dress with the crystal-and-gold buttons and zigzag gold belt is self-sustaining—has been, on many an occasion—but I was really overjoyed when I looked into the box of "flowers" the Desk said had been sent me and found the gardenias. I did not know you knew what I would wear! did not think I had told you I was going to the Inn and when. I had thought it would be warm and that I might have to wear my Navy taffeta. Gladys' face fell when I mentioned it. She said, "Not the blue?" So I took *it*. (It has just been washed, you know and did not shrink or fade.) I had feared I would have to give it up. For the least soiled look ends its romantic rightness?

That *fragrance*! and they stayed white all evening. I have them on my hall bookcase (held upright by a strange little "gold" statuette I received recently.) College florists are the peak of attention to business. Amherst's "Robert's Flowers" had my gardenias (tied with white) in white ribbon grass—on a bed of wet cotton cobweb with a pliofilm hood of dew-drops over the stem part, and this little card at the side (made by the John Henry Co. 2719!)

My May 12 *music-case*, Hildegarde—(the pin seal!). It might have gone to the College alone, it so embodied me—my notes, papers, books, pencils—except that I could not reach it after the President & Mrs. Cole's reception (it was in the cloak room) and I used a borrowed pen which sprayed two specks of ink right on the front of my blue skirt. On reaching the Inn, I put water on them & they *spread;* but bless the non-permanent ink. They washed entirely out and you would not know today, that the skirt had ever had them. "*Better dead* than spotted" this time. (They would have *ruined every good* of my trip.)

18. Performer in the New York City Ballet.

My watch, my hand-bag, my jacket! You and Sibley really armed me for the combat. When I see you I shall tell you about it all.

"How I go on" you say. *I:* it is I,—all this flutter,—while *you* have been been made an honorary member of the National Guard and Naval Militia! You and Major Case[19] "together" each with a sword, cutting the cake, after the lecture! the *only* woman—"first woman to be made a member" of the Old Guard! initiating the lecture, listening to it, shaking hands and fraternizing with the comrades. It was dear of you. (Here is a picture of you on horseback, armored and sworded but so halcyon by comparison, your countenance.)

The work of the writing-class was worth real study. If it isn't pleasing,—a recreation—something is wrong and I was much entertained by the originalities of a certain Robert Bagg[20]—some serious work and then a few lines about a girl with pigtails—

> *. . . let out like rope*
> *To trim a coming storm,*
> *She stepped into an easy lope.*

Kenneth Eisol[21] memorialized a (his) mechanic's lunch, a noble toadstool, roadside trees and how "ants descend a sandwich bag."

This class was in the Library from two to four—presided over by James Merrill. Amherst is nothing if not choice,—and apparently studious. The former observatory (now the music building) consists of three octagons, best seen from the back—a kind of fawn or putty grey in tint.

James Merrill and friend,—a Mr. [David] Jackson with whom he is going round the world in a baby Volkswagen—live four miles from town in the house of a Professor Bain whose place on the Faculty, Mr. Merrill is taking this year. These young bachelors are most remarkable—I never ate such a meal as they had prepared yesterday (Thursday) evening—roast beef, (rare) small round potatoes, beans, French salad and a very delicate custard baked in a shallow pan with raw sugar browned on top by the broiler. Some kind of Moselle wine; after cocktails to which the guests did *ample justice.* Professor Armour Craig & Mrs. Craig, Professor B. Barber & Mrs. Barber were the other guests. The view, of shadowed blue mountains and blossoming trees and emerald grass, was peace & beauty personified. Beside the road is an old old maple, the trunk growing up in a spiral, with many huge warts on it like a lime's.

We drove, from dinner—to Johnson Chapel where I was to read—a perfect, ideal little church, the oldest College building—big white columns in front and huge stone door sills. The pews are white with apricot nosing

19. Curator of the Rochester Historical Society.
20. Amherst undergraduate poet (1935–).
21. Amherst professor.

along the backs and arms and apricot velvet cushions. Speaking from a pulpit is always a pleasure,—*help*, I should say. I don't like to be recorded and did not start off well but then forgot the recording and all went well,—ending with about six short fables.

A touching, spare, intensive English teacher from Brattleboro had brought four school-children fifty miles to the Chapel—their & his solemnity went to my heart. It is just as if it were a matter of life and death to get this meeting and departure achieved. It made me think of Thomas Hardy, the look of the teacher and the rural big attentive eyes of the children.

Mr. Merrill had prepared an introduction which was so perfect intrinsically it indeed did justify tape-recording—he mentioned *The Dial*—(Acting Editor) and my various services to poetry "formal pattern with freedom of rhythm" and so on.

I like his "For a Second Marriage" (written for his mother indeed): (*Poetry:* February 1956).

> *How a tall trunk's cross-section shows*
> *Concentric rings, those many marriages*
> *That life on each live thing bestows.*

Enough.

Oh! I should say President and Mrs. Cole had a reception after my reading—very handsome. I met Mrs. [Harriet] Whicher, and Cynthia Walsh came,—and Mrs. [Pearl] Kazin from Northampton. Robert Francis,—a nature poet whom Macmillan has published several times,—overwhelmed me by having gone into the woods in the rain and managed to gather enough arbutus to make a small bouquet, had wound wet moss round the stems, & tinfoil and put the treasure in a cracker box encased with great exactness in tissue paper,—all so painstaking and accurate!—I'll stop. I don't want you not to want me to go anywhere again!

"Your loving very loving,"   Marianne

To Elizabeth Bishop   *260 Cumberland Street   Brooklyn 5*
                            June 9, 1956

Dear Elizabeth,

The Prize![22] I am delighted; and you must have no regrets. Nobody else should have had it. I should think it would have been very painful to anyone to take it away from you! Everybody seems pleased. I was much complimented to be called by Harvey Breit,[23] a friend. Indeed I have seen

---

22. EB won the 1956 Pulitzer Prize for *Poems: North & South—A Cold Spring*.
23. Editor of *The New York Times Book Review*.

"Manuelzinho." It is one of your best. Mysterious yet natural—and a departure without the suggestion of an effort to be novel. I have wished to write to you about it. I immediately removed it from *The New Yorker* and put it in *North & South*. (A confession, Elizabeth; I never did receive your new book, with Loren's violet leaf on it! Various letters to Boston led me to think it was a certain slender book, I found on coming home from Maine—in its wrappings from Boston. I explored everything when I found the book inside was something else, and have not told you lest you send me another. *I shall get one*—can do it better than you can—am nearer.) I nominated Loren, as you know, and was seconded by Karl Knaths and Lyonel Feininger. Lyonel F. has died and I asked for another second; Andrew Wyeth seconded me, but the Committee thought Loren should be nominated for a grant ($1000 for next year). I agreed and they said after she is given the grant, I should nominate her again & I shall.

"Nicey nice" is perfect. How accurate you are, Elizabeth. That is just how *I* have felt.

I went to Amherst with misgiving and it was raining; but James Merrill counteracted everything. He really is a blessing. And imagine how happy I am that I was compared with Robert Frost. He was there, (Robert Frost), asked me to visit with him a while before he took a train for New York, and he was everything we like, peaceful, direct and very deliberate, said he hated professionalists, spoke of never having been offered money, except three times, the last time by a cowboy who was not bookish but felt sympathy with him. I am very fond also, of Robert Francis, who lives near James Merrill's and Mr. Jackson's house, grows soy-beans, has no telephone, no steam heat, and has several small books about flowers and country subjects published by Macmillan; nature poems.

Henrietta [Ford Holland] is still in St. Luke's Hospital, but is very soon to be transferred to St. Barnabas' Hospital for convalescents. She admires you fervently, said when you were given the Prize, "I do love that girl—and her work is *brilliant*." She quotes and dwells on this and that, the wagon, your stories, your colorings and wordings. We are anxious to see the translation; it is so like you to take that intense care, of going to Diamantina, making the long trip there. How touching, the "seamless garments." Religion and gambling! or its like, bullfights and "the moment of truth"? Alyse Gregory has written a stirring article, "Six Deaths in the Afternoon." It is in *The Countryman*. Spring, 1956. 10 Bouverie St., London, EC4. Perhaps you and Lota subscribe. The pictures and nature notes are beyond everything delightful.

I am intolerable, the way I jam things together. Anyhow, I so *thank* you, Elizabeth, for liking my arcs of seeds in a banana, and Palestrina. That piece is to come out in *Zero*, complete, in November, and is in my Viking collections (of 11 pieces), which I shall send you; (September, October or November) you will receive it. It may be later. I hope it won't seem flat and struggling. Could I see that interview, or *not*?? Herbert; I must find that "Rise heart; the lord is risen." Well—I think I have it. Yes, I have. Armadillos and the pinwheeling owls; wish I could see them.

Are you well, Elizabeth—most of the time? Since I have Dr. Laf Loofy, I seem to surmount my deadly threats. Am so glad you will have the High Fidelity radio.

With much love,   Marianne

To Lincoln Kirstein   *June 30, 1956*

Measure for Measure, Lincoln! It's a little too much for me to ask you to read as you run, but you should and *must* allow yourself a sense of triumph in having raised this Globe Theatre with its just, capacious considerate auditorium and in having a company that can act—and with polish. Nina Foch was most lovable—spirited—she has impact and conveys that essential urgency, with her steady gaze and natural postures. And thanks be, an elately nunnish nun's habit. (Her voice, Lincoln, was so conscientiously articulate, it has got a little harsh! Pardon this observation.) The Duke has the convincingly noble swirl and was fine as the friar. Simpleton that I am, I was taken in. Everything had to burst on me. The contrivances are epic—the ball-dugouts, for quick action. I think everything of these. The upper windows and let down facades, and lanterns are so very handsome and Jean Rosenthal deserves medal upon medal. She is a thrilling craftsman, so concentrated on the job.

Virgil [Thomson]'s music is ravishing; he gets a high mark from me for his romance and adaptiveness. It makes me think of his banquet music in the all-Negro *Hamlet* over here in Brooklyn. And Mariana's little boy was one of the most exquisite things in the whole performance. An inspired contrast, as in my little Oliver Andes (*Love's Labor's Lost*).

You have an affectionate admirer in Edwin Howard; and hasn't he done well? I was so pleased to have him named in the folder. His heraldry is so touching. And so are your rarities in the lobby and up in the gallery. He extols your houses, worries about your respites (lack of respites) was excited to hear of Fidelma's portrait of you and of the pony-cart. His own cottage is heart-rending, it is so ardent and ingenious—his economical ingenuities and un-economical splendor of pink porcelain bathroom. He shops, gets the meals, does the dishes, grows the herbs and tends the flowers. Miss Julie Gillespie seems to love her job—whatever it is. I want her to thrive, Lincoln; she is a humane girl. Edwin had us meet Helen Menken—lovely person and several men! Mr. Reed and others.

My love to you both.

To Hildegarde Watson   *August 5, 1956*

Dear Hildegarde,

I am back from Harvard and found your letter of Wednesday. Why am I always a suppliant! I don't know. I do know that you help me put up with my failures and strengthen my hopes. The lines in the [*Ladies' Home*] *Journal.* They seem to me the peak of the prosaic and are, besides, a riddle to several. That you and Sibley can approve them, anyhow, consoles me. You will see that they are not entirely ravings of a ne'er do well when you see the notes, in October (or whenever the book [*Like a Bulwark*] comes out). I don't know how anyone could want them without the Notes which really are the thing to read and the stanzas, just a schoolroom try at composition.

Last Sunday you gave the party for Claire and Michael. How blessed you are, Hildegarde, in your way of telling—of enshrining a person and occasions. That little child—Bronwyn. I hope these rare young things make up to you and Sibley for some of your injustices—the mortal stress of certain desperate moments. And brave Michael. If he weren't St. Peter,—a rock of endurance, all could have been bitterness.

I hope that little B. does look like you, Hildegarde. (I doubt it! but perhaps she can *be* like you. And they will *all*, have an ear!)

Mr. Fred Barry. He benefits me, inspires with a desire to speak with him a few words. You make him so real to me. I am sure it *was* the nicest of the parties given for Claire and Michael. And what *presents*, Hildegarde, Michael's evening scarf with his initials in black; and C's black sweater with white fox collar. Romance and helpfulness in one. No one understands the superb impossible as you do, Hildegarde. Whenever I get anything "good," I always think: "Would Hildegarde think it odious, or appropriate?" My luggage went with me to Cambridge. (When I won't be seen, I sometimes save it and take my *straw* suitcase!) It was intensively *seen scrutinized*, and its maker *inquired* about. I am Mr. Anthony's live advertisement. Both bags suffered slight bumps and I have spent an hour effacing the injuries—(with British Museum rare book oil which Monroe Wheeler did not give me for travelling-bags). I think they are better bare, don't you? than in plastic skins. The conductor said he would make my car a No Smoking car. Rushed in presently and said he must put me in the forward car. In about ten minutes returned and said, "they changed their minds; I'll take you back." In all these hasty tugs and jerks, the racks *hit* my royal gear. (I always brow beat the porter into taking time: "Now *careful*. I *don't* want them battered.") (Of course my original seat was taken but another was empty.) I may have to travel first class.

The taxi man took me from Dana Palmer House (next to the Faculty Club) to S. Station in 12 minutes, darting along the Charles as if to save life, in the morning sun, so I barely had time to see the little knots of white sails on the River. I then had half an hour to wait for the 42nd Streeter.

Harvard. I can hardly account for the hypnotic effect the place has on me. Towering trees—I never noticed the lacy fronds of the honey-locusts as this time, high overhead, a few curly pods lying on the grass despite assiduous rakings and grass-cutting. Sprinklers keeping the lawns green, and now and then a student reading, with his back against a large elm by Lamont Library which my Quincy Street windows faced. I was in room 5 this time, in Dana Palmer House,—upstairs. Robert Giroux (of Farrar, Straus & Cudahy) had the room across from me, and lent me a Minneapolis paper's transcript of T. S. Eliot's big address; *The Frontiers of Criticism* (like a presidential message. It took me three nights "after hours" to read it.) It might be called, "Certain Scholastic Misapprehensions Corrected"—a very pleasing un-pontifical discussion.

In the Conference meetings, on Small Magazines (*"les jeunes revues"*?) *The Dial* was constantly being referred to with respect—a kind of awe, indeed, and I may, yes think I was present in a reflexive sense. A man from the state of Washington, was especially earnest, after one of the sessions, and said, "I still have a complete file." William Alfred was active director for Professor William Elliott; Allen Tate, Chairman. Robert Giroux started things off—said "a classic is a book that stays in print." He blent nicely with the Harvard decorum and sense of proportion, was brief—followed by Philip Rahv. I have shaken Philip R.'s hand numerous times in coming and going, to & from a party at his house, shudder at and occasionally save a *Partisan Review*, but he made a real dent in my armor this time. His discourse on the uncompromisable service rendered by a free magazine was worth all my trouble in going to the Conference. Perhaps I exaggerate, for my notes are not electrifying, but he was impassioned, and conservative in terms used, and had the untrivial air of a condemned man throughout the Conference and all this was sympathetic to me. I had breakfast Tuesday morning with the Levins, on their stone pavement by the dining-room—induced Marina (who is 14) to play for me, (a familiar very difficult concert piece. What was it?). Well, the piano is in the dining-room, Marina has a tape-recorder and plays duets with herself. Harry is a real teacher, thinker shall I say and so lively in conversation. Elena (Mrs. Levin) accompanied me to the Faculty Club—to an iniquitous "reading," conceived by Allen Tate, (your first printed piece & your most recent). Most visitors to the Conference participated. (In an upstairs reception room with an oriel window. Luncheon in the adjoining room.) Then a buffet luncheon—of great elegance and magnitude—ham or turkey or veal loaf or ragout (or all); deviled eggs, chicken salad, hot rolls, pie, ice cream, or jello with whipped cream. A Mr. Selzer (graduate s. from Princeton) sat by me. He knows George Garrett,[24] winner of prize (Glascock Memorial Poet Mt. Holyoke) when I was there once—a very pleasant fellow. Samuel French Morse was by me also, literary executor for Wallace Stevens. *And* as His Majesty said so formally, et cetera et cetera et cetera.[25]

(You will *abandon* me.)

The point of it all to me was a painting behind the refectory array of food;—*Strong Limbed Pine* by Charles Hudson who died 5 years ago, the Fogg catalogue says—an oil of trunk & half the branches with a blue ridge and suggested plain behind. I gazed and gazed upon it, as best I could amid the Carnival.

Harvard's generosity is quite unnerving. My friend and interviewer, Kathleen Cannéll, was to have luncheon with me at the Faculty Club. When I asked what I owed, was told "positively not"—as part of the Conference I was entitled to a guest! *Washcloths* are supplied at Dana P. House! though I've learned to take one. (Nowhere else). When I arrived—met at Back Bay by Mr. Alfred and Arthur S. ?—I found in my room a great bouquet of crimson carnations and gypsophila. Nothing said, but I learned by a parenthetic remark of Mrs. Prebles' that "the young man who had brought [me] from Back Bay sent them" on behalf of the Conference. I tried to get a little box of Wheaties at the Union for my room. The cashier smiled benignly & said, "*I think* the Union could *give* you those." Superb management—the inexorable procedure on entering, 4 newspapers side by side & a dish for nickels,—plastic plates in sectors and as much [of] each kind of food as you like, 2 eggs, two glasses of milk if you need them, and a row of enhancers, marmalade and so on, at the end of the breakfast foods on a separate table against the fireplace. Sternly indeed, I was *made* to sort my implements & left-overs (but I had none) on departing; juice-glass here, milk-glass here, silver in basket, napkin in trash bin, plate to the man in authority! Think how efficient that is!

And the *hunting-trophies* against the upper wainscot;—had never noticed them—a 7-foot stag-horns, elk, moose, prong-horned antelope, big horn sheep. Also—a little mysteriously unless prizes are awarded on occasion, the big brass laurel wreath, set in the flooring as you enter the main hall.

The airy summer attire, the really neat wash coats of the students, the college bells resounding through the stillness, impressed me deeply. I have been over-busy since back, did not touch the book review I must do (while in Cambridge) a manuscript to read, (two imposed ones as well)—some committee business. Well, I am grateful—and *above* all to you and Sibley.

Marianne

24. George Palmer Garrett (1929–), novelist, poet, and playwright.
25. MM may be mimicking Yul Brynner's line in *The King and I.*

I go away, resenting my imprudence. I have [never] gone to Harvard that I have not come back fortified, and more equable. The decorum of the place and actual serviceableness—everyone deep in his own business, the quiet unfrenzied heartiness of the sociabilities. Mr. [William] Alfred, Mr. "S." who transported us in his car, here and there—and a Harvard student Ralph Blume, invited me to dinner at the Beacon Hill Kitchen on Joy Street, (known only to Ralph Blume, a kind of bar through which we progressed to a garden with tall ailanthus trees above table umbrellas, with a square fountain-pool in the center and birds there. The waitresses were much oppressed and a dish crashed, but it was not noisy, and the food, perfect. Joy Street is so steep, I should think no car could ascend it, let alone park. We loitered then returned to the Conference in Alston Burr Hall—a new steep little amphitheatre w. green blackboards and disappearing writing leafs hinged to the arm of the chair. This meal, was after a tea at the Lowells'—Robert's & Elizabeth's. The house, on Marlborough Street is of early Bostonian grandeur with black and white marble entrance (and a flat stone dish of the most exquisite flowers on the table), spacious stairs up to the drawing-room—the walls, entirely books. There, a *multitude*. Dr. Merrill, his wife and friend, (or mother?) a Mr. Starr, friend of Pierre Emmanuel, who likes my fables Mr. Starr said quite circumstantially. John Holmes[26] and Mrs. Holmes, (weighted by my 5, 6 or is it 7 books to sign.) This was considered philistine by the Lowells, and Mr. Alfred who stood over me with controlled tolerance, as it was time to *go*.

Now,—have you been reading? My feelings can not be hurt, since I lack wisdom! Harvard goes to my head.

Lovingly,   Marianne

(I was *anything* but an asset, in Alston Hall, my discourse, bathos.)

To H.D.   *August 27, 1956*

Dear Hilda,

I am reading the Freud.[27] And what artistry brings visibly, to my very eyes, the paper-weight! "a set of prismatic triangles; . . . the peak, where one set of triangles met, pointed to the north pole or the south pole," "The Ark-like door of the outer study" and "The pear-branch cast its late-summer shadow toward the crab-apple tree," the amphorae and the *ankh*. Such personal, such considerate poetry, Hilda. Not to mention "Build thee more stately mansions, O my soul."

What good you do me, making emotion alive; "The glory that was

26. John Clellon Holmes (1926–), poet.
27. H.D.'s *Tribute to Freud*, published in 1954.

Greece" "The tripod of classic Delphic" . . . "It's a shadow thrown." The magic that is *written*! Yours only. So graphic the place, it is mysterious.

I am a rude reader, dear Hilda but no one is more susceptible to (of ?) excitement. You know this, or you wouldn't put up with me, would you?

There is so much of my own past here, the transfers, the calcomanias! The temple of Karnak! I am told that there are some to be had still, calcomanias. None I am sure, like those past ones.

Shall I see you? It is too soon to know perhaps. Doris Long says Bryher will be coming—& that she, Doris, is to be godmother for E. B. A blessing is it not, that the mind has wings—that the page is the person. Could I live if it were not so?

Affectionately,　Marianne

To Ezra Pound　　*Dec. 22 [19]56*

Very strange, Ezra, that someone doesn't want to meet me!!![28]

I b'long to *People to People*—(Eisenhower Harvey Breit Committee to create good feeling between peoples) and I did for a while contribute to Reinhold Niebuhr's committee to rescue intellectuals in foreign lands, and attended one meeting.[29] Anything wrong with these?

I *strongly* reprehend *Eleanor Roosevelt* for her *purblind* endeavor to elect Stevenson.[30] The whole man is what matters. That defamatory egomaniac and bad loser would have been a great savior of the day and of mankind, wouldn't he? Mrs. R. did *one thing* which has had my gratitude; ages ago she exposed Vishinsky for filibustering; V.: a monkey wrench persistently posing as a statesman—a continuously hissing steam-valve, with no one to oppose him—(*before* Ike consented to help us grapple with the Washington model of the welfare state).[31]

(Oh, yes, and she *is* "fair to Negroes.")

I hated George Meany till he said he was agoing to get to Washington to tell Nayroo to his face that he is a Russian Agent.[32] No kind of Balinese

---

28. In a letter to MM dated December 17, 1956, EP mentioned having met a visiting European who declined to meet MM because of her affiliation with certain cultural and political groups.

29. Reinhold Niebuhr formed Americans for Democratic Action immediately after World War II. During the 1950s Niebuhr emerged as a major intellectual spokesman for anti-Communist liberalism.

30. Adlai Ewing Stevenson (1900–1965) received the Democratic nomination for president in 1952. He lost to Eisenhower in 1952 and again in 1956.

31. Andrei Vishinsky (1883–1954), Soviet delegate to the UN and prosecutor in the Great Purge trials of the Stalinist era.

32. George Meany (1894–1980), president of the AFL and later of the AFL-CIO, actively opposed Communist affiliations in the international labor movement, often

mask can hide the face of compromise which *always* is supporting the baser cause.

I speak unguardedly and undefinedly because I am reely sick of those who make the worse cause appear the better. Somewhat elementary Teddy Roosevelt, and the kind of parents who believe in corporal punishment are really needed sometimes.[33]

With affectionate regards to you and remarkable Dorothy.   Marianne

P.S. That Georgetown Gentleman has not appeared.

P.P.S. Be *very careful* what kind of animal you send me. I'm a white,[34] very neurasthenic, allergic to zoos rather. Theo at the Bronx Zoo died from being looked at.

To Lincoln Kirstein   *January 24, 1957*

Dear Lincoln,

I wish I had arrived at Monroe [Wheeler]'s a little earlier; however, you *know* it was considerate to not settle Fidelma—was even a little violent to ring. When you got home, you needed space! I think Fidelma is the most sublime knight-in-armor-knight-laying-off-the-armor, always making it seem a happy thought for me to have come and dynamited privacy.

The ballet;[35] I marvel at the almost unanimous élan, precision, faultless timing, appropriate faces and torsos. The theme of "The Unicorn," (GORGON and M,) is really rich, poetic, valuable, I feel, and the settings and colors, a romance. I am a bungler where technique is concerned, but I thought some of the devices a little forced—in the management of the matador-cape skirts. All, however, was knit together eloquently at the end. The deep blue background was lived up to in the next one, by Impresario Mr. [André] Eglevsky, I thought, and the experienced nymphs. But—debar me if you must—the event of the evening to me was Arthur Mitchell; as Monroe said, "he has the right face and doesn't have to worry about what expression to wear." He is a dream come true, the little things he does, pawing the air and backing away; and his lightly bouncing-ball serenity and

through CIA cooperation; Jawaharlal Nehru (1889–1964), prime minister of India, presented a policy of "neutralism" that was attacked in 1956 by Secretary of State John Foster Dulles and Vice President Richard Nixon.

33. MM is referring to Roosevelt's famous maxim "Speak softly and carry a big stick."

34. *Oxford English Dictionary:* "an animal or species of a white color." MM may mean a white elephant. MM's letters to EP include many playful allusions to elephants and poetry, perhaps originating with her poem "Black Earth," which she sent to Pound in 1918.

35. Gian Carlo Menotti's "madrigal fable" was presented by the New York City Ballet on January 15, 1957.

pleasure also, a certain modesty and deference to prominence and space-demands of the others. So very genuine; he has genius, (doesn't have to achieve the whole thing, *Abandón!*). Melissa H[ayden] couldn't have been better or brassier? and the razzmatazz continuity to the utmost bedlam is perfection—a little like the *b fantastique*—you know the one I mean, in which Tanaquil LeClercq was so arch and elegant.

I can just hardly stand the absence of Tanaquil who used to be the one person I went to see.

I admire the Gorgon's little double-faced movable wings. I have always wanted flexible wings in the "Swan Lake" but I guess it wouldn't work out; it would take Fabergé to mount each swan. (I had no thought of seeing "The Unicorn" till I had finished my California work—detached the albatross that hangs from my neck. Monroe sprang this on me, Lincoln.

With love,   Marianne

To Hildegarde Watson   *January 25, 1957*

Hildegarde, the Historical Society Report. *Thank* you. How modest you are, never to have complained of this heavy task. All this complicated detail, formal, graceful, accurate, vivid; presented with such skill; and you doing so many things besides. "Mrs. George Selden's help was invaluable." (Couldn't Mrs. George do more of the hard work?!) But no one else could have managed the Report so well, enhanced by our careful corrections. The inventory of acquisitions is fascinating,—the portrait-statue of Master Russell and the scrolls and rosettes on the comb; and the part about Jenny Lind,[36] and dressing the figures.

And your chivalry and sense of decency, in protesting against the dictatorial egotist who was so wrong about "the artist." If the artist is maladjusted, badly "brought up," and an offense, nobody kills him. But were Sir Walter Scott, Maria Edgeworth, Anthony Trollope, Robert Southey, and Lord Morley, Earl Balfour, W. H. Hudson,[37] and Bach not artists? Then today,—Myra Hess,[38] Dr. [Albert] Schweitzer and for the machinery of sensibility, Henri Cartier-Bresson for whom Monroe Wheeler gave a party Wednesday,—natural, responsive, spontaneous, with an undercurrent of humor, so considerate, and finished, in every respect. I really don't know

36. Swedish soprano (1820–1887) who was brought to the United States by P. T. Barnum in 1850.

37. William Henry Hudson (1841–1922), Argentine-born English naturalist and novelist; author of *Green Mansions*.

38. Myra Hess (1890–1965), English pianist; Henri Cartier-Bresson (1908–), French photographer; Morris Graves (1910–), American artist living in Ireland; Mary Meigs, painter and writer, Bryn Mawr class of 1939 and friend of MM's through Louise Crane.

how to tolerate a paranoic like that one you so nobly opposed. Look at your-selves—Sibley an inventor, writer, and "all round" artist, and *you,*—por-traits, music, co-ordinating every useful thing. Loren MacIver, Morris Graves, Mary Meigs, Thornton Wilder and Robert Frost. This is beginning to be a diatribe.

I see that Alec Wilder composed the music for the Schweitzer film.

Got all tangled up and had to destroy this first page, Hildegarde. Make allowance for me, am incapable of getting anything right in my miscellany of detail, social and personal, a small questionnaire, references for my Cali-fornia paper, belated excuses & attacks on impious thesis-writers. Well, we know what artists can be like; and needn't struggle with intellectual mad bombers.

I see that Alec Wilder wrote the music for the Schweitzer film. My druggist says the whole thing is magnificent. (did say it)

After the party for Henri Cartier-Bresson, Monroe took me to *The Unicorn, the Gorgon, and the Manticore.* The music is very fine, some of it—especially toward the end when it becomes elate and ecclesiastical. The set-ting and costumes are romantic,—early Italian, with [Giorgio de] Chirico arches and towers as enclosing a plaza or courtyard, and the theme holds the attention—the unicorn; dreams in youth; the Gorgon, middle age; & the Manticore, old age.

The real feature of the evening was Arthur Mitchell a Negro dancer (in dungarees & cowboy hat), in the *Western Symphony.* His resilience, his ease, his pleasant face, his joyous boundings and sudden dignity, as light [as] a bouncing ball; (besides the little things he did, backing away and fighting the air, winding it all up with a snappy stamp)—are formula, I know, but done with a grace and sense of timing that no old time cakewalker could surpass. Part of an ensemble, he was, outrageous girls and other boys.

I am *immersed,* Hildegarde, in my interminable typings, YMHA con-test, and perpetual letters; am only on page 4 of my 11-page discourse—or I would have written at once, returning the Report. You may have needed it! I hope not. And yesterday, I felt I must go to the party for William Carlos Williams to whom we gave the $5000-award of the Mrs. Lamont,—Mr.-I.B.M.-Watson-Academy-of-American Poets—(not the Academy of Arts & Letters). It was a very regal party given by Mrs. Clark Williams (no relative of WCW)—150 Central Park South. She is a dear lady, very old with snow white hair, very strong, and a skilled hostess—in black velvet with two large salmon roses at the waist. Chinese bird and butterfly wall paper, china figurines; "rare" Martha Washington plates and tea-pots, jade dishes; and pale Chinese brocade settees. William & Florence Williams, their two sons and d.s in law were impressive, pleasing, and really pleased about the Award. The boys were wonderfully brought up;—one is a doctor and one, a manager at A & S our large department store here in Brooklyn. I joined them for dinner at a steak and chop house nearby. Such fine, natural lovable people. This great digression did not seem to me a calamity, but will I *ever* get my paper done!

With much love,   Marianne

P.S. I attacked William Carlos W. for having said (*Time* last week) that he practiced medicine and so in his writing could "do as he damn pleased." He begged me to believe that he deplored it too, had impulsively said it offhand when *Time* was nearby, and that it entirely falsified his feeling about the Award. I, we, had been told that he needed it—(and his right hand *is* paralyzed. He can move it but not use it, write or drive a car) and (we, several of us) have worked for two years to get it to him. (To have our paragon brush us off seemed a little cool.) I am also a great fool as you know, recklessly "sincere" and get myself in all kinds of dilemmas; and had no fundamental quarrel with William. And Florence is sublime; never morbid, injudicious, out of control or carelessly dressed. I'd do anything for *her*—her monumental goodness, all self-evident in the boys, Paul & William, and their attitude to their wives.

M.

To William Carlos Williams   *July 7, 1957*

Dear William:

I *am* interested in John Napier's letter and thank you for lending it to me.[39] (Am enclosing it.) Have transcribed some of it since it expresses what I think. (The rhythm is the person.)

I do not know Sidney Lanier's *Science of English Verse;* must see it; but how nicely Mr. Napier gives the core of it.

I am, always have been fanatically interested in rhythm; but did not know much about it—terms and controversies—until I came to work at the La Fontaine fables—try to translate them. La Fontaine's defying Boileau [Nicolas Boileau-Despréaux], his authorizing departures from precedent, has been a great pleasure to me, since I have some of the same fancies—I like the light rhyme and unaccented word rhymed with the accented. Not to mention mixed rhythms.

Babette Deutsch is my admiration!, in having compiled a real *Poetry Handbook*; her *Dictionary of Terms.* So neatly said, some things which I would have wrestled with in vain.

---

39. John Napier had written to WCW on June 26, 1957, to introduce himself; in this letter he wrote extensively about the importance of stress to rhythm, praising Sidney Lanier's *The Science of English Verse* and MM's rhythmical patterns, particularly in her poem "The Mind Is an Enchanting Thing."

I thank you for encouraging me—for Mr. Napier's reinforcing comments; and I thank you for your own letter, benevolent William. I did wish to go to Brandeis University to add my straw's weight to the honor shown you and Florence. You won all hearts, I hear. I did lend my straw to those of the voters on the award committee last autumn.

You are doing very much; consenting to be guests, not once but again and again; and the work you do! I couldn't begin to compass it—along with which, you are trying to get published "the work of an unknown woman." I hope the *Letters* are going to be satisfactory to you; anything biographic is a hazard; the letters are bound to reflect your individuality. I trust not *too* much space is devoted to American vs. English—about which we congenitally differ, do we not? I do not attack you, am to be depended on to reinforce you . . . never never can suggest how I relish and revere your magic with the boxwood acrid scent, and with the yellow flower and many another essence.

With love to you and to Florence,   Marianne

The boys are my notion of satisfactory "biography."

To Ezra Pound   *September 10, 1957*

Ezra, you are intolerable, to defy me, about the Jews who are not mine alone but everybody's benefactor; and foolish. And brazen, to risk a snipe at General Eisenhower who is, I think you should know, the best compound psychically whom we have had during our battered lives, and a real general. (My S. [Special] Delivery postman's buddy in Nîmes had no mud-boots. D. E. [Eisenhower] when inspecting, asked why, took off his fur-lined boots then and said, "Put these on."). You were a help when quoted—saying you never did curse the United States, or something like that. (And we leaving no stone unturned! Wm. Faulkner, Esquire post comment! etc.) BUT you are almost as bad as W. C. Williams whom it was not so simple to select for the American Poets $5000. He then said to *Time*, "I practised medicine so I could do as I damn please"; then repented to me, but doesn't he say it *again* on Television?[40] (They Say.)

I can't, i.e. don't like to** tell you about Tom except that visitors tell me "they" behave like newlyweds[41] ("which they are") *and he* seemed to note the fact that I had not replied in any way or sent any congratulation

40. Throughout 1957 Archibald MacLeish rallied a number of people from the literary world, including Faulkner and MM, to campaign for EP's release from St. Elizabeths. EP expressed his desire for the release, but continued to make remarks and maintain affiliations which obstructed this goal. MM submitted a statement in support of Pound during his trial in April 1958. He was released in May 1958.

41. T. S. Eliot and Valerie Fletcher were married January 10, 1957, in a private ceremony.

(very fine of you to write). I was only one of 2 people who did not write, he said. So I wrote, I think it was in July. I think he should be let be.

Yes, everything I do, say, or think, is garbled. I am drove—will be till November 1st. The good thing by W. H. Auden was in the region of

> *And now the mystery of our time*
> *surrounds us like a baffling crime.*[42]

MM

**I have nothing to tell—I don't write, don't hear, all I possess is gossip. (That, I despise.) He did one good thing in this curious leap (amongst many another at other times).
The Bermuda rig!

To Dorothy Pound and Ezra Pound   *April 19, 1958*

Dear Dorothy and Ezra,

Something to make us happy! I venerate Robert Frost, Tom [T. S. Eliot], and one or two others. Mr. Meacham![43] quite a treat, however curious—perhaps incommoding but what of it! since he is a just man.

Decent money is hard to get—even near the Bureau of Printing and Engraving—so I enclose a few *pour boires* for Dorothy to administer? or for a taxi.

With love,

No answer; kindness in showers, in letter-form is a cruelty. All so contradictory. Nothing, when a word would be of value, and then when "occupied," notes like chaff from the thresher.

My Negro houseworker, Gladys B., never telephones except when some frightful calamity has befallen her, but just now: "Miss Moore? Have you seen the paper this morning?" "Not yet." "Ezra Pound has been freed and I knew you would want to know *that*." Yes indeed.

Contingent possibilities. Oh my!

To Lota de Macedo Soares   *August 16, 1958*

Lota, always doing something exciting—dear thing—

I am so charmed by my tropical Gaufrettes—the most ethereal food ever to enter my matter-of-fact little home. All that delicate ribbon-grass

---

42. W. H. Auden, "New Year Letter (January 1, 1940)": "*The situation of our time / Surrounds us like a baffling crime.*"

43. EP had sent MM a copy of a newspaper clipping from the *Sunday Star* (Washington, D.C.). The article, by Harry Meacham, sent to Pound and signed "Let's hope this is it!," was headlined "Liberty Weighed for Poet Ezra Pound."

and the careful mailing brought them—the wafers—here whole—all but one or two, which of course needed to be eaten on *sight*! I *may* save a few; I may devour every one. I did part with several to a "Mrs. Olivari of Genoa," who towed me into her house and garden to give me some currants and a mauve nicotiana stalk, a snowball, and a bushy frond of asparagus fern. (The nicotiana-flowers are a faint claret or mauve on the back, pale on the face, and the fairy fuzz on the slender horns is so fine it is almost French suede.) Her back-yard is so nearly a greenhouse, that the bricks are all but obscured by vivid emerald pin-cushion moss. And it has rained heavily, so we were dappled by unintentional dew from the over-hanging cherry-boughs and some mammoth *fig*-leaves. (No figs.)

You do not seem quite so far away, Lota, since the magic package arrived. If *only* you were here—you and Elizabeth! My gems have brought me good fortune. It is years since I have had anything in *The New Yorker*. Now, after about 3 weeks of deliberation, Howard Moss (whom I met, do you remember, at your Gold-Fizdale-Mr. Pollit party), has taken a piece I wrote with much zeal, called "The Arctic Ox." I am much pleased. Elizabeth whom I have watched write (watched with veneration and envy) should have replaced several recent *N. Yorker* pieces which mystify me greatly.

I love the *Diary* [*of Helena Morley*] more and more. If I weren't in a constant blizzard of unsought, unliked tasks, I might have been trying to say in detail a little of how I treasure the book. I don't intend to be interfered with forever.

With my brother, sister-in-law, eldest niece and her husband, and two guests, I attended *The Winter's Tale* and the *M.-S.-Night's Dream* at the Shakespeare Theatre at Stratford, three days ago. The typhoon-like, Paul-and-Virginia storm in the *Tale*, with tattered foliage and lightning and mighty rumblings, and dashing rain,—while the babe lay on a rocky exposed spot to die, was almost unbearable, it was so good. There was some expert byplay of crossed garlands hung from rafters, and viands borne to the harvest-table, and ecloguelike fond behaviour in parenthesis, approved by the toddling shepherd foster-father of the rescued babe (now like one of the graces in Botticelli's *Spring*). Have I confused you beyond hope?

Coming away from the evening performance, I could not have liked better, the theatre sunk in gloom, with a diamond-spark of light on the tip of the cupola and fainter radiance indicating the angles of the roof. And near the exit from the grounds, there is an absolute giant beech, full of leaves, with a trunk I am sure six feet in diameter.

October first, I leave for the west, Oregon, Washington, and British Columbia; then in November attend a protracted festival in Baltimore. (Trying to be a traveller.) Aren't you coming here sometime soon—when I am home? How often I think of you and Elizabeth—imagining what you do and see—wishing I were as *positive* as you are. Lota. I think and hope I am getting to be so. I am too easily a victim—heart rent by all too much.

No parties for a month or so; then yesterday a big one given by David MacDowell and Ivan Obolensky. Leo Lerman was king, and several unknown ladies, queen, with sheath-umbrella-cover silk skirts and floating panels and violetted eyes. Father Fly(?), and a novelist, Mr. O'Connell, the Williamses, Wm. and Florence, so real and un-ephemeral. Oh, yes, I was at a buffet supper for Janet Flanner[44] at Monroe Wheeler's, where I met William Maxwell (of *The New Yorker*)—who wrote *The Folded Leaf.* Janet is certainly a novel in herself—so intense I could scarcely believe that America can own so omni-interested a person—attended by Natalia Murray who told me how gentle and delightful a guest Walter Gieseking had been, a special friend of her husband, Natalia Murray Denisi [*sic*]. I congratulated René d'Harnoncourt on having owned and loaned Nelson Rockefeller's Museum of Primitive Art a bronze pot traversed by six chameleons with beaded back-ridge. He said, "*Elephants.*" "Oh, no I was thinking of their trunks." (Their tails curved down!)

Much love, girls. Marianne

Now. I have to read a ms. purporting to be URGENT (Special D.).

To Hildegarde Watson   *November 29, 1958*

Your telephone-call, Hildegarde, did so much for me—to know that all was well with you. And yesterday—Friday—I had invited Dr. Wasser[strom][45] to lunch at Schrafft's 42nd & Lexington Avenue. He, without being intensive, told me so much about you and Sibley and seemed breathless to show me tributes (or tell of them) to you and Sibley and *The Dial.* He does have sensibility,? asking me one or two things that I wish had never trammeled existence—all the anomalies—Dr. Watson liked *The Little Review* and Margaret Anderson better than you did,?—Hart Crane excoriated (he used another word) *The Dial* for doing him a favor? Gilbert Seldes was to kidnap Scofield Thayer at Weehawken for Mrs. Thayer (his mother) as he went aboard the boat for England." I had not heard of that. "How is he now?" "How long ago was this? or that?" And, "I never knew much about Alyse Gregory except that she had a violent love affair before she married Llew-

44. Ivan Obolensky (1925–), London-born investment banker, publisher, and foundation consultant; Leo Lerman, writer, author of *The Museum: One Hundred Years at the Metropolitan Museum of Art*, and arts editor for *Mademoiselle* for many years; Janet Flanner (1892–1978), journalist and *New Yorker* columnist; Natalia Danesi Murray (1901–), journalist.

45. William Wasserstrom (1922–), author of *The Time of the Dial* and *A Dial Miscellany*; professor of English at the University of Rochester (1954–60).

elyn Powys." All this is alien to me, Hildegarde. I merely blinked and began
to breathe like a tuna on a fishing-boat. It had begun to rain and I had been
desperate coming down Park Avenue (in a taxi) to be passed and crowded
left by every taxi, truck, and pedestrian, because a highborn Japanese driver
believed in courtesy, caution and *moderation*. I needn't have taken a taxi at
all if I hadn't made a mistake in an address. But Dr. W. said he had arrived
a few minutes late, had only just come. I thought three hours enough discussion and several times put on my scarf. You and Sibley would *perish* before you entertained a person in the style I did—I demanded the check, "so
we could leave soon," (about 20 minutes after we received our food;) paid it
and then later Dr. Wasserstrom (not I) suggested more coffee as I rose to
leave; the incompetent, totally indifferent and slovenly girl, placed the 15¢
check upside down by the *cup*. I leaned way over and retrieved it. As we
finally emerged on the sidewalk, it was raining hard. Poor Dr. Wasserstrom
had a new smooth hat—in fact everything new, but he held my small umbrella over me to the subway and said he would go to the new Guggenheim
Museum & then the Museum of Modern Art.!

He seemed very grateful, Hildegarde, to you for asking him to the studio to a party, and Sibley for seeing him, would repeatedly shake his head,
draw a titanic breath and say, "they are magnificent." Then: "Dr. Watson is
a great *man*, and he was only 17 when he wrote those *good* stories in the
Harvard Monthly." (*Is* that the name?)

I had promised to go to Sneden's Landing [N.J.] today before I had
arranged to see Dr. W. so I *have* to go and am only half through my piece for
The [Christian Science] Monitor (for Dec. 1) but shall survive I guess.

Dear Hildegarde goodby,   M.

P.S. Sunday. *Maybe* I should mention, Hildegarde, that I am obliged to hibernate a few days—in case you had a thought of coming to N. York *now*.
Yesterday, having promised to autograph books at Palisades Library—Sneden's Landing—meant leaving before eleven to meet a car—drive to New
Jersey, have lunch, stay at the Library—till five (with the other door open
every little while to counteract "closeness")—have tea till seven—and arrive home about eight. If I hadn't worried along Friday with Dr. Wasserstrom and combatted the wind and rain afterward, I would have escaped. As
it is I *have* to disappear briefly till I get rested (and get used to the weather
maybe, too, which is 30).

I am just being *hyper* careful—not in misery; but I daren't "talk"!

There are always if's, aren't there? If I had been rushed to the Library
about three, and brought home by five, I wouldn't have been too tired but a
car for several, prevented anything in the way of individual initiative.

The sun is blazing and there is just ordinary wind. (And I am "*obliged*"
to be at Church today,—no ifs or buts—; but I'll just stay in bed!)

I am writing my very determined cousin Sue [Stauffer] that I *may* be able to see her Tuesday.

Am annoyed, Hildegarde, beyond anything *expressible at words*, but previous experience makes me a little careful! Shouldn't it?

Marianne

To Sarah Eustis Moore   *February 23, 1959*

Dear Sallie,

It is a very poor thing, to give a birthday present in advance of the day; and very coarse to enclose no line in one's own writing, but when I had a chance to have Isak Dinesen's *Anecdotes of Destiny* sent you by Doubleday, I *did* on account of the story, "Tempests" which I hope you will like.

You gave us *Out of Africa*, (you, Bee, "Johnnie," and Mark, April 11, 1938, remember?) and it seems to me part of life, so real and affecting it is. I thought of you all the time when at a dinner for I. D. at Monroe's not long ago, she is so better in every way than one could imagine (except that she is thin to emaciation and when not taking a taxi, uses a wheel-chair). She said a great deal about the Farm—Africa—about Kamante and Farah and much else. The Duke of Windsor came to see her; left in haste (a Wednesday?) and said he would come Saturday to dinner he so hoped to see some of the native dances she had described. Dismay! The dances can be given only after harvest, yet to fail to produce them! Farah turned pale then said, "I will go to all the chiefs. They must help you. I will tell them you helped them, they must help you." After two days, he came back exhausted, the car very dusty, and said the dancers *would come*. 2000 came and presents were given them and the chiefs were pleased, then one said, "We like the presents but we liked best your dress. It was more beautiful than the dresses of all the white ladies." (A chiffon with streamers and wide skirt from measurements in Paris.)

Then the story of publishing the first stories after *Out of Africa*. After returning to Denmark, the Baroness said to her brother, "If you will finance me for a year, I will be all right. I can do three things, I can cook, I can take care of mad people, and I can write." He said, "There are a great many cooks out of employment. You have not facilities to take care of mad people, you must write." "After working two years, I took my stories to London. I knew Lady Islington who knew—Hamish Hamilton—to whom I could show them. He said, 'Madame, no stories. Write a novel.' I said, 'Won't you even *look* at them?' He said, 'No.' I knew Dorothy Canfield Fisher: *she* sent them to her and she sent them to Robert Haas of Random House and he took them.

"Mr. H. (in London) said to me not long after, *'How* can I meet Isak Dinesen? I must *meet* him.' I said, 'You *have* met him. I am he.'"

I had no thought of writing you so long a letter, Sallie. It needs no answer. Neither does the book. (If you can't be burdened with books, give it away.)

The Baroness is endearing in many ways; she has *no* manner, slightly smiles, but her earnestness and deep feeling shame effusiveness or even emphasis. She wore a lustrous medium gray taffeta with billowing skirt, three-quarter sleeves, covered up neck and a white tulle rose right in the front of the neck, also a tiny black hat with a pompom of black and white uncurled ostrich feather which threatened her left eye a little, like Skye terrier-bangs.

Anything in the way of "attitude" seems out of the question, in connection with her. For two years she was ill—had spinal operations and lay prone, obliged to dictate all she wrote. (Miss Clara Swensen, her companion and secretary, was with her, always is. The other guests were Fred Adams, Director of the Morgan Library, [&] Glenway Wescott.)

I hope, Sallie, that you aren't over-straining yourself. I would rather be lean than over-heavy; but as Dr. Laf Zoofy, my Lebanese doctor says, "When *tall*, you have to weigh commensurately."

With love (and let me sometime tell you the ingenious story I.D. told me!),

Craig

To Fidelma and Lincoln Kirstein   *June 15, 1959*

Dear Fidelma and Lincoln:

Nothing could have made up to me for not seeing the Imperial Household. They strengthen my every fanaticism in favor of hyper-acute color. Just the properties would have been a day of drama. I was in K on the aisle but if I had not known, Fidelma, to do it, I would not have gone up to the mezzanine to see the emerald platform vermilion and gold fence. Then the pace, the decorum, the tea-toned faces, the slow continuing resonance of the big drum in the suspended frame, and the quick pattering and intervals of the little one, were an everlasting impression; also the pendant gold ball on the fishbeak or noses of the masks, the precisely tied chin-bows, and weighty magnificent tassels, the placing without a slip, of the mirrors addorsed.

Martha Graham—my first sight of her dancing, could it have been better! with garb as imperial as any oriental could wish, the gallows, scaffold steps and the agonies; all high drama.

Francisco Moncion continues the Chagall firebird mood in a wonderful manner, against the faint glow of moon in the backdrop. His speed, his birdlike ways and that Karinska? cerise and violet costume, I would never tire of; Patricia Wilde just doesn't suit me, in fact grates on me—too sway-backed and scientifically thinned, hackney-gaited. Mechanically automatic Swiss toy Maria Tallchief, better and more impersonal as I recall. Plenty-rehearsed, limber Diana Adams, running about as if tearing ribbon from the bolt, had that man-dancer command of recourses, I thought; (the one with a kind of Margaret Miller-shaped face)? I don't want to extoll a store-mannikin. Then Violette Verdy, *was* it she? in the Firebird pastoral, was perfection, whirling spontaneously with the continuousness of an accordion, and so charming and girl-like.

How unsparing you are, dear Fidelma and Lincoln—getting me treasure essential to me.

I went to the side "mezzanine ticket-window"—got there by a quarter of two and was handed a ticket instantly with a little yes-sir looking-for-you cordial nod. And let me say, that I think the wash-room facilities and matron and facilities [*sic*], home-done enamelled look, do the Center the utmost credit.

Hairfine, precise, *lovely friends*, this thing I've written looks like rubbish. If I could help it, I would.

With love,   Marianne

To James Sibley Watson   *July 16, 1959*

Dear Sibley, The ring —

The emerald is of a color that disables comment—I suppose varied by the adjoining of the many triangular facets that extend deep enough to profit by the small triangles of each;—in a way, subdividing the hexagon of the original prism. In any case, an "attraction!" Then the diamonds are so compact they are like the indivisible stones of the walls of Cuzco, that seem in the ring to extend oval like the emerald—perhaps by making right to left prongs—opposite rather than oblique. Or has it gone to my head?

It is like putting an imperial crown on a toad, for me to possess, let alone wear, such a thing—a dilemma—yet it might be safer for me to wear it than to take care of it in the box—which is also very elegant. It is so delicate, special and un-"*novelty*," the refinement is indescribable.

As I said to Hildegarde, I have been struggling with some needful revision of my will, and seem not to be giving you and Hildegarde anything—having hoped I might hand you something that might have a meaning. It is hardly logical to be receiving a jewel.? But it may "do something for me," battered as I have been by combined physiological enemies. And your lack of solemnity—having said to Hildegarde that if I were "robbed" or lost it, you and she could get me another! does a great deal for me—(passing over the fact that there *is* no other). This getting of emeralds in pairs is not usual!! It should prolong life. (*MARAGADA: SMARAGDUS!*)[46]

Hildegarde told me after you telephoned, of the death of Elsey. Death may be "a friend" to the dead but what insupportable intensifying of the significant to us—living. He—for Mrs. Lasell—took Mother and me from the Farm to Annisquam: what competence and care—and veiled interest. (The last great enemy—death.)

(Pardon me, Sibley.) With love,   Marianne

To Monroe Wheeler   *December 20, 1961*

Dear Monroe,

I am grateful; but you did send me candy, Monroe! *You* should be present, to benefit and help me eat it—magnificently purveyed,—with a scarlet pompom of satin ribbon—two pounds. I shall not be the slender wheat straw I was a year ago, but could live on candy.

The clippings are here! The information—amount raised and sums paid—are of interest?; but the casual, self invented erroneous reportings of a helpless guest, cause one to become an eremite forever. A crashing, incompatible vagrant, and stranger to the drawing-room I surely seem! in these write-ups.

A business touch, here, Monroe. (As they say in the east, "both pilgrimage and business.")

Hildegarde tells me that there is no item by e. e. cummings in the Museum of Modern Art. She says she would buy and present if *permitted* by you, e.e.'s recent *Christmas Tree*—a really magical thing, with glints of tinsel and a *veritable* chic scarlet ribbon below the boughs. Of course it may look too like what it is to seem "modern." But it certainly is contemporary.

The best 3 drawings of e. e. c.'s that I have seen, (of his early caricatures) are truly Daumier-esque, some of them, don't you think? A certain 3 belong to Hildegarde; and since Sibley Watson is not exhibitionist, he might obstruct my wishing you to consider them but they are gems—three

---

46. *Maragdos* is Greek for emerald; *smaragdus* is Latin for emerald, borrowed from the Greek.

line drawings incisive, and unhelped by so much as an after touch, —of Sibley Watson taking pictures under a cloth as in early days. The spiral of uninterfering wistaria-twined legs in one, is irresistibly funny yet unliteral. No face in any of them.

I live under an endless threat of importunate beggars, Monroe—persons who have done me colossal favors, who have turned poet or *littera-teur* (spell it) and want to be exhibited or advertised or reviewed; or just want money and I *won't* compromise. So, be emancipated. I am not waiting & *waiting* till you oblige me! But those "Daumier"ly Cummings are remarkable—(as neat as Toulouse-Lautrec) and "funny," executed very boldly.

I *hope* Christmas will not be a festive anxiety for you, if you go home or stay here. I said to Louise I'll be with her mother & her on Christmas,—Christmas Eve with Edward Darlington, Henrietta Holland and the Zullis of N.Y. University.

Condone my rackety ways. I was shocked to know that Cummings isn't Modern—had to say so. That done, I'll not bother you with the scandal again.

Gratefully, Marianne

[on envelope flap:] "You're taking time to collect those notices, I appreciate tremendously."

To James Laughlin   *March 20, 1962*

Dear Mr. Laughlin:

You help everyone; you never "impose" and it pains me not to feel enriched by Charles Reznikoff;[47] but the rhythms seem tenacious, not felt—halt the mind, failing to afford the joy that poems should create.

I could say the "fly" has pathos but a writer does not like to be pitied. Certainly it may be I who am at fault. Anyhow, I can't feel honest in selecting plausible lines. The battle to be accepted is bitter, exasperating; from 1910 I have been aware of being disapproved of—enheartened by the fact that you and one or two others "saw something" in me, and if anyone should put himself out to ease the path for another, it is I; but the doggerel and untranscended misery here should be offset by impudence or virtuosity of some sort? Let me again some time try to be of use. I grew to like Dylan Thomas, in fact, very fast; but this is not work that suffers from momentum or defiance.

In any case, condone me; you will never find me indifferent—or high "browed!"

47. American poet of the objectivist school (1894–1976), whose manuscript Laughlin had sent to MM.

I do admire your valor. And the worst of it, protégés can be thankless. So thoughtful of you to enclose an envelope.

Marianne Moore

To John Warner Moore   Grande Bretagne Hotel, Athens
                                                    Sept[ember] 20th [1962] Thursday II[48]

Cruise to the Islands, 2-dogs. 1st *Delos* and its 5 lions facing the same way with mouth open—saw a lizard a kind of horned gecko on a tumble-down wall—heard a meadow-lark. A pale gray bird like a mourning dove flew over the lions—Temple of Dionysus with 2 wings from his shoulders, riding on (or preceded by) a panther, the Greek girl guide Niké said, "the animal sacred to *him*" in very broken English—says Pelo*pón*nesus, the way everyone does.

The same day Mikonos—extolled by everyone, but we got there only at 8 PM. Frances wouldn't go ashore. Norvelle, S. [Sister] and I descended the side of the ship (gangplank) into a chugging motor boat, and landed on a big quay and wandered past Petros a famous old pelican site, and paused by the shops. I bought MYSELF a small olive wood box, 2 wooden spoons of pine, hastened back to the boat—not hunting out Vianula a well known aged dyer & weaver. A very American American hatless, in shorts said, "*Delos* this way—though I don't want to be the Pied Piper leading you all astray." He was right & we got safe aboard.

Tuesday Sept. 18. Rhodes—I am sending you the Apostle P's Harbor where he was wrecked. Donkeys for some. *We* walked up the mosaic of black & white pebbles to the Crusaders Citadel—the best thing yet. Magnificent sheer walls—ramparts—a dim crude carving of a ship with curved sail on the face of the rock in shadow made by the rocky angles. [MM sketches the scene.] (A small wonderful Byzantine church. Mrs. Hawthorne bought & lit a thin brown candle: "For the pleasure of being with you.") We tarried there some time—saw no viper though men & women wear boots to protect them from snakes. We drank lemonade at the foot of the ramparts, the town of Lindos—under a vine 10 or more inches thick shading 20 or 30 feet—from which big blue grapes hung down. (Oranges & lemons.)

Next day, Crete—the palace of Gnossos, lily prince with 3 peacock feathers drooping from his crown—and lilies & a butterfly in the fresco. We drove round the old city park & saw immense stone cannon balls in pyramids, went (in the taxi) through narrow streets, peeped into a mosque—saw 2 plane trees of huge girth, 800 yrs old.

48. The first letter of this sequence, dated September 16, was numbered I; MM mailed them in the same envelope.

There was a roadside paddock of donkeys and mules—about 40—of which Mrs. Hawthorne took a picture for me.

Afternoon of the day we visited the excavations & restorations by Sir Arthur Evans, we visited Santorini. Your brother rode donkeyback up the sizzagging cobbled road to the top—the driver holding an arm and calling constantly to the donkey *Dah, dah, dah*—now and then beating the beast lightly and my leg at the same time occasionally. I asked Niké to tell him to get me a bell like his donkey's but 2 hours later coming down in the dusk he helped me off, then got out his knife & cut the bell from the rope on the donkey's neck. The perspective from that steep mountain I'll never forget. From the very top saw the sun sink in gold and rose pink. An old fellow in the museum on top, gave me in parting a white rose & some lemon verbena. Mr. Nomékos who owns the *Delos* shipline has a house on the summit of many pillars & veranda in front, had everyone come in, wander through the rooms & up 4 sets of stairs.

On Crete, I forgot to say we saw crenelated towers, perfect round battle-towers & 2 minarets.

Back on the *Delos*, we packed for Athens & arrived at 8 or 9 AM delighted to have our easeful rooms again. The sea on the cruise especially at Lindos was a burning blue,—too intense to imagine.

I am not agoing to the 3-day Poetry Festival in Washington—MAY let *The Tribune* visit me.

Frances and I had a stateroom together on the *Delos*, Sister & Norvelle. F. & N. have just given me an octopus bureau scarf—(design of an octopus). We leave on the 24th to visit 4 places ending the 28th on the Saturnia.

F. & N. are determined I see Greece if I never see another thing in my life! I'll send a few cards to you & Constance. I got the checks, money is holding out good.

Haven't yet finished my article.

> *Dearest love,* toadlet

To T. S. Eliot and Valerie Eliot   260 Cumberland Street   Brooklyn 5, N.Y. *December 25, 1962*

Dear Tom and Valerie,

Dejected and deprived—told we are not to see you in January, I was wishing you could be saturated by the sun which makes even our bare twigs look warm, when I received your Fra Angelico *Coronation of the Virgin* and all my ponderings became gratitude.[49] A really holy thing: the absorbed eye and reticent hand,—so quiet and so exalted. The pink sleeve and inconspicuously regal cloak.

49. Christmas card sent by TSE to MM.

Dear Valerie and Tom, *please* be able to come to New York. It is an inconsequential, dull place if you can't.

And I want to tell you about my wanderings in Greece; and living next door to Desdemona's palace in Venice.

Fondly,   Marianne

To Mary Markwick Moore Reeves   The Lodges, Inc.,
                                         Prouts Neck, Maine
                                         August 28, 1963

Dear Mark,

The weather was torrid when I sent you the box and I hoped you would bear with me, and keep it patiently till winter.

I wish I were to see you when you come—or came—to [Carol?] Reeve's wedding. I am at Prouts Neck with Malvina Hoffman and will be going home the 4th of September.

You pay a penalty for being *related to me,* Mark! I wish I could hear your commentary. It is most unusual for me to be helped by a knowledgeable speaker instead of being asked to *prepare* the paper, *myself.* You are one of my few literary relatives who knows the material and other material, not to mention my [Guandi] Italian versions—my *Reader & Fables.*

Ezra Pound's daughter, Mary de Rachewiltz, who has translated E. E. Cummings very astutely, is scandalized by Giovanni Galtieri's equivalents for some of my lines. I know so little Italian, I am a [crass?] critic. You are a judge.

I cannot think of better helpers for reference on me than the writers you speak of, Mark. My regulation advice to young writers, I quote from George Grosz about drawing and painting.

> *Endless curiosity*
> *observation and a*
> *great amount of joy in the thing.*

Also *Be as clear* as your natural reticence allows you to be. I am always quoting Ezra P.'s "Imagist don't's": Natural order of words, no unnecessary word etc. (avoiding adjectives)—and his saying "Never never never use any word that under powerful emotion you could not conceivably use"—misquoted but I think I quote it correctly in the Donald Hall interview.

I say: Exercise *Patience*! (Ever since 1945 I have wished I had a suitable equivalent for "The Grasshopper & Ant"

> *Grasshopper: instead of* "ease" *&* "please"
> *Ant:* "*I sang please do not be* repelled"

G.: Ant. Sang? I am delighted when someone has *excelled.*)

Well, THANK YOU, dear Mark for the "pamphlet"—and for telling me that *John* has been asked to teach the upper class in Shakespeare—the *crowning honor* in any university or college.

Spare yourself all you can. I never resent "no letter" or card. Midway stored possessions mean concentrated toil,—dishes silver!!! I myself am suffocated by books and trying to assort memorabilia so I understand *any* seeming lapse of letter or card—I even send cards to strange professors.

Much love, Craig

Such pretty stationery and Air Mail label.

To John Warner Moore and family   The Royal York Hotel, Bath
September 11, 1964

Dear Constance, JWM, Sallie, and Bee,

After *The Lamb* for F. & N. [Frances and Norvelle], dinner for us all warm French bread, brook trout, and peaches, and The Grosvenor Arms Hotel for Miss Nesbitt and me at Hindon near Salisbury, Avebury and Stonehenge we came to Bath, stopping sometime at Wardour Castle with a shaven lawn and unbelievable history of Lady Elinor and her Arundel husband. She with a grandchild and 25 retainers, (starving), withstood a siege of Roundheads who after a long time blew up the Castle so she fled. Only a variety of steep spiral stairs and a few walls remain with coats of arms over various doorways.

The trees are the finest ever seen, Cedars of Lebanon, one redwood, a grotto and stonemasons busy repairing damage to the walls and windows. It was F. 80 and more in the sun outdoors and little birds twittering—one creeping up the redwood. The Brownes and Miss N.—all with various bird-books for the trip—couldn't tell what it was—a little like a nuthatch. A flock of swans on the small stream were cruising about—a large party. Two riders opened a wooden gate without dismounting, closed it and rode on. Despite the hot lawn, the castle was as frigid as any Armour Refrigerating plant.

Our favorite Inn is The Black Horse—a Clydesdale with white feet painted on the front wall of the Inn—an effigy of a racehorse on the garden high signpost as you go in. Fine food and a parlor fireplace with a stone inglenook that had cushions on the stone close to the fire. Laurel filled the fireplace now.

Stonehenge was a great sight. We went twice, thinking of Thomas Hardy and Tess. It was lowering the first time—evening, the stones pale gray and closer together than they seem in pictures, with a low dull lapis blue line of clouds and trees against which they were silhouetted. Norvelle, our historian who knows every king and episode—could not find the dagger and sword on an inner stone of the circle—finally found it, [MM sketches a knife] dimly discernible and sword bigger and dimmer [MM sketches a sword] found when we went a second time—next morning in bright sun; and who should be there but Ellen Thayer and her friend, Hildegard Nagel who had come by taxi.

I mix up sequences but a real thrill was the Abbey at Glastonbury and Kg. Arthur's and Queen Guinevere's original tomb site 1101. Much dry shaven grass—very green near the grave and after lunch, we visited Wells—a little jaded but persevering. The inverted arch (and cope-chest) and matchless central pillar of the Chapter-house were hard to leave. Under a crimson pseudo leather flap in a locked case in the collegiate school was one groat bearing the head of Henry VIII found by chance among cathedral contributions long ago.

My pleasantest memory of a verger or supervising prelate was a hospitable, quite old man with Roman features & white hair with an initiate smile bending down pleasantly to listen, who led me to the foot of the chapter house stairs. Frances, ever contributing shillings or pound (for upkeep of the Cathedral)—followed. The stairs were not shallow Mellon Gallery stairs; but deep, hollowed out aslant by many feet—and there was the pillar expanding to the roof in a flawless lily or trumpet. The ecclesiastic had said the Cathedral College another flight up was open. We ascended and found Q. Elizabeth's big presentation document as Founder of the College—and the groat; also two firedogs—with knowing pointed heads a good deal like a rat but with tapered ears—a wonderful piece of wrought iron work. We then continued to The Royal York Hotel; on the way saw Queen Square and the Francis Hotel where M. [Mole] & I stayed in 1937 ("more like us" Frances said but we like the R. York).

I have made no notes of these places (Black Horse at Treffont Magna & Glastonbury and Wells)—so if it is not *too* much trouble to save me this letter?

Love, and plenty more to tell you,   "Rat"

(P.S. Miss Nesbitt is away for 3 days at a nephew's wedding.)

To Constance Moore and John Warner Moore
                    260 Cumberland [Brooklyn]   *February 5, 1965*

Dear Constance and JWM,

Sallie has just telephoned me and made me really feel that you are having a good time and a safe time, that JWM was [not?] fit to visit when just back from the Hospital but that now he has recovered or *is* recovering vitality and that you are among suitable people and can "play games." This does an enormous amount for my morale.

Fight Nite quite an excitement in New York and here. George Plimpton may have got me a ticket but is discreet and said "I have an extra ticket and wondered if you would like to join us." He said first "My illness is letting up and I thought I'd make my first serious foray on Monday night—to see the Floyd Patterson–[George] Chuvalo prize-fight at Madison Square Garden. A number of [us] are going—Peter Matthiessen,[50] the qiviut expert, Bob Silvers of the *N.Y. Review of Books*, John Phillips, Marquand's son; etc. wondered if you'd care to join us. I thought we'd have supper at eight— perhaps in the Coffee House—and start in time for the main event which starts, I believe, about ten. I will come with a limousine for you—though I doubt the same chauffeur. I do hope you can arrange it. The fight should be interesting—the Garden a sellout . . .

"I am staying at my parents, 1165 5th Avenue and the telephone there is AT 9 6365. Very best wishes."

Toni Palmieri asked permission to take pictures and was allowed but requested not to mention the Coffee Club. Mr. Plimpton backed away but I said, "oh, you must be in this." I don't know how good Toni is. George Plimpton had never heard of *The Women's Wear Daily* and seemed much amused. I said my Bryn Mawr friends call it *The Underwear Daily*. We had very good soup, slightly thick barley I guess with shreds of parsley and lettuce and carrot in it, steaks, French beans and French salad with skinned tomatoes and baked Alaska on meringues—talked to some editors of Harper and Row (Willie Morris among them) before dinner. It was snowing large wet flakes and I had on my best tricorne but the car was close by. The garden was a mass of rather battered felt hats and heavy faces, arms waving $100 bills and men shouting, Pay you double, pay you double right in sight of the brass buttons of policemen. I had to be led by the hand through the squeeze of humanity; ticket-taker vigilant looking at your face and ticket, strong thumb on the ticket. Inside the air was dense with cigarsmoke, jammed from eaves to floor and from wall to wall, reporters with typewriters close to our side of the ring and when Cassius and his party came in Cassius sat against the right back corner of the ring. It looked very official, smooth hard canvass, thick scarlet ropes and two low red stools in diagonally opposite corners of the ring with buckets and bottles and towels near the stools.

The fighters rinsed their mouths, spit out the water, and the crowd kept shouting more and more vociferously, "Let's go, Floyd." *The Times* said, the seediest and toniest crowd the G. has seen and the richest non-title fight in ring history. George Plimpton kept explaining what went on, how good Zack Clayton was (the referee) and how he kept following the fighters, lean and limber, careful also not to stay planted so the crowd's view wouldn't

50. American novelist (1927–).

be obstructed. He said Chuvalo was feet on the ground the entire time and Floyd hopping and retiring in dancing motion most of the time. No one was knocked down. Chuvalo planted blow after blow on Floyd's lower waist (kidney) and Mr. Plimpton said "he's going to feel this; it's dangerous." One could see them tire and the bell rang too soon every time. Was panting so I could hardly breathe.

[words missing] and one of the party right opposite the middle of the ring and George Brown who trained George P., A. J. Liebling, Harvey Breit and Ernest Hemingway. Others kept leaning out and smiling—pointed out Don Newcombe down on the floor. The seats there the most expensive, G. P. said, but we could see much better. Harvey and a girl were next to me (not part of our group; the girl in a quilted blue oilskin parka and very pretty thin wool lace brown stockings—which she insisted were very warm).

There was a little discussion about the rounds. George Plimpton said 6–5. One judge said 7–5 and the other, 8–4. But the decision was a win for Floyd. He put his arm around Chuvalo and then came back and said something. I know just how you feel. Said "Cassius, who would spring up on the canvas, helped me more than the coach; I did everything he said to do. He helped me a great deal." Under the bragging, I think there's a nice fellow.

George P. then said to me, "It's traditional to go [to] the Toots Shor's Club and see some of the former fighters and trainers. Or would you rather go straight home?" "By no means," I said, so as the crowd thinned, we slowly got downstairs and to the car in a wet big-flake snow. The driver was not in the car but there was no other car, so we got in and it proved to be the right one.

The club has a low ceiling dotted with yellow discs of light in the ceiling, some green foliage by the counter and cashier. It is built in an L. George P. said Norman Mailer had invited us to sit at his table. George said we'd sit a few minutes and then move to the table by the back wall, there were so many of us. I liked Norman Mailer immensely—and on getting home read his article in the Jan 31 *Times;* "Cities Higher than Mountains"—in which he says "Man has always been engaging the heavens. Now the jungle is being replaced by a prison." Really ingenious article. He lives at 128 Willow. George P. is always alluding to him. I now see a reason.

I sat between Mr. J. [Joe] Fox, a Random House Editor and George Brown who is *most* pleasant and refined, waved his hand to us when we left—after a "pushing person" had sketched a black and white of me on a giant note book about newspaper size. It was examined by all, Gene Tunney and others and I said timidly, "Could *I* see it?" The face was like a starving antelope's but the hat very stylish and graceful.

We then met Toots Shor—a tall, solid, quiet fellow—very formal. Nobody tweaks him. I then when G. P. had finished paying the bill, said "no, Mr. Plimpton. If you would do me a favor, have the driver take you home and then take me to Brooklyn." "It's just a little way across the bridge" he said. "I am going to see you right to your door." At the door, I said, "*Don't get out. I don't want you to have a backset. These are exceptional circumstances.*" He got out and said something about the zoo trip. Peter Matthiessen has been elected to the Zoo Board of Directors and thought he could show us round when it's warmer and there would be more baby animals to see.

The Brownes after these many weeks still have a nurse for Norvelle's broken heel which I mentioned at Greenwich. It occurred to me I should *give* them something. They say nothing—they have no chance to expand or have any gifts and don't want financial help which I felt or any cheer-up thoughtful present. So I do as they say.

You can hardly have been with me all through my fite notes but I assure you the whole thing was stupendous—to me anyhow.

With love,

To Mary-Louise Schneeberger   *35 West 9th Street, NY, NY*
                                     [postmarked February 16, 1968]

Dearest Mary-Louise,

A Lincoln's Birthday shared by St. Valentine. You have the biggest heart dear warm hearted snow-bird—double check for me to divide, snow-bird, right now and do you know? Last evening at the Craftsmen Poetry evening Cousin Edith's friend, Mrs. H. (someone carried off the poem on the back of which I wrote her name) came up to me and won my heart, she spoke so lovingly of Cousin Edith and of the poetry-program yesterday. Come see me, dear Mary-Louise, after this polar weather abates.

You say, I may keep the *Life* picture if I haven't it and I haven't. And I do feel that way oftentimes when not writing an overdue article as at present.

I am so happy that Harry Belafonte happened to pick me for his show—so handsomely surprising me by his end-dance: "Marianne, Carry On."

I love the thought of Carmel and you, Mary-Louise in your Chinese vermilion dress! Much love, dear Cousin Edith and Mary-Louise, when this polar weather abates, if you'll visit me in your car!

The huge check, so rescuing this snowbird.

Lovingly,   Marianne

To Elizabeth Bishop and Roxanne[51]   *35 W. 9th St. [New York]*
January 3, 1969

Dear Elizabeth and Roxanne,

I am much delighted, proud of the grasshopper and his apparatus. How novel! I ought to abandon state scenes and go West.

I wonder and wonder, Elizabeth, if your hand has got right, if you are thinking of visiting us. You know I never have been at one of your readings Elizabeth. I must "examine" one. I have been reading [Jean Baptiste Pierre Antoine de Monet de] Lamarck, [Frédéric] Cuvier and [Alexander] von Humboldt—such impassioned scientists and Darwin; working under difficulties, all of them—, and so beneficial; in fact indispensable! All their journeys, in days when travel was not easy, all like ants when their hill has been stepped on.

Art seems to have desisted? I still want to paint—all the fur on my bushy best paintbrush-brush eaten up by a moth.

I so thank you for the grasshopper. Summer seems less indispensable since we have oil.

Come back!

My lizard in a curve is much admired.

Love, Marianne

---

51. The addressee Roxanne prefers to remain anonymous.

Glossary of Names

FAMILY GLOSSARY

*A name in italics indicates the subject appears
also as a main entry.*

ANNIE ISABELLA ARMSTRONG, MWM's cousin on paternal side.

ANN BORDEN ("AUNT ANN," ALSO REFERRED TO AS "FANNY BORDEN"), family friend and Vassar librarian, who arranged for *Elizabeth Bishop* to meet MM.

MARY WATSON CRAIG ("COUSIN MARY"), married to Ira Shoemaker. MWM's first cousin and MM's first cousin once removed. MWM wrote to her frequently, and MM and JWM maintained close ties with her after MWM's death.

MARY WATSON CRAIG ("MARY WATSON"), second cousin of MM's. Her father, John Orr Craig, was MWM's first cousin. Married Clifford Heindel and lived near Greencastle, Pa. Sister of *Sue Brewer Craig*.

SUE BREWER CRAIG, only sister of *Mary Watson Craig* and MM's second cousin. Married to Dr. Ralph Stauffer.

MAY ("MARY") EUSTIS (Mrs. P. B. Wightman), one of three sisters of *Constance Eustis Moore*. Owned a house in Woodbury, Ct., that MM and MWM visited.

EDITH HOWARD ("AUNT EDITH"), *Edwin Howard*'s mother, who attended the Mary Institute (St. Louis) with MWM when she lived in Kirkwood, Mo. "Aunt" was an honorific title, marking the close friendship.

EDITH MOORE LOVE (Mrs. Will), first cousin of John Milton Moore (MM's father) and MM's first cousin once removed. MM corresponded with her in the 1950s and 1960s after MWM's death.

CONSTANCE EUSTIS MOORE (1890–1984), ("Consence" or "Teddy"). Married to JWM in July 1918. They had four children: Mary ("Mark") Markwick Moore (Mrs. John D. Reeves); Sarah ("Sallie") Eustis Moore; Marianne ("Bee") Craig Moore; and John Warner Moore, Jr. See *John Warner Moore*.

JOHN WARNER MOORE (1886–1974), brother of MM. B.A. Yale, 1908; B.D. Princeton Theological Seminary, 1914; chaplain, U.S. Navy, 1917–48, retiring as captain. Thereafter became chaplain at boys' preparatory school, The Gunnery, Washington, Ct. Married *Constance Eustis*, 1918 (see above). Primary family nicknames: "Biter" and several other names suggesting dogs; "Turtle"; "Badger"; "Toad"; "Fish"; "Bible"; referred to himself in the third person as "Porker."

MARIANNE MOORE (1887–1972). Primary family nicknames: "Uncle"; "Gator"; "Fangs"; "Rat"; "Basilisk"; "Feather"; "Weaz." Referred to herself in the third person as "Barca" ("Barka") and as "Willow."

MARY WARNER MOORE (1862–1947), mother of MM and JWM. Daughter of the Reverend John Riddle Warner and Jane ("Jennie") Craig Warner. Married John Milton Moore (1885); separated from him before the birth of MM. English teacher at Metzger Institute, Carlisle, Pa. (1899–1916). Primary family nicknames: "Bunny" and other names suggesting rabbits; "Fawn"; "Mouse"; "Mole"; "Bear"; "Cub."

GENERAL GLOSSARY

CONRAD AIKEN (1889–1973), American poet, novelist, and *Dial* contributor; MM reviewed his work for *The Hound & Horn*, and they corresponded between 1930 and 1944.

RICHARD ALDINGTON (1892–1962), British poet who also published translations, an autobiography, and critical essays. As an associate editor of *The Egoist*, he accepted two of MM's early poems for publication. Married to *H.D.* (1913–38).

MARGARET ANDERSON (1886–1973), American who founded and edited *The Little Review*.

W[YSTAN] H[UGH] AUDEN (1907–1973), British poet, playwright, librettist, and essayist; immigrated to America in 1939, became an American citizen in 1946. A friend of MM's who visited her in Brooklyn and with whom she corresponded between 1939 and 1963.

MARY BARNARD (1909–), American poet, prose writer, and translator of Sappho. MM began reading her poetry in the mid-thirties; they later became acquainted, and corresponded between 1949 and 1971.

SYLVIA BEACH (1887–1962), American publisher, editor, and translator who owned and managed Shakespeare and Company, a bookshop and lending library in Paris. MM wrote to her during the *Dial* years, when Beach sponsored James Joyce's work; they later met through *Bryher* in the mid-thirties and corresponded between 1936 and 1963.

THE BENÉTS, friends of MM's who spent summers in Carlisle.

LAURA BENÉT (1884–1979), American poet and sister of *William Rose Benét* and *Stephen Vincent Benét* and a casual friend of MM's; they corresponded between 1912 and 1971.

STEPHEN VINCENT BENÉT (1898–1943), American poet, novelist, and writer of libretti; author of *John Brown's Body* (1928).

WILLIAM ROSE BENÉT (1886–1950), American poet, critic, and editor of the *Saturday Review of Literature;* he also edited, with *Norman Holmes Pearson, The Oxford Anthology of American Literature* (1938). Classmate of JWM's at Yale and friend of MM's; he and MM corresponded between 1916 and 1950. Married to Elinor Wylie (1885–1928), American poet and novelist.

GLADYS GRANBY BERRY (Mrs. Wallace Berry), MM's part-time housekeeper from 1946 on, who became a friend.

ELIZABETH BISHOP (1911–1979), American poet, fiction and prose writer, and translator. MM met Bishop in New York in 1934 through the efforts of *Ann Borden*. They carried on a close correspondence between 1934 and 1971.

BLAST (June 1914–July 1915), little magazine published in London and edited by Wyndham Lewis. Contributors included Rebecca West, Ford Madox Hueffer [Ford Madox Ford], *T. S. Eliot*, and *Ezra Pound*.

MAXWELL BODENHEIM (1893–1954), American poet, novelist, and playwright; he contributed to *The Dial* and MM reviewed his work for *The Dial*.

LOUISE BOGAN (1897–1970), American poet, essayist, and poetry critic for *The New Yorker* (1931–70). She and MM favorably reviewed each other's work and corresponded between 1944 and 1968.

BROOM (1921–24), international monthly magazine of the arts published in Rome, Berlin, and New York. Edited by Harold A. Loeb (with *Alfred Kreymborg*, Slater Brown, Matthew Josephson, and *Malcolm Cowley*). *Lola Ridge* was the American editor. Contributors included MM, *Malcolm Cowley*, *Conrad Aiken*, *Kreymborg*, Jean Toomer, *Lola Ridge*, *William Carlos Williams*, *E. E. Cummings*, and others.

FRANCES BROWNE, college and lifelong friend of MM's with whom she corresponded between 1906 and 1971. Traveled with her to Greece, Italy, England, and Ireland in the 1960s. Sister of Norvelle Browne, Bryn Mawr class of 1909.

BRUNO'S (January–April 1917), weekly little magazine, edited by Guido Bruno, which published early work by MM. Superseded *Bruno's Weekly* (July 1915–September 1916).

BRYHER (Winifred Ellerman) (1894–1983), British writer of poetry, fiction, and nonfiction; an important patron of the arts who supported individual artists, publishing ventures, and the journals *Life and Letters To-day* and *Close-Up*. Introduced to MM by *H.D.*, who was then Bryher's companion; Bryher and MM became close friends and corresponded extensively between 1920 and 1970. Marriages of convenience to *Robert McAlmon* (1921–27) and *Kenneth Macpherson* (1927–48).

KENNETH BURKE (1897–1993), American literary critic and philosopher, who also wrote fiction and poetry. He was music critic for *The Dial* (1927–29) and for *The Nation* (1934–36). He received the Dial Award in 1928. As a *Dial* editorial assistant, he became a friend of MM's; they corresponded between 1925 and 1971. He also reviewed MM's work.

MARY BUTTS (1892–1937), English novelist and short-story writer.

CAMERA WORK (January 1903–June 1917), photographic quarterly published in New York and edited by *Alfred Stieglitz*.

MARCIA CHAMBERLAIN, close friend of MM's; they corresponded from 1942 until Chamberlain's death in 1955. MM became acquainted with her through *Kathrine Jones*, Chamberlain's companion, and frequently visited both at their home in Maine.

THE CHIMAERA (May–July 1916), bimonthly little magazine published in Port Washington, N.Y., and edited by *William Rose Benét*. Contributors included MM, *Amy Lowell*, Helen Hoyt, the *Benéts*, and others.

CLOSE-UP (1927–33), film journal started by *Bryher* and *Kenneth Macpherson*, who edited it. Printed in Switzerland, it was first a monthly and then a quarterly. MM published there a review-essay on contemporary films of the time and a review of *James Sibley Watson*'s and Melville Webber's *Lot in Sodom*.

COLLEGE VERSE (November 1931–May 1941), monthly sponsored by the College Poetry Society of America and published in Grinnell, Iowa. Edited by Eda Lou Walton (1931–33), Arthur H. Nethercot (1933–35), and others.

CONOVER FAMILY. J. Dey Conover and his wife, Lillian, were close family friends of the Moores'. JWM taught their son in Elizabeth, N.J. The Conovers visited MM and her mother in Carlisle and, later, frequently in New York.

CONTACT (December 1920–June 1923), irregular little magazine published in New York; started in 1920 by *William Carlos Williams* and edited by him and *Robert McAlmon*. Contributors included MM, *Kenneth Burke*, Williams, McAlmon, *Mina Loy, Marsden Hartley, Wallace Stevens*, and *Glenway Wescott*. The "new series" of *Contact* ran for three issues in 1932 and was edited by Williams.

CONTEMPO (May 1931–February 1934), irregular literary review of ideas and personalities published in Chapel Hill, N.C. Editors included M. A. Abernethy, S. R. Carter, Phil Liskin, V. N. Garoffolo, A. J. Buttitta, and others.

CONTEMPORARY POETRY AND PROSE (1936–37), monthly surrealist magazine published in London and edited by *Roger Roughton*. Contributors included David Gascoyne, *E. E. Cummings, Wallace Stevens*, and others.

JOSEPH CORNELL (1903–1972), American artist best known for his boxes made of found objects, maps, photographs, engravings, and other materials. An acquaintance of MM's with whom she corresponded between 1943 and 1961.

JOHN COURNOS (1881–1966), born in Russia and lived in the United States from 1891 on; novelist and translator, who also wrote biographical sketches and his autobiography. MM began following his work in 1916.

MALCOLM COWLEY (1898–1989), American critic, poet, novelist, *Dial* contributor, and editor of *The New Republic*. An acquaintance of MM's who advised her on her translation of La Fontaine's *Fables* and was on the board that awarded her the Bollingen Prize. They corresponded between 1925 and 1954.

GORDON CRAIG (1872–1966), English author, editor, theorist, director, and stage designer, with whom MM corresponded between 1926 and 1927. She had a keen interest in his work.

LOUISE CRANE (1917–), Vassar classmate and friend of *Elizabeth Bishop*'s; Bishop introduced her to MM. Crane became a close friend and patron of MM's; they saw each other regularly in New York and corresponded extensively between 1937 and 1969. MM named Crane and her lawyer coexecutors of her estate.

THE CRITERION (October 1922–January 1939), quarterly literary review published in London and edited by *T. S. Eliot*, which published MM's poems and reviews in the 1930s. Known as *The New Criterion* (January 1926–January 1927) and as *The Monthly Criterion* (May 1927–March 1928).

E[DWARD] E[STLIN] CUMMINGS (1894–1962), American poet, prose writer, occasional playwright, and painter. A close friend of the *Watsons'* who became a friend of MM's; they corresponded between 1921 and 1962. MM also reviewed his work.

DECISION (January 1941–February 1942), a "review of free culture," was a monthly little magazine published in New York and edited by Klaus Mann. In 1941 Muriel Rukeyser became associate editor.

BABETTE DEUTSCH (1895–1982), American poet, translator, and critic, with whom MM was acquainted and corresponded between 1950 and 1969.

THE DIAL (1880–1929), reviving the earlier nineteenth-century periodical by that name (1840–44), which was edited by Margaret Fuller and Ralph Waldo Emerson. *Scofield Thayer* and *James Sibley Watson* became co-owners of *The Dial* in 1920, publishing it as a monthly of art and literature between 1920 and 1929. Edited by MM between 1925 and 1929.

LUCY MARTIN DONNELLY (1870–1948), Bryn Mawr English professor.

MARION DORN (1931–), artist and textile designer; friend of MM's whom MM saw regularly in New York and with whom she corresponded between 1948 and 1964. Married to *Edward McKnight Kauffer*.

T[HOMAS] S[TEARNS] ELIOT (1888–1965), American poet who immigrated to England in 1914, first encountering MM's work as an associate editor of *The Egoist*. Eliot became a friend of MM's, with whom she corresponded extensively between 1921 and 1964, though she did not meet him until 1933. Eliot reviewed and promoted MM's work, and as her editor at Faber & Faber, he was closely involved in the arrangement of her *Selected Poems*. MM also reviewed Eliot's work.

THE EGOIST (1914–19), British bimonthly edited by Dora Marsden (January–June 1914) and *Harriet Shaw Weaver* (July 1914–1919); *Richard Aldington, H.D.,* and *T. S. Eliot* were assistant editors. Superseded *The New Freewoman* (June–December 1913). MM began publishing poems in *The Egoist* in 1915.

ALFEO FAGGI (1885–1966), Italian-born sculptor who became a naturalized American in 1927; MM admired his work and reviewed it for *The Dial*.

MEI LAN FANG (1894–1961), Chinese traditional actor whom MM saw perform in New York in the thirties.

FIFTH FLOOR WINDOW (April 1931–May 1932), irregular little magazine of creative and critical writing, published in New York and edited by Harvey N. Foster, Ulrick Sullivan, Marianne Brown, and others.

DUDLEY FITTS (1903–1968), American poet, critic, and translator; he was a friend of *Ezra Pound*'s and a member of the committee that selected MM for the first award given by the Bryher Foundation in 1949.

LLOYD FRANKENBERG (1907–1975), American poet and critic who was a friend of MM's. Married to *Loren MacIver*.

FURIOSO (1939–53), irregular little magazine of verse edited by James Angleton and E. Reed Whittemore, Jr., with Carmen Mercedes Angleton. Published in New Haven, Ct. Contributors included *William Carlos Williams, E. E. Cummings,* John Peale Bishop, *W. H. Auden,* MM, and *Wallace Stevens,* among others.

ALLEN GINSBERG (1926–1997), American poet who sent the manuscript of *Empty Mirror* to MM for her comments, through the efforts of his father, *Louis Ginsberg,* who was acquainted with MM.

LOUIS GINSBERG (1895–1976), American poet and educator.

JOSEPH ("JOE") FERDINAND GOULD (1889–1957), American author of *Oral History,* a compilation of his thoughts and material overheard in the houses, bars, and streets of New York.

ALYSE GREGORY (1884–1967), American novelist and managing editor of *The Dial* who preceded MM as editor. A friend of MM's, with whom she corresponded between 1922 and 1966. Married to *Llewelyn Powys*.

HORACE GREGORY (1898–1982), American poet, translator, critic, editor, and teacher of classical literature; he and Moore were acquainted and corresponded between 1952 and 1956.

YVETTE GUILBERT (1868–1944), French popular singer whom MM admired.

MARCET HALDEMAN, close college friend of MM's during the Bryn Mawr years; they corresponded frequently between January and May 1908, while MH was on a temporary leave from Bryn Mawr. Bryn Mawr class of 1909.

MARSDEN HARTLEY (1877–1943), American painter and poet; acquaintance of MM's whom she attempted to assist in the publishing of his poetry, transcribing his manuscript, *The Pressed Foot*, and sending his poems to *Poetry* in 1937.

C. BERTRAM HARTMAN (1882–1960), American artist whose work MM admired.

ELINOR BLAINE ("HONEY") HAYS, daughter of a prominent family in Carlisle. MWM was friendly with Mrs. Hays, and MM was a close friend of "Honey" throughout her life, corresponding with her between 1906 and 1969.

H.D. (Hilda Doolittle; 1886–1961), American poet, novelist, and prose writer. H.D. and MM spent time together at Bryn Mawr, although they were not friends at the time. In 1915 they began corresponding when MM sent her poems to *The Egoist*. This would be the beginning of a long friendship; they exchanged work and corresponded between 1915 and 1960. In 1921 H.D. and *Bryher* arranged to have MM's *Poems* published by the Egoist Press. She and MM reviewed each other's work. Married to *Richard Aldington* (1913–38).

JANE HEAP (1887–1964), American editor, critic, and painter who was coeditor, with *Margaret Anderson*, of *The Little Review*.

ROBERT HERRING, film critic for The Manchester *Guardian*, whom *Bryher* appointed editor of *Life and Letters To-day* in 1935. MM corresponded with him between 1936 and 1940.

ROBERT HILLYER (1895–1961), poet, critic, and contributor to *The Dial*; founder of the Poetry Society.

MALVINA HOFFMAN (1887–1966), American sculptor and painter, who also wrote on sculptural methodology and published a memoir, *Yesterday Is Tomorrow: A Personal History*, with which MM assisted her. A close friend of MM's with whom she corresponded between 1950 and 1965.

THE HOUND & HORN (1927–34), Harvard miscellany edited by Varian Fry and *Lincoln Kirstein* (1927–29), Bernard Bandler II (January 1929–September 1933), R. P. Blackmur (1929), *Lincoln Kirstein* (January 1929–September 1934), Varian Fry (October/December 1929), and A. Hyatt Mayor (October/December 1931–September 1933). Severed its ties with Harvard in 1929 and moved to New York in 1930.

EDWIN HOWARD, American architect and semiprofessional photographer in New York; designed the American Shakespeare Theatre in Stratford, Ct. He and his family were close personal friends of the Moores'. Edwin had two siblings, Gladys and Richard.

PEGGY JAMES, daughter of William James and friend of MM's during the Bryn Mawr years. Bryn Mawr class of 1910.

KATHRINE JONES (1882–1952), close friend of MM's whom she acknowledged in the foreword to her *Fables of La Fontaine* and with whom she corresponded between 1942 and 1952. Companion of *Marcia Chamberlain*.

EDWARD McKNIGHT KAUFFER (1890–1954), American painter, graphic artist and illustrator; he was a close friend of *T. S. Eliot*'s and became a close friend of MM's; he and MM corresponded between 1943 and 1954. Married to *Marion Dorn*.

THE KENYON REVIEW (Winter 1939–), quarterly published at Kenyon College and originally edited by John Crowe Ransom. Early contributors included John Berryman, Muriel Rukeyser, Allen Tate, MM, and others.

JOHN BARRETT KERFOOT (1865–1927), literary editor of *Life* magazine and associate editor of *Camera Work*, whose writing MM admired and whom she met at *Alfred Stieglitz*'s gallery during her 1915 trip to New York.

LINCOLN KIRSTEIN (1907–1996), founder and editor of *The Hound & Horn* (1927–34) and American dance authority; founded the New York City Ballet in partnership with George Balanchine. He became a friend of MM's and regularly invited her to performances. They corresponded between 1931 and 1969.

ALFRED KREYMBORG (1883–1966), American poet and playwright who edited *Others*. MM met Kreymborg in 1915 in New York, where he introduced her to several leading artists, editors, and writers.

GASTON LACHAISE (1882–1935), French artist and sculptor; acquaintance of MM's whose work she admired. His alabaster head of her is in the Metropolitan Museum of Art in New York. Illustrations of his work appeared in *The Dial*.

THE LANTERN, Bryn Mawr College and alumnae literary magazine in which MM published poems during and immediately following her college years.

RONALD LANE LATIMER, whose given name was James G. Leippert (–1960), was an American editor and publisher who also wrote poetry. He frequently adopted pseudonyms, including Mark Jason, Mark Zorn, Martin Jay, and, of course, Latimer. Best known for his editing of the *Alcestis Quarterly* (1934–35) and the Alcestis Press (1934–38), he also edited *The New Broom and Morningside* (1932) and *The Lion and Crown* (1932–33). MM corresponded with him between 1932 and 1938.

JAMES LAUGHLIN (1915–), American poet who edited and published *New Directions in Prose and Poetry* in 1936, which led to his founding of the publishing company New Directions. An acquaintance of MM's, with whom she corresponded between 1937 and 1969.

D. H. LAWRENCE (1885–1930), English novelist, poet, essayist, and *Dial* contributor; MM admired his poetry.

JAMES G. LEIPPERT: see *Ronald Lane Latimer*.

HARRY LEVIN (1912–1994), critic and scholar of comparative literature at Harvard University; he and MM corresponded between 1945 and 1969. Advised MM on her translation of La Fontaine's *Fables*.

LIFE AND LETTERS TO-DAY (1935–50), literary magazine originally called *Life and Letters*, it was bought by *Bryher* in 1935, renamed *Life and Letters To-day*, and absorbed the London *Mercury,* May 1939. *Robert Herring* edited it; MM contributed to it.

THE LION AND CROWN (1932–33), quarterly little magazine edited by *James G. Leippert* and published at Columbia University. Contributors included *Conrad Aiken, Carl Rakosi,* Gertrude Stein, and others.

THE LITTLE REVIEW (March 1914–May 1929), little magazine published irregularly and edited by *Margaret Anderson* and *Jane Heap* (1922–29). *Ezra Pound* was the foreign editor (1917–21). Published Joyce's *Ulysses* from 1918 to 1921.

LESTER LITTLEFIELD, bibliographer and friend of MM's; they corresponded between 1939 and 1970. Advised MM on her unpublished novel and typed parts of it for her. A Pound enthusiast and a friend of *Louise Crane*'s.

AMY LOWELL (1874–1925), American poet; casual acquaintance of MM's during the 1920s.

MINA LOY (1882–1966), English poet, painter, playwright, and actress with whom MM was acquainted.

GEORGE PLATT LYNES (1907–1955), photographer who did several portraits of MM, including the jacket photo for *The Marianne Moore Reader.*

ROBERT McALMON (1896–1956), American expatriate who wrote poems and fiction and edited *Contact* with *William Carlos Williams.* An acquaintance of MM's with whom she corresponded between 1921 and 1952. Marriage of convenience to *Bryher* (1921–27).

HENRY McBRIDE (1867–1962), American artist and critic who contributed to *The Dial.* He was also an art critic for the New York *Sun.* MM corresponded with him between 1939 and 1959.

LOREN MacIVER (1909–), American painter; friend of *Elizabeth Bishop*'s. MM admired her work and they corresponded between 1943 and 1968. Married to *Lloyd Frankenberg.*

KENNETH MACPHERSON, writer, filmmaker, and editor of *Close-Up.* Marriage of convenience to *Bryher* (1927–48).

LINCOLN MacVEAGH (1890–1972), friend of *Scofield Thayer*'s and director of the Dial Press (1923–33), which published MM's *Observations* (1924).

DR. ALVIN EDWIN MAGARY (1879–1964), pastor of Lafayette Avenue Presbyterian Church in Brooklyn.

MANIKIN, which ran for only three issues in 1923, was edited by *Monroe Wheeler.* Each issue was devoted to a single author; published MM's "Marriage."

THE MARIONETTE (1918–19), little magazine of the puppet theater edited by *Gordon Craig.*

THE MASSES (1911–17), monthly magazine combining an interest in socialism with the arts. Superseded by *The Liberator* in 1918. Editors included Thomas Seltzer, Horatio Winslow, Piet Vlag, and Max Eastman.

ELIZABETH MAYER (1908–?), introduced to MM by *W. H. Auden,* she became a friend of MM's. MM assisted her with her translation of *Rock Crystal,* a fable by the German author Adalbert Stifter.

MESURES, French little magazine founded and edited by Jean Paulhan and Henry Church.

STEWART MITCHELL (1892–1957), poet and managing editor of *The Dial* between

1919 and 1920. In 1933 he was managing editor of the *New England Quarterly*. MM reviewed his poems for *The Dial* and corresponded with him between 1922 and 1957.

HARRIET MONROE (1860–1936), American poet, critic, and founding editor in 1912 of *Poetry: A Magazine of Verse*, who began publishing MM's poetry in 1915. An acquaintance of MM's, who visited MM and her mother in New York.

GEORGE MOORE (1852–1933), Anglo-Irish novelist whose work MM reviewed enthusiastically.

MARION MOREHOUSE, painter and friend of MM's; they corresponded between 1944 and 1965. Married to *E. E. Cummings*.

FRANK MORLEY, friend of *T. S. Eliot*'s and editor at Faber & Faber; he and MM corresponded between 1934 and 1946.

SAMUEL FRENCH MORSE (1916–1969), poet, critic, and educator; director of the Cummington School of the Arts (1946–47). *Wallace Stevens* scholar and his literary executor.

EDWARD NAGLE (1893–1963), artist and stepson of Gaston Lachaise; contributed to *The Dial*.

THE NEW ENGLISH WEEKLY (1932–49), review of public affairs, literature, and the arts edited by Alfred Richard Orage (1932–34) and Philip Mairet (1934–48). Published *T. S. Eliot*'s "East Coker."

REINHOLD NIEBUHR (1892–1971), American theologian and social and political activist; MM admired him and they corresponded between 1952 and 1962.

YONÉ NOGUCHI (1875–1947), Japanese-born poet, essayist, and *Dial* contributor; MM reviewed his essays for *Poetry*.

NORCROSS FAMILY, close friends of the Moores' in Carlisle.

DR. GEORGE NORCROSS ("Dockey"), minister of the Second Presbyterian Church of Carlisle, doctor of divinity from Princeton Theological Seminary, and instrumental in establishing the Carlisle Indian School (1879). Lived with his family in the "Manse."

LOUISE JACKSON NORCROSS, wife of *Dr. George Norcross* and sister of Sheldon Jackson.

MARY JACKSON NORCROSS ("Beaver" or "Rustles"), Bryn Mawr 1899, third daughter of the Norcrosses, and very close friend of MWM's, often referred to in MM and JWM's college letters as part of the family. Designed and helped to build an Arts and Crafts house in Sterrett's Gap, Pa., which the Moores referred to as "the Nest" at "the mountain."

OTHERS (July 1915-July 1919), monthly little magazine edited by *Alfred Kreymborg* and William Saphier. Associate editors included *William Carlos Williams*, Helen Hoyt, *Maxwell Bodenheim, Lola Ridge*, and Orrick Johns. Published early poetry of MM, *Williams, Ezra Pound, Wallace Stevens, T. S. Eliot*, and others.

PAGANY (1930–33), quarterly little magazine edited by Richard Johns.

CHESTER HALL PAGE (1912–), pianist, who became secretary to *Louise Crane* in the 1930s; acquaintance of MM's with whom he corresponded.

NORMAN HOLMES PEARSON (1909–1975), American educator and scholar who taught at Yale University; author and editor of books on English and American literature. An acquaintance of MM's with whom she corresponded between 1937 and 1966.

GEORGE PLANK (1883–1965), American illustrator and designer of magazine covers; MM knew him from Carlisle and they corresponded between 1925 and 1952. At her request, he illustrated *The Pangolin and Other Verse* (1936).

POETRY (1912–), monthly magazine of verse published in Chicago and edited by *Harriet Monroe* (1912–35), *Morton Dauwen Zabel* (1936–37), George Dillon (1937–42), and others. MM began publishing poems in *Poetry* in 1915.

DOROTHY POUND (née Dorothy Shakespear) (1886–1973), acquaintance of MM's with whom MM corresponded during *Ezra Pound*'s incarceration at St. Elizabeths Hospital. Married to *Pound* in 1914.

EZRA POUND (1885–1972), American poet who immigrated to England in 1908. Through his relationship with *The Egoist* and as "foreign editor" of *Poetry*, Pound became acquainted with MM's work, writing to her for the first time in December 1918. They became close friends, corresponding extensively between 1918 and 1968, though she did not meet him until 1939.

LLEWELYN POWYS (1884–1939), English essayist and novelist. Married to *Alyse Gregory*.

CARL RAKOSI (1903–), American poet of the objectivist school.

HERMANN P. RICCIUS (1883–1965), Scofield Thayer's family business manager and representative.

LOLA RIDGE (1871–1941), Irish-born poet who came to New York in 1908. Part of *Alfred Kreymborg*'s *Others* group. A friend of MM's; MM helped in typing and publishing her work.

ELIZABETH MADOX ROBERTS (1886–1941), American poet and novelist who published in *The Dial*.

A. S. W. ROSENBACH (1876–1952), American dealer in rare books and manuscripts, who also wrote bibliographies and satires. His Philadelphia home was converted into a museum under the auspices of the Rosenbach Foundation, and now holds the major archive of MM's manuscripts and letters.

PAUL ROSENFELD (1890–1946), American critic of music, art, and literature; wrote the "Musical Chronicle" for *The Dial* (1920–27). He was a casual friend of MM's; when he died, she commemorated his life and work in *The Nation*.

W. W. E. ROSS (1894–1966), Canadian poet and geophysicist, whose work MM admired and reviewed.

ROGER ROUGHTON (–1941), English poet and editor of *Contemporary Poetry and Prose;* he solicited work from MM.

PIERRE ROY (1880–1950), French painter and graphic artist whose work MM followed.

BERTRAND RUSSELL (1872–1970), British mathematician, philosopher, and social and political critic who contributed to *The Dial*.

GEORGE SAINTSBURY (1845–1933), English critic and historian; from 1895 to 1915, professor of rhetoric and English literature at the University of Edinburgh. Saintsbury was an acquaintance of MM's; his work was published in *The Dial* and they corresponded between 1925 and 1930.

MAY SARTON (1912–1995), Belgian-born American poet, novelist, and prose writer who also published her journals. MM corresponded with her between 1948 and 1970.

PERDITA SCHAFFNER (1919–), *H.D.*'s daughter, who was later legally adopted by *Bryher*. A friend of MM's; they corresponded between 1932 and 1960. Married to John Schaffner.

SCRUTINY (1932–), quarterly critical magazine published in Cambridge, England, and edited by F. R. Leavis, L. C. Knights, Denys Thompson, and D. W. Harding.

SECESSION (Spring 1922–April 1924), irregular little magazine edited by Gorham B. Munson, with Matthew Josephson and *Kenneth Burke*. First published in Vienna and Berlin, then moved to New York. Contributors included MM, Hart Crane, and *Malcolm Cowley*.

SEED (January–July 1933), quarterly little magazine published in London and edited by Herbert Jones and Oswell Blakeston. Contributions by *H.D., Mary Butts, Bryher*, and others.

GILBERT VIVIAN SELDES (1893–1970), associate and managing editor of *The Dial* (1920–23) and *Dial* contributor; he and MM corresponded between 1920 and 1967. An important theater critic who wrote *The Seven Lively Arts* (1924).

CHARLES SHEELER (1883–1965), American painter, photographer, and *Dial* contributor whose work MM followed.

THE SITWELLS, acquaintances of MM's.

DAME EDITH SITWELL (1887–1964), English poet and critic whose work MM admired and reviewed and with whom she corresponded between 1949 and 1964.

SIR OSBERT SITWELL (1892–1969), English author with whom MM corresponded between 1949 and 1965.

THE SMART SET (1900–30), monthly magazine published in New York and edited by Willard Huntington Wright (1912–14) and by George Jean Nathan and Henry Louis Mencken (1914–23).

LOTA DE MACEDO SOARES (1910–1967), prominent Brazilian who became *Elizabeth Bishop*'s companion in 1951.

THE SOIL (1916–17), monthly magazine of art edited by Robert J. Coady and Enrique Cross and published in New York. Published early poems by *Wallace Stevens* and *Maxwell Bodenheim*.

THE SOUTHERN REVIEW (1935–42), quarterly published at Louisiana State University and edited by Charles W. Pipkin (1935–41), Cleanth Brooks, Jr. (1941–42), and Robert Penn Warren (1941–42). New series (1965–), edited by Donald Stanford and Lewis P. Simpson at LSU. Since 1983, various editors. Published work by Allen Tate, *Yvor Winters*, R. P. Blackmur, Eudora Welty, and Katherine Anne Porter, among others.

WALLACE STEVENS (1879–1955), American poet and essayist. An acquaintance of MM's whose work she admired and reviewed extensively, soliciting it for *The Dial*. Stevens also reviewed MM's work. She corresponded with him between 1933 and 1955, though they did not meet until 1943.

ALFRED STIEGLITZ (1864–1946), American photographer and promoter of modern painting. Editor of the *American Amateur Photographer* (1892–96), *Camera Notes* (1897–1903), and the quarterly *Camera Work* (1903–17). MM met him in 1915 when she visited his Gallery 291 during a visit to New York.

ELLEN THAYER, office assistant at *The Dial*. Cousin of *Scofield Thayer* and college friend of MM's. Class of 1907 at Bryn Mawr College. MM worked with her at *The Dial* and corresponded with her between 1932 and 1952.

SCOFIELD THAYER (1890–1982), American poet and co-owner of *The Dial* with *James Sibley Watson*. Editor of *The Dial* from 1920 to 1925, at which point MM became editor. A friend of MM's with whom she corresponded throughout the twenties.

MARTHA CAREY THOMAS (1857–1935), American educator and feminist; dean and professor of English (1884–94) and president (1894–1922) at Bryn Mawr College. Thomas was instrumental in creating the rigorous standards for which Bryn Mawr became known.

VIRGIL THOMSON (1896–1989), American composer. Gertrude Stein wrote libretti for his first opera, *Four Saints in Three Acts* (1928), and also for his opera *The Mother of Us All*. MM corresponded with him between 1954 and 1964. He set MM's poem "My Crow Pluto" to music.

TIPYN O'BOB, Bryn Mawr College literary magazine, in which MM published stories and poems during her college years. Often referred to by MM as *Typ* and *Tip*.

THE TRANSATLANTIC REVIEW (1924–25), monthly little magazine published in Paris and edited by Ford Madox Ford. Published poetry by *E. E. Cummings, Ezra Pound,* and *William Carlos Williams*, among others.

TRANSITION (1927–38), monthly little magazine published in Paris and The Hague and edited by Eugene Jolas and Elliot Paul. Influenced by the surrealists, they published excerpts of Joyce's *Finnegans Wake;* other contributors included Franz Kafka, Gertrude Stein, *William Carlos Williams,* and *H.D.*

THE TYRO (1921–22), little magazine devoted to the arts of painting, sculpture, and design, published in London and edited by Wyndham Lewis. Contributors included *T. S. Eliot, Robert McAlmon,* and Lewis.

MARK VAN DOREN (1894–1972), American poet with whom MM corresponded between 1939 and 1963.

VIEW (1940–47), quarterly little magazine of the arts published in New York and edited by Charles Henri Ford.

JEAN WAHL (1888–1974), existential philosopher who fled Hitler's occupation of France, later organizing a conference series in America, based on the Entretien de Pontigny of the prewar years, which MM attended in 1943 at Mount Holyoke.

HILDEGARDE [LASELL] WATSON (1888–1976), musician and concert soprano, who became a close friend of MM's; they corresponded extensively between 1933 and 1972. Married to *James Sibley Watson*.

JAMES SIBLEY WATSON, JR. (1894–1982), co-owner, with *Scofield Thayer*, of *The Dial;* contributor, under *W. C. Blum;* creator of experimental films; M.D. and innovator in field of radiology. MM frequently addressed him as "Doctor Watson." A friend of MM's whose work she admired and with whom she corresponded between 1921 and 1970. Married to *Hildegarde Watson*. Their children are: Michael Lasell Watson (1918–) and Jean Iseult Watson (1921–).

HARRIET SHAW WEAVER (1876–1961), English editor of *The Egoist* between 1914 and 1919, who assisted *Bryher* and *H.D.* in publishing MM's *Poems* (1921) with the Egoist Press.

GLENWAY WESCOTT (1901–1987), American poet and fiction writer. An early admirer of MM's work, Wescott wrote favorably about her poems for *The Dial*; they became friends, corresponding between 1922 and 1971. Companion of *Monroe Wheeler*.

THE WESTMINSTER MAGAZINE (1911–44), literary quarterly published at Oglethorpe University in Georgia. The Spring/Summer 1935 issue was *The Westminster Anthology*, edited by *T. C. Wilson* and *Ezra Pound*.

MONROE WHEELER (1899–1988), American director of exhibitions and publications at the Museum of Modern Art and editor of the little magazine *Manikin*. A good friend of MM's whom she saw often and with whom she corresponded extensively between 1923 and 1971. Companion of *Glenway Wescott*.

WILLIAM CARLOS WILLIAMS (1883–1963), American poet, prose writer, and pediatrician; he and MM met in 1917. Admirers and reviewers of each other's work, they became good friends, corresponding between 1916 and 1961.

EDMUND WILSON (1895–1972), American poet, novelist, essayist, playwright, and literary critic; he and MM corresponded between 1949 and 1969. Nicknamed "Bunny."

T[HEODORE] C. WILSON (1912–1950), American poet, critic, and editor of *The Westminster Anthology* (1935). *Ezra Pound* arranged for MM to meet Wilson in the thirties; they became friends, and corresponded between 1934 and 1950.

ANN WINSLOW (1894–1974), American editor, whose given name was Verna Elizabeth Grubbs; edited *Trial Balances* (1935), an anthology of poetry from the 1930s which was accompanied by critical comments written by older poets and critics. MM commented on *Elizabeth Bishop*'s poetry for the anthology.

YVOR WINTERS (1900–1968), American poet and critic who taught in the English department at Stanford University from 1928 until his death. MM became acquainted with him in 1921 when he sent her some poems; they corresponded between 1921 and 1930. Contributed to *The Dial*.

KURT WOLFF, founder of Pantheon Books.

MORTON DAUWEN ZABEL (1901–1964), American professor of English at the University of Chicago; poet, critic, and associate editor (1928–36) of *Poetry*. After *Harriet Monroe's* death in 1936, he became the editor (1936–37) of *Poetry*. MM met Zabel in 1931; he became a friend with whom she corresponded extensively between 1931 and 1963.

THE ZORACHS, acquaintances of MM's.

MARGUERITE ZORACH (1887–1968), American artist who painted MM and her mother.

WILLIAM ZORACH (1887–1966), American sculptor who did an oil portrait and a sculpture of MM.

LOUIS ZUKOFSKY (1904–1978), American poet of the objectivist school; MM began reading his work in the early thirties, and corresponded with him between 1936 and 1967. MM was an enthusiastic supporter of his son, virtuoso violinist Paul Zukofsky.

Appendix

ABBREVIATIONS

B	Bryher	JWM	John Warner Moore
BM	Bryn Mawr (Canaday Library)	MDZ	Morton Dauwen Zabel
		MH	Marcet Haldeman
EB	Elizabeth Bishop	MN	Mary Norcross
EP	Ezra Pound	MW	Monroe Wheeler
HD	Hilda Doolittle	MWM	Mary Warner Moore
HM	Harriet Monroe	RM	Robert McAlmon
HRHRC	Harry Ransom Humanities Research Center	RML	Rosenbach Museum and Library
HW	Hildegarde Watson	TSE	T. S. Eliot
JSW	James Sibley Watson	WCW	William Carlos Williams

KEY

A	autograph (handwritten)	pc	postcard
C	carbon	S	signed
D	draft	T	typed
L	letter		

to JWM   6/16/05   ALS RML
to MWM   9/24/05   ALS RML
to MN   10/8/05   ALS RML
to MWM and JWM   11/2/05   AL RML
to MWM and JWM   12/11/06   AL RML
to MWM and JWM   1/17/07   ALS RML
to MWM and JWM   1/31/07   ALS RML
to MWM, JWM, and MN   2/14/07   ALS RML

to MWM and JWM   2/19/07   ALS RML
to MWM, JWM, and MN   3/17/07   AL RML
to MWM   5/9/07   ALS RML
to MWM and JWM   10/24/07   ALS RML
to MWM and JWM   1/12/08   ALS RML
to MWM, JWM, and MN   1/13/08   ALS RML
to MH   1/26/08   ALS BM
to MH   2/9/08   ALS BM

to MH   2/11/08   ALS BM

to MH   2/28/08   ALS BM

to MH   3/15/08   AL BM

to MWM, JWM, and MN   3/29/08   ALS RML

to MWM and JWM   4/2/08   AL RML

to MWM and JWM   4/5/08   ALS RML

to MH   5/17/08   ALS BM

to MWM and JWM   10/28/08   ALS RML

to MWM and JWM   12/12/08 or 12/13/08   ALS RML

to MWM and JWM   2/1/09   ALS RML

to MWM and JWM   2/14/09   ALS RML

to MWM and JWM   3/16/09   ALS RML

to MWM and JWM   5/2/09   ALS RML

to MWM, JWM, and MN   5/6/09   ALS RML

to JWM   4/22/10   ALS RML

to MWM and JWM   7/6/10   ALS RML

to MWM and JWM   7/31/10   ALS RML

to MWM and JWM   8/18/10   ALS RML

to MWM and JWM   8/21/10   AL RML

to MWM and JWM   8/23/10   ALS RML

to JWM   11/13/10   ALS RML

to JWM   3/3/11   ALS RML

to JWM   6/20/11   ALS RML

to JWM   7/5/11   ALS RML

to JWM   7/9/11   ALS RML

to JWM   8/13/11   ALS RML

to JWM   11/23/13   TLS RML

to JWM   1/11/14   ALS RML

to JWM   10/4/14   ALS RML

to HM   4/8/15   ALS Chicago

to JWM   5/9/15   ALS RML

to JWM   9/22/15   ALS RML

to JWM   10/3/15   ALS RML

to JWM   10/10/15   ALS RML

to JWM   12/12/15   ALS RML

to JWM   12/19/15   ALS RML

to JWM   3/9/16   ALS RML

to HD   8/9/16   TLC RML

to HD   11/10/16   TLC RML

to WCW   4/16/17   ALD RML

to HM   5/10/18   ALS Chicago

to EP   1/9/19   TLS Beinecke

to JWM   11/2/19   ALS RML

to JWM   1/16/20   ALS RML

to JWM   6/11/20   ALS RML

to JWM   9/19/20   ALS RML

to B   10/15/20   ALS Beinecke

to JWM   10/17/20   ALS RML

to B   11/29/20   TLS Beinecke

to B   12/13/20   TLS Beinecke

to HD   1/11/21   TLC RML

to JWM   1/23/21   ALS RML

to B   1/23/21   ALS Beinecke

to JWM   2/13/21   ALS RML

to JWM   2/20/21   ALS RML

to HD   3/27/21   TLS Beinecke

to JWM   4/4/21   ALS RML

to TSE   4/17/21   ALD RML

to B   4/18/21   TLS Beinecke

to JWM   4/24/21   ALS RML

to JWM   5/1/21   ALS RML

to B   5/3/21   TLS Beinecke

to B   5/9/21   TLS Beinecke

to RM   5/9/21   TLS Beinecke

to EP   5/10/21   TLD RML

to RM   6/18/21   TLS Beinecke

to B   7/7/21   TLS Beinecke

to RM   7/8/21   TLS Beinecke

to JWM   7/10/21   ALS RML

to TSE   7/15/21   ALD RML

to HD   7/26/21   TLC RML

to B   7/27/21   TLS Beinecke

to B   8/31/21   TLS Beinecke

to RM   9/2/21   TLS Beinecke

to B and HD   11/10/21   TLS Beinecke

to JWM   12/18/21   ALS RML

to JWM   1/1/22   ALS RML

to RM   7/28/22   ALS Beinecke
to HD   11/18/22   TLS Beinecke
to Yvor Winters   12/20/22   TLC RML
to JWM   1/14/23   ALS RML
to JWM   3/25/23   ALS RML
to JWM   4/8/23   ALS RML
to B   5/5/23   TLS Beinecke
to JWM   5/10/23   ALS RML
to JWM   7/5/23   AL RML
to B   7/5/23   TLS Beinecke
to JWM   8/5/23   ALS RML
to MW   8/25/23   ALS Berg
to MW   10/1/23   ALS Berg
to JWM   11/30/23   ALS RML
to TSE   12/10/23   ALS Faber
to Alyse Gregory   2/5/24   TLS Beinecke
to B   9/9/24   TLS Beinecke
to WCW   10/9/24   TLS Beinecke
to HD   10/26/24   ALS Beinecke
to Alyse Gregory, JSW, and Scofield Thayer   12/23/24   ALS Beinecke
to George Plank   3/15/25   ALS Beinecke
to MW   4/19/25   ALS Berg
to Maxwell Bodenheim   7/6/25   TLC Beinecke
to WCW   12/16/25   TLS Beinecke
to Scofield Thayer   12/28/25   TLC RML
to Alyse Gregory   12/29/25   TLC RML
to JSW   1/7/26   TLS BM
to George Saintsbury   2/2/26   TL[C?] Beinecke
to Yvor Winters   2/3/26   TLC RML
to JSW   2/13/26   TLC RML
to JSW   4/12/26   TLC RML
to Scofield Thayer   5/1/26   TLS Beinecke
to George Saintsbury   5/18/26   TLC Beinecke
to MW   7/18/26   ALS Berg
to JSW   3/3/27   TLS Beinecke
to JSW   3/10/27   TLD RML

to JSW   5/10/27   TLC RML
to JWM   7/31/27   ALS RML
to TSE   8/10/27   TLS Faber
to JWM   1/22/28   ALS RML
to JWM   3/15/28   ALS RML
to JWM   5/4/28   ALS RML
to JWM   7/29/28   ALS RML
to JWM   1/27/29   ALS RML
to JWM   2/24/29   ALS RML
to EP   3/8/29   TLS Beinecke
to JWM   3/27/29   ALS RML
to D. H. Lawrence   3/28/29   TLC Beinecke
to D. H. Lawrence   6/22/29   TLD HRHRC
to JSW   7/12/29   ALD RML
to MW   3/18/30   ALS Berg
to JWM   6/24/31   TL RML
to HM   10/1/31   ALS Chicago
to EP   11/9/31   TLS Beinecke
to MDZ   12/7/31   TLS Chicago
to HM   3/14/32   TLS Chicago
to B   4/4/32   TLS Beinecke
to JWM   6/25/32   TLS RML
to MW   7/11/32   TLS Berg
to JWM   7/19/32   TLS RML
to JWM   7/24/32   ALS RML
to EP   7/29/32   TLS Beinecke
to B   10/3/32   TLS Beinecke
to Alyse Gregory   10/17/32   TLC RML
to MW   11/20/32   ALS Berg
to Kenneth Burke   11/30/32   TLS Pa. State
to John W. Moore, Jr.   12/9/32   TLS RML
to JWM   12/18/32   TL RML
to EP   1/18/33   TLS Beinecke
to JWM   2/12/33   TL RML
to MDZ   2/15/33   TLS Chicago
to B   2/22/33   TLS Beinecke
to MDZ   2/22/33   TLS Chicago
to EP   3/2/33   TLS Beinecke
to MW   3/3/33   TLS Berg
to MDZ   3/14/33   TLS Chicago
to B   5/16/33   TLS Beinecke

to MDZ   5/23/33   TLS Chicago
to HW   5/25/33   transcript BM
to JWM   6/11/33   TLS RML
to HW   7/22/33   ALS BM
to William Rose Benét   7/28/33
   TLS Beinecke
to William Rose Benét   8/21/33   TLS
   Beinecke
to HW   9/3/33   ALS BM
to HW   10/25/33   ALS BM
to TSE   1/18/34   TLS Faber
to WCW   1/26/34   TLC RML
to JWM   3/1/34   TLS RML
to Mr. Samuel French Morse   3/7/34
   TLS Rotella
to Ann Borden   3/8/34   ALS Vassar
to MDZ   3/31/34   TLS Chicago
to TSE   5/16/34   TLS Faber
to HW   5/23/34   ALS BM
to TSE   6/16/34   TLS Faber
to B   7/24/34   TLS Beinecke
to B   8/27/34   TLS Beinecke
to TSE   10/23/34   TLS Faber
to T. C. Wilson   11/8/34   TLS Beinecke
to JWM   11/27/34   T and ALS RML
to EP   1/5/35   TLS Beinecke
to HD   1/6/35   ALS Beinecke
to T. C. Wilson   1/18/35   TLS Beinecke
to EP   3/4/35   TLS Beinecke
to TSE   3/12/35   ALS Faber
to T. C. Wilson   4/15/35   TLS Beinecke
to WCW   6/22/35   ALS Buffalo
to George Plank   6/25/35   ALS Beinecke
to TSE   6/27/35   TLS Faber
to T. C. Wilson   7/5/35   TLS Beinecke
to Wallace Stevens   7/11/35   ALS
   Huntington
to HW   8/8/35   ALS BM
to B   8/9/35   TLS Beinecke
to George Plank   8/14/35   ALS Beinecke

to EB   9/8/35   ALS Vassar
to T. C. Wilson   9/29/35   TLS Beinecke
to Ronald Lane Latimer   10/3/35
   TLS Chicago
to Ronald Lane Latimer   10/7/35
   TLS Chicago
to T. C. Wilson   11/29/35   TLS Beinecke
to EB   12/20/35   TLS Vassar
to B   1/18/36   TLS Beinecke
to Wallace Stevens   3/10/36   TLS
   Huntington
to EB   3/14/36   TLS Vassar
to EB   8/28/36   ALS Vassar
to EB   9/20/36   TLS Vassar
to EB   10/1/36   ALS Vassar
to MDZ   10/1/36   TLS Chicago
to EB   10/19/36   TLS Vassar
to JWM   10/20/36   TLS RML
to Wallace Stevens   10/29/36   TLS
   Virginia
to B   11/7/36   TLS Beinecke
to EP   11/24/36   TLS Beinecke
to WCW   12/7/36   TLC RML
to WCW   12/15/36   TLC RML
to EB   12/17/36   ALS Vassar
to HW   12/19/36   ALS BM
to EP   12/26/36   TLS Beinecke
to JWM   1/4/37   AL RML
to EB   1/24/37   TLS Vassar
to JWM   1/30/37
to Louise Crane   2/21/37   ALS RML
to EB   3/1/37   TLS Vassar
to EB   3/7/37   TLS Vassar
to HW   8/15/37   ALS BM
to EB   late August 1937 TLD RML
to Wallace Stevens   10/20/37   TLS
   Huntington
to Alfred Stieglitz   1/28/38   ALS Beinecke
to E. E. Cummings   3/5/38   TLC
   RML
to E. E. Cummings   4/12/38   ALS
   RML
to EB   5/1/38   TLC RML

to B   6/10/38   TLS Beinecke

to Louise Crane and EB   12/26/38   ALS RML

to JWM   11/19/39   ALS RML

to JWM   1/20/40   ALS RML

to Louise Crane   2/14/40   ALS RML

to EB   3/17/40   ALS Vassar

to Louise Crane   5/2/40   ALS RML

to HD   9/23/40   TLS Beinecke

to JWM   10/6/40   ALS RML

to EB   10/16/40   TLS Vassar

to JWM   11/22/40   ALS RML

to B   12/8/40   TLS Beinecke

to Marsden Hartley   1/2/41   ALS Beinecke

to WCW   1/7/41   TLS Beinecke

to James Laughlin   1/7/41   TLS Laughlin

to MW   1/19/41   ALS Berg

to JWM   1/21/41   ALS RML

to HW   5/23/41   transcript BM

to Louise Crane   6/5/41   ALS RML

to JWM   6/21/41   ALS RML

to EB   1/31/42   ALS Vassar

to Kathrine Jones   3/19/42   RML draft

to Marianne Craig Moore   5/5/42   TLS Moore family

to Carl Rakosi   9/7/42   TLS HRHRC

to WCW   9/7/42   TLS Beinecke

to EB   9/8/42   ALS Vassar

to Joseph Cornell   3/26/43   TLC RML

to EB   8/20/43   ALS Vassar

to HW   8/27/43   ALS BM

to Lloyd Frankenberg   9/19/43   ALS RML

to MW   10/9/43   ALS Berg

to EB   11/16/43   AL Vassar

to Lloyd Frankenberg   12/26/43   ALS RML

to JWM   3/9/44   TLS RML

to HD   3/13/44   TLS Beinecke

to JWM   4/21/44   ALS RML

to W. H. Auden   10/12/44   TLC RML

to JWM   10/31/44   ALS RML

to WCW   11/12/44   TLS Beinecke

to JWM   1/8/45   ALS RML

to George Plank   3/23/45   ALS Beinecke

to Elizabeth Mayer   4/30/45   ALS Berg

to EB   9/27/45   ALS Vassar

to MW   4/24/46   ALS Berg

to EP   7/31/46   TLS Lilly

to B   10/29/46   TLS Beinecke

to EP   6/22/47   TLS Lilly

to Louise Crane   7/9/47   ALS RML

to HW and JSW   7/16/47   ALS BM

to JWM   late summer 1947 ALS RML

to George Meals   11/6/47   CL RML

to EB   8/24/48   ALS Vassar

to Wallace Stevens   9/18/48   ALS Huntington

to MW   1/7/49   ALS Berg

to WCW   2/21/49   TLS Beinecke

to EP   6/10/49   TLS Lilly

to Louise Crane   6/27/49   TLS RML

to JWM   7/1/49   AL RML

to EP   7/30/49   TLS Lilly

to WCW   2/2/50   ALS Beinecke

to EP   6/21/50   ALS Lilly

to HW and JSW   8/24/50   ALS BM

to HW   9/11/50   ALS BM

to E. E. Cummings and Marion Morehouse Cummings   11/15/50   ALS Houghton

to JWM   11/16/50   ALS RML

to MW   12/29/50   ALS Berg

to Edith Love   1/10/51   ALS Denison

to EB   1/26/51   ALS Vassar

to Glenway Wescott   2/3/51   ALS Berg

to HW   3/7/51   ALS BM

to WCW   6/22/51   TLS Beinecke

to WCW   9/23/51   TLS Beinecke

to Edward McKnight Kauffer   12/11/51   TLS RML

to Lincoln Kirstein   1/11/52   ALS Kirstein

to Malvina Hoffman   1/12/52   ALS Getty

to WCW   1/27/52   TLS Beinecke

to Robert McAlmon   2/23/52   TLS Beinecke

to Allen Ginsberg   7/4/52   TLS Stanford

to Louis Ginsberg   7/11/52   TLS Columbia

to Dorothy Pound and EP   7/31/52   TLS Lilly

to Louise Crane   8/2/52   TLS RML

to HW   11/19/52   ALS BM

to Glenway Wescott   12/10/52   ALS Berg

to Edith Sitwell and Osbert Sitwell   12/19/52   ALS HRHRC

to W. H. Auden   2/16/53   TLC RML

to HW   8/14/53   ALS BM

to Mary Shoemaker   2/16/54   ALS RML

to HW   3/6/54   ALS BM

to Mary Shoemaker   4/9/54   ALS RML

to Edward McKnight Kauffer   Easter Day, 1954   ALS   Schulman

to HW   9/8/54   ALS BM

to TSE   10/27/54   TLS Faber

to Chester Page   1/10/55   ALS Page

to EP   undated—June 5–7, 1955   TpcS Beinecke

to Malvina Hoffman   7/5/55   ALS Getty

to Kenneth Burke   7/7/55   TpcS Penn State

to Louise Bogan   10/8/55   ALS Amherst

to MW   11/5/55   ALS Berg

to Lincoln Kirstein   11/24/55   ALS Kirstein

to HW   5/11/56   ALS BM

to EB   6/9/56   TLS Vassar

to Lincoln Kirstein   6/30/56   TLC RML

to HW   8/5/56   ALS BM

to HD   8/27/56   ALS Beinecke

to EP   12/22/56   ALS Beinecke

to Lincoln Kirstein   1/24/57   ALS Kirstein

to HW   1/25/57   ALS BM

to WCW   7/7/57   TLS Beinecke

to EP   9/10/57   TLS Beinecke

to Dorothy Pound and EP   4/19/58   TLS Beinecke

to Lota de Macedo Soares   8/16/58   TLS Vassar

to HW   11/29/58   ALS BM

to Sarah Eustis Moore   2/23/59   TLS Moore family

to Lincoln Kirstein   6/15/59   ALS Kirstein

to JSW   7/16/59   TLC Berg

to MW   12/20/61   ALS Berg

to James Laughlin   3/20/62   TLS James Laughlin

to JWM   9/20/62   ALS RML

to TSE and Valerie Eliot   12/25/62   ALS Faber

to Mary Markwick Moore Reeves   8/28/63   ALS Moore family

to JWM and family   9/11/64   ALS RML

to Constance Moore and JWM   2/5/65   TLC RML

to Mary-Louise Schneeberger 2/16/68   TLS RML

to EB and Roxanne   1/3/69   ALS Vassar

Index

A NOTE ABOUT THE EDITORS

Bonnie Costello teaches at Boston University and is the author of *Marianne Moore: Imaginary Possessions* and *Elizabeth Bishop: Questions of Mastery.*

Celeste Goodridge teaches at Bowdoin College. She is the author of *Hints and Disguises: Marianne Moore and Her Contemporaries.*

Cristanne Miller teaches at Pomona College and is the author of *Emily Dickinson: A Poet's Grammar* and *Marianne Moore: Questions of Authority.* She is also a co-author, with Suzanne Juhasz and Martha Wellsmith, of *Comic Power in Emily Dickinson.*